THE FBI
A Comprehensive Reference Guide

Edited by
Athan G. Theoharis
With
Tony G. Poveda
Susan Rosenfeld
Richard Gid Powers

Oryx Press
1999

The rare Arabian Oryx is believed to have inspired the myth of the unicorn. This desert antelope became virtually extinct in the early 1960s. At that time, several groups of international conservationists arranged to have nine animals sent to the Phoenix Zoo to be the nucleus of a captive breeding herd. Today, the Oryx population is over 1,000, and over 500 have been returned to the Middle East.

© 1999 The Oryx Press
4041 North Central at Indian School Road
Phoenix, Arizona 85012-3397

Published simultaneously in Canada
Printed and bound in the United States of America

♾ The paper used in this publication meets the minimum requirements of American National Standard for Information Science—Permanence of Paper for Printed Library Materials, ANSI Z39.48, 1984.

Library of Congress Cataloging-in-Publication Data

Theoharis, Athan G.
   The FBI : a comprehensive reference guide / edited by Athan G.
Theoharis with Tony G. Poveda, Susan Rosenfeld, Richard Gid Powers.
     p.   cm.
   Includes bibliographical references and index.
   ISBN 0-89774-991-X (alk. paper)
   1. United States. Federal Bureau of Investigation. 2. United
States. Federal Bureau of Investigation—History.   I. Title.
HV8144.F43T48   1999
363.25'0973—dc21
                                              98-26642
                                                 CIP

CONTENTS

ILLUSTRATIONS

Exhibits

Figures

Tables

CONTRIBUTORS

Tony Poveda received his D.Crim. in criminology from the University of California, Berkeley. He is currently a professor of sociology at the State University of New York–Plattsburgh where he served as chair of the sociology department and coordinator of the criminal justice program. Poveda is the author of *Lawlessness and Reform: The FBI in Transition* (1990) and *Rethinking White Collar Crime* (1994), and he has also published numerous articles in scholarly journals, including *Crime, Law and Social Change, Justice Quarterly, Crime and Delinquency, Psychiatry, Adolescence,* and *Issues in Criminology.*

Richard Gid Powers received his Ph.D. in American civilization from Brown University. He is currently a professor of history at City University of New York–Staten Island and is a member of the graduate faculty of the City University of New York. Powers is the author or editor of *G-Men: Hoover's FBI in American Popular Culture* (1983), *Secrecy and Power: The Life of J. Edgar Hoover* (1987), *Handbook of Japanese Popular Culture* (1992), and *Not Without Honor: The History of American Anticommunism* (1996). He has also published numerous articles in scholarly and popular journals, including *Insight, Perspectives* (American Historical Association), *Dictionary of American Biography, Collier's Encyclopedia, Encyclopedia of the Presidency, Aethelon, American Quarterly, Journal of American Studies, Southwest Review, Journal of Popular*

Culture, Mass Communications Review, Human Behavior, American Studies, and *Art Journal.* Powers has received numerous research grants; held a Fulbright Lectureship (Kyoto University) and a Fulbright Fellowship (University of Hiroshima); and his books and articles were awarded the Outstanding Book Selection (Gustavus Myer Center), Ray Brown Award (Popular Culture Association), Russel B. Nye Award *(Journal of Popular Culture),* and DeGolyer Institute Award *(Southwest Review).* He is author of a forthcoming history of the FBI, titled *Politics and Power: The History of the FBI,* to be published by The Free Press.

Susan Rosenfeld (prior to 1992, Susan Rosenfeld Falb) received her Ph.D. in history from Georgetown University. She has lectured at the FBI Academy and taught at various universities (including Georgetown University, American University, Cornell University, Virginia Commonwealth University, and Howard University); was a fellow in the American Studies division of the Smithsonian Institution; held archival appointments in the Civil Archives and in the Machine-Readable Archives Divisions of the National Archives and Records Administration (including serving on the National Archives's FBI Records Appraisal Task Force in 1981); and was appointed the FBI's first official historian (serving from 1984 to 1992). Rosenfeld is the author or editor of *Advice and Assent: The Development of the Maryland Assembly, 1635–1689* (1986), *Federal History*

Programs: A Guide for Heads of Government Agencies (1987), *Conducting Research in FBI Records* (1984–1992), *Significant Dates in FBI History* (1985–1992), *The History of the J. Edgar Hoover FBI Building* (1987, 1992), and *Abridged History of the FBI* (1992). She has also published numerous articles in scholarly and FBI journals, including *The Chronicle of Higher Education, Dictionary of American Biography, The Investigator, Maryland Historical Magazine, William and Mary Quarterly*, (Organization of American Historians) *Newsletter, Reviews in American History*, and (Conference on Women's History) *Newsletter*. Rosenfeld has received numerous research grants and was specially commended by the National Archives for her service on the FBI Records Appraisal Task Force and for her Survey of Machine-Readable Records. She is currently completing a history of federal surveillance since World War II.

Athan G. Theoharis received his Ph.D. in history from the University of Chicago. He is currently a professor of history at Marquette University. Theoharis is the author or editor of *Anatomy of Anti-Communism* (1969), *The Yalta Myths: An Issue in U.S. Politics, 1945–1955* (1970), *Seeds of Repression: Harry S. Truman and the Origins of McCarthyism* (1971), *The Specter: Original Essays on the Cold War and the Origins of McCarthyism* (1974), *The United States in the Twentieth Century* (1978), *Spying on Americans: Political Surveillance from Hoover to the Huston Plan* (1978), *The Truman Presidency: The Origins of the Imperial Presidency and the National Security State* (1979), *Beyond the Hiss Case: The FBI, Congress, and the Cold War* (1982), *Imperial Democracy: The United States since 1945*

(1982, 1988), *The Boss: J. Edgar Hoover and the Great American Inquisition* (1988), *From the Secret Files of J. Edgar Hoover* (1991), *The FBI: An Annotated Bibliography and Research Guide* (1994), *J. Edgar Hoover, Sex, and Crime: An Historical Antidote* (1995), and *A Culture of Secrecy: The Government versus the People's Right to Know* (1998). He has also edited nine discrete FBI files on microfilm (ranging from former FBI Director Hoover's secret office file to the FBI's sensitive break-in, wiretap, and bugging files) and has published numerous articles in popular and scholarly journals, including *Political Science Quarterly, Journal of American History, Nation, Intellect, USA Today, Judges' Journal, Wayne Law Review, Cornell Law Review, First Principles, Rights, OAH Newsletter* (Organization of American Historians), *Chicago Journalism Review, Journalism History, Dictionary of American Biography, Encyclopedia of the Presidency, Encyclopedia of the American Legislative System, Encyclopedia of American Foreign Policy, Author's Guild Bulletin, Access Reports, Midwestern Archivist, Public Historian, Crime and Justice: A Historical Review, Criminal Justice Review, History Teacher*, and *Government Publications Review*. Theoharis has received numerous research grants, and his books and articles were awarded the Outstanding Book Selection (Gustavus Myer Center), Achievement Certificate (Wisconsin Library Association), Gavel Award Certificate (American Bar Association), and Binkley-Stephenson Award (Organization of American Historians). He is currently writing a history of the FBI from 1939 through 1956.

INTRODUCTION

The Federal Bureau of Investigation has emerged during the twentieth century as a powerful agency—playing a central role in law enforcement and the maintenance of domestic internal security while shaping American popular culture and reflecting the public's changing concerns about law enforcement.

Until the 1980s, few scholarly publications based on research in FBI records have comprehensively surveyed the agency's history, its important personalities and cases, the controversies in which it has been involved, or its portrayal in the media and in popular culture. For the most part, the books, articles, comics, radio and television shows, and movies about FBI cases and its long-time director, J. Edgar Hoover, have covered only the "public" activities of the FBI—chiefly, its investigation of suspected federal crimes. Until the late 1970s, media stories and movies rarely covered the FBI's "secret" activities, such as intelligence-gathering on the legal activities of citizens and the purposeful disruption of targeted political activities and organizations.

Moreover, before the 1970s, most books published about the FBI were written by journalists or former FBI agents and officials. Their writings present either incomplete or slanted versions of the FBI's history, based on the authors' limited understanding of the FBI's various programs and procedures or guided by the purposeful assistance of high-level FBI officials. However, the absence of scholarly, research-based history and analysis was due neither to indifference nor to a pro-FBI bias—the necessary information simply was not available.

Prior to the enactment of key amendments to the Freedom of Information Act (FOIA) in 1974, prospective historians of the FBI could not research FBI records. Not a single FBI document had been deposited in the National Archives until the late 1970s. The 1974 FOIA amendments enabled researchers to obtain, for the first time, specified FBI files. This increased accessibility of FBI records did not, however, lead immediately to a more comprehensive and nuanced portrayal of the FBI and the contributions of its agents and officials.

The FOIA's exemption from release of (1) classified information, (2) information that might reveal FBI sources or methods, and (3) information that might violate the privacy rights of individuals referenced in FBI records, as well as the cost of obtaining FBI documents under the FOIA (processing fees are 10 cents per page), has made it necessary for research projects either to be narrowly conceived or to rely on heavily censored records. The result has been an uneven elucidation of the FBI's history: comparatively complete coverage of the Palmer Raids of 1920 and the John Dillinger case of the 1930s, somewhat slanted accounts of the assassination of President John F. Kennedy (owing to heavily censored records), and virtually nothing about FBI counterintelligence programs or the highly sensitive espionage and organized crime cases of the World War II and Cold War eras. Furthermore, very little has been written about FBI investigations that did not result in prosecution—often because it is difficult to know what organizations and individuals were monitored in FBI operations whose activities were not known outside the Bureau.

Our recent knowledge of FBI practices and procedures has also expanded as the indirect by-product of research not directly related to the FBI. Virtually every recent biographer of an important twentieth-century figure has filed an FOIA request for that person's FBI file. Interestingly, the FBI had compiled files on many well-known individuals—and not because information had been uncovered associating them with criminal activities. The released records provide fascinating information about various people's political and personal activities and the reasons for the FBI's interest in that information.

Individuals with FBI files include composers Leonard Bernstein and Aaron Copland; singers Pete Seeger, John Lennon, and Elvis Presley; Hollywood producers Walt Disney, Frank Capra, and Orson Welles; Hollywood actors Ronald Reagan, Katharine Hepburn, Burt Lancaster, Helen Gahagan Douglas, Rock Hudson, and Frank Sinatra; baseball player Mickey Mantle; Supreme Court justices Abe Fortas, Potter Stewart, and Earl Warren; reporters and columnists Joseph Alsop, Harrison Salisbury, Don Whitehead, and Courtney Ryley Cooper; writers Ernest Hemingway, Lillian Hellman, John Steinbeck, Robert Sherwood, Pearl Buck, Archibald MacLeish, Norman Mailer, Jessica Mitford, Max Lowenthal, and Carl Sandburg; feminists Gloria Steinem and Bella Abzug; and liberal and radical activists Eleanor Roosevelt, Margaret Sanger, Dorothy Day, Adlai Stevenson Jr., John F. Kennedy, Martin Luther King Jr., Norman Thomas, Emma Goldman, and Eugene Dennis.

Despite this recent increase in publications about various facets of the FBI and the agency's investigative and monitoring activities, work has only begun to provide readers with an understanding of the complex reality of the FBI's historic role—synthesizing these disparate and discrete stories to develop an overview that does not treat events or personalities in isolation.

For that reason, *The FBI: A Comprehensive Reference Guide* is written in essay format. Each essay provides an integrated overview of FBI-related developments and personalities, placing in broader context each important

case, legislative or policy decision, personality, media portrayal, or FBI relationship with a president, member of Congress, or law enforcement agency. Scholars with research-based knowledge (see "Contributors") have been commissioned to write the essays that make up this book.

The opening essay on the Bureau's role and powers traces the evolution of the FBI and provides context for understanding the impact of particular cases and the basis for specific controversies, covered in separate chapters. The essay on popular culture surveys the changing public image of the FBI and discusses the more important movies, books, and radio or television shows that helped shape that image. The essays on the FBI's facilities and its organization convey the Bureau's growth, portray the complexity of its mission and organizational structure, and provide needed background to an understanding of the role of bureaucracy in twentieth-century America—as does the essay on relationships, which surveys the evolving character of the FBI's relations with the White House, the attorney general, Congress, and other police agencies. For readers having an interest in specific FBI personalities, the biographies chapter provides useful background information, identifying each individual's status at specific times (helpful to researchers of FBI files in identifying whether a referenced Bureau staff member is an agent, the head of a field office, or a senior FBI official). An extensive chronology lists key events from 1789 to the present.

Numerous photographs throughout the book illustrate the essays, along with graphs and tables that present such key information as annual statistics on personnel and appropriations, addresses and other contact information for FBI field offices, top FBI executives since the agency's founding, and FBI "firsts"—the names and accomplishments of groundbreaking employees. An authoritative annotated bibliography, with separate sections for books, articles, and accessible FBI files, guides readers to additional resources.

To aid the reader seeking information on a specific individual, case, controversy, legislation, or policy, two finding aides are provided: a comprehensive index and a contents listing at the beginning of each essay. For example, the famous pursuit and capture of John Dillinger is covered in the essay on notable cases, but this case had more extensive reverberations: It was a catalyst to the enactment of legislation expanding the FBI's powers during the 1930s, it contributed to the image of the G-man, it helped shape the culture of the FBI, and it was important to the careers of individual agents and officials—thus, it is discussed in the essays on the FBI's role and powers, popular culture, internal traditions, and biographies.

The FBI: A Comprehensive Reference Guide is an invaluable finding aid and reference book that includes never-before-published information on FBI facilities, the FBI's organizational structure, and background information on FBI personalities. It also provides fascinating detail to supplement other sources on twentieth-century America (capturing, for example, the history of anticommunist politics, the nation's changing conceptions of law enforcement, and the evolution of privacy rights).

This *Guide* will be useful not only to those having an interest in the FBI—it will also be an excellent resource for those interested in twentieth-century U.S. history, American popular culture, criminal justice, bureaucracy, national security policy, McCarthyism, states' rights issues, civil liberties, and dissent in general.

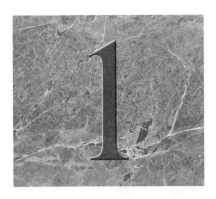

A BRIEF HISTORY OF
THE FBI's ROLE AND POWERS

Athan G. Theoharis

1

Introduction

Created as a minor division of the Department of Justice in July 1908, the Federal Bureau of Investigation (originally named the Bureau of Investigation) grew steadily over the next decades as its role and powers were enlarged. The increase in the FBI's total personnel reflects this: from 34 in 1908 to 23,323 by 1994 (see Table 1.1, page 4). Two complementary developments triggered this growth: (1) Congress enacted legislation that dramatically expanded federal law-enforcement responsibility, and (2) the executive branch became increasingly interested in investigating political radicals and subversives.

Between 1910 and 1996, the United States Congress enacted a series of laws that increasingly regulated personal, political, and economic activities. By expanding the definition of crimes of interstate commerce, Congress extended federal law enforcement responsibilities to areas that previously were exclusively local and state responsibilities (bank robbery, theft, extortion, fraud, and gambling). Other federal laws narrowed the scope of privacy rights by criminalizing such things as the mailing of obscene literature or the crossing of state lines to engage in nonmarital sexual activities. Still other laws proscribed speech and associations that could threaten the existence of the U.S. government or promote the interests of foreign powers (espionage, acting as an agent of a foreign power, engaging in international terrorism, or promoting violent revolution).

The latter national security concerns provided the second catalyst to the FBI's growth. In an effort to anticipate and thereby to preclude "subversive," "communist," and "terrorist" activities—even when such activities violated no federal law—presidents and their attorneys general directed the FBI to investigate individuals and organizations engaged in what others might characterize as political advocacy. To assist in the implementation of various federal employee loyalty and security programs and to provide intelligence (to the White House; to the Justice, State, and War Departments; or to other federal intelligence agencies), the FBI monitored the personal activities and political associations of individuals who were considered a potential threat to the nation's security. FBI officials also disseminated information about the personal lives and political activities of alleged sub-versives to favored members of Congress, congressional committees, news reporters and columnists, and prominent civic and business leaders. These dissemination activities, intended to influence public opinion, were first instituted informally during the 1940s but were refined into formal programs during the 1950s. Thus, the FBI's role

eventually grew beyond law enforcement to include a mission to limit the influence of radical political activists. This "containment" role encountered public and congressional objections during the mid-1970s. Many members of Congress and the public reacted to disclosures of the scope and abuses inherent in the FBI's intelligence mission by demanding tighter restrictions over—and more effective oversight of—the FBI.

The Early Bureau (1908–19)

Creation of the Department of Justice

The framers of the U.S. Constitution of 1787 intended to create a more effective national government than had been possible under the Articles of Confederation, but nonetheless one having limited powers. At first, the federal government's principal role was to promote national economic growth: whether through protective tariffs, land and monetary subsidies to fund road and railroad construction, land grants to state universities to ensure the training of engineers and the teaching of scientific agriculture, or the distribution of federal lands to encourage western settlement and mining. The new federal government was granted the power to tax, to conduct foreign relations and negotiate tariffs, and to raise and maintain a standing army. The scope of these powers, however, was not specifically defined.

The Constitution barred the federal government from intruding on state powers, and although the distinction between federal and state responsibilities was not clearly defined, law enforcement was principally (if not exclusively) a local and state responsibility until the mid-twentieth century. Accordingly, when establishing the positions of secretaries of state, treasury, war, and navy in the 1790s, Congress provided that these secretaries would also head departments and command the personnel essential for fulfilling delegated responsibilities to conduct foreign relations, collect taxes and disburse federal funds, and protect the nation from foreign and Indian attack. In contrast, when authorizing the office of the attorney general in 1789, Congress did not create an associated department. The U.S. attorney general's responsibilities were simply to represent the federal government in cases before the Supreme Court and to advise the president and the cabinet on the constitutionality of proposed legislation.

However, federal responsibilities changed during the late nineteenth century in response to the nation's rapid industrialization, the attendant rise of large national corporations, and the development of a nationwide transportation system that broke down regional barriers. Congress enacted legislation regulating business, its actions reflecting a growing conviction that local and state regulation could not alone advance societal interests. Railroad rates were regulated (the Interstate Commerce Act of 1887), mergers were prohibited that restrained trade or commerce by promoting monopoly (the Sherman Anti-Trust Act of 1890), and obscene literature and advertisements—including literature promoting birth control and abortion—were banned from the postal system (the so-called Comstock Law of 1873).

Enforcement of these laws soon required a new administrative structure: the Department of Justice. When the department was created in 1870, the limited number of federal criminal statutes and the nature of the crimes they proscribed created no immediate need for a special division of skilled investigators. In most cases, when deciding whether to seek indictments, U.S. attorneys themselves could interview witnesses and review relevant documents. In rare situations, when they needed the services of skilled investigators, Justice Department officials temporarily hired private detectives (primarily from the Pinkerton Detective Agency) or relied on operatives from the Secret Service (this Treasury Department agency, created in 1869, investigated violations of pay, bounty, and counterfeiting laws). Congressional actions of 1892 and 1907–08, however, permanently changed the Justice Department's investigation procedures.

Creation of the Bureau of Investigation (1908)

In 1892, Congress responded to revelations that the Pinkerton Detective Agency had been involved in strike-breaking activities during the Homestead strike by enacting legislation prohibiting government agencies from temporarily hiring individuals currently employed in the private sector. Congress's purpose was to prevent conflicts of interest, but its actions meant that the Justice Department could no longer hire private detectives to conduct any needed investigations.

Then, in May 1908, Congress restricted the use of Treasury Department appropriations to enforcing pay, bounty, and counterfeiting laws and to protecting the president (the assigned responsibilities of the Secret Service) following a series of revelations that Secret Service agents had been used by the Navy Department to spy on the amorous activities of a naval officer on leave and by the

Justice Department during a land fraud investigation of two U.S. congressmen from Oregon. This restriction effectively barred the Justice Department from contracting for the services of Secret Service agents.

Concurrently, during congressional hearings on Justice Department appropriations in 1907, and again in 1908, Attorney General Charles Bonaparte (see Exhibit 1.1)

Exhibit 1.1 **Charles J. Bonaparte,** *Courtesy of the FBI*

unsuccessfully attempted to secure funding for a "small detective force" within the Department of Justice. Members of the House Appropriations Subcommittee rejected Bonaparte's requests, some condemning the proposed creation as a "spy system," others warning darkly about the consequences of forming "a general system of espionage . . . conducted by the General [federal] Government," and still others fearing the consequences should executive branch officials "employ secret-service men to dig up the private scandals of men."

After Congress's initial rejection of Bonaparte's funding request in 1907, the Justice Department was not prevented from turning to the Secret Service for investigative assistance—but Bonaparte felt compelled to take action when Congress, in 1908, restricted Secret Service appropriations and again refused to approve his request to fund a special investigative force. Accordingly, on June 29, 1908, Bonaparte hired 10 former Secret Service agents as Justice Department employees and funded this through a "miscellaneous expense fund." Then, on July 26, 1908, Bonaparte appointed Stanley W. Finch to head this new, permanent investigative division within the Department of Justice. At the time, Congress was not in session, having adjourned for that year's presidential and congressional campaigns.

Thus, the establishment of the Bureau of Investigation contravened the spirit of Congress's actions of 1907 and 1908, and Bonaparte's decision alone did not ensure the Bureau's status—Congress could have countered his move by restricting the use of contingency funds or by rescinding the "detection" section of the 1870 statute defining the Justice Department's power.

TABLE 1.1

NUMBER OF FBI PERSONNEL AND FBI APPROPRIATIONS ANNUALLY, 1908–97

Year	Agents	Support Staff [1]	Appropriation
1908	34	—	no figure available
1909	64	—	no figure available
1910	64	9	no figure available
1911	81	33	$329,984 [2]
1912	158 [3]	12	$354,596 [2]
1913	335 [3]	27	$415,452 [2]
1914	122 [3]	39	$455,698 [2]
1915	219 [3]	29	no figure available
1916	234 [3]	26	$510,000 [2]
1917	265	305	$617,534 [2]
1918	225	268	$1,746,224 [2]
1919	301	329	$2,272,658 [2]
1920	579	548	$2,457,104 [2]
1921	346	294	$2,342,751 [2]
1922	401	194	$1,892,077 [2]
1923	401	189	$2,166,997 [2]
1924	441	216	$2,245,000
1925	402	99	$2,184,688
1926	380	237	$2,294,500
1927	386	208	$2,154,280
1928	359	223	$2,250,000
1929	339	242	$2,250,000
1930	400	255	$2,307,720
1931	383	324	$2,781,419
1932	388	433	$2,978,520
1933	353	422	$2,775,000
1934	391	451	$2,589,500
1935	568	714	$4,626,508
1936	609	971	$5,000,000
1937	623	1,064	$5,925,000
1938	658	1,141	$6,223,000
1939	713	1,199	$6,578,076
1940	896	1,545	$8,775,000
1941	1,596 [4]	2,677 [4]	$14,743,300
1942	2,987 [4]	5,000 [4]	$24,965,000
1943	4,591 [4]	7,743 [4]	$38,836,000
1944	4,886 [4]	8,305 [4]	$42,768,000
1945	4,370 [4]	7,422 [4]	$44,197,146
1946	3,754 [4]	6,020 [4]	$37,078,000
1947	3,170 [4]	4,692 [4]	$34,900,000
1948	3,741	5,559	$43,900,000
1949	4,005	5,615	$48,588,709
1950	4,155	5,789	$52,635,919
1951	4,962	6,573	$69,947,000
1952	6,451	8,206	$90,665,000
1953	6,459	7,525	$84,400,000
1954	6,073	7,558	$77,000,000
1955	6,269	8,128	$81,002,000
1956	6,246	7,866	$93,826,000
1957	6,185	7,590	$95,510,000
1958	6,147	7,839	$105,562,000
1959	5,988	7,285	$112,111,000

Year	Agents	Support Staff [1]	Appropriation
1960	5,889	7,862	$114,600,000
1961	5,899	8,062	$125,550,000
1962	5,968	8,147	$127,216,000
1963	6,045	7,942	$135,925,000
1964	6,142	8,220	$146,900,000
1965	6,336	8,533	$161,080,000
1966	6,508	8,948	$169,100,000
1967	6,675	9,399	$182,325,000
1968	6,703	9,320	$194,986,000
1969	7,177	9,233	$219,670,000
1970	7,600	10,428	$256,857,000
1971	8,548	11,130	$294,565,000
1972	8,659	11,252	$336,116,000
1973	8,767	11,357	$358,915,000
1974	8,658	11,122	$392,294,000
1975	8,441	10,846	$449,546,000
1976	8,619	11,405	$485,950,000 [5]
1977	8,149	11,203	$513,377,000
1978	7,931	11,547	$553,954,000
1979	7,800	10,780	$584,483,000
1980	7,857	10,562	$621,942,000
1981	7,751	10,582	$680,723,000
1982	7,885	11,234	$767,009,000
1983	8,340	11,362	$854,254,000
1984	8,760	12,013	$1,063,936,000
1985	8,925	11,940	$1,160,388,000
1986	9,012	12,541	$1,156,143,000
1987	9,434	12,910	$1,303,989,000
1988	9,640	13,570	$1,401,492,000
1989	9,599	13,463	$1,439,100,000
1990	9,851	12,729	$1,684,444,000
1991	10,314	13,369	$1,697,121,000
1992	10,479	14,118	$1,927,231,000
1993	10,273	13,834	$2,007,423,000
1994	9,785	13,538	$2,038,705,000
1995	10,285	13,797	$2,138,781,000
1996	10,702	14,602	$2,307,201,000
1997	10,074	13,611	$2,548,583,000

Notes

1. Support staff includes clerks; craft and maintenance workers; technicians; secretaries at FBI field offices, resident agencies, foreign liaison offices, and FBI headquarters at Washington, D.C.; and some administrators at FBI headquarters.
2. Prior to 1924, Congress did not specifically appropriate funds for Bureau personnel and operations. These were funded out of appropriations to promote Justice Department "detection and prosecution of crimes." These figures thus might overstate or understate Bureau expenditures: overstate, in that not all the funds appropriated for the "detection and prosecution of crimes" were necessarily allocated to the Bureau; understate, in that some Bureau operations may have been funded through other appropriations to the Department of Justice.
3. Prior to 1917, Bureau personnel were not broken down into the categories of agents and support staff, with the latter including clerks, secretaries, and technicians, as well as supervisors. Such employees were included within the agent figure.
4. FBI employees assigned to the Special Intelligence Service (SIS) to conduct foreign intelligence operations in South America were listed under the agent and support staff categories for the years 1941 through 1947.
5. Prior to 1976, the federal government's fiscal year ran from July 1 through June 30. In 1976, the fiscal year was changed to run from October 1 through September 30. Accordingly, Congress approved a special transitional appropriation of $128,741,000 to fund FBI operations for the period July 1, 1976, through September 30, 1976.

Appearing before a House Appropriations Subcommittee in January 1909, Bonaparte justified his independent action while attempting to allay concerns that this new bureau would monitor political and personal activities. He characterized the detective force as "absolutely indispensable to the proper discharge of the duties" of the Justice Department. Investigations conducted by this force, moreover, would be confined to uncovering violations of antitrust, postal, and banking laws, or involving criminal acts directed at the federal government, therefore, Congress need not enact legislation defining the scope of Bureau investigations. Such micromanagement, he argued, would also contravene sound administration, as the attorney general was responsible for ensuring that agents would not stray beyond their law enforcement mission to monitor personal and political conduct. Bonaparte had no objection, however, to Congress limiting the use of appropriated funds to the "detection and prosecution of crimes against the United States." In addition to antitrust violations, these involved postal fraud, impersonation of government officials with intent to defraud, thefts and murders committed on Indian reservations, destruction of government property, and violation of federal banking laws. In 1909, Congress adopted this limitation, but in 1910, the restriction was lifted, and Congress permitted the use of appropriated funds "for such other investigations regarding official matters under the control of the Department of Justice as may be directed by the Attorney General."

Congress's relaxed standard for Justice Department investigations was triggered by its action in 1910, and then again in 1919, expanding the definition of interstate commerce crimes. Technology, the sharp increase in immigration dating from the 1880s, and an internal population flow from rural America to the nation's cities caused many in Congress and in the broader public to question whether local and state police could adequately protect societal interests in curbing crime. With these increased federal responsibilities for law enforcement, congressional funding for Bureau activities was increased 7-fold from $329,984 in 1911 (the earliest date for which appropriations can be estimated) to $2,457,104 in 1920, and the number of agents increased 17-fold from 34 in 1908 to 579 in 1920 (see Table 1.1).

The Mann Act (1910) and the Dyer Act (1919)

In 1910, Congress enacted the White Slave Traffic Act (or Mann Act). The Mann Act made it a federal crime to transport women across state lines "for the purpose of prostitution, or for any other immoral purpose." Enacted to curb organized prostitution, the act reflected the concerns at that time that young rural women attracted to the exciting life of the nation's cities were being lured into prostitution, and further, that local and state police alone could not safeguard community morals and protect innocent but vulnerable women. The act's chief proponent, Congressman James Mann, starkly warned that "most of these girls are enticed away from their homes in the country to large cities. The police power exercised by the State and municipal governments is inadequate to prevent this—particularly when girls are enticed from one State to another."

In contrast to other interstate commerce and antitrust investigations, which involved publicized corporate rate practices or mergers and thus could be triggered by Justice Department officials in Washington, D.C., violations of the Mann Act could be uncovered best through the initiative of Bureau agents. In addition, such investigations necessitated the stationing of Bureau agents outside Washington, D.C., in the nation's larger cities. Bureau agents visited known houses of prostitution to solicit the cooperation of their owners and employees in identifying either clients or the local political and police officials who illegally provided protection. Over time, agents acquired vast amounts of sensitive information that bore little relationship to the development of federal criminal cases—since political payoffs or the prominence of customers were not directly prohibited by the act.

The number of Mann Act investigations increased steadily, abating temporarily in 1917 following U.S. involvement in World War I and the priority assigned to espionage investigations. They intensified after the war during the moralistic 1920s, but were reduced thereafter, first because of the adverse public and press reaction to FBI Director J. Edgar Hoover's controversial leadership of vice squad raids in 1937 and 1940 in Miami, Florida, and second because of changed priorities for the Bureau created by the crises of World War II and the Cold War.

The Bureau's role expanded further with the passage of the Motor Vehicle Theft Act (or Dyer Act) in 1919. Enacted at a time of a surge in the sale of automobiles—with an attendant increase in auto theft crimes—the act authorized

Bureau investigations whenever stolen automobiles were transported across state lines. Like the Mann Act, the Dyer Act reflected concerns that local and state police officials lacked the resources and capabilities to apprehend interstate criminals.

The Dyer Act proved to be a public relations bonanza for the Bureau of Investigation. Bureau officials, on their own and through cooperation with local police, were able to compile an impressive record of arrests and recovered property. During 1922 congressional testimony, Bureau Director William Burns emphasized that the value of stolen automobiles recovered by the Bureau "amounts to more than our appropriations," and Director J. Edgar Hoover in 1970 cited the FBI's impressive record of recovering 30,599 stolen vehicles the previous year and winning convictions in 3,694 stolen vehicle cases.

World War I and Internal Security Concerns (1914–19)

The outbreak of war in Europe in 1914, and U.S. involvement beginning in April 1917, further increased the Bureau's stature and role. Since 1914, many German Americans, Irish Americans, pacifists, socialists, and radical labor union activists had vociferously opposed U.S. involvement in the military conflict between England, France, and Russia and the Central Powers of Germany and Austria-Hungary. Congress's declaration of war on the Central Powers on April 6, 1917, did not silence this dissent, and the administration of President Woodrow Wilson feared that its efforts to mobilize the nation—to ensure an effective military role quickly (and at a time when a German military breakthrough seemed imminent)—could be weakened by continued domestic opposition. Opposition to the nation's war effort could also undermine support for the potentially controversial policies of raising a conscript army and increasing federal spending (from a prewar annual average of $750 million, the federal budget rose to $12.5 billion by 1918 and to over $18 billion by 1919).

Moreover, the administration feared that the Central Powers might recruit American citizens and alien residents to commit espionage and sabotage (given the large immigrant population in the United States, immigrants from Europe having averaged one million annually during the years 1900–14). Prior to 1917, Bureau agents had investigated suspected German agents (including German consular officials) who, it was thought, might sabotage the shipment of military goods from Canada and the United States.

American ports and factories were monitored when, between 1915 and 1917, explosive devices were discovered on 47 ships bound for Allied countries, and suspicious fires of July 30, 1916, and January 11, 1917, exploded a munitions dump at Black Tom Island (in New York City's harbor) and a munitions firm in Kingsland, New Jersey. Suspecting that the Black Tom explosion was the work of German operatives, Congress appropriated funds in 1916 for Bureau investigations of foreign-directed activities when requested by the Department of State.

U.S. involvement in World War I intensified concerns about foreign sabotage and influence. In response, Congress enacted the Espionage Act of 1917. This law proscribed the stealing of government secrets with the intent of aiding the nation's enemies, required the fingerprinting and registration of alien residents from enemy nations, and prohibited oral and written statements that "willfully" or "falsely" "interfere[d] with the operation or success of the military or naval forces of the United States or to promote the success of its enemies . . . cause insubordination, disloyalty, mutiny, or refusal of duty" within the armed services or "willfully obstruct" military recruitment. Congress also enacted the Selective Service Act of 1917 (requiring men aged 21 to 30 to register to be drafted for military service); the Sedition Act of 1918 (forbidding oral or written expression of "any disloyal, profane, scurrilous, or abusive language" about the U.S. government, Constitution, or armed services, "or any language intended to . . . encourage resistance to the United States, or promote the cause of its enemies"); and the Immigration Act of 1918 (requiring the deportation of alien residents who were members of organizations promoting anarchy or violent revolution).

Armed with these new federal laws to strengthen the nation's internal security, Bureau investigations secured the convictions of over 2,000 individuals—but none involved espionage or sabotage by German operatives or their American sympathizers. Instead, Bureau investigations focused on members of labor unions, members of the Socialist Party, and pro-German and pro-Irish activists (the latter because of the Irish rebellion of 1916 to obtain independence from Great Britain). Owing to the Espionage Act's broad restrictions, those convicted even included the producer of a Hollywood movie on the American Revolution—*The Spirit of '76*—a film that portrayed the nation's wartime ally, Great Britain, in a negative light.

The Bureau's personnel, however, did not increase proportionately with these newly acquired internal security responsibilities. Justice Department officials, for budgetary reasons and because they believed that the need for investigators was only temporary, did not dramatically expand the permanent force of agents (between 1917 and 1919, total personnel increased from 570 to 630; see Table 1.1). Instead, on March 22, 1917, Bureau Chief A. Bruce Bielaski (with Attorney General Thomas Gregory's consent) implemented a liaison relationship with the American Protective League (APL), a conservative businessmen's organization headquartered in Chicago, in which APL members agreed to obtain "information of activities of agents of foreign Governments or persons unfriendly to this Government for the protection of public property, etc." In actuality, however, APL members uncovered no instances of espionage, but instead monitored radical, antiwar, and trade union activities. In their most controversial action, in September 1918, APL members (who had no authority to make arrests and falsely represented themselves as Secret Service operatives) assisted Bureau agents in arresting thousands of New Yorkers suspected of violating the Selective Service Act of 1917 (see pages 104–05).

The Bolshevik Revolution in Russia of November 1917 and the revolutionary government's funding of the Third International (proclaiming the inevitability of worldwide revolution) further heightened Wilson administration interest in the plans and activities of American radicals. These concerns seemed justified following a series of bombing attempts in 1919. In one case, a bomb exploded at the home of Attorney General A. Mitchell Palmer, and in a second case, New York postal authorities discovered 24 bombs addressed to prominent business and civic leaders. On August 1, 1919, Attorney General Palmer created a special Radical Division (subsequently renamed the General Intelligence Division, GID) to collect and collate all information about radical political activities uncovered by the Bureau of Investigation, other government agencies (the State Department's consular service and military and naval intelligence), local police, and patriotic organizations and citizens. Palmer appointed an attorney in the Justice Department's anti-radical alien enemy unit, J. Edgar Hoover, to head the GID.

The GID quickly amassed over 200,000 dossiers on radical activists and organizations, on the role of radicals in the 1919 steel and coal strikes, on some 500 foreign-language newspapers (to keep up with "radical propaganda"), and also on progressive senator and antiwar critic Robert La Follette, settlement house reformer and pacifist Jane Addams, the pro-Irish *Chicago Tribune* and Hearst newspapers, militant black nationalist and founder of the Universal Negro Improvement Association (UNIA) Marcus Garvey, members and officers of the National Association for the Advancement of Colored People (NAACP), and editors of black newspapers and periodicals whom Bureau officials suspected were "exciting the negro element of this country to riot and to the committing of outrages of all sorts."

The GID was created to promote an intensified antiradical campaign that Bureau Director William Flynn initiated in April 1919. Flynn had ordered "a vigorous and comprehensive" investigation of all anarchists, communists, and "kindred" alien resident agitators. Cognizant that the Bureau's authority to investigate radicals would terminate with the formal end of the war (the Espionage and Sedition Acts applied only during wartime and required proof of intent to assist the nation's enemies), Flynn nonetheless ordered agents to secure evidence "which may be of use in prosecutions under the present existing statutes or under legislation of that nature which may hereinafter be enacted."

Flynn may have expected that Congress would eventually enact a peacetime sedition law, but without it, the burgeoning Bureau files on radical activities supported no official Justice Department responsibility. Such information, however, could be used by Immigration Bureau officials seeking to deport alien radicals under provisions of the 1917 and 1918 immigration laws. Accordingly, on November 7, 1919, Bureau of Investigation agents raided the offices of the Union of Russian Workers (URW) in New York and 11 other cities. Relying on GID reports summarizing the URW leaders' advocacy of anarchism and violent revolution, Immigration Bureau officials were able to deport 249 of the arrestees on December 21, 1919.

Abuse of Power and Scandal (1920–24)

The Palmer Raids (1920)

The URW raid and deportation proceedings precipitated a second and more massive coordinated attempt to curb radical activities. For this objective, the alien deportation provision of the 1918 immigration statute continued to prove useful. Bureau investigative reports could assist Immigration officials in deporting alien radicals, and the results of this cooperative effort could also help promote interest in the peacetime sedition legislation the Bureau hoped would be enacted—arresting large numbers of alien radicals would publicize the seriousness of the radical threat. Accordingly, Bureau of Investigation officials worked closely with their counterparts in the Bureau of Immigration to implement a plan that relied on the simultaneous arrest of members of the Communist and Communist Labor Parties, organizations proscribed by the attorney general, both of which had many alien members and both of which followed the Russian Bolsheviks in proclaiming the necessity of violent revolution.

Attorney General A. Mitchell Palmer did not personally engineer the so-called Palmer Raids of January 2 and 6, 1920. Only after the raids were conducted did Palmer attempt to ride the initially favorable publicity (based on the belief that a radical revolutionary threat had been aborted) to the Democratic presidential nomination that summer. The principal strategists, instead, were Bureau of Immigration head Anthony Caminetti and GID head J. Edgar Hoover. To ensure maximum effect, Bureau of Investigation agents, who had infiltrated both communist organizations, ensured that their local branches held meetings on the night of January 2—enhancing the numbers of those who could be arrested. In addition, Caminetti convinced Acting Secretary of Labor John Abercrombie (enforcement of the immigration laws was a Labor Department responsibility) to revise departmental rules to permit the use of "telegraphic warrants" (blank arrest warrants with the name of the alien to be filled in by the arresting officer) and to suspend a provision known as Rule 22 (which would have provided arrested aliens the right to legal counsel during deportation hearings).

On the night of January 2, 1920, Bureau of Investigation and Immigration Bureau agents, assisted by local police, simultaneously arrested 4,000 Communist Party and Communist Labor Party members and sympathizers in 33 cities. To ensure success and preserve the element of surprise, between 6,000 and 10,000 individuals were taken into custody that night and in a follow-up raid on January 6, including many who were either citizens (and thus not subject to deportation) or were not actually members of these organizations (these individuals were released without undergoing interrogation in the hastily assembled deportation hearings).

Initially, the Palmer Raids received positive publicity. Reporters were invited to view and photograph the unkempt and bearded radicals (confirming the stereotypical image of mad bombers). Photocopies of radical publications were released to the press, seemingly confirming that the arrestees were planning a violent revolution. Press reports glowingly characterized the raids not as deportation proceedings but as the successful containment of a potential revolutionary threat. Indeed, the *New York Times* article on the raids was headlined "Revolution Smashed"; its article praised the "clarity, resolute will, and fruitful intelligence" of those planning the raids, while the legal periodical *Bench and Bar* affirmed that "the need for repression is great, and the time for repression is now" and Massachusetts Secretary of State Albert Langley proclaimed, "If I had my way, I'd take them out in the yard every morning to shoot them, and the next day would have a trial to see whether they were guilty."

Within weeks, however, the tide shifted. On January 26, Secretary of Labor William Wilson reinstated Rule 22, precluding Immigration Bureau officials from using statements obtained from the arrested aliens during interrogations conducted without the presence of legal counsel. In addition, Assistant Secretary of Labor Louis Post, after examining the rationale for deporting the arrestees, and concluding that the law's standard of "knowing membership" had not been met, ordered the release of the vast majority of arrestees (only 556 of the original 4,000 arrestees were eventually deported). Then, in May 1920, the liberal National Popular Government League published the findings of 12 distinguished lawyers who had reviewed the planning and execution of the raids. Titled *Report Upon the Illegal Practices of the United States Department of Justice*, this booklet detailed the "continued violation of [the] Constitution and breaking of . . . Laws by the Department of Justice" in the execution of the raids and their aftermath. The Bureau's use of *agent provocateurs* and the lack of legal authority to enforce immigration laws were sharply criticized, as were the inhumane conditions under which many of the detainees were held.

Congress's attempt during that period to impeach Assistant Secretary of Labor Post also backfired. Attorney General Palmer had publicly denounced Post's rulings (which led to the release of the vast majority of Palmer Raid arrestees) as threatening the nation's security—criticisms that precipitated a congressional impeachment inquiry of Post's conduct. During the resultant hearings conducted by the House Rules Committee in May, Post rebutted his critics, and in the process highlighted the Bureau's abusive conduct in planning and executing raids. A companion

Senate Judiciary Committee inquiry denounced Palmer's "deliberate misuse of his office," and observed that he had abandoned the prosecution of suspected violators of federal statutes to go "into the field of propaganda against radicals." Combined, the negative post-raid publicity tarnished the Bureau's reputation. Moreover, instead of enacting peace-time sedition legislation as Bureau officials had hoped, in 1921 Congress repealed the Sedition Act of 1918. Addition-ally, after 1920, Bureau appropriations and personnel were reduced, although not to the prewar level (see Table 1.1).

Investigating Strikers, Communists, and Other Radicals

Rebuffed in the attempt to expand their investigative authority, Bureau officials nonetheless continued monitoring political radicals, trade union activists, and civil rights activists, in part because they were convinced that the arrest of Communist and Communist Labor Party members during the Palmer Raids had resulted in "a marked cessation of radical activities in the United States." Responding to the flurry of trade union strikes that threatened to paralyze the economy in 1919, Bureau agents sought to ascertain the role of radicals in agitating labor unrest and to determine whether labor organizing and strike activities were a forerunner to a planned revolutionary overthrow of the U.S. economic system. Indeed, in October 1920, GID Director J. Edgar Hoover broadened the role of his division from its original focus on "radical activities in the United States and abroad" to cover "the studying of matters of an international nature, as well as economic and industrial disturbances incident thereto."

Bureau officials were also concerned about the upsurge of protest activities by black Americans during the postwar period, culminating in the race riots that erupted in 26 cities during the summer of 1919. Convinced that the NAACP's encouragement of black protest was influenced by commu-nists and that the militant black nationalist Marcus Garvey upheld "Soviet Russian rule" and endorsed Bolshevism, Bureau agents closely monitored the NAACP's and Garvey's activities. The Bureau failed to uncover any evidence of criminal conduct by the NAACP. At first seeking to ensure Garvey's deportation (he was an alien resident), Bureau officials eventually secured his conviction in 1923 for mail fraud during his administration of the Black Star steamship line and other business enterprises he had formed to promote economic independence among black Americans.

Bureau investigations of the white supremacist Ku Klux Klan had a similar result. The Bureau began investigating the Klan in response to Louisiana governor John Parker's protest that state authorities were unable to curb the increas-ingly powerful Klan. Stymied by Southern juries' refusals to return indictments against Klan members for a series murders, Bureau officials shifted tactics and secured the March 1924 conviction of Klan leader Edward Y. Clarke for violating the Mann Act (see page 47).

No comparable statutes permitted the use of the Bureau's extensive files on radical political activists. Accordingly, Bureau officials sought other ways to use this intelligence. Information uncovered about communist influence and the labor movement's organizational strategies was shared with business leaders (thereby providing them with helpful intelligence about union organizers). In September 1922, moreover, Bureau agents investigated members of the railroad workers union. That month, Attorney General Harry Daugherty obtained a sweeping injunction against the union for promoting a nationwide railroad strike. The strike was broken when the Bureau identified over 1,200 workers who were then arrested for violating the court's anti-strike injunction.

Bureau officials also assisted state officials. Having learned of Communist Party plans to hold a secret national convention on a farm near Bridgman, Michigan, Bureau agents raided the meeting on August 22, 1922, seizing party records and capturing some of the individuals in attendance. Since no federal law had been broken, Bureau officials turned over this information to the Michigan state police, who unsuccessfully sought to convict party secretary Charles Ruthenberg and the party's liaison to the labor movement, William Foster, under state laws against anar-chism and syndicalism. Bureau officials also shared this information with Richard Whitney (the director of the American Defense Society), who wrote a series of articles for the *Boston Evening Transcript*. Although failing to secure convictions in the Bridgman case, the Bureau's cooperative assistance with other state authorities (notably in New York and Arizona) did result in 115 convictions of communists by 1922 under state anti-anarchist and anti-syndicalist statutes.

The Teapot Dome Scandal (1923–24)

In 1923, a Senate committee initiated an investigation, championed by Democratic senators Burton Wheeler and Thomas Walsh, into Secretary of the Interior Albert Fall's decision to lease to businessmen Edward Doheny and Harry Sinclair—without competitive bidding—oil reserves in Teapot Dome, Wyoming, and Elk Hills, California. Suspecting collusion, the senators questioned whether Fall had been bribed and why Attorney General Daugherty had quashed a Justice Department investigation into this deal.

Prior to the inception of the committee's hearings, Bureau Director Burns dispatched agents to Montana to uncover any damaging information about Wheeler. Bureau operatives also closely monitored Wheeler's and Walsh's activities in Washington, D.C., including tapping their phones, opening their mail, and breaking into their offices and homes to gather information. These latter surveillance activities were uncovered during publicized congressional hearings, as was the Bureau's monitoring of other congressional critics of the Harding administration—Senators Robert La Follette, Thaddeus Caraway, and William Borah and congressmen Roy Woodruff and Oscar Keller. To stanch this scandal, President Calvin Coolidge (who became president in August 1923 following Harding's death) demanded Attorney General Daugherty's resignation. Daugherty's replacement, Harlan F. Stone, fired Bureau Director Burns on May 9, 1924.

Reform and Retrenchment (1924–32)

J. Edgar Hoover Appointed Director (1924)

Attorney General Stone quickly sought to restore public confidence in the Bureau and to squelch the evolving political scandal. In addition to firing Bureau Director Burns, he dissolved the GID (formally ending what was to have been a wartime program), banned wiretapping, and issued new guidelines intended to preclude any future political spying by the Bureau. Henceforth, Bureau investigations were to be confined to enforcing federal laws, and noncriminal information would not be shared with business leaders and state authorities. The Bureau would not be "concerned with political or other opinions of individuals . . . only with their conduct and then only with such conduct as is forbidden by the laws of the United States." A properly restrained federal investigative capability, Stone argued, was essential to law enforcement, given the "enormous expansion of Federal legislation, both civil and criminal, in recent years."

Last, to ensure tighter discipline within the Bureau's ranks and a more professional staff, on May 10, 1924, Stone appointed then Assistant Director J. Edgar Hoover as acting director of the Bureau (see Exhibit 1.2). Stone made this appointment permanent in December 1924, having been impressed by Hoover's leadership in implementing the ordered reforms.

Exhibit 1.2　**J. Edgar Hoover,** *Courtesy of the National Archives (65-H-369-1)*

Hoover had a reputation of being a stern taskmaster. Although involved in the planning and execution of the Palmer Raids and in the surveillance of Senator Wheeler, he had done so as a loyal subordinate who was obligated to comply with the orders of his superiors.

Because of the prevailing belief that the Teapot Dome scandal stemmed from the ability of individuals of low character to act independently, Hoover's unquestioned integrity and demanding leadership were expected to result in the needed administrative reforms. The new Bureau director immediately initiated a house-cleaning in Bureau ranks, firing time-servers and part-time employees (many of whom were political appointees and viewed their Bureau posts as opportunities for self-enrichment). In addition, stricter hiring standards were instituted consistent with Attorney General Stone's requirements: individuals of "known character and ability, giving preference to men who have some legal training."

Administrative Reforms

Hoover inherited an agency steeped in scandal and inspiring little public confidence, at a time when a fiscally conservative Republican administration and Congress demanded reduced federal spending. The new Bureau director responded astutely to these political realities. By the end of 1924, 62 employees had been dismissed, 5 of the Bureau's 53 field offices were closed, and $300,000 of that year's $2.4 million appropriation was returned to the U.S. Treasury. Hoover further reduced the force levels between 1924 and 1929 from 441 agents and 216 support staff to 339 agents and 242 support staff (the increased support staff was to ensure stricter supervision); Bureau appropriations remained essentially unchanged ($2,245,000 in 1924 and

$2,250,000 in 1929). By 1932, the number of Bureau field offices was reduced further to 22. Higher standards for Bureau appointments were imposed, and a special training school for new agents established in the New York field office (training responsibility was transferred to the Washington, D.C., field office in 1928 then to a specially created training facility in Quantico, Virginia, in 1972). Sensitive to prevailing states' rights beliefs, in 1924 Hoover established a nationwide Fingerprint Division (a clearinghouse enabling local police to identify criminals who had committed crimes in other locales) and in 1932 a Crime Laboratory that employed the latest technology to identify crime suspects and their methods. By 1974, 159,000,000 sets of fingerprints had been amassed, with the collection increasing at the rate of 3,000 sets a day.

New rules were issued to ensure a more disciplined and professional corps. Agents had to meet rigorous dress, deportment, and personal conduct standards. Appointments were removed from political influence, and clear rules were established to evaluate agent performance. A *Manual of Regulation* was provided to agents to proscribe standards for the conduct of investigations, and the Bureau director advised agents and heads of field offices (special agents in charge, SACs) of new or revised rules (through the *SAC Letter* and the *Bureau Bulletin*). A special inspection division was established to ensure compliance with these rules, and derelict agents and heads of field offices were given letters of reprimand for poor performance—and were fired for serious breaches or repeated rules violations.

Hoover's administrative reforms refurbished the Bureau's image, in part because they corresponded to the priorities shaping the conservative politics of the 1920s stressing efficiency, rationality, and limited government. The Bureau's fingerprint clearinghouse division, for example, embodied these priorities: An essential service was provided—applying technology to solving crimes—a service that local and state police could not replicate. The Bureau's role was limited and consistent with states' rights principles: promoting cooperation among geographically dispersed and independent local police agencies at the same time that law enforcement remained a local and state responsibility.

Another Bureau practice, instituted in 1930, also promoted local law enforcement. An annual summary of crime statistics, *Uniform Crime Reports*, was compiled and published, thereby providing local and state police (and the public and Congress, since the annual statistics were extensively reported) with quantified evidence of crime trends and the incidence of serious crime.

The Bureau of the 1920s, thus, was a leaner, more professional agency—yet a minor player in the field of law enforcement. This constricted role did not mean that the Bureau's interest in radical political activities had been abandoned. Bureau agents continued to monitor radical activists and organizations. In addition, reports detailing political activities and associations volunteered by a conservative citizenry were welcomed. Bureau officials also accommodated the political interests of Presidents Calvin Coolidge and Herbert Hoover. In October 1931, for example, Bureau Director Hoover initiated an intimidating investigation of George Menhinick, the editor of a financial newsletter whom President Hoover believed was contributing to financial panic (following the stock market crash of October 1929, a severe economic depression occurred). In 1932, Bureau agents infiltrated the so-called Bonus March (thousands of World War I veterans converged on Washington, D.C., to pressure Congress to pay their veterans' bonuses that year, rather than in 1945) and sought information that the beleaguered president (up for reelection) could use to discredit the marchers as criminals or communists.

These practices were exceptional, however. During the 1920s, Bureau activities primarily involved law enforcement. This did not include enforcing Prohibition—a special Prohibition Bureau having been established for that purpose—but Prohibition had promoted a climate of lawlessness and was one element that catalyzed the growth of crime gangs. Warring gangs engaged in violent turf battles, which seemed to demonstrate the inability or lack of will of local police agencies to curb this crime menace. Although an alarmed citizenry demanded a more effective policing role, these demands did not automatically lead to an expansion of the Bureau's powers.

The New Deal Era (1932–39)

The stock market crash of October 1929 and the ensuing Great Depression through the 1930s ushered in a new era in American politics and changes in the role and powers of the Bureau of Investigation. In the 1932 presidential election, Franklin Delano Roosevelt, the Democratic nominee, decisively defeated Republican incumbent Herbert Hoover. Following his inauguration, Roosevelt exploited the political and economic crisis of the depression to steer through Congress a series of laws to promote economic recovery and alleviate social and economic distress. This so-called

New Deal rejected an earlier policy of laissez-faire, limited federal government wherein the private sector was ceded primary responsibility for managing economic growth and setting the standards governing prices, production, hours and wages, pensions, and labor negotiations. The New Deal unleashed a further assault on the prevailing states' rights tradition, as increasingly the federal government assumed social welfare responsibilities, formerly the province of the states. And, because the economic crisis of the Great Depression occurred at a time of a sharp increase in crime, New Deal principles rejecting limited government also revolutionized law enforcement.

During the Prohibition Era of the 1920s, notorious gangsters seemed to violate the law with impunity, frustrating the efforts of local and state police to maintain law and order. Then, during the early 1930s, a series of highly publicized kidnappings and bank robberies lent further credence to fears that local and state police were incapable of protecting the public. An expanded federal role seemed essential to resolving the nation's crime problem—and not simply as a clearinghouse and coordinator. Thus, between 1932 and 1939, Bureau personnel and appropriations more than doubled: from 801 (of which 388 were agents) to 1,912 (of which 713 were agents) and from $2,978,520 to $6,578,076 (see Table 1.1). Agents acquired the popular identity of the G-man: the highly professional and apolitical hero who "always got his man." The Bureau's professionalism contrasted sharply with the popular image of overwhelmed state and local police forces, seemingly unable to protect the citizenry from the criminal exploits of brazen and violent gangsters.

The Lindbergh and Dillinger Cases and the G-Man

On March 1, 1932, the young son of famed aviator Charles Lindbergh and his wealthy wife, Anne Morrow Lindbergh, was kidnapped from the family estate at Hopewell, New Jersey. The kidnapper demanded a $50,000 ransom, which the Lindberghs paid on April 2 in return for information on the location of their child. The information proved to be false, and on May 12, the Lindbergh baby's body was found in a shallow grave near their home. Because of Lindbergh's fame, the kidnapping captured nationwide interest and seemed to document the public's vulnerability to such crimes.

At the time, kidnapping was not a federal offense, and responsibility for apprehending the kidnapper was the province of the state police. Months passed, and on October 19, 1933—since the New Jersey police were no closer to solving the crime—President Franklin Roosevelt ordered the Bureau to take charge of the investigation, including coordination of the efforts of local and state police and federal agencies (notably, the Secret Service and the IRS). Even with a joint effort, law enforcement authorities did not identify Bruno Hauptmann, an unemployed carpenter, as the kidnapper until September and October 1934. (Hauptmann was tried on state charges; was convicted of kidnapping and murdering the Lindbergh baby; and on April 3, 1936, was electrocuted.)

The drama of the Lindbergh case coincided with the upsurge of a "crime wave." The nation's news media and the Hollywood film industry graphically described the crime spree of a host of colorful characters (characterized by memorable nicknames such as George "Machine Gun" Kelly, Lester Gillis aka "Baby Face" Nelson, Alvin "Creepy" Karpis, and Charles "Pretty Boy" Floyd).

Notable among these gangsters was "Handsome" John Dillinger. Between May 1933 and July 1934, Dillinger robbed 10 banks in five states; he even robbed a police station of weapons and ammunition and, on another occasion, successfully escaped from jail. Dillinger's well-publicized crime spree earned him the title of Public Enemy Number One. At this time, bank robbery was not a federal crime, so—responding to the clamor for federal action—Bureau agents sought Dillinger's capture for violating the Dyer Act (crossing state lines in stolen motor vehicles). Ultimately, Bureau agents shot and killed Dillinger during a stakeout (see pages 54–55).

The Dillinger and Lindbergh cases provided an unprecedented opportunity for the Roosevelt administration to enlarge the federal government's role in law enforcement, followed as they were by other highly publicized criminal activities of Kelly, Nelson, Floyd, and Karpis (all of whom were apprehended by Bureau agents amid great fanfare) and a dramatic gun battle in the Kansas City, Missouri, railroad station (between the criminal associates of convicted bank robber Frank Nash and the state police and Bureau agents escorting him as he was being transported to the federal penitentiary in Leavenworth, Kansas). These high-profile crimes both heightened public alarm and seemingly confirmed that local and state police were incapable of protecting the populace.

President Roosevelt effectively exploited this public fear in his annual address to Congress on January 3, 1934. Crime posed a serious threat to "our security," Roosevelt argued, and the "strong arm of Government" was required to combat it. The President demanded congressional enactment of Attorney General Homer Cummings's Twelve Point Crime Program. In July 1933, Cummings had announced his intention to draft legislation extending federal jurisdiction to include kidnapping, bank robbery, and extortion. "The safety of our country," Cummings warned, was threatened by the "organized forces of crime" operating "across State lines." An increased federal role was required to meet this serious crime threat: "The police of the great cities were hopelessly corrupt. The rural system of crime control which was lodged in the sheriff and the constable was unsuited to modern conditions. If the elements of an offense were not all committed in a single State, such criminals might sometime escape prosecution altogether."

Interstate gangs had made crime a national problem, but the federal government could not act without legislative authority. Roosevelt's and Cummings's lobbying efforts succeeded because they tapped into the conviction—which the nation's newspapers, periodicals, and movies promoted—that a more vigorous assault on crime was needed. As stated in a *Philadelphia Record* editorial, only "a central agency can supervise our national battle against organized crime." Although his Twelve Point Crime Program was not enacted in its entirety, by June 1934 Attorney General Cummings had convinced Congress to make kidnapping a federal crime when the victim was transported across state lines or when the perpetrators used telephones or the mail in their ransom demands; also, to extend federal jurisdiction to interstate racketeering, transporting stolen property across state lines, bank robberies, and extortion. Bureau agents were also empowered to carry firearms, execute warrants, and make arrests.

The Federal Bureau of Investigation (1935)

In 1935, the refurbished Bureau of Investigation was appropriately renamed the Federal Bureau of Investigation, a title aptly capturing its new role as the nation's principal law enforcement agency (see Table 1.2). FBI officials promoted this sense of the agency's primacy when establishing the FBI Police Training School in 1935 (renamed the FBI National Police Academy in 1936 and then the FBI National Academy in 1945). Police officers and sheriffs from around the country were invited to this school to be instructed in the most up-to-date policing techniques. In addition, the FBI's Crime Laboratory was modernized, and FBI press releases regularly emphasized the agency's use of modern technological and methodological advances to identify criminals and convict them for their crimes.

TABLE 1.2

NAMES USED FOR THE JUSTICE DEPARTMENT'S INVESTIGATIVE DIVISION

Official Name	Date
No official name	July 26, 1908
Bureau of Investigation	March 16, 1909
United States Bureau of Investigation	July 1, 1932
Division of Investigation	August 10, 1933
Federal Bureau of Investigation	March 22, 1935

Cognizant of the importance of publicity in undercutting still-powerful states' rights beliefs and fears of centralized bureaucracies, the FBI's Crime Records Division was given the additional responsibility to improve communication with Congress and the media. Favored reporters, writers, and members of Congress were "assisted" in publicizing the FBI's successful war on crime by being supplied with privileged information that enhanced the Bureau's reputation. The reported exclamation of the notorious gangster George "Machine Gun" Kelly when apprehended by FBI agents—"Don't shoot, G-men!"—was particularly effective in promoting the image of the super-efficient FBI agent. The G-man myth quickly entered popular lore.

Monitoring Radicals and Subversives

The Great Depression (from 1929 to 1939) had created a political climate that impelled an expanded federal role in both the economic realm and in crime fighting. The seeming collapse of capitalism and the attendant loss of public confidence in established institutions also spawned American fascist and communist movements. Tapping the same vein of frustration and alienation as European fascist and communist organizations, American fascists and communists drew inspiration—and in some cases, direct support—from Nazi Germany and Soviet Russia. The Roosevelt administration—and to different degrees, many American liberals and conservatives—regarded the American fascist and communist movements as a "fifth column"—an internal threat that, through stealth and betrayal, intended to promote the policy interests of hostile foreign governments.

Prior to the outbreak of World War II in Europe in 1939, high-level U.S. government officials pressured President Roosevelt to adopt measures to curb what they claimed was a potentially serious internal security threat—communist and Nazi sympathizers. The president shared these concerns and, following a May 1934 cabinet meeting, he requested a limited FBI investigation of the American fascist movement, to focus particularly on whether its racialist and "anti-American" activities had "any possible connection with official representatives of the German government in the United States."

In January 1936, Secretary of War George Dern advised Attorney General Cummings that the War Department had uncovered "definite indication" of foreign espionage and that "some [domestic] organizations would probably attempt to cripple our war effort through sabotage." A civilian counterespionage service should be established, Dern felt, to "prevent foreign espionage in the United States and to collect information" so that in the event the United States went to war, federal officials could detain "any person intending to cripple our war effort by means of espionage or sabotage."

President Roosevelt did not accede to Dern's recommendation to establish a special counterespionage service but instead solicited the counsel of FBI Director J. Edgar Hoover. Impressed by a detailed FBI report that right-wing business leaders had purportedly financed a military coup to overthrow the government and by other intelligence reports that American fascist and communist movements threatened the nation's security, Roosevelt invited Hoover to the White House on August 24, 1936, to discuss "the question of subversive activities in the United States, particularly Fascism and Communism." During this private meeting, Hoover briefed Roosevelt on "recent developments in the Communist activities." The FBI had acquired evidence that the communists planned to gain control of the International Longshoremen's Union, the United Mine Workers Union, and the Newspaper Guild, Hoover asserted, and "by doing so they would be able at any time to paralyze the country." Furthermore, communists influenced other subversive activities "within Governmental service . . . particularly in some of the Departments and in the National Labor Relations Board."

Roosevelt's 1936 Directive

Hoover's alarming report complemented similar reports that the president had received from military intelligence. In response to this briefing, Roosevelt asked Hoover how he might obtain "a broad picture of the general [fascist and communist] movement and its activities as may affect the economic and political life of the country as a whole." The FBI director thereupon claimed that under a 1916 appropriation statute, the FBI was empowered to conduct noncriminal investigations involving the activities of foreign governments when requested by the State Department. Incorporated in the U.S. Code, this appropriation provision authorized the FBI "to conduct such other investigations [beyond crimes against the United States] regarding official matters under the control of the Department of Justice and the Department of State as may be directed by the attorney general."

Interested in ensuring secrecy and concerned that a formal departmental request might be leaked to the press, Roosevelt arranged a meeting the next day with Hoover and Secretary of State Cordell Hull. During this meeting, Roosevelt reminded Hull of the 1916 statute, adding that because the communist and fascist movements "were international in scope and that Communism particularly was directed from Moscow . . . the State Department would have a right to request an inquiry to be made." Hull concurred. The secretary of state and the president decided that Hull would not make this request in writing, in order to ensure confidentiality. Hoover was further directed to brief Attorney General Cummings about this matter.

Hoover promptly took advantage of this request and the opening provided by President Roosevelt's interest in secrecy. On September 5, 1936, the FBI director ordered all FBI field offices "to obtain from all possible sources information concerning subversive activities conducted in the United States by Communists, Fascisti, and representatives or advocates of other organizations or groups advocating the overthrow or replacement of the Government of the United States." A broad-based surveillance program was implemented, one focusing on: the maritime industry; "Government affairs"; the steel, coal, newspaper, clothing, garment, and fur industries; "general strike activities"; the armed services; educational institutions; and "general activities—Communist and Affiliated Organizations, Fascist, Anti-Fascist movements, and activities in Organized Labor organizations."

It is noteworthy that the program Hoover implemented exceeded the president's more limited request for a "broad picture" to determine whether the American fascist and communist movements were subject to foreign direction and control. Furthermore, the program was actually initiated prior to Hoover's briefing of Attorney General Cummings. Belatedly, on September 10, 1936, Hoover informed Cummings of his joint meeting with the president and the secretary of state (misdating this as having occurred on September 1). Equally sensitive to the need for secrecy, Cummings verbally directed Hoover to proceed and to coordinate the FBI's investigation with military and naval intelligence and the State Department.

The Rumrich Case and Counterespionage

In 1935, predating the inception of the broad surveillance program initiated by President Roosevelt in September 1936, FBI agents uncovered a German spy ring that had been operating in New York City since 1927. Leaders of this ring had recruited pro-Nazis (including both German Americans and German alien residents) to infiltrate defense plants and the U.S. military in order to obtain U.S. military secrets. The fruits of this intelligence operation were forwarded to Germany by couriers who either used false passports or were employed in the shipping industry. The FBI's resultant investigation ultimately led to the indictment on June 20, 1938, of 18 members of the so-called Rumrich spy ring. Recognizing the publicity value of this spy plot, Justice Department officials sought to impress the public "with its dangers." Indeed, at a June 24, 1938, press conference, President Roosevelt cited the indictments as the rationale for increasing congressional appropriations for FBI counterespionage investigations. The case did heighten internal security concerns by offering seeming confirmation of the divided loyalties of ethnic Americans and their adherence to foreign ideologies (see page 58).

The Rumrich case had also precipitated a review within the Roosevelt administration of existing counterespionage operations. Although generally aware of the FBI's monitoring of fascist and communist activities, Attorney General Cummings was not fully informed of their scope and focus. Thus, when briefing Hoover about the review ordered by Roosevelt, Cummings advised the FBI director of his intention to seek direct congressional authorization for future counterespionage operations. Hoover objected. The FBI was currently investigating "various forms of activities

of either a subversive or a so-called intelligence type," Hoover reminded Cummings, and could expand these investigations to meet any future threats. Such expansion "can be covered" under provisions of the 1916 statute even though these "matters do not in themselves constitute a specific violation of a Federal Criminal Statute, such as subversive activities." The FBI director emphasized to the attorney general the need for "the utmost degree of secrecy" in order to "avoid criticisms or objections which might be raised for such an expansion by either ill-informed persons or individuals having some ulterior motive." Many Americans find the term espionage "repugnant," he noted, and thus it would be "undesirable to seek any special legislation [i.e., congressional authorization] which would draw attention to the fact that it was proposed to develop a special counterespionage drive of any great magnitude."

President Roosevelt and Attorney General Cummings endorsed Hoover's preference for secrecy. Opting for the recommended low-key strategy, in November 1938 Roosevelt merely requested increased appropriations from Congress for the FBI, the Military Intelligence Division (MID), and the Office of Naval Intelligence (ONI) to "handle counterintelligence activities." Although the president had recommended increasing FBI appropriations by $150,000, reducing Hoover's proposed increase of $300,000, in 1939 Congress approved the higher amount. The impetus was Hoover's alarmist testimony of May 1939 before a House Appropriations Subcommittee, in which he cited the dramatic increase in FBI spy cases: from an annual average of 35 prior to 1938 to 634 in 1938 and a projected total of 772 in 1939.

Increased Autonomy for FBI Intelligence Activities

Although Congress increased FBI appropriations, it had not directly expanded the FBI's authority to conduct counterespionage operations. The sole authority for such noncriminal investigations rested on the 1916 statute (see "Roosevelt's 1936 Directive," page 15), which necessitated a State Department request. This requirement posed unanticipated problems for Hoover when, in early 1939, State Department officials insisted on having a controlling voice in coordinating such investigations.

To neutralize the State Department's role, in March 1939, Hoover urged Attorney General Frank Murphy (Cummings's successor) to approve a plan to ensure control by the FBI director—not the State Department—over expanded FBI investigations "intended to ascertain the identity of persons engaged in espionage, counter-espionage, and sabotage of a nature not within the specific provisions of prevailing statutes." Under current policy, Hoover explained, the State Department's "specific authorization" was required, and State Department officials had recently instituted a cumbersome committee system headed by Assistant Secretary of State George Messersmith—a system that might result in State Department control over all federal surveillance activities. Murphy immediately raised the matter with President Roosevelt, who (after consultation with military and naval intelligence officials) issued another secret directive on June 26, 1939. Dissolving the State Department's interdepartmental committee, Roosevelt ordered that the investigation of "all espionage, counterespionage, and related matters" was to be "controlled and handled" only by the FBI, MID, and ONI. All other agencies were thereafter to forward to the FBI "any data, information, or material" they might obtain "bearing directly or indirectly on espionage, counterespionage, or sabotage."

Thus, even before the outbreak of war in Europe in September 1939, the FBI's powers had expanded. The process by which this was done, moreover, ensured a more independent agency. When secretly authorizing the FBI's investigations of noncriminal "subversive activities" in 1936, the president had first approached Hoover directly, and in the process bypassed the FBI director's ostensible superior, the attorney general (see "Roosevelt's 1936 Directive," page 15). Even though Hoover and Cummings had excellent rapport, the FBI director's direct access to the president undercut the ability of Attorney General Cummings and his successors to oversee FBI activities. The underlying interest in secrecy further hampered the ability of the attorney general to evaluate and curtail FBI investigations of "subversive activities." This was all the more compromising since no law triggered these investigations and therefore the normal Justice Department review process was not required. Thus, there was no outside review of these FBI investigations to ascertain whether sufficient evidence of a criminal violation had been uncovered to warrant seeking an indictment—or whether the investigation was proving fruitless and should be terminated.

President Roosevelt's June 1939 decision to terminate the State Department's interdepartmental committee eliminated another external check over FBI activities. Convinced at first of the need to base FBI "intelligence"

investigations on federal statutes, Roosevelt had accepted a system wherein FBI investigations of "subversive activities" would be responsive to specific requests from the State Department, ensuring that State Department officials could determine their inception and duration. When changing course in 1939 and authorizing FBI officials themselves to initiate "espionage" and "counterespionage" investigations and to coordinate all information obtained by other federal agencies and departments, Roosevelt enabled FBI officials to determine independently their control and direction. The president's strategy of working with sympathetic members of the House Appropriations Committee rather than risking a debate over legislation authorizing FBI counterespionage operations also ensured that FBI officials' own criteria would determine the scope and purpose of FBI investigations.

FBI Director Hoover privately outlined these criteria when distinguishing between FBI investigative and intelligence activities. An *investigation* was "conducted when there is a specific violation of a Criminal Statute involved, always presuppose an overt act and is proceeded upon with the very definite intention of developing facts and information that will enable prosecution under such legislation." In contrast, "an entirely different premise" underpinned *intelligence* activities; namely, "Much of the activity indulged in by Communists and subversive elements does not, in the original stage, involve an overt act or violation of a specific statute. These subversive groups direct their attention to the dissemination of propaganda and to the boring from within processes, much of which is not a violation of a Federal Statute at the time it is indulged in, but which may become a very definite violation of the law in the event of a declaration of war or of the declaration of a national emergency."

Hoover's phrasing when referring to the need to monitor those disseminating "propaganda" and "boring from within" ensured that intelligence investigations would focus on attempts by labor union and civil rights activists, political dissidents, and radical journalists to change public policy or to oppose the president's foreign policy and internal security decisions. Because intelligence investigations did not lead to prosecution, they precluded the two possible deterrents resulting from court review: (1) the openness of judicial proceedings could create adverse publicity, and (2) judicial proceedings could permit defense attorneys to question FBI methods and evidence in terms of fairness and lawfulness. In effect, the FBI's "intelligence" investigations subverted the checks on abuses of power otherwise integral to the American constitutional system.

The World War II Era (1939–45)

The trend toward a more powerful and more autonomous FBI accelerated with the onset of World War II following Germany's September 2, 1939, invasion of Poland. Occurring weeks after the conclusion of a nonaggression pact between the Soviet Union and Germany, the European war heightened Roosevelt administration concerns about the political influence of American fascists and communists. The administration recognized the political difficulties it would encounter in seeking to change the course of the nation's international role from isolationism to more active intervention—the influence of right-wing and left-wing critics who had shaped the public and congressional debates over the neutrality laws of 1935–37. To ensure a more active U.S. role in international affairs after 1939, Roosevelt would have to rescind these laws' limitations on U.S. commercial and financial relations with belligerent powers, as well as their limitations on the president's freedom to conduct foreign policy at a time of international war.

The German invasion of Poland at first altered the terms of the foreign policy debate from whether to ensure neutrality to how to preserve it. Although many Americans feared Germany's power and objectives, the predominant public sentiment favored noninvolvement. Organizations representing that sentiment (notably, the predominantly conservative America First Committee and the communist-dominated American League for Peace and Democracy) lobbied Congress and the public to avoid international commitments that were unneutral. For many leaders of America First, already suspicious of President Roosevelt's expansion of federal and presidential powers under the New Deal, domestic issues were as crucial as the foreign policy crisis—the nation's interests were not affected by this war, but military involvement could lead to a dictatorship and regimented economy. President Roosevelt's foreign policy initiatives of 1940–41 (the destroyer-bases deal, Lend-Lease, and the Argentia Conference) intensified conservative opposition. On the left, pacifists and radicals (who identified with the then-neutral Soviet Union) rejected the need for U.S. involvement in the European conflict and criticized the

administration's initiatives as promoting militarism and imperialism. Already worried that the American fascist and communist movements were influenced by, if not subject to the direction of, Germany and the Soviet Union, the administration now perceived these movements to be a sinister fifth column.

FBI Reports to the Roosevelt White House

Beginning in May 1940, President Roosevelt and senior White House aides forwarded to FBI Director Hoover the names of individuals who had written or telegraphed to protest the president's unneutral foreign policy. "It was the President's idea," presidential press secretary Stephen Early wrote Hoover, that the FBI "might" record the "names and addresses of the senders." The FBI director expanded upon the president's proposal, and that month forwarded to the White House reports detailing whatever derogatory information the FBI had already collected on the identified critics. When the FBI had no preexisting file, a special FBI inquiry was initiated with the results also sent to the White House. These reports detailed the individual's association with suspected fascist or communist groups and general political activities (particularly, positions on foreign and military policy, civil rights, and labor strikes). Hoover's reports provoked no protest from the White House, even though they confirmed that the FBI was monitoring political activities that did not violate federal statutes. The Roosevelt White House, instead, expressed appreciation and invited further submissions of information. There ensued a continuous flurry of FBI reports.

Thus, after 1940, not all of the FBI's "intelligence" mission could be characterized as counterespionage; many political activists were monitored who, at worst, could undermine national unity by raising public doubts about the consequences of the president's foreign policy. Quite independently, FBI agents were also monitoring German and Soviet agents who might seek to disrupt military planning or acquire defense information; additionally, they monitored and wiretapped "diplomatic representatives [German, Italian, Japanese, and Soviet] at the sanction of the State Department." Insofar as many of the adherents of the anti-Roosevelt America First Committee were prominent American civic and political leaders, including Charles Lindbergh and U.S. senators Burton Wheeler and Gerald Nye, FBI intelligence reports on their speeches and strategies furthered the president's political interests—providing information about planned lobbying and congressional initiatives.

The FBI also began, sometimes in response to White House pressure, to monitor profascist publications and the editors and reporters of mainstream conservative newspapers. The latter caused particular concern to the president, owing to their prominence and their long-term adversarial stance—since 1933, they had consistently criticized the Roosevelt administration, first for its New Deal reforms and then for its interventionist foreign policy. Moreover, when Attorney General Francis Biddle refused to initiate the prosecution of some of these publications and individuals, Hoover protested to White House aide Stephen Early that "until some of the Attorney General's instructions had been changed [FBI] agents could not operate," having been "blocked by the Attorney General time and time again." Early advised Hoover to inform Biddle of the president's "desires," and Roosevelt followed up by demanding that the attorney general "speak to me" about the matter of "seditious publications in the United States—the clear and present danger." The attorney general did subsequently attempt to prosecute profascist periodicals, but he could not secure indictments of the president's most effective critics, who had become subject to FBI surveillance: *Washington Times-Herald* publisher Eleanor Patterson and columnist Inga Arvad, *New York Daily News* publisher Joseph Patterson and reporter John O'Donnell, and *Chicago Tribune* publisher Robert McCormick and reporters Chesly Manly and Stanley Johnston.

Delimitation Agreements Enlarge the FBI's Role

The Roosevelt administration's concerns about national security set the stage for the FBI's expanded role and resultant autonomy. Internal security concerns led Roosevelt to bypass the attorney general to work instead directly with FBI Director Hoover. This changed administrative relationship was highlighted both when presidential press secretary Stephen Early directly contacted Hoover to submit names of administration critics and when Hoover urged Early to have the president pressure the attorney general to prosecute those responsible for "seditious" publications.

FBI officials exploited this special access to the president to limit the roles of potential rivals, agencies that might otherwise have capitalized on the foreign-relations neutrality crisis to expand their own powers. Stressing the need to curb vigilante activities, in September 1939, Hoover advised Attorney General Frank Murphy of the plans of New York City police to monitor subversive activities. In response, on September 6, 1939, and then again on January

8, 1943, President Roosevelt publicly directed the FBI—instead of local law enforcement—to "take charge of investigative work in matters relating to espionage, sabotage, and violations of the neutrality regulations." To ensure that this critical national need would be met, "all police officers, sheriffs, and other law enforcement officers" were to "promptly" forward to the FBI any information they acquired "relating to espionage, sabotage, subversive activities, and violations of the neutrality laws." In addition, "all patriotic organizations and individuals [must] likewise report" to the FBI all information relating to "espionage and related matters." As in the cases of interstate prostitution and theft, a successful counterespionage program required a centralized federal system to coordinate all accumulated information. Although issued to avert vigilante activities by limiting the role of local police, Roosevelt's orders had the effect of ensuring FBI dominance. Moreover, the directives disarmed potential opposition to the FBI's expanded role: couched in terms of averting espionage, sabotage, and violations of the neutrality laws, the fact that the FBI was monitoring political activities did not seem improper.

Administration concerns about internal security underpinned additional executive directives in 1940 and 1942. These expanded the FBI's powers into areas of foreign intelligence and counterintelligence at the expense of the State, War, and Navy Departments. Deeply concerned that German agents might exploit neutralist sentiments within the United States and anti-Yankee sentiments within Latin and South America, the president secretly authorized the FBI in June 1940 to conduct foreign intelligence and counterintelligence operations in South America. In response, FBI Director Hoover created a special FBI division, the Special Intelligence Service (SIS). And, when by executive order of June 1942 Roosevelt created a wartime foreign intelligence agency, the Office of Strategic Services (OSS), to "plan and operate such special services as may be directed by the United States Joint Chiefs of Staff," this spy agency was excluded from operating in the Western Hemisphere—already the bailiwick of the SIS. Independently, during the 1940–41 period, FBI agents worked closely with British security officers to monitor German consular officials and members of the business community within the United States and in the Western Hemisphere who might attempt to promote German foreign policy interests.

Far more important in the long run, since foreign intelligence did not remain an FBI responsibility after World War II—when the SIS was dissolved and its records and sources turned over to the Central Intelligence Agency (after that agency was created in 1947)—decisions made by President Roosevelt and Attorney General Robert Jackson enlarged the FBI's powers while curbing attempts by the Military Intelligence Division (MID) and the Office of Naval Intelligence (ONI) officials to expand their agencies' domestic surveillance roles. For example, in November 1940, Attorney General Jackson sidetracked a proposal by American Legion officials to monitor suspicious activities in defense plants and their communities and to report their findings to military intelligence; instead, Jackson authorized the American Legion Contact program, whereby FBI agents recruited and directed Legionnaires in their monitoring activities. By the end of the war, over 40,000 Legionnaires had served as FBI informers. (The FBI continued many of these contacts after 1945. Intensified following the outbreak of the Korean War in 1950, this program was terminated only in 1966.) FBI officials also established the Plant Informant program, in which FBI agents recommended steps to guard against espionage and sabotage to factory owners having defense contracts, with FBI agents investigating all reports concerning employees suspected of involvement in espionage or sabotage.

Delimitation agreements of June 5, 1940, and February 9, 1942, concurrently excluded MID and ONI from the domestic security arena. Under these agreements, the FBI was to coordinate all information developed by any agency "relating to subversive movements"; was to chair the Interdepartmental Committee on Intelligence; was responsible "for ascertaining the location, leadership, strength and organization of all civilian groups designed to combat 'Fifth Column' activities"; was to monitor the "activities and developments of Un-American groups whose activities are aimed to frustrate or interfere with the national defense program"; was to conduct all investigations involving American citizens and alien residents not directly employed by the War and Navy Departments "who attempt to frustrate plans for national defense." ONI and MID were barred from investigating "civilians," could only investigate military personnel and conduct investigations for base security, and had to rely on the FBI for information about "important developments . . . including the names of individuals definitely known to be connected with subversive activities."

Custodial Detention Index and Security Index

The FBI's monopoly in internal security investigations encouraged FBI officials to initiate other programs, some of which lacked statutory authority and endangered constitutional liberties. For instance, following the outbreak of war in Europe in September 1939, FBI Director Hoover devised a program directed at "individuals, groups and organizations engaged in . . . subversive activities, or espionage activities, or any activity that was possibly detrimental to the internal security of the United States." Under this program, FBI agents were to identify "discreetly" all "persons of German, Italian, and Communist sympathies," whether alien residents or citizens, and others whose "interest may be directed primarily to the interest of some other nation than the United States." Those "whose presence at liberty" at time of war "would be dangerous to the public peace and safety of the United States Government" were to be listed in what was known as the Custodial Detention index. The controlling criteria for these listings was not conduct but *anticipated* conduct. The listed individuals could not be detained, of course, since Hoover's unilateral action lacked statutory authority. Accordingly, in June 1940, the FBI director sought Attorney General Jackson's approval to compile "a suspect list of individuals whose arrest might be considered necessary in the event the United States becomes involved in war." Jackson approved the Custodial Detention program, including a measure that, following a declaration of war, warrants would be issued to arrest the foreign aliens listed in the index. Because no statute existed that would have authorized the internment of listed citizens, if war were declared, a special Justice Department committee would be formed to decide if they might be prosecutable under the Smith Act of 1940 (see "Curbing Fascism, Communism, and German Spying," pages 22–23) "or some other appropriate statute." In addition, the attorney general agreed that the FBI's "counter-espionage" activities and confidential sources (both individuals who provided information and information obtained through wiretaps, bugs, break-ins, and mail opening) were not to be publicly compromised "without the prior approval of the Bureau."

Once the United States had joined in World War II, Attorney General Francis Biddle (Jackson's successor) authorized the detention of dangerous German and Italian aliens. (Japanese aliens and Japanese Americans were detained in residential "camps" during the war, pursuant to President Roosevelt's February 1942 executive order.) However, Biddle did not authorize the detention of "Communist" aliens (by then, the Soviet Union was a wartime ally), nor did he consider prosecuting U.S. citizens who were listed in the Custodial Detention Index. In July 1943, moreover, Biddle ordered Hoover to discontinue the Custodial Detention program, having concluded that this "classification system is inherently unreliable." For all cases in which individuals had been listed on this index, Biddle required that their files include a stamp stating that the listing was unreliable and thus canceled. "There is no statutory authorization or other present justification" for such a list concerning citizens, the attorney general concluded, adding that the Justice Department's "proper function" was to investigate persons "who may have violated the law," which purpose "is not aided by classifying persons as to dangerousness."

Hoover's response to Biddle's order indirectly confirms how FBI secrecy and President Roosevelt's interest in having the FBI conduct noncriminal investigations undermined the attorney general's ability to oversee the Justice Department's investigative division. In a highly confidential directive to FBI officials of August 1943, the FBI director technically complied with Biddle's order terminating the Custodial Detention listings, but added, "Henceforth, the cards known as Custodial Detention cards will be known as Security Index." FBI agents were to continue "to investigate dangerous and potentially dangerous" citizens and aliens and to list them in the Security Index. Sensitive that his insubordination could be discovered, Hoover admonished FBI officials that this renamed list was to be "strictly confidential and should at no time be mentioned or alluded to in investigative reports or discussed with agencies or individuals outside the Bureau," with the exception of MID and ONI officials, "and then only on a strictly confidential basis."

Wiretapping and Break-in Policies

In 1934, Congress had formally banned wiretapping when enacting the Communication Act's regulation of the telephone and communication industries. This law and the congressional hearings and debate that accompanied its passage did not explicitly apply this ban against the "interception and divulgence" of communications "transmitted by wire" to federal agents. Therefore, federal agents continued to employ wiretaps during criminal investigations. In rulings of 1937 and 1939, however, the Supreme Court, *in Nardone v. U.S.,* held that the wiretapping ban did apply to federal

agents, and furthermore that whenever an indictment had been based on illegally obtained wiretapped evidence, that case was tainted and its dismissal was required.

President Roosevelt privately concluded that the Court's rulings governed only criminal cases, and then because the intercepted information would be "divulged" to effect prosecution. This limitation, Roosevelt believed, did not apply to "national defense" investigations, whose purpose was not prosecutorial but to obtain advance intelligence. Accordingly, on May 21, 1940, the president secretly authorized FBI wiretapping of persons "suspected of subversive activities against the United States, including suspected spies." To limit FBI wiretapping to "national defense" investigations, Roosevelt required the attorney general's advance approval "after investigation of the need in each case" and specified that the FBI confine its use of wiretaps "to a minimum and to limit them insofar as possible to aliens."

FBI wiretapping remained illegal, however, despite President Roosevelt's secret directive. This meant that for cases in which the FBI wiretapped suspected spies, information obtained in that way could not be used for prosecution under the espionage statutes. Furthermore, the president's unwillingness to disclose his private determination that wiretapping for intelligence purposes lay outside the Court's ruling placed his attorney general in a delicate position. Jackson responded by adopting a procedure to minimize the risk of public discovery. During a follow-up meeting with the FBI director, the attorney general informed Hoover of his intention to "have no detailed record kept concerning the cases in which wiretapping would be utilized." The only records of wiretaps were to be maintained in the FBI director's "immediate office, listing the time, places, and cases in which this procedure is utilized."

However, Jackson's decision to keep no separate records of the FBI wiretaps he had approved subverted his ability (and that of subsequent attorneys general) to monitor FBI wiretapping practices. Just as important, Jackson did not issue guidelines governing "national defense" wiretaps, such as proscribing the length of their use or requiring reauthorization of ongoing wiretaps after a defined period. Thus, once obtaining the attorney general's approval, FBI officials could continue a wiretap indefinitely (even when no evidence of a "national defense" threat was found).

Jackson's concern with deniability and his lack of interest in monitoring FBI intelligence investigations closely enabled Hoover to employ other illegal investigative techniques without seeking the attorney general's authorization, or even advising him of them. In 1940, for example, FBI officials initiated a mail-opening program, code-named Z-Coverage, first targeting Axis embassies in Washington, D.C., and then extended to include Axis consulates in New York City and the embassies of Axis-aligned governments (Spain, Portugal, and Vichy France) and the Soviet Union. Similarly, following the 1941 Japanese attack on Pearl Harbor, FBI officials effected an arrangement whereby the international telegraph companies (Western Union, RCA, and ITT) would delay transmitting for 24 hours all telegraph messages of identified Axis-aligned countries and the Soviet Union so that the Army Security Agency and the FBI could copy them.

Also deemed permissible by the FBI—though illegal—were break-ins, either to install bugs or to photograph the records of individuals and organizations suspected of "subversive activities." Conducted sporadically before 1942, that year, Hoover decided that the regular use of this "invaluable technique" was necessary "in combating subversive activities of a clandestine nature aimed at undermining and destroying our nation." Conceding that break-ins were "clearly illegal," the FBI director was unwilling to "obtain any legal sanction" (that is, to seek the approval of the attorney general or the president). Instead, Hoover simply required FBI agents to obtain his (or a designated senior FBI official's) advance authorization beforehand, outlining the safeguards they would adopt to preclude discovery. His purpose was to ensure that agents did not conduct break-ins indiscriminately and recklessly.

Hoover's approval requirement, however, necessitated the creation of written records, which might need to be produced in response to a congressional subpoena or court-ordered discovery motion. Hoover minimized this risk through a Do Not File procedure. Documents captioned "Do Not File" were not to be indexed in the FBI's central records system but instead were to be routed to the office files of senior FBI officials at the FBI's Washington, D.C., headquarters for review and approval (and were then to be regularly destroyed). The head of an FBI field office, in turn, created an "informal" memorandum (that is, a nonofficial record) of each authorization and filed it in the office safe "until the next inspection by Bureau Inspectors, at which time it [the informal memo] is destroyed" (see Exhibit 5.7, pages 184–86). The Do Not File procedure refined another special records procedure that Hoover had devised in 1940 to safeguard sensitive communications among senior FBI

officials. To distinguish these more sensitive informal memoranda from official memoranda that were to be serialized and indexed in the FBI's central records system, an informal memorandum was to be written on pink paper (official memoranda were written on white paper) and to contain the notation that the memorandum was "to be destroyed after action is taken and not sent to files."

Curbing Fascism, Communism, and German Spying

Separate records procedures safeguarded certain FBI records from discovery: those describing deliberate approval of illegal activities and those confirming FBI officials' authorization of politically sensitive investigations (whether monitoring the political activities of First Lady Eleanor Roosevelt or servicing the personal interests of prominent citizens, such as John D. Rockefeller III). Secrecy immunized Bureau operations from scrutiny and permitted an unprecedented expansion in the FBI's autonomy. Ironically, this independence and focus on political activities occurred at the very time, 1939–40, when Congress enacted a series of laws directed at averting violent revolution and precluding German and Soviet agents from influencing U.S. policy.

In 1939, Congress enacted the Hatch Act, which barred from federal employment anyone who was a member of "any political party or organization which advocated" the violent overthrow of the government. That same year, Congress amended the Foreign Agents Registration Act of 1938 to require that any individual "who, within the United States, acts at the order, request, or under the direction of a foreign principal" register as a foreign agent with the Justice Department. Then, in 1940, Congress enacted the Alien Registration Act (or Smith Act), under which alien residents of the United States had to be fingerprinted and, more important, were forbidden to "knowingly or willfully advocate, abet, advise or teach the duty, necessity, desirability or propriety of violently overthrowing" the government, assassinate any government official, or print, write, or disseminate publications advocating such doctrines or organizing such groups. Combined, these acts proscribed radical speech and association, and they empowered the FBI to monitor, in particular, those who joined or organized the Communist Party and the German-American Bund.

These laws seemingly provided the authority to prosecute political radicals for activities that the FBI had already been monitoring; ironically, however, there was no marked increased in prosecutions. Furthermore, some of the cases that were prosecuted precipitated criticisms of the FBI's professionalism and methods.

In the most notorious World War II case prosecuted under the Smith Act, 26 American fascists (notably, Gerald Winrod, Elizabeth Dilling, and Gerald L. K. Smith) were indicted in July 1942. During the resultant trial, U.S. attorneys were unable to prove that the 26 had conspired together to overthrow the government. Securing a second indictment in 1944 (expanded to 30 individuals, including Lawrence Dennis), the Justice Department eventually moved to dismiss the charges following a raucous trial aborted by the death of the presiding judge. The U.S. government suffered a further defeat in 1945 when the Supreme Court overturned the convictions of leaders of the German-American Bund who had been indicted for counseling resistance to the wartime Selective Service Act. Earlier, in January 1940, FBI agents had arrested 17 members of the pro-German Christian Front on the charge of stealing arms and ammunition from a National Guard armory as part of a "vast plot" to overthrow the government and establish a fascist dictatorship. The government lost this case, as well, for the FBI's evidence was essentially ideological, and defense attorneys successfully challenged the truthfulness of the FBI's key informer, Denis Healy. In a further embarrassing development in February 1940, FBI agents arrested 12 individuals for having violated the Logan Act of the 1790s when recruiting volunteers in 1937 to serve in the Abraham Lincoln Brigade to fight on the side of the Spanish government against the pro-fascist forces of General Francisco Franco. Liberals in the Congress and the media denounced this action as politically motivated. The Justice Department defended the Bureau's role but decided to forego prosecution.

Not all FBI investigations provoked controversy. Between 1940 and 1942, FBI investigations led to the conviction of a number of American fascists and fascist sympathizers who were directly linked with German intelligence operations. The first case of 1940–41 stemmed from the defection of William G. Sebold. German intelligence had recruited and trained Sebold, a naturalized American citizen, to become a German spy during his 1939 visit with his family in Germany. Sebold, however, immediately contacted the FBI on his return to the United States. FBI officials thereupon devised an elaborate scheme intended to identify others whom the German government had recruited as spies. With FBI assistance, Sebold estab-

lished a radio transmitter station in Centerpoint, Long Island, New York, with the FBI screening messages. This operation led to the conviction of 33 German agents in 1941, including the leader of German intelligence's New York–based spy ring Frederick Duquesne.

Then, in June 1942, FBI agents arrested eight individuals who had been sent by German intelligence to sabotage American transportation and industrial facilities, code-named Operation Pastorius. The saboteurs had been transported by German submarines and landed in two teams of four in Jacksonville, Florida, and in the town of Amagansett, on Long Island, New York, but they were apprehended before they could even attempt to implement their sabotage mission. Tried in military courts (six of the arrestees were German citizens), this case highlighted the FBI's efficiency and professionalism, as proclaimed in one typical newspaper headline: "FBI Captures 8 German Agents Landed by Subs" (see page 60).

Overall, and despite questions raised by the Smith Act, Selective Service Act, and Logan Act cases, the FBI's publicized successes in curbing German espionage and sabotage during the crisis of World War II overrode any concerns that the FBI might become a secret police agency that could threaten individual rights and constitutional government. Congress's enactment of the Hatch Act, the Foreign Agents Registration Act, and the Smith Act during the period when the United States was officially neutral confirmed a far-reaching shift in public policy—the surveillance of political radicals had come to be seen as essential to curbing movements committed to advancing the interests of foreign governments. However, influential congressional leaders did not attempt to ascertain the FBI's definition of an internal security threat, and during these years, Congress essentially abandoned any meaningful oversight of FBI operations.

Although Congress had never established a formal oversight system—dating from the Bureau's creation in 1908—the House Appropriations Committee had informally assumed this function during its annual review of proposed FBI appropriations. In March 1943, however, the chair of the House Appropriations Committee, Clarence Cannon, proposed a liaison relationship, whereby a total of three FBI agents would be assigned (for three-year terms) to assist the Appropriations Committee's staff in their review of the proposed budget requests of federal departments and agencies. This arrangement, which continued from then on, exempted the FBI's budgetary requests from critical scrutiny.

The Cold War Era (1945–56)

The defeat of the Axis powers and the end of World War II in 1945 did not usher in an era of peace or a retrenchment in the nation's international role. Almost immediately, the United States became involved in a cold war with the Soviet Union. Although direct military conflict never occurred, U.S. officials viewed the Soviet Union as a hostile adversary. However, the Soviet threat was not perceived primarily as that of an ordinary "great power" capable of compromising U.S. security interests by means of its military and industrial strength. Rather, postwar U.S. national security policy and the foreign policy of containment were based on the premise that the Soviet Union was a subversive adversary. Success in safeguarding U.S. security interests required measures that could anticipate and then stymie Soviet leaders' attempts to achieve their goal of world domination by stealth, by exploiting socioeconomic discontent, and by capitalizing on the pro-Soviet orientation of revolutionary movements. Thus, containing communist expansion necessitated both a major military build-up and costly foreign aid programs and, just as important, a vigilant countersubversive policy. At home, this meant that the FBI needed to be given the tools and freedom to anticipate attempts by American communists and communist sympathizers to steal military and diplomatic secrets and to undermine national unity or promote policies that advanced Soviet interests.

Because of the intensity of concerns about the internal security threat posed by international communism, the FBI's role and powers in the post-1945 period grew even beyond what had been triggered by the crisis of World War II. This expansion cannot be perceived by comparing FBI staff levels of the World War II and Cold War eras, however. FBI force levels essentially stabilized: from a peak of 13,191 at the end of 1944, FBI personnel declined temporarily to 11,792 in 1945 and 7,862 in 1947 but rebounded to 9,620 by 1949 and to 14,112 by 1956 (see Table 1.1).

What these personnel levels do not reveal, though, is the FBI's shift of focus to internal security investigations, at the expense of criminal investigations. Even so, the result was not a substantial increase in espionage convictions. Thus, although FBI investigations resulted in a limited number of highly publicized espionage (or espionage-related) cases, the number of FBI case files by the 1980s in the espionage, sedition, treason, domestic security, and foreign intelligence assets classifications exploded to reach 660,000. (This figure does not include case files in the foreign counterintelligence classification, the contents and even the number of which remained classified in 1997.)

Thus, intelligence investigations dominated the FBI caseload and focused on monitoring radical activists and organizations and their efforts to influence public policy (specifically, their opposition to U.S. foreign policy and internal security initiatives). Although intended to weed out potentially disloyal government employees, these investigations extended to individuals employed in the private sector—notably, artists, writers, college and university professors, and news reporters—targeted because they "might influence others against the national interest or are likely to furnish financial aid to subversive elements."

Counterintelligence and American Communism

Since the Bolshevik Revolution of 1917, the American communist movement became a principal target of FBI investigations. Monitoring did not cease in the aftermath of the Palmer Raids of 1920 or following Attorney General Stone's 1924 ban on political surveillance. President Roosevelt's 1936 oral directive and the heightened concern about "fifth column" activities following the outbreak of war in Europe in 1939 made FBI investigations of communists and communist movements a high priority in the pre–World War II era. There was no relaxation of this surveillance role after 1941 when the United States became formally aligned with the Soviet Union against the Axis powers of Germany, Italy, and Japan. Thus, in the Cold War era, the FBI merely intensified ongoing "intelligence" investigations. Counterintelligence investigations were made high priority, and specially trained FBI agents were assigned to monitor Soviet agents, to anticipate and subvert their attempts to recruit as spies American communists, communist sympathizers, or military and government officials motivated by greed.

Highly classified, and dependent on secrecy for their success, the nature, scope, and results of FBI counterintelligence operations during the Cold War era are the least known of FBI activities. The following accounts hint of a larger, successful FBI counterintelligence mission, beyond what has been made public. It is known that in cases when prosecution resulted, FBI officials intentionally did not disclose all obtained evidence, even when disclosure would have confirmed Soviet perfidy. Their main priority was to avoid compromising the FBI's most sensitive programs, procedures, and recruited informers. A discussion of three known cases (Elizabeth Bentley, *Amerasia*, and Judith Coplon) and the recently disclosed code-named Operation Solo program indirectly confirms the limits to our current knowledge of FBI counterintelligence operations.

The Elizabeth Bentley Case

In August and then November 1945, Elizabeth Bentley decided to break from her communist past. She approached FBI agents and disclosed that from 1938 through 1945, she had served as a courier for a wartime Soviet spy ring, formerly headed by her lover, Jacob Golos (a Soviet agent who operated under the cover of World Tourist, a Soviet travel business headquartered in New York City). As a courier for the communist underground, Bentley claimed to have obtained U.S. government documents from communist federal employees recruited by Golos. In her interviews with FBI agents, she named her contacts in the War Production Board and the Treasury Department (notably, Nathan Silvermaster, William Remington, Victor Perlo, Frank Coe, Harold Glasser, and Harry Dexter White). Bentley's uncorroborated allegations triggered an intensive FBI inquiry. In 1948, a federal grand jury convened to consider her charges and the fruits of the FBI's investigation, but no indictments were returned.

Bentley's allegations were almost immediately leaked to the media, and in 1948 and 1950 they precipitated three highly publicized House and Senate investigations. At the time, conservatives championed Bentley's contentions of the existence of a wartime Soviet spy ring. Their principal objective, however, was to impugn the loyalty of New Dealers and thereby discredit the Roosevelt and Truman administrations. Significantly, these congressional hearings did not even attempt to evaluate FBI counterintelligence operations; to discover, for instance, why the FBI had failed to uncover the Golos ring during World War II and then, following Bentley's defection, had failed to uncover enough evidence to secure indictments. This did not mean, however, that the FBI had not monitored the federal employees identified by Bentley, either before or after 1945, or that it had no knowledge of communist underground activities—FBI efforts in this area remain unknown, as relevant records are (in 1997) classified.

The *Amerasia* Case

The *Amerasia* case of June 1945 raises similar questions. In January 1945, an analyst for the wartime Office of Strategic Services (OSS) was struck by the fact that an article

published in *Amerasia,* a journal of Far Eastern affairs, was an almost verbatim summary of a classified OSS report. Concerned over this breach in security, OSS agents broke into the offices of *Amerasia* and thereupon discovered thousands of pages of classified OSS, ONI, and State Department documents. Their break-in was illegal; furthermore, responsibility for domestic security was the province of the FBI. Accordingly, OSS officials advised the FBI of this security breach.

In the subsequent investigation, FBI agents conducted additional break-ins and wiretapped the offices of *Amerasia*, the hotel of one of its editors, and the apartment of one of the identified State Department contacts. Eventually six individuals were arrested: *Amerasia* publisher Philip Jaffe, editor Kate Mitchell, freelance reporter Mark Gayn, ONI employee Andrew Roth, and State Department employees Emmanuel Larsen and John Service. Only three of the six were indicted by a federal grand jury—Jaffe, Roth, and Larsen. Prosecution of these three was circumvented, however, when Larsen discovered that FBI agents had broken into his apartment preceding his arrest. Recognizing the vulnerability of their case, Justice Department officials entered into a plea bargain with Jaffe's attorney (before he could learn of Larsen's discovery).

Although prosecution failed, the *Amerasia* case indirectly highlights the difficulties FBI agents encountered in ascertaining how *Amerasia* editors acquired classified documents. They could legally monitor the office of *Amerasia* and the movements of their editors, but illegal investigative techniques permitted the expeditious identification of the individuals who had provided the leaked documents. By doing so, however, prosecution was undermined. Originally, Justice Department attorneys sought to obscure this problem by a strategy of timing the arrests— whether at *Amerasia*'s office or private residences—and thereby to "discover" pilfered documents through a warranted search. This strategy was subverted by Larsen's inadvertent discovery—struck by the FBI arresting agents' ability to locate easily where he had secreted the documents in his apartment, Larsen queried his janitor, who admitted having earlier allowed the agents to enter his apartment.

The Judith Coplon Case

The same problem recurred in the Judith Coplon case. A low-level Justice Department employee, Coplon was arrested on March 4, 1949, at a time when she had planned to deliver 28 FBI documents to Valentin Gubitchev, a member of the Soviet Union's United Nations staff in New York. Having earlier obtained (through U.S. military intelligence, in a program code-named Venona) deciphered Soviet consular communications, by 1948, FBI counterintelligence specialists were able to identify Coplon as a Soviet spy. Intensively monitoring her activities (including wiretapping her phone), FBI agents uncovered her relationship with Gubitchev. FBI officials then devised a plan to ensure her conviction, which involved permitting her access to selected FBI reports and arresting her at a time when she sought to pass these documents to Gubitchev. During her trial in 1949, the FBI never introduced the evidence obtained through the Venona project—having a greater interest in preserving this sensitive source. Furthermore, Coplon's conviction was eventually overturned. The FBI's illegal wiretapping of Coplon was uncovered, and the Supreme Court's 1939 ruling in *Nardone v. U.S.* required dismissal of the case.

The Bentley, *Amerasia,* and Coplon cases highlight why FBI counterintelligence operations cannot be fully reconstructed at this time. First, the FBI's interest in safeguarding sensitive sources ensured that, when prosecution was considered or actually took place following an investigation, not all the evidence that the FBI had obtained was introduced. Furthermore, in the cases where prosecution was not possible because the FBI had resorted to illegal investigative techniques (which provided otherwise unobtainable information), the prosecutive strategy was to avoid disclosing these illegal activities and win convictions on the basis of legally admissible evidence. The FBI's use of wiretapping and break-ins during counterintelligence investigations, moreover, was not unusual—what *was* exceptional was the inadvertent discovery of information without making use of those means. Continued classification restrictions preclude a full understanding of the extent of FBI wiretapping and break-in activities during counterintelligence investigations and, as important, what information was obtained and what actions were taken to contain Soviet operations (without having to resort to prosecution, risky because FBI methods could be compromised).

Operation Solo

The recent disclosure of one of the FBI's most sensitive counterintelligence programs, code-named Operation Solo, further confirms that prosecution was not the principal objective of FBI counterintelligence operations. Under this program, between 1951 and 1954, FBI agents recruited two high-level Communist Party officials, Morris Childs and

Jack Childs, as double agents. The Childs brothers were a particularly valuable source. As trusted party members, they served as couriers for transmitting Soviet funds to the U.S. Communist Party. Morris Childs also met periodically with high-level Soviet officials in Moscow and with other communist leaders in Soviet bloc countries. Through Operation Solo, then, the FBI acquired invaluable information about communist plans in general and about Soviet contacts with their American counterparts. The sensitivity of the Childses' positions of trust within the Communist Party and their access to Soviet officials necessitated that FBI officials safeguard this source not only during the program's operation but also after the brothers ceased to function as double agents. Significantly, the Childs brothers' roles were never revealed during Smith Act or Subversive Activities Control Board proceedings, even though such evidence on Soviet funding of the U.S. Communist Party would have been invaluable. Furthermore, even though it was probably one of the FBI's most dramatic counterintelligence successes, Operation Solo became known recently only through interviews granted by former FBI agents and the Childs family.

It is indisputable that FBI agents successfully infiltrated the Communist Party and obtained advance intelligence about communist plans, but historians of the FBI still do not have a firm sense of what FBI officials learned and how this intelligence was used. At minimum, Communist Party leaders and recruited Soviet agents could have been prosecuted under the Foreign Agents Registration Act of 1939. But to do so would have required "surfacing" or exposing double agents like the Childs brothers, which would have conflicted with the principal purpose of FBI counterintelligence operations: to understand Soviet plans and objectives.

Cold War Smith Act Cases

Espionage for the Soviet Union by U.S. residents was difficult to establish. Through Operation Solo, the FBI had been able to confirm Soviet funding of the U.S. Communist Party, but not necessarily that the party's leaders directly recruited individuals to spy for the Soviet Union. Elizabeth Bentley's description of a Soviet spy ring did not establish that the Soviet Union had acquired highly sensitive military and diplomatic secrets (her testimony was uncorroborated and her identified sources held low-level positions in the federal bureaucracy). In the *Amerasia* case, in contrast, the editors had acquired classified documents for the purpose of publishing this information in order to influence U.S. foreign policy, but the FBI had not uncovered evidence that these classified reports were forwarded to the Soviet Union. Only the Coplon case—and the Julius and Ethel Rosenberg atomic bomb espionage case (see pages 64–66) and the intercepted Soviet consular messages of 1942–45 of the Venona project—uncovered evidence of Soviet espionage by U.S. residents. The Alger Hiss case of 1948–50 (see pages 62–63) has also been characterized as involving espionage; Hiss, however, was convicted only of perjury—denying to a federal grand jury in 1948 that he had given classified State Department documents to communist functionary Whittaker Chambers in 1938 (at a time when Hiss was a low-level State Department employee). Hiss became the subject of an intensive FBI investigation in 1945, triggered by allegations that he might be a Soviet spy. Significantly, the FBI's investigation of Hiss in 1945–46 (which included tapping his phones) had been initiated later, when Hiss held an important policymaking position in the State Department and could either influence U.S. policy or acquire sensitive diplomatic secrets. This investigation uncovered no evidence of espionage on Hiss's part.

The publicity surrounding the Hiss, Rosenberg, Coplon, Bentley, and *Amerasia* cases, nonetheless, reinforced the popular perception of the 1950s that the U.S. Communist Party was a "Trojan horse," part of a dangerous conspiracy that promoted Soviet communist interests through stealth and subterfuge. Ironically, despite the FBI's successes in obtaining some of the U.S. Communist Party's most sensitive secrets—whether through break-ins, bugs, wire-taps, mail opening, and the recruitment of disgruntled Party members to serve as informers—Communist Party leaders were not prosecuted for espionage, treason, or sedition. Instead, when the top 12 leaders of the U.S. Communist Party were indicted in 1948 for allegedly participating in a conspiracy to promote the violent overthrow of the U.S. government, they were prosecuted under the Smith Act of 1940.

This case *(Dennis v. U.S.)* went to trial in 1949. The FBI evidence focused on communist publications (primarily Marxist classics), and FBI informers testified about how communist leaders planned to promote revolutionary change—thereby violating the Smith Act's prohibition against organizing or teaching the violent overthrow of the U.S. government. Exploiting this broad anti-conspiracy statute, Justice Department attorneys sought convictions of the Communist Party leaders not for overt actions but for

intent (through publications and speech) to effect violent revolution. This effort succeeded as all 12 were convicted—and the Supreme Court, in 1951, upheld their convictions and the constitutionality of the Smith Act.

In contrast to the earlier failed attempts of 1942–44 to prosecute American fascists, the Cold War Smith Act cases against the Communist Party leadership enhanced the FBI's reputation as an effective bulwark against foreign spies. In addition, the latter Smith Act cases silenced criticisms of the scope and purposes of the FBI's monitoring of radical activities—indeed, FBI Director Hoover effectively lumped those who criticized the FBI with those who sought to undermine the nation's internal security. By successfully silencing criticism of FBI operations, Hoover—for a time—subverted any meaningful scrutiny of the FBI's investigative priorities, including whether adequate resources were being devoted to monitoring the postwar upsurge in white collar and organized crime.

The McCarran Act (1950) and the Communist Control Act (1954)

Passage of the Internal Security Act of 1950 (the McCarran Act) and the Communist Control Act of 1954 seemingly provided additional opportunities for FBI prosecutions. The McCarran Act authorized the forced deportation of alien radicals; barred communists from employment in defense industries and from securing passports; required communist, communist-front, and communist-action organizations to register as foreign agents with a specially created Subversive Activities Control Board (SACB), to submit lists of their members to the SACB, and to label their publications as communist propaganda; and authorized the detention of "dangerous radicals" during presidentially declared national emergencies.

The Communist Control Act extended the McCarran Act's registration requirements to include "Communist-infiltrated" organizations; it denied to communist and communist-infiltrated organizations the "rights, privileges, and immunities attendant upon legal bodies," including the right to appear on election ballots; and it denied to communist-infiltrated organizations the right to petition the National Labor Relations Board for union elections and certification.

These laws did not, in fact, shift the FBI's role from intelligence gathering to law enforcement. Instead, the prosecutive option was foreclosed by a series of Supreme Court rulings, in particular the Court's rulings of 1956 and

1965 in *Communist Party v. Subversive Activities Control Board* and *Albertson v. Subversive Activities Control Board.* The Fifth Amendment right against self-incrimination, the Court held (while conceding that the McCarran Act was constitutional), meant that the SACB could not compel members of the Communist Party or front groups to register. Other Court rulings, notably two 1957 decisions in *Yates v. U.S.* and *Jencks v. U.S.,* further deterred prosecution. In *Yates,* the Court, in effect, reversed its earlier ruling in *Dennis v. U.S.,* which had upheld the conviction of the Communist Party leadership under the Smith Act. Reinterpreting and thereby narrowing the effect of this earlier ruling, the Court held that the Smith Act had not prohibited advocacy of violent overthrow of the government per se—only advocacy that led to illegal conduct. The government thus had to prove that indicted communist activists intended to organize a revolution to overthrow the U.S. government. In *Jencks,* moreover, the Court ruled that defense attorneys had the right to examine the pretrial statements that government witnesses had made to the FBI—a ruling that would have breached the confidentiality of FBI files if the Justice Department chose to prosecute based on allegations of FBI informers. Moreover, FBI informers would have to be surfaced during any trial, ending their usefulness for continuing FBI surveillance. In combination, the Court's rulings discouraged the prosecution of Communist Party officials and members.

Containment of Communism and Radical Activism

Having concluded that legal prosecution carried greater costs than benefits, FBI officials sought other ways to contain communism and radical activism. Capitalizing on the heightened internal security concerns of the Cold War years, they instituted a number of secret, but extra-legal programs having this containment purpose.

The deterioration of U.S.-Soviet relations after 1945 and the prospect that tensions could escalate into military conflict created a propitious opportunity for one such program, which had the additional benefit of ensuring ex post facto authorization for the FBI's ongoing Security Index program (see pages 20–21). In March 1946, FBI Director Hoover recommended that Attorney General Tom Clark "determine what legislation is available or should be sought" to institute a program to detain all listed "members of the Communist Party and any others who might be dangerous" in the event the United States went to war or broke diplomatic relations with the Soviet Union. Hoover identified the "others" as including those holding "important positions" in organized labor and civil rights movements, education, churches, and the media "who have shown sympathy for Communist objectives and policies." Such a program, Hoover argued, required "statutory backing."

Attorney General Clark concurred on the need for a detention program but was unwilling to seek congressional authorization, fearing that this "would only bring on a loud and acrimonious discussion." After lengthy deliberations, on August 3, 1948, Clark instead ordered FBI officials to identify and list such dangerous individuals. Clark realized that congressional authorization would be needed in order to detain these individuals, but he concluded that a campaign should first be orchestrated to educate the public to accept "the proposition that Communism is dangerous," and in the crisis atmosphere that would follow the outbreak of war, the government could then seek ex post facto authorization. To effect this strategy, Justice Department officials drafted a presidential proclamation recommending an appropriate congressional resolution authorizing the already instituted program. These were to be released at the time of war to ensure speedy congressional action.

Such legislative authorization seemingly was obtained in September 1950 when Congress enacted the preventive detention title of the McCarran Act—although not because Justice Department officials had lobbied for this provision. Justice Department officials, however, did not welcome this congressional initiative, owing to the fact that the McCarran Act's standards for listing and then detaining individuals were less stringent than those of the ongoing Security Index program. Unwilling to conform to Congress's mandate, FBI and Justice Department officials at first lobbied Congress to amend the McCarran Act to correspond to the Security Index program. When this failed, Attorney General J. Howard McGrath decided to ignore the congressional standards and directed the FBI to continue listing individuals and to base apprehension and detention planning on the 1948 authorization. If a war crisis developed, FBI and Justice Department officials again concurred, Congress would be more inclined to amend the McCarran Act to correspond to their Security Index program.

The detainment title of the Security Index program never became operational, despite U.S. involvement in the Korean War in June 1950 and that war's escalation following Chinese Communist intervention in November 1950.

Regardless, it remains an example of how FBI officials—on their own—sought alternative extra-legal means to contain the possible influence of radical activists.

On August 28, 1956, FBI Director Hoover—on his own—authorized a project code-named COINTELPRO–Communist Party. COINTELPRO is a contraction for "counterintelligence program," and the purpose of the program was to undermine communist "influence over the masses, ability to create controversy leading to confusion and disunity, penetration of specific channels in American life where public opinion is molded, and espionage and sabotage potential." Through tactics such as anonymously sending letters with disruptive contents to party members or allowing carefully camouflaged leaks to sympathetic reporters and members of Congress, FBI officials attempted to "disrupt" and discredit the Communist Party. Basically, COINTELPRO–Communist Party refined and extended tactics that FBI officials had adopted as early as 1946, but the more aggressive stance constituted an even sharper departure from the FBI's law enforcement mission than programs such as the Security Index. COINTELPRO activities, based on a self-determined mission of defining the parameters of permissible political conduct, were unknown even to the president and the attorney general, and they were not subject to public or judicial challenge as to their purpose and legality.

"Educational Campaign" and Other Information Dissemination

Concurrent with their March 1946 decision to secure Attorney General Clark's approval of a Security Index program, FBI officials in February 1946 launched an "educational campaign" so that "in the event of an emergency we will have an informed public opinion." By releasing through "available channels" "educational material" demonstrating the "basically Russian nature" of the U.S. Communist Party, FBI officials believed they could undermine communist support from the trade union movement, from within the liberal religious community, and more generally from political and social liberals. "Available channels" included reporters, columnists, editors, members of Congress, and congressional committees. The sole condition was that the recipient of material intended for dissemination not disclose that it originated with the FBI.

At first implemented informally, the FBI's educational campaign was refined and expanded during the 1950s. A formal effort, code-named the Mass Media program, was implemented in 1956. The FBI's liaison relationship with members of Congress and congressional committees differed, shaped by the political opportunism of recipient collaborators, notably the chief counsels and chairs of the House Committee on Un-American Activities (HUAC), the Senate Internal Security Subcommittee (SISS), and Senator Joseph McCarthy.

Responding to a request from the chairman and chief counsel of HUAC for FBI assistance for planned hearings into communist influence in Hollywood, FBI Director Hoover ordered FBI officials to "expedite" the requested assistance. In response, the HUAC staff was first provided with the names of directors, writers, and actors who should be called to testify, distinguishing between individuals willing to identify which of their associates were communists and those who were or had been Communist Party members. In addition, FBI officials subsequently prepared for the HUAC staff a detailed report on communist influence in Hollywood, summary memoranda on subpoenaed witnesses, and photocopies of their Communist Party membership cards. The FBI's assistance proved crucial to the committee's highly publicized hearings of October 1947 that led to contempt charges of 10 subpoenaed producers and writers. Thereafter, FBI officials provided various kinds of assistance to HUAC members and staff. The propensity of some committee members and staff to betray the source of this assistance complicated what was intended to be a secret arrangement. In response, FBI Director Hoover terminated FBI assistance, then resumed limited assistance, and eventually honored certain requests he considered meritorious (as in the case of the committee's 1960 attempt to discredit those calling for HUAC's abolition).

The same ambivalence characterized the relationship between FBI officials and Senator Joseph McCarthy during the period from 1950 through 1953 (see Exhibit 1.3). When the senator catapulted to national prominence in February–June 1950 by accusing the Truman administration of knowingly harboring "Communists in the State Department," FBI officials cautiously provided information (but not FBI reports) to the senator. By 1952, McCarthy was able to exploit this informal relationship to obtain advice on strategy and recommendations on possible staff appointees. FBI assistance ended abruptly in July 1953 when McCarthy hired an FBI supervisor, Francis Carr, to serve as staff counsel to the Senate Committee on Government Operations, which he then chaired. The FBI director opposed this appointment, advising McCarthy's aides that should the

Exhibit 1.3   *Left to right:* **Joseph McCarthy, Clyde Tolson, unidentified, and J. Edgar Hoover,** *Courtesy of the National Archives (65-H-1414-1)*

senator subsequently publicize FBI-related information, the Carr appointment would inevitably raise questions about McCarthy's "pipeline" to the FBI. When Senator McCarthy, nonetheless, went ahead with the Carr appointment, Hoover terminated FBI assistance.

In contrast, in February 1951, the FBI (this time with the approval of Attorney General J. Howard McGrath) instituted a secret liaison program with the SISS. FBI officials processed "name check" requests submitted by SISS staff (searching FBI files for information on the identified individuals) and provided background information on public and private organizations (ranging from labor unions and the Institute of Pacific Relations to the film, radio, and publishing industries). The FBI's assistance proved crucial to SISS's objective of educating the public about the seriousness of the communist threat—not the threat of espionage, but the ability of communists and other radicals to promote change or influence public opinion. However, in 1953–54, when Republican SISS members and staff violated Hoover's condition of confidentiality and threatened to involve the FBI in what became a partisan conflict with their Democratic counterparts, Hoover drastically cut back FBI assistance to "public source" information. Eventually, FBI officials bypassed the SISS staff to work directly with those SISS members, such as Senator James Eastland, who could be trusted to respect the FBI director's insistence on confidentiality.

FBI officials instituted other information-dissemination programs; notably, one in February 1951 that was code-named the Responsibilities program. Under this program, state governors and prominent civic leaders (e.g., officials in the Red Cross, members of police departments, and individuals such as former Republican President Herbert Hoover) were given FBI reports on suspected subversives employed in state agencies, in public or private colleges, or as elementary or high school teachers. Hoover privately rationalized this intelligence-dissemination program as deriving from the FBI's responsibility to safeguard the nation's internal security. Because "public utilities, public organizations and semi-public organizations" served "large portions of the public," the FBI had "an obligation for the protection of the facilities when we have information of a subversive nature affecting them." The Responsibilities Program was terminated in 1955, again when Hoover's condition of confidentially was breached by some of the governors.

FBI efforts also extended to disseminating information about homosexuals. In June 1951, Hoover unilaterally authorized a code-named Sex Deviates program to purge suspected homosexuals from government service, on the premise that the widespread intolerance and condemnation of homosexuality by most of U.S. society at that time made homosexuals vulnerable to being blackmailed into betraying national secrets. FBI officials had begun collecting information about homosexuals as early as 1937 but had not used this information systematically. Under the Sex Deviates program, "allegations concerning present and past" federal employees were to be forwarded to designated officials in the executive, legislative, and judicial branches. In time, Hoover expanded these dissemination efforts to include "information concerning sex deviates employed either by institutions of higher learning or law enforcement agencies."

The FBI's various "educational" initiatives had no law enforcement purpose. In addition, they contradicted the image the Bureau projected—of a highly disciplined, apolitical agency committed both to safeguarding the nation from criminals and spies and to respecting constitutional rights. Ironically, the success of these educational programs depended on the ability of FBI officials to employ illegal investigative techniques and, in the process, minimize any meaningful oversight of FBI practices. The evolution of FBI wiretapping and bugging policies highlights this.

Wiretapping and Bugging Policies

Dating from 1940 (despite the Communication Act's ban, in 1934), FBI wiretapping had been authorized under President Franklin Roosevelt's secret directive (see page 21). Roosevelt, however, had intended that FBI wiretaps would be limited to "national defense" investigations and, to ensure this, had required the attorney general's advance approval of each FBI wiretap. The decision of Attorney General Robert Jackson (and his successors) to not maintain records of FBI requests had the unanticipated result of enabling FBI wiretapping to extend beyond Roosevelt's specified limit. But this rendered the FBI even more vulnerable. To head off possible future problems and to sustain an expanded use during "subversive activities" investigations, in July 1946, by misrepresenting Roosevelt's intentions, FBI Director Hoover obtained President Truman's approval of FBI wiretapping in cases "vitally affecting the domestic security, or when human life is in jeopardy."

FBI officials' surveillance extended beyond wiretapping to the use of hidden microphones (bugs). Because bugs normally were installed after a break-in at an office or residence, and thus posed Fourth Amendment problems, FBI officials had—on their own—authorized such practices since the early 1940s. In October 1951, J. Edgar Hoover for the first time directly sought the policy guidance of the attorney general (at the time, J. Howard McGrath) concerning the FBI's break-ins for the installation of microphones to obtain "intelligence information highly pertinent to the defense and welfare of the country." Responding on February 26, 1952, McGrath stipulated, "I cannot authorize the installation of a microphone *involving a trespass* under existing law."

The attorney general thus did not directly ban such practices but created a written document of his conclusion that such installations were illegal. The sole effect of this reply was to cause a scaling back, not a termination, of such FBI activities.

The election of the more sympathetic Eisenhower administration in 1952 provided an opportunity to revisit this matter. The administration's interest in expanding FBI surveillance led FBI officials in March 1954 to recommend that Attorney General Herbert Brownell authorize FBI break-ins to install bugs during national security investigations. The same procedure was to be adopted as that governing FBI wiretapping: FBI officials were to seek the attorney general's prior approval, and decisions would be made on a case-by-case basis. Brownell concurred that hidden microphones were an invaluable investigative technique. Seeking to minimize the possible discovery of this authorization, he further concluded that he "would be in a much better position to defend the Bureau in the event there should be a technical trespass if he had not heretofore approved it." Accordingly, Brownell's broadly worded secret directive of May 1954 empowered FBI officials to break into homes and offices, to install surveillance microphones without having to notify him and obtain his advance approval in each case.

Attorney General Brownell's willingness to defer responsibility to the FBI director effectively subverted the ability of Justice Department officials to review the targets of FBI break-ins and bugging and the duration of such surveillance operations. As a result, Brownell and his successors were unaware of the vast number of FBI microphone installations. Within days of Brownell's secret directive, FBI officials decided also to use bugs during "important" crime cases, on the understanding that such installations "will only be approved by high Bureau officials."

Recognizing the political risks inherent in employing recognizably illegal investigative techniques and disseminating information to influence public opinion, FBI officials adopted safeguards to preclude the discovery of these actions. Although attorneys general might have willingly declined to monitor FBI activities and deliberately did not create records of what they had authorized, Hoover's own oversight rules created a risk that such activities could be discovered inadvertently. To avert this eventuality, additional records procedures were instituted. In June 1949, Hoover approved the JUNE mail procedure. Whenever reporting information obtained from "highly confidential sources" (i.e., wiretaps, bugs, break-ins, or mail opening) or from "the most sensitive sources, such as Governors, secretaries to high officials who may be discussing such officials and their attitude," FBI agents were to caption these reports "JUNE." Thus captioned, these reports were to be routed to the Special File Room at FBI headquarters to be "maintained under lock and key." Hoover supplemented these restrictions in July 1949 when issuing *Bureau Bulletin* number 34. Whenever uncovering information that "could cause embarrassment to the Bureau, if distributed," agents were not to include this information within the text of their report but instead "on administrative pages attached to the regular report." Officials at FBI headquarters could detach the administrative pages whenever the report was "distributed to agencies outside the Bureau"—and no one would know that information was being withheld.

Hoover, in time, concluded that additional rules were needed to prevent discovery of these separately filed records. Dating from their inception as a special recordkeeping method, informal and Do Not File memoranda were to be destroyed "after action is taken." FBI assistant directors retained these memoranda in their office files and decided when to destroy them. In March 1953, Hoover ended this discretionary arrangement and ordered FBI assistant directors to "destroy them as promptly as possible but in no case shall they be retained in excess of six months."

From Anticommunism to "Law and Order" (1956–72)

The Cold War reshaped the FBI's role and mission, making internal security and counterintelligence high priorities. Closely monitoring identified or suspected Soviet agents during the 1950s and after, FBI agents uncovered a number of cases of Soviet spying activities, the most notable involving the 1957 arrest of Soviet spy Rudolf Abel and the 1958 apprehension of another Soviet spy, Kaarlo Tuomi (who was turned into a double agent).

The breakdown of the nation's anticommunist consensus during the 1960s, however, both altered and redefined the FBI's role. Increasingly, during this tumultuous decade, American liberals as well as radicals organized to challenge U.S. policy toward Cuba, nuclear weapons testing and the arms race, racial and sexual discrimination, and, most dramatically, the controversial Vietnam War. Religious beliefs and social justice principles underpinned this new and broader political activism. Rejecting the premises of the containment policy—in which revolutionary movements were identified with communist subversion—liberals and radicals organized to challenge the nation's foreign policy and national priorities. Inevitably, the new organizations they formed (ranging from the Southern Christian Leadership Conference to the Women's Strike for Peace, Students for a Democratic Society, and Clergy and Laity Concerned About Vietnam) became the subjects of FBI surveillance, ostensibly to ascertain whether communist infiltration had occurred.

The militancy of some of these groups soon led FBI officials to move beyond simple monitoring. In October 1961, FBI Director Hoover launched another counterintelligence program: COINTELPRO–Socialist Workers Party. Hoover's action was triggered by concerns that the revolutionary Socialist Workers Party (SWP) had sought to promote "its line on a local and national basis through running candidates for public office and strongly directing and/or supporting such causes as Castro's Cuba and integration problems arising in the South." Under its "disruptive" COINTELPRO–Socialist Workers Party program, FBI agents attempted to sow dissension within the SWP's ranks and to promote a hostile public opinion by leaks to favored reporters—despite the fact that the SWP had a minuscule membership and never commanded public support for (or even awareness of) its message of violent revolution. The COINTELPRO–Socialist Workers Party, nonetheless, became the forerunner of additional COINTELPROs. These subsequent COINTELPROs targeted militant organizations that—unlike the SWP and the Communist Party—had the potential to undermine public support for official policy and to promote disorder.

The violent resistance to racial equality by white supremacist groups in the South during the 1960s precipitated the code-named COINTELPRO–White Hate. Under this program, FBI agents were ordered on September 2, 1964, to take steps to "frustrate any effort" by the Ku Klux Klan and other white supremacist organizations to "recruit new or youthful adherents." FBI agents should miss no "opportunity" to expose the "devious maneuvers and duplicity" of white supremacist groups. This was to be done "through the cooperation of reliable news media sources" and by seeking to "capitalize upon organizational and personal conflicts of their leadership."

The concurrent upsurge of urban race riots and the emergence of black nationalist groups commanding broad support among many embittered African Americans led to another program, COINTELPRO–Black Nationalist Hate. Instituted in August 1967, this program sought to "expose, disrupt, misdirect, or otherwise neutralize the activities of black nationalist, hate-type organizations and groupings, their leadership, spokesmen, membership, and supporters, and to counter their propensity for violence and civil disorder."

Then, in reaction to the growth of radicalism on college campuses and student opposition to the Vietnam War, in October 1968 Hoover authorized COINTELPRO–New Left to "confuse and disrupt New Left activities by misinformation" and other disruptive and harassment tactics. FBI agents were ordered to implement this program "with imagination and enthusiasm," with the objective being to reduce or contain "their violent and illegal activities."

The secrecy shrouding FBI activities permitted the expansion of the COINTELPROs. In the tense climate of the Cold War, members of Congress willingly granted broad latitude to FBI officials, based on the assumption that FBI efforts would be directed to containing foreign-directed subversion. By overstepping those understood limits, FBI officials became vulnerable to congressional restrictions on their powers if their full range of activities became known.

Intelligence Arm of the White House

FBI Director Hoover unilaterally authorized the various COINTELPROs. Nonetheless, with the exception of the COINTELPRO–Socialist Workers Party, the FBI director's decisions had been made, in part, in response to pressures from the White House. Presidents might not have known of the FBI's specific harassment activities, but they had demanded that the FBI investigate violent groups and individuals for purposes of prosecution. Unable to prosecute, FBI officials instead opted to "disrupt" and "harass." Thus, COINTELPRO–White Hate was prompted by President Lyndon Johnson's demand for an intensification of FBI investigations in the South, after he concluded that local police officials were unwilling to protect civil rights activists from violent attacks by white supremacists. Eager to discredit those responsible for urban race riots and antiwar demonstrations, Presidents Johnson and Nixon demanded increased FBI surveillance, triggering the creation of COINTELPRO–Black Nationalist Hate and COINTELPRO–New Left.

Since 1940, moreover, presidents had also pressured FBI officials to provide them with useful intelligence about the strategies of radical activists and other critics who sought to undermine public support for their policy objectives. This reporting relationship thereafter continued to shape the FBI's role.

Throughout the 1950s, FBI Director Hoover regularly forwarded to the Eisenhower White House reports on the planned activities of right-wing and left-wing activists and on the political and personal activities of such individuals as former first lady Eleanor Roosevelt, Democratic presidential candidate Adlai Stevenson, Supreme Court Justice William O. Douglas, *New York Times* reporter Harrison Salisbury, and syndicated columnists Joseph Alsop and Stewart Alsop.

Sensitive to the president's political concerns, in March 1956, Hoover briefed Eisenhower's cabinet on the "explosive" racial situation in the South, attributing this to the Supreme Court's 1954 desegregation decision. Behind this Southern concern over "mixed education," Hoover warned, "stalks the specter of racial [sic] marriage." The National Association for the Advancement of Colored People (NAACP), in particular, was exacerbating these tensions by preaching "racial hatred." Then, referring to an upcoming NAACP conference on civil rights, Hoover raised the possibility of communist influence, emphasizing that "the Communist Party plans to use this conference to embarrass the administration and Dixiecrats [Southern Democrats] who have supported it, by forcing the Administration to take a stand on [currently proposed] civil rights legislation, with the present Congress." The resulting rift this would create between the administration and Southern Democrats could "affect the 1956 election." Hoover's briefing of President Eisenhower's cabinet in March 1956 occurred in the presence of the attorney general, although Hoover's usual practice had been to bypass the attorney general and submit reports directly to the White House. These reports, after all, might be met with disapproval by the Justice Department head; they confirmed that political activities were being monitored and that the acquired information had not been used for law enforcement purposes.

Hoover's direct link to the president changed during the Kennedy administration, owing to the unique circumstance that the president's brother served as attorney general. Thus during Kennedy's presidency, FBI intelligence reports to the White House declined. The most sensitive of these reports, moreover, were triggered by specific requests from the White House or the attorney general. For example, responding to White House demands to identify the sources of leaked classified information to *Newsweek* and the *New York Times* in 1961 and 1962, the FBI investigated and wiretapped reporters Lloyd Norman and Hanson Baldwin. Also in 1961 and again in 1962, the FBI wiretapped three Agriculture Department officials, the secretary to House Agricultural Committee chairman Harold Cooley, and a Washington, D.C., law firm hired by the Dominican Republic to lobby the Congress on sugar quota legislation. After learning that Cooley was to meet representatives of the Dominican Republic government in New York City,

Hoover authorized FBI agents to bug the meeting. This initiative was triggered partly by foreign policy concerns: the Kennedy administration had sought to deny Dominican sugar exports to the U.S. market in order to pressure that country's authoritarian government to institute democratic reforms.

A new era in FBI–White House relations was ushered in under Presidents Lyndon Johnson and Richard Nixon. Having reached the mandatory retirement age of 70 on January 1, 1965, J. Edgar Hoover was able to continue as FBI director only because of a waiver President Johnson granted in 1964 (which President Nixon continued) and Hoover became far more subservient to the White House. Compounding this situation, both Johnson and Nixon unhesitatingly demanded that the FBI investigate their foreign policy critics and domestic adversaries. Because public opposition to the Vietnam War had broadened, FBI reports grew to include prominent reporters, members of Congress, and civic leaders.

The scope of the FBI's assistance soon expanded to unprecedented levels. President Johnson—insecure over having acceded to the presidency through Kennedy's assassination and distrustful of the loyalty of Kennedy holdovers on the White House staff and in the Justice Department—welcomed and solicited reports about the plans of suspected Kennedy loyalists from FBI Director Hoover during the crucial months of January through March, 1964. After Robert Kennedy resigned as attorney general and won election to the U.S. Senate, Hoover continued to exploit Johnson's concerns about the former attorney general; Johnson bitterly resented Kennedy's criticisms of his Vietnam War policies and Kennedy's influence among liberals in the Democratic Party and Congress.

Johnson's personal concerns also underlay his request—and Hoover's agreement—to send a special FBI squad to the 1964 Democratic National Convention. This squad kept the White House abreast of the plans of civil rights activists and their liberal supporters who sought to ensure the seating of the Mississippi Freedom Democratic Party delegation (which could adversely affect Johnson's candidacy in the South during the upcoming presidential election).

With the formal split between President Johnson and Senator J. William Fulbright over the administration's Vietnam War policy, in 1966 the FBI responded to another White House request and monitored the hearings held that year by the Senate Foreign Relations Committee on the Vietnam War, which Fulbright chaired. In 1966–68 the contacts of members of Congress and congressional staff with Soviet and Soviet bloc embassies also were monitored. President Johnson was particularly interested in information that "sets out the Communist Party line concerning some of the issues" raised by members of Congress during the hearings. Responding to other White House requests to link antiwar critics with subversion, FBI officials briefed members of Congress "so that they might not only make speeches upon the floor of Congress but also publicly," drafted a speech for delivery by a congressman, provided information to "be used by prominent officials of the administration whom the President intends to send in various parts of the country to speak on the Vietnam situation," and forwarded to the White House derogatory information on administration critics in the public and the media.

The FBI's reporting relationship was further refined and expanded during Nixon's presidency under the code-named INLET program. Beginning in 1969, at the request of the White House, the FBI also wiretapped certain members of the Nixon White House and National Security Council (NSC) staffs and four Washington-based news reporters. The initial purpose of these wiretaps was to ascertain the source of a leak to the *New York Times* concerning the administration's decision to bomb Cambodia (at a time when this escalation was intentionally withheld from Congress and the media). The FBI investigation never uncovered the source of the leak, but the wiretaps continued until 1971 insofar as they provided valuable political intelligence (two of the tapped NSC staffers joined the campaign of prospective Democratic presidential aspirant Senator Edmund Muskie in 1970). To promote President Nixon's strategy of discrediting the national media, in November 1970, Hoover processed a particularly sensitive presidential request for damaging personal information (concerning homosexuality and "any other stuff") about members of the Washington press corps.

Despite the magnitude of the FBI's assistance, Nixon remained dissatisfied with the extent of the FBI's surveillance reports. In June 1970, the president decided to enhance FBI monitoring activities while making the FBI (and the other intelligence agencies) more subservient to the White House. To achieve these objectives, a special interagency committee was appointed (composed of representatives from the FBI, CIA, National Security

Agency, and military intelligence agencies) to evaluate the intelligence collection methods then in place and to recommend needed changes. The resultant plan authorized the FBI and the other intelligence agencies to employ wiretaps, bugs, mail opening, and the interception of international messages to obtain information that could link radical antiwar and civil rights activists to foreign governments. Aware of the risks if it were disclosed that he directly authorized (in the language of the plan) "clearly illegal" activities, President Nixon had the authorization memorandum for the plan sent out under the signature of White House aide Tom Charles Huston.

FBI Director Hoover had originally resisted the proposed changes, concluding that they were too risky in the climate of opinion of the times and that "leaks to the press . . . would be damaging." Thus, when the so-called Huston Plan was instituted despite his objections and without direct presidential authorization, Hoover feared that the FBI had been put in a vulnerable position. Accordingly, he notified Attorney General John Mitchell of his willingness to "implement the instructions of the White House at your direction." Hoover added that he "would continue to seek [Mitchell's] specific authorization" each time the FBI conducted an illegal activity. Because Hoover's proposal subverted his strategy of deniability, President Nixon recalled Huston's authorization memorandum. Nonetheless, the FBI continued to employ illegal investigative techniques during its intensive monitoring of radicals, and it forwarded to the White House "general intelligence information" about internal security developments, planned demonstrations and riots, and "items with such an unusual twist or concerning prominent personalities which may be of special interest to the President or the Attorney General."

Organized Crime and the Top Hoodlum Program

During the Cold War era, the overwhelming primacy of internal security and counterintelligence matters diverted FBI resources from prosecuting organized crime and other more mundane law enforcement pursuits. In consequence, during the 1940s and 1950s, state and local police assumed the major responsibility for combating the increasingly sophisticated and powerful crime syndicates. This might seem paradoxical, considering the belief that evolved during the 1910–35 period that local and state police forces could

not, without federal assistance, safeguard the nation from organized prostitution, interstate car theft, bank robberies, and kidnapping.

The FBI's apparent dereliction of duty in the war against organized crime had encountered muted criticism during the 1940s and 1950s, to which the FBI director responded by emphasizing his aversion to the creation of a "national police force" and citing the FBI's limited legislative authority. Hoover conceded that crime was a serious societal problem, but denied the existence of a nationwide crime syndicate, a Mafia controlled and directed by Italian and Italian American crime families. "No single individual or coalition of racketeers," he asserted, "dominates organized crime across the nation." This stance became untenable after November 1957.

On November 14, 1957, New York state trooper Edgar Croswell observed the arrival of a procession of limousines with out-of-state license plates at the secluded estate of New York crime boss Joseph Barbara Sr., in Apalachin, New York. Establishing a road block—ostensibly to determine (under New York motor vehicle law) whether drivers and occupants had valid identification—Croswell discovered a gathering of 63 reputed crime bosses from around the country (see pages 119–20). That an ordinary New York state trooper could discover a conclave of crime leaders of Italian descent raised questions about the FBI's vaunted efficiency. Were FBI officials as completely uninformed about the links between crime families as it appeared? At a minimum, FBI officials were under great pressure to wage a more effective war on organized crime and rebut the notion of their seeming indifference.

Within days after the Apalachin story broke, FBI Director Hoover instituted a program code-named Top Hoodlum. FBI field offices were ordered to intensify their monitoring to identify and prepare reports on the activities and associations of the "top 10 hoodlums" in their area. These investigations were to be a high priority.

The Top Hoodlum program did not substantially increase federal prosecution of organized crime leaders, however. FBI agents could not develop evidence to ensure convictions, in large part because they could neither infiltrate tightly controlled crime families nor recruit informers from within their ranks. As a result, the Top Hoodlum program evolved into an intelligence operation that utilized the same illegal investigative techniques (wiretaps, bugs, and break-ins) as had been employed in monitoring political radicals.

Through these techniques, FBI officials uncovered invaluable intelligence about the general plans and associates of organized crime leaders. Indeed, through a bug installed in a mob hangout in Chicago, FBI agents confirmed the existence of a national "Commission," La Cosa Nostra, and learned the names of its members. But this discovery served no prosecutive purpose. Furthermore, FBI officials could not risk using wiretap or break-in information to ensure convictions—crime bosses hired high-powered attorneys who were alert to the possibility of illegally obtained evidence. Thus, ironically, the FBI's use of wiretaps, bugs, and break-ins immunized their Top Hoodlum subjects from criminal prosecution. This very fact also deterred FBI officials from disseminating much of the intelligence to the Justice Department—lest attorneys general (who neither knew about nor authorized the FBI bugging and break-ins) inquire how the information had been obtained.

The Top Hoodlum program, however, did have a limited by-product. FBI agents were able to pierce the protective shield created by the oaths of *omertà* among crime syndicate members by, in rare cases, recruiting informers—most notably, Joseph Valachi. A member of New York City's Vito Genovese crime family, Valachi had been convicted for heroin trafficking, and in June 1962 agreed to become an FBI informer in return for a reduced sentence. Although Valachi could provide no direct evidence to ensure convictions of his crime associates, he offered an insider's account of the organizational setup and tactics of La Cosa Nostra, as well as titillating commentary on rituals of silence and honor.

Historically, FBI officials had resisted surfacing the Bureau's highly placed counterintelligence and internal security informers (for example, the Childs brothers; see page 26). In contrast, they decided to disclose Valachi's successful recruitment. Valachi's testimony was publicized in the Sunday newspaper supplement, *Parade,* and during hearings conducted in September 1963 by a Senate subcommittee. The publicity refurbished the FBI's reputation. Indeed, *Parade*'s article began, "La Cosa Nostra, the secret, murderous underworld combine about which you have been reading in your newspaper, is no secret to the FBI."

While the Valachi testimony offset the embarrassment of Apalachin, it marked no departure in the FBI's law enforcement role. Organized crime investigations had become a higher priority, but until the 1970s and 1980s, few convictions resulted. The underlying problem was that

Valachi's recruitment as an FBI informer was an exception, and the FBI's most productive sources of information remained illegal investigative techniques. This situation changed in the late 1960s when Congress enacted legislation providing FBI officials with the tools essential to a successful war on crime—rescinding the legislative ban against wiretapping and instituting less restrictive standards for conviction under federal law.

The OCCSS Act (1968) and the RICO Act (1970)

Upon assuming office in 1961, Attorney General Robert Kennedy launched a major assault on organized crime. Exploiting the limited authority of federal antiracketeering laws, the attorney general sought to convict prominent crime bosses (Angelo Bruno, Louis Gallo, Stefano Magadinno, Joseph Aiuppa, Sam Giancana, and Carlos Marcello) and the corrupt president of the Teamsters' Union (James Hoffa). For the most part, Kennedy's ambitious objectives failed—Hoffa's conviction, for example, was for jury tampering, while Louis Gallo and his father were convicted for making false statements in a Veterans Administration application and Joseph Aiuppa for violating the Migratory Bird Act (he possessed more than the legal limit of mourning doves). The attorney general had also created a special organized crime task force in the Justice Department to coordinate this intensified anticrime initiative and unhesitatingly approved FBI requests to wiretap suspected crime bosses. Approving FBI wiretap requests, however, could not promote law enforcement and, thus, in 1961 and 1962, Attorney General Kennedy lobbied Congress to legalize wiretapping.

Kennedy's efforts to repeal the Communications Act's ban on wiretaps were unsuccessful. The upsurge of urban race riots during the mid- and late 1960s, the open disdain for the law and for traditional moral values by militant student antiwar and radical activists, and the increase in crimes of violence in the nation's cities created a new political dynamic. By the late 1960s, Southern Democrats and conservative Republicans abandoned their traditional opposition to expanding the federal government's law enforcement powers. Championing "law and order," they secured enactment of the Omnibus Crime Control and Safe Streets (OCCSS) Act of 1968 and the Racketeer Influenced and Corrupt Organization (RICO) Act of 1970.

These acts revolutionized law enforcement, centering responsibility at the federal level. A key section of OCCSS legalized the use of wiretaps and bugs during criminal investigations, subject to court-approved warrants (although broad permissive language affirmed the president's constitutional right to authorize wiretaps unilaterally during "national security" investigations and to safeguard the nation from revolutionary or "unlawful" change). As importantly, RICO criminalized the acquisition, maintenance, or control of a business funded through illegal activities and the use of a business to conduct an illegal activity. These laws effectively subverted the principal obstacles to an effective federal war on crime.

The OCCSS's legalization of wiretaps and bugs made it easier for the FBI to obtain hard evidence: sophisticated criminals did not create paper trails, and they also adopted procedures making it difficult to infiltrate and obtain information about their criminal enterprises. Along with OCCSS, RICO's permissive standards allowed a more effective attack on organized gambling, prostitution, misuse of union pension funds, narcotics trafficking, and loansharking, since many criminals laundered the funds they acquired illicitly through legitimate businesses or used legitimate businesses as fronts for their criminal activities. RICO also provided a further avenue to attack white collar crime, notably influence peddling and other forms of political corruption.

Scandal and Reform (1972–80)

The political crisis of the Watergate affair of 1972 undermined Richard Nixon's presidency, and in the process, affected the FBI's role and powers. In the spring and summer of 1973, a special Senate committee, chaired by Democratic senator Sam Ervin, initiated a highly publicized inquiry into the president's role (and that of his key aides) in the Watergate break-in and cover-up. In June 1972, five individuals had been apprehended when attempting to bug (and photocopy papers in) the headquarters of the Democratic National Committee at the Watergate apartment and office complex. The resultant investigation linked them and two other individuals—G. Gordon Liddy and E. Howard Hunt—to the 1972 Nixon reelection committee. Further revelations raised questions about whether the seven had acted alone and whether White House aides and the president were involved in an attempted cover-up to preclude discovery of other illegal activities conducted under the direction and authorization of the Nixon administration.

The Senate investigation uncovered evidence of these (Nixon administration) abuses of power (notably, the aborted Huston Plan and the FBI's wiretapping of NSC and White House aides and prominent reporters between 1969 and 1971). Seeking to contain the evolving scandal, President Nixon justified his refusal to comply with congressional requests for White House records on "executive privilege" and "national security" grounds. This strategy proved counterproductive and, instead, raised questions whether secrecy was being employed to preclude discovery of presidential abuses of power.

Further developments during 1973 increased public and congressional skepticism, culminating in a House of Representatives inquiry on whether to impeach President Nixon. However, Nixon resigned in August 1974 before the Senate voted on the impeachment resolution. Questions were also raised about the relationship between the president and the FBI—had the FBI been politicized, and had it wittingly employed "clearly illegal" techniques? These concerns intensified following a series of congressional and press revelations of 1974–75. These included disclosures of the FBI's various COINTELPROs and the fact that FBI Director Hoover (who had died in May 1972) had maintained a secret office file containing derogatory personal and political information on presidents, members of Congress, cabinet officials, and other prominent Americans. Similar questions had been raised about the Central Intelligence Agency (CIA), since five of those indicted for the Watergate break-in had ties to the Agency. Then, in December 1974, *New York Times* reporter Seymour Hersh dramatically publicized the CIA's massive and illegal Operation CHAOS program, in which Vietnam War opponents and civil rights activists were monitored.

In response, in 1975 special Senate and House committees (chaired respectively by Senator Frank Church and Representative Otis Pike) were established to investigate—for the first time—the scope, nature, and authorization of FBI (and CIA) activities. These investigations uncovered and publicized how, since the 1930s, the FBI had intensively investigated the political activities of American citizens, had employed illegal investigative techniques, had sought to harass targeted organizations and citizens, had operated as the intelligence arm of the White House, and had not been subject to the strict oversight of either the president or the attorney general.

The Levi Guidelines and FBI Charter Legislation

By the mid-1970s, a new consensus had evolved concerning the FBI's role and powers, one rejecting the post-Roosevelt development of deference to the chief executive. Indeed, in its final report, the Church Committee recommended that Congress enact a legislative charter for the FBI spelling out the parameters of FBI investigative authority. FBI charter legislation was intended to preclude the recurrence of politically motivated investigations and attendant violations of privacy and constitutional rights.

But this consensus masked fundamental differences. Liberals and conservatives might have concurred that delimiting the FBI's role should no longer remain exclusively an executive responsibility, but they differed over whether specific legislated restrictions were desirable. Many conservatives objected to proposals intended to spell out precisely the limits to FBI investigative authority and to confine FBI investigations to suspected violations of federal statutes. The potential recurrence of internal security threats, they argued, necessitated giving FBI officials some discretion to initiate investigations of individuals and organizations advocating violent or unlawful activities. They further believed that Justice Department officials (and not legislation) should establish the rules and procedures that would prevent internal security investigations from evolving into political surveillance. These differences over the specificity of charter restrictions delayed enactment of any FBI charter legislation during the 1976–80 period.

In the interim, in March 1976, Attorney General Edward Levi issued new guidelines to govern FBI "domestic security" investigations—that is, investigations pertaining to perceived internal security threats. (The attorney general concurrently issued secret guidelines governing FBI counterintelligence and foreign intelligence investigations.) The Levi Guidelines sought to achieve two objectives: (1) to provide some latitude to permit the initiation of FBI investigations based on political advocacy and not criminal conduct, but to limit their scope and duration to a provable intent to commit violence or crime, and (2) to subject such potentially noncriminal investigations to the supervision of the attorney general.

Under the Levi Guidelines, FBI officials could initiate investigations based on "allegations or other information that an individual or group may be engaged in activities which involve or will involve the violation of federal law." These "preliminary" investigations were to be confined to 90 days and were limited to confirming or refuting the "allegations or other information." In contrast, "full" investigations had to be based on "specific and articulable facts giving reason to believe that an individual or group is or may be engaged in activities which involve or will involve the use of force or violence and which involve or will involve the violation of federal law."

The Levi Guidelines also required that FBI officials' decisions pass Justice Department scrutiny. Full investigations had to be authorized by Justice Department officials who, at least annually, had to "determine in writing whether continued investigation is warranted." Vesting responsibility in the Justice Department for determining whether the standard of illegal conduct had been met, this requirement for written authorization in effect precluded the earlier practice wherein attorneys general, seeking deniability, evaded responsibility by deliberately ignoring FBI intelligence-gathering practices (see pages 21 and 31).

Diversity Issues

FBI officials were subject to other political pressures, as well. During the 1960s, demands for racial and sexual equality commanded broad public support, and in 1964, Congress enacted legislation prohibiting racial and sexual discrimination. To redress previous discrimination, President Nixon in 1969 instituted affirmative action programs that gave preference in hiring and in the awarding of government contracts to women and members of racial minorities. Because few blacks and no women served as FBI agents at that time—none as senior officials—FBI hiring and promotion practices became subject to critical scrutiny. In response to initiatives of FBI Acting Director L. Patrick Gray III and his successors, blacks and women were actively recruited and promoted to ensure a more diverse Bureau. The new hiring and promotion policies encountered some resistance within Bureau ranks, and frustrations over this resistance precipitated a series of lawsuits by black and Hispanic FBI agents during the 1980s (see pages 135–37).

Changes in Domestic Security Investigations

Changes in the national political environment in the 1960s and 1970s also forced FBI officials to reduce FBI domestic security investigations, although document classification restrictions preclude a definitive assessment of the actual extent of this reduction. Hints of the pressures the Bureau felt are offered by such evidence as a 1978 court case brought to enjoin FBI political surveillance activities in

Chicago, in which FBI officials admitted that 258 FBI informers in the Chicago area formerly classified under the category "domestic security" had been reclassified "foreign counterintelligence."

Reduction in domestic security investigations also followed the dissolution of the Soviet Union and the end of communist control over Eastern Europe during the years 1989–91. The 1980s, however, witnessed the emergence of a new internal security concern: the threat of "terrorism." Conceivably, investigations formerly classified as "domestic security" (to monitor communist or other subversive activities) were reclassified as "terrorist" and "foreign counterintelligence." In any event, the supposed scaling-back of FBI domestic security and counterintelligence activities did not substantially reduce FBI force levels: from 20,024 in 1976, FBI personnel temporarily declined to 18,419 in 1980 and then rebounded to 23,323 in 1994 (see Table 1.1). Partly, the maintenance of force levels resulted from a sharp increase in FBI criminal investigations. White collar and organized crime became FBI priorities during the 1970s and subsequent decades.

During the 1980s, under Operation ABSCAM and Operation GREYLORD, FBI agents uncovered the political corruption of local officials and members of Congress (ABSCAM) and of police officers and judges in the Cook County, Illinois, circuit court system (GREYLORD). Six U.S. representatives, one U.S. senator, and numerous local officials were convicted for accepting bribes in return for political favors, while 82 Cook County judges, clerks, lawyers, and police officers were implicated in fixing cases. Other FBI investigations resulted in convictions for corrupt Boston police officers and Philadelphia city council members (1986), a California state senator (1989), and 10 South Carolina state legislators (1990).

Armed with new authority to wiretap and the more permissive RICO standards, FBI agents also succeeded in winning convictions of organized crime leaders in New York, Boston, Philadelphia, Milwaukee, Tampa, New Orleans, Kansas City, and Las Vegas. In 1973, for example, FBI organized crime investigations led to more than 1,250 convictions. Furthermore, in the so-called Pizza Connection case, the FBI broke a nationwide crime ring, with ties to Italy, that used pizza parlors as fronts for heroin trafficking. In this intensified campaign, FBI agents went undercover to infiltrate crime syndicates and succeeded in recruiting high-level informers who provided critically important

information (notably Teamsters' Union official Jackie Presser and mafioso Gregory Scarpa). Beginning with the Pizza Connection case, FBI officials also worked closely with police officials in Italy and Russia—given the international character of crime and the connections that American criminals had forged with their overseas counterparts.

Furthermore, the FBI assumed a more active role in resolving hostage situations. In 1983, FBI Director William Webster created a special Hostage Rescue Team, a squad of specially trained sharpshooters and individuals skilled in hostage negotiations who could be dispatched quickly to rescue hostages. The actions of the FBI's Hostage Rescue Team (notably in controversial hostage situations in Ruby Ridge, Idaho, and Waco, Texas) precipitated congressional criticism in 1995 of the FBI's excessive use of force. In response, FBI Director Louis Freeh instituted new guidelines that emphasized negotiations rather than force, a tactic that proved successful during the 81-day siege of the so-called Freemen compound in Jordan, Montana, in 1996. Surrounding and isolating the individuals in the compound, FBI agents avoided violence and, after patient negotiating and pressure, secured the surrender of 16 Freemen wanted on federal and state fraud charges and for threatening the life of a federal judge.

The FBI's reputation and power were not enhanced by these successes, in contrast to the luster the Bureau's image acquired during its widely admired handling of the crime gang crisis of the 1930s and the communist crisis of the 1940s and 1950s. Media coverage had become more balanced, and reporters did not hesitate to raise questions about FBI methods—not only in the Ruby Ridge and Waco hostage situations, but also in the ABSCAM case. Some journalists, for instance, questioned whether certain members of Congress had been purposefully targeted. If in the past, such questions had been ignored, in the 1980s and 1990s they triggered congressional inquiries (ultimately, the suspicions proved groundless).

A Reorganized Bureau (1980 to the Present)

That FBI activities were conducted under stricter scrutiny and were regarded with less reverence did not mean that FBI agents ceased monitoring dissident movements. Recent disclosures of the FBI's Library Awareness program (wherein FBI agents asked librarians to identify individuals having foreign accents who borrowed scientific periodicals) and the Bureau's monitoring of ACT-UP (a homosexual rights organization) indirectly confirm this continued interest. The new foreign policy concerns of the 1980s, moreover, precipitated demands from Congress (as well as from the conservative media) that the FBI continue to monitor groups suspected of "terrorism." Ironically, these demands (for the monitoring of terrorists) were also prompted by the appearance of conservative political movements openly hostile to certain governmental policies, notably gun control and income tax. Countervailing pressures encouraged FBI officials both to resume "intelligence" investigations in areas where there were possible foreign connections and yet to act cautiously to avoid involvement in political controversies that were strictly domestic in nature.

The Smith Guidelines

During the 1980 presidential campaign, Republican presidential nominee Ronald Reagan criticized the Carter administration for having failed to curb the threat to American security interests posed by Soviet expansionism and Islamic fundamentalism. Pledging to restore American influence internationally, candidate Reagan specifically demanded "unleashing" the intelligence agencies. The implication of his unleashing pledge was that the reforms instituted under Attorney General Levi in the aftermath of the Church Committee revelations of 1975–76 (see page 37) had crippled the nation's security apparatus, leaving the nation vulnerable. Reagan's electoral victory—and that of the Republicans, who gained control of the Senate in 1980—sounded the death knell for FBI charter legislation (and companion proposals to govern the CIA). The new president, moreover, announced his intention to rescind the executive restrictions on CIA and FBI powers instituted during the mid-1970s. By Executive Order 12333 in 1981, President Reagan lifted his predecessor's restrictions on CIA counterintelligence and foreign intelligence activities. Then, in March 1983, Attorney General William French Smith rescinded the so-called Levi Guidelines governing FBI "domestic security" investigations.

Under Smith's revised guidelines, FBI officials could initiate "domestic security/terrorism" investigations whenever "facts or circumstances reasonably indicate that two or more persons are engaged in an enterprise [to further] political or social goals wholly or in part through activities that involve force or violence and a violation of the criminal law of the United States." Smith's permissive standard of reasonableness extended to advocacy. Not only did he empower the FBI to "anticipate or prevent crime," but FBI officials could initiate investigations whenever information was uncovered that individuals or organizations "advocate criminal activity or indicate an apparent intent to engage in crime, particularly crimes of violence."

Attorney General Smith also rescinded the requirement in the Levi Guidelines that Justice Department officials "at least annually" review and determine "in writing" whether continued investigation was warranted. Under Smith's relaxed standards, FBI officials only had to "notify" the Justice Department's Office of Intelligence Policy whenever initiating a "domestic security/terrorism" investigation. The attorney general, moreover, could once again avoid the responsibility of ensuring that, once instituted, investigations did not evolve into politically motivated monitoring. The attorney general's role instead became discretionary: "may, as he deems necessary, request the FBI to prepare a report on the investigation."

Counterintelligence and the Politics of Terrorism

During the 1980s and 1990s, FBI counterintelligence investigations—governed by still-classified guidelines—remained a high priority. Although the FBI's counterintelligence staff was sharply reduced after the collapse of the Soviet Union in 1991, and agents were shifted to organized crime and white collar crime cases, counterintelligence remained an important FBI responsibility. Both before and after 1991, FBI agents monitored Soviet—and then Russian—efforts to steal U.S. military, diplomatic, and industrial secrets. Indeed, a number of Soviet espionage operations were uncovered, the most dramatic involving the arrests of former naval intelligence officer John Walker in 1985 and CIA official Aldrich Ames in 1994. Walker was arrested for selling sensitive Navy information to the Soviet Union. His activities occurred during the period of the Cold War. In contrast, Ames's spying activities confirmed the need for an ongoing counterintelligence role. Recruited as a Soviet spy in 1986, during a period in which U.S.-Soviet relations had improved, Ames continued his spying activities even after the dissolution of the Soviet Union. The need for counterintelligence was further confirmed by the FBI's 1985 arrest of naval intelligence officer Jonathan Pollard, who had been recruited to spy on behalf of Israel, a U.S. ally.

During the 1980s and 1990s, moreover, U.S. security interests expanded to include international trade and industrial technology. Thus, FBI (as well as CIA) intelligence operations focused on subverting attempts, whether by friendly or adversary powers, to obtain U.S. industrial secrets. In one case, FBI agents uncovered the bribery attempt of a Polish agent to obtain industrial secrets that could promote Poland's economic development and ability to compete in international markets.

These international changes, combined with the shattering of the earlier Cold War security consensus, also blurred the distinction between FBI counterintelligence and domestic security investigations, as the following example illustrates. In his campaign for the presidency, Ronald Reagan pledged to project U.S. power abroad and to wage a more effective war against Soviet expansionism. Upon winning the presidency, Reagan lobbied intensively for a sharp increase in U.S. defense spending, particularly in the area of nuclear missiles. The president justified the need for a stronger defense and nuclear superiority as essential to meeting the magnitude of the Soviet threat. In response, domestic opponents organized the so-called "nuclear freeze" movement to promote disarmament, claiming that a costly arms buildup would increase international tensions and lead to a suicidal nuclear war. Their lobbying efforts became subject to FBI surveillance—although no evidence of foreign direction and control was uncovered.

The Reagan administration's anti-Soviet objectives also influenced its policy toward Central America. In 1979, the Marxist-influenced Sandinista rebels overthrew the military-dominated government of Anastasio Somoza in Nicaragua. This revolutionary government, in turn, supported rebels in neighboring El Salvador, who sought to overthrow that country's conservative, military-dominated government. Fearing the appeal of radical revolutionary movements, the Reagan administration both financed and encouraged the attempt of former members of the Nicaraguan National Guard, the so-called Contras, to overthrow the Sandinista government and directly supported the El Salvadoran government against the rebels. These policies encountered domestic opposition, from radical activists and also the American religious community (particularly Roman Catholics influenced by the tenets of liberation theology). The most influential of these dissident groups was the Committee in Solidarity with the People of El Salvador (CISPES).

In 1981, FBI officials authorized a limited investigation of CISPES, based on allegations of an FBI informer that the organization was involved in international terrorism. This investigation intensified after 1983 under the more permissive Smith Guidelines (see page 40) and was eventually terminated in 1985. The FBI investigation uncovered no evidence that CISPES was a terrorist organization or was controlled by a foreign terrorist power or movement. Furthermore, the FBI's investigation had expanded beyond CISPES to target over 100 domestic groups opposed to the Reagan administration's Central American policy. These included the National Council of Churches in New York, New York City's Riverside Church, student and faculty organizations at 18 college campuses, the Norfolk (Virginia) Women's Peace Center, the Lutheran Christian Leadership Conference, United Automobile Workers and National Educational Association locals, and two Roman Catholic orders—the Maryknoll Sisters and the Sisters of Mercy.

The FBI's massive CISPES inquiry resembled the investigations of the Cold War years. FBI agents sought to identify individuals "actively involved in demonstrations" and focused on the political philosophy of these activists—indeed, an FBI agent characterized the writings of one church leader as evidence of a "mind totally sold on the Marxist Leninist philosophy." Confirming an underlying containment purpose, one FBI agent emphasized that it was "imperative at this time to formulate some plan of attack against CISPES and specifically against individuals . . . who defiantly display their contempt for the U.S. government by making speeches and propagandizing their cause." Furthermore, when another agent concluded that a targeted group was nonviolent, was committed to educating public opinion, and thus "it does not appear that further investigation is warranted," he was rebuffed. FBI officials ordered him to "consider the possibility" that the group "may be a front organization for CISPES."

During the 1980s, FBI investigations broadened beyond Marxist movements (whether or not Soviet-oriented) to include the Arab American and Muslim communities. Influenced by the Islamic fundamentalism that led to the overthrow of the shah of Iran and to the Islamist rebellion against the Soviet-imposed government in Afghanistan, many American Muslims (recent immigrants and alien residents) criticized U.S. Middle East policy, deeming it hostile to Arab interests. During the Gulf War against Iraq in 1990, FBI agents began monitoring Arab American leaders and groups, ostensibly to preclude terrorism. This surveillance intensified following the February 1993 bombing of the World Trade Center in New York City by Islamic fundamentalists.

Following an intensive investigation, FBI agents apprehended those responsible for the attack on the World Trade Center and uncovered a second plot to blow up the Lincoln and Holland Tunnels, the United Nations building, and various federal buildings in New York. In the latter case, the conspirators were apprehended before they could implement their plan.

The new FBI investigations of terrorists did not mean that one foreign enemy (the Soviet Union and communism) was displaced by another (Iran and Islamic fundamentalism). During the 1980s and 1990s, various new antigovernment groups were formed in the United States, many of them militant. Strictly domestic in origin, these so-called militia groups' orientation is conservative, though motivated by hatred of the federal government. Some of these groups adhere to an ideology of white supremacy and Christian fundamentalism. Others are convinced that the federal government seeks to deprive the citizenry of the constitutional right to bear arms, in order to impose "a new world order" under the United Nations. Others fear a Zionist conspiracy. Self-described as patriots, militia groups sprang up, particularly in the Midwest, Great Plains, and Western states, and engaged in paramilitary training activities modeled after the citizens' militia of the American Revolution.

The FBI began monitoring some of the activities of members of these militia groups—but did not target the groups per se. In 1985, members of a white supremacist group, The Order, were convicted for their commission of a string of bank robberies intended to finance the group's planned white supremacist revolution. In 1996, FBI agents arrested members of another militia group, the Freemen, for mail and bank fraud and threatening the life of a federal judge. Significantly, these investigations were prompted not by the antigovernment ideology of the groups but by the criminal conduct of some adherents.

The 1980s also witnessed an intensification in the political conflict over abortion, with the formation of anti-abortion groups that advocated violence (whether bombing or impeding access to abortion clinics or killing abortion providers). Following passage in 1993 of federal legislation criminalizing attacks on abortion clinics, pro-choice activists demanded that the FBI monitor anti-abortion groups, such

as Operation Rescue, citing their rhetoric as evidence of a conspiracy. FBI officials resisted these demands for broad-based investigations.

In both areas—anti-abortion and militia activities—FBI investigations focused on the illegal activities of individuals, not radical rhetoric. The Freemen and The Order were targeted for their violation of federal statutes, not their anti-government diatribes and advocacy of revolution (many militia leaders quoted Thomas Jefferson's remark on the possible need for revolution to preserve liberty). Ironically, the FBI's more restrained role precipitated criticism. After the bombing of the Alfred P. Murrah Federal Building in Oklahoma City, Oklahoma, on April 19, 1995, there was a call for reassessment of the need for a strengthened, autonomous agency. This terrorist attack resulted in the destruction of the building and the deaths of 168 individuals (including children at a daycare center). Following the World Trade Center bombing and the highly publicized arrest of Islamic fundamentalists for conspiring to blow up buildings in New York City, initial press reports and commentary blamed the Oklahoma City bombing on Islamic fundamentalists. Instead, the FBI's investigation led to the arrest of Timothy McVeigh and Terry Nichols, Army veterans who shared the anti-government and anti–gun control philosophy of the militia movement.

At first, many—both conservatives and liberals—demanded revisions of the guidelines governing FBI terrorist investigations, claiming that this heinous bombing could have been averted. But these criticisms soon abated, given the reality of the permissive standards of the Smith Guidelines, as well as the concerns of many conservatives that broadening FBI authority could lead to targeting critics of gun control laws. The Clinton administration, moreover, announced its intention to "clarify" the Smith Guidelines to permit increased FBI surveillance of terrorist groups and their adherents. The specific clarification has not been publicly disclosed, although in 1996, Attorney General Janet Reno created a special rapid response team, headed by the FBI, to deal with potential terrorist bombing attacks.

Concurrently, the Clinton administration pressured the Congress to enact counterterrorism legislation to extend FBI investigative powers (roving wiretaps; access to bank, credit, and financial records; and "tagging" explosive materials) and to expedite the deportation of suspected terrorists. Broad opposition to this legislative initiative delayed enactment and eventually led to major changes in the proposed law. When finally approving the Anti-Terrorism

Act of 1996, Congress dropped the sections extending FBI wiretapping authority; requiring the tagging of explosives; and providing warrantless access to bank, credit, and financial records, but approved the provisions making it easier to deport suspected terrorists.

Empowered by laws to investigate proscribed economic, political, and personal activities, the FBI of the late 1990s was a vastly different agency than that created in 1908. Its personnel and operations were refined to incorporate new administrative crime-fighting strategies and to exploit new technologies. Its powers had also expanded in response to presidential directives issued during periods when the public and the Congress feared radical movements and dissent. Yet, although the periodic abatement of this sense of crisis temporarily resulted in skepticism and then criticism of FBI activities, no attempt was made either to dissolve the FBI or to enact legislation confining the agency's role to law enforcement.

NOTABLE CASES

Tony G. Poveda

Introduction

A central legacy of the Federal Bureau of Investigation has been a long series of notable cases, many celebrated in American popular culture. The cases discussed in this chapter are organized according to three major eras in the FBI's history: (1) the early years (1908–24), when the Bureau had only a limited and uncertain mandate; (2) the Hoover years (1924–72), when FBI authority in both law enforcement and domestic security grew rapidly; and (3) the modern era (from 1972 to the present), characterized by the development and refinement of new proactive and high-tech investigative methods.

The Early Years (1908–24)

During its first years as a federal agency, the Bureau of Investigation (as the agency was called until 1935; see Table 1.2) was limited in its investigations to cases involving antitrust laws, interstate commerce laws, land frauds, and miscellaneous statutes that were not the province of other federal agencies. The Bureau's first major investigative responsibilities, directly assigned by Congress, arose from the passage of the White Slave Traffic Act of 1910. This legislation, also known as the Mann Act, outlawed the interstate transportation of women for immoral purposes; specifically, it targeted commercialized prostitution. Following United States entry into World War I in 1917, the Bureau also became responsible for enforcing the Selective Service Act, which required the pursuit of individuals avoiding conscription (or "slackers" as they were called) and the investigation of other war-related matters. The Bureau focused its efforts on apprehending foreign agents and spies operating within the United States, preventing the disruption of wartime production by radical workers, and containing the influence of antiwar activists. In the aftermath of the war, a new fear replaced the wartime concern over German spies, slackers, and antiwar radicals: "Reds" (communists) and alien anarchists. The notable cases of the Bureau's early years emerged from these limited responsibilities.

Mann Act or White Slave Traffic Act Cases

The main reason for enacting the Mann Act or White Slave Traffic Act of 1910 was to curb organized prostitution. Nonetheless, the Justice Department (and Bureau of Investigation) almost immediately interpreted this act to apply, as well, to cases of private "immorality," even when no profit motive was involved. In 1917, the U.S. Supreme Court upheld this broad interpretation.

Bureau agents pursued White Slave Act cases vigorously, exploiting the publicity to promote the Bureau's professionalism and indispensability—given the perceived seriousness of the crime and the inability of local police to track those involved (see Exhibit 3.1, page 103). Two of the most famous cases involved prominent public figures, Jack Johnson and Edward Y. Clarke. Both men were convicted for transporting an unmarried woman across state lines for immoral purposes.

Jack Johnson

At about the time the Mann Act was passed, Jack Johnson had risen to the top of the boxing world, becoming the first black heavyweight champion. His flamboyant life-style and open association with white women touched a sensitive chord among members of both races and made him a controversial public figure.

In October 1912, Chicago police arrested Johnson, charging him with abducting a 19-year-old white woman, Lucile Cameron, from Minneapolis. The abduction accusation had been brought by Cameron's mother, however, and was never corroborated by the alleged victim. In fact, about a month and a half after his arrest, Johnson and Lucile Cameron married. Racial prejudice shaped this case throughout: an angry white mob threatened to lynch Johnson, white inmates objected to his incarceration in their section of the county jail, and many (of both races) opposed his interracial marriage.

Concurrently, in a separate case, the assistant U.S. attorney in Chicago opened an investigation conducted by the Bureau to determine whether Johnson had violated the Mann Act, and on November 7, 1912, a federal grand jury indicted him. The victim and key witness in this case was a white woman named Belle Schreiber, a former prostitute, who claimed that Johnson had paid her way to Chicago from Pittsburgh for immoral purposes. Johnson acknowledged knowing Schreiber and helping her financially, but denied having paid her for sex. In May 1913, however, he was convicted by an all-white jury and sentenced the following month to one year in prison and a $1,000 fine. While appealing his case, Johnson jumped bail and fled to Europe where he and his wife, Lucile, took up residence in Paris. After living abroad for several years, Johnson returned to the United States in 1920 and served out his sentence at Leavenworth penitentiary.

Edward Y. Clarke

Revived during the 1920s, the Ku Klux Klan was a secret society that proposed to defend the nation not only against blacks, but also recent immigrants (Southern and Eastern Europeans, who were predominantly Jewish or Catholic), radicals, and immoral women, all of whom were perceived as threats to traditional American values. Its white supremacist, anti-Semitic, and anti-Catholic themes resonated with a public threatened by the social and economic changes transforming a formerly rural, traditional, and predominantly Protestant society. In 1920, Edward Y. Clarke joined the revived and increasingly powerful Klan and soon became its chief publicist/recruiter and eventually the acting imperial wizard.

The Klan's vigilante justice (including lynchings and intimidation tactics) disturbed many state and national leaders, leading one Southern governor to request federal assistance. The Bureau did investigate Klan activities, but it was unable to develop evidence of any federal violation—no federal law proscribed acts of violence, and the Klan's criminal activities were covered only by state and local laws.

Newspaper revelations about Edward Y. Clarke's financial and personal relations with Elizabeth Tyler, another Klan leader, provided a different opening for a Bureau investigation. One report claimed that the two had been arrested by the police and charged with disorderly conduct after being found inebriated and not fully dressed.

Clarke's and Young's indiscreet personal conduct, moreover, coincided with growing factionalism and conflict within the group: Clarke was aligned with Imperial Wizard William Simmons and the "old guard" against insurgents led by Hiram Evans. In the midst of this struggle within the Klan, Clarke was indicted for violating the Mann Act on March 1, 1923. He was charged with having taken a woman named Laurel Martin to New Orleans from Houston in February 1921 for immoral purposes. Several days after Clarke's indictment, Hiram Evans, who had become imperial wizard, removed Clarke from the Klan, using the charges as a pretext to purge his powerful rival. Clarke pled guilty to the charge on March 10, 1924, and was fined $5,000 for violating the Mann Act. The publicity engendered by Clarke's trial (revealing behavior that contradicted the morality espoused by the Klan) and by intra-Klan factionalism served to undercut the organization's mystique, and by the end of the decade, it had declined as a force in Southern and national politics.

Radicals and Aliens

During World War I and the postwar years, the Bureau of Investigation emerged as one of the key federal agencies in the promotion of a powerful crusade against spies, enemy aliens, and radicals. A wartime alarm over German spies and enemy aliens spilled over to encompass opponents of the war and those who interfered with the war effort by hampering conscription or disrupting war-related industries. One of the prime targets of the federal government's wartime activities was a radical labor organization known as the Industrial Workers of the World (IWW). Alien anarchists were also pursued under the Espionage and Sedition Acts of 1917 and 1918. Among these wartime and postwar sedition cases was the conviction of Jacob Abrams, a Russian Jewish immigrant. Then, in the immediate aftermath of the war, the Justice Department's antiradical crusade mushroomed into the Red Scare of 1919–20. In an attempt to prevent what Justice Department officials believed was an impending Bolshevik revolution in the United States, thousands of radicals were rounded up nationwide for deportation. One of the targeted groups was the Union of Russian Workers. Some of the Bureau's more notorious cases came out of this period, both in the Justice Department's prosecution of the IWW during the war and in its postwar effort to deport alien radicals.

IWW Arrests and Trial

During the early years of World War I, the radical IWW sought to exploit the economic boom produced by the war to increase its support among disgruntled miners, migrant farm workers, lumberjacks, and textile workers. Founded in 1905 to bring about the organization of all workers for the purpose of overthrowing a capitalist economic system, the IWW's membership at first remained small. Between 1916 and 1917, however, IWW membership increased from approximately 40,000 to about 100,000. Centered in the mining and lumber industries of the West, the IWW had the potential to radicalize the American labor force and impede wartime production.

United States entry into World War I in April 1917 reversed the fortunes of this radical labor movement. In the spring and summer of 1917, the IWW mounted strikes in the wheat fields of the Dakotas, in the lumber industry of the Pacific Northwest, and in the copper mines of Montana and Arizona. Ironically, the IWW's success in organizing workers in these three important economic sectors proved to be its undoing. Major newspapers called for government action against members of the IWW, or "Wobblies," as they were known. The union's critics alleged that IWW strikes threatened war production and, during wartime, such actions could be tantamount to treason and sabotage. Members of Congress, especially in the Western states where the IWW was the strongest, denounced the Wobblies, while Western governors demanded that President Woodrow Wilson intern the leadership of the Wobblies as a war measure. The Justice Department, however, rejected this suggestion, and vigilante groups sprang up throughout the West, taking the law into their own hands. In one case, a group of Butte, Montana, vigilantes lynched Wobbly organizer Frank Little. Western business leaders affected by the IWW strikes, through their local contacts with sympathetic U.S. attorneys, pressured the Justice Department to act to curb the IWW.

As pressure for federal action against the Wobblies mounted during the summer of 1917, Attorney General Thomas Gregory directed Bureau agents to gather evidence for prosecution. The Bureau did not launch investigations proving criminal conduct but, instead, on September 5, 1917, Bureau agents and local police raided IWW offices throughout the country, seizing correspondence, organization minutes, financial records, membership lists, pamphlets, and other materials that could be used against the Wobblies. In Chicago alone—the site of the IWW's national headquarters—Bureau agents seized about five tons of documents.

Justice Department officials originally sought to establish a financial link between Germany and the IWW, but uncovered no such connection. Nonetheless, wartime statutes provided another legal basis for prosecution, as Congress had made it a federal crime to interfere with conscription or with war-related industries. Under wartime presidential proclamation, moreover, enemy aliens could be detained. Based on a review of the seized IWW records, a federal grand jury in Chicago on September 28 indicted 166 IWW members, including the national leadership of the organization, among them its president, William D. "Big Bill" Haywood.

When the Chicago trial opened on April 1, 1918, 113 Wobblies were tried on more than 100 counts. The prosecution argued that the IWW constituted a massive criminal conspiracy to overthrow the government and impede the war effort, citing as evidence the IWW's literature seized by Bureau agents. The government's attorneys cited no actual crimes committed or actually planned by IWW members. The defense's strategy was to present testimony from IWW organizers about their life experiences and the working conditions they encountered in the field. George Vanderveer,

the lead attorney for the defense team, argued that the IWW as an organization had never taken an official position on conscription, leaving this to be a matter of personal choice for members. Vanderveer denied that the purpose of IWW-sponsored strikes was to interfere with the war effort and instead was to improve working conditions.

After less than an hour of deliberation, the jury found each defendant guilty on all counts. On August 31, Judge Kenesaw Mountain Landis sentenced 35 of the defendants to 5 years in prison; 33 to 10 years in prison; and another 15 to the maximum of 20 years. The remaining 30 defendants received clemency because of their tenuous ties to the IWW.

The conviction of the national leadership in the Chicago trial (including Haywood, Vincent St. John, and Ralph Chaplin, the editor of *Solidarity*, the IWW's newspaper) was followed by regional trials of IWW members throughout the West—in Sacramento, Fresno, Wichita, and Omaha. The resultant federal prosecution transformed the IWW from a militant labor movement to an organization preoccupied with its own defense, as legal expenses depleted its limited resources.

The Abrams Case and Anarchism

In May 1918, Congress passed the Sedition Act, which amended the espionage laws to make it easier to prosecute wartime critics of the Wilson administration. It became a federal crime to "willfully utter, print, write, or publish" disloyal language about the U.S. government, and to "willfully urge, incite, or advocate" actions that would interfere with the U.S. government's waging of war, including war production.

In one of the first applications of this statute, on August 23, 1918, Jacob Abrams and four of his anarchist associates (Mollie Steimer, Hyman Lachowsky, Samuel Lipman, and Jacob Schwartz) were arrested in East Harlem by New York City police for having distributed leaflets denouncing President Woodrow Wilson's decision to send troops to Russia at the end of World War I. The leaflets protested this action as a disguised effort to overthrow the Bolshevik government. As a Jewish immigrant from czarist Russia in 1908, Abrams had a personal interest in the government of Russia. Like many Russian Jews, he had fled the czar's regime because of its anti-Semitic policies and initially welcomed the Bolshevik Revolution of November 1917.

A federal grand jury indicted the five defendants on September 12, 1918, charging them with four counts of conspiracy under the espionage and sedition laws. The anarchists were charged with conspiring to publish disloyal language about the U.S. government and with conspiring to encourage resistance to U.S. efforts to wage war against Germany. The day before the trial, one of the defendants, Jacob Schwartz, died at Bellevue Hospital. The official cause of death was pneumonia, but Schwartz's friends maintained that his death resulted from a beating he had received during the initial police interrogation.

The thrust of the prosecution's case was to prove that the defendants had written, printed, and distributed the two leaflets. The defense did not challenge the accuracy of this testimony, but instead argued that these were not criminal acts. In addition, the defense attempted to show that U.S. intervention in Russia was misguided, but presiding judge Henry DeLamar Clayton did not allow this line of inquiry. In his summation, defense attorney Harry Weinberger offered a defense of anarchism: His main point was that his clients had a right to free speech, including the right to protest U.S. foreign policy. The trial itself lasted only a week and a half, and after deliberating for slightly more than an hour, the jury found the defendants guilty on all counts. Abrams, Lipman, and Lachowsky each received 20-year prison sentences and $1,000 fines; Steimer received a 15-year sentence and a $500 fine.

Since the defendants were not U.S. citizens, they could have been deported after conviction. However, they appealed the verdict to the U.S. Supreme Court, which did not issue a ruling until November 10, 1919. The main issue before the Court involved whether the defendants' "seditious" speech fell within the bounds of the First Amendment and how the interests of security could be balanced against the right of the individual to change the structure of the government. The Court's majority upheld the conviction, with Justices Oliver Wendell Holmes and Louis Brandeis dissenting. Soon after the Supreme Court's decision, Abrams and Lipman fled to New Orleans where they intended to take a ship to Mexico. Before they could depart, Bureau agents apprehended them and returned them to New York City. Abrams, Lipman, and Lachowsky were then sent to federal prison in Atlanta (Steimer to a state prison in Missouri) where they remained until they were deported to Russia in November 1921.

Emma Goldman and the Union of Russian Workers

The Bureau of Investigation's surveillance of radical groups had begun following U.S. involvement in World War I. The end of the war did not terminate Bureau surveillance; instead, the Bureau's antiradical activities intensified during the immediate postwar period. A number of factors contributed to this postwar resurgence. The Bolshevik Revolution in Russia in November 1917 had raised the possibility that revolutionary change could erupt elsewhere in Europe and in the United States. In addition, in 1919, a sharp increase in labor unrest occurred throughout the United States, including nationwide strikes in the steel and coal industries and a general strike in Seattle.

However, the factor that galvanized this antiradical action involved a series of bomb plots and bombings in the late spring of 1919. One of those bombings occurred at Attorney General A. Mitchell Palmer's Washington, D.C., residence on the night of June 2. Although Palmer and his family were not injured, the bomber was killed in the explosion, and anarchist leaflets were found outside the Palmer residence. This botched bombing attempt was never solved—nor were any of the other bombings that occurred that night in eight cities across the country.

About two weeks later, top-level Justice Department officials decided on a strategy to combat the feared threat of revolution, as well as the more general menace of radicalism and anarchism. Since the United States was no longer at war, the Espionage and Sedition Acts could not be invoked to arrest or detain citizens for their "seditious" speech, so their strategy focused on alien radicals. The Immigration Act of 1918 provided broad authority to deport aliens on the basis of their beliefs and associations, particularly if they believed in anarchism or revolutionary change, or belonged to organizations that advocated those principles, although these laws could not be invoked against citizens. Additional purposes were to heighten awareness of the danger of radicals and mobilize public support for peacetime sedition legislation. The Justice Department's strategy of deporting alien radicals, however, required the cooperation of the Immigration Bureau, a division of the Labor Department, which had jurisdiction over matters pertaining to immigrants and aliens. A measure of cooperation was obtained, but differences between Justice and Labor Department officials later undermined Palmer's deportation strategy.

To promote its campaign against radicals, on August 1, 1919, the Justice Department established a new unit, the Radical Division (in 1920, renamed the General Intelligence Division or GID), headed by J. Edgar Hoover. The first target of the Radical Division's crusade was the Union of Russian Workers (URW), an anarchist group of approximately 4,000 Russian immigrants. This particular deportation effort, in addition, focused on two prominent anarchists, Emma Goldman ("Queen of the Reds" or "Red Emma") and Alexander Berkman, both of whose highly public activities personified the radical alien threat.

Emigrating from her native Russia in 1889, Emma Goldman spent most of her years in the United States as a radical activist—feminist, anarchist, and birth control reformer (see Exhibit 2.1). A charismatic speaker, she also edited the anarchist journal *Mother Earth.* During World War I, Goldman and fellow anarchist Alexander Berkman were

Exhibit 2.1   **Emma Goldman,** *Courtesy of the National Archives*

arrested in June 1917 for violating the Selective Service Act. The No-Conscription League that they had organized, which assisted those who resisted draft registration, was found to constitute a conspiracy in violation of the law. Convicted in July, Goldman was sentenced to two years in prison and fined $10,000. Just prior to her release from prison in September 1919, the Immigration Bureau issued a warrant for her arrest. Her anarchist beliefs and associations made her subject to deportation under the 1918 Immigration Act. J. Edgar Hoover wrote the legal brief as head of the GID and argued the government's case for Goldman's deportation. Hoover documented Goldman's advocacy of violence, referring to back issues of her journal. Since Goldman claimed to be a U.S. citizen—through her father and husband—Hoover also challenged the validity of her naturalization. He also indirectly implicated her in the 1901 assassination of President McKinley, citing statements made by McKinley's assassin, Leon Czolgosz, that he had been influenced by her writings. On November 29, 1919, the Immigration Bureau announced its decision to deport her.

At about the same time that Emma Goldman's deportation was being determined, Bureau agents, with the assistance of local police, raided the meeting places of the URW in 12 cities across the country (on November 7, 1919). Although arrest warrants had been issued for 600 of its members, far more than that number were rounded up during the raids. The URW was targeted because Hoover and the Labor Department had concluded, relying on provisions of the Immigration Act of 1918, that membership in the organization made any alien deportable. Two clauses in the URW's constitution, which had been drafted in 1907, advocated the violent overthrow of government. These

references, however, were to the Russian czar, who had since been overthrown by the Bolsheviks. By 1919, the URW had evolved largely into a cultural organization of Russian immigrants.

The raids received favorable publicity in major newspapers, as did the Immigration Bureau's success in obtaining rulings ordering the deportation of the alien radicals a month later. A troop transport ship, rechristened the *Buford* and dubbed by the press the *Soviet Ark,* was commissioned to return the Russians to their homeland. On December 21, 1919, the *Buford* sailed from New York harbor, carrying on board 249 aliens, including 184 members of the URW—and Emma Goldman and Alexander Berkman. GID Director Hoover was present for the sailing, as were members of the press and congressmen whom he had invited. The deportation of Emma Goldman and the other Russian aliens marked an early success for the GID and the Palmer Justice Department. But the favorable publicity proved to be short-lived. Massive dragnet raids of radicals—the Palmer Raids of January 1920—soon provoked mounting and debilitating criticisms (see pages 107–10).

The Hoover Years (1924–72)

During J. Edgar Hoover's lengthy tenure as FBI director, the FBI's investigative responsibilities grew enormously, in the areas both of law enforcement and domestic security. During the 1930s, this expansion primarily involved law enforcement, as Congress enacted crime legislation nearly doubling the Bureau's investigative authority. Some of the FBI's most famous cases derive from this so-called gangster era, involving such criminals as John Dillinger, George "Machine Gun" Kelly, Frank Nash, and Charles "Pretty Boy" Floyd. During World War II, espionage cases became paramount as FBI officials focused on spies and internal security. Following the war, the national panic over communism gave further impetus to shifting FBI priorities from law enforcement to domestic security, giving rise to celebrated cases concerning spying, the stealing of atomic bomb secrets, and questions about the loyalty of federal employees. During Hoover's last decade as FBI director, cases in a wide range of investigative areas became major priorities, reflecting the turbulent period of the 1960s: organized crime, civil rights, and assassinations, as well as internal security cases involving antiwar dissent, black power, and white supremacist politics.

The Early Hoover Years

Two celebrated cases in the early Hoover years, occurring prior to the expansion of federal authority in crime control during the 1930s, highlight the FBI's limited jurisdiction at that time. Both served as catalysts to the expansion of federal law enforcement responsibility. One case involved Al Capone, a major organized crime figure; the other, the kidnapping of the infant son of famed aviator Charles Lindbergh.

Alphonse Capone

Alphonse Capone ("Scarface"), one of the most notorious mobsters of the Prohibition era, rose to prominence during the 1920s as the chief boss of the famed Chicago crime syndicate. From humble origins as a street gang member and bouncer at a bar in New York City, Al Capone was brought to Chicago by Johnny Torrio, head of the Italian crime syndicate in Chicago during the early 1920s. In 1925, Capone succeeded Torrio, who by then dominated most organized bootlegging, prostitution, and gambling operations in Chicago. At its peak during Prohibition, the Capone organization's annual revenue from various illegal operations has been estimated as hundreds of millions of dollars.

During the Prohibition era (1920–33), organized crime and Chicago politics were closely intertwined. Even before Prohibition, Mayor William ("Big Bill") Thompson underscored this relationship between crime and politics, promising to make Chicago a "wide-open city." Vice operations were permitted to flourish, and organized crime became even more widespread with the proliferation of bootlegging enterprises during Prohibition. Because of this unofficial alliance between local politicians and gangsters, Al Capone and his syndicate were largely untouchable by local law enforcement officials during most of the 1920s, and federal agents were never able to amass sufficient evidence to secure Capone's indictment for violating the Volstead Act, the law implementing Prohibition.

However, a 1927 U.S. Supreme Court ruling that unlawful income was subject to income taxes (*United States v. Sullivan*) provided another avenue for federal prosecution of Capone and other organized crime figures. Accordingly, in 1929, Secretary of the Treasury Andrew Mellon, under pressure from President Herbert Hoover, ordered an Internal Revenue Service investigation of Capone. Treasury Department officials eventually secured Capone's indictment for income tax fraud, and on October 17, 1931, the Chicago gangster was found guilty in federal court of five counts of tax evasion on income earned between 1924 and 1929. A

week later, Capone was sentenced to 11 years in federal prison, fined $50,000, and ordered to pay court costs and back taxes, plus interest.

The Bureau of Investigation's limited role in the Capone case (investigating and prosecuting tax evasion was a Treasury Department responsibility) occurred when the crime boss failed to comply with a subpoena ordering his appearance as a witness before a federal grand jury in Chicago on March 12, 1929. Capone, who was in Miami at the time, claimed to have been suffering from bronchial pneumonia and to have been bedridden for six weeks. He produced a doctor's statement that travel to Chicago would have been dangerous to his health. Although Capone testified before the federal grand jury later in March, Bureau agents arrested him on March 27 for contempt of court. The Bureau had uncovered evidence that Capone's claims that he could not initially appear before the grand jury were false. Agents obtained statements from witnesses that Capone had gone to the racetrack in Miami, flown to the Bahamas, and taken a boat trip during the time he maintained he was sick and in bed.

Capone was convicted on the contempt of court charges—for filing a false affidavit—and, on February 28, 1931, was sentenced to six months in the Cook County Jail. His six-month contempt sentence was served concurrently with the tax evasion sentence. Capone was released from the federal prison on Alcatraz in November 1939, having served over seven years of his sentence and having paid all fines and back taxes.

Although law enforcement officials hailed Capone's contempt of court conviction as the beginning of the notorious gangster's downfall, major newspapers ridiculed the contempt of court and tax evasion convictions as mere technicalities. Indeed, in light of the far more serious crimes that Capone had committed—for which he had never been charged (murder, racketeering, gambling, prostitution, and extortion)—tax evasion and contempt of court were trivial. But this misses the point: the failure to prosecute Capone for these more serious crimes was a function of the federal government's (and the Bureau's) limited jurisdiction, for Capone's criminal activity fell principally within the jurisdiction of local authorities.

The Lindbergh Kidnapping

The second famous case that occurred during Hoover's early years as director of the Bureau was the kidnapping of Charles Lindbergh's son. On the night of March 1, 1932, the Lindberghs' 20-month-old child was abducted from the second floor of their home, near Hopewell, New Jersey. A ransom note was left, demanding $50,000. Because of Lindbergh's celebrity status as an aviator, the case drew national and international attention and was widely publicized in the media. Primary responsibility for the investigation to apprehend the kidnapper(s), however, rested with the New Jersey State Police, headed by Colonel Norman Schwartzkopf. As the investigation proceeded, other agencies became involved, including the New York City Police Department, the Treasury Department's Secret Service, and the Bureau of Investigation.

Thousands of volunteers offered to assist in the search. When the child was not immediately found, the investigators were inundated with clues called in from around the country.

A retired school principal in New York City, John F. Condon, offered to act as an intermediary to ensure the ransom exchange between the kidnapper(s) and the Lindberghs, and on the night of April 2, acting on behalf of the Lindberghs, Condon paid the $50,000 ransom to a man with a German accent at St. Raymond's Cemetery in the Bronx. In exchange, Condon received a receipt and information about the location of the Lindbergh baby: he was on a boat called *Nellie* near Martha's Vineyard, Massachusetts. The boat was never located, and about six weeks later, on May 12, the baby's body was found in a shallow grave about four and a half miles from the Lindberghs' New Jersey home.

Exhibit 2.2   **Bruno Richard Hauptmann,** *Courtesy of the National Archives (65-HN)*

Discovery of the child's body increased public pressure on federal authorities, especially President Herbert Hoover, to intervene. Because kidnapping was not then a federal crime and the Bureau had no jurisdiction, Bureau Director Hoover had initially offered unofficial assistance to the Lindberghs and to local investigators. This offer was, at first, rejected. On the day after the body was found, President Hoover authorized all federal investigative agencies to cooperate with the New Jersey State Police, if so requested, and he announced that Bureau Director Hoover would coordinate the efforts of the various federal agencies. A month later, Congress passed a kidnapping statute, and in

October 1933, Herbert Hoover's successor as president, Franklin Roosevelt, placed the Justice Department in charge of federal investigative efforts in the Lindbergh case, in effect giving the FBI principal jurisdiction.

The Lindbergh case remained unsolved for two-and-a-half years, until September 1934. At that time, an alert gas station attendant in New York City became suspicious when a customer used a $10 gold certificate to pay for his gas—all gold certificates were to have been turned in to banks by April 1933, when the United States went off the gold standard. The attendant made a note of the customer's vehicle license number on the certificate, although at the time, he did not link it to the Lindbergh kidnapping. A few days later, a teller at a Manhattan bank recognized the gold certificate as one of the marked bills in the Lindbergh ransom and reported it to the Bureau's New York City office. Checking the automobile license number recorded by the gas station attendant with the Department of Motor Vehicles, Bureau investigators found a vehicle registered to Bruno Richard Hauptmann, an unemployed carpenter who lived in the Bronx.

At the time of the ransom payment in 1932, the head of the Secret Service, Elmer Irey, had insisted that marked gold certificates be used. Accordingly, Bureau agents distributed pamphlets to banks and selected retail businesses in the New York City area listing the serial numbers of the gold certificates used in the ransom payment. These actions, along with the gas station attendant's recording of the license number and the bank teller's recognition of the ransom bill, led to Hauptmann's arrest on September 20, 1934 (see Exhibit 2.2).

During the ensuing trial, the prosecution succeeded in linking Hauptmann to the kidnapping through the marked ransom bills, a wooden ladder that had been found at the scene of the crime, eyewitness testimony, and handwriting analysis. At the time of Hauptmann's arrest, investigators found he also possessed another gold certificate that had been part of the ransom money, and further discovered an additional $14,600 of the ransom payment in his garage. Arthur Koehler, a wood expert employed in the Forest Service of the Department of Agriculture, linked the wood in the home-made ladder left at the crime scene to Hauptmann—based on peculiarities of the wood and the tools used to construct the ladder. John F. Condon, the go-between in the ransom payment, identified Hauptmann as the recipient of the ransom (though initially he had been unable to make a positive identification). A Bureau handwriting expert, moreover, testified that the ransom note had been written by Hauptmann. Defense attorneys unsuccessfully sought to raise doubts about Hauptmann's guilt, focusing on conflicts in eyewitness testimony and fingerprint evidence. Convicted on April 3, 1936, Hauptmann was electrocuted for kidnapping and murdering Charles Lindbergh Jr. Hauptmann maintained his innocence throughout, and subsequent studies have questioned his guilt. Recent critics of the verdict claim that Hauptmann's conviction had been based on suppressed evidence, perjured testimony, witness intimidation, and a near-hysterical trial atmosphere.

The Lindbergh case marked a turning point in the federal role in crime control. Despite President Herbert Hoover's reluctance to commit federal resources and to assume federal jurisdiction in crime matters, Congress passed a statute on June 22, 1932, making kidnapping a federal crime when the victim was transported across state lines. Enacted a little more than three months after the Lindbergh kidnapping, this legislation was popularly designated the Lindbergh Law. Nearly two years later, on May 18, 1934, the law was amended to establish federal jurisdiction, and the presumption of interstate transportation, if a kidnapping victim was not found within seven days.

Gangster Cases of the 1930s

The Capone and Lindbergh cases were harbingers of how federal law enforcement powers changed during the 1930s. As a by-product, the FBI was transformed from a small, relatively obscure investigative bureau with limited authority to a high-profile agency with expanding powers. That transformation was triggered by a series of celebrated gangster cases that brought broad public recognition to the FBI and helped shape the FBI's public identity as the foremost law enforcement agency in the United States.

The Depression-era gangsters provided the occasion for the Roosevelt administration's successful "war on crime." At the time, Roosevelt and Attorney General Homer Cummings sought legislative approval for a Twelve Point Crime Program to expand federal authority in crime control. In the politics of crime, gangsters like John Dillinger and "Baby Face" Nelson were dramatically portrayed as "public enemies," and the Bureau agents pursuing them were G-men crime fighters. Attorney General Cummings's anticrime crusade of 1933–35 persuaded the public that these gangsters were not ordinary criminals but a dangerous threat

worthy of federal attention—and therefore that new legislation was needed to expand the federal (and FBI) role in crime control.

The Kansas City Massacre

The case that most persuasively demonstrated the need for an expanded national crime-fighting role began on the morning of June 17, 1933, in front of Union Railway Station in Kansas City, Missouri. Frank Nash, an escaped federal prisoner who was being transported to Leavenworth penitentiary, had just arrived from Arkansas on the 7:15 a.m. train, under police and Bureau guard. As seven law enforcement officers (including four Bureau agents) were transferring Nash from the train to an automobile in front of the station, they were ambushed by three gunmen who opened fire with machine guns and pistols, then fled. In approximately 30 seconds, four of the lawmen were killed. Among the casualties was Agent Raymond Caffrey, who died shortly after the assault. Nash was also killed in this violent attack, which has raised the possibility that the gangsters may have been trying to execute Nash because of his knowledge of underworld activities, rather than to free him.

A Bureau investigation following the ambush, which came to be called the Kansas City Massacre, alleged that the gunmen were Vernon C. Miller, Adam C. Richetti, and Charles "Pretty Boy" Floyd. All had lengthy criminal records: Miller had served time in a South Dakota prison for embezzlement and was reputed to have ties with Midwest underworld gangs; Richetti had served prison time for several robberies; Floyd had a history of bank robbery, and at the time of the Kansas City shoot-out, he was a fugitive from the law following his escape enroute to an Ohio penitentiary where he was to serve a 12- to 15-year sentence. Floyd later denied that he had been involved in the Kansas City ambush, although FBI officials have consistently maintained that he was a participant.

Bureau Director Hoover ordered a national manhunt for the three gunmen. Miller was found dead a few months later in a ditch just outside of Detroit, Michigan, apparently killed during an altercation between gangster associates. Bureau agents eventually caught up with Richetti and Floyd near Wellsville, Ohio, in October 1934, the criminals having been spotted by the local police chief. Following a brief shoot-out, local police apprehended Richetti, but Floyd escaped. On the following day, October 22, a squad of local police and Bureau agents located Floyd a few miles away on a farm. A gun battle ensued, and Floyd died shortly thereafter. Richetti, the only surviving suspect in the Kansas City

Massacre, was returned to Kansas City where he was tried and convicted for the murder of the four lawmen. Richetti was executed in the gas chamber on October 7, 1938.

The Kansas City Massacre evoked public outrage at the arrogance of gangsters in so boldly assaulting legally constituted authority. Attorney General Cummings capitalized on this incident to launch his crusade for more federal crime legislation, emphasizing that the murder of a Justice Department agent was a direct challenge to the federal government, while Bureau Director Hoover also attempted to mobilize public opinion against the forces of the criminal underworld. The shoot-out in Kansas City became the opening round in what proved to be a decade-long struggle between the FBI (and the Justice Department) and the rural outlaws who, during the Depression era, came to be portrayed as "public enemies."

John Dillinger

John Dillinger rose to national notoriety during a 14-month period, from May 1933 to July 1934, when he and his gang embarked on a crime spree throughout the Midwest. The exploits of the Dillinger gang immediately commanded the attention of the media, of law enforcement officials in several states, and of the Bureau of Investigation. The city of Chicago, the state of Indiana, and the Bureau all established special "Dillinger squads" in a concerted effort to capture Dillinger and his gangster associates. Dillinger's exploits, moreover, became a source of embarrassment to law enforcement officials, as newspapers publicized his jail escapes and raids of police stations for weapons, and his slipping away from authorities at the last moment. He became the stereotype of the 1930s gangster; a folk hero to some, but a notorious criminal to others. In June 1934, Bureau Director Hoover dubbed Dillinger "Public Enemy Number One."

Dillinger's criminal career began ordinarily enough as a high school dropout who had numerous brushes with the law as an adolescent. His first major criminal offense occurred in 1924, at the age of 21, when he and an accomplice unsuccessfully attempted to rob a grocery store in his hometown, Mooresville, Indiana. Arrested shortly thereafter, Dillinger pled guilty and received a 10- to 20-year prison sentence, of which he served nearly 9 years in an Indiana prison.

Soon after his release in May 1933, Dillinger robbed a bank in Ohio. A few months later, he was arrested and held in the county jail in Lima, Ohio, to await trial. Three associates—men whom he had met while in prison—helped him escape from the Lima jail on October 12, killing the sheriff in the process. These men formed the original Dillinger gang, robbing banks throughout the Midwest and sometimes raiding police arsenals for machine guns, revolvers, and ammunition.

In early 1934, the Dillinger gang killed a police officer during a robbery of a bank in East Chicago, Indiana. The gang fled to Tucson, Arizona, where local authorities recognized them from photographs, and they were arrested on January 23, 1934. One gang member, Harry Pierpont, was extradited to Ohio for the murder of the sheriff in Lima, and Dillinger was returned to Crown Point, Indiana, to be tried for the killing of the East Chicago policeman. Under considerable media fanfare, Dillinger was locked up in the Crown Point jail. Escaping on March 3 by using a wooden gun he had carved to secure his release, he then stole the sheriff's car and fled to Illinois. When he crossed the Indiana-Illinois state line, Dillinger had committed his first federal offense and thus provided an opening for official Bureau involvement. At that time, neither bank robbery nor interstate flight were federal crimes, but by transporting a stolen car across state lines, Dillinger had violated the Motor Vehicle Theft Act (or Dyer Act) of 1919.

The Bureau thereupon joined the hunt for Dillinger, which continued throughout the spring and summer of 1934. On two occasions, Bureau agents were on the verge of capturing Dillinger when he slipped away. In late March, agents determined that Dillinger was in an apartment in St. Paul, Minnesota, where he was recuperating from wounds received during another bank robbery. After a brief surveillance of the apartment, agents knocked on the front door; Dillinger's girlfriend answered but quickly shut the door. Following a call for reinforcements, a shoot-out ensued—but Dillinger escaped, although further wounded.

About three weeks later, on April 22, agents received a tip that the Dillinger gang, joined by another notorious gangster, Lester Gillis (aka "Baby Face" Nelson), was at the Little Bohemia Lodge in northern Wisconsin. Agents from the FBI's St. Paul and Chicago field offices were immediately dispatched to the scene. Prior to their arrival, Bureau officials prematurely announced to reporters that agents had Dillinger surrounded and to expect some "good news." As the agents approached the lodge at nightfall, barking dogs signaled their arrival. Three guests, local residents who had stopped at the lodge for drinks, became alarmed, ran out the front, and attempted to drive away—whereupon agents opened fire, killing one man and wounding the other two.

Thus alerted, the Dillinger gang escaped. A short while later, "Baby Face" Nelson encountered three lawmen a few miles away and immediately started shooting, killing one agent and wounding a second agent and a local police officer.

The Little Bohemia incident was a major embarrassment for Bureau officials, who intensified the Bureau's manhunt for Dillinger. Director Hoover dispatched Samuel Cowley to Chicago to head the Bureau's investigative efforts and to coordinate operations with Melvin Purvis, head of the Bureau's Chicago field office. Attorney General Cummings also added to the drama of the search by announcing that Bureau policy was: "Shoot to kill—then count to 10."

On July 21, 1934, Bureau agents received what proved to be the tip that led to Dillinger's demise. Anna Sage (whose real name was Anna Cumpanas), madam of a brothel in Gary, Indiana, informed local police that she was willing to make a deal to turn in Dillinger, a friend and customer. The Immigration and Naturalization Service was in the process of deporting Sage as an undesirable alien. In exchange for the reward money and a halt to deportation proceedings, she offered to provide information on Dillinger's whereabouts. After consulting with Hoover, Cowley and Purvis agreed that she would receive some of the reward money and that the Justice Department would intercede with the Labor Department (which had jurisdiction over immigration matters) in an effort to prevent her deportation. Sage thereupon informed Purvis that she, a woman companion, and Dillinger would be viewing a movie at the Biograph Theatre in Chicago the following night, and that she would be dressed in red for easy recognition. Bureau agents staked out the theater, but decided not to confront Dillinger until the show was over. Exiting the theater with his two women companions at 10:30 p.m., Dillinger apparently became suspicious and began running. Warning Dillinger that he was surrounded, Purvis ordered him to surrender, whereupon Dillinger reached for his pistol. When Purvis lit his cigar (a prearranged signal), agents fired and killed Dillinger.

Following Dillinger's death, "Baby Face" Nelson and John Paul Chase, another long-time Dillinger criminal associate, fled Chicago for California. Their apprehension remained a Bureau priority, and Cowley was assigned responsibility to locate Nelson and Chase, who periodically returned to the Chicago area. On November 27, 1934, agents spotted Nelson driving a stolen vehicle just outside Barrington, Illinois, and informed Cowley. In a shoot-out between Nelson, Chase, and several agents, two agents were killed, including Cowley. A mortally wounded Nelson

managed to escape with Chase in a Bureau car. Agents found Nelson's body the following day near a cemetery in Niles Center, Illinois.

During 1934, and in rapid succession, Bureau agents first killed John Dillinger, then "Pretty Boy" Floyd, and finally "Baby Face" Nelson in highly publicized shoot-outs. Attorney General Cummings's anticrime crusade paralleled and effectively exploited the manhunts for these notorious gangsters. Indeed, on March 20, 1934, when first outlining his proposed anticrime agenda, Cummings cited Dillinger's escape from the Crown Point jail as demonstrating the limits of local law enforcement. Each episode in Dillinger's Midwest crime spree became further evidence of the challenge that gangsters posed to the nation's safety and the need to expand federal authority in crime control. Cummings's publicity campaign succeeded. Congress approved most of the attorney general's Twelve Point Crime Program in May and June 1934. This legislation made bank robbery and interstate flight federal crimes, amended the Lindbergh Law, and authorized Bureau agents to carry weapons and make arrests.

Bonnie and Clyde

In the midst of the Dillinger manhunt, Bureau agents also sought another band of outlaws who were involved in their own highly publicized crime spree. This gang, headed by Clyde Barrow and Bonnie Parker (see Exhibits 2.3 and 2.4), roamed the southern Midwest, where they committed a series of bank robberies, engaged in shoot-outs with local

Exhibit 2.3 **Clyde Barrow,**
*Courtesy of the National Archives
(65-HN)*

police, and on occasion even kidnapped local peace officers—making headlines along the way.

Bonnie and Clyde had first met in Texas in 1930 when they were 19 and 21, respectively. Their criminal career together began in February 1932, when Barrow was paroled from prison after serving a two-year sentence in Texas for auto theft and burglary. They were soon joined by three other associates, including Clyde's brother Buck and Buck's wife, Blanche. By November 1933, the other gang members had been either captured or killed as their crime spree took them through several states, including Texas, Iowa, Missouri, and Oklahoma.

Despite the depletion in the ranks of their gang, Bonnie and Clyde continued on their own, with lawmen in hot pursuit. In November 1933, they narrowly escaped capture near Grand Prairie, Texas. Two months later, they helped five prisoners escape from a prison farm in Waldo, Texas. In early April 1934, Bonnie and Clyde were involved in shoot-outs with police in Grapevine, Texas, and Miami, Oklahoma, but again escaped.

Exhibit 2.4   **Bonnie Parker,**
Courtesy of the National Archives (65-HN)

Murder and robbery were state charges. Nonetheless, the Bureau had first entered the case in May 1933, when a federal judge in Dallas issued an arrest warrant charging Bonnie and Clyde with violation of the Motor Vehicle Theft Act, transporting a stolen vehicle across state lines (from Texas to Oklahoma). Bureau agents began their pursuit of the two fugitives, along with lawmen from several states.

Bonnie and Clyde's luck soon turned. In April 1934, Bureau agents and local authorities learned of their presence in Louisiana. They did not, however, immediately locate the infamous pair. Instead, Frank Hamer, a former Texas Ranger who had pursued the outlaw couple for months, received a tip that eventually led to Bonnie and Clyde's final encounter with police. Informed that Bonnie and Clyde would be traveling on a highway outside Sailes, Louisiana, Hamer organized a small posse of local deputies to capture the fugitives. On the morning of May 23, 1934, the couple's vehicle, traveling at high speed, attempted to breach the posse's barricade. Hamer's posse opened fire on the moving vehicle, and Bonnie and Clyde were both killed in a hail of gunfire as their car went off the road. Officers found an arsenal of weapons inside the car, along with the dead bodies of the two outlaws, who had been shot approximately 50 times. At the time of his death, Clyde Barrow had been accused of 12 murders in the preceding two years, with 8 of the victims either police officers or guards. Bonnie Parker was wanted as an accomplice.

The Urschel Kidnapping and George "Machine Gun" Kelly

Another headline-making crime occurred about a month after the Kansas City Massacre and two months after Dillinger was paroled from prison in Indiana. On July 23, 1933, a wealthy oilman, Charles F. Urschel, was abducted from his Oklahoma City home by two kidnappers armed with a machine gun and a pistol. Urschel's wife immediately reported the kidnapping to the Bureau on its newly instituted kidnapping phone line. Owing to recent passage of the Lindbergh Law, the Bureau now had its first major kidnapping case.

Four days after the kidnapping, E. E. Kirkpatrick, a friend of the Urschels, received a ransom note demanding $200,000 and directing him to travel to Kansas City, Missouri, to make payment. The stranger who received the ransom informed Kirkpatrick that Urschel would be released within 12 hours. The next night, Charles Urschel was released by his kidnappers near Norman, Oklahoma.

When interviewed by Bureau agents about the abduction, Urschel was able to provide a wealth of detail. Although he had been blindfolded, he could report a good deal: how he and his kidnappers traveled, peculiarities about where they stayed, and conversations that transpired. In what proved to be of critical importance, Urschel recalled that on the farm where he was being held captive, he could hear a plane flying overhead each morning and evening, but that one morning when it rained, he had heard no morning plane. Checking weather reports and airport schedules in the Oklahoma City vicinity, in combination with other clues, agents were able to establish an approximate location. On August 10, agents raided a farm near Paradise, Texas, owned by a family named Shannon, in-laws of the notorious gangster George "Machine Gun" Kelly. The Shannons were arrested and implicated themselves by admitting to a role in guarding Urschel. They identified Kelly and Albert Bates as the kidnappers.

Bureau agents traced Bates to Denver and soon arrested him. Kelly and his wife, Kathryn, were located at a house in Memphis, Tennessee. Raiding this house on September 26, 1933, Bureau agents and Memphis police caught Kelly by surprise. As he gave up without a fight, he allegedly pleaded with the agents, "Don't shoot, G-men! Don't shoot!" Transported to Oklahoma City, Kelly and his wife were tried for the kidnapping of Charles Urschel. Following a three-day trial, they were convicted on October 12 and sentenced to life in prison. Albert Bates and the Shannons, who were tried separately, also received life sentences.

The quick solution of the Urschel kidnapping and the capture of "Machine Gun" Kelly reinforced an emerging image of the Bureau as a skillful investigative agency. Agents soon acquired a new nickname: "G-men." Whether Kelly had actually referred to arresting agents in this manner or not, journalists, radio broadcasters, and movie scriptwriters quickly adopted the term when reporting on Bureau cases—replacing the more innocuous and impersonal "the Feds."

The Karpis and Buchalter Cases

As the gangster era of the 1930s drew to a close, two other cases proved noteworthy—mainly because of FBI Director Hoover's personal role in them. Hoover directly participated in the arrests of kidnapper-robber Alvin Karpis in 1936 and of New York City gangster Louis Buchalter in 1939. Both arrests became headline-making events and brought favorable publicity to the FBI director while enhancing the emerging reputation of the FBI.

Alvin Karpis, known by his underworld associates as "Creepy," had been a member of the "Ma" Barker gang, which had carried out bank robberies, murders, and kidnappings throughout the Midwest between 1931 and 1935. Following the death of Barker and her sons, who were killed by agents in January 1936, Karpis became the last of the major "public enemies" of the gangster era. At the time of the FBI search for Karpis in 1936, he was wanted for numerous robberies and for the kidnapping of two wealthy executives in St. Paul, Minnesota—William Hamm Jr., president of Hamm Brewing Co., and Edward Bremer, president of a local bank.

In late 1935, agents were ordered to inform the FBI director if they located Karpis, for Hoover indicated that he might want to get involved in the case personally. The first opportunity came in March 1936 when agents tracked Karpis to Hot Springs, Arkansas. However, before Hoover and a squad of agents could raid his hiding place, Karpis left town, apparently tipped off by local police. The following month, agents again located Karpis, who then was staying in an apartment in New Orleans. Hoover and some of his top aides, including Clyde Tolson and Louis Nichols, immediately flew to New Orleans to carry out the arrest. On April 30, 1936, agents surrounded the Canal Street apartment. Before they could approach the building, Karpis and an associate walked out of the apartment and got into a car. In the FBI version of the arrest, Hoover and another agent approached the car, confronted the suspects, and made the arrests. In Karpis's version of the arrest, he and his associate had been arrested and disarmed by agents, and only then did

Hoover and Tolson appear at the arrest site. All accounts agree, however, that in the rush to get to Karpis's apartment, none of the agents had brought along handcuffs, and that an agent's necktie had to be used to tie Karpis's hands behind his back. Karpis was flown to St. Paul where he was charged with kidnapping Hamm and Bremer. He was convicted and sentenced to life imprisonment, serving 33 years.

Why had Hoover decided play a personal role in apprehending Karpis? He had not participated in any earlier arrests. One explanation is that Karpis had threatened Hoover's life in retaliation for Bureau agents killing "Ma" Barker. Another is that Hoover sought to silence his congressional critics. In hearings conducted by the Senate Appropriations Committee in April 1936, Senator Kenneth McKellar persistently questioned the FBI director about his qualifications and investigative experience, including whether he had ever made an arrest. Hoover defended his professional experience in the Justice Department and Bureau, but conceded that he had never personally made an arrest—agents, in fact, did not have that power until 1934. Both of these incidents—the Karpis threat and the McKellar criticism—presented personal challenges to Hoover.

Three years later, Hoover made headlines in another high-profile case when arresting Louis "Lepke" Buchalter. Buchalter headed a protection racket that largely controlled the garment industry in New York City and was linked to an alleged nationwide hit squad, Murder Incorporated. For two years, Buchalter, had been aggressively pursued by New York state and city police. In August 1939, Walter Winchell, the noted New York City columnist and broadcaster, received an anonymous call that Buchalter might be interested in surrendering to federal authorities (Buchalter knew of Winchell's friendship with J. Edgar Hoover). Since he was wanted by federal agents for less serious offenses than those for which the state authorities sought him, Buchalter hoped to make a deal with federal officials. Responding to a radio appeal by Winchell for Buchalter to give himself up, Buchalter negotiated the terms with Winchell. He agreed to surrender on the corner of 28th Street and Fifth Avenue on the night of August 24, 1939. In the FBI version of the arrest, Hoover met Buchalter alone at this corner and single-handedly made the arrest. An unofficial version, however, has agents placing the intersection under surveillance, Winchell meeting Buchalter at the corner, and then the two of them driving to Hoover's limousine, parked several blocks away, where both entered the director's vehicle.

Tried and convicted on federal narcotics charges, Buchalter was sentenced to 14 years. Subsequently, he was turned over to state officials, who convicted him on murder charges. On March 5, 1944, Buchalter was electrocuted at Sing Sing Prison in New York.

The Karpis and Buchalter arrests had been carefully orchestrated to bring favorable publicity to both Hoover and the emergent Bureau of the 1930s. In Buchalter's case, the FBI arrested its first major organized crime figure. Ironically, given that the FBI's war on gangsters had enhanced the FBI's authority and reputation, the Buchalter arrest proved to be the Bureau's last arrest of a major crime boss until the 1960s and marked the end of the so-called gangsters era.

The Buchalter case differed markedly from the Bureau's other gangster cases. The "public enemies" of the gangster era, whom the FBI aggressively pursued, were predominantly rural outlaws who traveled the country (especially the Midwest) in small, mobile gangs; Buchalter, in contrast, was an urban gangster whose crimes were rooted in the crime syndicates of big-city life.

Sabotage and Espionage Cases of World War II

With the approach of World War II, the nation encountered new threats to its domestic security—threats that redefined the Bureau's mission and investigative priorities. As early as 1934, the Bureau was secretly authorized by President Franklin Roosevelt to investigate Nazi groups in the United States. Then in 1936 and 1938, the president again secretly directed the Bureau both to intensify its monitoring of German and Soviet agents and to ascertain whether native American fascists and communists were directed by, or acting on behalf of, Nazi Germany or Soviet Russia. Sensitive to public concerns about political spying, the president intentionally sought to avoid any publicity regarding the scope and purpose of the Bureau's expanded surveillance activities.

Roosevelt changed tactics in September 1939 following the outbreak of war in Europe that month with the German invasion of Poland. On September 6, the president publicized the FBI's responsibility to oversee domestic security investigations. The Bureau, the president announced in a directive to local police officials, was to become the clearinghouse for all information pertaining to espionage, sabotage, and subversive activities.

The World War II era (both prior to and following U.S. military involvement in December 1941) proved to be a period of rapid expansion for the FBI: its agents increased from about 896 in 1940 to 4,370 in 1945, and its appropriations from $8.8 million to $44.2 million in those years (see Table 1.1). The Bureau's responsibilities also shifted dramatically: from apprehending gangsters to monitoring spies and saboteurs; from seeking information to promote law enforcement to collecting and disseminating intelligence. These new priorities determined the FBI's notable cases of the war years.

The Rumrich Case

The first major prewar espionage case occurred when federal agents of the State and Justice Departments uncovered a German spy ring operating in the United States. This espionage ring inadvertently came to the attention of federal authorities in February 1938 when New York City police and State Department agents arrested one of the lesser figures in the operation, Guenther Gustav Rumrich (see Exhibit 2.5). Rumrich had attempted to obtain 50 passport application forms from the Passport Office in New York City, an action that immediately aroused suspicion and brought the FBI into

Exhibit 2.5   **Guenther Gustav Rumrich,** *Courtesy of the National Archives (65-CC)*

the investigation. Following an intensive investigation, Rumrich and three of his associates (Erich Glaser, Johanna Hofman, and Otto Herman Voss) were arrested for espionage, the FBI having learned that these suspects had intended to obtain secret military plans regarding the defense of the U.S. east coast and sell the plans to Germany.

Rumrich, 27 at the time of his arrest, had been a sergeant in the U.S. Army but deserted in 1935. Although born in the United States, he had been educated in Germany. Unable to obtain gainful employment in the United States, Rumrich offered to work for the German espionage service and was accepted. When his trial opened in October 1938, Rumrich pled guilty and testified as the government's key witness in the case. In addition to the three other defendants who had been arrested at the beginning of the investigation, 14 codefendants were also named, but they escaped to Germany when news of the arrests was leaked.

In his trial testimony, Rumrich outlined the plot to obtain U.S. military plans to defend the east coast and the Panama Canal, along with other military secrets. In his opening statement, U.S. Attorney Lamar Hardy claimed that the plot had been directed from Germany. All of the defendants were found guilty following several days of testimony and were sentenced by Federal Judge John Knox on December 2: Voss to six years in prison, Hofman to four years, and Glaser and Rumrich to two years each. In announcing the sentences, Judge Knox commented on the ineptitude of the spies, asserting that their biggest achievement was "to stir resentment" against Germany. He also criticized the "protective agencies," which included the FBI, for allowing some of the more important German agents to escape.

The Duquesne-Sebold Case

Just prior to the United States entry into World War II, on June 29, 1941, FBI Director Hoover announced the roundup of 33 German spies. This second espionage case seemed to confirm the scope of German spying in the United States and the FBI's success in monitoring German espionage. Among those arrested was Frederick Joubert ("Fritz") Duquesne, the head of a German espionage ring. The arrests culminated a 16-month investigation that involved an FBI double agent, William G. Sebold (see Exhibit 2.6).

Born in Germany, William Sebold emigrated to the United States in 1922. He established permanent residence, married, and eventually became a U.S. citizen. In 1939, he returned to Germany to visit relatives in Hamburg. When war broke out in Europe, Sebold, who was still in Germany, was approached by Gestapo officials and asked to "cooperate" with the German government upon his return to the United States. Initially ignoring these requests, he later expressed disinterest, but the requests persisted and turned into threats. Sebold was warned that if he did not cooperate with the Gestapo, they would inform U.S. authorities of his German criminal record (Sebold had been jailed for offenses committed around 1920)—unreported information that might jeopardize his U.S. citizenship. Should he refuse, they also threatened to send him to a concentration camp. Sebold

Exhibit 2.6 **FBI Surveillance Photos of Frederick Duquesne,** *Courtesy of the National Archives (65-M)*

agreed to cooperate and was sent for a seven-week training program so that he could operate a clandestine shortwave radio when he returned to the United States. Sebold returned to the United States, arriving in New York in February 1940 with instructions to meet with four "collectors," who would provide him with messages that he would transmit back to Germany. He was further instructed to open an office in Manhattan, which would serve as the location for these meetings, and set up a shortwave radio station on Long Island to transmit the messages (as well as to receive instructions from Germany). Sebold was known as "Tramp" to his German espionage associates.

Unknown to the German authorities, upon his return to the United States, Sebold contacted State Department officials and revealed the nature of his assignment. They, in turn, informed the FBI. FBI agents recruited Sebold as a double agent, setting up his Manhattan office and securing a house in Centerport, Long Island, to serve as a shortwave radio station. In fact, the shortwave transmissions to Germany were sent by FBI agents, not Sebold. The first transmission, approved and censored by the FBI, went out on May 31, 1940.

Following 16 months of monitoring German espionage activities in this manner, FBI officials decided to round up the spies who had transmitted messages through Sebold's operation—hence the June 29, 1941, arrests. Of those arrested, 19 pled guilty, 14 (including Duquesne) did not. Their trial on the charge of furnishing military secrets to Germany (including the Norden bombsight, a secret device to aid bombardiers in hitting their targets) opened in federal court in Brooklyn on September 3, with Sebold as the government's star witness. Although Duquesne and the other defendants denied the charges, Sebold's testimony implicated them. All 14 defendants were convicted on December 12 after a 14-week trial for violation of the Espionage Act. On January 2, 1942, Judge Mortimer Byers sentenced the 33 defendants (including the 19 who earlier had pled guilty) to a combined 310 years and 9 months in prison. Herman Lang, who had been charged with sending plans of the Norden bombsight to Germany, received a 20-year sentence, as did Frederick Duquesne, the head of the espionage operation.

George John Dasch and the Long Island Saboteurs

The most sensational World War II case occurred in June 1942 when FBI agents arrested two teams of German saboteurs. The sabotage teams, comprising four members each, had been transported by German submarines to the U.S. mainland. One team landed on a beach near Amagansett, Long Island (New York) on June 13; the other team landed on Ponte Vedra Beach, near Jacksonville, Florida, on June 17. The eight saboteurs had been selected for their prior experience of living in the United States and their familiarity with American customs and geography. They had then been trained at a Nazi sabotage school near Berlin. Their mission was to sabotage industrial plants and transportation facilities at various sites in the East, including an aluminum plant in Tennessee and locks on the Ohio River. In addition to causing physical destruction, the mission's additional objective was to strike a psychological blow to the U.S. civilian population by disrupting the home front. It was to be the first of several sabotage missions.

The mission, however, quickly unraveled when the first team landed on Long Island. John Cullen, a Coast Guardsman who was patrolling the beach around midnight,

encountered the four German agents. Although they claimed to be fishermen, Cullen's suspicions were aroused when one spoke in German, and the leader of the group, George John Dasch, offered him a bribe for his silence. After accepting the bribe out of concern for his own safety, Cullen immediately reported the incident upon returning to the Coast Guard station. Later that morning, several Coast Guardsmen returned to the beach and discovered that the "fishermen" had buried their German uniforms and other equipment. This discovery was reported to Coast Guard superiors, who immediately informed the FBI's New York City field office around noon that same day.

Dasch and his team took the Long Island Railroad into New York City, where they separated into pairs. The following day, Dasch began to have doubts about the mission and became concerned that he would be captured. In an anonymous call to the New York City FBI office, he reported having some information, but then hung up. A few days later, he surrendered to federal agents in Washington, D.C., who were initially skeptical about his claims. After a lengthy interrogation, Dasch revealed the whereabouts of the other members of his team, and informed the agents that a second team had landed on the Florida coast. He also provided a list of the possible contacts and the cover names that the other would-be saboteurs might use. FBI agents arrested the remaining members of his Long Island team on June 20 in New York City. The members of the Florida team were arrested a few days later—two in New York City on June 23 and the other two in Chicago on June 27. Within two weeks of the Long Island landing, all eight saboteurs had been taken into custody.

The eight German agents were tried before a military tribunal in July 1942, and all eight were convicted and sentenced to death. Because of their cooperation with the FBI, President Roosevelt commuted the sentences of Dasch and another traitor, Ernest Burger, to 30 years and to life, respectively. The others were executed on August 8. At the end of the war, in April 1948, President Harry Truman granted clemency to Dasch and Burger, and they were promptly deported to Germany.

The full details of the Dasch case were not revealed during the war. In part, FBI Director Hoover's announcement of the quick capture of the eight saboteurs was intended to deter future German sabotage missions. By not mentioning Dasch's role in the undoing of the mission, the implication was publicly conveyed that owing to the FBI's superior investigative skills, the case was solved. The quick capture of the German saboteurs bolstered the FBI's image at home and abroad as the protector of U.S. domestic security. Indeed, for the rest of the war, there were no documented incidents of German sabotage in the United States.

Throughout the war years, FBI agents also closely monitored the activities of Soviet consular officials; Soviet purchasing agents assigned to Washington, D.C., and New York City (under the Lend-Lease program); and American communists (some of whom had obtained employment in various federal agencies). For a variety of reasons, none of these investigations resulted in prosecution—thus, the scope and intensity of FBI investigations is not reflected in known FBI espionage cases. These wartime investigations acquired a different importance during the Cold War era—not in effecting prosecution, for the information about Soviet espionage activities was disseminated only within the executive branch. This evidence strengthened the central tenet of postwar internal security policy: Soviet perfidy and the disloyalty of U.S. communists and communist sympathizers necessitated an enhanced FBI surveillance role.

Cold War Security Cases

The wartime espionage and sabotage cases marked a turning point in the FBI's investigative responsibilities and priorities, as the Bureau became more enmeshed in intelligence work. With the end of World War II, the president and the attorney general had to decide whether this war-related intelligence authority should be curtailed. Although President Harry Truman terminated the FBI's foreign intelligence responsibilities in the Western Hemisphere in 1946, he nonetheless endorsed that domestic security continue as a top FBI priority. In part, these concerns led President Truman, in March 1947, to authorize the Federal Employee Loyalty Program to pursue any disloyal federal employee. In part, FBI counterintelligence agents sought to uncover spy rings believed responsible for divulging top U.S. government secrets to the Soviet Union. During the Cold War era, from the late 1940s through the 1960s, the FBI closely monitored communist activists and alleged subversives, who had become the main targets in a nationwide search for "subversives." The FBI's notable cases reflected these security concerns. As one result, the FBI's budgetary resources increased from $44.2 million in 1945 to $114.6 million in 1960.

From *Amerasia* to the Trials of Remington, Hiss, and Coplon

Some of the more celebrated cases of the McCarthy era brought attention to important domestic security issues; still others revealed illegal FBI investigative practices, like break-ins and wiretaps. Some of these cases embroiled the FBI in controversy and are discussed in greater detail in Chapter 3.

The first major postwar espionage case involved a journal on Far Eastern affairs, *Amerasia*. In January 1945, an article was published in *Amerasia* that had been based on a classified report of the Office of Strategic Services (OSS). This aroused the suspicion of Kenneth E. Wells, an OSS analyst who had written the original report. His discovery triggered an OSS investigation into the source of this leak. During this investigation, on March 11, 1945, OSS agents broke into the New York offices of *Amerasia,* where they discovered dozens of photocopied State Department, Navy, and OSS documents (some marked "Top Secret"). OSS officials referred the matter to the FBI (investigating espionage was an FBI responsibility). The FBI's investigation identified three federal employees (John S. Service, Emmanuel Larsen, and Andrew Roth) as the suspected sources of these pilfered documents. In the course of conducting this investigation, however, FBI agents again broke into and wiretapped *Amerasia*'s offices, obtaining evidence that later proved to be inadmissible. The three federal employees, *Amerasia*'s two editors (Philip Jaffe and Kate Mitchell), and a freelance reporter (Mark Gayn) were arrested on June 6, 1945, and were eventually charged for the crime of unauthorized possession of classified documents (evidence of espionage was not uncovered). A federal grand jury returned indictments against only three of the arrestees (Jaffe, Larsen, and Roth). None of these three was tried. Instead, on September 28, 1945, two (Jaffe and Larsen) reached a plea bargain; in return for pleading no contest, they would receive small fines but no imprisonment. The prosecution had been stymied by Larsen's post-indictment discovery that FBI agents had earlier broken into his apartment. Because Larsen's attorney had filed a motion on September 28 to quash the indictment of his client (on the grounds that the FBI's earlier break-in required suppressing all the evidence obtained at the time of his client's arrest), Justice Department attorneys quickly proposed a seemingly lenient plea bargain to Jaffe's attorney, Albert Arent. At the time, Arent was unaware of Larsen's motion and the break-in problem. He accepted—and even when learning of this development, honored the terms. The third defendant, Roth, was never prosecuted.

Shortly after the *Amerasia* case, in November 1945, Elizabeth Bentley, a former member of the U.S. Communist Party, walked into the FBI's New Haven, Connecticut, field office and recounted her participation as a courier for a wartime Soviet spy ring in the United States. Bentley named the low-level government officials in the Treasury Department and wartime agencies whom she claimed had provided her with copies of government documents. She presented herself as a disillusioned communist who had broken from the party following the death of her lover, Jacob Golos, the Soviet espionage agent who headed this spy ring. Her courier role entailed delivering to Golos classified information that had been given to her by American communists who worked in the federal government. Bentley, however, could not produce any document or confederate to substantiate her claims. An intensive FBI investigation was launched (code-named Gregory). The results of this inquiry were presented to a federal grand jury in 1948, but no indictments were returned. It remains unclear what the FBI uncovered in this investigation—recently released FBI reports are heavily censored. In 1995, however, the CIA made public highly sensitive records—intercepted Soviet consular messages of the period 1943–45—which confirmed the substance of some of Bentley's allegations and the Soviets' recruitment of many of those she named (notably, Nathan Silvermaster, Frank Coe, Victor Perlo, and William Ullman).

Bentley's allegations were soon brought to the attention of congressional investigators and became public in highly partisan hearings in July 1948, conducted first by the Senate Committee on Expenditures in the Executive Department and then by the House Committee on Un-American Activities (HUAC). Bentley's personality and inability to corroborate her charges—combined with the fact that those she named refused to testify, citing the Fifth Amendment—led congressional investigators to seek additional testimony from other communist defectors.

Bentley's congressional testimony did lead to a highly controversial perjury case involving one of the individuals whom she had named, William Remington, at the time employed by the Commerce Department. In testimony before HUAC, Remington admitted meeting Bentley and providing her with information during the war years, but he maintained that the information was not classified and that he believed she was a researcher. Two years later, in April 1950, two other former communists, Howard Bridgman and Kenneth McConnell, testifying during a HUAC hearing, claimed that Remington had been a member of the U.S. Communist Party in 1937. In testimony of May 4, Remington denied this charge. On June 8, 1950, a federal grand jury indicted Remington for perjury: his denial of Communist Party membership. He resigned from the

Commerce Department the next day. Following a six-week trial. Remington was convicted of perjury on February 7, 1951. Upon appeal, the Circuit Court of Appeals reversed the conviction because of the trial judge's improper instructions to the jury regarding what constitutes Communist Party membership. In addition, the appeals court cited the judge's failure to provide the defense with minutes of the grand jury testimony of Remington's former wife, a key government witness.

Rather than retry the case, federal prosecutors sought a new indictment from another grand jury, which they obtained on October 25, 1951. Following a second trial that began on January 13, 1953, the jury found Remington guilty on two of five counts of perjury—when he swore that he had not known of a Young Communist League at Dartmouth, where he had been an undergraduate, and that he had not supplied Bentley with classified documents. Remington was sentenced to three years in prison, which he began serving on April 15, 1953. His appeals to the Circuit Court of Appeals and the Supreme Court were unsuccessful.

Remington's case paralleled that of Alger Hiss, a former State Department official. In early August 1948, HUAC subpoenaed Whittaker Chambers, another ex-communist turned FBI informer, who at the time was a senior editor of *Time* magazine. In dramatic public testimony before HUAC on August 3, Chambers accused Hiss of having been a member of a communist cell in Washington, D.C.; he also named eight other federal employees whom he claimed had sought to promote communist influence in government. At this time and in succeeding months, however, Chambers denied that Hiss had engaged in espionage. In response to Chambers's accusations, Hiss demanded and was granted the opportunity to appear before the committee on August 5, at which time he denied Chambers's allegations under oath and conveyed the impression that he did not know Chambers (although he later admitted to having known Chambers, but under a different name). Hiss dared Chambers to repeat these allegations in public, and when he did, brought a suit for libel.

The resultant libel proceedings transformed the case. In November and then in December 1948, Chambers produced a series of documents that he claimed to have received from Hiss in the 1930s, when Hiss worked for the State Department. On November 17, 1948, Chambers turned over to Hiss's attorneys, who were taking depositions from him in Hiss's libel suit, summaries of State Department reports (in Hiss's handwriting) and typewritten copies of State Department reports. Hiss's attorneys immediately referred these documents to the Justice Department. In a more dramatic development, this time in response to a HUAC subpoena, on December 2, 1948, Chambers brought HUAC investigators to a garden on his Maryland farm where he retrieved five rolls of microfilm from a hollowed-out pumpkin (subsequently dubbed the "Pumpkin Papers"). At this point, Chambers abruptly modified his allegations about Hiss, describing their relationship during the 1930s as involving espionage and claiming to have received the "Pumpkin Papers" from Hiss during this Soviet espionage operation.

This new evidence dramatically changed the context of an ongoing grand jury inquiry—initially convened merely to ascertain whether Chambers or Hiss had committed perjury in their HUAC testimony, given their conflicting accounts. On December 15, 1948, the grand jury indicted Hiss on two counts of perjury: the first for denying having met Chambers after 1937, and the second for denying having passed classified documents to Chambers. Despite the documents that Chambers produced, the three-year statute of limitations on espionage had expired, and the Justice Department's only legal recourse against Hiss was to prosecute him for perjury. Although the trial was formally a perjury case, it was publicly understood to involve espionage. It assumed particular importance because of Hiss's subsequent career. Although a low-level State Department employee in 1938, Hiss had won a series of promotions, and in 1945 headed State's postwar planning staff and was a member of the U.S. delegation to the controversial Yalta Conference. Hiss resigned from the State Department in December 1946 to accept an appointment to head the Carnegie Endowment.

During Hiss's two trials in 1949 and 1950, the defense strategy focused on character: emphasizing Chambers's questionable truthfulness (given the dramatic conflicts between the accounts given in his HUAC testimony, his original October 1948 testimony, and then his December 1948 grand jury testimony) and Hiss's impeccable reputation. In addition, the defense claimed that the handwritten notes were appropriate in the context of Hiss's official duties and implied that Chambers had acquired them from another source. However, the defense was unable to explain the typed documents, which FBI experts during the trial confirmed had been typed on a machine once owned by Hiss but subsequently given away. Although the first trial ended in a hung jury on July 7, 1949, Hiss was convicted in a second trial, on January 21, 1950, and was sentenced to five years in prison (serving 44 months in a federal penitentiary).

In the years following Hiss's conviction, the question of his guilt or innocence continued to be debated. During the 1950s, both Hiss and Chambers wrote books about the case, reasserting their claims. During the 1970s, FBI documents (some with heavy text obliteration) were released under the Freedom of Information Act (FOIA), but these records have not conclusively resolved the controversy. Based on these and other documents released under the FOIA, Hiss appealed his conviction in 1982, claiming the newly revealed information showed that there had been prosecutorial misconduct. A federal judge rejected Hiss's appeal to reopen the case, and the Supreme Court refused to hear the case the following year. The issue of Hiss's guilt again resurfaced in the early 1990s following the collapse of the Soviet Union. Dmitri Volkogonov, a Russian general and historian who was in charge of KGB and military archives, claimed that a search of those files found no reference to Hiss (although he later admitted that some records may have been missing or destroyed). Until his death in November 1996, Alger Hiss maintained his innocence just as adamantly as partisans on the other side insisted on his guilt.

Hiss's trial coincided with another espionage case involving Judith Coplon, a low-level Justice Department employee. In March 1949, FBI agents arrested Coplon in New York City. At the time of her arrest, she possessed 28 FBI documents that she intended to deliver to a Soviet agent, Valentin Gubitchev. Indicted in Washington, D.C. (for unauthorized possession of classified documents), and also in New York City (for intent to deliver classified documents to an agent of a foreign power), Coplon was subsequently tried and convicted.

During Coplon's Washington trial, the judge required the prosecution to produce the originals of the 28 "raw" FBI files on which the government's case was based. The judge's order embarrassed FBI officials since the files revealed that FBI reports contained unsubstantiated rumors and gossip. Because 15 of the 28 documents contained information clearly obtained from wiretaps, Coplon's attorneys requested a discovery hearing to ascertain whether Coplon's phone had been tapped. The judge rejected this request, endorsing the government's contention that this was a "fishing expedition."

In the subsequent New York trial, however, the presiding judge did order a pretrial hearing to ascertain whether Coplon's phone had been tapped. In response, Justice Department lawyers admitted that Coplon's home and office phones had been wiretapped, both prior to and after her arrest (in the process intercepting privileged conversations between Coplon and her attorney).

Although Coplon was convicted and received prison sentences in both cases, in December 1950, a federal appeals court overturned her convictions in both the New York and Washington trials because of the illegal wiretaps and her arrest without a warrant. Remanded for a new trial, Coplon remained subject to criminal prosecution until 1967 when Attorney General Ramsey Clark formally dropped prosecution.

The Smith Act and Clinton Jencks Cases

At about the same time as Whittaker Chambers publicly accused Hiss of membership in the Communist Party, the Justice Department, at the urging of FBI officials, turned its attention to the leadership of the U.S. Communist Party and initiated prosecution of its top leadership. The legal basis for this prosecution was the Smith Act of 1940, which made it illegal to advocate the violent overthrow of the U.S. government.

On June 29, 1948, a grand jury in New York City indicted the 12 members of the party's national board, and FBI agents arrested them about a month later. During the ensuing nine-month trial, which ended in October 1949, Justice Department attorneys relied on FBI informants who had infiltrated the party, some of whom rose to positions of influence in the party's leadership. In addition, federal prosecutors used party publications and literature, as well as the testimony of ex-members (such as Louis Budenz) to support their case: that the party was committed to the violent overthrow of the U.S. government. Eleven defendants were convicted (the twelfth defendant was tried separately due to illness), and all but one received the maximum sentence of five years. In 1951, the Supreme Court, in *Dennis v. United States,* upheld their convictions and the constitutionality of the Smith Act.

Justice Department officials then proceeded with a second round of prosecutions in which they convicted another 93 Communist Party members, this time, the second-level leadership. In 1957, however, the Supreme Court in *Yates v. United States* overturned these latter Smith Act convictions. Effectively reversing the *Dennis* decision, the Supreme Court concluded that the government needed to prove advocacy "of action and not merely abstract doctrine" to convict individuals for violating the Smith Act. In effect, the Court held that it was not sufficient to show that communists advocated the violent overthrow of the U.S. government in their writings or in their literature, but that it

was necessary to demonstrate that they intended to act on these beliefs. This ruling essentially ended further Smith Act prosecutions.

Two weeks before the *Yates* decision, on June 3, 1957, the Supreme Court issued another landmark ruling pertaining to the use of FBI informants in criminal prosecutions. The Court's ruling in this case, *Jencks v. United States,* had serious implications for future criminal prosecutions of communists under the Smith Act, or any other federal statute. The case involved an appeal of Clinton Jencks, a New Mexico labor leader who had been convicted of perjury for filing a false affidavit regarding his membership in the U.S. Communist Party—in violation of the Taft-Hartley Act. The prosecution's key witnesses were two former communists, both of whom were also paid FBI informants, who recounted Jencks's positions and activities in the Communist Party. During the trial, the presiding judge had denied a defense motion to obtain access to reports that these paid informants had regularly submitted to the FBI. The defense had intended to use the reports to impugn the credibility of these government witnesses—contrasting their original accounts with their trial testimony. In overturning Jencks's conviction, the Supreme Court ruled that the trial judge had erred, and that informant reports that pertain to trial testimony should be made available to the defense.

All these postwar cases—most notably, the *Amerasia*, Hiss, and Smith Act prosecutions—lent credibility to a growing public anxiety over the loyalty of federal employees and the existence of Soviet spy rings. Indeed, within a month of Hiss's conviction, Senator Joseph McCarthy's often-cited speech in Wheeling, West Virginia, in which he claimed to possess a list of 205 "known" communists in the State Department, catapulted him to national prominence. At the time, the media and the public found the senator's claim to be credible: that communists were employed in sensitive policy positions and that the Truman administration had known about this serious problem, but did little to correct it.

Thus, another effect of these notable cases against Communist Party members and alleged communists was to usher in the so-called McCarthy era and to intensify the federal government's aggressive pursuit of communists in government and communist influence in American life.

"The Crime of the Century": The Rosenberg Case

Yet another case involving Soviet spying captured the nation's attention and further fueled this rising alarm over domestic security. It was the most sensational espionage case of the Cold War era and involved the Soviets' success in stealing design information during the development of the atomic bomb, acquired through the disloyal actions of U.S. Communist Party members who recruited scientists employed during the wartime Manhattan Project (the U.S.-sponsored effort to develop the atom bomb during World War II) to spy in behalf of the Soviet Union. FBI Director Hoover subsequently termed this case "the crime of the century." This Cold War case centered on the roles of Julius and Ethel Rosenberg in recruiting a low-level military officer to steal atomic bomb research secrets for the Soviets during World War II. The Justice Department (based on the FBI's investigation) claimed that Julius Rosenberg headed a Soviet spy network during the war, and that he and his wife, Ethel, had been key members of a conspiracy to steal secrets relating to the production and development of the atom bomb. The Rosenbergs and their defenders denied these charges, claiming that they were framed by the government because of their communist beliefs and were victims of the excesses of McCarthyism.

The trail leading to the Rosenbergs (see Exhibits 2.7 and 2.8) began in 1949 when the FBI agents successfully identified Klaus Fuchs as a Soviet spy. The possibility that Fuchs spied had been uncovered from cryptic references in Soviet consular messages that military intelligence had intercepted during World War II but was unable to decipher until 1948–49. (This top secret message-interception program, code-named Venona, became key to FBI and National Security Agency counterintelligence efforts during the Cold War years.) A German-born British physicist, Fuchs had worked on the Manhattan Project both in New York and at the Los Alamos laboratory in New Mexico.

Exhibit 2.7   **Ethel Rosenberg,**
Courtesy of the National Archives (65-CC)

FBI officials alerted British counterintelligence to their identification of Fuchs as a Soviet spy. Since Fuchs had returned to England after the war, British authorities pursued the lead, and in 1950 they questioned him on whether he had committed atomic espionage. FBI counterintelligence experts were also allowed to interrogate Fuchs to uncover

whether he had worked with any other sources in the United States. Fuchs ultimately confessed to providing the Soviets with information on the design of the atomic bomb and

Exhibit 2.8   **Julius Rosenberg,**
Courtesy of the FBI

identified his Soviet contact as "Raymond." He was tried in Britain in March 1950 on espionage charges, convicted, and sentenced to 14 years in prison.

The FBI then attempted to learn the full name of "Raymond" and whether others were involved in this Soviet espionage operation. FBI agents eventually were able to identify this individual as Harry Gold, a Communist Party member then employed as a chemist in Philadelphia. In May 1950, Gold confessed to having acted as a courier and was indicted on espionage charges. Gold further admitted to agents that, in addition to Fuchs, he had a second source of information at the Los Alamos laboratory, a soldier whom the FBI identified as David Greenglass, the brother-in-law of Julius Rosenberg.

When FBI agents questioned Greenglass in June 1950, he implicated both his wife, Ruth, and Julius Rosenberg in his espionage activities, claiming that Rosenberg had recruited him. Although Greenglass did not at first implicate his sister, Ethel, 10 days prior to the trial, he maintained that she had been present and had taken notes at meetings when information was passed to her husband.

FBI agents arrested Julius Rosenberg on July 17, 1950, and Ethel about a month later, on August 11. Although FBI officials and federal prosecutors believed Ethel had only been an accomplice in her husband's espionage activities, her arrest and prosecution became part of their "lever" strategy to get Julius to confess and to provide the names of other Soviet spies. A third defendant believed to be part of Julius Rosenberg's spy network, Morton Sobell, was also charged with conspiracy to commit espionage and was tried with the Rosenbergs.

The trial began on March 6, 1951, with David Greenglass and Harry Gold testifying as key witnesses for the prosecution. Greenglass reasserted his previous claims about Julius Rosenberg's central role in the espionage activities (modified to include Ethel's complicity) and discussed the nature of the information he had supplied to them: a sketch of a spherical lens mold design and a description of a series of plutonium experiments—all bearing on the development of the atom bomb. Gold, who was already serving a 30-year sentence, offered testimony linking Julius to a Soviet contact agent, Anatoli Yakovlev, a connection that was necessary for an espionage conviction. Both Julius and Ethel Rosenberg took the stand in their own defense, hoping that at least one of the jurors would believe their claims of innocence. On March 29, 1951, the jury found all three defendants (Julius Rosenberg, Ethel Rosenberg, and Morton Sobell) guilty.

Federal Judge Irving Kaufman delayed sentencing until April 5, as he considered whether to apply the death penalty. In his report to the attorney general prior to sentencing, FBI Director Hoover had opposed the death penalty for Ethel (because of his concern over public reaction to the execution of a mother of two small children), but Judge Kaufman thought otherwise. He sentenced both Rosenbergs to death and Sobell to 30 years in prison. Greenglass had previously pled guilty and was later sentenced to 15 years.

The Rosenbergs appealed their conviction to the U.S. Court of Appeals, Second Circuit. Although disagreeing with the severity of the sentences, the court ruled on February 25, 1952, that their trial had been fair. The Supreme Court denied a subsequent appeal when it voted on October 13, 1952, not to review the case. Having exhausted their appeals, and denied clemency by President Dwight Eisenhower, the Rosenbergs were executed at Sing Sing Prison on June 19, 1953.

In the years following the Rosenbergs' conviction, some have questioned their guilt, while others have questioned the significance of the information they might have conveyed to the Soviet Union. At the time of the trial, the prosecution claimed that the Rosenbergs had stolen the secret of the atom bomb. Judge Kaufman, at the time of sentencing, also maintained that the Rosenbergs had put the atom bomb in the hands of the Soviets, and that they were indirectly responsible for "communist aggression in Korea," which had resulted in thousands of deaths. Although FBI Director Hoover publicly emphasized the significance of the secrets that the Rosenbergs had helped convey to the Soviets, in internal memoranda, he acknowledged that the Soviets had probably obtained the secrets of the atom bomb by other means.

Critics, including Nobel Prize–winning physicist Harold C. Urey, argued that Greenglass, a machinist, did not have the background to understand and transmit the secrets of the atom bomb. Other critics pointed out that physicist Klaus Fuchs had transmitted vital information about the bomb's design to the Soviets through Harry Gold before Greenglass's espionage activities; what information could Greenglass have added to this? But others emphasized that Greenglass's recruitment came at a time when Fuchs had broken off contact with the Soviets, suggesting that Soviet officials might therefore have had some questions about the trustworthiness of Fuchs's information. An additional twist was added to the controversy in March 1997 when a former Soviet spy, Alexander Feklisov (who claimed to have had at least 50 meetings with Julius Rosenberg during the 1940s), provided his account of the Rosenbergs' role in espionage in interviews with the *New York Times* and *Washington Post* and in a television documentary aired on the Discovery Channel. He confirmed that during the 1940s, Julius had been involved in establishing a Soviet spy ring and had passed secrets involving military electronics, but not the secrets of the atom bomb. He also maintained that Ethel was never directly involved in spying but probably had been aware of her husband's activities.

The atomic bomb espionage case served to reinforce popular concerns about the Soviet threat and about the disloyalty of American communists. Congress, moreover, amended the espionage statute, making peacetime espionage a capital offense—the so-called Rosenberg Law of 1954. (The espionage of the Rosenbergs had been committed during wartime.) On the whole, FBI Director Hoover championed the case as a triumph for FBI investigative methods in combating Soviet espionage. His *Reader's Digest* article, "Crime of the Century," further popularized the FBI's successes in combating Soviet espionage. The spy trail ended with the Rosenbergs' convictions, however, since they refused to implicate others.

Colonel Rudolf I. Abel, Soviet Master Spy

The last of the major postwar espionage cases involved Soviet spy Rudolf Ivanovich Abel, who had been operating in the United States for about nine years before his arrest in 1957. Unlike the other Cold War security cases, which had involved the compromised loyalty of American citizens, Rudolf Abel was a colonel in the KGB, the Soviet intelligence service.

The defection of Reino Hayhanen, another Soviet agent and a collaborator of Abel's, led to the FBI's discovery of Abel. When ordered by his KGB superiors to return to the Soviet Union (apparently for incompetence and excessive drinking), Hayhanen defected to the CIA at the U.S. embassy in Paris in May 1957, while en route to Moscow. FBI agents interrogated Hayhanen upon his return to the United States, to obtain information about his espionage activities. Hayhanen could not name his superior, knowing him only as "Mark." From his description of "Mark" and their activities, FBI agents narrowed their search to a building in Brooklyn, New York, where a man called Emil Goldfus was a tenant and operated a photograph studio. After several days of surveillance and Hayhanen's positive identification of Goldfus as "Mark" (i.e., Abel) from a photograph taken by agents during the surveillance, FBI officials arranged to have the Immigration and Naturalization Service (INS) arrest Abel as an illegal alien on June 21 at the Hotel Latham in Manhattan, where he had registered. Following his arrest, an FBI search of his person, studio, and hotel room uncovered a variety of espionage equipment and materials (including shortwave radios, hollowed-out objects, and microfilm). FBI agents eventually established that he was Rudolf Abel, a Russian citizen.

Charged with conspiracy to commit espionage, Abel was tried in federal court in October 1957 on three counts of espionage, with his former subordinate, Hayhanen, testifying against him. Convicted on all counts on October 25, Abel was sentenced three weeks later to 30 years in prison on the most serious charge. Although appealed, his conviction was upheld by the Supreme Court in March 1960. Abel served four years in prison until he was returned to the Soviet Union in February 1962 in exchange for American U-2 pilot Francis Gary Powers, who had been shot down while on a reconnaissance flight over Soviet territory and captured by the Soviets. Hayhanen was given a new identity and established residence somewhere in New England.

As a postscript to the Rosenberg case, among Hayhanen's revelations to the FBI was a statement that indirectly linked Abel to the Rosenbergs. Abel had instructed him, Hayhanen said, to deliver some money to Helen Sobell (code-named "Wife of Stone"), the wife of Morton Sobell, one of the codefendants in the Rosenberg case. A deciphered message later found in Abel's possession seemed to confirm Hayhanen's claim of a link between Abel and the Rosenberg spy network.

The notable McCarthy-era cases and the crisis of the Cold War firmly established the FBI as *the* federal agency responsible for protecting the nation's security—from both internal subversion and foreign spies. What had begun as a temporary, World War II–related responsibility had become a permanent assignment. These cases marked the FBI's transformation from an agency involved exclusively in law enforcement (in the gangster era) to one with a central mission that included both counterintelligence and domestic surveillance.

Organized Crime

Joseph Valachi and La Cosa Nostra

The official FBI line prior to the 1960s was that organized crime was primarily a local police problem committed by independent gangs of "hoodlums" and "gangsters," and thus outside the jurisdiction of the Bureau. Embarrassed by FBI ignorance of the 1957 Apalachin conclave (a high-level meeting of national Mafia leaders, discovered by New York state troopers), J. Edgar Hoover immediately intensified FBI investigations of organized crime leaders under what was called the Top Hoodlum program. Few convictions ensued, however, as the FBI lacked both the resources and the interest to wage a vigorous war on organized crime. This began to change during the "law and order" politics of the 1960s.

In the early 1960s, Attorney General Robert F. Kennedy lobbied Congress to expand federal efforts to combat organized crime. His proposed federal campaign required new legislation, new initiatives from federal law enforcement agencies, and the mobilization of public opinion. As part of this effort, Attorney General Kennedy prodded Hoover to intensify the FBI's organized crime enforcement further.

In 1963, the appearance of Mafia informer Joseph Valachi before a Senate subcommittee and a national television audience marked a turning point in the federal war on organized crime. Valachi's testimony highlighted the national character of organized crime activities—and thus the importance of the FBI's role in the effort to combat them.

Born in New York City in 1904, Valachi was the son of Italian immigrants. He grew up in a rough neighborhood in Manhattan's East Harlem, dropping out of school by the age of 15. His long criminal career included 18 arrests in New

York State on various charges—burglary, robbery, assault, gambling, and narcotics. By his own admission he became a "soldier" in the Mafia around 1930.

A 1959 conviction on federal narcotics charges led to Valachi being committed to the Atlanta Penitentiary to serve 15- and 20-year sentences. During his incarceration in Atlanta, Valachi concluded that Vito Genovese, head of one of the Mafia families and also imprisoned in Atlanta, had "marked" him for execution, suspecting that he had become a government informer. Anticipating attack by a Mafia enforcer, Valachi killed a fellow inmate in June 1962, incorrectly believing him to be the Mafia's "hit man."

Shortly after this murder, Valachi expressed a willingness to cooperate with federal authorities in return for a reduced sentence on the murder charge (life imprisonment instead of execution) and protection from the Mafia. A further motive was revenge against his former organized crime associates. Valachi was secretly transferred to the Westchester County Jail (New York), where he was initially interrogated by Federal Bureau of Narcotics agent Frank Selvagi. But it was an FBI agent, James P. Flynn—not Selvagi—who ultimately elicited from Valachi his story of life in the Mafia. Beginning in September 1962, Flynn made almost daily jail visits to Valachi who, for security reasons, had been transferred to Fort Monmouth, New Jersey. Over the next eight months, Flynn won Valachi's confidence and elicited from him a detailed description of the organization and activities of the Mafia as he had experienced them. During one of these interrogation sessions, Valachi used the term "La Cosa Nostra" to refer to organized crime (an Italian phrase meaning "our thing," or "our family"). He said that La Cosa Nostra was the name used by insiders; "Mafia" was used only by outsiders.

During the summer of 1963, Senator John McClellan (chair of the Senate Permanent Subcommittee on Investigations) and Attorney General Kennedy decided that the subcommittee's hearings on organized crime and narcotics would provide the forum for Valachi to "go public" as a witness. At the time, Kennedy was lobbying for passage of new legislation to provide immunity to witnesses from prosecution in racketeering cases and to revise the legislative ban on wiretapping to enhance federal law enforcement authority. Two years earlier, the same Senate subcommittee's hearings on gambling had successfully mobilized support that led to the passage of federal legislation to curb gambling in interstate commerce.

Beginning on September 27, 1963, Valachi testified about La Cosa Nostra before the McClellan subcommittee, for six days in public and for one day in a closed session. He described the structure of organized crime "families" in the United States and their hierarchy, with bosses or *capos* at the top, and he named the heads of the New York families. Valachi claimed that a national organized crime cartel existed, ruled by a 12-man commission, and he graphically described La Cosa Nostra's criminal activities.

Valachi's testimony commanded widespread media coverage—although some skeptics disputed Attorney General Kennedy's characterization of Valachi's revelations as a breakthrough in the government's information about organized crime (and a break in the underworld code of silence). These skeptics questioned the veracity and significance of Valachi's testimony. Officials of the New York City Police Department, for example, characterized Valachi as "a small, publicity-loving bum" whose testimony consisted of nothing more than "stale rumors and underworld gossip." Given that Valachi was a lowly "soldier" in the Genovese crime family, other observers questioned his knowledge of the high-level decisions about which he claimed to have information. In fact, much of Valachi's testimony conformed to information that the FBI had already (if illegally) obtained from wiretaps of targeted crime leaders.

Valachi's cooperation with federal authorities produced evidence leading to the successful prosecution of only one criminal case (prosecution was complicated by the FBI's illegal wiretap). Nonetheless, his Senate testimony brought national publicity to the organized crime problem. The monolithic, conspiratorial picture of organized crime that he presented gained ascendance during the 1960s, with its acceptance by President Johnson's Crime Commission in 1966–67 and its popularization in Peter Maas's 1968 book *The Valachi Papers* and in the *Godfather* novel and movies. Although Congress did not immediately pass the new legislative measures that Attorney General Kennedy desired (legislation legalizing wiretapping was enacted in 1968 and legislation facilitating the prosecution of racketeering in 1970), federal efforts against organized crime thereafter intensified, and the FBI was gradually drawn into organized crime enforcement.

Valachi's introduction to the public of the term "La Cosa Nostra" also gave FBI Director Hoover a measure of face-saving, since he had previously denied the existence of the "Mafia" as an organization. Since 1963, "La Cosa Nostra"

(LCN)—but not "Mafia"—entered the FBI lexicon, and to the present day, it is the Bureau's term of preference to describe the organized crime syndicate.

Civil Rights Cases of the 1960s

Federal civil rights laws have existed since the post–Civil War Reconstruction Era, including laws that provided federal jurisdiction in police brutality cases. Prior to the 1960s, however, the FBI had avoided involvement in such cases. FBI Director Hoover explicitly expressed this reluctance during a 1956 briefing to President Dwight Eisenhower's cabinet, when he argued against any expansion in civil rights enforcement. In that briefing, in which he read from a lengthy FBI report titled "Racial Tensions and Civil Rights," Hoover sympathetically presented the South's view on civil rights matters—opposition to integration and "mixed" education—and, furthermore, claimed that the Ku Klux Klan had become defunct. Hoover portrayed segregationists as prominent Southern citizens, and at the same time suggested that civil rights groups were subject to subversive or communist influences. The FBI director, moreover, emphasized that the FBI was not a "national police force" and that it lacked the resources to investigate civil rights violations across the country; these were more properly handled by local authorities.

Some critics of the FBI have attributed Hoover's reluctance in civil rights enforcement to his own biases as a Southerner. A more important reason was Hoover's awareness that FBI agents worked closely with local police to solve cases, and that FBI appropriations were highly dependent on Southern members of Congress who controlled important committees (notably, appropriations and judiciary). More aggressive civil rights enforcement might jeopardize the FBI's political base in Congress, as well as its relations with local law enforcement agencies, and thus its ability to solve cases.

The "Freedom Summer" of 1964 proved to be a turning point, as civil rights workers from across the country, including many white college students, came to Mississippi to register blacks to vote. This voting rights project heightened racial tensions in the South, as most Southerners, not just white supremacist groups like the Ku Klux Klan, opposed these "outside" efforts to upset the region's traditional race relations.

FBI and Justice Department officials had been criticized for their failure to protect civil rights demonstrators from mob violence and police brutality in various well-publicized

incidents throughout the South during the early 1960s. For example, the Freedom Riders, a group of civil rights activists who sought to integrate public transportation in the South, had been beaten on several occasions by local mobs when they arrived at bus terminals. In one notorious incident at the Montgomery, Alabama, bus terminal in 1961, Freedom Riders were beaten by an anti-integration mob as they disembarked from the bus. Local police were conspicuously absent, and although an FBI agent was present, his mission was simply to witness the violence and take notes. Among those beaten at the Montgomery bus terminal was John Seigenthaler, a Justice Department official there to witness events.

At the same time as they maintained this non-interventionist policy in the protection of civil rights activists, federal officials sometimes prosecuted civil rights demonstrators for "obstruction of justice." The sharp increase in racial tensions during the summer of 1964 soon brought federal civil rights enforcement policy to a critical juncture. The national media's focus on racial violence and conflict in the South, along with mounting pressure from President Lyndon Johnson, forced a more interventionist federal policy. By the mid-1960s, the FBI's role in civil rights cases began to change. Several nationally publicized murders of civil rights workers brought the FBI into the limelight, as Bureau officials, under pressure from the public and the president, mobilized resources and agents to solve these crimes. The most notable of these cases were the murder of Medgar Evers in 1963, the killing of three civil rights workers in the summer of 1964, and the murder of Viola Liuzzo in 1965.

These murders both raised national consciousness on civil rights issues and led to a fundamental shift in the FBI's and Justice Department's enforcement and prosecution of civil rights statutes. From a federal policy of avoidance, the Justice Department of the Johnson administration increasingly adopted a policy of intervention, especially when local authorities failed to pursue cases in state courts. The FBI's presence in the South increased, symbolized by the opening of a field office in Jackson, Mississippi. In addition, FBI officials launched a major initiative to combat Ku Klux Klan violence, initiating in July 1964 a COINTELPRO (counterintelligence program) against the group, with the aim of disrupting and neutralizing various "white hate groups." Under this program, FBI agents made widespread use of informants within the Klan to obtain intelligence and to promote disruption and dissent. Between 1964 and 1971,

FBI officials authorized 287 separate COINTELPRO actions against the Klan, and by 1970, Klan violence in the South had subsided.

The Murder of Medgar Evers

On the evening of June 12, 1963, President John F. Kennedy went on national television to make a moral appeal to the nation, calling for an end to segregation and racism. Medgar Evers and other black civil rights leaders in the South were favorably impressed by the president's speech, despite Kennedy's failure to provide details on his to-be-proposed civil rights legislation. Returning home that night after listening to Kennedy's address, Evers—who at the time was Mississippi's field secretary for the National Association for the Advancement of Colored People (NAACP)—was shot and killed outside his home in Jackson.

The FBI opened an investigation of the case as a federal civil rights violation—that the murderer(s) had conspired to deprive Evers of his civil rights. FBI agents gathered ballistic and fingerprint evidence and traced a rifle and scope found near the scene of the crime to Byron De La Beckwith, an ardent segregationist who lived in nearby Greenwood. (A former FBI agent later claimed that agents actually identified Beckwith after making a deal with a robbery suspect, "Julio," to discover who had been the assassin. Julio kidnapped a segregationist who knew the identity of Evers's killer and coerced him—by putting a gun in his mouth—to divulge the gunman's name.) FBI agents arrested Beckwith on June 22. Rather than file federal charges, agents turned Beckwith over to Jackson police for prosecution in state court for Evers's murder.

At the time of his assassination, Evers was the most prominent civil rights leader in Mississippi and was leading a drive for fair employment and integration. His funeral was attended by civil rights leaders from across the country, including Martin Luther King Jr.; Roy Wilkins, the national executive director of the NAACP; and government officials, including John Doar of the Civil Rights Division of the Justice Department. Evers was buried several days later in Arlington National Cemetery.

Beckwith was tried twice in 1964 for the murder of Evers, but all-white juries were deadlocked both times. Beckwith claimed to have been 90 miles away at the time of the killing, and three police officers testified to that effect. In addition, the Mississippi State Sovereignty Commission (a state-funded agency created in 1955) secretly assisted Beckwith's attorneys in screening potential jurors to weed out Jews and civil rights sympathizers. Nearly 30 years later,

state prosecutors developed new evidence in the case (including the disclosure in 1989 of the State Sovereignty Commission's role). In December 1990, a grand jury reindicted Beckwith. In 1993, after several years of appeals by defense lawyers who raised issues of the right to a speedy trial and double jeopardy, the Mississippi Supreme Court paved the way for a new trial by denying those appeals. Following an eight-day trial in Jackson, Beckwith was convicted of murder on February 5, 1994, and sentenced to life imprisonment. Beckwith, 73 at the time of the third trial, still claimed innocence. As in the two previous trials, three police officers (two from the 1964 trial transcript) again testified that he had been 90 miles away at the time of the shooting. The prosecution's case was strengthened by the testimony of six witnesses that Beckwith had bragged to them at various times about killing Evers and getting away with it. This testimony supplemented the fingerprint evidence from Beckwith's rifle found at the scene of the crime and the testimony of a witness who saw a car similar to Beckwith's near the scene that night. In the end, the jury, consisting of eight blacks and four whites, found Beckwith guilty.

"Mississippi Burning": Schwerner, Goodman, and Chaney

One year after Evers's murder, another high-profile case received national media attention. It involved the disappearance of three civil rights workers near Philadelphia, Mississippi, on the night of June 21, 1964. These three men—Michael Schwerner and Andrew Goodman, both white and from New York; and James Chaney, black and from Meridian, Mississippi—had been arrested earlier that day by a Neshoba County deputy sheriff for speeding and had been jailed. Following their release from jail that night, around 10:00 p.m., they disappeared.

When it became apparent that local authorities were not seriously pursuing the case, Attorney General Kennedy announced that the FBI would enter the case, initially regarding it as a kidnapping. Code-named MIBURN (for Mississippi burning, a reference to the church-burning that the three civil rights workers had visited just prior to their arrest), the case became a high FBI priority. At that time, the FBI did not have a field office in Mississippi, so agents were brought in from other states to begin the search for the three missing civil rights activists. Eventually, 258 agents were involved in the massive investigation, interviewing over 1,000 Mississippians including 480 Klansmen.

The burned car of the three young men was found in a swamp, but not the bodies of the three activists. FBI agents ultimately broke open the case after paying an informant $30,000 to reveal the location of the bodies and to disclose the identities of those who had been involved in their murders. It was revealed that on the night of their disappearance, the three young men had been abducted from their car by 19 members of the Ku Klux Klan who shot and killed them. The informant, a Klan member who was also a participant in the crime, led agents to a dam construction project on the Ollen Burrage farm near Philadelphia, where the bodies of the three civil rights activists were recovered, having been buried under hundreds of tons of earth (see Exhibit 2.9).

In the weeks following the discovery of the bodies of Schwerner, Goodman, and Chaney, state authorities failed to bring murder charges against any of the alleged coconspirators. Accordingly, FBI and Justice Department officials decided to proceed with federal civil rights charges and, on December 4, FBI agents arrested the 19 suspects, including Sheriff Lawrence Rainey and Deputy Sheriff Cecil Price. All 19 were indicted in January 1965, and after much legal wrangling, the trial was held in October 1967. An all-white jury found seven of the defendants guilty but acquitted Sheriff Rainey. The severest penalty went to Klan leader Sam Bowers, who received a 10-year sentence; in contrast, Deputy Sheriff Price was given a 3- to 10-year sentence.

The Philadelphia murders triggered a demand for a greater federal presence in Mississippi to control Klan violence. This had also been the recommendation of Allen Dulles, who headed a fact-finding team sent by President Johnson to Mississippi in the midst of the search for the missing civil rights activists. Acting on this report, President Johnson ordered FBI Director Hoover to open an FBI field office in Jackson as soon as possible, stipulating that the director participate in the opening ceremonies. On July 10, 1964, the Jackson, Mississippi, field office was officially opened, with Hoover and his assistant, Clyde Tolson, presiding. A veteran agent, Roy K. Moore, was selected to head the Jackson office, where he served until his retirement in 1974.

The Murder of Viola Liuzzo

In early 1965, national attention shifted to Alabama, where a voter-registration drive was underway, a drive that culminated in a four-day march from Selma to Montgomery between March 21 and 25. Earlier attempts by civil rights activists to march from Selma to the Alabama capital had been rebuffed by the local police, the most notable incident occurring on "Bloody Sunday," March 7, 1965, when civil rights marchers were tear-gassed by state troopers led by Sheriff Jim Clark.

On the last day of the Selma-Montgomery march, a car driven by Viola Liuzzo, a white Detroit housewife who had been transporting marchers back to Selma, was approached by a car carrying four members of the Ku Klux Klan. As the car pulled alongside, Liuzzo was shot and killed by one of the Klansmen. On the following day, March 26, President Johnson held a nationally televised news conference, with FBI Director Hoover at his side, to announce the arrest of the four Klansmen. Johnson did not mention at the news conference that the quick arrest of the suspects was made possible by an FBI informant, Gary Thomas Rowe, who had been riding in the car with the Klan members.

The suspects were tried on state murder charges in state courts. Despite the testimony of Rowe (who witnessed the shooting) and the ballistics testimony of FBI agents, the three defendants, Collie Leroy Wilkins, Eugene Thomas, and William Eaton, were acquitted. Federal prosecutors then decided to prosecute the suspects for federal civil rights violations. In December 1965, the three Klansmen were convicted on the federal charges and received the maximum sentence of 10 years in prison.

Thirteen years later, in a renewed investigation by Alabama authorities of racial killings in the 1960s, new information surfaced linking FBI informant Rowe to various racially motivated killings and other acts of violence, including the shooting of Viola Liuzzo. The Liuzzo family thereupon filed a wrongful death action against the U.S. government in July 1979, seeking damages on the grounds that Rowe, who was under FBI supervision, could have

Exhibit 2.9 **Excavation of the Remains of Michael Schwerner, Andrew Goodman, and James Chaney,** *Courtesy of the National Archives (65-CC)*

prevented, and may have participated in, the murder of Liuzzo. A federal judge dismissed the suit in May 1983, maintaining that the FBI was not liable for her death. The Justice Department conducted its own inquiry into the allegations against Rowe in 1979. Although finding no conclusive evidence that Rowe had been involved in murder, the Justice Department inquiry did document six incidents of racist violence that Rowe participated in, including attacks on blacks, civil rights activists, and journalists.

Assassination Cases of the 1960s

Three prominent public figures were assassinated within a five-year period during the 1960s: President John F. Kennedy, civil rights leader Martin Luther King Jr., and Senator (and former attorney general) Robert F. Kennedy. Each murder generated shock and outrage throughout the nation and precipitated a corresponding public outcry to solve these crimes. In each instance, even though it appeared the assassination had been committed by a lone gunman, conspiracy theories proliferated that linked the lone assailant to co-conspirators (including foreign governments, dissident groups, federal agencies, and organized crime). Although these assassination cases involved complicated jurisdictional questions between local and federal authorities, the FBI became the lead federal agency in the investigation of each. Substantial FBI resources were committed to these crimes; in fact, the Bureau assigned more resources to investigating President Kennedy's assassination than to any other case in its history up to that time.

Some conspiracy theories have implicated the FBI in two of the assassinations. Questions about the adequacy of the Bureau's investigation of Lee Harvey Oswald, President Kennedy's alleged assassin, and allegations that Oswald was an FBI informant, have fueled suspicions of the FBI's role in the president's assassination. Similarly, the FBI's extensive surveillance of Martin Luther King Jr., and revelations that FBI officials had covertly attempted to discredit King (by leaking damaging personal and political information to reporters, members of Congress, and the White House) up to the day he was killed, aroused further suspicions about the FBI. These assassination-conspiracy notions acquired additional credibility in light of the publicized antagonisms between FBI Director Hoover and all three of the murdered public figures.

The FBI played a prominent investigative role in all three assassination cases. Its assistance to local law enforcement officials served to bring the offenders in question to justice. In each case, the FBI concluded that a lone assailant was responsible. The intense public interest in these cases sustained doubts—not just about who fired the shots, but whether the assassins had acted alone or as part of a broader conspiracy. A second set of questions surfaced as to whether there had been a government cover-up. Indeed, conspiracy proponents have variously attributed responsibility for these murders to the FBI, the CIA, President Johnson, Cuban premier Fidel Castro, organized crime, and white supremacists. The FBI's investigative efforts, and those of the Warren Commission and the House Select Committee on Assassinations, failed to put these suspicions about all three assassinations to rest. The establishment of the Kennedy Assassination Records Review Board in 1992, empowered to review and order the release of classified FBI and CIA records, should allay some of these suspicions.

President John F. Kennedy

Early in the afternoon of November 22, 1963, as President John F. Kennedy's motorcade passed Dealey Plaza in downtown Dallas, Texas, several shots rang out and the president was fatally shot in his open limousine. Later that afternoon, Dallas police took Lee Harvey Oswald into custody following an extensive manhunt in which Dallas patrolman J. D. Tippit was also killed, apparently by Oswald. A rifle found shortly after the assassination on the sixth floor of the Texas School Book Depository Building, near Dealey Plaza, was later determined to have belonged to Oswald. Oswald was thereupon arraigned for the murder of both Kennedy and Tippit. But within 48 hours of his arrest, as he was being transferred to the county jail, Oswald was shot and killed in the basement of the Dallas Police Department headquarters by Jack Ruby, a Dallas nightclub owner—in the midst of police protection and during a live national television broadcast.

At the time, no law made the killing of the president a federal crime. Nonetheless, President Lyndon Johnson, who was quickly sworn in after Kennedy's death, demanded a complete FBI report on the assassination. Following an intensive investigation, the FBI delivered a five-volume report to Johnson on December 5. In it, the FBI concluded that Lee Harvey Oswald had been the lone assailant in President Kennedy's assassination.

During the course of this inquiry, Hoover learned that Oswald had been under FBI investigation prior to the assassination. Hoover immediately ordered an internal inquiry into the adequacy of that investigation. An FBI security file had been opened on Oswald in October 1959, following his defection to the Soviet Union. This investigation was closed in August 1962, after Oswald was interviewed by agents upon his return to the United States (after defecting to the Soviet Union, Oswald became disillusioned and, after contacting the U.S. embassy, secured permission to return to the United States).

In March 1963, FBI agents had initiated another investigation of Oswald, having uncovered information about his association with communists and other suspicious activities (notably, his involvement in activities criticizing the Kennedy administration's anti-Castro policies). Moreover, about two months prior to Kennedy's assassination, Oswald had traveled to Mexico City, where he met with a KGB officer at the Soviet embassy. Then, two or three weeks before the assassination, Oswald visited the Dallas FBI office where he left a note threatening to blow up the FBI office or the Dallas Police Department if agents did not stop bothering his wife, Marina (a Soviet national whom Oswald had married while in the Soviet Union and who had received permission to leave with him). Marina Oswald had been interviewed by an agent a few days earlier.

FBI agents, however, had taken no action on these danger signals. Stunned by the deficiencies in the pre-assassination investigation of Oswald, FBI Director Hoover disciplined 17 agents, including FBI Assistant Director William Sullivan. However, FBI officials disclosed neither these disciplinary actions nor Oswald's threatening note, which was destroyed shortly after Oswald was killed, to President Johnson or to the commission assigned to investigate the assassination.

One week after Kennedy was killed, by Executive Order 11130, President Johnson established a blue-ribbon panel headed by Chief Justice Earl Warren to investigate the events surrounding the assassination of President Kennedy. The Warren Commission, as the panel was known, relied heavily on the FBI's investigative efforts. FBI agents conducted approximately 25,000 interviews and over 2,300 FBI reports were submitted to the commission. FBI Assistant Director Alan Belmont headed this investigation, with two FBI divisions looking into different aspects of the case. The Domestic Intelligence Division investigated Oswald's background and pre-assassination activities; the General Investigative Division looked into the criminal aspects of the case surrounding the shooting of the president. In the end, the Warren Commission's 26-volume report, submitted to President Johnson on September 24, 1964, concluded that Oswald had acted alone in assassinating President Kennedy.

Chapter 8 of the Commission's final report did, however, criticize the FBI's pre-assassination domestic security investigation of Oswald, concluding that the FBI had taken too restrictive an interpretation of its responsibilities and should have alerted the Secret Service that Oswald could pose a threat to the president.

Fifteen years later, a House Select Committee on Assassinations reexamined the earlier (FBI and Warren Commission) investigations of Kennedy's assassination and arrived at somewhat different conclusions. Although concurring that Oswald fired the shots that killed the president, the committee's 1979 report also concluded that "Kennedy was probably assassinated as a result of a conspiracy." However, the evidence available to the committee was not sufficient to identify the extent of the suspected conspiracy. Having obtained access to FBI reports of its investigations of organized crime bosses (including wire-tapped conversations), the committee suggested that organized crime leaders might have been motivated to assassinate the president (the intercepted conversations recorded various crime bosses' displeasure with Attorney General Robert Kennedy's "war on crime" and contained verbal threats). The committee, nonetheless, rejected allegations that the FBI or any other federal agency was involved.

The committee's report did not fault the FBI's pre-assassination investigation of Oswald and consequently disagreed with Hoover's disciplining of the 17 FBI agents and officials for their handling of Oswald's security file. Indeed, the committee concluded that the Bureau had conducted a "thorough and professional investigation" into Oswald's role in the assassination, but had been deficient in pursuing the possibility of a conspiracy. Finally, the committee report criticized the FBI for not cooperating fully with the Warren Commission—particularly for not sharing information such as the Oswald note, which did not become publicly known until 1975.

The Reverend Martin Luther King Jr.

In April 1968, black civil rights leader Martin Luther King Jr. traveled to Memphis, Tennessee, to lead a march in support of striking sanitation workers. At around 6:00 p.m. on April 4, while standing on the second-floor balcony of the Lorraine Motel, King was shot by a sniper and died an hour later. Although FBI Director Hoover was initially reluctant to get involved in the case (again, the FBI lacked jurisdiction for what was a local crime), Attorney General Ramsey Clark ordered the FBI to investigate the shooting. Over 3,075 agents were eventually involved in tracking leads to identify and apprehend King's assassin.

From fingerprints left on the rifle found near the scene of the crime, FBI agents identified James Earl Ray as the prime suspect (see Exhibit 2.10). Ray, however, had fled the country soon after King's murder, first traveling to Canada

and then to Great Britain on a false Canadian passport. With the assistance of the Royal Canadian Mounted Police, who had traced him to England, Ray was arrested at London's Heathrow Airport on June 7. A 40-year-old convicted robber, Ray had escaped from a Missouri prison in April 1967. He had a long arrest and conviction record going back 20 years, mainly for

Exhibit 2.10   **James Earl Ray,**
Courtesy of the National Archives (65-CC)

robberies. In the days preceding King's shooting, Ray purchased a rifle in Birmingham, Alabama, then traveled to Memphis where he rented a room near the Lorraine Motel. No trial was held as Ray, on the advice of his attorney, agreed to plead guilty to first degree murder on March 10, 1969, and Judge W. Preston Battle sentenced him to 99 years in a state prison.

Ray subsequently claimed to have been the victim of a conspiracy. His revised alibi was that a man called "Raoul" had directed his pre-assassination activities, and that he had been several blocks away from the Lorraine Motel at the time of the shooting. Until his death from kidney failure on April 23, 1998, Ray made numerous requests from prison in Nashville for a new trial, recanting his previous confession and blaming the assassination on an unidentified band of white supremacist conspirators.

The House Select Committee on Assassinations that reviewed the Kennedy assassination investigation also reexamined the shooting of King and the adequacy of the associated FBI and local police investigations. The committee's 1979 final report concluded that Ray had fired the single shot that killed King; that Ray's later version of events and implication of "Raoul" was not believable, given the varying and inconsistent accounts of the shooting he had

offered over the years. Moreover, no witness had ever seen Ray and "Raoul" together. The committee, however, did conclude that "there is a likelihood" that Ray acted as part of a conspiracy, and it faulted the FBI for not adequately exploring that possibility (the consensus among FBI and Justice Department officials had been that Ray acted alone and was motivated by racial hatred). Finally, the committee rejected the charge that any federal, state, or local government agency had been involved in King's assassination.

By then, additional questions had been raised about the FBI itself that seemed to have a bearing on the case. During the mid-1970s, extensive hearings conducted by the Senate and the House (the Church Committee and the Pike Committee, respectively) had publicized the extensive scope of FBI domestic intelligence operations, including its surveillance of Martin Luther King Jr. and its attempts to discredit him. Most disturbingly, FBI reports that came before the committees revealed that the purpose of these FBI efforts had been to contain King's growing influence, and they further documented J. Edgar Hoover's resentment that King had been awarded the Nobel Peace Prize in 1964. The public disclosure of the scope and political purpose of this harassment mission, in turn, raised speculation as to the possibility of FBI involvement in King's assassination. The committee, however, found no evidence to support this allegation. It concluded that FBI agents had no advance knowledge of the assassination and no contact with James Earl Ray beforehand. The respected historian and King biographer David Garrow, who carefully studied the FBI's extensive surveillance of King, has also emphatically rejected the possibility of FBI involvement in King's murder.

Senator Robert F. Kennedy

Two months after King's assassination in Memphis, Senator Robert F. Kennedy was shot and killed in Los Angeles. Kennedy had just finished delivering a victory speech at the Ambassador Hotel, having that day won the California Democratic presidential primary. As he was exiting through the hotel's kitchen, several shots were fired at close range and Kennedy fell, fatally wounded. Rushed to a nearby hospital, Kennedy died the following day, on June 6. His security guards, however, immediately subdued the assailant, Sirhan Bishara Sirhan, who was then taken into custody by the Los Angeles police.

Attorney General Ramsey Clark invoked the 1968 Civil Rights Act and the Voting Rights Act of 1965 to bring the FBI into this case. Provisions of the Civil Rights Act made it a federal crime to injure persons campaigning for public office. Although the case was ultimately prosecuted in state court, FBI agents from all over the country produced some 4,000 pages of reports.

The 24-year-old suspect was a Palestinian Arab. In 1957, his family had moved to the United States from Jerusalem to take up residence in Pasadena, California, where Sirhan attended school and aspired to be a jockey until he was injured in a fall.

On June 7, a Los Angeles County grand jury indicted Sirhan for first-degree murder. He subsequently pled not guilty. His trial opened on January 8, 1969, with the prosecution maintaining that Sirhan had acted alone in the murder of Senator Kennedy. Sirhan's attorneys did not dispute his having fired the shot, but based their case on psychiatric testimony that he could not have premeditated the act, which was a necessary condition for a first-degree murder conviction. Sirhan was "out of control with reality" and in a trance-like state at the time of the shooting, they argued, and the killing was unplanned and the "product of a sick and obsessed mind." Nonetheless, Sirhan was convicted of first-degree murder on April 18 and sentenced to die in the gas chamber. In June 1972, after the California Supreme Court banned the death penalty, Sirhan succeeded in having his sentence reduced to life imprisonment.

Although the assassination of Robert Kennedy was generally viewed as the act of a lone, disturbed gunman, some conspiracy-theory advocates have attempted to link Sirhan to other conspirators. For example, some witnesses claim to have seen Sirhan with a mysterious unidentified woman in a polka-dot dress on the night of the shooting. Early in the investigation, however, Attorney General Clark emphasized that the FBI had uncovered no evidence of a conspiracy. Moreover, as recently as 1992, a Los Angeles County grand jury declined to open a new investigation in response to claims that additional information had been uncovered and that some of the ballistics evidence might have been altered and destroyed, suggesting a police cover-up.

Domestic Security Cases

After (and during) World War II, FBI investigative emphasis shifted from law enforcement to intelligence, from crime-fighting to the pursuit of both foreign intelligence operatives and their suspected domestic adherents, including communists and others considered to be subversive. During the Cold War years, substantial Bureau resources were invested in domestic intelligence operations, although most of these

activities were concealed from public scrutiny until the 1970s. Since the purpose of FBI domestic intelligence investigations was not to prosecute targeted individuals or groups for suspected criminal activities but rather to monitor and sometimes to disrupt them, the findings of these domestic security investigations were typically kept secret. Notable exceptions were the high-profile prosecutions of Alger Hiss, the Rosenbergs, and the American Communist Party leadership during the McCarthy era.

Not until congressional inquiries in the mid-1970s (the Church and Pike Committees) were the nature and scope of FBI domestic intelligence operations publicly revealed: the extensive surveillance of domestic political groups, the institution of aggressive containment programs (COINTELPROs) to disrupt some of them, and the compilation of secret dossiers on public officials and others.

In the waning years of Hoover's directorship, however, two cases foreshadowed the massive disclosures that were made following his death in 1972. First, in 1973, it was revealed during the Watergate hearings that the FBI had wiretapped 17 individuals (prominent reporters, as well as members of President Nixon's White House National Security Council staffs) between 1969 and 1971 to identify leaks of classified information to the media from within the Nixon administration. Second, in 1971, an FBI regional office was broken into by an activist group that stole FBI files and circulated them to members of the media and certain politicians.

These two cases proved to be a "sign of the times." The Bureau was subjected to intense public and congressional scrutiny during the mid-1970s, following Hoover's death and the evolving Watergate scandal of the Nixon administration. The regional office break-in, while damaging in itself, eventually led to the release of still other FBI documents, particularly those associated with the Bureau's highly secret counterintelligence program against domestic political groups. Similarly, the discovery of the 17 wiretaps during Daniel Ellsberg's trial provided an early hint of the manner in which the FBI had been politically misused, not just by the Nixon administration but by earlier presidential administrations as well.

Ironically, the Nixon White House's growing disenchantment with FBI Director Hoover's performance in the domestic security field, especially the Bureau's failure to discover the sources of security breaches in the government, indirectly contributed to politically risky decisions culminating in the Watergate scandal. The FBI's failure to pursue the investigation of Ellsberg (for leaking the Pentagon Papers) as seriously as Nixon and his top advisers demanded, and Hoover's decision to document FBI operations pursuant to the Huston Plan (a secret Nixon White House set of recommendations to relax intelligence gathering aimed at domestic dissenters) triggered these decisions—and underlay discussions within the White House in October 1971 to pressure Hoover to retire as FBI director. Beginning in the late 1960s, Hoover became more concerned about the "flap potential" of certain practices (break-ins, wiretaps, bugs, mail-opening, and the recruitment of college-age informants) routinely conducted by the FBI. Particularly in his later years, Hoover was reluctant to allow the Bureau to engage in activities that, if disclosed, might taint the reputation of an agency he had spent a lifetime building. The end result was that the Nixon White House created its own "investigative" unit, the Plumbers, who were to be deployed when questionable tactics needed to be used. For example, they broke into the office of a Los Angeles psychiatrist who once treated Daniel Ellsberg to acquire embarrassing information to discredit the former Defense Department analyst. And in June 1972, employees of the (Nixon) Committee to Re-Elect the President orchestrated (and funded through campaign contributions) the break-in to the Democratic National Committee headquarters in the Watergate office building in Washington, D.C.

The 17 National Security Wiretaps

In 1969, the Nixon administration was deeply involved in a risky strategy to bring to an end the costly and unpopular Vietnam War. To avoid antiwar criticism and at the same time advance U.S. military objectives, President Nixon authorized the secret bombing of suspected North Vietnamese supply bases in Cambodia. Because secrecy was imperative, the president and his National Security Adviser, Henry Kissinger, became alarmed by an article published on May 9, 1969, on the front page of the *New York Times,* in which reporter William Beecher disclosed this secret bombing operation. President Nixon and National Security Adviser Kissinger requested FBI Director Hoover's assistance in locating the source of the leak, fearing the impact of further publicity on U.S. public opinion and in heightening antiwar demonstrations. Hoover delegated this sensitive assignment to William Sullivan, the assistant director who headed the FBI's Domestic Intelligence Division. On May 10, Colonel Alexander Haig, a member of Kissinger's National Security Council (NSC) staff, gave Sullivan the names of four White House and NSC aides suspected of leaking the information to reporter Beecher, along with the official White House

request to wiretap any suspects. Sullivan was also informed that Attorney General John Mitchell had approved the wiretaps.

Between May 1969 and February 1971, the FBI installed a total of 17 wiretaps: 13 of the wiretaps were on the telephones of government employees (White House, State Department, and Defense Department staff members) suspected of leaking information, and four were on members of the press (including *New York Times* reporters William Beecher and Hedrick Smith, London *Times* reporter Henry Brandon, and CBS correspondent Marvin Kalb) suspected of receiving classified information.

Despite an intensive investigation that lasted nearly two years, FBI agents were unable to identify who inside the Nixon administration had disseminated classified information about the bombing in Cambodia. Moreover, although the FBI's investigation had been initiated to identify the source of leaks, these wiretaps soon acquired another value as they were found to be a source of invaluable political intelligence for the Nixon White House (some detailing the political strategies and plans of the president's Democratic adversaries, two of the wiretapped NSC aides having subsequently resigned to join the staff of the leading Democratic aspirant for the presidency in 1972, Senator Edmund Muskie). Indeed, the FBI continued to tap these two aides even after their resignations, when they no longer had access to classified information. These wiretaps were discontinued in 1971 on orders from FBI Director Hoover. The FBI director had been willing to continue this no-longer-legal investigation until then, but decided in 1971 to terminate these taps, as he was scheduled to testify before a congressional committee on FBI wiretapping practices and had ordered a review to discontinue unneeded taps.

The 17 wiretaps might have remained secret had it not been for Daniel Ellsberg's 1973 trial in the aftermath of the Pentagon Papers case. Although the Nixon administration had lost its case to enjoin the *New York Times* and other newspapers from publishing the Pentagon Papers in June 1971, it had then sought to discourage future leaks. Having identified Ellsberg as the individual responsible for leaking the Pentagon Papers, it had sought to convict him for conspiracy, espionage, and theft of government property. A former Defense Department analyst who joined the staff of the NSC in 1969, Ellsberg had helped compile the Pentagon Papers and, after leaving the NSC staff, had retained a security clearance and access to a copy of the Papers deposited at the Rand Corporation in California. Ellsberg was indicted and tried on the charge of the unauthorized disclosure of classified information.

During Ellsberg's trial and that of a co-conspirator, Anthony Russo, the press learned and reported that the Nixon administration had wiretapped news reporters in a search for leaks. Ellsberg's and Russo's attorneys brought these reports to the attention of the trial judge, W. Matt Byrne, who ordered the prosecution to reveal whether the defendants or their lawyers had been wiretapped. Initially, the Justice Department prosecutors were unable to locate any records of these alleged wiretaps. Their difficulty stemmed from the fact that, owing to their sensitivity, records relating to the 17 FBI wiretaps had not been filed among the FBI's national security wiretap records. Because of their recognized sensitivity, the originals of the FBI reports derived from these wiretaps had been hand-delivered to the White House by FBI agents while the one copy of each of these reports was maintained by FBI assistant director Sullivan in his secret office files. Again unlike other FBI national security wiretap records, the FBI's ELSUR file (recording all authorized wiretaps) contained no record either of Attorney General Mitchell's approval or of the names of the individuals whose conversations had been intercepted.

After an FBI internal inquiry ordered by Acting Director William D. Ruckelshaus on May 4, 1973, FBI agents who had, in 1969–71, been involved either in installing these 17 wiretaps or preparing the reports based on them recalled that Ellsberg had been overheard on one of these taps, the one installed on the phone of former NSC aide Morton Halperin. This information was reported to Judge Byrne, who ordered the prosecution to produce the logs and records of the Halperin wiretap. Head prosecutor David Nissen responded that the records had been missing since 1971 (the FBI's copy having been delivered to the Nixon White House) and, therefore, that he could not comply with Byrne's request. On May 11, Byrne dismissed the charges against Ellsberg and Russo, basing his ruling on the prosecution's failure to produce the necessary logs and records.

Meanwhile, Ruckelshaus continued his investigation into the missing records of these 17 wiretaps. From Sullivan, who as head of domestic intelligence had kept the logs in his office, Ruckelshaus learned that in October 1971, the FBI's copies of the wiretap logs had been given to Assistant Attorney General Robert Mardian for safekeeping. Sullivan's action had been triggered by FBI Director Hoover's demand

for his own resignation as assistant to the director that month. Sullivan had then advised Mardian of his concern that Hoover might use these sensitive records to blackmail Nixon and Kissinger to ensure his continued tenure at the Bureau. In 1973, Mardian informed Ruckelshaus that the wiretap logs might still exist—at the White House. By 1973, Mardian had left the Justice Department. The wiretap logs were eventually located in the safe of John Ehrlichman, one of Nixon's closest advisers who had recently resigned due to the Watergate scandal. Ruckelshaus and an FBI agent personally retrieved the logs and records of the 17 wiretaps on May 12. Two days later, Ruckelshaus, who had been acting FBI director for about two weeks, held a press conference to explain the discovery of the wiretap logs and records.

The Media Break-in

About the same time as Bureau officials terminated the 17 national security wiretaps in 1971, on the night of March 8, 1971, an activist group calling itself the Citizens' Commission to Investigate the FBI broke into the Bureau's resident agency office in Media, Pennsylvania (outside Philadelphia) and stole hundreds of FBI files. The following day, this group anonymously took credit for the raid. Then, two weeks later, the Citizens' Commission began to selectively release the stolen documents to the press and certain politicians.

The documents revealed that the FBI had extensively monitored numerous left-wing political groups, including antiwar and black militant organizations. The "Media files," as they came to be called, also revealed the FBI's widespread use of informants, especially on college campuses. Although left-wing political activists had long claimed that the FBI was monitoring dissident political activities, the stolen Media files for the first time documented the scope and purpose of these FBI domestic intelligence operations. Among the pilfered FBI files were memoranda involving the FBI's COINTELPRO–New Left—a 1968 program whose stated purpose was to "disrupt, harass, and discredit" radical activists in order to minimize the influence of their political activities. These memoranda, in turn, triggered a request filed under the Freedom of Information Act by NBC correspondent Carl Stern that eventually led to the public discovery of this and other controversial FBI containment programs.

FBI officials immediately became alarmed over the Media break-in, both as a major breach of Bureau security and as potentially tarnishing the FBI's reputation of apolitical professionalism. Former FBI Acting Associate Director W. Mark Felt later referred to the break-in as a "watershed event" that adversely affected the public's image of the Bureau.

In response, FBI Director Hoover disciplined the agent in charge of the Media office and closed over 100 resident agencies for security reasons. Hoover, moreover, launched a major investigation, code-named MEDBURG, to identify the Media burglars, and designated Roy K. Moore, head of the Jackson, Mississippi, field office, to lead the investigation. Agents were brought from all over the country to Philadelphia, where the investigation was centered. Other FBI field offices were alerted to assist in identifying possible suspects, especially those in the antiwar movement. After several months of intensive work, Moore and his investigators believed that they had identified the burglars—members of the Catholic left. They had not, however, developed enough evidence to arrest and prosecute them. The case was never solved.

The Modern Era (1972 to the Present)

In the years following J. Edgar Hoover's death in May 1972, the Federal Bureau of Investigation went through a period of turmoil and transition. Congressional inquiries of the mid-1970s forced a rethinking of FBI investigative priorities and increased congressional oversight of Bureau activities. The Department of Justice instituted new guidelines for the Bureau's domestic security and counterintelligence investigations. A "new" FBI emerged, with a new style of leadership, different priorities, new investigative techniques—and closer monitoring by both the legislative and executive branches.

Under these new priorities, domestic intelligence activities were dramatically reduced, although domestic security and terrorism remained important investigative areas. Foreign counterintelligence, organized crime, and white-collar crime became top priorities, as did drug enforcement and terrorism (in 1982) and violent crime (in 1989). With the collapse of the Soviet Union in the 1990s, the FBI gave increased attention to international crime, especially given the international character of drug trafficking and terrorist operations.

This new modern FBI also developed new techniques to improve the quality of its investigations (undercover work, artificial intelligence, psychological profiling, DNA testing) and began to exploit new technologies (computer databases and digitized fingerprints). A proactive, high-tech mystique was fashioned, replacing the G-man image of the Hoover FBI. The notable cases of the post-Hoover Bureau reflect the turmoil of this transition period and the new priorities and techniques adopted to meet the new threats of the modern era.

The Watergate Investigation

The Watergate investigation best symbolizes the turmoil shaping the post-Hoover FBI. The June 1972 break-in of the national headquarters of the Democratic National Committee (DNC) soon involved the FBI in an investigation both of high-level officials in the Nixon administration and members of President Nixon's reelection committee (Committee to Re-elect the President, or CRP), who were suspected of either planning the break-in or covering up their involvement.

The FBI's investigation of the Watergate break-in became the largest Bureau investigation since the assassination of President Kennedy, involving over 300 agents in 51 field offices. As the Watergate scandal (as the events surrounding the break-in and cover-up came to be called) unfolded in 1973, members of Congress questioned whether the Justice Department's (and the FBI's) investigation had been—and might continue to be—compromised by White House aides. This concern was reinforced by Acting FBI Director L. Patrick Gray's admission in April 1973, during his confirmation hearings as FBI director, to having destroyed, in 1972, Watergate-related documents given to him by White House aides. Ultimately, a special prosecutor was appointed in May 1973 to carry on the Justice Department's investigation into the Watergate break-in and cover-up.

The Watergate scandal began with the discovery by Washington, D.C., metropolitan police of five "burglars" in the DNC headquarters at the Watergate hotel and office complex in Washington, D.C., in the early morning hours of June 17, 1972. A security guard, who had detected this burglary in progress, alerted Washington, D.C., police. They arrested five men (Bernard Barker, Virgilio Gonzalez, Eugenio Martinez, James McCord, and Frank Sturgis) on the sixth floor, carrying electronic surveillance equipment. Because of possible federal wiretapping violations, the FBI opened an investigation. The FBI investigation led to the indictment, on September 15, of the five burglars arrested at DNC headquarters and their two accomplices (E. Howard Hunt and G. Gordon Liddy) on charges of conspiracy, burglary, and interception of communications violations. At the time, McCord was CRP's security officer, Liddy held a high-level appointment at CRP (having moved over from the White House staff), and Hunt (a former CIA agent and former White House aide) was a consultant to the Nixon White House.

At that point, the FBI was unable to establish that the break-in and bugging operation was known to or authorized by higher-level officials in CRP or at the White House. The FBI was able to confirm, however, that funds contributed to the Nixon campaign had funded the break-in. By tracing the serial numbers of $100 bills found on those arrested, the FBI had discovered that their source was contributors' checks that had been cashed and laundered through a bank in Mexico.

Publicly and in their grand jury testimony, the arrestees claimed to have acted alone. They had broken into the DNC headquarters for national security reasons: to ascertain whether Cuban premier Fidel Castro might have sought to fund the election campaign of the Democratic nominee, Senator George McGovern. Their testimony and that of other White House and CRP officials succeeded in containing the FBI investigation—and limiting the indictments to the seven. Although not known at the time, some of the White House and CRP officials had committed or suborned perjury while White House legal counsel John W. Dean III had closely monitored the FBI investigation and the Justice Department attorneys' presentation of the case to the grand jury.

The seven were tried in January 1973, and all were convicted, five by guilty pleas. Sentenced on March 23, Liddy received the stiffest punishment—a minimum of six years in prison. On the day of the sentencing, the presiding federal judge, John Sirica, who had threatened to impose severe sentences and expressed disbelief that the seven had acted alone, revealed the contents of a letter he had received from one of the defendants (McCord), which alleged that others (in addition to the seven) had been involved, and that the defendants had been pressured to plead guilty. At this point, the Watergate investigation ceased being an inquiry into a minor burglary, and became a major investigation into a political cover-up that would eventually reach into the Nixon White House.

As events unfolded, raising new questions about higher-level involvement, President Nixon nominated L. Patrick Gray III as permanent FBI director (Gray had been acting director since Hoover's death in May 1972). Gray's confirmation hearings before the Senate Judiciary Committee began on February 28, 1973. (Under 1968 legislation, FBI directors were to be confirmed by the Senate, and their tenure was limited to 10 years.)

The Watergate case, and particularly Gray's role in directing the FBI investigation, immediately became a central part of the hearings. Questions were raised when Gray admitted to having regularly provided copies of FBI investigative files on the Watergate case to John Dean, the president's legal counsel, and—to the dismay of many—he even offered to share some of these documents with members of the Judiciary Committee. This controversial admission was soon followed by Gray's further acknowledgment of having destroyed two files of Watergate-related documents that had been given to him on June 28, 1972, by Dean and John Ehrlichman, Nixon's domestic policy adviser. These documents had been retrieved from the White House safe of E. Howard Hunt, one of the Watergate burglars. It was later disclosed that their contents included State Department cables that Hunt had altered in an effort to implicate President John F. Kennedy in the 1963 murder of South Vietnam's president (and that Hunt had unsuccessfully attempted to get *Life* magazine reporter William Lambert to publish a major exposé of the "true story behind the Diem coup"; Lambert passed, having insisted on authenticating the faked document). In response to this heightened controversy over his actions, Gray withdrew his nomination on April 27, 1973.

Gray's confirmation hearings and resignation marked the beginning of a period of turmoil in the Justice Department—and for the Nixon White House, as a result of events in the evolving Watergate scandal. Three days after Gray's resignation, President Nixon accepted the resignations of Attorney General Richard Kleindienst and three top White House aides (H. R. Haldeman, John Ehrlichman, and John Dean), all of whom had become publicly enmeshed in the Watergate scandal. In less than two weeks, on May 10, a federal grand jury indicted two former Nixon cabinet members (former Attorney General John Mitchell and former Commerce Secretary Maurice Stans) on obstruction of justice charges relating to an alleged Watergate cover-up.

These events caused both the public and members of Congress to question the independence of the Justice Department's investigation of the Nixon White House and CRP. The FBI's culpability, if any, proved to have been limited to Acting FBI Director L. Patrick Gray III, who had formerly served in the Nixon Justice Department and had played a role in Nixon's 1960 and 1968 campaigns for the presidency. Indeed, Gray admitted during his confirmation hearings to having shared files with Dean, to having destroyed documents on behalf of the White House, and to having allowed CRP attorneys to be present during agent interviews with members of the Nixon re-election committee—which was not standard Bureau procedure. The Senate Watergate Committee subsequently learned that Gray had allowed the FBI's Watergate investigation to trace the source and laundering of the $100 bills to be circumscribed, and to have delayed FBI interviews with several White House aides, though he later permitted them, agreeing to the White House condition that presidential counsel Dean be present. Senate investigators further learned that President Nixon and White House chief of staff H. R. Haldeman had pressured CIA officials to ask Gray not to pursue its efforts to trace the laundering of campaign contributions (through Mexico) by claiming that this might compromise CIA methods and sources.

In their testimony before the Senate Watergate Committee, Attorney General Kleindienst and Assistant Attorney General Henry Petersen (the head of the criminal division and the Justice Department official responsible for supervising the investigation and presenting the case to the grand jury) maintained that the Justice Department's investigation had been handled properly and carried out effectively. Nonetheless, the Gray disclosures, the high-level personnel changes in the Nixon administration, and indictments of key officials increased congressional pressure for the appointment of an untainted prosecutor. On May 23, 1973, Elliot Richardson, who had succeeded Kleindienst as attorney general, appointed Archibald Cox as the special prosecutor in charge of the Watergate investigation. Under Richardson's guidelines, the special Watergate prosecutor was empowered to select a staff, have a separate budget, and exercise wide discretion and authority in the conduct of the now radically expanded investigation.

Paralleling the special prosecutor's investigation, a Senate Watergate Committee (officially, the Senate Select Committee on Presidential Campaign Activities) began hearings, during the spring and summer of 1973, into the 1972 presidential campaign. Although these hearings focused on wrongdoing by high-level officials of the Nixon administration and CRP, some of the testimony also raised questions about whether the FBI had been misused by presidential administrations, past and present. During his June testimony, former White House counsel John Dean (who by then had been dismissed by President Nixon) submitted documents to the committee confirming both Nixon's (the Huston Plan, NSC wiretaps, the Fielding break-in) and past presidential misuse of the FBI for political purposes. Among these documents were two memoranda, which Dean had solicited from former FBI assistant director William Sullivan in 1972, that cited examples of political misuse of the FBI during the Roosevelt and Johnson administrations. (These memoranda had been solicited from Sullivan to buttress President Nixon's strategy to contain the Watergate scandal, by documenting that earlier presidents had more brashly employed the FBI for partisan purposes.) Because its mandate was limited to the 1972 presidential campaign, the committee did not publicly disclose these memoranda at the time—though they were leaked to members of the Washington press corps and proved central to the later, 1975, investigation of the FBI by the so-called Church and Pike committees. The Watergate Committee did publicize the documents showing the Nixon White House's political uses of the FBI and CIA between 1969 and 1971.

During July, the Senate Watergate Committee received additional surprising testimony from White House aide Alexander Butterfield that, since 1971, all of President Nixon's conversations in the White House Oval Office had been taped. This revelation offered the opportunity to resolve conflicting accounts about President Nixon's knowledge and authorization of the Watergate break-in and cover-up.

Almost immediately, the Senate Watergate Committee and the special prosecutor's office sought tapes and transcripts of specified Watergate-related conversations. A major constitutional crisis ensued when President Nixon refused to turn over all the tapes, claiming the right of "executive privilege." Although Nixon did voluntarily release some tapes and transcripts, a July 1974 Supreme Court ruling forced him to surrender additional tapes to the special prosecutor. In *Nixon v. U.S.*, the Court rejected Nixon's claim to an absolute right to withhold documents relating to conversations with White House aides, affirming that the president must disclose information essential to a inquiry into suspected criminal conduct of White House officials. One of the transcripts released in August 1974 in the aftermath of the Court's ruling—the so-called "smoking gun" transcript—proved especially damaging to the president. It recorded Nixon's conversations with Haldeman during a June 23, 1972, meeting (six days after the break-in) at which Haldeman proposed a plan that could limit the FBI Watergate investigation by invoking "national security" reasons, specifically by importuning CIA officials to ask Gray to "call off his men." President Nixon, under threat of impeachment by the Senate (the House had voted articles of impeachment), resigned from office a few days later—on August 9.

The outcome of the Watergate investigation—the result of the combined efforts of the Justice Department and the special prosecutor—produced numerous indictments and convictions of high-level officials in the Nixon administration. In addition to the seven Watergate burglars and accomplices, approximately 40 government officials were indicted on conspiracy, obstruction of justice, and perjury charges. Among those ultimately convicted and sentenced to prison terms were former Attorney General John Mitchell, presidential counsel John Dean, White House chief of staff H. R. Haldeman, and domestic policy adviser John Ehrlichman. President Nixon did not admit to any wrongdoing when announcing his resignation. His successor, Gerald Ford, nonetheless pardoned him for any crimes that he may have committed as president. Moreover, the Watergate affair prompted a new interest in the FBI—particularly raising questions about the Bureau's relationship with the White House and whether political criteria shaped FBI investigative priorities.

Radicals and Extremists

From 1965 to 1975, as confirmed by a 1976 General Accounting Office (GAO) study, FBI intelligence investigations (domestic and foreign) constituted approximately 20 percent of the Bureau's investigative workload. (The exact breakdown between domestic and foreign intelligence investigations remains classified information.)

Throughout the 1960s, the FBI responded to the upsurge in antiwar and civil rights demonstrations, by closely monitoring targeted civil rights activists, campus radicals, and anti–Vietnam War activists and organizations, and it continued to do so into the early 1970s. By the late 1960s, some of these groups, frustrated by the failure of mass protests and civil disobedience to achieve change, had adopted more militant stands and were willing to employ violence. The Students for a Democratic Society (SDS) was

founded in the early 1960s on a program of social reform and participatory democracy. During the late 1960s, SDS experienced a rapid growth in membership and support on college campuses, particularly as opposition to the Vietnam War mounted. By the end of the decade, SDS had collapsed as a mass-based student organization and only a small faction remained active—the Weathermen (later renamed the Weather Underground). This radical faction resorted to robberies and bombings to further its new revolutionary agenda. As it had since their emergence, the FBI continued to monitor antiwar, civil rights, and feminist movements; by the early 1970s, however, FBI investigations focused on radical new-left groups like the Weather Underground and militant black nationalist groups like the Black Panther Party.

While FBI investigations predominantly involved collection of intelligence about these groups' tactics and plans, in some cases evidence was uncovered of illegal conduct. In March 1970, three members of the Weather Underground were killed in a Manhattan townhouse explosion while manufacturing bombs. The resultant FBI investigation identified those involved but produced no convictions. A few months later, in August, four students (Dwight Armstrong, Karleton Armstrong, Leo Burt, and David Fine) at the University of Wisconsin at Madison, who were protesting the university's involvement in war research, blew up a campus laboratory, killing a graduate student. In this second episode, FBI agents, after a lengthy and painstaking inquiry, were able to identify and eventually apprehend and convict the perpetrators. These cases, however, paled in importance to two others that dominated media attention during the 1970s. One of them involved the kidnapping of the granddaughter of newspaper tycoon William Randolph Hearst by a small, and virtually unknown, revolutionary group calling itself the Symbionese Liberation Army (SLA). The other case involved the arrest of Leonard Peltier and three other members of the radical American Indian Movement, or AIM, who were indicted for killing two FBI agents on the Pine Ridge Reservation in South Dakota.

The Hearst and Peltier cases involved high-profile FBI investigations of radical groups (SLA and AIM) for their criminal conduct (kidnapping and murder). These cases differed from Hoover-era domestic security investigations, wherein radical groups had been targeted for surveillance and/or disruption (not criminal prosecution). FBI domestic security operations were substantially curtailed during the late 1970s; nonetheless, radical groups remained subject to investigation as criminal enterprises. Indeed, the reforms of FBI domestic intelligence instituted in 1976 transferred responsibility for overseeing investigations of domestic radical groups from the Intelligence Division to the General (Criminal) Investigative Division. By the late 1970s, "terrorism" had become the primary designation for FBI investigations that formerly had been labeled "domestic security," "domestic intelligence," or "domestic subversion." In 1982, moreover, terrorism was added to the list of top FBI investigative priorities. The Hearst and Peltier cases reflected this shift in FBI focus and tactics.

Patricia Hearst and the SLA

On the evening of February 4, 1974, Patricia Hearst was kidnapped from her Berkeley, California, apartment by three people (one woman and two men) who were later revealed to be members of the Symbionese Liberation Army (SLA). The SLA was a small revolutionary group, consisting of about a dozen members, mostly white and middle class. However, two of their leaders were black, and escaped convicts. A few months earlier, the SLA had claimed responsibility for the murder of Marcus Foster, the school superintendent in Oakland, California. At the time of her abduction, Patricia (or Patty) Hearst was a 19-year-old sophomore at the University of California; her father, Randolph Hearst, was the president and editor of the *San Francisco Examiner*.

About a week after the kidnapping, the SLA demanded from Hearst's parents a ransom of $2 million in free food for the poor in the San Francisco Bay Area. When the Hearst family complied with this demand, the SLA demanded another $4 million. The Hearsts agreed to this demand by the end of March, placing $4 million in an escrow bank account to be used for free food when their daughter was released. Shortly after these ransom arrangements had been made, the Hearsts received a surprise tape-recorded message from their daughter: she had joined the SLA and her name was now Tania. About two weeks later, FBI agents identified her as a participant in an April 15 San Francisco bank robbery; the bank's videotape showed her toting an automatic weapon. The videotape did not enable investigators to determine conclusively whether she had been coerced by the SLA into participating in the robbery. A subsequent tape-recorded message from Patty (alias Tania), however, stated that she had been a willing participant in the bank robbery

and that her weapon had been loaded. The FBI thus classified Patricia Hearst as a fugitive ("armed and dangerous"), and in June she was indicted on federal bank robbery charges.

At first, the FBI was unable to locate Hearst and her SLA abductors. At a May news conference, FBI Director Clarence Kelley conceded that the Bureau was "stumped" in the kidnapping investigation. A week later, however, on May 17, local police officers discovered an SLA hideout in Los Angeles and surrounded the house. A lengthy shoot-out ensued, during which the police used automatic weapons and tear gas. The house caught fire and burned to the ground. During this siege, five SLA members were killed—but Patricia Hearst's whereabouts remained unknown. It was not until September 18, 1975, that Charles Bates, the FBI agent in charge of the investigation, announced her capture in San Francisco.

At her trial in February and March of 1976, Hearst was defended by the noted criminal lawyer F. Lee Bailey, who argued that she had been a "prisoner of war" for nearly 20 months and that she had been coerced and brainwashed into committing criminal acts during her captivity. Nonetheless, the jury convicted her on March 20 and she was sentenced by Federal Judge William Orrick to a seven-year prison sentence. Patricia Hearst served 22 months at a federal correctional facility in Pleasanton, California, before President Jimmy Carter commuted her sentence.

Leonard Peltier and AIM

During the 1970s, the Pine Ridge Reservation near Wounded Knee, South Dakota, became the site of two major confrontations between FBI agents and members of the American Indian Movement (AIM). Founded by a group of Native Americans in Minneapolis in 1968, AIM endorsed a militant approach in the struggle to recover Indian lands, reclaim rights guaranteed by past treaties, and protect current Indian holdings from further government encroachment. By the early 1970s, the FBI identified AIM as a domestic security threat, and it was designated an "extremist" organization and its leaders as "key extremists."

The first of the two confrontations between FBI agents and AIM activists occurred in February 1973 at Wounded Knee, the site of an 1890 massacre in which approximately 200 Indian men, women, and children had been killed by the U.S. Cavalry. On February 28, a caravan of about 300 Indians, including AIM members, occupied the village of Wounded Knee in a protest against intolerable conditions on the reservation. Spokespersons for the group demanded hearings on an 1868 treaty, an investigation of the Bureau of Indian Affairs (BIA), and declared an independent Oglala Nation. A large federal force of FBI agents, U.S. marshals, and BIA police was dispatched to end this occupation, and they surrounded Wounded Knee, equipped with automatic weapons, armored personnel carriers, and helicopters. The ensuing standoff between the two camps lasted for seven weeks, with occasional shoot-outs that resulted in the killing of two Indians and the wounding of others. The occupation ended on May 6, when the few protesters remaining at Wounded Knee surrendered to federal agents. Other government representatives agreed to conduct investigations into the conditions at Pine Ridge and alleged treaty violations. More than 100 Native Americans who participated in the Wounded Knee occupation were eventually indicted on various federal charges, including arson, theft, assault, and interfering with federal officers.

The second confrontation on the Pine Ridge Reservation occurred two years later at the Jumping Bull Ranch, about 20 miles from Wounded Knee near the village of Oglala. In the aftermath of the Wounded Knee occupation, by May 1975, the FBI had increased its presence on the reservation to about 60 agents (compared with 3 before the occupation), reinforcing the BIA police. The FBI's authority derived from provisions of the Major Crimes Act of 1885, which granted the federal government jurisdiction over major crimes committed on Indian reservations.

On the morning of June 26, 1975, FBI agents at Pine Ridge instituted a search for a robbery suspect, Jimmy Eagle. Shortly before noon, the agents believed they had spotted Eagle traveling in a vehicle on the reservation, accompanied by several other Indians whom the agents believed were armed. During their pursuit of this vehicle, the agents were fired upon and immediately called for reinforcements. Additional agents and BIA police soon arrived, and the resultant shoot-out continued throughout the afternoon. By the end of the day, two FBI agents (Ron Williams and Jack Coler) and one Native American (Joe Stuntz) had been killed.

Exactly what transpired remains a subject of controversy. On the one hand, AIM members claimed that FBI and BIA agents provoked the shoot-out as part of a well-planned raid that went awry. In contrast, FBI officials claimed that the shoot-out was the result of a cold-blooded ambush by well-armed Indians. An intensive FBI investigation (code-named RESMURS, for reservation murders) was conducted over the next several months under the direction of the head of the FBI's Minneapolis field office, Richard Held, with about 200 agents participating in the search for the individuals who had killed the agents. The FBI's conduct during this investigation was subsequently criticized by various sectors. Indeed, the chair of the U.S. Civil Rights Commission protested to Attorney General Edward Levi the FBI's aggressive investigative tactics (entering homes without warrants and intimidating potential witnesses) and paramilitary presence on the reservation.

The FBI investigation identified four members of AIM (Leonard Peltier, Jimmy Eagle, Bob Robideau, and Dino Butler) as responsible for the murder of the two agents. Indicted on November 25, 1975, two of the four, Robideau and Butler, were tried in Cedar Rapids, Iowa, in June and July of 1976 and acquitted. The charges against Eagle were dropped in September. Peltier, who had fled to Canada, was eventually arrested and extradited to the United States. Subsequently tried in Fargo, North Dakota, in March and April 1977, Peltier was convicted of two counts of first-degree murder and was sentenced to two consecutive life sentences. Peltier appealed his conviction, arguing that there had been a pattern of misconduct by FBI agents, including fabricated evidence, coerced testimony, and possibly perjury. Nonetheless, his conviction was upheld by the Court of Appeals, and in March 1979, the Supreme Court refused to review the case. The U.S. Parole Commission denied Peltier parole in 1993 and again in 1996.

Undercover Operations

The public first became aware that a "new" or modernized FBI was emerging in the early 1980s. No event contributed more to this awareness than the February 1980 disclosure of the FBI's Operation ABSCAM. Under ABSCAM, an undercover "sting" operation, FBI agents posed as representatives of a fictitious Arab sheik seeking political favors, for which he was willing to pay. ABSCAM exposed political corruption, extending even to members of Congress. ABSCAM was the first in a series of FBI undercover operations publicized in the media, typically by their code-name acronyms. These included BRILAB (involving the bribery of labor officials), MIPORN (pornography in the Miami area), RECOUP (stolen car racketeering), COLCOR (corruption and drug trafficking in Columbus County, North Carolina), and FRONTLOAD (organized crime in the construction industry). In all of these investigations, FBI agents went undercover, sometimes setting up bogus legal or illegal businesses, in order to ensnare criminals.

Although ABSCAM was the most celebrated of these cases, two other FBI undercover operations of this period also highlighted the Bureau's new investigative techniques and its new focus on public corruption: Operation UNIRAC and Operation GREYLORD. These investigations were significant because of the individuals who were targeted: union officials, the judiciary, and politicians.

Operation UNIRAC

In June 1978, 22 labor-union officials and shipping executives were indicted by a federal grand jury in Miami, thereby disclosing an FBI undercover investigation into waterfront corruption that had been conducted for nearly three years. This operation, code-named UNIRAC (union racketeering), discovered how union officials had been able to control business activities through racketeering in several Atlantic and Gulf Coast ports. Businesses operating on the docks had been required to make payoffs, failing which they would become subject to extortion and intimidation by the waterfront unions, particularly, the International Longshoremen's Association (ILA). During the course of the investigation, FBI agents posed as officials for businesses making payoffs to union officials.

Several months after the Miami indictments, in January 1979, a federal grand jury in New York City also indicted for labor racketeering and extortion Anthony Scotto, a vice president of the ILA and head of the Brooklyn local. During Scotto's trial, the prosecution described the illegal payments that he had received. In his defense, Scotto claimed that the payments had been political contributions, not for his personal gain. During his nine-week trial, a number of prominent character witnesses, including New York governor Hugh Carey and two former mayors of New York City, offered testimony on Scotto's behalf. Nonetheless, Scotto was convicted in November 1979 on 33 of 60 counts, and was sentenced to five years in prison and fined $75,000. Scotto and George Barone, an ILA vice president in Miami, were the more prominent among the more than 110 convicted as the result of Operation UNIRAC.

Operation ABSCAM

The ABSCAM investigation was initiated by the FBI's New York City field office in mid-1978. This investigation involved three phases over a period of two years. It began as a "sting" operation, with agents setting up a bogus "fencing" business (Abdul Enterprises) to recover stolen securities and paintings. Mel Weinberg, a convicted swindler, was recruited as an intermediary whose job was to convince thieves to bring stolen property to these fencing fronts, which were located on Long Island. There, undercover FBI agents posed as representatives of a fictitious wealthy Arab sheik (Kambir Abdul Rahman) who was interested in purchasing stolen goods.

During the fall of 1978, this investigation shifted from one focusing on stolen property to political corruption in New Jersey. As a result of leads provided by Weinberg, FBI agents were authorized to extend their investigation to the office of the mayor of Camden, New Jersey, Angelo Errichetti. According to Weinberg's sources, Errichetti had been soliciting bribes for political favors. Accordingly, in a new undercover scam, FBI agents approached Errichetti to propose a deal for their Arab sheik. They described the sheik as interested in investing money in the Camden seaport and possibly in opening a casino in Atlantic City if he could obtain the needed licenses and authority. Errichetti willingly offered his services, initially accepting a $25,000 bribe from the undercover agents, and he soon involved other public officials, including Harrison A. Williams Jr., a U.S. senator from New Jersey.

As word of the Arab sheik's investment plans (and the political favors that he required) spread from local politicians to members of Congress, the focus of the FBI's investigation shifted again—from New Jersey to Washington, D.C., and to Congress. In this third phase of ABSCAM, agents rented a two-story house on W Street in Washington for their new operational site. Members of Congress were brought to this location, where undercover agents expressed an interest in obtaining political favors for the sheik, who was now portrayed as seeking asylum in the United States. Meetings at the W Street site were videotaped, and Justice Department lawyers in an adjacent room closely monitored the transactions on a closed-circuit monitor as various seemingly cooperative public officials were offered $50,000 payments in exchange for their services. Operation ABSCAM abruptly ended on February 3, 1980, when the *New York Times*, in a front-page article, reported that members of Congress had been the subject of an FBI undercover operation. It is suspected that Justice Department insiders leaked information about ABSCAM to the press, but this was never conclusively determined.

During ABSCAM's third phase, FBI officials authorized bribe meetings with 27 public officials, based on the allegations of middlemen in the investigation (only 20 of the

27 actually came to such meetings). Twelve convictions on charges of bribery and conspiracy resulted, involving seven members of Congress and five other public officials. The convicted members of Congress were Senator Harrison A. Williams Jr. (NJ), and Representatives Frank Thompson (NJ), John Murphy (NY), Richard Kelly (FL), Raymond Lederer (PA), John Jenrette (SC), and Michael Myers (PA). Some of the defendants unsuccessfully appealed on the grounds of entrapment and that their civil rights had been violated during the course of the investigation; their convictions were upheld.

Operation GREYLORD

Operation GREYLORD, one of the FBI's most successful undercover operations, began in early 1980 when Terrence Hake, a prosecutor in Cook County, Illinois, became disillusioned with the corrupt judicial system that he saw around him. Hake agreed to work undercover for the Bureau, first posing as a corrupt prosecutor and later, when he left the state attorney's office, as a corrupt defense lawyer. His taped conversations revealed a widespread pattern of bribery among court officials.

When the FBI's 42-month GREYLORD investigation of the Cook County Circuit Court was publicly disclosed in August 1983, in the process, the controversial investigative techniques that FBI agents used to detect judicial corruption were also revealed. In addition to Hake's undercover role, FBI agents had posed as prosecutors, defense lawyers, and defendants who bribed judges. One judge's chambers had been bugged, and phone conversations had been secretly recorded. In some cases, agents had been authorized to testify falsely under oath. All together, approximately 100 bogus cases were brought to court as part of this undercover operation.

Over the course of the next eight years, the U.S. attorney in Chicago successfully prosecuted more than 90 judges, lawyers, police officers, and court personnel. Twenty of those indicted were judges—out of 334 judges on the Cook County Circuit Court in 1983. The last conviction in the GREYLORD case occurred on December 31, 1991. It involved a court bailiff, Lucius Robinson, who had passed hundreds of bribes to corrupt judges. Although granted immunity for testifying, Robinson was convicted of lying to a grand jury about the corruption and was sentenced to three years of probation. The convicted judges all received prison sentences for accepting bribes.

Organized Crime Cases

During the 1980s, the FBI (and the Justice Department) launched a major assault against organized crime, the infamous La Cosa Nostra (LCN). LCN crime families throughout the United States were targeted under the RICO (Racketeer Influenced and Corrupt Organizations) statute, part of the Organized Crime Control Act of 1970.

RICO provided federal investigators and prosecutors, for the first time, the legal tools needed to pursue patterns of criminal activity, criminal organizations, and crime profits, and not, as formerly, individual criminals. The statute prohibits the use of profits derived from illegal activity in any enterprise and the use of any enterprise to commit a pattern of criminal activity. The concept of "enterprise" is broadly constructed to include legal and illegal enterprises; as defined in the statute, an enterprise can be "an individual, a partnership, a corporation, an association, a union, or any legal entity capable of holding a property interest." "Patterns of criminal activity" encompass a wide variety of both state and federal violations, including racketeering, fraud, bribery, and narcotics.

Empowered after 1970 to focus on criminal conspiracies, FBI organized crime investigations also began to employ a variety of investigative techniques, not only recently legalized wiretapping but also sting operations, and the recruitment of informants who were promised protection under the Witness Protection Program. The result, as Attorney General William French Smith testified in 1983 before the President's Commission on Organized Crime, was the conviction, between 1981 and 1983, of more than 2,500 members and associates of organized crime.

In the most famous of these undercover operations, FBI agent Joseph Pistone (using the alias Donnie Brasco), infiltrated, for the first time, an LCN enterprise—the Bonanno crime family in New York City. In 1982, after six years undercover posing as a jewel thief and con man, Pistone's participation in this risky undercover operation was ended by the FBI, owing to concerns about his life. In the ensuing four years, Pistone became a key government witness and his testimony led to prosecution and convictions in numerous organized crime cases. Pistone provided some of the early information that triggered the "Pizza Connection" investigation, a case that involved international drug smuggling. Because of death threats from LCN, Pistone was obligated to change his identity after his undercover work, and he is no longer an FBI agent.

The FBI's successful assault on La Cosa Nostra during the 1980s, culminating in crime boss John Gotti's conviction in 1992, represented a major change in the Bureau's investigative priorities. At the time of the Apalachin incident in 1957, the FBI maintained that "the Mafia" did not exist. Not until the 1960s, with the Valachi hearings and the influence of Attorney General Robert Kennedy, were FBI resources gradually committed to the investigation of organized crime. The cases against La Cosa Nostra in the 1980s highlight this new commitment. At about the same time, federal authorities began to realize that the problem of organized crime extended beyond La Cosa Nostra, with the rise of other "non-traditional" organized crime groups, such as motorcycle clubs, prison gangs, Japanese "Yakuza" groups, Colombian cocaine rings, and Cuban crime cartels. These groups were also targeted by the FBI.

Operation BRILAB

Operation BRILAB (initially involving bribery of labor-union officials) was disclosed about one week after ABSCAM. It started out as an investigation into political corruption and bribery in the Southeast and eventually ensnared the reputed head of the LCN family in New Orleans, Carlos Marcello. In a year-long investigation, the FBI set up a sting operation in which agents and a convicted insurance-fraud perpetrator posed as insurance dealers offering bribes and kickbacks for state business.

As a result of BRILAB, Marcello and Charles Roemer, commissioner of administration for the governor of Louisiana, were indicted and convicted in April 1981: Marcello for bribing state officials to obtain lucrative insurance contracts and Roemer for receiving illegal payoffs. Both were sentenced to seven years in prison. In a separate federal case a few months later, Marcello was also found guilty of conspiring to bribe a federal judge.

The Pizza Connection Case

The so-called Pizza Connection case, one of the FBI's most famous international drug trafficking investigations, derived its name from the pizza parlors used by drug traffickers as fronts for heroin distribution in various locations in the East and Midwest—in New York, New Jersey, Pennsylvania, Michigan, Illinois, and Wisconsin. This international drug ring, which involved the collaboration of the Sicilian Mafia and the Bonanno crime family (in New York City), bought morphine base in Turkey, processed it in Sicily, and imported heroin into the United States.

The FBI's investigation began in 1979 and was part of a federal coordinated task force (Organized Crime Drug Enforcement Task Force Program).

Eventually tracing these links, the FBI developed evidence that led the Justice Department in April 1984 to bring heroin trafficking charges against 31 persons who had been arrested as participants in this international narcotics conspiracy. The more notable of the arrestees were Gaetano Badalamenti (a Sicilian Mafia leader) and Salvatore Catalano (head of the New York operations of the drug ring and member of the Bonanno family). Badalamente was arrested in Spain and was later extradited to the United States.

Only 22 of the defendants were tried when the trial began on September 30, 1985. Some of those initially indicted were not prosecuted because they were fugitives, dead, or were being held in other countries. Lasting 17 months, the trial became one of the longest and most complex federal criminal trials in U.S. history. The prosecution team, which included Louis J. Freeh, then an assistant U.S. attorney in Manhattan, introduced evidence uncovered by the FBI that included the testimony of hundreds of witnesses, wiretapped conversations, and financial and other documents. Prosecutors claimed that the drug smuggling ring had imported 330 pounds of heroin a year (for the previous five years), with a street value of $1.6 billion, and that the heroin had been distributed in major U.S. cities, such as New York, Philadelphia, Chicago, Detroit, and Newark. The prosecution also claimed that the defendants had transferred approximately $60 million of their illegal profits into overseas accounts. On March 2, 1987, all 17 of the defendants were convicted of participation in a narcotics conspiracy and a continuing criminal enterprise (of the remaining 5 from the original 22, 4 pled guilty and 1 was murdered after the trial started).

In June 1987, Federal Judge Pierre Leval sentenced the defendants to lengthy prison terms. Four of the convicted offenders were also ordered to contribute $2.5 million to a fund for the treatment of drug addicts.

The Commission Case

In yet another Manhattan case involving the LCN, U.S. attorney Rudolph Giuliani brought charges in February 1985 against members of the LCN's ruling body, known as the Commission. Leaders of the most powerful LCN families in the United States formed the Commission, whose function was to settle disputes among the approximately 24 LCN families nationwide. Prosecutors characterized them as the Mafia board of directors.

Eight Commission members were charged under the RICO statute for running the activities of the LCN in a racketeering pattern. These members included the top leadership of three of New York City's crime families: Anthony Salerno (Genovese family boss), Anthony Corallo (Lucchese family boss), Carmine Persico (Colombo family boss), Gennaro Langella (Colombo family underboss), Salvatore Santoro (Lucchese family underboss), Ralph Scopo (Colombo family soldier), Christopher Furnari (Lucchese family counselor), and Anthony Indelicato (Bonanno family captain). Prosecutors maintained that the eight had coordinated LCN criminal activities (such as loan-sharking, bribery, and extortion), resolved interfamily disputes, and ordered executions.

During the 10-week trial, the prosecution relied on the fruits of the FBI's intensive investigation of the Commission members, presenting numerous witnesses, over 100 secretly taped conversations, and surveillance photographs to support their claims about the defendants. In November 1986, all eight defendants were convicted on all charges. Federal Judge Richard Owen sentenced seven of the LCN leaders to 100-year prison sentences while Indelicato received a 40-year sentence for the 1979 murder of a crime boss (although the eight would be eligible for parole in 10 years).

The Patriarca Case

In March 1990, 21 members and associates of the Patriarca crime family in New England were indicted. Federal authorities maintained that since the 1940s the Patriarca family had controlled loan-sharking and gambling in New England. Among those indicted were Nicholas Bianco and Raymond J. Patriarca, two rival heads of the New England LCN. They faced a long list of charges under the RICO statute, including racketeering, drug trafficking, gambling, and murder in support of the Patriarca family enterprise.

The indictments were the by-product of an FBI investigation that had relied on the extensive use of wiretaps and bugs. One such bug intercepted a 1989 initiation ceremony in which Patriarca presided over the induction of 4 new recruits. In two subsequent trials in 1991 and 1992, one in Hartford and the other in Boston, 15 defendants were convicted of racketeering (6 of the original 21 charged pled guilty). Tried in Hartford, Bianco and 7 other defendants were convicted, with Bianco sentenced to 11 years and fined $125,000. Three of the other defendants (Gaetano Milano,

Frank Colantoni, and Louis Pugliano) were convicted of murdering Connecticut crime boss William Grasso as part of a factional dispute. Tried in Boston, Patriarca and 6 others were convicted with Patriarca receiving an 8-year prison sentence and a fine of $122,344 (the cost of confinement).

The John Gotti Case

On December 11, 1990, FBI agents arrested John Gotti, the alleged boss of the Gambino crime family in New York City, on racketeering and murder charges—the latter for the 1985 murder of Paul Castellano, his predecessor as head of the Gambino family. In three previous trials (in 1986, 1987, and 1990), Gotti had escaped convictions, earning him the nickname, the "Teflon Don." However, in the 1992 trial, held in Federal District Court in Brooklyn, the jury remained anonymous and sequestered, as the judge feared the possibility of jury tampering.

In their investigation leading to Gotti's arrest and ultimate conviction, FBI agents had uncovered Gotti's racketeering activities as head of the Gambino family. These activities included the resort to murders, extortion, and gambling. In the course of this investigation, the FBI wiretapped Gotti's conversations with associates (evidence from which was extensively used during the trial). In addition, FBI officials successfully recruited the cooperation of Gotti's underboss, Salvatore ("Sammy the Bull") Gravano, who turned informer in a plea bargain with federal authorities. Gravano detailed and helped corroborate Gotti's criminal activities, including ordering the murder of Castellano. Gravano's veracity as a witness was somewhat questionable, however, since he was implicated in many of the same crimes as Gotti, including murders, and was testifying to save himself from punishment—an argument that Gotti's defense lawyers did not overlook. Nonetheless, on April 2, 1992, Gotti was convicted on all counts. In June, Federal Judge I. Leo Glasser sentenced him to life imprisonment without the possibility of parole. For his cooperation, Gravano was sentenced to five years in prison and placed in the Witness Protection Program.

Espionage Cases of the 1980s

The FBI's long history of spy cases dates from the World War I period, a time of widespread public concern about German spies and enemy aliens. Just before and during World War II, the Rumrich and Dasch cases captured public interest, and in the Cold War era, concerns intensified again with the Rosenberg and Abel cases. Nonetheless, the decade producing an unprecedented number of spy cases was the 1980s. In fact, it was in 1985 that more suspects were charged with espionage against the United States than ever before—in that year, 11 were in custody—while during the previous four years, an additional 11 people had been charged. In contrast, a total of 46 people had been convicted of espionage during the preceding 40 years.

Of the espionage cases of the 1980s, the most notable began in 1984 with the first arrest ever of an FBI agent for spying (Richard W. Miller). Two cases were prosecuted in 1985 involving current or former Navy personnel accused of selling classified information to foreign nations (John A. Walker and Jonathan Jay Pollard). Then, in 1994 (although his spying began in the mid-1980s), Aldrich H. Ames, a CIA counterintelligence officer, was arrested for espionage. These defendants seriously compromised the nation's security interests by transmitting significant military secrets to the Soviet Union (or Israel, in the case of Pollard) and, in the case of Ames, jeopardized the lives of other intelligence agents.

The espionage cases of the 1980s coincided with the end of the Cold War. The collapse of the Soviet Union eliminated the nation's major intelligence adversary—and internal security threat. This did not mean, however, that the FBI could abandon its domestic security role. The United States would remain an espionage target of world powers, whether allies or potential adversaries. Furthermore, in the 1990s, the nature of the security threat, and espionage possibilities, also derived from the interest of foreign nations in acquiring industrial and technology secrets, rather than military or diplomatic information. One by-product of these cases, particularly the Ames case, was the institution of reforms to broaden U.S. monitoring activities and to improve CIA-FBI relations—thereby promoting the two agencies' complementary intelligence and counterintelligence missions.

Richard W. Miller

A 20-year veteran FBI agent, Richard W. Miller was assigned to the counterintelligence squad in Los Angeles. During the course of his duties, he became sexually involved with a Soviet immigrant, Svetlana Ogorodnikov, who was also a KGB agent. Having learned of this affair, FBI agents in the Los Angeles field office launched an investigation into Miller's activities. Confronted by superiors with evidence of his actions, Miller confessed to the sexual liaison and later admitted having given a classified document, an FBI manual, to Ogorodnikov. He was arrested on October 3,

1984, and subsequently charged with espionage in Federal District Court in Los Angeles. Svetlana Ogorodnikov and her husband, Nikolai, were also charged; they pled guilty in June 1985, with the expectation that they would testify in Miller's trial.

During Miller's first trial, his defense lawyers argued that his affair with Ogorodnikov had been part of an amateurish plan to infiltrate the KGB. Prosecutors rebuffed this defense, emphasizing that Miller's activities were unauthorized and therefore constituted spying. The defense also attempted to challenge Miller's confession, claiming that it had been coerced during his interrogation by FBI agents. This trial ended in a deadlock; the judge declared a mistrial in November 1985 after two weeks of deliberation.

Miller was convicted, however, in a second trial, on June 19, 1986, on six counts of espionage. The jury apparently rejected Ogorodnikov's testimony that neither she nor Miller were spies, and that Miller had never passed classified documents to her. Miller was sentenced to two concurrent life sentences. A federal appeals court overturned his conviction in April 1989, ruling that the trial judge had erred when admitting evidence on the results of Miller's failed lie detector test. The case was returned to Federal District Court in Los Angeles for retrial.

In the third trial, in October 1990, Miller was reconvicted on all six counts of espionage. This time, the U.S. Court of Appeals in San Francisco in January 1993 upheld his conviction and 20-year prison sentence. Miller was the first FBI agent ever to be convicted for espionage. (Earl Pitts became the second; he was convicted in 1997 for spying for the Soviets, and then the Russians, between 1987 and 1992.)

John A. Walker

Following a tip to the FBI from his former wife, Barbara, John A. Walker was placed under FBI surveillance in 1985. Barbara Walker claimed that when they were still married (about 10 years earlier), she had witnessed her husband leaving classified documents in wooded areas in northern Virginia in exchange for cash. At the time, Walker was a U.S. naval intelligence officer and was stationed at the Norfolk naval base. Walker retired from the Navy in 1976 but continued to live in the Norfolk area where he operated his own private detective agency.

Initially, FBI agents had dismissed these allegations as the complaints of a disgruntled ex-wife. Three months later, however, agents at the FBI's Norfolk, Virginia, office followed up on this report. For about six weeks, FBI agents kept Walker under both physical and electronic surveillance, wiretapping his home and business. On May 19, 1985, FBI agents followed him as he made a series of suspicious deliveries, arresting him in the early morning hours of May 20 for espionage.

As the investigation unfolded, agents learned that Walker—during and following his retirement—had recruited a number of other naval personnel to assist him in his lucrative spying operation. These included his son, Michael; his brother, Arthur; and a close friend, Jerry Whitworth. All had access to classified materials of interest to the Soviets. Walker's motivation was mercenary, not ideological. Indeed, during the course of his 18-year spy operation, which included the last 8 years of his naval service, he passed regular Navy security checks. The extent of his spying has not been conclusively reconstructed, but among the sensitive military secrets that Walker admitted selling to the Soviets were top-secret codes of U.S. naval communications.

Indicted on October 28, 1985, Walker reached a plea agreement with federal authorities. In this plea bargain, John Walker pled guilty to espionage charges and agreed to a life sentence in exchange for a reduced sentence for his son, Michael (25 years in prison). Walker also agreed to describe the contents of the classified materials that he had supplied to Soviet agents. Arthur Walker and Jerry Whitworth were convicted, as well, and were sentenced to lengthy prison sentences—life and 365 years, respectively.

Jonathan Jay Pollard

Jonathan Jay Pollard was employed as a civilian counterintelligence analyst for the Navy in the mid-1980s when he decided to sell classified documents to Israel. In contrast to Walker, whose motivations were pecuniary, Pollard believed that this information was essential for Israeli national security. Alerted to Pollard's activities, FBI agents arrested him and his wife, Anne, on November 21, 1985, in Washington, D.C., on espionage charges.

The case became a major embarrassment for the Israeli government since its own security officers had been caught spying on a major ally. Israeli officials insisted that the mainstream Israeli intelligence agencies had not recruited Pollard, and that the country's political leaders were unaware of his spying—even though four Israelis were also accused of being co-conspirators with Pollard, but were not indicted. (The alleged Israeli co-conspirators were Rafael Eitan, who once headed the secret intelligence-gathering unit that supervised Pollard's activities; Air Force colonel Aviem Sella; Joseph Yagur; and Irit Erb—the latter two had been assigned to the Israeli consulate and embassy in New York.) In December 1985, Prime Minister Shimon Peres apologized to the United States for the Israeli espionage "to

the extent that it did take place." He also said that Israel would dismantle the secret counterterrorism unit that had directed Pollard's activities. According to State Department officials, Israel also later agreed to return any documents that had been provided by the Pollard espionage.

In a plea agreement signed on June 4, 1986, Pollard pled guilty to espionage, and his wife pled guilty as an accessory. In addition, Pollard agreed to provide the Justice Department with information about Israeli espionage operations in the United States. In 1987, Pollard was sentenced to life in prison; Anne Pollard received a 40-month sentence. A federal appeals court upheld Pollard's conviction and life sentence in March 1992.

Several years later, Israeli officials appealed to President Bill Clinton to release Pollard. The Israeli government had been criticized from within for leaving one of its spies "out in the cold." To strengthen Israel's case for his release, Pollard, an American Jew, was made an Israeli citizen in November 1995. However, in July 1996, President Clinton rejected this appeal for clemency.

Aldrich H. Ames

A career CIA official, Aldrich H. Ames worked at the Central Intelligence Agency for 31 years, his last 9 years as a double agent for Soviet, and then Russian, intelligence. As a CIA counterintelligence officer in the Soviet and East Bloc section, Ames had access to classified information about U.S. intelligence operations and the identities of both CIA agents and Soviets whom it had successfully recruited as spies. On February 21, 1994, Ames was arrested on espionage charges—for selling classified information to the Soviet Union (and then Russia) for more than $2.5 million.

In 1991, the FBI and the CIA began a joint investigation in response to the suspicious loss of Soviet intelligence agents working for the CIA and FBI in 1985 and 1986. Two Soviet officials who had been recruited as spies by the FBI, for example, were recalled to Moscow in 1985 and executed shortly thereafter. Hesitant at first to cooperate with the FBI, CIA officials originally mishandled the agency's own inquiry to identify a suspected Soviet "mole." Ames escaped CIA suspicion, despite his flamboyant and lavish life-style (exceeding his salary), which he attributed to his wife's inheritance; questionable work habits; access to sensitive reports; failed polygraph tests during regular security reviews required of all CIA employees; and frequent foreign trips. Only after 1991, when CIA officials requested FBI assistance in the inquiry, did Ames finally come under suspicion. The FBI's initial identification of Ames as a suspect was the result of a May 1993 tip from a former KGB intelligence officer (who had defected). In the months prior to his arrest, FBI agents placed Ames under both physical and electronic surveillance. Agents tapped his telephone and were able to retrieve evidence of the activities conducted from his computer. Inspection of his household trash revealed a torn-up note from Ames to his Russian contact.

Indicted on April 26, 1994, Ames eventually accepted a plea agreement. He accepted a life sentence without the possibility of parole in exchange for leniency for his wife, Rosario, who was also charged and was given a relatively light sentence of five years and three months in federal prison. Ames also agreed to assist federal authorities seeking to assess the extent of his espionage activities. He admitted to compromising more than 100 intelligence operations, and FBI and CIA officials estimated that at least 10 Soviet agents who had been recruited by U.S. intelligence were executed because of Ames's disclosures to the Soviets.

The Ames case precipitated harsh criticism of the CIA and FBI, both for their failure to apprehend Ames earlier (given the five-year delay between the suspicious loss of their Soviet double agents and the onset of an investigation) and the jealousy that compromised the formation of an effective FBI-CIA liaison. In response to an internal inquiry, 11 CIA officials were reprimanded in September 1994. A two-year investigation conducted by the Justice Department's inspector general, Michael Bromwich, criticized FBI officials for not responding sooner. Only a brief summary of the classified 400-page report was released in April 1997. Bureau officials took issue with Bromwich's report, stating that it had "the benefit of hindsight" and had been written "with the outcome already known."

Militias and Religious Sects

Not only had the nation's foreign threats changed by the 1990s, but so, too, did the sources of domestic violence and antigovernment activities. The rise of heavily armed citizen groups soon involved the FBI in three major standoffs; two involved militias (survivalist, white supremacist, antigovernment activists), and the third, a religious sect. One standoff (with the Freemen, in Montana) was settled peacefully, but the other two (Ruby Ridge and Waco) resulted in significant loss of life. These three cases had important long-term consequences and served to define how the Bureau would handle future armed confrontations between citizen groups and federal authorities.

In the aftermath of the Ruby Ridge and Waco incidents, FBI and Justice Department officials instituted several reforms in the fall of 1995. These changes centered on the

rules for use of deadly force, review of shooting incidents, and management of crisis situations. In any siege, senior FBI officials were to take a direct part in the management of the operation, and an effort would be made to integrate the operation's tactical and negotiation components. With the onset of the Freemen confrontation, FBI officials had the first opportunity to employ these reforms—called the "Montana model" by the *Washington Post* and a policy of "patience and resoluteness" by FBI Director Freeh. Although some newspapers and local officials criticized the FBI's conduct in Montana as too patient and too slow-moving, the successful outcome of the Freemen standoff seemed to vindicate the new, less confrontational strategy.

Ruby Ridge

Randall (or Randy) Weaver, a survivalist and antigovernment activist, first came to the attention of federal authorities during an ATF (Bureau of Alcohol, Tobacco and Firearms) investigation of the Aryan Nation, a white supremacist group. ATF officials had initiated an investigation of this group, suspecting it of violating federal weapons laws. In the course of this investigation, ATF agents learned of Weaver's association with this group. An ATF informant, posing as an illegal arms dealer, accordingly sought to buy weapons from Weaver. After three years of such attempts, the informant succeeded in October 1989, when Weaver sold him two illegal sawed-off shotguns. Indicted for this illegal weapons sale, Weaver was arrested in January 1991. Released on his own recognizance, he failed to appear for his trial a month later. Weaver's case was then referred to the U.S. Marshals Service, which designated him a "dangerous fugitive."

At the time, Weaver and his family lived in a remote mountain cabin in northern Idaho, near Ruby Ridge. Although aware of his residence, it was not until more than a year later that six marshals were first sent to arrest Weaver. On August 21, 1992, during their surveillance of the cabin area, the marshals became involved in a shoot-out that resulted in the deaths of Weaver's 14-year-old son, Samuel, and one of the marshals, William Degan. Federal authorities at the scene thereupon requested the assistance of the FBI's Hostage Rescue Team. The following day, a recently arrived 50-member FBI team placed the cabin under surveillance.

Eleven FBI sharpshooters were stationed around the cabin on August 22 with orders to "shoot on sight." Although the question of who authorized these orders provoked controversy later, the snipers were instructed to shoot any armed adult in the vicinity of the cabin. Pursuant to these orders, sharpshooter Lon Horiuchi shot and wounded

Randall Weaver as he was walking outside the cabin. Horiuchi later claimed that he had believed Weaver was about to shoot at a helicopter overhead. As Weaver and a friend, Kevin Harris, ran back to the cabin, Horiuchi fired a second shot at the cabin entrance, seriously wounding Harris. The same bullet also fatally wounded Weaver's wife, Vicki, who had been standing behind the cabin door, not visible to Horiuchi. A 10-day standoff ensued, culminating with the peaceful surrender of Weaver and his three daughters (aged 16, 10, and 10 months). Harris had been removed on the ninth day and flown to a hospital for treatment. During this standoff, hundreds of FBI agents and other law enforcement officials were brought to the remote cabin site, reinforced by helicopters and armored personnel carriers.

Weaver and Harris were charged for the murder of U.S. Marshal Degan. Both were acquitted of this murder in their July 1993 trial in Idaho. Weaver was also acquitted of all major weapons charges, except for his failure to appear in court after his arrest for the sale of the illegal shotguns. In Weaver's subsequent wrongful death lawsuit for the killing of his son and wife, the Justice Department agreed in 1995 to pay $3.1 million, but admitted to no wrongdoing.

The shoot-out and standoff precipitated a series of investigations (by the FBI, the Justice Department, and Congress) that focused on the FBI's conduct of the siege at Ruby Ridge, and questioned whether excessive force had been used by the FBI's Hostage Rescue Team. An ancillary issue was whether FBI officials at the scene had given "shoot on sight" orders and questioned whether these orders had been approved by FBI officials in Washington. Additional controversy surfaced over whether FBI officials had orchestrated a cover-up to justify their initial assessment or to protect supervisory FBI officials who had responsibility for this operation. Based on the FBI's own administrative review of the facts of the case in January 1995, FBI Director Freeh (who was not director at the time of the Ruby Ridge incident) announced disciplinary actions against 12 FBI officials. Freeh concluded that no criminal conduct had occurred, but he did find evidence of "inadequate performance, improper judgment, neglect of duty, and failure to exert proper managerial oversight."

Several months later, Eugene Glenn, one of the disciplined agents who had served as a field commander at Ruby Ridge, complained to the Justice Department that there had been a cover-up. Glenn maintained that the official FBI inquiry had exonerated the high-level FBI officials in Washington (notably Larry Potts, whom Freeh later promoted to deputy director) and instead placed the blame for

deficiencies in the operation on agents in the field. In response to Glenn's allegations, the Justice Department's Office of Professional Responsibility (OPR) initiated a review; then, in August 1995, it opened a criminal investigation into the role of six high-level FBI officials (including Potts) during the siege and their response to subsequent inquiries. Pending the result of this inquiry, Freeh suspended the six officials.

Responding to pressure from conservatives and antigun activists, in 1995, Congress launched its own investigation into the FBI's conduct at Ruby Ridge. Although uncovering no new facts, the resultant subcommittee report sharply criticized the FBI for the use of excessive force—and welcomed FBI Director Freeh's new rules governing hostage operations.

The OPR investigation was concluded in August 1997. Only one of the suspended officials, Michael Kahoe, was charged with a crime—obstructing justice (for destroying an "after-action" report of November 1992 critical of the FBI agents' role in the shoot-out). His action, in effect, kept this report from both the prosecutors and defense attorneys in Weaver's 1993 trial. The OPR report found that there was "insufficient" evidence to support further prosecutions. A high-ranking FBI official in Washington, Kahoe pled guilty to the obstruction of justice charge in October 1997 and was sentenced to 18 months imprisonment, a $4,000 fine, and two years probation after his release from prison.

Several days after the Justice Department announced that it would not seek further prosecutions, a state prosecutor in Idaho filed criminal charges against FBI sharpshooter Lon Horiuchi for the killing of Vicki Weaver (manslaughter) and against Kevin Harris for the death of Deputy U.S. Marshal William Degan (first-degree murder). Horiuchi petitioned to have the case taken over by a federal court since he had been acting in an official capacity. In January and then in May 1998, Federal District Judge Edward Lodge ruled in Horiuchi's favor, foreclosing state prosecutors from pursuing the case further.

Branch Davidians at Waco
On February 28, 1993, federal Alcohol, Tobacco and Firearms (ATF) agents attempted to raid a Branch Davidian residential compound located about 12 miles outside of Waco, Texas. The Davidians, a religious sect, are an offshoot of the Seventh Day Adventists, and their leader, David Koresh, was a charismatic figure who believed that the second coming of Christ was imminent and would result in an "apocalyptic showdown" with government agents.

Earlier, ATF agents had initiated an investigation into whether members of the sect illegally possessed firearms and explosives, and they decided to conduct a surprise raid on the compound to execute arrest and search warrants. Apparently tipped off, the Davidians anticipated this raid, and a shoot-out broke out in which 4 ATF agents and 6 Davidians were killed, and about 26 others were wounded.

Immediately following the failed raid, ATF officials requested FBI assistance, and the Bureau's Hostage Rescue Team was dispatched to Waco. Unwilling to attempt another raid against the heavily armed Davidians, more than 700 FBI and ATF agents in armored vehicles cordoned off the compound. Their "waiting" strategy led to a 51-day standoff. In this siege operation, the FBI became the lead agency, and FBI negotiators attempted to arrange a peaceful surrender with Koresh. These negotiations were sometimes complemented by pressure tactics, such as cutting off electricity, playing loud music at night, illuminating the compound with bright lights, and tightening the perimeter.

During the standoff, 35 sect members were released at various times. FBI negotiators had intermittent conversations with either Koresh or one of his top lieutenants, but as the negotiations proceeded, Koresh's tactics frustrated them. Indeed, at one point, Koresh promised to surrender and then recanted. In an attempt to pressure Koresh, FBI negotiators issued various ultimatums and threats, and resorted to acts of harassment. By early April, FBI officials concluded that the standoff could go on indefinitely. Accordingly, they drafted a plan for a tear-gas assault, as a way to flush the Davidians out of the compound. The plan was presented to Attorney General Janet Reno, who approved it on April 17, after first rejecting it the day before. As originally proposed, CS tear gas would be gradually injected into the Davidian compound over a 48-hour period, thereby allowing the Davidians to exit through non-gassed areas.

On April 19, at about 6:00 a.m., an FBI tank (a combat engineering vehicle or CEV) with an attached boom began inserting tear gas into the Davidian compound. The Davidians responded by shooting at the vehicle. Tear gas continued to be injected throughout the morning hours, until 12:07 p.m., when the Davidians deliberately started fires at several locations within their compound. Nine Davidians fled from the compound at that time and were arrested. At about 12:25 p.m., gunfire was heard from within the compound. The fire, moreover, began to spread quickly and soon engulfed the entire compound, which burned to the ground. Unable to escape, an estimated 80 Davidians lost their lives, including Koresh and 25 children under the age of 15. Medical examiners subsequently concluded that most of the deaths resulted from asphyxiation from the smoke and fire, that others were killed by falling debris during the fire, and that still others had been shot to death.

The conflagration at Waco, and the deaths of women and children, precipitated widespread criticism. In response, numerous congressional hearings and a Justice Department investigation were launched to ascertain responsibility for the tragic outcome of the Waco standoff. In 1993, the House Judiciary Committee held hearings; two years later, two House subcommittees held joint hearings, issuing their report in 1996. The Justice Department conducted its own inquiries, issuing a series of reports in 1993.

The several official reports resulting from the House hearings and Justice Department inquiries placed "ultimate responsibility" for what happened at Waco on David Koresh. Nonetheless, these reports severely criticized both the ATF and FBI: the ATF for its conduct in the initial raid, and the FBI for its management of the standoff and the tear-gas assault. One of the Justice Department reports, prepared by an outside expert, criticized FBI officials for rejecting their own behavioral science experts' advice in their negotiating strategy with Koresh, and concluded also that Reno had been "ill-advised" in approving the assault. In addition, the 1996 House report criticized Attorney General Reno for approving the tear-gas plan, and President Clinton for not accepting her resignation.

Despite these criticisms, ATF and FBI officials suffered few legal consequences. The ATF director resigned for his role in the initial raid, and the two ATF agents in charge of the raid were fired, but were later reinstated. No FBI officials or agents were disciplined. Indeed, Attorney General Reno consistently defended both the tear-gas plan and the FBI's implementation of it.

Nine members of the Branch Davidians who left the compound during the standoff were subsequently prosecuted and convicted on various charges, including voluntary manslaughter and weapons violations. In June 1994, Federal Judge Walter Smith sentenced five of the defendants to 40 years in prison for their role in the shoot-out with ATF agents; three other defendants received prison sentences ranging from 5 to 20 years. A ninth defendant, who testified for the government, received a three-year prison sentence.

Surviving relatives of some of the Branch Davidians filed lawsuits against law enforcement officials, among these a 1994 lawsuit brought by Koresh's father and grandmother on behalf of three of Koresh's children who died in the fire. Attorney General Reno and six law enforcement officials were named in the $153 million lawsuit, which is currently pending.

The Freemen in Montana

The FBI became involved in another standoff in the spring of 1996 with a small group of armed citizens calling themselves the Freemen. A group of right-wing, antigovernment militants, the Freemen rejected the legitimacy of the U.S. government. They specifically rejected federal law, taxes, and U.S. currency, and claimed that the federal government was controlled by Zionists. The Freemen first entered the public spotlight in 1994 when an armed group took over the county courthouse in Jordan, Montana, and held a meeting. Shortly thereafter, they began issuing arrest and death warrants for various local, state, and federal officials. In September 1995, the Freemen moved their headquarters to a ranch, which they dubbed Justus Township, just outside of Jordan (population 450). Their actions led a federal grand jury in 1995 to indict many of the Freemen on 51 counts of fraud and threats to public officials.

Federal authorities did not attempt to arrest the indicted Freemen until March 25, 1996, when—as part of an undercover sting operation—FBI agents arrested two Freemen leaders (LeRoy Schweitzer and Daniel Petersen) on the perimeter of their 460-acre ranch. A standoff ensued as other Freemen, numbering approximately 21, prepared to repulse any further attempts to arrest them. About 100 FBI agents were brought in to set up roadblocks, but for the most part, they stayed at some distance from the ranch's perimeter. The agents avoided wearing the military-style outfits worn by other FBI agents during the confrontations at Ruby Ridge and Waco.

Not until April 4 were FBI agents able to initiate negotiations with the Freemen, but these efforts proved unproductive. FBI officials then recruited outside intermediaries in an attempt to achieve a peaceful end to the standoff. Two of the more notable mediators were, themselves, right-wing sympathizers: Charles Duke (a Colorado state senator) and James "Bo" Gritz (a former Green Beret colonel). Duke and Gritz were also unable to negotiate a settlement. By early June, the FBI increased its pressure tactics, bringing in armored vehicles and a helicopter on June 1, and cutting off electricity to the ranch on June 3. At about this time, FBI agents transported one of the Freemen, Edwin Clark, from the ranch to meet with Schweitzer, the Freemen leader who had been arrested on the first day of the standoff and had

been jailed. During the course of the standoff several people were allowed to leave the ranch. By the time of their peaceful surrender to FBI agents on June 13, only 16 Freemen remained. It is still not entirely clear why the Freemen, after 81 days, decided to end the standoff. Federal officials denied having made any deals for leniency; some believe that the Freemen simply decided to continue the struggle in court.

The still-defiant Freemen were taken to Billings, Montana, in government vans, where they faced federal charges that included mail and bank fraud, weapons violations, and threatening to kill a federal judge. The fraud charges related to their having defrauded banks and businesses of nearly $2 million. Because of threats made against Montana judges, two out-of-state federal judges were called in to handle the case. In the resultant trial, the Freemen refused to recognize the government's right to try them. Nonetheless, in July 1998, 6 of the 12 Freemen defendents were convicted on several charges of financial fraud, while 3 (including Schweitzer and Petersen) were convicted of threatening to kill Montana's chief judge, Jack D. Shanstrom.

Terrorism Cases of the 1990s

In 1982, anti-terrorism was elevated to a national priority program in response to the Reagan administration's heightened interest in domestic and international terrorism. In fact, the actual incidence of terrorist acts within the United States remained low. This changed dramatically during the 1990s with the 1993 World Trade Center bombing and the 1995 bombing of the federal building in Oklahoma City. The World Trade Center and Oklahoma City bombings marked a new, unprecedented threat, reflecting a willingness by U.S. residents (in one case, alien residents; in another, U.S. citizens) to employ violence to achieve political or social objectives. Domestic security investigations, which had been curtailed, became once again a prominent FBI priority—classified now as terrorism investigations, both domestic and international.

In response to these highly publicized domestic (and international) terrorism incidents in the 1980s and 1990s, some members of Congress and the public raised questions about the adequacy of FBI authority to conduct domestic security and terrorism investigations. In March 1983, the Reagan administration had revised the guidelines governing domestic security investigations, which had originally been implemented by Attorney General Levi in 1976. The 1983 guidelines (the so-called Smith Guidelines) gave the FBI more latitude to open domestic security and terrorism investigations.

In the wake of the World Trade Center and Oklahoma City bombings, concerns were again expressed about the adequacy of the FBI's domestic intelligence authority. The Smith Guidelines were not formally changed; indeed, during 1995 congressional testimony, FBI Director Freeh indicated that the Bureau did not need broader authority, and that it would be sufficient to reinterpret the existing guidelines.

In the aftermath of the Oklahoma City bombing, the FBI pursued a more aggressive antiterrorism strategy, trying to detect domestic terrorist conspiracies in the planning stages. It remains unclear, however, how extensively the FBI has monitored groups of Islamic fundamentalists, militant white supremacists, right-wing militias, and radical revolutionaries.

World Trade Center Bombing

On February 26, 1993, at 12:18 p.m, a massive car bomb exploded in the underground parking garage of the World Trade Center (WTC) in New York City. The explosion created a crater five-stories deep, killed 6 people, injured more than 1,000, and trapped thousands of office workers in the twin-towers complex in lower Manhattan. At the time, the cause of the explosion was not immediately known; the initial theory was a transformer explosion.

The New York City police (NYPD), the ATF, and the FBI immediately launched a joint investigation of the explosion. The FBI code-named its investigation TRADEBOM, and deployed about 300 agents, including a highly trained bomb squad dispatched from Washington, D.C., the day after the bombing. The FBI bomb squad's initial assessment attributed the explosion to a bomb. This was confirmed the following day when an ATF explosives expert and an NYPD investigator found metal parts of a truck van in the rubble of the WTC underground parking garage. Explosive marks on the metal suggested that a bomb might have been inside the van. The investigators also discovered the vehicle identification number (VIN) on one of the fragments. Using the VIN, FBI agents traced the destroyed vehicle to the Ryder Truck Rental Company in Alabama. Ryder officials, in turn, identified the Ford Econoline van as having been rented on February 23 from its Jersey City, New Jersey, office to a Mohammed A. Salameh.

The FBI's discovery of the truck's VIN and identification of Salameh marked the beginning of the unraveling of the WTC bombing. From interviews with the Ryder staff at the Jersey City office, FBI agents learned that a few hours after the bombing, Salameh had come to the office seeking a refund of his cash deposit and reporting that the vehicle had been stolen. Salameh was informed that to obtain his refund, he would have to produce a copy of the police report. FBI agents conducted a background check on Salameh, using the Bureau's computerized terrorism files, and discovered that the 25-year-old Palestinian from Jordan had taken part in a demonstration a year earlier on behalf of El-Sayid Nosair, who had been accused, but acquitted, in the murder of Rabbi Meir Kahane, the founder of the Jewish Defense League. Agents also discovered that Salameh attended the Jersey City mosque where Sheik Omar Abdel Rahman preached. Rahman, who had been expelled from Egypt in 1981, advocated the violent overthrow of the Egyptian government. Since the 1990 murder of Kahane, FBI agents had placed many of Rahman's followers under surveillance. Six days after the WTC bombing, Salameh returned a second time to the Ryder office, seeking his $400 refund. The evidence linking him to the van, along with the expiration of his immigration visa, provided FBI agents with sufficient basis to arrest him shortly after he left the Ryder office. A search of Salameh; his apartment; and later, a storage unit that he had rented uncovered additional evidence, including chemicals that were components in the WTC bomb and a business card that led agents to a second suspect, Nidal Ayyad.

Ayyad, a 25-year-old chemical engineer, was also associated with the Jersey City mosque and had a number of ties to Salameh, including a joint bank account. When arresting Ayyad, agents found a letter, saved in his computer files, similar to one received by the *New York Times* four days after the explosion. This letter, which officials initially believed to be a hoax, was reportedly sent by a so-called Liberation Army Fifth Battalion, which claimed responsibility for the bombing. The letter stated, "This action was done in response for the American political, economical and military support to Israel, the state of terrorism, and to the rest of the dictator countries of the region."

Two other suspects were subsequently arrested by FBI agents: Mahmud Abouhalim, who had left the United States the day after the bombing and was captured in Egypt by Cairo police, and Ahmed Mohammed Ajaj, who was actually in prison at the time of the bombing. These four arrestees, all Muslim fundamentalists, were charged with conspiracy, explosive destruction of property, and interstate transportation of explosives. Their five-month trial began in September

1993, during which 207 witnesses testified and 10,000 pages of transcript were compiled. Convicted on March 4, 1994, the four were sentenced by federal judge Kevin Duffy in May to 240 years in prison with no possibility of parole.

Despite the quick arrest and conviction of the four defendants in the WTC case, many unanswered questions remained about the bombing: Had these four acted alone? If not, who ordered and financed the attack? Was this a terrorist attack, funded and directed by foreign governments or Muslim extremists? Fearing that this was not an isolated incident, but could be part of an ongoing conspiracy, FBI agents intensified their monitoring of Islamic fundamentalists in the New York area.

In this surveillance effort, FBI agents enlisted the services of Emad Salem, a U.S. citizen of Egyptian ancestry who had previously served as a Bureau and NYPD informant on the Islamic community. Salem succeeded in infiltrating the Jersey City mosque attended by Sheik Rahman's followers, gaining their and the Sheik's confidence and taping many of their conversations. He soon discovered that the WTC was only the first of several landmarks in New York City that these militant Muslims planned to bomb. Other sites included the United Nations building, the federal office complex where the FBI field office is located, the Holland and Lincoln Tunnels, and the George Washington Bridge. To provide cover for his role as informant/conspirator, Salem aided the Muslim group in their preparations for these planned acts, including renting a safe house that FBI agents bugged. On June 24, as some of the conspirators were assembling bombs in a Queens warehouse, FBI agents moved in and arrested five of them. Other arrests followed, including Sheik Rahman. The arrestees were subsequently indicted on a wide range of conspiracy charges involving plans to bomb the aforementioned facilities and to assassinate a number of prominent individuals (both U.S. and Egyptian).

The resultant bombing conspiracy trial of Rahman and his followers began on January 30, 1995, in the U.S. District Court in Manhattan. Although the defendants in this second terrorist bombing trial were not specifically accused of carrying out the WTC bombing, the planned conspiracy— for which they were indicted—was portrayed as constituting part of a wider plot to destroy New York City landmarks in order to change the U.S. government's Middle East policies. Sheik Rahman was charged as the spiritual leader of the conspirators who had given religious sanction to their terrorist plot.

Defense lawyers denied the charges, arguing that the defendants were being framed, and that Salem and the FBI had fabricated the plots to salvage the Bureau's sagging reputation (after Waco). Prosecutors presented a detailed case, relying in part on hours of Salem's secretly recorded conversations with the defendants, transcripts of Rahman's speeches, and FBI videotape of the conspirators making bombs in a warehouse. The trial lasted nine months. On October 1, 1995, the jury convicted Rahman and nine of his Muslim followers. One of those followers, El-Sayid Nosair, had been acquitted in 1991 in a New York State trial for the murder of Rabbi Meir Kahane. (Three others pled guilty and a fourth testified for the government.) Sentenced in January 1996, Rahman and Nosair received life sentences without the possibility of parole, while the sentences of the other eight defendants ranged from 25 to 57 years in prison.

During the trial of Sheik Rahman and his followers, FBI agents arrested two additional individuals who were charged for involvement in the WTC bombing: the alleged mastermind of the operation, Ramzi Ahmed Yousef, and the alleged driver of the van, Eyad Ismoil. Both had fled the country just hours after the WTC bombing. Yousef, a 27-year-old electrical engineer, was arrested in Pakistan on February 7, 1995, and returned to the United States to stand trial. An Iraqi and a militant Muslim, before fleeing in February 1993, Yousef had resided in the United States for only a few months. Prosecutors described Yousef, a roommate of Salameh prior to the bombing, as the only professional terrorist in the Rahman group. (Before his trial for his role in the WTC bombing, Yousef was first tried and convicted in 1996 for conspiring to blow up an American airplane in Asia.) Yousef and Ismoil's trial for their role in the WTC bombing opened in August 1997 in federal court in Manhattan. They were both convicted of conspiracy on November 12, 1997, by an anonymous jury that deliberated for three days.

Oklahoma City Bombing

On April 19, 1995—on the second anniversary of the FBI's tear-gas assault on the Branch Davidian compound at Waco—another major act of terrorism occurred: the bombing of the Alfred P. Murrah Federal Building in Oklahoma City, Oklahoma. At 9:02 a.m., a 4,800-pound bomb placed in a parked truck in front of the federal building exploded, causing the nine-storied structure to collapse, killing 168 people and injuring 850 others (see Exhibit 2.11).

Exhibit 2.11 **Alfred P. Murrah Federal Building,** *Courtesy Agence France Presse/Corbis-Bettmann*

More than 1,000 ATF and FBI agents were committed to investigating the case, in addition to personnel of local police and rescue agencies. Initially, investigators and the public suspected the bombing to be the work of Middle Eastern terrorists, not unlike the World Trade Center bombing. However, attention soon focused on domestic suspects. The first major clue was discovered before noon on the day of the bombing: a large piece of twisted metal, which was the rear axle of a truck. This axle was found a block and a half away from the site of the explosion. FBI agents were able to identify a vehicle identification number found on the axle, and were then able to trace the vehicle to its owner, Ryder Rental Inc., in Miami. That same afternoon, Ryder officials identified Elliott's Body Shop in Junction City, Kansas, as the agency that, on April 17, had rented the truck to an individual who called himself Robert Kling. The vehicle had not been returned. Still later that afternoon, FBI agents interviewed employees at Elliott's Body Shop in Junction City and obtained descriptions of "Robert Kling" and another suspect. An FBI artist produced composite drawings of the two suspects, and these sketches were widely circulated in the national media and were used by FBI agents when interviewing people in Junction City and elsewhere. The owner of the Dreamland Motel in Junction City identified the FBI's drawing of "Robert Kling" as portraying Timothy McVeigh, a man who had registered at the motel on April 14 under what turned out to be his real name. McVeigh had given as his address a farm in Decker, Michigan, owned by James Nichols, whose brother, Terry, was an Army friend of McVeigh.

Coincidentally, about 90 minutes after the explosion, Timothy McVeigh was stopped by an Oklahoma state trooper on Interstate 35 for driving without a license plate. The trooper discovered that McVeigh was carrying a concealed weapon. The trooper arrested McVeigh and took him into custody, without realizing that McVeigh would soon become the prime suspect in the Oklahoma City bombing case. The trooper automatically checked the county's terminal link with the FBI's NCIC computer to determine whether McVeigh had any outstanding warrants—which he did not. Two days later, however, when FBI agents obtained McVeigh's name from the owner of the Dreamland Motel, they immediately entered his name into the NCIC computer. At this time, agents discovered that McVeigh had been arrested by the Oklahoma trooper, tracked him to the Noble County Jail, and on April 21, arrested him for the Oklahoma City bombing at the jail in Perry, where he remained in custody.

The ongoing FBI investigation also sought to locate and identify any other suspects. Based on McVeigh's listing of the Decker, Michigan, address in his motel registration, FBI agents searched the Michigan farm of James Nichols. They immediately took both James Nichols and his brother, Terry, into custody as material witnesses. The FBI learned little from James Nichols, except that McVeigh had visited and was a friend of his brother. Terry Nichols had been an Army buddy of McVeigh's, and they remained friends after leaving the service. Terry Nichols told agents that he had been with McVeigh three days before the bombing and had driven McVeigh to Junction City from Oklahoma City. Terry Nichols claimed ignorance of the impending bombing. An FBI search of Terry Nichols's home in Herington, Kansas, however, uncovered additional evidence: explosives, blasting caps, blue plastic barrels similar to fragments found at the bombing scene, and a receipt for the purchase of 2,000 pounds of ammonium nitrate. Based on this evidence, Terry Nichols was formally charged on May 10 as a co-conspirator in the bombing. James Nichols was released, and charges against him were later dropped. On August 11, McVeigh and Terry Nichols were indicted on murder and conspiracy charges. Because of the extensive media coverage of the case in Oklahoma, U.S. District Judge Richard Matsch moved the trial to Denver on February 20, 1996, and in October he ruled that McVeigh and Nichols would be tried separately.

McVeigh's trial began on March 31, 1997, with jury selection, and on April 24 opening statements were presented. A 29-year-old Army veteran who had served in Operation Desert Storm in Kuwait, McVeigh had no previous criminal record. Since leaving the Army, he had drifted from state to state, attending gun shows and traveling in right-wing militia circles, but apparently never joined any specific group. He had become increasingly disillusioned with the federal government, and his antigovernment views had been reinforced by the federal raid and standoff at Waco. When he was arrested on April 19 by the Oklahoma trooper, he had among his possessions a copy of *The Turner Diaries,* a far-right novel that describes the bombing of FBI headquarters, which, in turn, set off a white "Aryan" revolution.

The prosecution's case against McVeigh was based on the FBI's extensive investigation that involved 25,000 interviews and some 7,000 pounds of physical evidence. During the trial itself, the prosecution presented a streamlined case, calling only 137 witnesses over 18 days. Federal prosecutors alternated between producing witnesses who testified about the horrors of the bombing and those who were able to link McVeigh to the explosion. Among these were forensic experts and other specialists who identified the truck and the explosives and traced them to McVeigh.

In the months just prior to and during the McVeigh trial, a major controversy surrounding the FBI Crime Laboratory erupted. In response to allegations by a chemist employed in the explosives unit, Frederic Whitehurst, the Justice Department's inspector general (IG) conducted an 18-month investigation. The IG's report, released in April 1997, corroborated many of Whitehurst's criticisms of laboratory procedures: the mishandling of evidence, the role of non-scientists in the management of the lab, and the occasional altering of lab findings to support the prosecution. Moreover, some of the findings in the report pertained specifically to the Oklahoma case. An examiner in the explosives laboratory, David Williams, had based some of his conclusions about the bombing on speculation rather than scientific analysis, and some of his findings were "tilted" to incriminate the defendants. In response to the IG's report, FBI officials reassigned Williams and two other laboratory employees who had worked on the Oklahoma City bombing case. In order to contain criticism of the FBI lab by McVeigh's defense team, prosecutors deliberately chose not to call these FBI forensic experts as witnesses.

The most damaging testimony against McVeigh came from his sister, Jennifer, and Michael and Lori Fortier, two friends with whom he had spent time in the months preceding the bombing. Jennifer McVeigh reluctantly testified about a document agents found on her computer that her brother had written; a letter blaming ATF agents for the deaths at Waco and warning that they "will swing in the wind one day." Jennifer further testified that her brother had told her to expect "something big." The Fortiers testified that McVeigh had confided in them about his bombing plans, and

that Michael Fortier had accompanied McVeigh on a practice run to Oklahoma City that included planning where he would leave his getaway car.

McVeigh's defense team, which consisted of 14 court-appointed lawyers, offered an abbreviated defense, presenting 25 witnesses in three and a half days. The defense strategy initially had been to blame the bombing on a wider conspiracy of international or domestic terrorists, but because they had uncovered no evidence supporting this theory, Judge Matsch did not allow them to develop that line of inquiry during the trial. Defense lawyers attempted to discredit the Fortiers' testimony, arguing that their statements were self-serving since one (Lori) was given immunity and the other (Michael) pled guilty to reduced charges. McVeigh's lawyers also questioned the integrity of evidence handled by the FBI Crime Laboratory, and called former FBI chemist and whistleblower Frederic Whitehurst as a witness. Whitehurst, however, testified that he was not aware of any specific evidence in the Oklahoma City bombing case that had been contaminated. McVeigh never took the stand in his own defense.

On June 2, after four days of deliberation, the jury convicted McVeigh on all 11 counts of conspiracy and murder in the Oklahoma City bombing. Eight of the counts involved the murder of eight federal law enforcement agents who were killed by the explosion, the only killings that fell under federal law. Eleven days later, the same jury recommended the death sentence for McVeigh, a sentence (along with the verdict) that his lawyers have appealed. McVeigh's conviction, however, has not put to rest all questions about a wider conspiracy.

The trial of Terry Nichols, McVeigh's co-conspirator, began on November 3, 1997. During this trial, prosecutors presented a circumstantial case against Nichols, tying him to McVeigh, to the purchase of some of the bomb components, and to a robbery to help finance the bombing. Prosecutors were unable to place Nichols at the bombing site. Nichols's defense lawyers attempted to cast doubt on the government's case by presenting witnesses who either reported having seen other Ryder trucks in Kansas or having seen McVeigh with other men in Junction City. Following six days of deliberation, on December 23, 1997, Nichols was convicted but only on the conspiracy charge and the eight counts of involuntary manslaughter (but not on the murder charges). Nichols was acquitted of the two counts of using a weapon of mass destruction and destruction by explosives. In the sentencing phase, the jury was unable to reach a verdict (whether Nichols should receive the death penalty, life imprisonment, or imprisonment without parole), delegating responsibility to Federal Judge Matsch on the appropriate penalty of life imprisonment.

Other Bombing Cases

In addition to the two major terrorist bombings of the 1990s—of the World Trade Center in New York and the Murrah Federal Building in Oklahoma City—the FBI investigated a number of other bombings that resulted in loss of life. However, these other bombings were not investigated as terrorist acts, as there was no evidence or suggestion that they had been intended to achieve political or social objectives. One notable case involved the mail-bomb killing of a federal judge and a civil rights lawyer in the Southeast. Another celebrated case involved a serial bomber who, over an 18-year period, killed three people and injured 23 others. These two cases were code-named VANPAC and UNABOM.

The VANPAC Case

In December 1989, several pipe bombs were mailed to a number of locations in the Southeast, two of which exploded, fatally injuring their recipients. One killed a federal appeals court judge, Robert S. Vance, and seriously injured his wife, when Vance opened a package in his home in Birmingham, Alabama. A second package killed Robert E. Robinson, a prominent civil rights attorney and NAACP official in Savannah, Georgia. Two other mail bombs, moreover, were intercepted and disarmed before they reached their intended targets: the NAACP office in Jacksonville, Florida, and the 11th Circuit Court headquarters in Atlanta, Georgia. Apparently, the motivation for the bombing was racial, although no individual or group claimed responsibility. Alternatively, investigators suspected drug dealers. The FBI, however, identified another suspect: Walter Leroy Moody Jr.

More than 100 FBI agents were assigned to the case, along with investigators from the ATF and other law enforcement agencies. The FBI's investigative efforts were coordinated in the field by Inspector Larry A. Potts, while Louis J. Freeh was appointed by Justice Department officials as special prosecutor to present the case to the grand jury. (As such, VANPAC brought Freeh and Potts together, was an important reason Freeh promoted Potts to deputy director, and later proved embarrassing to the FBI director when questions were raised about Potts's role in the Ruby Ridge operation.)

Moody lived in Rex, Georgia (about 50 miles from Atlanta). In 1972, he had been convicted on a bombing charge. In that case, a bomb that was intended for an Atlanta auto dealer who had repossessed Moody's car exploded prematurely, injuring Moody's wife. Moody was convicted in this earlier case on the charge of possession of a pipe bomb and served three years in prison. More than a decade later, Moody appealed his 1972 conviction and, in 1988, his appeal was reviewed by the 11th Circuit Court. Robert Vance was one of the three judges on the panel who denied Moody's appeal.

As FBI agents pursued the investigation of the 1989 bombings, they learned that Moody had coached and bribed witnesses for his 1988 appeal. These criminal acts became a second line of investigation and prosecution. Investigators further focused on the unusual design of the 1989 bombs, which resembled Moody's 1972 bomb, leading them to suspect Moody. In November 1990, Moody was indicted for murder in the 1989 bombings.

Before Moody was tried for the murders of Vance and Robinson, federal prosecutors charged him with obstruction of justice for witness tampering in his 1988 appeal. Following a five-day trial in December 1990, he was convicted on all 13 counts. Moody was sentenced to 15 years in prison for that conviction; his wife, Susan, pled guilty to witness-tampering and agreed to cooperate with prosecutors.

Moody's trial for the 1989 bombings opened on June 4, 1991. Because of the pretrial publicity in the Southeast, the venue was changed to St. Paul, Minnesota. During the trial, Moody took the stand, against the advice of his court-appointed lawyers. Blaming the Ku Klux Klan for the bombings, Moody claimed to have been in Florida when the pipe bombs were mailed in Georgia. Prosecutors argued that Moody's frustration at being unable to overturn his 1972 conviction led him to commit the bombings. Moreover, FBI agents had intercepted, under a court-authorized electronic bug, a particularly self-incriminating conversation of Moody's in his jail cell while awaiting trial on the obstruction charges. Moody was recorded saying to himself: "Kill those damn judges . . . I shouldn't have done it, idiot." After a three-week trial, Moody was convicted on all 71 counts and, in August, he was sentenced to seven life terms plus 400 years with no possibility of parole.

Moody was subsequently indicted in Alabama on state murder charges for the mail bombing in Birmingham of Vance, and after four and a half years of delays, this case came to trial in October 1996. In November, the jury found him guilty, and he was subsequently sentenced to die in Alabama's electric chair.

The UNABOM Case

Between 1978 and 1996, a total of 16 bombings were attributed to a serial bomber who came to be known as the Unabomber, after the FBI's code name for the case. Some of the bombs were sent by mail, while others were left in public places, often at universities. The first four bombing incidents occurred in the Chicago area: two bombs were left at universities, another was detonated on an airplane, and the fourth was mailed to an airline executive. These bombings, which took place between May 1978 and June 1980, resulted in minor injuries to the unsuspecting persons opening the packages. Because the bomber's early targets were associated with universities and airlines, in 1980, the FBI code-named its investigation UNABOM.

In 1982, the targets of the bombs were on the West Coast, beginning when a bomb was found in Cory Hall at the University of California at Berkeley. The first death occurred in December 1985 when the owner of a computer rental store in Sacramento, California, picked up a device outside the entrance to his business. He was fatally injured when the package exploded. Another bombing incident occurred in 1987, followed by a lull until 1993 when the bombings resumed. In December 1994, a New York City advertising executive was killed when he opened a package mailed to his New Jersey home, and in April 1995, a California forestry official was killed when he opened a parcel mailed to his office. All together, the bombing incidents attributed to the Unabomber killed 3 and injured 23 in eight states.

Three federal agencies coordinated a joint investigation of this 18-year bombing spree: the FBI, the ATF, and the U.S. Postal Service. Although having interviewed thousands of people during the course of the investigation, investigators were able to identify few serious suspects. The explosions ensured that any physical evidence would be piecemeal, and hotline tips frequently sent agents in unproductive directions.

With the resumption of bombings in 1993, a special FBI task force was established in San Francisco, the number of agents assigned to the case increased, and a $1 million reward offered to anyone providing information that might lead to the apprehension and conviction of the Unabomber. Behavioral science experts were assigned to develop a new psychological profile of the bomber, the result of which became a source of controversy among investigators. An early profile had characterized the Unabomber as a white male in his mid-thirties to early forties, likely a blue-collar airline employee. In contrast, the new profile pointed to a somewhat older person, well educated, with an engineering or math background and an anti-technology bias.

In 1995, the UNABOM case took a critical turn. That summer, in a public letter, the Unabomber offered to stop the bombings if the *New York Times* and the *Washington Post* published a manifesto he had written, a 56-page essay on the ills of modern industrial society. This proposal created discord within the UNABOM Task Force. Some officials argued that publishing this document would simply reinforce the conduct of the serial bomber; others argued that publication could become a source of new clues. In September 1995, the *Times* and *Post* published the 35,000-word manifesto, "Industrial Society and Its Future."

The first break in this difficult investigation came in early 1996. David Kaczynski, who read the manifesto, became suspicious about similarities in the anti-technology,

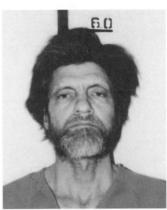

Exhibit 2.12   **Theodore Kaczynski,** *Courtesy Agence France Presse/ Corbis-Bettmann*

anti-modernity writings of the Unabomber and his brother's writings. Acting on David Kaczynski's behalf, a lawyer approached the FBI to report these suspicions. This tip ultimately led FBI agents to begin surveillance of David's brother, Theodore (Ted), who lived as a recluse in a remote cabin in Montana, 50 miles from Helena. Following several weeks' surveillance, FBI agents arrested Theodore J. Kaczynski on April 3, 1996, as the Unabomber suspect—although initially only charging him with possession of bomb components (see Exhibit 2.12).

FBI agents then conducted an intensive search of Kaczynski's primitive 10-foot by 12-foot cabin, which had neither electricity nor running water. The search uncovered additional evidence: chemicals, electrical wiring, manuals on making bombs, a partially completed pipe bomb, a diary, and a manual typewriter that agents believed had been used to type the manifesto. Kaczynski closely fit the 1993 FBI profile. He was 53 at the time of arrest and was well educated. He had graduated from Harvard in 1962, after which he attended graduate school at the University of Michigan, where he received a Ph.D. in mathematics. Kaczynski had then accepted an appointment as an assistant professor of mathematics at the University of California at Berkeley, where he remained for two years in the late 1960s before withdrawing into a hermit-like life-style.

On June 18, 1996, a federal grand jury in Sacramento indicted Kaczynski for the two California killings (in 1985 and 1995), and on October 1, 1996, he was indicted in Newark for the 1994 killing of an advertising executive. He pled not guilty to both indictments. Jury selection in the Sacramento trial began in November 1997 and lasted five weeks. Just as opening statements were to begin, Kaczynski (in a written statement to the judge) expressed dissatisfaction with his lawyers and their anticipated line of defense: that he is mentally ill, but not evil. Kaczynski, moreover, had refused to be examined by government psychiatrists. Following Kaczynski's last-minute request to defend himself, Federal Judge Garland Burrell Jr. ordered a psychiatric assessment of Kaczynski's competence. While the court-approved psychiatrist found him competent to stand trial, she raised questions about his mental health. No trial was held, however, because on January 21, 1998, Kaczynski accepted a plea bargain—to plead guilty of committing the bombings in return for a sentence of life imprisonment without parole.

Summary

Throughout the FBI's existence, its most notable cases have paralleled significant events in U.S. history. They also reflect the evolution of public concerns throughout this century. These concerns have been expressed in an ongoing series of "top" crime dangers (kidnappers, gangsters, the Mafia, serial murderers) and in public alarm over threats to the nation's security, whether foreign spies or violent domestic activists. Cases often reflected moralistic concerns, as in the Mann Act prosecutions, which are emblematic of the "white slavery" scare of that era.

The expansion in the FBI's role marked a shift away from an earlier view that saw law enforcement as primarily a local and state responsibility. The final breakdown in this view came in the 1960s with a public demand that the FBI investigate the serious problem of "law and order," symbolized by the assassinations of three prominent Americans: President John F. Kennedy, the Reverand Martin Luther King Jr., and Senator Robert F. Kennedy. The ensuing Watergate scandal further focused public attention on this problem, seen as encompassing corruption by public officials, as well.

The FBI's notable cases have left a rich legacy. Since 1908, FBI investigations have invariably intersected with major events and public issues in American life. Sometimes, FBI cases and investigations have simply responded to those events and issues; other times, the FBI has been a force in shaping key events and the national debate over crime and national security. Whatever the Bureau's role in public and political affairs, the cumulative effect of its diverse and celebrated cases tells an important story about the FBI's place in American society and about major changes that have influenced U.S. law enforcement during the twentieth century.

CONTROVERSIES AND ISSUES

Tony G. Poveda

Introduction

From its inception, the Federal Bureau of Investigation has been the subject of controversy. Concerns have most often centered on the Bureau's law enforcement and intelligence functions and have primarily involved questions about the limit and scope of FBI authority.

The history of FBI controversies can be divided into three main eras: (1) the early years, 1908–24, when the Bureau operated as a detective-style agency; (2) the period 1924–72, during the directorship of J. Edgar Hoover, when the FBI's investigative authority expanded and consolidated; and (3) the modern era, since 1972, characterized by the development and use of high-tech and undercover techniques.

This chapter will trace the main controversies in the Bureau's history chronologically and will focus on critical turning points in that history: those signaling new mandates, changes in authority, or the advent of new investigative techniques. Although these controversies typically centered on the disclosure of questionable FBI conduct, they also reflected wider public concerns in American society during this century. As such, the controversies surrounding the formation and evolution of the Federal Bureau of Investigation are best understood as an integral part of this larger history.

The Early Years (1908–24)

During the Bureau of Investigation's first two decades, controversies centered around the agency's formation; the uncertainty of its jurisdiction; its collaboration with private citizens and detective agencies; and its zealous pursuit of draft evaders, aliens, and political radicals.

Born in Controversy

On July 26, 1908, Attorney General Charles Bonaparte, with the authorization of President Theodore Roosevelt, organized a small investigative force within the Justice Department that, by the end of the year, consisted of 34 men. Bonaparte's successor, George W. Wickersham, officially named this investigative force the Bureau of Investigation the following year. It was not until 1935, however, that the Bureau acquired its present name, the Federal Bureau of Investigation (FBI) (see Table 1.2).

Creating an agency to conduct Justice Department investigations might not seem controversial. Bonaparte had acted, however, in the face of considerable congressional opposition. The attorney general had twice proposed to

congressional appropriations committees, in 1907 and 1908, that they fund a small departmental detective force. Both times, his proposal was rejected. Since its creation in 1870, the Justice Department had at times temporarily hired private detectives to conduct any needed investigations, but Congress terminated this practice in 1893 following the Homestead Strike, when private detectives from the Pinkerton Detective Agency shot striking workers. The Justice Department then turned to borrowing Secret Service agents from the Treasury Department whenever needing skilled investigators. However, this practice provoked controversy when Attorney General Bonaparte used Secret Service agents to investigate an Oregon land fraud case that led to the conviction of two congressmen from that state.

Resenting executive-branch investigations of members of Congress and seeing the potential for presidents to target their congressional critics for criminal inquiry, Congress attached a rider to the 1908 Justice Department appropriations prohibiting the Justice Department from borrowing Secret Service agents—effective July 1, 1908. This restriction produced a serious dilemma for Bonaparte: How was the Justice Department to conduct investigations without an investigative force of its own and without detectives from other agencies? His response was to create a detective force within the Justice Department by executive fiat and to finance it from the department's general funds.

Even before the Oregon land fraud case (and the resulting investigation of members of Congress) had triggered congressional opposition to a Justice Department investigative agency, members of Congress had articulated their fears that a federal police force might be abused by the president and attorney general. Congress worried that a federal investigative division could become a spy agency—not unlike that of czarist Russia—infringing on the rights and liberties of Americans. They also were concerned that such an agency, even if initially small and with limited powers, could grow rapidly. Some feared the kind of men who might be hired for such a police force, given the low esteem at the time for private detectives.

Attorney General Bonaparte sought to allay these concerns during the congressional session following the Bureau's creation, reassuring members of Congress on all of these points. To minimize abuses, he promised that only high-quality recruits would be sought for the new force and that he would monitor closely all agents and their activities. Investigations would be limited to violations of antitrust, interstate commerce, and miscellaneous other laws not already investigated by other federal agencies such as the

Secret Service and the Post Office. Although many in Congress remained dissatisfied, the Sixtieth Congress drew to a close in March 1909 without imposing any restrictions on the new agency—or attempting to abolish it. In fact, President Theodore Roosevelt had put the Bureau's congressional critics on the defensive, suggesting that their failure to authorize the new agency in the first place had protected criminals. Thus, if Congress had considered abolishing the Bureau in the year following its establishment, legislators would have been vulnerable to criticism; any restrictions on the new-found agency could be depicted as aiding criminals, and abolition could also have been dismissed as self-serving—to cover up corruption in Congress's ranks.

The original controversy over the Bureau's origins was thus closely linked to conflicts between the executive and legislative branches, at a time when Congress was committed to containing presidential power. President Roosevelt had fashioned himself the public defender of the nation's natural resources, and Congress's unwillingness to authorize an investigative force to pursue land frauds was a clear threat to the responsible exercise of executive power. Born in the midst of this political struggle between Congress and the president, the newly created national police force soon confronted other criticisms involving the scope and possible misuse of its power.

Mann Act Excesses

A moral panic, sometimes referred to as the "white slave scare," erupted in the early 1900s, reflecting public fears that girls and women from farms and small towns were being transported to the larger cities, and to other states, for purposes of prostitution. Support mounted for federal intervention, and in 1910, Congress passed the White Slave Traffic Act, more commonly known as the Mann Act (after its principal sponsor, Congressman James Robert Mann of Illinois). The Mann Act, which outlawed the interstate transport of women for immoral purposes, had as its chief aim the control of organized or commercialized prostitution (see Exhibit 3.1).

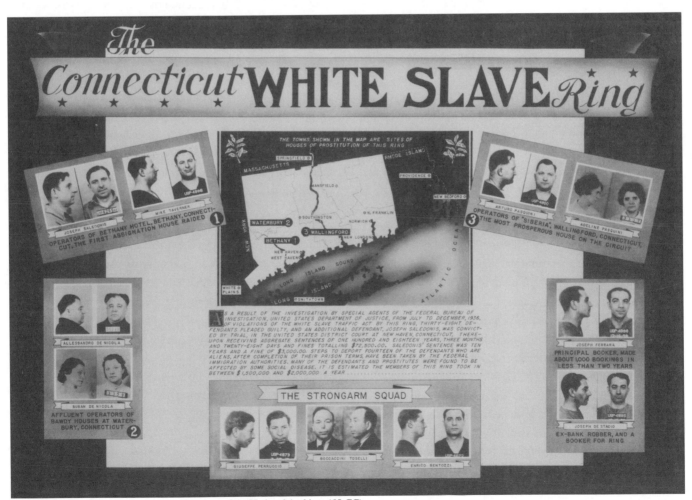

Exhibit 3.1   **Mann Act Enforcement,** *Courtesy of the National Archives (65-CC)*

Passage of the Mann Act had the immediate result of expanding the Bureau of Investigation's authority. By passing the new legislation, Congress had acknowledged the need for a federal policing role to supplement state and local law enforcement. Many states' rights conservatives opposed this change, maintaining that prostitution and vice should remain state responsibilities, but moral and progressive reformers prevailed. The Mann Act also led to Bureau agents being assigned to work outside of Washington, D.C. By 1914, the number of agents had grown to 122. Transformed into a truly national agency, Bureau agents were thereafter stationed around the country.

Before the Mann Act, the prosecution of prostitution, like the vast majority of crime, had been a local responsibility. The justification for a federal role in prosecuting this crime was based on the Constitution's commerce clause, which enabled Congress to enact laws regulating interstate commerce. Contending that this clause could be interpreted to include interstate prostitution, Congress expanded federal investigative responsibilities accordingly. The Supreme Court upheld this interpretation when ruling in cases in 1913 and 1917. This clause later formed the basis for extending federal police powers to other areas of "interstate commerce": auto theft (1919), kidnapping (1932), and bank robbery (1934).

In Mann Act investigations, Bureau agents surveyed postmasters and chiefs of police throughout the country to determine which communities had houses of prostitution. In each city where brothels were located, Bureau agents, along with a local lawyer and police officer, personally visited the establishment to conduct a census of the residents. They inquired as to their identities and personal histories (watching for out-of-state arrivals), the names of their customers, and the owners of the brothel. The madams of these establishments often became important sources of information for other Bureau investigations; for example, on the whereabouts of fugitives. This national vice survey uncovered massive amounts of information unrelated to commercial prostitution, including information about local public corruption and the private affairs of prominent customers. However, much of this information, including discoveries about local criminal activity, fell outside the Bureau's jurisdiction; nonetheless, it became incorporated into the Bureau's permanent records system.

Congress had intended for the Bureau of Investigation to prosecute organized prostitution that involved the interstate transportation of prostitutes, but the Bureau began also to use the Mann Act to police noncommercial, personal immorality. Bureau agents were soon arresting unmarried couples who had crossed state lines and had sexual relations, even when no monetary transaction was involved (see pages 46–47).

During the 1930s, Bureau agents conducted highly publicized raids of vice establishments in cities across the country—in Atlantic City, Philadelphia, Baltimore, Chicago, Miami, and Trenton, New Jersey—during which hundreds of customers were arrested, including prominent politicians and businessmen. Although they received generally favorable press coverage, the raids in Baltimore (in 1937) and Miami (in 1940) sparked criticism. The Miami raid came a few weeks after congressional testimony by Bureau Director J. Edgar Hoover requesting additional appropriations and claiming that the FBI lacked the resources to handle national defense cases. Citing this testimony, some newspapers questioned the FBI director's priorities, editorializing that treason and espionage should be given priority over vice. Conservatives were particularly concerned about the expansion of the FBI's federal powers under the Roosevelt New Deal, and complained that vice enforcement should be a local responsibility. The Bureau's vice raids were curtailed after 1940 and this focus became a less prominent part of operations.

The Mann Act, nonetheless, had expanded federal law enforcement powers, a change that remained controversial until the 1940s, as conservatives objected to federal involvement in what they felt should be a local matter, and liberals feared that the Bureau might use this authority to monitor labor unions and political dissent.

"Slacker" Raids of 1918

Soon after United States entry into World War I on April 6, 1917, Congress passed the Selective Service Act, requiring men between the ages of 21 and 30 (whether resident alien or citizen) to register for military service. Those eligible for the draft had to register with local draft boards by June 5. Enoch Crowder, judge advocate general in the War Department and the Army's top legal officer, was the main architect of the conscription plan. Following the law's enactment in May 1917, Crowder became provost marshal general in charge of selective service. To assist Crowder in enforcing the Selective Service Act, Attorney General Thomas W. Gregory directed the Bureau of Investigation, then under Chief A. Bruce Bielaski, to investigate those suspected of noncompliance (the so-called "slackers"). The Bureau's pursuit of draft evaders during the war, especially indiscriminately rounding up young men in major cities across the country during so-called slacker raids, soon provoked controversy over the legality of many of the arrests, the detention of innocent civilians, and the role of the American Protective League (APL).

In July 1917, Bielaski ordered Bureau agents to identify men who had failed to register for military service. At that time, it was not known how many draft evaders existed or who they were, and citizens were encouraged to assist the Bureau in this effort. Crowder later instituted a bounty-hunting policy, offering a $50 reward to anyone who turned in Army deserters, which included young men who had been drafted but failed to report, as well as those who had not registered in the first place.

At the time, the Bureau had developed a relationship with one of the more prominent volunteer-vigilante organizations that sprung up during the war, the APL. Self-described patriots, APL members, primarily businessmen and professionals who were not of draft age, volunteered to assist their country on the home front. APL's founder, Albert M. Briggs, a Chicago advertising executive, persuaded Bielaski that the APL could assist with wartime activities, and Bielaski and Briggs reached an understanding whereby the APL became an auxiliary to the Bureau. This quasi-official status gave the APL new standing, and its numbers grew rapidly, by the end of 1918 reaching approximately 250,000. In contrast, at the beginning of the war, the Bureau had 265 agents (and 305 support staff).

As the United States mobilized for war, the slacker problem became more critical, and some estimated the number of draft evaders by January 1918 to be approximately 350,000. In the spring and summer of 1918, Crowder (as head of the Selective Service) pressured the Justice Department to identify and arrest these draft dodgers. Adopting a new strategy in late March, the Bureau and its APL auxiliary staged the first citywide raid to round up slackers in Minneapolis. Although legal questions were raised concerning the power of APL members to make arrests, the raid's apparent success in locating slackers overshadowed these concerns. Dragnet raids were soon conducted in many other cities around the country, including Cleveland, Detroit, Philadelphia, San Francisco, Birmingham, Dayton, and St. Louis, leading to the identification of approximately 20,000 slackers. The methods employed were the same: draft-age men were stopped in various public locations—parks, bars, pool rooms, dance halls, and bus stops—and held by Bureau agents or APL members until

they could produce evidence of their draft status. If they did not possess draft cards, they were detained until they could produce them; otherwise, they were arrested as slackers.

As the need for military personnel continued to mount, only New York City had not been raided. This changed on September 3, 1918. On that day, 35 Bureau agents, 2,000 APL volunteers, and several hundred police officers and military personnel confronted young men in public places throughout the metropolitan area. Those who could not produce either draft cards or birth certificates proving they were not of draft age were arrested, some at the point of a bayonct, and then jailed. Approximately 75,000 men were detained after three days of raids. It was not immediately known how many of these detainees were actually draft evaders, but information later leaked to the press revealed that of every 200 detainees, only 1 proved to be a slacker. Moreover, in their zeal, agents rounded up far more suspects than could reasonably be accommodated, and many of those detained went without food and sanitary facilities for a day or two. Some detainees were not even of draft age or physically fit, including one 75-year-old man with crutches.

Unlike the earlier slacker raids, the New York City raid was immediately criticized. New York newspapers variously characterized the raids as "illegal" and "inexcusable"; some referred to the federal government's actions as "mob rule." Some senators criticized the tactic of rounding up large numbers of innocent civilians. Others challenged the legality of the arrests and detention without warrant or probable cause. And still others questioned whether APL members and military personnel could legally make arrests. A few senators did defend the raids, however, arguing that the inconvenience of some was necessary to enforce the conscription law.

President Woodrow Wilson responded to the Senate criticisms by requesting that Attorney General Gregory investigate the allegations. Gregory, in turn, designated Assistant Attorney General John Lord O'Brian, head of the War Emergency Division, to conduct this inquiry. O'Brian completed his report within two days. In publicly accepting responsibility for the raids, Attorney General Gregory acknowledged that some actions had been illegal and violated his instructions, specifically the use of APL members and military personnel to arrest suspects. Although Gregory admitted that the APL had no official authority, the Justice Department continued to use APL members during slacker raids throughout September 1918, most notably in a three-day raid in the state of Washington.

Collaboration with the APL

The Bureau's collaboration with the APL during World War I marked one of its more controversial actions. For, in addition to assisting Bureau agents during the slacker raids from April to September 1918, APL members provided their Bureau contacts with information they had gathered on those they suspected of being foreign agents and spies operating in the United States, and also on persons (especially aliens and dissenters) whom they considered potentially disloyal to the federal government or possibly a threat to industrial facilities.

This collaboration both predated and continued after the slacker raids. This initiative dated from February 1917, when Albert M. Briggs, founder of the APL, approached the head of the Bureau's Chicago office, Hinton Clabaugh, to offer the APL's assistance to Bureau agents investigating German aliens and spies by acting as chauffeurs. Since the Chicago office had no cars at the time, and had a staff of only 15 agents in the entire state of Illinois, Clabaugh readily accepted this offer. About a month later, Briggs offered to donate 75 cars for the Bureau's use during wartime investigations. Since this proposal had implications beyond the Chicago office, Clabaugh arranged a meeting in Washington, D.C., between Briggs and Bureau Chief Bielaski. At this meeting, Bielaski accepted the vehicles. Briggs, moreover, proposed that his nationwide organization of volunteers—the APL—assist the Bureau's wartime investigations by supplying information on the suspicious activities of aliens, dissenters, and possible spies. Bielaski accepted this proposal, as well.

Following Congress's declaration of war in April 1917, in the atmosphere of mounting fear of espionage and sabotage, Bureau officials solidified their relationship with the APL. When the initial hysteria over the threat of German espionage and sabotage never materialized (no spies were prosecuted during World War I), the APL focused instead on radical labor activities, believing they threatened the security of industrial facilities and could harm the war effort. A principal target was the Industrial Workers of the World (IWW)—the "Wobblies"—owing to the IWW's labor-organizing activities, its avowed anarchism and denunciations of imperial capitalists, and its opposition to the war. APL members infiltrated and disrupted IWW meetings and in general attempted to undermine this radical labor group.

The culmination of this attempted suppression were raids Bureau agents conducted at the IWW's Chicago headquarters in September 1917 and at more than 60 regional IWW offices across the country. Bureau agents and APL members seized correspondence, organization minutes, financial records, membership lists, pamphlets, and any other materials that could be used in the prosecution of the IWW. Some 166 IWW members were subsequently indicted in Chicago on various criminal charges, including conspiring to oppose by force the execution of the laws of the United States and to obstruct prosecution of the war.

By the beginning of 1918, the American Protective League, moreover, had developed an elaborate organizational structure with the Chicago APL chapter serving as the prototype for other cities. The APL's organizational chart provided for an extensive intelligence section with divisions in insurance, finance, hotels, public utilities, transportation, and various industries. A large investigation section was also established to carry out any specific Bureau requests. The APL, in fact, succeeded in obtaining information on "suspicious" persons from all kinds of records: bank, phone company, real estate, medical, and legal. APL investigators questioned friends and neighbors of suspects, and, on occasion, broke into homes and offices.

Nonetheless, until the New York City slacker raids in September 1918, the APL's activities had not generated controversy. Even then, criticism centered on the lack of discipline among rank-and-file APL members and the national organization's poor control of local chapters. Despite the APL's resort to illegal arrests and harassment of dissidents and enemy aliens, Bureau officials continued to use the organization as an auxiliary until the end of the war. Their concern focused on the threat posed by radicals and enemy aliens, especially German Americans. As a result, several thousand enemy aliens were interned for the duration of the war. This alarm about the German threat also extended to dissident groups who criticized the war or the Wilson administration's policies. Indeed, the Socialist Party leader, perennial presidential candidate Eugene Debs, was arrested and convicted for delivering an antiwar speech in June 1918 in Dayton, Ohio. Debs's arrest was one of the most celebrated Espionage Act cases of this period. Shortly after the signing of the armistice in November 1918, Bureau chief Bielaski reduced Bureau personnel to the prewar level, and both Bielaski and Attorney General Gregory called for the dissolution of the Bureau's special relationship with the APL by the end of the year. The termination of World War I formally brought to an end the Bureau's association with the APL.

Through its wartime APL liaison program, the Bureau had acquired an extensive national spy apparatus and had substantially increased its ability to investigate wartime statutes, such as the Selective Service and Espionage Acts. This questionable association with a volunteer-vigilante group had, in part, been prompted by Congress's limited funding of the Bureau, even during the war period. States' rights conservatives remained concerned about a national police force—and feared that even a temporary wartime expansion of the Bureau might become permanent. Ironically, this concern—that an enlarged Bureau might abuse its authority—led to excesses resulting from the Bureau's reliance on the assistance of civilian volunteers.

These concerns were compounded by the bureaucratic rivalries between civilian and military agencies that shared responsibility for maintaining wartime security. The Treasury Department (Secret Service), the War and Navy Departments (the Military Intelligence Division and the Office of Naval Intelligence), and the Justice Department (Bureau of Investigation) were all involved in monitoring suspected spies and radicals during the war years. In addition, wartime anxieties created a public relations problem—federal officials felt compelled to convince the public that all was under control on the home front. In this context, the Wilson administration preferred the Justice Department's greater use of civilian auxiliaries than relying on military forces to handle domestic security.

Antiradical Raids of 1919–20

In the months following the end of World War I, the wartime alarm over German spies and slackers was replaced by a new threat: Reds (communists), alien anarchists, and radical workers who might launch a revolution. These fears precipitated what came to be known as the Red Scare of 1919–20. The culmination of the Red Scare was the Palmer Raids of January 1920, when Bureau agents arrested and detained several thousand resident aliens and citizens nationwide, ostensibly for the purpose of enforcing the 1918 immigration law. The excesses employed in conducting the Palmer Raids, as in the case of the wartime slacker raids, plunged the Justice Department and the Bureau of Investigation into controversy. This controversy centered on the legality and brutality of the Bureau's conduct during these raids, and on

the Justice Department's seeming purpose to contain individuals and organizations because of their adherence to radical political beliefs.

A number of converging events fueled the postwar Red Scare. These included a wartime concern over pro-German influences on enemy aliens, the outbreak of the Bolshevik Revolution in Russia in November 1917 (and fear that it might spread to other European nations and the United States), and the outbreak in 1919 of over 3,600 labor strikes in the United States, involving 4 million workers. The 1919 strikes, in particular, heightened popular concerns because of their disruption of the economy. Two of the most dramatic resulted in national labor stoppages in basic industries, such as steel and coal; a general strike in Seattle in January 1919, which began with shipyard workers and spread, closing schools, public transportation, and various businesses; and a strike by the Boston police in September 1919, resulting in outbreaks of vandalism and rioting in parts of the city. The press was quick to link these strikes to Bolshevism and to raise the prospect of an impending revolution.

Furthermore, in late April 1919, a mail bomb delivered to the Atlanta home of U.S. Senator Thomas Hardwick blew off the hands of a servant. In the ensuing days, postal inspectors in New York City discovered over 30 bomb packages that were addressed to various public figures, including prominent political officials (Postmaster General Albert Burleson, Secretary of Labor William Wilson, and Attorney General A. Mitchell Palmer) and business leaders (John D. Rockefeller and J. P. Morgan). Newspapers and Justice Department officials were quick to blame anarchists and radical revolutionaries for these bomb plots. Then, on the night of June 2, a bomb exploded at the front door of Attorney General Palmer's home in Washington, D.C., killing the bomber (who apparently had stumbled). That same night, explosions occurred in eight other cities. None of these bombings were ever solved, but anarchist leaflets were found outside Palmer's residence.

The June 2 bombings provoked Attorney General Palmer to mobilize the Justice Department against radicals. During a top-level strategy meeting two weeks later, Justice Department officials decided to round up and deport alien radicals. Such raids would heighten public concerns about the radical threat and could create pressure leading to the passage of a peacetime sedition law—legislation that would enable the Justice Department to continue to monitor and prosecute radical activists. To implement this dual strategy, on August 1, 1919, Palmer established a new unit within the

Justice Department, the Radical Division (renamed the General Intelligence Division, the GID, in 1920), and appointed J. Edgar Hoover to head it. By January 1920, about one-third of the Bureau's investigative personnel was involved in antiradical matters.

GID Director Hoover quickly began collecting the literature of radical groups—their books, newspapers, periodicals, pamphlets, and speeches—to document their beliefs and identify their leaders and members. He created a card index system to list every identified radical. In the first three months, files were established on some 60,000 individuals; by 1920, more than 200,000 persons and organizations were included in the records.

These lists served no prosecutive purpose. Indeed, with the end of the war, the sole legal authority to act against "radicals" rested on the provision of the Immigration Act of 1918 that authorized the deportation of aliens who believed in anarchism or revolutionary change, or who were members of organizations advocating those principles. Citizen radicals, however, were exempt from arrest—unless a peacetime sedition statute were to be enacted.

The 1918 immigration statute might have been a thin reed, but it nonetheless underpinned the antiradical strategy crafted by Justice and Bureau of Investigation officials in 1919–20. In their resultant planning of dragnet raids, Justice and Bureau officials operated under severe legal limitations. Under the immigration laws, deportation proceedings were subject to administrative safeguards that protected the rights of any deportee. Furthermore, deportation hearings and arrests fell within the jurisdiction of the Immigration Bureau in the Department of Labor—not Palmer's Justice Department. Justice and Labor Department bureaucrats, nonetheless, effected a secret arrangement whereby the Justice Department would supply the names of alien radicals to the Labor Department, which would then issue arrest warrants. Justice personnel would then arrest the designated deportees, while Labor would handle the deportation hearings.

Two raids were eventually conducted. The first targeted the Union of Russian Workers (URW), an organization composed of Russian immigrants; its original constitution contained clauses advocating revolutionary change. GID Director Hoover provided the names of 600 URW members to the Immigration Bureau, which issued arrest warrants. On the night of November 7, 1919, Bureau agents—with the assistance of local police—raided URW meeting places in 12 cities. Everyone present at these sites was detained,

whether alien or citizen, member or visitor. In some cases, suspects were arrested in their homes, and anything that might be construed as evidence was seized. Famed anarchists Emma Goldman and Alexander Berkman were concurrently arrested for possible deportation.

Of the 250 arrestees, only 39 were finally held. Simultaneously, New York City police raided 73 radical centers, arresting 500 individuals (turning over any alien arrestees to federal authorities). Not all were ordered deported. On December 21, 1919, a former Army ship, renamed the *Buford,* sailed from New York harbor, transporting 249 Russian aliens back to their homeland. These included 184 arrested during the November 7 raids, along with Goldman and Berkman. The URW raid encountered no controversy, and initial newspaper coverage praised the deportations, designating the *Buford* "the Soviet Ark" and congratulating Attorney General Palmer for his actions against radicals.

GID Director Hoover, however, had become concerned during the execution of the November 7 raids about Rule 22 of the Immigration Bureau regulations governing deportation proceedings. This rule outlined the rights of aliens during such proceedings, and in particular guaranteed them the right to legal counsel. Hoover convinced Commissioner of Immigration Anthony Caminetti of the need to change Rule 22 prior to initiating the more massive raids scheduled for January 1920, emphasizing that the presence of lawyers during deportation hearings would make it difficult, if not impossible, to secure confessions from the detainees of their belief in anarchism or revolution. Commissioner Caminetti, in turn, persuaded John Abercrombie, who had become acting secretary of labor due to Labor Secretary Wilson's illness, to revise this rule.

On December 27, Abercrombie signed 3,000 arrest warrants, which were to be served during the upcoming raids, and Bureau assistant director Frank Burke informed agents in the field of the date for the raid. The raids were to be conducted nationwide, in 33 cities in 23 states, with simultaneous arrests during the night of January 2, between 7 p.m. and 7 a.m. Because the Bureau's total personnel of 579 agents was insufficient to execute the raids, assistance was sought from local police and from some veterans of the American Protective League. The Bureau had so successfully infiltrated the targeted organizations (the Communist Party and the Communist Labor Party) that its undercover agents and informants managed to arrange for the two organizations to both hold nighttime meetings on that date, to ensure the maximum number of arrests. Throughout the night, individuals were arrested at the meeting halls of the two organizations, at small shops and businesses operated by suspected radicals, at restaurants and recreation rooms frequented by radicals, and at some homes. All present were indiscriminately rounded up, whether aliens or citizens. Approximately 10,000 persons were arrested nationwide; of these, 6,500 were immediately released (primarily citizens not subject to deportation), with the remaining 3,500 held over for deportation hearings. Ultimately, only 556 were deported.

Initially, the press praised the raids; the *New York Times* front-page headline proclaimed that revolution had been averted, while the *Washington Post* argued, "There is no time for hairsplitting over infringements of liberty." Bureau Chief William Flynn reinforced this view, boasting that the raids had avoided a revolutionary uprising. As details of the raids surfaced, however, praise gave way to criticism. News stories soon reported the rough treatment of detainees and that many had been arrested without warrants. Other stories told how the searches accompanying the arrests often involved ransacking premises and seizing anything that might be regarded as evidence, and that many detainees were held for two or three weeks before being allowed to see their families or lawyers.

The Bureau's conduct of the raids encountered its first serious challenge from Assistant Labor Secretary Louis F. Post, who became acting secretary in March 1920 when Labor Secretary Wilson again became ill. A few weeks earlier, in late January, Secretary Wilson—having learned of Abercrombie's revision of Rule 22 in his absence—restored the previous requirement of the right to counsel during deportation hearings. This reinstatement of Rule 22 became significant when Post began reviewing deportation cases in March and April. He canceled hundreds of arrest warrants and refused to allow evidence to be admitted during the deportation hearings if it had been obtained without the alien having benefit of counsel. Post also ruled that membership in one of the two communist parties was not, in itself, a sufficient basis for deportation. Immigration officials would have to show that each individual alien had voluntarily become a member and was aware of the organization's purposes. By mid-April, Post had canceled about 70 percent of the deportation warrants under consideration.

Hoover and Palmer immediately and harshly criticized Acting Labor Secretary Post's actions, linking him to radical organizations. In response, in late April 1920, a House Rules Subcommittee initiated impeachment hearings against Post, ostensibly because his actions undermined the nation's security by freeing dangerous aliens. The subcommittee's initial inquiry found no basis for impeachment, although it did recommend that the House censure Post. Post responded by requesting the opportunity to appear before the subcommittee, whereupon he offered an impressive defense of his actions and successfully called the conduct of Hoover and Palmer into question. Although the subcommittee took no formal position, the hearings marked a turning point in the tide of public opinion against the Justice Department and the Red Scare.

Furthermore, concurrent with Post's impeachment defense, a private citizen group, the National Popular Government League (NPGL), initiated an inquiry into the Palmer Raids and, on May 28, 1920, published a 67-page pamphlet, *Report Upon the Illegal Practices of the United States Department of Justice.* This study, signed by 12 of the most distinguished lawyers of the day (including Felix Frankfurter, Roscoe Pound, Zechariah Chafee, and Ernst Freund), documented a host of abuses: warrantless arrests of citizens and aliens, lengthy detention in inadequate facilities, and the use of coerced confessions and illegal searches and seizures. The report also questioned Palmer's use of the attorney general's office to propagandize against radicals and to intercede in matters not related to the Justice Department's jurisdiction (enforcement of immigration laws being a Labor Department responsibility).

Attorney General Palmer and GID Director Hoover concurrently attempted to defend their actions in several forums: at a federal court habeas corpus hearing in Boston in April 1920 (which examined the arrest and detention of 18 radicals during the January raids), before the House Rules Subcommittee in June 1920, and before the Senate Judiciary Committee, which held hearings from January 19 to March 3, 1921. Although Hoover did not testify in the Boston case, he assisted the prosecution, and a number of Bureau agents were called upon to testify. Judge George Anderson, outraged at the government's misconduct and concerned that Bureau undercover agents and informants had acted as agents provocateurs, released the 18 defendants. At the House Rules Subcommittee hearings on June 1 and 2, Palmer, closely assisted by Hoover, sought to rebut the accusations that the Justice Department had acted illegally, as detailed in Post's earlier testimony and the NPGL report. His presentation emphasized the threat of Bolshevism and communists in the United States and defended the Justice

Department's role in curbing this menace. Unimpressed by Palmer's testimony, the subcommittee concluded its hearings without censuring anyone.

In its later hearings of January 1921, the Senate Judiciary Committee invited the testimony of Palmer and many of the same lawyers who had signed the NPGL report. Palmer's defense was a combination of denials, stone-walling, and buck-passing. He questioned the character and integrity of the lawyers who were his main accusers, in some instances suggesting that they, too, were radicals or associates of radicals. Although the Judiciary Committee never released its report, Senator Thomas Walsh of Montana, who had demanded the hearings, characterized the raids as "the lawless acts of a mob."

The controversy over the Justice Department's (and Bureau of Investigation's) conduct in the Palmer Raids involved questions of how to safeguard security and liberty in times of crisis without endangering democratic principles. Can the rule of law be maintained during periods of domestic turmoil and insecurity? Can the pursuit of law violators justify not obtaining warrants for arrests and searches, securing coerced confessions, holding persons in illegal detention, and overlooking procedural safeguards, such as the right to counsel and bail? Should federal officials monitor American citizens and resident aliens because of their beliefs and associations?

Teapot Dome and Its Aftermath

During the early 1920s, Bureau of Investigation and Justice Department operations became closely linked with the widespread corruption of the administration of President Warren G. Harding. The unraveling Teapot Dome scandal of 1923 and 1924 raised questions of whether the attorney general had failed to investigate and prosecute official corruption. Additional revelations documented misuse of the Bureau to retaliate against the administration's congressional critics. The conclusion to this series of events came with the forced resignation in April 1924 of Attorney General Harry M. Daugherty and his successor's firing of Bureau Director William J. Burns. By that time, the Bureau's reputation had reached the low point of its 16-year history, and the Justice Department had come to be known as the "Department of Easy Virtue." The incoming attorney general, Harlan F. Stone, responded by instituting new rules intended to preclude future abuses.

The Teapot Dome scandal began with allegations that two oilmen, Harry Sinclair of Mammoth Oil and Edward Doheny of Pan American Petroleum, had bribed Secretary of the Interior Albert B. Fall to obtain valuable oil reserves without competitive bidding. As secretary of the interior, Fall had stewardship over the nation's natural resources. These protected resources included three oil reserves that had been set aside during World War I for the emergency needs of the Navy. In 1921, Fall secretly leased two of these reserves to Sinclair and Doheny, one at Teapot Dome, Wyoming, the other at Elk Hills, California. Subsequently, it was learned that Fall had received $100,000 in exchange for granting these leases. Indicted and convicted of bribery (in 1929; his trial was delayed owing to his illness), Fall was sentenced to one year in prison. Although Sinclair and Doheny were also indicted, neither was convicted. Nonetheless, a 1927 Supreme Court decision annulled as illegal the leasing of the oil reserves at Teapot Dome and Elk Hills.

The corruption surrounding the secret oil leases had first been exposed during two Senate inquiries. Both were headed by Montana Democrats, one by Thomas J. Walsh and the other by Burton K. Wheeler. The hearings initiated by Walsh began in October 1923 and focused on the oil leases; they were low-keyed but systematic in uncovering damning evidence about the practices of the Harding administration. In January 1924, Wheeler conducted follow-up hearings that publicized additional allegations regarding Attorney General Daugherty's conduct. These hearings were highlighted by the dramatic testimony of flamboyant witnesses like Gaston Means, who claimed to have been recruited to spy on members of Congress. Means, a "special employee" for the Justice Department, testified that he had volunteered to bomb Daugherty's home to create another Red Scare, but that Daugherty had declined the offer. Much of the sensational testimony in the hearing was unverifiable.

While the initial controversy centered on Secretary of the Interior Fall's questionable leasing of Teapot Dome and Elk Hills, attention soon shifted to the conduct of Attorney General Daugherty and the Justice Department's failure to investigate Fall's approval of the oil leasing arrangement. The senators further questioned why the department had not investigated and prosecuted other frauds, notably the sale of war materials. The implication of all these questions was that politics and business interests had improperly shaped the Justice Department investigations and prosecutions. Daugherty refused to testify during the Senate hearings or to release Justice Department records.

Before the Senate inquiry took place, Attorney General Daugherty had set out to discredit the two senators slated to head the hearings. Bureau Director William Burns was authorized to send agents to Montana to investigate them, and Bureau agents in Washington, D.C., closely monitored the senators' offices, homes, and families—tapped their phones, intercepted their mail, and broke into their homes and offices. Agents even tried to lure Senator Wheeler into a compromising situation with a woman. The underlying purpose was to defame the two senators and thereby cast doubt on their credibility in the hearings.

Using Bureau resources for this politically driven investigation, Justice Department attorneys were able to obtain sufficiently damaging information about Senator Wheeler to convince a Montana grand jury to indict the senator on charges of a wartime conflict of interest. In the ensuing trial, which began in March 1924, Wheeler was acquitted; his Montana colleague, Senator Walsh, acted as his defense counsel. During this trial, two key witnesses admitted that they had perjured themselves, and other evidence that Walsh presented showed that the entire case had been manufactured by Daugherty to discredit Wheeler and thereby to undermine his critical inquiry into the Justice Department.

Finally—with the Justice Department under a cloud of suspicion—President Calvin Coolidge, who had become president following Harding's death in August 1923, dismissed Attorney General Daugherty (on March 28, 1924), replacing him on April 8, 1924, with Harlan F. Stone, a former dean of the Columbia Law School. Daugherty was subsequently tried twice on charges of conspiracy to defraud the U.S. government. Both trials resulted in hung juries and the charges were eventually dismissed.

About a month after assuming office, Attorney General Stone fired Bureau Director Burns. In testimony during the Senate hearings, Burns had admitted to a variety of questionable acts, including sending agents to Montana to investigate Wheeler. Burns was never charged with any crimes, but two of his subordinates were convicted of jury tampering, and Gaston Means, the Justice Department's most notorious operative, was convicted on larceny and conspiracy charges and was sentenced to two years in prison.

The Teapot Dome scandal exposed both a Justice Department improperly influenced by political and business interests and a Bureau of Investigation that had been misused for political purposes. Gaston Means, Burns's associate from their days of monitoring antiwar and radical activities during World War I, became a symbol of the corruption of the Daugherty Justice Department and the Bureau under Burns. Burns had recruited Means to the Bureau when appointed director in August 1921, using him for "special assignments," which included spying on Democratic members of Congress. Means also became notorious for having misused his Bureau position to sell information from Bureau files and to "fix" cases.

The man whom Attorney General Stone appointed on May 10, 1924, as the new acting director of the Bureau, J. Edgar Hoover, had served as assistant director under Burns and had headed the General Intelligence Division (GID) during the controversial Palmer era. Hoover's mandate was to divorce Bureau operations from politics and to select and promote agents solely on the basis of merit. Hoover thereupon confronted an enduring dilemma for both the Bureau and the Justice Department: How can politics and improper influence be kept out of the decision-making process that guides investigations and prosecutions when both the attorney general and the Bureau director are political appointees, subject to removal by the president?

The Hoover Years (1924–72)

During the Hoover era, the most contentious issues centered on the FBI's surveillance of citizens involved in radical political activities and the targeting of allegedly "subversive" groups. Another source of controversy involved the political misuse of the FBI by Hoover and various presidents—from Franklin Roosevelt to Richard Nixon. Moreover, dating from 1924, FBI Director Hoover compiled and maintained secretly in his office dossiers on public officials. Disclosures of these practices in the mid-1970s provoked a controversial debate about FBI power.

The Gangster Era and the New Federalism

One of the underlying controversies inherent in the creation of a federal investigative agency centered on the role of a national police force in American life. From the Bureau's inception in 1908, Congressional critics had warned of the dangers of such a force: it could develop into a national spy agency; it could be misused for political purposes; and, once established, it could grow rapidly in size.

Prior to the 1930s, the Bureau of Investigation's mandate had been uncertain and limited. Although Congress had expanded the Bureau's responsibilities by enacting statutes—such as the Mann Act (organized vice and prostitution), the Espionage Act, the Selective Service Act, and the Dyer Act (interstate auto theft)—it had also been careful to limit the Bureau's role and appropriations. Except for the Espionage and Selective Service Acts (which involved federal crimes), the commerce clause of the Constitution provided the sole basis for a federal law enforcement role in the area of interstate commerce. Except for this constitutional provision, the prosecution of crime remained a local and state responsibility.

This long-standing division between local and federal responsibilities in crime control began to change during the early 1930s. President Franklin D. Roosevelt's New Deal initiated a major shift in the federal government's involvement in addressing the nation's economic problems. Formerly, private businesses and local charities were responsible for promoting economic recovery and relief, but New Deal social and economic policies gave the federal government a central role. The Roosevelt administration rejected the principle that the best government is that which governs least. This change also extended to crime. During the Great Depression of the 1930s, the federal government began to assume a leading role in dealing with the serious threat of gangsters.

This expanded federal role in crime-fighting became the subject of heated controversy. Those who advocated expanding federal law enforcement authority argued that Prohibition had created crime gangs that operated on an interstate basis, and that the automobile and airplane enabled criminals to operate beyond the range of local police. In addition, many criticized local police and sheriffs as often incompetent, corrupt, or both. Proponents of this new federalism included powerful business groups and public officials who, during the 1920s, had formed the National Crime Commission (NCC). They endorsed federal laws to protect their interests in the national arena and urged passage of "get tough" measures, such as the Baumes Law in New York in 1926, which provided for a life sentence for a fourth felony conviction. Franklin Roosevelt, as governor of New York during the late 1920s, had been a member of the NCC's executive committee.

Defenders of the traditional wisdom, in contrast, argued that expanding federal crime-control authority would undermine local law enforcement and therefore could prove to be counterproductive. Expanding federal authority would also intrude on local and state power, an issue about which states' rights advocates felt very strongly. Critics further pointed out that federal authorities had not distinguished themselves either when enforcing Prohibition or during the Palmer era, and that federal agents had a poor record in

working with local law enforcement. The 1931 Wickersham Commission (the National Commission on Law Observance and Enforcement), which had been appointed by President Herbert Hoover, conceded that crime and lawlessness were national problems but favored greater support for local law enforcement.

The turning point in this debate came in March 1932 when the infant son of the famed aviator Charles A. Lindbergh was kidnapped from the family's New Jersey home. This celebrated kidnapping attracted national and international attention—shocking the public as a threat to family values and security. Two months after the family's $50,000 ransom payment for the child's return, the Lindbergh baby's dead body was found.

At the time, the Bureau had no jurisdiction to investigate kidnapping, although Bureau Director Hoover asked to be kept informed about developments in the case. For over two years, local and state police unsuccessfully struggled to solve the Lindbergh kidnapping. Finally, President Roosevelt ordered the FBI to take the lead in the investigation. Eventually, Bruno Richard Hauptmann was arrested and convicted; he was electrocuted on April 3, 1936.

The Lindbergh baby abduction precipitated quite a different controversy than had the Palmer Raids or the Teapot Dome scandal: public and congressional pressure mounted to expand federal powers. Proponents argued that if prostitutes and automobiles were properly federal responsibilities, so, too, was the kidnapping of children. In response, on June 22, 1932, Congress enacted the so-called Lindbergh Law, making kidnapping a federal crime if the victim was transported across state lines. Succumbing to the resultant national frenzy, President Herbert Hoover, a long-time states' rights proponent, reluctantly signed the bill. His attorney general, William Mitchell, shared the president's lack of enthusiasm, emphasizing the local nature of crime and that the public should not expect too much from federal involvement.

The Lindbergh Law proved to be a portent of changes to come. The Roosevelt administration that followed the Herbert Hoover era had no aversion to expanding federal powers. From 1933 to 1935, Attorney General Homer S. Cummings attempted to mobilize public opinion against the gangsters and racketeers of the day and led an anticrime crusade to pressure Congress to enact an ambitious legislative agenda. Indeed, journalists characterized this attempt to create panic over a crime crisis as "Mr. Cummings's crime wave."

Cummings's war on crime was aided by a further dramatic development, the so-called Kansas City Massacre. On June 17, 1933, Bureau agents and local police became involved in a shoot-out with several gangsters in Kansas City, Missouri. These gangsters ambushed Bureau agents and Frank Nash, an escaped bank robber who had been captured and was being transported to Leavenworth penitentiary. One Bureau agent, three police officers, and Nash were killed in the machine-gun attack, and two other agents were wounded (see pages 53–54).

The Kansas City Massacre symbolized the brazenness and ruthlessness of gangsters, who had been transformed in the public mind, as the result of Cummings's publicity effort, into national enemies. John Dillinger was the most notorious of these Depression-era criminals. In 1933, Dillinger had just been released after a nine-year prison sentence when he and his associates, whom he had met in prison, embarked on a robbery spree throughout the Midwest. The news media, however, treated the Dillinger story as a kind of Keystone Cops comedy, emphasizing police bungling in the various phases of Dillinger's criminal career. Most embarrassing to the Bureau was Dillinger's escape from a hideout after Bureau officials prematurely announced that he had been caught (see pages 54–55).

Dillinger's humiliation of the Bureau made his capture a top priority for both Cummings and Hoover. Cummings told the press that agents had orders to "shoot to kill—then count to 10," while Bureau Director Hoover pressured agents to locate and arrest him. On July 22, 1934, acting on a tip, Bureau agents shot and killed Dillinger in Chicago.

The exploits of other gangsters provided further evidence that the nation confronted a serious crime crisis. These included Charles "Pretty Boy" Floyd, whom federal authorities claimed had been a member of the gang perpetrating the Kansas City Massacre; George "Machine Gun" Kelly, the kidnapper of wealthy Oklahoma oilman Charles Urschel; the Barker-Karpis gang, wanted for robberies in the Midwest, as were Clyde Barrow and Bonnie Parker ("Bonnie and Clyde"); and "Baby Face" Nelson, who had escaped from prison while serving a sentence for murder. These notorious gangsters made the attorney general's list of public enemies—their pursuit by Bureau agents was publicized extensively, and most of them met Dillinger's fate: killed in a hail of gunfire by federal agents or local police.

Arguing that society was being threatened by a ruthless, criminal underworld, Cummings championed the need to strengthen the forces of law and order. A "super police force" was needed, with the powers to take on gangsters and racketeers. He proposed a merger of the Prohibition Bureau and the Bureau of Investigation. After some initial dissension, including objections by Bureau Director Hoover to including the Prohibition unit, on August 10, 1933, Cummings created a new Division of Investigation to be headed by Hoover. Since Prohibition was drawing to a close with the repeal of the Eighteenth Amendment, Cummings's new agency was nothing more than a name change—and that, too, was short-lived. On March 22, 1935, the Division of Investigation was renamed the Federal Bureau of Investigation.

Cummings concurrently lobbied for additional legislation—his Twelve Point Crime Program to expand the federal role in crime prosecution. Nine of his proposed bills were approved by the Seventy-Third Congress in May and June 1934. The Lindbergh Law was amended to create a presumption of interstate transportation if the victim was not discovered after seven days, and to subject the perpetrators of such crimes to the death penalty. Bank robbery became a federal crime, as did the transportation of stolen property across state lines, the flight of felons across state lines to avoid prosecution, and racketeering in interstate commerce. Killing or assaulting a government agent became a federal offense. Furthermore, Bureau agents were empowered to make arrests, execute warrants, and carry firearms. By approving this crime legislation, Congress greatly expanded the Bureau's mandate, providing the federal government with a comprehensive criminal code for the first time. The outcome of Cummings's war on crime and successful legislative agenda was greater public acceptance of a federal role in crime control, and, more enduringly, the founding of a more powerful Federal Bureau of Investigation.

States' rights arguments might have been defused, but the FBI's expanded law enforcement powers soon precipitated other criticisms. These were circulated by the chair of the Senate Appropriations Subcommittee having oversight over Justice Department (and Bureau) budgetary requests, Senator Kenneth McKellar. During hearings in 1936, McKellar caustically questioned Hoover about FBI operations. McKellar asked whether Bureau appropriations were spent on advertising, particularly the making of motion pictures (a score of G-man movies glorifying the exploits of Bureau agents were produced in 1935). Conceding that the

G-man pictures promoted the FBI's image, Hoover insisted that FBI officials had not participated in their production. McKellar also questioned Hoover about the Bureau's role in solving the Lindbergh kidnapping case and whether it had cooperated with local police in that and other cases (McKellar's line of inquiry implied that Bureau officials had sought to deny other police agencies proper credit for solving cases). Hoover again disputed McKellar's version of what had happened. Finally, McKellar probed Hoover's qualifications for the FBI directorship, specifically questioning his expertise in crime investigation and noting his failure to have personally executed any arrests. In the course of this exchange, Hoover admitted that he had never personally made an arrest (although before 1934, Bureau agents did not have this power). One month after the McKellar hearings, Hoover rectified this situation by personally effecting the capture of Alvin Karpis, Public Enemy Number One and a member of the "Ma" Barker gang, in New Orleans.

J. Edgar Hoover successfully countered the various criticisms of FBI operations and the Bureau's expanded authority during the New Deal era; indeed, Bureau appropriations increased from $2.8 million in 1933 to $6.2 million in 1938 (see Table 1.1). Despite the initial controversies involving the FBI's expanded role, by the late 1930s, the G-man myth had taken root and the FBI's role as a powerful federal law enforcement agency had become firmly established. By the end of the decade, the conservative, states' rights opponents of federal expansion in law enforcement were clearly on the defensive.

The Revival of Antiradicalism

The expansion of federal crime control powers during the 1930s did not include authorizing FBI monitoring of radical political activities. Nonetheless, as early as 1934, President Franklin Roosevelt secretly requested a Bureau investigation of Nazi groups in the United States. Later, in 1936, Roosevelt secretly directed the FBI to gather intelligence on the American fascist and communist movements. These intelligence assignments were unknown to Congress and the public until September 1939, following the outbreak of World War II with the German invasion of Poland. At that time, Roosevelt publicly directed all local law enforcement officials to turn over to the FBI any information pertaining to espionage, sabotage, violations of the neutrality laws, and subversive activities. This was the first indication that the FBI's mission included a domestic security capability—

through a new unit called the General Intelligence Section. These surveillance activities provoked controversy, triggered by FBI raids in Detroit, Milwaukee, and New York City.

In February 1940, FBI agents arrested 12 activists in Detroit and Milwaukee on the charge of having earlier illegally recruited volunteers to fight in the Spanish Civil War with the Abraham Lincoln Brigade. The Brigade had been formed in 1937 to fight on behalf of the Loyalist government (backed by the Soviet Union) against the forces of Generalissimo Francisco Franco (who was heavily backed by the European fascist leaders Adolf Hitler and Benito Mussolini). Although Franco's forces were eventually victorious (indeed, the civil war had already ended in March 1939), the Justice Department nonetheless had belatedly decided to pursue criminal cases against the Brigade recruiters. Those arrested had violated a federal statute prohibiting the recruitment of Americans to fight in foreign wars. In effecting the arrests during the night (around 5 a.m.), FBI agents in some cases broke down doors to enter premises and searched homes and offices without warrants. The Detroit defendants were not allowed to call lawyers until just prior to their court appearance later that afternoon, and on their way to court, they had been chained together and paraded in front of photographers. The FBI's tactics precipitated harsh press criticism. The *Milwaukee Journal* likened the Bureau's behavior to that of the Gestapo, while the *New Republic* compared its methods to the Soviet secret police. The *New York Daily News* declared that "Mr. Hoover is widely believed nowadays to be building up a secret police organization of un-American, anti-American complexion." In addition to press criticism, liberal activists called upon Attorney General Robert Jackson to investigate the FBI. The most prominent proponent of such an inquiry was a liberal Republican, Senator George Norris, who publicly criticized FBI Director Hoover and wrote to Jackson demanding that he restrain the FBI to preserve the rule of law. In an effort to quell the mounting furor over Hoover and his agents' conduct, Attorney General Jackson dismissed the charges against the Brigade recruiters, stating that he did not see the wisdom in reviving this past conflict and in pursuing an outdated case.

The next month, a Senate committee chaired by Burton Wheeler of Montana, an old Bureau nemesis from the Daugherty-Burns era, issued a report cataloguing police misconduct in the first six months of World War II. Although the report did not mention the FBI by name, Wheeler later indicated that its main subject was the Bureau. Expressing concern over the "resurgence of a spy system" that targeted persons for their radical beliefs, the committee's report criticized the practices employed in effecting arrests: illegal searches and seizures, use of high-pressure tactics in interrogation, and detention of suspects without the benefit of counsel. The combination of the Senate committee report, press accounts of Bureau misconduct in the Brigade arrests, and growing outrage in the liberal community over restoration of the FBI's intelligence function raised serious questions about FBI Director Hoover's leadership of the Bureau.

In a series of speeches to conservative groups in 1940 and 1941—including the Daughters of the American Revolution, the International Association of Chiefs of Police, and the American Legion—Hoover responded to his critics. Claiming that the Bureau was the target of a widespread "smear" campaign by anti-American forces, the FBI director argued that the purpose of these criticisms was to cripple national security. The FBI (and law enforcement), Hoover argued, represented the first line of defense against anti-American forces seeking to discredit the Bureau as part of a sinister plan to disrupt and overthrow the United States government. The FBI director did not specifically identify these anti-American forces, characterizing them as "international confidence men" and "scoundrels," and other times as "conspiring Communists, their fellow travelers, mouth-pieces, and stooges" or a "fifth column." Hoover thus succeeded in turning a potential controversy into a public relations triumph.

The FBI was not without its defenders in Congress. Influential congressmen, including Senator Pat McCarran, the senior member of the Judiciary Committee, defended the FBI director's integrity and character, praised the FBI's work, and denounced the Bureau's critics—Senators Norris and Wheeler, in particular.

After some delay, Attorney General Jackson also publicly defended Hoover and the FBI. In a letter released to the press, Jackson reaffirmed his (and the FBI director's) commitment to civil liberties, emphasizing that FBI investigations were confined to violations of federal law. A Justice Department report, released in May 1940, concluded that the allegations against the FBI had been exaggerated and that the charges of misconduct were unwarranted. In addition, at a White House dinner in March 1940, President Roosevelt publicly defended FBI Director Hoover.

Although criticism of his leadership continued, Hoover mounted a successful public relations counteroffensive, capitalizing on his new-found popularity as head of the G-men and using his own powerful political connections. Furthermore, because these were war years, the espionage and sabotage menace about which Hoover warned seemed more critical than alleged irregularities in FBI operations. In the end, neither the Senate nor the House initiated a full-scale investigation of the FBI. A more limited inquiry into wiretapping was conducted instead, but this sidestepped the issues raised by the Abraham Lincoln Brigade raids.

The controversies of the period from 1939 to 1941 resembled those of 1908, at the time when the Bureau was first created, and 1920, when the Justice Department conducted the Palmer Raids. The recurring issue was whether a national police force should investigate the opinions and beliefs of Americans. In 1924, Bureau investigations were restricted to criminal matters, but during the 1930s, President Roosevelt—through a series of secret directives—restored the FBI's intelligence function to include investigating radical activities and the political opinions of certain Americans.

Cold War Anticommunism

In the years immediately following the end of World War II, it became clear that the Bureau's domestic security function was neither temporary nor war-related. Throughout the late 1940s and early 1950s, internal security issues became central FBI responsibilities and a major part of that period's political agenda. The resultant internal security controversy differed from that of the 1930s and 1940s, however; the central question focused less on suspected foreign spies than on the loyalty of Americans (notably, federal employees), many of whom were accused of having communist sympathies. By the 1950s, the issue of communists in government provoked a second Red Scare, popularly known as McCarthyism, named after the U.S. senator from Wisconsin, Joseph R. McCarthy (see Exhibit 3.2). In a February 9, 1950, speech in Wheeling, West Virginia, McCarthy catapulted to national prominence when claiming to possess a list of 205 "known" communists employed in the State Department. (The "known" reference was to the Truman administration, and the intended implication was that the president was unwilling, or unable, to initiate a needed purge.) McCarthy's influence peaked following Republican victories in the 1952 congressional elections, at which time he chaired the Permanent Subcommittee on Investigations.

Exploiting this powerful forum, the senator promoted the need to institute more effective security measures (at minimum, the dismissal of disloyal federal employees) and to "expose" both communists and those who were indifferent to the communist threat.

Exhibit 3.2   **Joseph R. McCarthy,**
Courtesy of The Milwaukee Journal

Beyond McCarthy's personal crusade against communism, the loyalty issue reflected deeper tensions in American life in the postwar era. In particular, New Deal Democrats and the Truman administration were pitted against Republican partisans and conservatives. To many conservatives, the New Deal policies of the Roosevelt and Truman administrations threatened traditional American values. They attributed the decline of family, church, and school to the liberal policies of the 1930s and 1940s, which enlarged the role of the federal government and, in the process, introduced subversive, un-American influences into American life. Their attack on communists in the government, and on the Truman administration for failing to address the serious loyalty threat, succeeded in redefining national politics—and during the tense Cold War era, effectively silenced any criticisms of FBI monitoring of radical activists and federal employees.

J. Edgar Hoover and the FBI had not been neutral bystanders in this postwar debate over internal security. In February 1946, FBI officials initiated a campaign to educate the public about the dangers of communism. This FBI campaign was carried out in two ways: overtly, through the speeches of FBI Director Hoover, and indirectly, through FBI officials in Washington and agents in the field, who, through their contacts in Congress, state government, and the media, promoted alarm about the communist threat. FBI officials, for example, covertly assisted congressional committees, such as the House Committee on Un-American Activities (HUAC) during the late 1940s and later Senator McCarthy's subcommittee, by helping them prepare

hearings to expose communist influence in American life. The FBI's assistance to these committees was done secretly, by leaking information from FBI files to committee members. Also, former FBI agents were hired by these committees to perform investigations, providing another means of access to FBI files. The FBI's educational efforts, because not known, were not controversial. Ironically, the sole controversy about FBI activities that surfaced during the early Cold War years involved isolated court cases, cases that inadvertently disclosed the FBI's resort to illegal investigative practices, such as break-ins and wiretaps. These cases both provoked controversy and lent credibility to anticommunist security themes.

The first of these was the 1945 *Amerasia* case (see pages 25 and 61). The FBI's role first in arresting six individuals affiliated with *Amerasia*, a journal of Far Eastern affairs, and then in the failure of any of the arrested to have been convicted of the seeming crime of espionage, provoked little controversy in 1945.

In 1950, however, the *Amerasia* case resurfaced in controversy during the inquiry conducted by the so-called Tydings Committee into Joseph McCarthy's 81 cases of "Communists in the State Department." Since one of the six *Amerasia* defendants was John Service, McCarthy and his supporters questioned why the Justice Department had failed to prosecute him and the other *Amerasia* spies. When the Justice Department attempted to defend its non-prosecution decision of 1945, citing the FBI's illegal activities (break-ins and wiretaps), FBI officials worked quietly to neutralize this defense and threatened to disclose information obtained through a wiretap of prominent Washington attorney Thomas Corcoran, a disclosure that could prove embarrassing to the Truman administration. FBI officials' close but covert relationships with conservatives in Congress and the news media effectively silenced any potential controversy about FBI illegal activities and, instead, highlighted another issue: Had the Truman administration hamstrung the FBI and thereby harmed a needed internal security prosecution?

The *Amerasia* case paralleled another major controversy involving the Truman administration's responses to the allegations of Elizabeth Bentley, a one-time member of the U.S. Communist Party, who in November 1945, reported to agents in the FBI's New Haven, Connecticut, field office tht she had been a courier for a communist espionage ring during World War II. A Vassar graduate who had spent time in Italy doing postgraduate work, Bentley described herself as a disillusioned communist who had broken from the party following the death of her lover, Jacob Golos, a Soviet espionage agent. She claimed that during the war, she had acted as a courier for Golos, to whom she provided classified information that she received from American communists who worked in wartime federal agencies and departments (notably the Treasury Department, the Bureau of Economic Warfare, the Office of Strategic Services, and the War Production Board). Bentley named the government officials whom she alleged were part of this Soviet espionage network. These included Harry Dexter White, Nathan Silvermaster, William Ullman, Victor Perlo, Donald Wheeler, Charles Kramer, Harold Glasser, Edward Fitzgerald, Frank Coe, and William Remington.

Although Bentley could neither document her claims nor describe the contents of all the materials she had delivered, her allegations led FBI officials to initiate an intensive inquiry, code-named Gregory, to investigate them and seek indictments. This initial effort failed, as a specially convened federal grand jury returned no indictments in 1948. Bentley's allegation of a wartime Soviet spy ring, however, seemed to have been corroborated by other wartime FBI investigations of Soviet consular officials and American communists, and by a Soviet defector, Igor Gouzenko, who had worked as a clerk in the Soviet embassy in Ottawa, Canada. In September 1945, Gouzenko informed the Royal Canadian Mounted Police that during the war, the Soviets had operated spy networks in Canada, Great Britain, and the United States, and had relied on members of the Canadian Communist Party to further their spy activities.

In a November 1945 memorandum, and in a flurry of follow-up memoranda in 1946, FBI Director Hoover informed President Truman and other senior administration officials of the Bentley allegations, in particular, her charges that Treasury Department official Harry Dexter White had been part of this wartime spy ring. Truman ignored Hoover's warning, and in January 1946, nominated White to be one of the executive directors of the International Monetary Fund.

Truman's dismissal of the FBI reports questioning White's loyalty resurfaced as a public issue in November 1953. In a speech before a Chicago businessmen's organization, Republican Attorney General Herbert Brownell cited Truman's earlier handling of the White nomination as an example of the laxity of that administration's security policies and its disregard of the FBI's careful work. The new Republican administration would be more diligent and responsible, Brownell pledged. When Truman responded by accusing Brownell of McCarthyism, the attorney general,

accompanied by Hoover, was able to repeat and amplify these charges in a forum provided by the Senate Internal Security Subcommittee. Hoover's public testimony in the highly charged partisan hearings infuriated many southern Democrats—who believed that the FBI director should have avoided becoming drawn into a partisan controversy. Nothing came out of this controversy—and the FBI's reputation for nonpartisanship and apolitical professionalism remained intact. The prevailing sentiment was that the communist threat required a vigorous response—concerns fortified by the government's prosecution of the leadership of the U.S. Communist Party.

In 1948, at the urging of FBI officials, the Justice Department secured indictments of the top leadership of the U.S. Communist Party. The legal basis for this prosecution was the Smith Act of 1940, which made it illegal to advocate the violent overthrow of the United States government. On June 29, 1948, a New York grand jury indicted the 12 members of the party's National Board, and FBI agents arrested them about a month later. During the ensuing nine-month trial, which ended in October 1949, Justice Department attorneys relied, in part, on FBI informants who had infiltrated the party, some of whom rose to positions of influence in the party's leadership, to support their case. Eleven defendants were convicted (the twelfth defendant was tried separately due to illness), and all but one received the maximum sentence of five years. In 1951, the Supreme Court, in *Dennis v. United States*, upheld their convictions and the constitutionality of the Smith Act.

The Justice Department then attempted to prosecute the second-level leadership of the Communist Party, obtaining another 93 convictions. In 1957, however, the Supreme Court, in *Yates v. United States*, overturned these latter Smith Act convictions. Effectively reversing the *Dennis* decision, the Supreme Court required that the government prove advocacy "of action and not merely abstract doctrine" to convict individuals for violating the Smith Act; it was not sufficient to show that communists advocated the violent overthrow of the United States government in their writings. This ruling essentially ended further Smith Act prosecutions.

By 1954, FBI Director Hoover had already curbed Communist Party prosecutions because of his concern that legal action would necessitate the surfacing of FBI informants—which would adversely affect the Bureau's ability to continue to monitor communist activities. The Smith Act cases, moreover, did not contribute to a reappraisal of the quality of the evidence and the purpose of prosecuting

American communists. The FBI's and the Justice Department's successes in indicting and convicting the Communist Party leadership was viewed as legitimate and indirectly furthered the 1946-initiated FBI campaign to "educate" public opinion.

No case provoked more national attention and controversy during the Cold War era than that of Alger Hiss. Originally a low-level State Department aide, by 1945, Hiss had risen in prominence, attending the Yalta Conference as a member of the U.S. delegation and heading the State Department's postwar policy planning staff.

In August 1948, during testimony before the House Committee on Un-American Activities (HUAC), an admitted ex-communist, Whittaker Chambers, accused Hiss of having been a member of a communist cell in Washington, D.C. Hiss, and others whom Chambers named, had allegedly sought to promote communist influence and infiltration of the New Deal. In December 1948, Chambers revised his accusations, claiming then that Hiss had been engaged in espionage and had supplied him with classified government documents, which he then relayed to the Soviets. Chambers repeated these charges before a federal grand jury and produced State Department documents that he claimed had been given to him by Hiss (see pages 62–63). On December 15, 1948, the grand jury indicted Hiss on two counts of perjury; the first for denying that he met Chambers after 1937, and the second for denying that he had passed classified documents to Chambers. Hiss was convicted on January 21, 1950, and was sentenced to five years in prison.

Because of the partisanship of HUAC's August hearings and the reaction of many liberals (who believed Hiss was innocent and saw his case as an attempt to discredit New Deal liberalism), the Hiss case deeply divided Americans. The controversy surrounding the case at the time, however, never extended to FBI operations and procedures. The FBI's behind-the-scenes assistance to HUAC (and particularly freshman congressman Richard Nixon) was not generally known, however; Hiss's conviction, moreover, lent credence to allegations that the ineffectiveness of security procedures during the Roosevelt and Truman administrations had hampered FBI investigations and indirectly promoted communist spying.

At about the same time as the first Hiss trial, on March 4, 1949, FBI agents arrested Judith Coplon, at the time employed in the Justice Department's Foreign Agents Registration Section, for unauthorized possession of classified government documents. Coplon was apprehended as she was in the process of delivering 28 FBI documents to Valentin Gubitchev, a member of the Soviet Union's United Nations staff. Based on information that the FBI received from Army intelligence officers (who had successfully decoded Soviet consular messages from the 1944–45 period), FBI agents learned of Coplon's earlier recruitment as a Soviet spy. To counter her espionage activities and to identify her Soviet contacts, FBI officials developed an elaborate strategy to entrap her in 1949—alerting her to a manufactured FBI report that would be of interest to her Soviet contacts. Coplon fell into the trap, and FBI agents apprehended her during a planned rendezvous in New York City with Gubitchev.

Coplon was subsequently indicted and tried in both Washington, D.C., and New York City. Her first trial, in Washington, involved her indictment on charges of unauthorized possession of classified documents. During the trial, the presiding judge required the admission into evidence of the specific FBI reports on which the summaries in Coplon's possession had been based. The "raw" reports proved embarrassing to the Bureau because they included unsubstantiated rumors and gossip and confirmed that the FBI was monitoring political activities. Moreover, since information in some of the reports came from wiretaps, Coplon's attorneys sought a ruling to ascertain whether Coplon herself had been wiretapped (under a 1939 Supreme Court ruling, if evidence had been obtained by this illegal method, the case could be dismissed). The Justice Department's attorneys successfully repulsed this request, dismissing it as without foundation and merely a "fishing expedition." Coplon was ultimately convicted on June 30, 1949, and was sentenced to 10 years in prison.

Coplon was then tried in New York City for conspiring to transmit classified documents to a foreign agent. In this second trial, Coplon's defense attorney persuaded the judge to hold a pretrial hearing to ascertain whether her telephone had been tapped. During this hearing, Justice Department lawyers admitted that Coplon's home and office phones, along with her parents' home phone, had been tapped, both prior to her arrest and during the first trial (thereby intercepting her privileged conversations with her attorney). It was also admitted at the hearing that FBI officials had ordered the wiretap logs destroyed in view of the "imminence" of her trial. This disclosure also raised questions about Justice Department supervision of the FBI, given the unqualified dismissal of defense attorneys' request to have the possibility of wiretapping looked into during Coplon's first trial. In spite of these acknowledged irregularities, Coplon was convicted on March 7, 1950, and sentenced to 15 years in prison.

Nine months later, however, the U.S. Circuit Court of Appeals overturned Coplon's two convictions, owing to the FBI's improper wiretaps and warrantless arrest of Coplon in New York. Although its case against Coplon involved numerous legal problems (not only the problematic wiretap evidence, but the sensitivity of the intercepted Soviet consular messages that had first brought Coplon to the FBI's attention), the Justice Department did not officially dismiss its case against Coplon until 1967.

The Coplon case precipitated a flurry of demands for an investigation of FBI methods and priorities. Critics sought to use the evidence of FBI political surveillance and wiretapping to instigate stricter oversight and controls over FBI operations. However, given the heightened national concerns over internal security, these demands commanded little support—especially since their proponents were the radical National Lawyers Guild, civil libertarians, and liberal newspapers such as the *Washington Post* and the *New York Times*. Coplon's obvious guilt, moreover, suggested that security considerations should take precedence over libertarian concerns.

No sooner had the Hiss and Coplon trials concluded than an even more sensational espionage case made national news. In 1950, the FBI arrested Communist Party activists (Harry Gold, David Greenglass, Julius Rosenberg, Ethel Rosenberg, and Morton Sobell) on the charge of conspiring to obtain secrets on behalf of the Soviet Union (see pages 64–66). In the resultant trial, Julius and Ethel Rosenberg were convicted on March 29, 1951, without having confessed and based on the damaging testimony of David and Ruth Greenglass. David was Ethel Rosenberg's brother and he admitted during interrogation by FBI agents (and during the trial) to having been recruited by Julius Rosenberg to help steal atomic secrets for the Soviets. Convinced that the Rosenbergs were responsible for the Soviet's success in learning the secrets of the atom bomb, Judge Irving Kaufman sentenced both to death. They were executed on June 19, 1953.

Occurring in the midst of the Korean War, and given the seriousness of the charge of communist espionage, the Rosenberg trial precipitated little controversy at the time (except from those, primarily from abroad, who opposed the severity of the death sentence—or who contrasted the leniency of the 15-year prison sentence given to Greenglass, who had actually provided information).

The *Amerasia* case; the Bentley allegations; the Harry Dexter White affair; and the trials of the Communist Party leaders, Alger Hiss, Judith Coplon, and the Rosenbergs fueled a postwar internal security crisis, and for the most part, the FBI's activities and methods escaped critical scrutiny. In the virulently anticommunist atmosphere of the era, few questioned the fairness or legality of FBI procedures or sought to ascertain whether the FBI had moved beyond law enforcement to political containment. Even disclosures of FBI illegalities in the *Amerasia* and Coplon cases, and the publicized disclosures of the scope of FBI monitoring activities as documented by the release of FBI files in the Coplon case, did not raise questions about the FBI's methods and whether FBI investigations were politically motivated. Nor did the publication in 1950 of Max Lowenthal's critical book, *The Federal Bureau of Investigation*, which attempted to document FBI abuses going back to the Palmer Raids. Alerted to the imminent publication of Lowenthal's critical history, FBI officials attempted to prevent publication, and HUAC subpoenaed Lowenthal to appear before the committee.

Lowenthal's experience highlighted the risks of challenging FBI officials or criticizing their conduct during the tense climate of the early Cold War era. The controversy surrounding FBI domestic security operations during the Palmer era and Abraham Lincoln Brigade arrests—raising questions about whether the FBI should have an intelligence function and whether it should investigate radical activists—was no longer a legitimate matter for debate. Domestic security activities became accepted as essential FBI operations to protect the nation from the influence of communists, subversives, and other dangerous elements.

Organized Crime

On November 14, 1957, New York State Police Sergeant Edgar Croswell became suspicious upon observing a large number of black limousines approach the estate of Joseph Barbara Sr., located in the hills outside of the village of Apalachin, New York, in the Binghamton area. Croswell quickly set up a roadblock outside of Barbara's hilltop home; under New York law, he could stop all vehicles to inquire as to the identity of their occupants. As word of the roadblock and police presence reached those assembled at the Barbara estate, a mass exodus ensued, with some fleeing by car and others by foot. State police, nonetheless, identified (but did not detain) more than 60 of Barbara's guests, who turned out to be prominent organized crime figures from across the country and from outside the United States. Sergeant Croswell had stumbled upon an important meeting of Mafia crime families. His discovery made national headlines and captured the interest both of the public and of those in law enforcement. Its broader importance was its damaging effect on the FBI's image and reputation for efficiency and professionalism.

FBI Director Hoover was especially embarrassed by the national publicity surrounding the discovery of the Apalachin meeting, since he had repeatedly denied the existence of the Mafia or of a national organized-crime syndicate. In his view, gangsters were not members of a nationwide, interlinked criminal conspiracy. Hoover had characterized these crime figures as "just a bunch of hoodlums" and contended that their prosecution was a local law enforcement problem. The Apalachin incident, therefore, became a major public relations crisis: How could the foremost federal crime-fighting agency have been unaware of a national crime syndicate?

Almost immediately, the nation's newspapers called for a war on this new menace, while President Eisenhower's attorney general, William P. Rogers, endorsed federal action. Thus, FBI Director Hoover faced a major challenge both to his credibility as the nation's leading crime expert and to his authority to set the FBI's law enforcement priorities.

Although Hoover publicly insisted that the FBI had been furnishing information on organized crime figures to local police all along, he concurrently commissioned William Sullivan (at the time, head of the FBI's Research and Analysis Section) to conduct a study on organized crime. Sullivan and his small staff worked diligently over the next year and compiled a two-volume report that thoroughly reviewed the existing literature on the subject, tracing the history of the Mafia in Italy and its operation in the United States for several decades. After reading this internal study, Hoover privately conceded the existence of an organized crime syndicate but refused to circulate copies of the study outside the Bureau—publicly releasing the Sullivan study, even within the Justice Department, would have been tantamount to admitting that the FBI's official position on organized crime had been wrong.

Hoover also established a new initiative against organized crime, the Top Hoodlum program. Each field office was required to identify the 10 major mob members in its geographical area and closely monitor them. Primarily an intelligence effort, the program's purpose was to gather information about organized crime figures and their activities—a serious deficiency of the FBI in the 1950s—not necessarily to arrest and prosecute individuals. As in the internal security arena, FBI agents employed break-ins, wiretaps, and bugs to obtain the required intelligence. Because it was illegal to obtain information in this way, and thus it was not admissible in court, FBI officials neither informed Attorney General Rogers of these practices nor sought his approval.

In May 1954, Attorney General Herbert Brownell (Rogers's predecessor) had authorized FBI bugging installations, but only for cases in which "internal security and the national safety" were involved. FBI officials decided on their own, in the late 1950s, to employ bugging during criminal investigations, but not having cleared this decision with the attorney general, these practices ultimately limited their ability to contain the targeted criminals.

The Chicago field office was one of the first to use bugs under the Top Hoodlum program. In the summer of 1959, Chicago agents bugged one of the Chicago mob's meeting places, a tailor shop on North Michigan Avenue. The bug remained undetected for five years. From that one microphone, a wealth of information was learned about organized crime in Chicago and in the United States. This information included mob decisions, past and current, as told by the mobsters themselves; family problems; and the names of judges, police officers, and politicians who had been bribed to cooperate. In early 1960, this bug intercepted a conversation between Sam Giancana, a Chicago crime boss who had just returned from the East Coast, and an associate. Giancana updated his associate on the membership of "the Commission" (the Mafia's national executive council), and the FBI's hidden microphone duly recorded his listing of the names. This success led to the installation of bugs at other Mafia meeting places in Chicago and in the homes of Giancana and other Chicago crime figures. Soon, other FBI field offices installed hidden microphones for their surveillance of the top hoodlums in their regions.

The Justice Department had concurrently established the Special Group on Organized Crime, under the leadership of Milton R. Wessel, a former assistant U.S. attorney. This unit was in existence for only two years, however, primarily because of FBI Director Hoover's refusal to cooperate and share information. In part, Hoover's refusal to cooperate was so that he could conceal from Justice Department officials the illegal methods that FBI agents were using to gather intelligence on organized crime.

At this time, the Senate had initiated an investigation into the influence of organized crime on labor unions. During hearings in 1957 and 1959 chaired by Senator John McClellan, the Select Committee on Improper Activities in the Labor and Management Field, whose chief counsel was Robert F. Kennedy (John F. Kennedy was also a member of the committee), exposed the underworld ties of Teamsters' Union presidents David Beck and James Hoffa.

The organized crime issue, moreover, resurfaced at the annual convention of the International Association of Chiefs of Police (IACP) in 1960. At this convention, delegates introduced a resolution endorsing federal action in the war on organized crime. Although some police chiefs supported the resolution, FBI Director Hoover's criticism effectively prevented the proposal from reaching the floor. Hoover warned that a national police force could threaten civil liberties. A few months later, during annual testimony before the House Appropriations Subcommittee, the FBI director further responded to his critics, including the Special Group on Organized Crime, which had criticized the FBI's reluctance to become involved in organized crime enforcement. Organized crime was a local problem, Hoover stressed, and existed because of the failure or ineptness of local law enforcement. The FBI could assist local police, but it lacked jurisdiction to tackle what was a local problem. Unofficially, Hoover also resisted demands for a coordinated federal attack on organized crime since this could jeopardize Hoover's exclusive control over Bureau operations.

FBI officials' resistance to a federal attack on organized crime came to an end in 1961. The new Kennedy administration—particularly, Attorney General Kennedy—pressured FBI officials to enlist in the fight against organized crime. Keenly interested in expanding the federal role against organized crime, an interest dating from his tenure on the McClellan committee, Attorney General Kennedy enlarged the Justice Department's Organized Crime and Racketeering Section. This section served as a national clearinghouse for information on organized crime. In a July 1961 meeting with Courtney Evans, Hoover's liaison to the Justice Department, the attorney general pressured the FBI to use electronic surveillance in organized crime investigations. Furthermore, Attorney General Kennedy lobbied for the passage of legislation in 1961 to legalize FBI wiretapping and to empower the FBI to fight organized crime. In particular,

Kennedy proposed making the interstate transportation of gambling paraphernalia and the interstate transmission of gambling information by wire federal crimes.

Although new legislation was enacted to extend FBI jurisdiction in organized crime, Hoover remained reluctant to cooperate fully with other federal agencies. In 1967, when Attorney General Ramsey Clark developed federal anticrime strike forces, few FBI agents assisted this coordinated effort. John Ehrlichman, chief domestic policy advisor to President Nixon, similarly complained that Attorney General John Mitchell was "unsuccessful in asking Hoover to turn his agents loose on the Mafia."

Attorney General Kennedy's influence did prove pivotal in shifting the FBI's organized crime role. So, too, did the changing attitudes of the public and Congress. In a series of hearings in 1963 and 1964, the Senate Permanent Subcommittee on Investigations dramatically exposed Mafia operations—its national structure and criminal activities (gambling and narcotics). These hearings publicized the testimony of Joseph Valachi, a Mafia informer, who introduced a new term to describe the mob, "La Cosa Nostra" (LCN). Valachi graphically detailed the LCN's organization and activities, describing how the LCN controlled a nationwide crime cartel based in the nation's large cities. His testimony intensified public concerns about the menace of organized crime.

Senator Estes Kefauver had previously promoted this portrayal of a nationwide organized crime conspiracy during Senate hearings on organized crime in 1950–51, as had Harry Anslinger, head of the Federal Bureau of Narcotics (FBN). Until the 1960s, however, the idea of the existence of a nationwide crime conspiracy (the Italian Mafia) had not received widespread support from either the media or prominent political leaders. In contrast, not only were the Valachi hearings widely publicized, this theme of a nationwide crime syndicate received further support from President Lyndon Johnson's Crime Commission (1967). By the end of the 1960s, awareness of La Cosa Nostra had also entered popular culture, most notably in novels and movies like *The Godfather.*

Dating from the Apalachin incident, the FBI had become enmeshed in controversy as questions were increasingly raised both about FBI Director Hoover's adamant denial that the Mafia existed and the FBI's seeming failure to recognize organized crime as a national problem.

Some have suspected that Hoover had been blackmailed by the mob. In a recent version of this hypothesis, writer Anthony Summers claimed in a 1993 biography that organized crime leaders possessed a compromising photograph of Hoover engaged in a homosexual act, and that they used it to blackmail him for hands-off treatment of their activities. Summers, however, offered no documentary evidence for this theory beyond rumors and the accounts of not-very-credible witnesses.

In 1969, criminologist Donald Cressey attributed the FBI's failure to lead a war against organized crime to the Bureau's lack of statutory jurisdiction until the Kennedy years. Cressey's explanation has been challenged by others who point out that, since the 1930s, the Bureau did have jurisdiction in many areas of interstate crime. Moreover, had Hoover wished to move against organized crime, he could have commanded the necessary support. Furthermore, in other areas in which the FBI's legal authority was questionable, such as the political surveillance of "subversives," the FBI had not been reluctant to commit resources.

Journalist Fred Cook, in contrast, attributes the FBI's avoidance of organized crime prosecution to a number of factors related to the costs of combating a powerful and politically risky adversary. First, the G-man myth of efficiency and invincibility had been built on an apparently impressive statistical record involving mundane federal crimes—with citations to the amount of stolen property recovered and the number of fugitives located. Tangling with a formidable adversary, like the Mafia, could jeopardize this carefully crafted image. Second, because crime bosses relied upon corrupt public officials for much of their activity, any attack on organized crime would inevitably involve revelations of political corruption. Exposing the connections of members of Congress and other leading politicians to organized crime could affect the FBI's legislative power base. Third, Hoover feared that given the enormous profitability of organized crime, FBI agents might—like local police officers—be corrupted.

The Hoover-King Controversy

During the late 1950s and early 1960s, moreover, the FBI's seeming avoidance of civil rights enforcement raised quite different questions. FBI Director Hoover was then criticized for failing to protect civil rights activists and those involved in various demonstrations challenging segregation laws or seeking to register black voters in the South. Civil rights activists were subjected to mob violence and threats,

sometimes with the sanction of local police authorities. Responding to these criticisms, Hoover justified the FBI's passivity as due to the lack of federal jurisdiction—no federal laws were violated—and that the FBI was an investigative agency, not a peacekeeping one.

But the reasons may have been more complex. In their efforts to promote desegregation and ensure racial equality and voting rights, civil rights activists frequently became involved in brutal conflict with the same local police officers with whom FBI agents worked in solving federal crimes. The FBI's strongest congressional supporters, moreover, were conservative Southerners who vigorously opposed the civil rights movement and its demands for racial integration and equality. Furthermore, FBI Director Hoover, a product of a segregated Washington, D.C., personally did not sympathize with the struggle for black civil rights and had developed a strong disdain for one of the movement's principal leaders, the Reverend Martin Luther King Jr. Ultimately, King was subjected to one of the most extensive programs of surveillance and harassment in FBI history. When this became known during the 1970s, the resultant controversy over Hoover's public conflict with King and with the civil rights movement provoked debate over FBI priorities and how they were set, and the FBI's methods in pursuing investigative targets.

In a January 1962 report, an Atlanta-based civil rights organization, the Southern Regional Council (SRC), criticized the FBI for failing to act against local officials who sought to repress civil rights demonstrations in Albany, Georgia. This report emphasized the distrust between blacks in Albany and local FBI agents, and criticized FBI agents' failure to make arrests in spite of clear evidence of police brutality or to act on complaints by blacks that their civil rights had been violated. Following an updated release of the SRC report in November 1962, the *Atlanta Constitution* quoted Martin Luther King Jr. as agreeing with its conclusions. Elaborating, King further alleged that because FBI agents in the South were white Southerners, they sympathized more with Southern segregationist views and were friendlier with local police. Albany, Georgia, had been the site of a major campaign led by King to desegregate public facilities.

Responding to King's remarks, FBI officials telephoned his Atlanta office—King was president of the Southern Christian Leadership Conference—to inform him that four of the five agents in Albany, Georgia, were Northerners. King did not return these phone calls (made by FBI assistant director Cartha DeLoach and the Atlanta special agent in charge). His failure to do so was regarded by Hoover and DeLoach as a serious affront to the Bureau. Accordingly, the thin-skinned Hoover—unaccustomed to criticism from any quarter—considered King a personal enemy, both of himself as director and of the Bureau.

FBI agents had been monitoring King and the SCLC since 1957 under its "racial matters" category. After 1967, these investigations intensified. Early that year, Hoover warned top Kennedy administration officials that two of King's advisers were linked to the U.S. Communist Party. In May 1962, King was listed in the FBI's Reserve Index, a secret list of individuals whom Hoover conceded could not meet the criteria for inclusion in the Security Index, but "who, in a time of emergency, are in a position to influence others against the national interest or are likely to furnish material financial aid to subversive elements due to their subversive associations and ideology." (Others listed on this Reserve Index included novelist Norman Mailer and a college history professor who had praised the Soviet Union in one of his classes.) In October 1962, an investigation of King and the SCLC was opened as part of an FBI effort code-named COMINFIL. COMINFIL was a Bureau program targeting organizations and persons believed to be under communist influence. Moreover, because of the Kennedy administration's continuing concerns about communist influence in the civil rights movement (and King, in particular), concerns fueled by FBI reports and memoranda, on October 10 and 23, 1963, Attorney General Robert Kennedy approved an FBI request to wiretap King's Atlanta home and SCLC offices. In addition, during a nine-hour conference on December 23, 1963, high-level FBI officials deliberated over various proposals to "contain" King's influence. The following month, the first of at least 15 FBI microphones was installed to monitor King's private life. These bugs were placed in hotel and motel rooms where King stayed during his frequent travels around the country. Installed without Attorney General Kennedy's knowledge, these microphones were intended to acquire information that could be used to discredit King personally and thereby undermine his leadership.

This campaign to uncover communist influence in the civil rights movement and to discredit King was largely clandestine, known at this time only within the Bureau and to a few members of the Kennedy and Johnson administrations. In April 1964, however, Hoover's conviction that civil rights activists were subversive, and his personal dislike of King, became public when he testified before the House Appropriations Subcommittee on the extent of communist influence in the civil rights movement. King responded by denying this assertion of communist influence, and then criticized the FBI's civil rights record.

This marked the first of several public exchanges between Hoover and King during 1964, culminating in a November 18 press conference. In the course of this meeting, one reporter asked Hoover about King's criticisms of FBI agents assigned to the South. Hoover responded by first citing King's failure to return his phone calls, and then characterized King as "the most notorious liar in the country." Off the record, Hoover added, "He is one of the lowest characters in the country." Appalled by Hoover's attack on his integrity, King responded publicly the following day in a telegram to the FBI director. King expressed interest in a meeting on civil rights matters, while attributing the FBI director's disparaging remarks to his apparent faltering "under the awesome burden, complexities and responsibilities of his office." Hoover's remarks also precipitated press demands for the FBI director's retirement, notably in a *New York Times* editorial and during questions at President Lyndon Johnson's press conference later that month.

Hoover and King met on December 1, presumably to discuss their differences. The meeting was cordial but was taken up by a 55-minute monologue in which Hoover recited the Bureau's achievements. None of the controversial matters were raised during this meeting—notably the implication of communist influence or Hoover's personal criticisms of King.

The Hoover-King public controversy subsided following this meeting, but not the Bureau's covert efforts to discredit the prominent civil rights leader. Throughout 1964, as King's reputation was enhanced by numerous awards and honors, FBI efforts to discredit King escalated. In December 1963, *Time* magazine had named King "Man of the Year." King was the recipient of honorary degrees from several universities and had an audience with the pope in Rome in 1964. On October 14, 1964, it was announced that King had been awarded the Nobel Peace Prize. On each of these occasions, FBI officials disseminated derogatory information about King—to the White House, Congress, churches, universities, and the media. The most extreme of these efforts to discredit King involved the mailing of a tape-recording to King's wife, Coretta. This tape was a composite of sexual activities and conversations intercepted by the microphones planted by FBI agents in King's hotel rooms. An unsigned, handwritten letter was included with this tape that threatened to expose King in 34 days: "King, there is only one thing left for you to do. You know what it is. . . . There is but one way out for you. You better take it before your filthy fraudulent self is bared to the nation." The date was significant—King was to receive the Nobel Peace Prize 34 days later. FBI surveillance, and FBI officials' clandestine efforts to discredit King, continued until his assassination in Memphis, Tennessee, on April 14, 1968.

FBI Director Hoover weathered this initial public controversy, but questions had been raised about the FBI's commitment to civil rights enforcement. These questions assumed greater importance owing to President Johnson's successes, in 1964 and 1965, in steering civil rights legislation through Congress. This new federal legislation, combined with the president's strong stance against racial violence in the South, necessitated a change in the Bureau's civil rights policies. Furthermore, the murder of three civil rights workers in Mississippi during the summer of 1964 and the killing of a Detroit housewife by Ku Klux Klan members in Alabama the following year heightened pressures on the FBI to enter the battle against Klan terrorism. In response, Hoover agreed to open an FBI field office in Jackson, Mississippi, in July 1964. That same month, FBI officials initiated a COINTELPRO (counterintelligence program) targeting the Klan and other racist groups.

The Hoover-King controversy also raised the issue of whether Hoover should retire. Under federal law, employees must retire when they reached the age of 70. Hoover's 70th birthday fell on January 1, 1965. Prior to the onset of the Hoover-King controversy, President Johnson had issued an executive order on May 8, 1964, exempting Hoover from the mandatory retirement law. Johnson's order did not specify the duration of this exemption, stipulating only "an indefinite period of time." Hoover's controversial press conference in November 1964, less than two months before his 70th birthday, led influential members of the press to demand that Johnson reconsider his earlier executive order. However, the president refused, and Hoover remained in office.

Bugging and the Fred Black Case

Since the early 1940s, FBI Director Hoover had authorized FBI agents to install hidden microphones (bugs) to collect intelligence about targeted individuals and groups. At first, such uses were confined to domestic security cases. In time, the use of bugs was expanded to include civil rights activists (such as Martin Luther King Jr.) and organized crime leaders

(under the Top Hoodlum program). Hoover's independent authorization of FBI microphone installations was not seriously challenged until the mid-1960s. On March 30, 1965, Attorney General Nicholas Katzenbach issued new guidelines requiring for the first time the attorney general's prior approval for all FBI microphone installations and stipulating that such approval would have to be renewed every six months.

Katzenbach's restrictive guidelines proved to be less important at first than in a case that came before the Supreme Court in 1966 (the Fred Black case), which precipitated a bitter conflict between the Justice Department and the FBI. This conflict began with a demand from the Supreme Court that the Justice Department submit a brief outlining the legal authority for the FBI bugs that had been installed in Black's office and home in 1962.

That year, an FBI investigation began into the gambling activities and influence peddling of Fred Black, a Washington lobbyist. This investigation uncovered evidence of Black's income tax evasion, for which he was convicted in 1964. At the time the tax-evasion case was tried, Justice Department attorneys did not know of the FBI's bugs (installed in 1962). They learned about them in 1965, inadvertently, when briefed by the FBI about another case. When Black's attorneys appealed his tax-evasion conviction to the Supreme Court in 1966, Attorney General Katzenbach (through Solicitor General Thurgood Marshall) informed the Court that the FBI had obtained information about Black through bugging his office and residence. The Court, in turn, ordered the government to present a brief outlining the legal authority for such installations.

When preparing the Justice Department's response, Attorney General Katzenbach consulted FBI Director Hoover and a bitter conflict ensued over the wording of the brief; in particular, whether the brief should explicitly stipulate that the FBI's bugging practices in the Black case had been authorized (and also whether such practices were generally reviewed and approved) by the attorney general. Because Katzenbach was unwilling to stipulate, Hoover exploited his contacts in the Johnson White House, the Supreme Court (Abe Fortas), and the Senate (Edward Long) to pressure Katzenbach to revise the language of the brief. This pressure did not work, and in the end, the Justice Department's response to the Court stated that the bug installed in the Black case had been authorized by FBI officials who were acting under independent authority previously granted by the Justice Department. The brief further conceded that no specific statute or executive order authorized FBI bugging.

Since planting microphones often involved a trespass (in violation of the Fourth Amendment, and thereby affecting the admissibility of any acquired evidence), until the early 1950s, FBI officials had not disclosed FBI bugging installations to the attorney general. In October 1951, Hoover for the first time directly briefed Attorney General J. Howard McGrath about FBI bugging practices. McGrath responded to this briefing by conceding that the use of microphones was permissible as long as no trespass was involved. He added that he could not authorize any microphones installed through trespass but did not directly prohibit or curb any such Bureau uses.

McGrath's ruling left the FBI vulnerable should it continue to install microphones by trespass until Attorney General Herbert Brownell, in a confidential memorandum of May 20, 1954, authorized FBI microphone installations "when uncovering the activities of espionage agents, possible saboteurs, and subversive persons." Brownell's directive emphasized this technique's importance in fulfilling the FBI's intelligence function in matters of "internal security" and the "national safety." Attorney General Brownell did not, however, require that FBI officials seek his prior approval for each bugging installation. Such prior approval was not required until March 30, 1965, when Attorney General Katzenbach issued new guidelines requiring the attorney general's prior approval for all FBI bugging installations. Katzenbach's guidelines (which, in effect, challenged Hoover's discretionary authority), combined with the conflict over the wording of the brief in the Black case, underlay the Hoover-Katzenbach conflict of 1966.

The Hoover-Katzenbach confrontation brought about substantive changes in FBI bugging policies and other FBI investigative practices that had been largely unmonitored. Ironically, these changes were instituted secretly by FBI Director Hoover. In response to Katzenbach's March 1965 guidelines, FBI Director Hoover sharply reduced the number of FBI wiretaps and bugs; he did not want the attorney general to discover how extensively these techniques were being used. Another factor in Hoover's decision to reduce bugs and wiretaps was an anticipated investigation (during 1965) of government eavesdropping, by Senator Edward Long's subcommittee of the Judiciary Committee. The combination of these hearings and Katzenbach's rules

heightened FBI Director Hoover's concern that his reputation, and that of the Bureau, might be tarnished if the FBI's use of questionable techniques become known. In addition to imposing numerical limits on FBI wiretaps and bugs, Hoover also banned the use of "clearly illegal" investigative practices that FBI agents had used extensively in the past—mail openings and break-ins; in Bureau terminology, "black bag jobs" (see Exhibit 5.7). Since 1942, FBI agents had illegally broken into homes and offices for the purpose of photocopying documents (letters, membership and subscription lists, financial records, and other information). Despite this ban, FBI agents continued to conduct break-ins, a practice that provoked controversy later in the 1970s.

The Media Break-in and COINTELPRO

During the early 1970s, FBI Director Hoover and the FBI became subject to mounting criticism. Throughout most of his tenure, Hoover had enjoyed virtual immunity from criticism and congressional scrutiny. There were some exceptions: the Abraham Lincoln Brigade arrests, the Judith Coplon case, the Apalachin incident, the harassment of Martin Luther King Jr., and the Fred Black case. But these controversies proved short lived and did not precipitate any kind of in-depth inquiry into the FBI's operations and objectives.

Events of 1971, however, combined to shatter this wall of secrecy and the attendant invulnerability. In one case, Senator George McGovern, who in 1972 became the Democratic presidential nominee, urged the Justice Department to probe FBI Director Hoover's punishment of agent Jack Shaw. Hoover had ordered Shaw and 15 other FBI agents to withdraw from a course at New York City's John Jay College of Criminal Justice following confidential remarks that Shaw had made to the instructor that were critical of the Bureau. Hoover had then transferred Shaw to the Butte, Montana, field office, knowing that he would resign rather than accept this transfer owing to his wife's serious illness (she was dying of cancer). Senator McGovern also made public an anonymous letter that he had received from 10 agents who charged that the FBI had lost its effectiveness because agents spent so much time polishing Hoover's image. At about the same time, on April 5, 1971, Democratic House majority leader Hale Boggs Jr. demanded Hoover's dismissal, accusing the FBI director of wiretapping members of Congress. Furthermore, a group of prominent scholars, lawyers, journalists, former Justice Department officials, and former FBI agents organized a two-day conference held at Princeton University on October 29 and 30, 1971. The conference, cosponsored by the American Civil Liberties Union's Committee for Public Justice and Princeton's Woodrow Wilson School of Public and International Affairs, sharply criticized FBI priorities, methods, and powers.

None of these events, however, equaled the effect of a March 8, 1971, burglary of an FBI office in Media, Pennsylvania, an FBI resident agency near Philadelphia. A group, calling itself the Citizens' Commission to Investigate the FBI, broke into this FBI office and stole hundreds of FBI files. (These files documented the scope of the FBI's monitoring of political activities and questionable practices.) Members of the group then released these files selectively and in stages, beginning approximately two weeks after the burglary, to carefully selected politicians, groups, and journalists whom they believed would be sympathetic to publicizing the contents of the stolen documents. Learning of this, Attorney General John Mitchell attempted to discourage publication, arguing that this "could endanger the lives or cause other serious harm to persons engaged in investigative activities on behalf of the United States." Some recipients did not disclose or publicize their contents, including Senator McGovern, who returned them, and an African American congressman, Parren Mitchell, who had received copies of files pertaining to the FBI's surveillance of black organizations.

Not all recipients returned the files, however, and publicity about their contents exposed a formerly secret side of FBI operations. The Philadelphia chapter of the Black Panthers had been sent a wiretap log showing that its headquarters was wiretapped. Other documents revealed that the FBI had conducted investigations on 22 college campuses in the Philadelphia area, focusing on black activism and student antiwar activities. The released files confirmed, for example, that Congressman Henry Reuss's daughter, a student at Swarthmore College, had been the subject of FBI inquiries about her antiwar activities, and that the campus police chief, switchboard operator, and a secretary in the registrar's office had been recruited as FBI informants. Those publishing the Media documents included the *Washington Post* and the *New York Times* (which reprinted segments of stolen files), and *WIN* magazine (published by the War Resisters League), which devoted an entire issue to the Media files, publishing the most complete record of the documents.

FBI Director Hoover reacted immediately and harshly to the Media break-in. The agent in charge of the Media office was suspended without pay for a month and was given a disciplinary transfer to the Atlanta field office. Within four months, 103 of the FBI's 538 resident agencies were closed, and security in the remaining ones was strengthened. Hoover also ordered a major FBI investigation, code-named MEDBURG, to track down the Media burglars. Agents from around the country were brought in to aid in this investigation, which focused on peace groups and antiwar activists. Although the investigators suspected that members of the Catholic Left antiwar movement were responsible, they never solved the case. The break-in, moreover, led Hoover on April 28, 1971, to terminate the FBI's secret counterintelligence program, COINTELPRO.

Although the Media break-in did not make major headlines, the public release of files documenting the extent of FBI political surveillance eventually led to further discoveries about secret FBI operations. FBI Assistant Director W. Mark Felt's phrase "a watershed event" is apt; the Media burglary unleashed a controversy that commanded widespread public, media, and congressional attention.

Some discoveries were triggered by NBC reporter Carl Stern's observation of the "COINTELPRO–New Left" caption on one of the released FBI documents. Since the code name COINTELPRO was unknown outside the Bureau, Stern asked the attorney general for documents pertaining to this program. Mitchell denied Stern's request. Stern thereupon filed a Freedom of Information Act (FOIA) lawsuit to obtain all FBI COINTELPRO documents. Stern's FOIA suit succeeded, and in December 1973 and March 1974, he obtained FBI records on the initiation of the various COINTELPRO programs. These releases were the first of a long series of disclosures compromising this once-secret operation to harass and disrupt targeted organizations. In 1975, the Church Committee (Senate Select Committee to Study Government Operations with Respect to Intelligence Activities) obtained additional documents about the FBI's COINTELPRO programs. Still other FOIA requests led to the release of over 50,000 pages of COINTELPRO files in November 1977.

The released COINTELPRO files documented the origins and growth of this FBI containment program. It began in 1956 by targeting the U.S. Communist Party, and expanded to target the Socialist Workers Party (in 1961); white hate groups, mainly the Ku Klux Klan (in 1964); black nationalist hate groups (in 1967); and the new left, youthful antiwar and student activists (in 1968). The techniques FBI agents employed in this campaign to "disrupt," "harass," and "neutralize" these targeted organizations replicated the tactics that had been employed during wartime operations against foreign intelligence agencies. These included the use of informants, propaganda, and disinformation—intended not to prosecute but to disrupt the targeted groups. Stories were also planted with "friendly" journalists to present the FBI's characterization of the motives, objectives, and personal immorality of the group's leadership or members. Anonymous mailings (letters, fliers, and pamphlets) were also disseminated to promote dissension within the targeted group. In some cases, a "snitch jacket" technique was employed, wherein a group member was identified as an informant through the planting of false information. Between 1956 and 1971, 2,340 COINTELPRO actions were approved and implemented.

Concurrent with the public release of the COINTELPRO files, Attorney General William Saxbe commissioned a committee, headed by Assistant Attorney General Henry Petersen and consisting of Justice Department lawyers and Bureau agents, to study COINTELPRO and report any recommendations. Saxbe released an abbreviated, 21-page version of this report in November 1974. The Petersen Committee concluded that many COINTELPRO activities "were entirely proper and appropriate law enforcement procedures," but that some involved "isolated instances" that "can only be considered abhorrent in a free society." The committee recommended against opening a criminal investigation, stressing the historical context of the Bureau's actions and that any violations of the First Amendment were "insubstantial."

Clarence Kelley, who became FBI director in July 1973, similarly attempted to contain the controversy precipitated first by the release of the COINTELPRO files and then by the Petersen report. In testimony before the House Judiciary Committee, Kelley defended FBI officials and agents as having "acted entirely in good faith and within the bounds of what was expected of them by the President, the Attorney General, the Congress, and the American people." He emphasized that the Bureau's actions had been undertaken in a different era, when college campuses were in turmoil, cities were in disorder, and revolutionary forces were threatening the social fabric.

Despite Saxbe's and Kelley's attempts to contain the damage of these revelations, the release of the Media files and the subsequent disclosures about COINTELPRO represented a turning point for the FBI. Since the 1930s, the FBI had commanded the positive image of a highly profes-

sional and apolitical agency. These disclosures highlighted the FBI's darker side of questionable and politically motivated operations. A series of national surveys conducted by the Gallup polling firm documented the devastating impact of these disclosures. Thus, whereas, in 1966, 84 percent of those polled expressed a "highly favorable" rating of the FBI, by 1970, this rating had declined to 71 percent; by 1973, to 52 percent; and by 1975, to 37 percent. Unlike earlier controversies, the Media break-in and its aftermath precipitated a wholesale rethinking of the FBI's role, administration, priorities, methods, and oversight.

The Modern Era (1972 to the Present)

More recently, the FBI's new investigative techniques, including undercover operations, computerization of criminal history databases, and digital telephony, have provoked controversy. In addition, FBI officials' decisions in several high-profile cases (the CISPES investigation, the standoff at Waco, Texas, and the shoot-out at Ruby Ridge, Idaho) raised additional questions about FBI procedures and provoked demands for greater public and congressional scrutiny.

FBI Domestic Intelligence and the Congressional Inquiries of 1975–76

The controversy over FBI surveillance activities, highlighted by the Media files, continued during the 1970s. The Watergate scandal of President Richard Nixon's administration and additional disclosures of FBI wrongdoing precipitated congressional hearings of 1975 on the FBI (and on other intelligence agencies—the CIA, NSA, and military intelligence). These hearings specifically inquired into what role, if any, the FBI should play in domestic intelligence. Revelations brought about by these hearings, in turn, intensified demands to reform FBI domestic intelligence operations, at the center of which was a call to establish a new administrative framework.

President Nixon's misuses of the FBI and the CIA played an important part in his forced resignation in August 1974. In fact, the second article of the House Judiciary Committee's impeachment resolution centered on such abuses of power. Earlier, Acting FBI Director L. Patrick Gray, Nixon's appointee to succeed Hoover (who had died in May 1972), admitted during his confirmation hearing that the FBI had given confidential files on the Watergate investigation to John Dean, President Nixon's counsel; he also admitted that, at Dean's request, he personally had destroyed other sensitive White House documents. In the wake of these admissions, Gray withdrew his candidacy for director in April 1973.

This controversy over the impropriety of the White House–FBI relationship soon escalated. During hearings Senator Sam Ervin's committee conducted into the Watergate affair in 1973, the committee obtained documentation from John Dean that showed how earlier presidential administrations had misused the FBI, and also that FBI Director Hoover maintained in his office files containing derogatory information on public officials. Dean's documentation consisted of two memoranda written by former FBI Assistant Director William Sullivan. Dean had originally solicited Sullivan's assistance for examples of earlier presidential uses of the FBI. Sullivan's memoranda detailed how the administrations of Lyndon Johnson and Franklin Roosevelt had also used the FBI for political purposes. President Nixon's strategy in having Dean seek Sullivan's assistance had been to show that other presidential administrations had engaged in similar practices and had also misused the FBI for political purposes. In addition, when attempting to justify the break-ins conducted in 1971 by the White House "plumbers" of Daniel Ellsberg's psychiatrist's office (for the purpose of obtaining damaging personal information to discredit Ellsberg, who had leaked the Pentagon Papers to the *New York Times*), during an August 1973 press conference, President Nixon offered that similar burglaries had also been conducted "on a very large scale" during the Kennedy and Johnson administrations. The following day, the Justice Department confirmed that FBI agents had conducted break-ins over a 30-year period. These "national security" break-ins, which officials characterized as employing an "old, established investigative technique," had been discontinued in 1966. Inadvertently, Nixon had leaked one of the FBI's closely guarded secrets: the practice of conducting "black bag jobs."

Many of the disclosures about FBI misconduct were unrelated to the Watergate scandal and, therefore, were not focused on during the 1973–74 Watergate hearings. Inadvertently, both Nixon's attempted justifications and the Ervin Committee's discoveries of Nixon's abuses of the intelligence agencies changed the political dynamic—shattering the mystique and wall of secrecy that had shrouded FBI operations. This increased skepticism was intensified as further revelations refocused attention on the FBI's abuses of

authority (and similar abuses by other intelligence agencies). In a *New York Times* article on December 22, 1974, Seymour Hersh disclosed that the CIA had engaged in domestic spying when attempting to link the American antiwar movement of the late 1960s to foreign sources and influence (Operation CHAOS). In November 1974, Attorney General Saxbe made public the abbreviated version of the Justice Department's report on COINTELPRO. Following up on the Sullivan memoranda, the Civil and Constitutional Rights subcommittee of the House Judiciary Committee had requested a Justice Department investigation of Sullivan's claims. In testimony on February 27, 1975, before the subcommittee, Attorney General Edward Levi confirmed that former FBI Director Hoover had maintained a secret Official and Confidential file in his office, which included derogatory information on prominent Americans (including presidents, cabinet officers, and members of Congress).

These post-Watergate revelations unleashed a new set of congressional inquiries. Unlike the Watergate investigations, which had centered exclusively on the Nixon administration, these investigations focused on the intelligence agencies (principally the FBI and CIA). On January 27, 1975, the Senate established the Select Committee to Study Government Operations with Respect to Intelligence Activities, more commonly known as the Church Committee, after its chair, Frank Church. In the following month, the House created a Select Committee on Intelligence, also known as the Pike Committee, after its chair, Otis Pike. Both committees pursued allegations of misconduct and inadequate oversight, held extensive hearings in 1975, and issued final reports in 1976.

The Pike Committee's investigation was assertive, subpoenaing documents and refusing to allow the executive branch to censor its final report. In the end, however, the House voted 246–124 to suppress the Pike Committee's 338-page final report, agreeing with President Ford and the intelligence agencies that the report should be subjected to prior review by the executive branch. Eventually, only the committee's 11 recommendations and the transcripts of its 1975 hearings were published.

The Church Committee's inquiry was more cooperative; committee members and staff negotiated with the intelligence agencies to obtain relevant records and submitted their final reports to them for review. At the request of the intelligence agencies, three chapters ("Cover," "Espionage," and "Budgetary Oversight") and sections of other chapters were deleted from the Senate's final published report. This report offered 183 recommendations to reform the intelligence agencies. Despite its limitations (it was denied complete access to all relevant agency records and it accepted censorship), the Church Committee's work represented the most thorough ever examination of the intelligence agencies. A staff of 100 assisted the 11 committee members. They conducted over 800 interviews and more than 250 executive hearings, and obtained over 110,000 pages of documents.

Book III of the Church Committee final report detailed the FBI's violations of the rights of Americans. These included COINTELPRO, surveillance of Martin Luther King Jr., and harassment of the Black Panther Party. The report also described the FBI's various intelligence collection techniques: the use of informants, electronic surveillance, surreptitious entries, and mail openings. Additionally, a nearly 200-page history surveyed FBI domestic intelligence, dating from World War I and the Red Scare era. Book III concluded with a discussion of the Huston Plan of 1970, a Nixon administration proposal authorizing the intelligence agencies to employ "clearly illegal" techniques when monitoring domestic dissenters (see pages 21–22).

The Church and Pike Committee inquiries centered on how the federal intelligence agencies had operated outside of a legal and constitutional framework and with minimal congressional oversight. Their revelations precipitated a policy debate over whether the FBI's domestic intelligence function should be terminated entirely or limited in scope—and, if limited in scope, whether continuing FBI investigations of violations of specific federal laws (the criminal standard) would deny the government the intelligence it needed to prevent terrorism and other violence.

Both committees supported a middle ground, recommending a modified FBI intelligence capability. The FBI would be permitted to conduct domestic security operations, as distinct from criminal investigations, but these should be administered by the FBI's Criminal Division, not the Intelligence Division. Foreign counterintelligence operations alone should remain the province of the Intelligence Division. The committees also recommended that Congress enact an FBI legislative charter, and thereby become involved, for the first time, in establishing legal boundaries for FBI operations. A legislative charter would delineate the FBI's powers, functions, and responsibilities, with the attorney general (and the president) having the discretion to issue specific rules governing how to carry out authorized investigations. Finally, the committees called for better congressional oversight of FBI operations.

Many of these recommended reforms were implemented. In August 1976, FBI Director Kelley transferred investigations of domestic radical and terrorist organizations from the Intelligence Division to the General Investigative Division, where they would be treated like other criminal cases. Kelley also ordered a review of the Bureau's domestic security investigations, with the aim of discontinuing those found to be unnecessary. The FBI's new investigation strategy would focus on organizations and key individuals in policy-making positions, not rank-and-file members. As a result of these changes, FBI domestic security investigations declined dramatically from 21,000 in mid-1973 to fewer than 300 by the end of 1976. About the same time, Justice Department officials began to draft guidelines to govern domestic security investigations, which were formally instituted on April 5, 1976. For the first time, the attorney general set the standards for the conduct of FBI domestic intelligence operations. These so-called Levi Guidelines (named after Attorney General Edward Levi) specified when investigations could be initiated, the three levels of investigations (preliminary, limited, and full), and the investigative techniques appropriate to each level. Concurrently, the Senate, in May 1976, and the House, in July 1977, established permanent intelligence committees to monitor the FBI's (and the other intelligence agencies') foreign intelligence and counterintelligence activities. FBI domestic activities (criminal and domestic security) were to be monitored by subcommittees of the House and Senate Judiciary Committees.

The major proposed reform that both the Church and Pike Committees had endorsed, and which ultimately was never implemented, involved congressional enactment of an FBI statutory charter. Such a charter would have codified FBI responsibilities and authority and, therefore, would have established an organizational structure that could not be changed easily, as historically had been the case whenever attorneys general or presidents issued revised guidelines or executive orders. Charter legislation was introduced as early as 1978; none ever passed.

The scope and purpose of FBI domestic intelligence, nonetheless, remains a source of controversy. For some, a principal concern centers on whether the FBI will resume its former lawless practices, especially during periods of domestic turmoil and dissent. The FBI's investigation of CISPES (Committee in Solidarity with the People of El Salvador) during the early 1980s heightened such concerns. Release of FBI records in 1988 involving the CISPES investigation seemed to confirm that groups opposed to the

Reagan administration's policies in Central America had been targeted for their political beliefs and opinions. For others, the restrictions imposed on FBI domestic security investigations after 1975 provoked concern that the Bureau's ability to apprehend and forestall terrorist or other violent activities had been compromised.

These conflicting views continued to create controversy and provoked sharp debate in the 1980s. Alarmed over the terrorist threat, the Reagan administration revised the Levi Guidelines in March 1983. The new guidelines, the so-called Smith Guidelines (named after Attorney General William French Smith) granted the FBI greater latitude to initiate domestic security and terrorism investigations. These concerns about international and domestic terrorism were further heightened by the bombing of the World Trade Center in New York City in February 1993 and the bombing of the federal building in Oklahoma City in April 1995. On both occasions, many in Congress and the media at first questioned the adequacy of the FBI's domestic intelligence authority. Ultimately, the Smith Guidelines were "clarified" in 1995, although the specific nature of these revisions was not disclosed. The policy issues that the Church and Pike Committees struggled with when confronted by the disclosures of past FBI lawlessness remain part of an ongoing controversy over the role and authority of the FBI.

Surreptitious Entries in the Early 1970s

In an unanticipated consequence, the 1971 Media break-in spawned a series of civil lawsuits by individuals who discovered that they had been targeted under FBI programs to harass and contain radical political movements. In 1973, one of these groups, the Socialist Workers Party (SWP), initiated a lawsuit seeking $27 million in damages for the FBI's violation of the organization's constitutional rights. The SWP suit resulted in still further disclosures of past FBI practices, with the release in 1975 of some 4,000 pages of FBI files, about 1,000 of which pertained to COINTELPRO. These documents confirmed that between 1960 and 1966, the SWP had been the target of at least 92 break-ins.

These released records contradicted the official estimates that FBI officials had provided to the Church Committee: that FBI agents had conducted "at least 239 surreptitious entries" ("black bag jobs" for purposes other than microphone installation) against all domestic subversive groups between 1942 and 1966. When conveying this low estimate in 1976, FBI officials conceded that this number might not be accurate, since the FBI maintained no central index systematically recording break-ins. In 1978,

however, a former FBI agent, M. Wesley Swearingen, who during the 1950s headed the FBI's break-in squad in Chicago, stated in an affidavit submitted in support of a Chicago lawsuit that the Chicago squad he led had committed thousands of break-ins during the 1950s and 1960s.

The resultant controversy over past FBI break-in practices assumed new proportions, this time centering on FBI officials' claims that the FBI had ceased conducting domestic security break-ins in 1966 due to former FBI Director Hoover's order banning such break-ins in July of that year. Following the July 1976 release of documents during the Socialist Workers Party suit, Justice Department attorneys inadvertently discovered FBI records confirming that FBI agents had continued to conduct break-ins after 1966, and that these records had been withheld from the current FBI director, Clarence Kelley. These disclosures prompted a Justice Department internal investigation, headed by Assistant Attorney General J. Stanley Pottinger. In conducting this investigation, FBI agents assigned to the case (derisively known as the "dirty dozen" by their FBI colleagues) conducted an unannounced visit to the FBI's New York City field office in August 1976. The investigators removed several file cabinets, which were turned over to Justice Department prosecutors.

These files documented break-ins conducted by the New York office between 1954 and 1973 (files that, under Hoover's 1942 order, should have been destroyed within six months of their creation). This discovery raised a new controversy over who controlled FBI operations. FBI Director Kelley admitted that FBI subordinates had lied to him when affirming that "black bag jobs" had been discontinued. Kelley further maintained that some FBI personnel "harbor a feeling that the good old days during the time that Hoover headed the organization will someday come back." Kelley's insistence that those days would not return did not silence concerns about the shakiness of his command and of the Justice Department's seemingly tenuous control over FBI operations.

The ordered Justice Department investigation of surreptitious entries focused on these newly discovered break-in records. Additional problems surfaced involving an FBI investigation of radical activists during the 1970s. During an investigation seeking to locate members of the radical Weather Underground group, who were fugitives from justice, a special Squad 47 in the New York City field office (about 68 agents under the supervision of John Kearney) had broken into the residences and opened the mail of friends of these fugitives between 1970 and 1974.

The records retrieved from the New York office documented these illegal practices. In response, Attorney General Griffin Bell initially sought to indict Kearney, who had resigned in 1972, for these break-ins. Bell's decision precipitated a storm of protest from rank-and-file agents, some of whom wrote letters to the attorney general while others picketed the New York City headquarters. In response to this criticism and declining agent morale across the country, the attorney general extended the Justice Department's inquiry and uncovered evidence that Squad 47's illegal activities had been authorized by high-level FBI officials (Acting FBI Director L. Patrick Gray, Acting FBI Associate Director W. Mark Felt, and FBI Assistant Director Edward Miller). Bell dropped the charges against Kearney, and in April 1978, a federal grand jury indicted Gray, Felt, and Miller for conspiring to violate the rights of citizens: for having approved surreptitious entries at the homes of friends and relatives of the Weather Underground. FBI Director William Webster exonerated the agents who had participated in the break-ins. Nonetheless, he disciplined four of their supervisors: he dismissed two (but later reinstated one), demoted another, and suspended a fourth.

Only Felt and Miller were tried in 1980—Gray, who claimed to not having been advised of Felt's and Miller's actions, succeeded in obtaining a separate trial. During their eight-week trial, Felt and Miller admitted authorizing the break-ins, but claimed that the FBI could legally search homes without a warrant in cases of national security involving foreign-directed terrorism. Felt claimed that Gray had given him blanket authority to approve surreptitious entries in such cases. Gray denied having given such approval. Five former attorneys general and former President Nixon testified during their trial. The attorneys general claimed that they had never approved such break-ins during their tenure in office. Nixon testified that in 1970 he had approved a proposal (part of the Huston Plan) that would have allowed warrantless searches, but revoked his approval four days later. Nixon further described his concerns about violent protests during the Vietnam War and his insistence that FBI agents apprehend fugitives of the Weather Underground. The former president did not admit to having specifically approved the Weather Underground break-ins. After deliberating over a two-day period, the federal jury convicted Felt and Miller on November 6, 1980. A month later, the judge fined them $8,500. The case against Gray was dropped shortly after the Felt-Miller trial, mainly due to insufficient evidence that Gray had approved these break-ins. Several months later, on March 26, 1981, President Ronald Reagan pardoned Felt and Miller. They had served the FBI and the country "with great distinction," Reagan asserted, and had acted in good faith in pursuing radical fugitives during the crisis of the Vietnam War, which was marked by violence and domestic turmoil.

The Gray-Felt-Miller case marked the first time that either an FBI director or high-level FBI officials had been indicted or prosecuted for conduct involving the performance of official duties. Their prosecution reflected the changing climate of the 1970s. It was a signal that lawless practices would no longer be condoned, and that Justice Department officials intended to set an ethical tone. Furthermore, at the heart of this controversy was the issue of control over the FBI. By prosecuting Bureau heads for apparently acting on their own authority, Justice Department officials made it clear that FBI officials would no longer have the autonomy and independence of action that had long been exercised.

ABSCAM and Other Undercover Operations

On February 3, 1980, in a front-page article, the *New York Times* reported that high-level public officials, including members of Congress, had been the subject of an FBI undercover operation code-named ABSCAM, for Abdul scam (Abdul was the name of a fictitious sheik). This disclosure, apparently leaked to the press by Justice Department insiders (although this was never confirmed), was covered by all of the major television networks and was the subject of feature stories in news magazines, such as *Time* ("The FBI Stings Congress") and *Newsweek* ("The New FBI Is Watching"). The prominence of those targeted by the FBI made the ABSCAM operation a major national news story, but ABSCAM was also newsworthy because of the entrapment issue raised by the investigation.

ABSCAM highlighted the further impact of the controversy precipitated by the Ervin, Church, and Pike Committees' hearings—resulting in a rethinking of FBI investigative priorities (to focus on white-collar crime, organized crime, and foreign counterintelligence) and the adoption and refinement of new investigative techniques (undercover operations, profiling). Since the mid-1970s, FBI investigations began to focus on complex criminal investigations in the white-collar crime and public corruption areas, in striking contrast to an earlier focus on kidnapping, auto theft, and bank robbery cases. This focus on white-collar crime was not in itself controversial, but ABSCAM's reliance on a new investigative technique—undercover operations—was. ABSCAM prompted questions of whether the FBI had been carrying out a vendetta against Congress. Were specific members of Congress selected for investigation because of their politics? Were they entrapped? Was the FBI out of control? Further issues were raised about FBI undercover investigations in general. Controversy swirled around questions of whether sufficient safeguards and guidelines governed such operations to preclude entrapment, and about the very necessity and appropriateness of undercover investigations. In response, a Select Senate Committee was established to study undercover activities, and the House Subcommittee on Civil and Constitutional Rights (CCR) of the Judiciary Committee conducted its own inquiry into ABSCAM and the more general issues raised by undercover operations. Both committees held hearings and published final reports in 1983 and 1984.

The ABSCAM investigation was initiated by the New York City field office in mid-1978, for the purpose of recovering stolen securities and paintings. In this operation, FBI agents recruited Mel Weinberg, a convicted swindler, as a middleman. Weinberg's role was to get thieves to bring stolen property to the Bureau's bogus fencing front, Abdul Enterprises, with offices on Long Island and a 62-foot yacht. At these locations, undercover agents posed as representatives of a wealthy Arab sheik interested in purchasing the stolen goods.

ABSCAM shifted from an investigation of stolen property during the fall of 1978 to an investigation of political corruption in New Jersey. From leads initially provided by Weinberg, FBI undercover agents approached Angelo Errichetti, the mayor of Camden, New Jersey. The agents indicated to Errichetti that the wealthy sheik was interested in investing in the Camden seaport and possibly in opening a casino in Atlantic City. Both of these ventures would require political favors that the sheik was willing to purchase. As Errichetti spread the word of the sheik's investment plans, other public officials became interested, including members of Congress.

At this point, around July 1979, the focus of the FBI's investigation into political corruption shifted to Congress. FBI agents rented a two-story house on W Street in Washington, D.C., as yet another operational site for their undercover operation. Members of Congress were brought to this location by middlemen and were told that an Arab sheik required assistance in his quest for asylum. The FBI agents posing as the sheik's representatives were advised that the going congressional bribe rate for such assistance

was $50,000. FBI agents videotaped these meetings at the W Street site while Justice Department lawyers, who were in an adjacent room, carefully monitored the bribery transactions on a closed-circuit screen. The ABSCAM operation ended in February 1980 when information about this investigation was leaked to the press.

Most of the resultant publicity and controversy centered on the third phase of ABSCAM, when the investigation had shifted to Congress. FBI officials had authorized bribe meetings with 27 public officials, based on the allegations of middlemen in the investigation (only 20 meetings were held). These meetings resulted in 12 convictions, involving one senator and six congressmen.

The Senate Select Committee issued its final report on the ABSCAM investigation in 1983. After weighing the benefits and risks of undercover operations, the report concluded that, on the whole, such operations "have substantially contributed to the detection, investigation, and prosecution of criminal activity." The report found that in some cases, undercover operations were "indispensable," but reached no conclusions about how many safeguards should be instituted or what these should entail. Although commending the FBI and the Justice Department for improving safeguards in its undercover activities, the report nonetheless uncovered deficiencies in the ABSCAM investigation: (1) problems with the selection and supervision of informants, (2) the virtually unlimited scope of the initial approval, (3) misconduct by informants, (4) reliance on corrupt middlemen, and (5) lax management and supervision.

The CCR, the House subcommittee chaired by Don Edwards, was much more critical of FBI undercover operations. Based on 21 hearings over a four-year period, its report of April 1984 discussed the threat of undercover operations to public institutions, third parties, and the proposed targets. The subcommittee was not reassured by the attorney general's 1981 guidelines on FBI undercover operations, finding that they were not always observed. Its investigation had uncovered "a pattern of widespread deviation from avowed standards, with substantial harm to individuals and public institutions." In a companion inquiry into Operation CORKSCREW (an FBI investigation into allegations of judicial bribery in Cleveland), the CCR concluded that "the safeguards in practice were little more than rhetoric, offering at best limited constraints upon the investigators."

As the CCR pointed out, undercover operations sometimes had damaging consequences for innocent third parties. A General Accounting Office report concurrently found that, as of December 31, 1982, the FBI's undercover operations had spawned 29 lawsuits against the federal government involving claims of $424.3 million. The FBI's Operation RECOUP, for example, a 1981 investigation of stolen car racketeering, involved establishing a bogus used car business with FBI agents acting as intermediaries in the sale of stolen cars. Those conducting the operation were fully aware that the innocent purchasers of these vehicles would eventually lose title to them. By October 1982, more than 250 cars had been confiscated from such innocent purchasers.

Responding to public and congressional concerns over undercover operations, the Justice Department developed guidelines on the FBI's use of the undercover technique. Issued on January 5, 1981, these guidelines provided three safeguards: (1) undercover operations could be initiated whenever there was reasonable suspicion that a pattern of criminal activity already existed, (2) targeted individuals should clearly understand the illegal nature of the operation, and (3) undercover operations should be modeled on the real world. An Undercover Operations Review Committee (UORC) was also established at FBI headquarters in Washington to serve as a centralized clearinghouse for reviewing and approving proposed major undercover activities. As noted, the Edwards House subcommittee (CCR) report expressed serious reservations about the FBI's adherence to these guidelines and did not consider the UORC to be a reliable check on FBI operations. Instead, the CCR report recommended legislation requiring judicial authorization before an undercover operation could be initiated, not unlike the judicial warrant that was required for most police searches. This recommendation was rejected by Justice Department officials and FBI Director Webster rejected it as an unreasonable constraint on executive and law enforcement discretion; it was never enacted.

The controversy surrounding the ABSCAM case differed substantially from the earlier controversies of the Cold War era. At its core were questions about the Bureau's new priorities (public corruption) and investigative techniques (the undercover operation), not about whether political activists were being targeted. The FBI's first undercover operations employed the anti-fencing "sting" technique (to catch thieves and recover stolen property), and were jointly conducted with local law enforcement, funded

through LEAA (Law Enforcement Assistance Administration). In 1975–76, 10 such operations were conducted. The Bureau's first explicit request to fund undercover operations was submitted in 1976, $1 million for Fiscal Year 1977. In subsequent years, FBI long-term undercover operations increased dramatically from 53 in 1977 to more than 300 by 1983; appropriations for these activities also increased from $1 million in 1977 to $12.5 million in 1984. By 1984, the undercover technique was extended to white-collar crime, public corruption, and organized crime, and was "nearly coextensive with the FBI's jurisdiction." Although undercover activities constituted a small proportion of total FBI investigations, they became an important technique in the FBI's investigative arsenal. During 1991, 245 major undercover investigations were conducted, a number that does not include many more short-term undercover operations.

This new reliance on the undercover technique began in the mid-1970s, in what FBI Director Kelley called the "quality-over-quantity" approach. Confronting dwindling resources, Kelley channeled FBI operations to areas where they would be most effective. FBI investigations thereafter focused on selected targets for maximum results. To further this approach, field offices implemented the "target squad" concept. Complementing an older strategy of reacting to crimes after they occurred (case squads), target squads sought to identify in advance particular crime figures or patterns of criminal activity (such as drug trafficking, organized crime, or political corruption). This proactive strategy was the catalyst to the undercover technique.

Although institutionalized in FBI operations, undercover activities remain controversial. Do such investigations encourage entrapment? Do undercover activities create rather than detect crimes? How are the subjects of such investigations selected? Others have questioned the adequacy of the (1981) attorney general guidelines for undercover operations. Should a judicial warrant be necessary as an independent check on such operations?

The CISPES Investigation

FBI files publicly released in January 1988 to a New York lawyers' group, the Center for Constitutional Rights, confirmed that during the early 1980s, the FBI had conducted an intensive investigation of CISPES (Committee in Solidarity with the People of El Salvador), a domestic political group critical of President Ronald Reagan's Central American policies. The FBI's 1,320-page CISPES file, released in response to a Freedom of Information Act request, revealed that 59 FBI field offices had monitored CISPES in a pattern of surveillance reminiscent of the Bureau during the Hoover era.

Concurrent with this release, the House Subcommittee on Civil and Constitutional Rights received reports of nearly 50 unexplained break-ins of churches, homes, and offices of opponents of the Reagan administration's Central America policy. During testimony before the subcommittee in February 1987, FBI Assistant Director Oliver Revell denied that any agents had conducted such break-ins. Revell pointed out, however, that the Bureau could legally conduct physical searches without warrants if done pursuant to a "higher executive authority" and involving foreign intelligence matters. These guidelines (Foreign Counterintelligence or FCI), Revell emphasized, were largely classified.

Revell's testimony and the release of the CISPES documents again brought up questions about the FBI's domestic surveillance practices. The contents of the released files showed that the FBI's investigation of CISPES had two phases. The first began in September 1981 as a criminal investigation, to determine whether CISPES violated the Foreign Agents Registration Act (FARA). FBI officials suspected that CISPES was acting as an agent of one of the El Salvadoran opposition groups which, if confirmed, would require that it register with the U.S. government. Although CISPES opposed the Reagan administration's policy of funding the El Salvadoran government and attempted to influence public opinion through conventional methods (demonstrating, lobbying, speaking, publishing newsletters, and occasionally engaging in nonviolent civil disobedience), the FBI's six-month investigation uncovered no evidence to support the "agent of a foreign power or group" allegation. Accordingly, this investigation was officially closed in February 1982.

In March 1983, a second FBI investigation of CISPES was opened, this time under the "foreign counterintelligence—international terrorism" guidelines. FBI officials' suspicion that CISPES was a terrorist group was initially based on CISPES's own admission that it supported opposition groups in El Salvador, such as the FMLN (Farabundo Marti Front for National Liberation). In addition, an FBI informant, Frank Varelli, reported to his Bureau contacts that this support not only included money, food, clothing, and

medical supplies, but also military aid. An unidentified source also claimed that the FMLN was responsible for terrorist activities in the United States.

The premise of the FBI's investigation was that CISPES's legitimate activities were a front for a covert terrorist program. To detect these activities, FBI agents began to monitor the organization's public activities. In doing so, FBI agents employed a variety of techniques: informers infiltrated the organization and its demonstrations; agents checked FBI files, police records, and various public records for information on CISPES members; individuals, residences, meetings, and offices were monitored; photographs were taken of demonstrations; license plate numbers of vehicles parked near demonstrations or meetings were recorded and traced; and CISPES members and leaders were interviewed. Although FBI headquarters instructed FBI field offices that "the purpose of the investigation was not to investigate the exercise of First Amendment Rights of CISPES members," in practice, the CISPES investigation monitored lawful political activities.

On October 28, 1983, moreover, FBI officials ordered all FBI field offices to develop "information on the locations, leadership, and activities of CISPES chapters within each field offices' jurisdiction." The resultant 27-month surveillance also encompassed more than 100 other groups having ties to CISPES and its members, including church groups and labor unions. When the FBI's massive investigation of CISPES was officially closed on June 18, 1985, no criminal charges were brought against CISPES or its members. Instead, FBI officials concluded that CISPES was involved in legitimate political activities and was not an international terrorist group.

In response to controversy precipitated by the disclosure of the CISPES files, FBI officials conducted an internal inquiry in 1988. The inquiry defended the propriety of the original focus and intent of the CISPES investigation: to determine whether CISPES was involved in terrorist activities. Nonetheless, during public testimony before a House subcommittee in September 1988, FBI Director William Sessions conceded that the initial (1981) investigation had been flawed because it relied heavily on faulty information provided by informer Varelli, whom FBI officials subsequently realized was unreliable. In addition, Sessions acknowledged that the "major problem" was that "the scope of the investigation was unnecessarily broadened" in October 1983. Overall, he argued that the CISPES investigation had been flawed, but "an aberration" in the

FBI's otherwise high standard of conduct. Sessions disciplined six FBI supervisors who had managed the CISPES investigation at FBI headquarters in Washington, D.C., and at the Dallas field office. Three supervisors were suspended for two weeks without pay and were placed on internal probation; three others received written reprimands.

These revelations spawned two congressional inquiries and a broader investigation into FBI investigations of terrorist organizations. In one of these inquiries, the Senate Intelligence Committee's (1989) report corroborated the FBI's conclusion that the CISPES investigation had been mismanaged, both in having originally been triggered by unfounded allegations when opening the case, and then in monitoring lawful political activities. This report further uncovered that, as the result of the FBI's CISPES investigation, the names of 2,375 individuals and 1,330 groups were indexed in the FBI's central records system. In its own more comprehensive inquiry, a General Accounting Office study revealed that during the period from January 1982 to June 1988, the FBI had conducted approximately 19,500 FBI terrorism investigations, and that in the majority of cases, FBI officials' explanations as to why cases had been opened were not always clear or were based on tenuous links to terrorists. In only 12 percent of the cases in the GAO sample had the FBI received information that the targeted individual or group had been directly involved in terrorist activity.

The CISPES case, which generated widespread press coverage, once again raised questions about the Bureau's intelligence activities and surveillance of Americans. Was the FBI being used for political purposes to silence critics of Reagan administration policies? Was "terrorism" the new rationale, replacing the earlier "subversive" and "communist" justifications for FBI surveillance? Had investigations been opened under the classified Foreign Counterintelligence Investigation guidelines as "international terrorism" matters in order to circumvent the more restrictive and public Domestic Security/Terrorism guidelines? FBI Directors Webster and Sessions denied such political purposes or that FBI terrorism investigations were linked to White House policy interests. Nonetheless, suspicions dating from the Hoover era continue to provoke controversies about recent FBI operations. Civil libertarian critics of the FBI have questioned the adequacy of the FBI reforms of the mid-1970s and have endorsed the need for an FBI legislative charter. In their view, attorney general guidelines and presidential executive orders are not sufficient to ensure Bureau compliance with the rule of law.

These concerns were heightened further by revelations around the same time about the FBI's Library Awareness Program. Under this program, FBI agents contacted librarians at 21 scientific and technical libraries in the New York City area to ascertain whether Soviet agents were using library materials—and which ones. FBI Director Sessions defended this program as necessary to thwart foreign intelligence activities by learning which technical articles Soviet spies were reading. Most librarians, and the American Library Association, protested this practice of having librarians report on the reading habits of library users. In addition, the practice was criticized as an infringement on First Amendment rights. The disclosures of CISPES and the Library Awareness Program brought renewed public attention to the FBI's surveillance activities.

Discrimination within the FBI Ranks

Most controversies in the FBI's history have centered on questions over the limits of authority or FBI investigative practices. These typically involved the FBI's relations with outsiders: "slackers," radical aliens, communists, subversives, and members of Congress. In the late 1980s and early 1990s, a different controversy surfaced, one involving the FBI's own ranks. A 1990 survey of Bureau employees, conducted at the request of FBI Director William Sessions, found that the majority of FBI employees (agents and support staff) were dissatisfied with Bureau personnel practices, particularly regarding assignments and promotions. This dissatisfaction was widespread, manifesting itself among blacks, Hispanics, women, and white males. Promotions were widely regarded as unfair, with about 70 percent of employees believing that assignments and promotions were not awarded to the most qualified. Based on a random sample of 4,172 employees (with 74 percent responding), this study also found that 26 percent of FBI employees reported discrimination on the job because of their race, color, national origin, religion, disability, sex, or age. Minority and women agents widely believed that an "old-boy network" excluded them from the best assignments, those that facilitated career advancement, and thereby disadvantaged them when it came to promotions. White male agents, on the other hand, viewed the FBI's affirmative action measures as reverse discrimination, with preferential treatment given to minorities and women. The study also uncovered allegations both of sexual harassment and of discrimination against homosexuals. These complaints were mirrored in a series of lawsuits against the FBI during the late 1980s and early 1990s, some brought by individuals and others by classes of Bureau employees: blacks, Hispanics, white males, women, and homosexuals.

The controversy reflected both ongoing FBI practices and the legacy of the Hoover FBI, when minorities and women had been systematically excluded from employment and promotion. At the time of Hoover's death, in May 1972, the FBI employed 143 minority agents and no women in an agent force of 8,659. Acting Director L. Patrick Gray first recruited women agents in 1972, although it was not until FBI Director William Webster's tenure (1978–87) that women and minority agents were actively recruited. Subsequent FBI directors (William Sessions, 1987–93, and Louis J. Freeh, 1993–) made minority recruitment a top priority. As a result, by 1997, minorities (African Americans, Hispanics, Native Americans, and Asian Americans) constituted 15.3 percent of all FBI agents, and women were 14.7 percent. By January 31, 1997, 1,617 agents were women of a total agent force of 10,816 (see Table 3.1).

The top positions in the Bureau, however, were filled disproportionately by white males. By the late 1980s, the resultant clash between new minority and women recruits, seeking career advancement, and many old-guard agents, wishing to preserve their positions and agent culture, inevitably led to charges of discrimination and harassment.

Two lawsuits brought by minority agents during the 1980s symbolized the FBI's internal problems. In one case, agent Bernardo Perez, in the early 1980s, filed a class-action suit on behalf of himself and more than 300 others (about three-fourths of the Bureau's Hispanic agents). The second lawsuit was filed in 1987 by an African American agent, Donald Rochon.

The Perez lawsuit alleged that Hispanic agents were discriminated against in assignments and promotions and were relegated to the so-called "taco circuit"—assignments in the Southwest where Spanish-language skills were

needed. The menial and unrewarding nature of these assignments, such as translating for non–Spanish speaking agents, excluded Hispanic agents from assignments having greater potential for career advancement.

In September 1988, Federal Judge Lucius D. Bunton ruled that Hispanic agents had been discriminated against in this pattern of assignments and, therefore, had been denied a fair opportunity for career advancement. Two years later, in September 1990, FBI Director Sessions accepted the recommendations of a special court-appointed panel and ordered the immediate promotion of 11 veteran Hispanic agents, including Perez. Each Hispanic agent was entitled to as much as $50,000 in additional salary and retirement benefits.

Donald Rochon's landmark case alleged harassment by fellow agents at the Omaha and Chicago field offices, where he had been assigned from 1983 to 1986. Rochon claimed to have been the object of racist "jokes" and "pranks"; for instance, a gorilla's face was pasted over a photo of his two children on his desk; he received numerous offensive letters and phone calls, some with insulting references to his white wife, and others implying death threats; he also received a bill for a life insurance policy he had not applied for. In August 1990, Sessions approved an out-of-court settlement in which Rochon would leave the Bureau and receive a benefit package of approximately $1 million. In addition, Sessions disciplined 11 white agents and supervisors for either harassing Rochon or failing to respond to his complaints. Sessions's disciplinary actions ranged from requiring agents to attend counseling, giving oral reprimands, and issuing formal censures, to suspending one agent without pay for 21 days.

Shortly following the Perez and Rochon settlements, 250 black agents, in a group known as BADGE (Black Agents Don't Get Equality), met to consider filing a class-action suit against the Bureau. Their allegations paralleled

TABLE 3.1

SPECIAL AGENT EMPLOYMENT STATISTICS (JANUARY 31, 1997)

Ethnicity/Race	Number of Men	Number of Women	Total	Percent of Total
American Indian	43	9	52	0.5
Asian	209	33	242	2.2
Black	507	104	611	5.6
Hispanic	648	98	746	6.9
Total Minorities	1,407	244	1,651	15.3
White	7,792	1,373	9,165	84.7

Source: Federal Bureau of Investigation Web Site <http://www.fbi.gov>, February 13, 1998.

those of the Perez case: that blacks were discriminated against in assignments and promotions, and that black agents were disproportionately assigned to black urban areas and to divisions and cases having less potential for career advancement. They also claimed that a white "old-boy network" made promotions less accessible to black agents. In April 1992, after a year of negotiations with BADGE, Sessions announced a settlement that averted a lawsuit. Ratified by a federal court in January 1993, this settlement included the following terms: a federal judge would monitor the FBI's personnel practices for five years to ensure that black agents receive fair treatment; the FBI would hire outside consultants to review the Bureau's promotion and disciplinary procedures; six black agents would be promoted to supervisor; and nine other black agents would be reassigned to FBI headquarters in Washington.

Almost immediately, the FBI Agents Association, a predominantly white agent group representing about two-thirds of the Bureau's agents, challenged the BADGE settlement. Instead of suffering discrimination, the association claimed, minority agents were receiving preferential treatment. In September 1993, Federal Judge Thomas Hogan rejected their request to block implementation of this plan. Hogan concluded that Bureau promotions over the years reflected a "manifest imbalance" favoring white agents and that the settlement sought to remedy that imbalance.

In June 1993, agent Suzane J. Doucette filed the first sexual harassment lawsuit against the FBI. She accused a superior at the Tucson field office of assault and sexual harassment—putting a chokehold on her and touching her "in ways that are very sensitive." Doucette subsequently resigned, ending her 10-year FBI career, and in February 1995 reached a $300,000 out-of-court settlement. In 1994, three other lawsuits were filed on behalf of female agents Heather Power-Anderson, Boni Carr Alduenda, and Joanne E. Misko, alleging sexual harassment, retaliation when they complained, and discrimination in promotion. In addition, in 1995, a group of female agents considered filing a class-action suit against the Bureau to challenge a pervasive culture of sex bias—in training, assignments, transfers, and promotions.

In another landmark case, Frank Buttino, a 20-year veteran agent, filed suit in 1990 challenging his dismissal as a security risk—responding to an FBI internal inquiry, he had admitted to being homosexual. (Like minorities and women, homosexuals had formerly been excluded from the FBI.) An anonymous source had previously informed Buttino's superiors that he was homosexual. As Buttino's class-action lawsuit was about to go to trial in San Francisco in December 1993, FBI officials agreed to a settlement. The terms included a pledge not to discriminate against gay men and lesbians as employees or as applicants and to grant Buttino nearly $100,000 in cash, legal fees, and a monthly pension ($1,746) when he turns 62. A federal judge approved this settlement in March 1994. Concurrently, FBI Director Freeh instructed all FBI field offices that homosexual conduct should no longer be regarded as misconduct. Attorney General Janet Reno had previously, on December 3, 1993, prohibited Justice Department agencies from discriminating against gays and lesbians.

These lawsuits and settlements occurred during the directorships of William Sessions and Louis Freeh. Both FBI directors instituted strong affirmative action hiring policies and measures to remedy past discrimination. Sessions appointed James Perez to head the FBI's equal employment opportunity (EEO) affairs office, and gave him wide discretion in handling complaints. Sessions also revised FBI applicant tests to ensure fairness in the selection of new agents. Sessions's actions provoked dissent among many white agents, with some privately criticizing the Bernardo Perez and Donald Rochon settlements as "caving in" to minority demands; these agents sarcastically dubbed the director "Concessions."

Since his nomination in 1993, Freeh has consistently emphasized the importance of diversifying the Bureau's agent force. He named the first woman, the first Hispanic, and the second and third African Americans to the top ranks (assistant director) of the FBI. In 1994 and 1995, Freeh publicly warned that sexual harassment and discrimination in the FBI "will not be tolerated," and that the Bureau's legacy of discrimination, "a very, very bad historical track record," was over.

Ruby Ridge and Waco

During the 1990s, two controversial incidents became symbolic of excesses in federal law enforcement and raised new questions about FBI operations, particularly whether agents had used excessive force in effecting arrests. Both incidents involved standoffs with heavily armed groups that resulted in the loss of life. The first resulted in a shootout and 11-day standoff at a cabin in Ruby Ridge, Idaho, in August 1992. FBI sharpshooters, attempting to arrest Randall Weaver, a survivalist and anti-government activist, accidentally killed members of his family. The second incident occurred about six months later, near Waco, Texas. A 51-day standoff occurred involving a religious cult (the Branch Davidians) and agents from the FBI and ATF (Bureau of Alcohol, Tobacco and Firearms of the Treasury Department). This standoff culminated on April 19, 1993, when FBI agents launched a tear-gas assault on the group's barricaded compound, during which more than 80 members of the sect died.

The controversy surrounding the Ruby Ridge and Waco incidents centered on how the federal government handled confrontations between law enforcement agents and citizens. In their aftermath, the FBI, the Justice Department, and the Treasury Department launched internal inquiries into the conduct of agents and the decision making of higher-level officials. In 1995, Congress also held hearings that were highly critical of FBI procedures and the militarization of law enforcement. In addition, in 1996, a federal grand jury was convened to consider criminal indictments against the FBI officials who had either supervised the Ruby Ridge raid or participated in the subsequent FBI inquiry (it had been alleged that FBI records were destroyed to protect senior FBI officials as part of a botched cover-up).

In contrast to past controversies involving questionable investigations, Ruby Ridge and Waco raised questions about the use of deadly force and the appropriate deployment of the FBI's elite Hostage Rescue Team in crisis situations. The tragic outcomes of both cases also raised questions about the agency's accountability and its apparent paramilitarism. Furthermore, the deaths at Waco and Ruby Ridge became linked with larger political issues of the 1990s, reinforcing the anti-government ideology of militia and right-wing groups who already saw the federal government as out of control.

The controversy over Ruby Ridge focused on two issues: first, the FBI's performance during the siege and, second, the integrity of its subsequent internal inquiries into the shoot-out. To understand these issues, it is necessary to review how the FBI became involved in the standoff at Randy Weaver's remote cabin in northern Idaho.

Weaver first came to the attention of ATF agents during an investigation of the Aryan Nation, a white supremacist group with members in several Western states. ATF officials believed that this group was in violation of federal weapons laws, and that Weaver was associated with this group. An ATF informant, posing as an illegal arms dealer, sought to buy weapons from Weaver. After attempting for three years to persuade Weaver to make such an illegal sale, the informant succeeded in October 1989, when Weaver sold him two

sawed-off shotguns. Weaver was indicted for this illegal weapons sale in December 1990, and was arrested about two months later. Released on his own recognizance, Weaver failed to appear for his trial date. At this point, Weaver's case was referred to the U.S. Marshals Service with the warning that he was a "dangerous fugitive."

Another year transpired before six marshals traveled to Weaver's mountain cabin to arrest him. During the marshals' surveillance of the cabin, a shoot-out occurred on August 21, 1992, that resulted in the deaths of Weaver's 14-year-old son, Samuel, and U.S. Marshal William Degan. Federal authorities at the scene thereupon solicited the assistance of the FBI's Hostage Rescue Team. The 50-member team arrived the following day, placing the cabin under surveillance.

The team's subsequent actions became the basis for controversy. At issue were the FBI's "rules of engagement" (the instructions given to the FBI sharpshooters regarding when they could use deadly force), and who had authorized the use of force. Under "shoot-on-sight" orders, snipers could shoot any armed adult in the vicinity of the cabin. Pursuant to these rules, on August 22, sharpshooter Lon Horiuchi shot and wounded Randall Weaver, who was walking outside the cabin and carrying a weapon. Horiuchi believed Weaver was about to shoot at a helicopter overhead. As Weaver and a friend, Kevin Harris, ran back to the cabin, Horiuchi fired a second shot at the cabin entrance, seriously wounding Harris and fatally wounding Weaver's wife, Vicki, who had been standing behind the cabin door but was not visible to Horiuchi. Weaver and his three daughters surrendered peacefully after a 10-day siege, during which hundreds of FBI agents and other law enforcement officers surrounded the remote cabin site and were reinforced by helicopters and armored personnel carriers.

Having arrested Weaver, the Justice Department prosecuted Weaver and Harris for the murder of U.S. Marshall Degan. Weaver and Harris were acquitted by a federal jury in July 1993. Weaver was also acquitted of all major weapons charges, except for having failed to appear in court. Two years later, the Justice Department announced an out-of-court settlement of $3.1 million with the Weaver family, but admitted to no wrongdoing.

In the aftermath of the shoot-out and standoff, FBI and Justice Department officials conducted a series of reviews of the operation. An FBI shooting-incident review (1992) concluded that no agency rule was intentionally violated when Horiuchi shot Vicki Weaver, but FBI Director Freeh later acknowledged that the agent in charge of the review had also been part of the FBI headquarters' team overseeing the handling of the siege, posing a potential conflict of interest.

In contrast, a Department of Justice task force, consisting of 19 FBI inspectors and 4 Justice Department lawyers, was much more critical of the FBI's performance. Its more than 300-page report, completed in the summer of 1994, found that the specific "shoot-on-sight" rules of engagement employed at Ruby Ridge departed from the FBI's deadly force policy, and that the shot that killed Vicki Weaver was illegal. The task force report precipitated further reviews by the Justice Department's Office of Professional Responsibility (OPR) and its Civil Rights Division, both of which concluded that no criminal prosecution of FBI personnel was warranted, and that Vicki Weaver's fatal shooting was not unlawful.

Based on these reviews and the FBI's own administrative review, in January 1995, FBI Director Freeh announced disciplinary actions against 12 FBI employees. Freeh concluded that there had been no criminal conduct, but he did find evidence of "inadequate performance, improper judgment, neglect of duty, and failure to exert proper managerial oversight." His disciplinary actions ranged from oral reprimands to written censure with suspension.

One of the agents most harshly disciplined, Eugene Glenn, complained to the Justice Department that the official inquiries were a cover-up, exonerating high-level FBI officials in Washington who had supervised the operation and blaming any shortcomings on agents in the field. As one of the FBI field commanders at Ruby Ridge, Glenn disputed his supervisors' claims, particularly those of Larry Potts, and denied that the agents in the field had been responsible for changing the rules of engagement. He also challenged the independence of those conducting the Bureau's administrative review, in light of their close ties to officials who supervised the operation.

Following another OPR interim report, the Justice Department opened a criminal investigation in August 1995. This investigation, which concluded in August 1997, focused on the role high-level FBI officials had played during the siege and subsequent inquiries. In the aftermath of this inquiry, FBI Director Freeh temporarily suspended six FBI officials, including Larry Potts, his former deputy director. No charges were brought against five of the FBI officials, except E. Michael Kahoe, who in October 1996 pled guilty to obstructing justice (for destroying copies of the FBI's internal "after-action" critique of its performance at Ruby Ridge). In August 1997, state officials in Idaho brought

charges against FBI sharpshooter Lon Horiuchi (for the death of Vicki Weaver) and Kevin Harris (for the death of U.S. Marshall Degan). In January and May 1998, Federal Judge Edward Lodge, however, ruled that Horiuchi could not be tried in state court because his conduct related to his official duties.

The Ruby Ridge incident also precipitated congressional action. On September 6, 1995, the Senate Judiciary Committee's Subcommittee on Terrorism, Technology and Government Information began hearings into the siege at Ruby Ridge and the FBI's conduct during the standoff. In October testimony before the subcommittee, FBI Director Freeh admitted to "serious deficiencies" in the FBI's conduct, and that FBI officials at Ruby Ridge and FBI headquarters were responsible for "a trail of serious operational mistakes." Freeh criticized the "shoot-on-sight" policy, but defended the lawfulness of Horiuchi's killing of Vicki Weaver. Freeh, who became FBI director after the Ruby Ridge and Waco incidents, then outlined the reforms he had instituted to preclude any recurrence. The FBI's deadly force policy was clarified to permit use of deadly force "only in the face of imminent death or serious physical injury to the officer or another person." The FBI's shooting incident review policy was also revised to avoid any appearance of a conflict of interest between those participating in the incident and those serving on the panel of inquiry. Freeh revised the management structure overseeing crisis situations and increased the training of crisis managers. Finally, Freeh reassured the subcommittee that the FBI could investigate itself. In its report of December 1995, the subcommittee praised Freeh's revised deadly force policy and restrictions on the use of the Hostage Rescue Team (HRT). Nonetheless, the subcommittee concluded that the FBI's shooting of Vicki Weaver was unjustified.

Several months after the Ruby Ridge incident, the FBI, along with ATF, was involved in a second major controversy involving a standoff with a heavily armed group, this time at the Branch Davidians' residential compound near Waco, Texas. An offshoot of the Seventh-Day Adventists, the Branch Davidians believed in the imminence of the Second Coming of Christ. Their leader at the time of the standoff, David Koresh, also anticipated an "apocalyptic showdown" with government agents.

The crisis had been triggered by an ATF investigation of the Branch Davidians' illegal purchase of weapons. In an attempt to serve arrest and search warrants, on February 28, 1993, ATF agents launched a raid on the group's compound. A shoot-out ensued between the ATF agents and the Branch

Davidians, resulting in the death of 4 agents and 6 Davidians and the wounding of 16 ATF agents. ATF officials immediately requested FBI assistance. Members of the FBI Hostage Rescue Team were dispatched to the compound (located about 12 miles outside Waco), and on March 1, the FBI became the lead agency in an ensuing 51-day standoff with the heavily armed religious sect.

FBI officials on the scene attempted to negotiate a peaceful surrender with Koresh and his followers. They complemented these negotiations with pressure tactics to bring the Davidians to the bargaining table—cutting off electricity, playing loud music, and tightening the perimeter around the compound. More than 700 law enforcement personnel participated in the 51-day standoff, with between 250 and 300 FBI agents at the scene at any given time. Unlike the seige at Ruby Ridge, the rules of engagement at Waco barred FBI agents from using deadly force unless they or others were in imminent danger. In fact, FBI agents never fired a shot during the entire standoff, including during the April 19 assault.

As the negotiations proceeded, Koresh promised to surrender but then recanted. Thirty-five sect members were released, and periodically, FBI negotiators issued ultimatums and threats and resorted to acts of harassment. By early April, FBI officials concluded that the standoff could go on indefinitely. Frustrated over the progress of negotiations, FBI officials developed a plan to conduct a massive assault on the well-fortified compound, using tear gas to force the Davidians out. Under this plan, tear gas would be gradually injected into the compound over a 48-hour period, allowing time for the Davidians to escape from the non-gassed exits. This plan was presented to Attorney General Janet Reno, who had assumed office on March 12. Reno rejected the plan on April 16, but reconsidered the following day after meeting with FBI Director Sessions and other officials.

On April 19, an FBI tank (combat engineering vehicle or CEV) with an attached boom began inserting CS tear gas into the Davidian compound at 6:02 a.m. The Davidians responded by shooting at the FBI vehicles. Tear gas continued to be injected throughout the morning hours until, at 12:07 p.m., the Davidians started simultaneous fires at several locations within the compound. Shortly thereafter, nine Davidians fled and were arrested; gunfire was also heard from within the compound. Owing to strong winds, the fire quickly spread and the compound was soon completely consumed by flames. An estimated 80 Davidians lost their lives, including Koresh and 25 children under the age of 15.

Responding to the public controversy over the tragic outcome of the Waco standoff, the Justice Department and Congress initiated inquiries into the FBI's conduct during this raid. The House Judiciary Committee convened an unusual hearing on April 28, 1993, receiving testimony from the key officials and agents who were involved in the Waco shootout and standoff—from ATF and the Treasury Department, as well as the FBI and the Justice Department. In her testimony, Attorney General Reno defended her approval of the tear-gas plan, arguing that it was the only workable, non-lethal option, given the stalemated negotiations, the fatigue of the FBI's Hostage Rescue Team, and the risk of physical and sexual abuse for children inside the compound.

These hastily convened hearings did not end the controversy, which was heightened by the published findings of the Justice Department's own inquiries. On October 8, two reports were released: "Report on the Events at Waco, Texas, February 28 to April 19, 1993" (the Scruggs Report), prepared by Richard Scruggs, an assistant to the attorney general, and five other Justice Department officials; and "Evaluation of the Handling of the Branch Davidian Standoff in Waco, Texas, by the United States Department of Justice and the Federal Bureau of Investigation" (the Dennis Report), prepared by Edward S. G. Dennis Jr., a partner with a Philadelphia law firm and former assistant attorney general. Both reports exonerated the FBI. The Dennis Report, for example, acknowledged mistakes in managing the crisis, such as conflicts between FBI negotiators and the tactical units at the scene, and FBI officials who ignored the advice of behavioral science experts (inside and outside the Bureau) on the possibility of mass suicide. Nonetheless, the Dennis Report concluded, FBI officials were not blameworthy, as the standoff was "a mass suicide choreographed by Koresh over a two-month period. . . . Under the circumstances, the FBI exhibited extraordinary restraint and handled this crisis with great professionalism." Both reports were sharply criticized by the press for failing to place any blame on high-level FBI or Justice Department officials. Indeed, an October 12 *New York Times* editorial labeled the Dennis Report a "whitewash."

A month later, the Justice Department released another report on the events at Waco. This 46-page report, prepared by an outside expert, Alan A. Stone (a professor of law and psychiatry at Harvard), criticized FBI officials for rejecting their own experts' advice in their negotiating strategy with Koresh. Stone also claimed that Attorney General Reno had been misinformed about the medical impact of tear gas and had been "ill-advised" when approving the assault.

Nearly two years later, in July 1995, two House subcommittees (the Crime Subcommittee of the Judiciary Committee; and the National Security, International Affairs and Criminal Justice Subcommittee of the Government Reform and Oversight Committee) held joint hearings on the Waco siege. With the House then controlled by Republicans, the hearings and the subcommittees' final report, released a year later, sharply focused not on the actions of the FBI and ATF but on the Clinton administration's handling of the Waco standoff. In their report of July 1996, the two subcommittees characterized Attorney General Reno's approval of the tear-gas plan as "premature, wrong, and highly irresponsible," and criticized President Clinton for his failure to accept her resignation. The report nonetheless concluded that David Koresh bore "ultimate responsibility" for what happened at Waco.

In the aftermath of this controversy, the ATF director resigned for his role in the initial raid, but no FBI agent or official was disciplined for their handling of the 51-day standoff or the tear-gas assault. Indeed, the Justice Department consistently defended the tear-gas plan and attributed the tragic outcome to Davidian leader Koresh.

Waco and Ruby Ridge proved controversial because they raised serious questions about the FBI's deadly force policy. Had the Bureau become a paramilitary force? Could the FBI (and Justice Department) police itself? And, more broadly, was federal law enforcement out of control? In 1994 and 1995, FBI Director Freeh instituted several reforms in response to these public and congressional concerns. The peaceful settlement of another confrontation between the FBI and an armed citizens' group (the Freemen in Montana, in June 1996) partially restored the Bureau's reputation in its handling of crisis situations. Militia and some right-wing groups, however, continue to see Waco and Ruby Ridge as "wake-up calls." In their view, these two incidents reveal a federal government and an FBI that are out of control.

Summary

Since its beginning in 1907, the Federal Bureau of Investigation has been involved in a series of controversies. The most significant controversies highlight the changing issues that have most concerned the American public, and many have led to major turning points in the FBI's history.

During the first two decades (1908–24), the major contoversies centered around the Bureau's creation as a federal investigative agency; its collaboration with private citizens and detective agencies; and its zealous pursuit of draft dodgers, aliens, and radicals. During those early years, the main fear was that, once established, a national police force might become large and powerful. Such a force could infringe on individual rights and liberties, and as a part of the Justice Department, could be misused by the executive branch.

At the turn of the century, the prevailing belief was that the prosecution of crime should be a local and state responsibility. The passage of the Mann Act in 1910 marked a limited departure from this view, as the act made commercialized prostitution involving the interstate transportation of prostitutes a federal crime. The Supreme Court's rulings of 1913 and 1917, which upheld the constitutionality of the Mann Act, established a constitutional basis for further extending federal policing—the interstate commerce clause of the U.S. Constitution. Nonetheless, the persistence of ongoing congressional concerns over a national police force effectively limited the Bureau's responsibilities and size. Congress's limited funding of the Bureau, even during the crisis of World War I, led Bureau officials to develop a controversial association with the American Protective League, whose members assisted the Bureau in enforcing wartime statutes. By the time of the Palmer Raids of 1920, earlier predictions that a federal police force would become too large and too powerful were apparently borne out when Justice Department agents rounded up radicals across the country. Yet, only the broader governmental scandal of Teapot Dome (1923–24) forced a rethinking of the Bureau's role, resulting in the implementation of reforms to insulate the Bureau from misuse by Justice Department and White House officials.

These reforms ushered in the second major era in the Bureau's history, dominated by the 48-year tenure of J. Edgar Hoover as the Bureau's director (1924–72). During the first decade of his directorship, Hoover insulated the FBI from political influences and created a professional agent force. By the 1930s, Hoover had become an outspoken advocate for an expanded federal role in crime control. The Lindbergh kidnapping in 1932 marked a turning point in the national debate; the case challenged the capability of local law enforcement, and the value of federal agents in crime control and investigation seemed clear. Federal law enforcement authority dramatically expanded owing to the efforts of the administration of Franklin Roosevelt, resulting in the passage of Attorney General Cummings's Twelve Point Crime Program. Public opinion was further mobilized by the Bureau's celebrated pursuit of John Dillinger and other gangsters, and the American public became convinced that a war on gangsters required an expanded federal presence.

The crises of World War II and the Cold War provoked controversy in response to the Bureau's domestic intelligence activities. Criticisms—whether of the FBI's arrests in 1940 of activists who had recruited volunteers to fight in the Spanish Civil War or of the FBI's wiretapping of Judith Coplon, prosecution of U.S. communist leaders under the Smith Act, and investigating "disloyal" federal employees during the Cold War era—commanded little public, media, or congressional support. Internal security concerns both immunized FBI operations from critical scrutiny and strengthened respect for the FBI.

The FBI's activities did not provoke controversy again until the 1970s with disclosures about COINTELPRO and the findings of the Church Committee. During that decade, FBI operations were critically scrutinized and some of the agency's more abusive practices were publicly disclosed: the widespread political surveillance of citizens, the targeting of certain domestic political groups for disruption, and the maintenance of files on prominent public officials. In addition, FBI priorities were criticized for failing to act against organized crime and to safeguard civil rights.

More recent controversies have focused on the adequacy of recent restrictions on the Bureau's domestic intelligence operations. Disclosures of the 1970s that FBI agents continued to conduct break-ins, and of the 1980s that the FBI targeted CISPES, again brought forth accusations of FBI abuses of power—and raised questions of whether reforms of the 1970s had successfully exorcised the ghost of FBI Director Hoover. Distinctly new controversies also arose. Operation ABSCAM raised questions about undercover operations and proactive investigative techniques developed during the late 1970s. The efforts to diversify the FBI's agent force also resulted in controversy about internal discrimination within the FBI, notably involving racial, ethnic, and gender discrimination in assignments and promotions. Finally, in the 1990s, the Waco and Ruby Ridge incidents raised questions about the FBI's paramilitarism.

None of these controversies, however, proved to be of sufficient magnitude to arrest the Bureau's steady increase in size and power. Shifting public concerns gave rise to questions about FBI investigative purposes, strategies, and methods, but underlying these controversies was a broad public consensus on the need for a strong federal law enforcement presence.

Ambivalence about the FBI's role—the demand for expanded powers and jurisdiction, yet the need for limits—has been at the heart of the basic dilemma of law enforcement in a democratic society: the conflict between crime control and due process. Controversial tactics or programs have not led to demands to abolish the FBI or to impose close public scrutiny. Instead, these controversies have centered on whether order and security can be maintained within the rule of law. This ongoing tension between law and order has been, and remains, an ongoing source of controversy in the work of the Federal Bureau of Investigation.

FBI OVERSIGHT AND LIAISON RELATIONSHIPS

Athan G. Theoharis

The Attorney General

The Official Role

When the Bureau of Investigation was created by executive order in July 1908, Attorney General Charles Bonaparte intended to assume personal responsibility over Bureau operations. His purpose was to confine Bureau activities to investigating violations of federal antitrust and interstate commerce laws and to allay congressional fears that a federal investigative force would monitor personal and political activities and subvert the constitutional system of checks and balances. (Some members of Congress had questioned whether a federal police force might target critics of the president for criminal investigation.) Bonaparte's administrative plan was feasible, given the Bureau's limited mission and its small size (numbering 34 agents in 1908 and increasing to 234 agents and 26 support staff by 1916).

The Bureau's relationship with the attorney general soon changed. United States involvement in World War I in April 1917 increased the Bureau's internal security responsibilities, and personnel were increased accordingly (570 in 1917 and 630 by 1919). In addition, under a liaison program approved by Attorney General Thomas Gregory in February 1917, Bureau agents were authorized to work closely with the American Protective League, a conservative businessmen's organization headquartered in Chicago, in monitoring political radicals and antiwar activists (see pages 105–07). Gregory's successor, A. Mitchell Palmer, extended this surveillance role in August 1919 when he created a special Radical Division within the Bureau of Investigation (later renamed the General Intelligence Division) to coordinate all information pertaining to radical activities.

As the Bureau's size and responsibilities increased, attorneys general (already overwhelmed with their newly acquired wartime responsibility to enforce the Espionage, Sedition, and Selective Service Acts) could no longer directly supervise Bureau operations. Accordingly, on June 30, 1919, Attorney General Palmer assigned supervisory responsibility over the Bureau to the assistant attorney general of the Division of Miscellaneous Matters.

Attorney General Harry Daugherty, Palmer's successor, modified this administrative arrangement. Committed to rationalizing departmental operations, on November 21, 1921, Daugherty established a new post, administrative assistant attorney general, to which he appointed his trusted aide Rush Holland. The Bureau and other departmental divisions were to report directly to Holland. Daugherty also sought to ensure that the Bureau would be responsive to the political interests of the Harding administration. His ensuing actions, when ordering Bureau investigations of striking railroad workers in 1922, as well as of the administration's congressional critics in 1923–24, eventually caused a major political scandal for President Calvin Coolidge (who became president following Harding's death in August 1923). To silence criticisms, Coolidge demanded Daugherty's resignation.

Daugherty's successor as attorney general, Harlan F. Stone, moved quickly to stanch this evolving scandal. In May 1924, he initiated a series of reforms in the Bureau's operations—most notably, prohibiting wiretapping and investigations of political activities. Then, on January 12, 1925, Stone reimposed the attorney general's direct control over Bureau operations. The director of the Bureau was required to report to the attorney general only his decisions "on the operations of the Bureau of Investigation as a whole" and otherwise to the particular assistant attorney general having jurisdiction over an "individual case or subject." Stone intended to limit Bureau activities "strictly to investigations of law, under my direction or under the direction of an Assistant Attorney General regularly conducting the work of the Department of Justice." In reality, this meant that William Donovan, the assistant attorney general whom Stone had appointed to head the Criminal Division, supervised Bureau operations.

This reporting relationship was slightly modified when Attorney General Homer Cummings reorganized the Department of Justice in 1933, renaming the Bureau the "Division of Investigation." (This name was changed again in 1935 to the Federal Bureau of Investigation; see Table 1.2.) On December 30, 1933, Cummings appointed William Stanley, then assistant to the attorney general, to head the Administrative Division. Stanley's duties were to "handle general administration, including supervision" of the Bureau.

Cummings's administrative change was in response to the Bureau's growth (total personnel tripled from 775 in 1933 to 2,441 in 1940) and increased investigative responsibilities. Attorneys general could no longer directly supervise Bureau operations to ensure that they were lawfully mandated and complied with the Roosevelt administration's policy priorities. The Bureau director became subject to the competing demands of the Justice Department's various administrative divisions (at the time: Anti-Trust, Tax, Claims,

Lands, Criminal, War, Customs, and Administration). Moreover, under presidential directives of 1936, 1939, and 1940, the FBI's mission expanded to include collecting intelligence about possible threats to the nation's internal security. The FBI's role changed further when, dating from 1940, the Roosevelt White House requested intelligence reports on individuals and organizations opposed to the president's foreign policy initiatives, an assignment that ensured FBI Director J. Edgar Hoover direct access to the White House.

This changed status led Hoover in August 1941 to propose to Attorney General Francis Biddle a change in procedure, emphasizing that to ensure secrecy, the FBI director should report "direct" to the attorney general and "not to some other Departmental official." Biddle agreed to this recommendation on November 27, 1941, "because so many of the matters being handled by the Bureau were of such a delicate nature, originating as they did in other departments, in the White House."

Biddle's order seemingly reinstituted the earlier arrangement (from 1908 to 1919 and from 1924 to 1933), in which the Bureau director reported directly to the attorney general. In reality, a fundamental change in the relationship had occurred. Thereafter, the FBI director continued to seek the attorney general's approval for any major changes in Bureau policies. Thus, in 1952 and 1954, FBI Director Hoover sought the permission of Attorneys General J. Howard McGrath, James McGranery, and Herbert Brownell to install surveillance microphones by means of break-ins. But this request for approval constituted only a part of the FBI–attorney general relationship; in other areas, the FBI director acted independently and authorized programs and procedures without the attorney general's advance permission.

In 1940, FBI officials began to receive and act upon requests from the White House (and other intelligence agencies) for reports on particular individuals and organizations. When servicing these requests, FBI officials bypassed the attorney general. The FBI director, however, did not merely service White House requests but submitted unsolicited reports directly to the White House (and to other intelligence agencies). Reports provided by the FBI to the White House included derogatory information about the president's foreign policy critics, and reports sent to military intelligence agencies included copies of code books, cipher strips, and enciphering and deciphering tables. Because of the sensitivity either of the requests or of the FBI's submis-

sions, the attorney general was never fully informed about these FBI activities—particularly when agents had employed illegal methods to obtain the information.

The so-called Huston Plan (see pages 34–35) highlights this situation of ignorance on the part of the attorney general. Dissatisfied with the quality of intelligence that the White House was receiving from the FBI and other U.S. intelligence agencies about radical political activities, President Richard Nixon established a special interagency task force in June 1970 (composed of representatives of the FBI and other federal intelligence agencies) to recommend changes in intelligence collection methods and procedures, but he did so without consulting Attorney General John Mitchell. Furthermore, Mitchell was not informed of the task force's recommendation that the president authorize "clearly illegal" investigative techniques; he learned of this recommendation inadvertently when FBI Director Hoover advised Mitchell of his intention to seek the attorney general's advance approval each time the FBI conducted any of the recommended "clearly illegal" activities. Mitchell then contacted President Nixon to brief him about Hoover's plans. Unwilling to sacrifice "deniability" (given Hoover's declared intention to create a written record that the particular illegal activity had been conducted pursuant to the president's program), Nixon recalled the Huston Plan authorization memorandum.

Nonetheless, the attorney general and the president remained committed to the concept of a centralized and presidentially directed intelligence community. Accordingly, in September 1970, Mitchell created a Special Intelligence Evaluation Committee. When this committee attempted to create a permanent staff composed of representatives from all the intelligence agencies, Hoover refused to permit FBI participation, claiming "manpower and budgetary" reasons. The FBI director's refusal killed the proposal—and Mitchell neither ordered nor sought to convince Hoover to cooperate.

Earlier, in 1942, FBI Director Hoover, on his own—without obtaining "legal sanction" (that is, the attorney general's approval)—authorized FBI break-ins, and then in 1956, he unilaterally authorized the COINTELPRO–Communist Party (expanded during the 1960s to other targeted organizations) to "harass and disrupt" dissident activists and organizations. Despite the formal reporting requirements of various attorneys general dating from the early 1940s, the FBI by the early 1940s had become an autonomous agency; in many of the FBI's sensitive programs and procedures, the FBI director operated independently of the attorney general.

The FBI Director–Attorney General Relationship

The personalities and politics of attorneys general also influenced the ambiguous FBI–attorney general relationship. At first, given the Bureau's limited federal law enforcement role, attorneys general did not directly monitor Bureau operations—a situation highlighted by Attorney General Palmer's highly publicized role in the so-called Palmer Raids of January 1920. Palmer had not been involved in the planning of these dragnet raids, but afterward—in response, first, to the resultant positive publicity, and then to Assistant Labor Secretary Louis Post's rulings freeing the vast majority of the arrested radicals—Palmer sought credit for them, seeking to promote his candidacy for the Democratic presidential nomination of 1920.

Palmer's criticisms of Post's actions triggered a House impeachment inquiry. In testimony before a House subcommittee considering an impeachment resolution in 1920, and later in 1921 in testimony before the Senate Judiciary Committee, the attorney general defended the actions of Bureau agents who had conducted the raids, arguing that "if . . . some of my agents out in the field . . . were a little rough or unkind, or short or curt, with those alien agitators whom they observed seeking to destroy their homes, their religion, and their country, I think it may well be overlooked." Palmer's after-the-fact rationalization backfired, and his presidential ambitions were shattered.

Palmer's actions, and questions raised about the Bureau's conduct of the raids, did not lead to intensified congressional oversight of the attorney general's administration of the Bureau. Accordingly, Palmer's successor, Harry Daugherty, who had served as Warren Harding's campaign manager during the 1920 presidential election, was emboldened to exploit the Bureau's resources politically. Daugherty's appointee as Bureau director, William Burns, maintained records on the party affiliations and political connections of Bureau agents and appointed to the force many agents whom friendly congressmen had recommended. In the wake of disclosures of these (and other) abuses of power, Daugherty and Burns were dismissed in 1924.

President Coolidge's appointee for attorney general, Harlan F. Stone, reinstituted tighter oversight over Bureau operations. These reforms included the banning of wiretapping and political surveillance, dismissal of "special employees," and basing appointments on merit and professionalism. As part of these reforms, Stone fired Burns and in May 1924 appointed J. Edgar Hoover as acting Bureau director. Stone required Hoover to institute the specified changes in personnel and procedures. Hoover dutifully complied and, to cement his personal relations with Stone, began what became a regular Bureau practice thereafter— agents were ordered to perform personal services for the attorney general. These services ranged from arranging transportation and accommodations for Attorney General Stone and his family when in travel status or on vacation to, years later, conducting security reviews of Attorney General John Mitchell's apartment in the Watergate complex. This valued assistance to the attorney general raised the Bureau's status in relation to other divisions in the Justice Department.

President Franklin Roosevelt's attorney general, Homer Cummings, sought to ensure the continuance of this superior-subordinate relationship. Cummings's purpose, however, was to expand the federal government's law enforcement role, a goal that required launching a public relations campaign to extol the necessity for a stronger, professional Bureau. Cummings's implicit trust in Hoover's loyalty, both to himself and to the Roosevelt administration's programs, created a new relationship wherein the attorney general also granted broad latitude to the FBI director both to investigate "subversive activities" and to allow the FBI to promote its own media campaign extolling the FBI's successes in combating gangsters.

Within these broad guidelines, Cummings was able to control FBI operations. His immediate successors—Frank Murphy, Robert Jackson, and Francis Biddle—were not. In their case, President Roosevelt's interest in having the FBI service his administration's policy interests undercut their oversight authority. The president issued a series of directives in 1939, 1940, and 1943, the purposes of which were to enable FBI monitoring of critics of his interventionist foreign policy and to curb a suspected "fifth column" threat. Although these presidential directives were issued after consultation and with the consent of Attorneys General Murphy and Jackson, the president's priorities (and attendant interest in secrecy) made it very difficult for them (and their successors) to monitor the FBI and to limit FBI investigative activities. Indeed, when Biddle in 1941 sought to proscribe FBI monitoring into liberal political and trade union activities, Hoover successfully resisted the attorney general's proposed rules, claiming that they would hamper FBI "investigations into situations involving potential danger to the Government of the United States" and "will make utterly impotent the work of the FBI in subversive fields." In the same preemptive fashion, Hoover dismissed Bureau critics as communist-influenced and stressed his own "experience in meeting and coping with law enforcement problems, on a national basis and meeting this with legal, efficient and honorable tactics."

Unwilling to challenge the FBI director, Biddle recognized that Hoover would operate independently anyway, having earned the president's support. Biddle's successor, Tom Clark, conceded that he faced the same dilemma, admitting that President Harry Truman oftentimes "would tell me things the Bureau was doing that I didn't know about." When Clark complained and requested that Hoover brief him about the FBI's reports to the White House, the FBI director "reluctantly gave me [Clark] copies of some of the things he was sending over to the White House . . . but not all of them." Clark's suspicions were well founded. In November 1945, for example, Clark approved an FBI request to wiretap prominent Washington attorney Thomas Corcoran. At the time, however, Clark was unaware that the FBI had been wiretapping Corcoran's phone since June 1945, a wiretap installed at the request of the Truman White House on the understanding that it was not to "become known," and that if it did, it "would be the FBI's baby" and the White House "would deny any knowledge." Moreover, even when Clark accidentally learned in 1948 that the FBI was leaking information to President Truman's critics in the House Committee on Un-American Activities (HUAC), he was unable to sever this covert FBI-HUAC relationship.

Clark's successors—Attorneys General J. Howard McGrath, James McGranery, Herbert Brownell, and William Rogers—also deferred to the FBI director. Their own limited influence reflected the politics of their appointments (McGrath and Brownell had served as campaign managers, respectively, for Truman during the 1948 and Eisenhower during the 1952 presidential elections) and the dynamics of Cold War internal security politics. Unwilling to challenge FBI Director Hoover, they willingly granted the FBI great latitude to conduct investigations of dissident activities, and they likewise raised no serious objections about the FBI's failure to investigate organized crime aggressively.

Actions of Attorneys General McGrath and Brownell demonstrate this passivity and deference. Embarrassed by the loss of the Judith Coplon case—following revelations that Coplon's phone had been tapped by the FBI and that Justice Department attorneys prosecuting the case had been unaware of it—McGrath required that, thereafter, FBI officials were to notify the Justice Department whenever referring "any case" for possible prosecution in which the subject had been wiretapped. But FBI officials resisted this requirement as placing an "intolerable burden" on the FBI and exacted a modified notification requirement, limiting it to cases "where the Department is seriously considering" prosecution.

In contrast, Brownell decided in 1954 not to monitor and require his own advance approval for all FBI microphone uses. Then, when briefed in 1956 about the FBI break-in activities and other tactics to "disrupt" communist activists, he raised no objections about their propriety and legality. Brownell's position was that the Justice Department's main priority should be to "back the Bureau" and that this could best be achieved without strict oversight. He concluded that any guidelines governing FBI microphone installations, for example, should "be sufficiently general to cover all situations." His resultant 1954 bugging directive was purposefully vague—intended to encourage FBI officials to interpret it broadly. Indeed, in 1959, after some deliberation, FBI officials decided not to seek the approval of Attorney General William Rogers (Brownell's successor) to use bugs during criminal investigations. They concluded that the broad language of Brownell's May 1954 directive "covered both Security and Criminal matters" and thus Rogers's approval was unnecessary.

Robert F. Kennedy and Nicholas Katzenbach

Politics and personality became central to the FBI–attorney general relationship during the tenure of Attorney General Robert F. Kennedy. Committed to a vigorous war on crime, and eager to advance the political interests of President John F. Kennedy (having served as campaign manager of his brother's 1958 senatorial and 1960 presidential campaigns), Robert Kennedy's aggressive style ensured a personality conflict with FBI Director Hoover. Hoover had become accustomed to deference from the attorney general, and thus he resented Kennedy's unintended slights, implicit in his public advocacy of a more effective war on organized crime. Kennedy's youth, his seeming disrespect for the seniority (in age) of his subordinate, and his attempts to impose his authority over FBI operations further rankled the sensitive Hoover.

As early as May 1961, Attorney General Kennedy apprised White House aides that he intended to "keep abreast of any contacts between the White House staff and [the Justice] Department," insisting that "any" meeting must "first" receive his approval. Additionally, Kennedy subverted another of Hoover's positions of influence, his chairmanship of the Interdepartmental Intelligence Conference, a subcommittee of the National Security Council established in 1949 to coordinate internal security activities among the various intelligence agencies. Attorney General Kennedy ordered that internal security policy would instead be the responsibility of the Justice Department. The attorney general's creation of Justice Department organized crime strike forces also indirectly suggested that the FBI had neither the will nor the purpose to curb this national crime menace.

This did not mean that Kennedy closely monitored FBI operations. To the contrary, he willingly avoided monitoring the FBI's wiretaps and installations of microphones, preferring not to know their extent and purposes. (Indeed, on August 17, 1961, the attorney general signed a form letter providing advance approval for all FBI requests to telephone company officials for "leased lines" to be used during microphone installations.) Furthermore, Kennedy was unwilling to challenge FBI wiretapping priorities—highlighted by his own initiative over whether the FBI could safely (that is, without discovery) wiretap civil rights leader Martin Luther King Jr.

In June 1963, the attorney general sounded out FBI officials over the feasibility of wiretapping King. Kennedy quickly concluded that this action would be too risky politically. Undaunted by the attorney general's hesitancy, FBI officials argued that a wiretap of King could be "conducted with full security," and they discounted Kennedy's concerns that tapping King could be discovered, arguing that the FBI had "years of experience in this field and we [the FBI] continually reviewed our procedures to insure that every measure possible to secure such installations was taken." Unwilling to rebuff FBI interest and despite his own reservations, in October 1963, Kennedy authorized an FBI wiretap of King "on a trial basis, and to continue it if productive results were forthcoming." Kennedy's approval was conditional: this tap would have to be evaluated "at the end of the 30 days." This evaluation never occurred. Kennedy apparently forgot his requirement in the midst of

the crisis that followed the assassination of his brother the next month. The King wiretap was not discontinued until March 1965, when Kennedy's successor as attorney general, Nicholas Katzenbach, first learned of its existence.

President Kennedy's assassination also changed the FBI–attorney general relationship. Recognizing how President Kennedy's assassination reduced Robert Kennedy's status, given President Lyndon Johnson's suspicions about the personal loyalty of Kennedy holdovers on the White House staff and in the Justice Department, senior FBI officials forwarded to the new president information about the disloyalty of key Kennedy associates. These behind-the-scenes reports to the White House, and Hoover's unsubtle refusal to act as Kennedy's subordinate, complicated Robert Kennedy's relations with Hoover until his resignation in August 1964 to seek election to the U.S. Senate. Nonetheless, Robert Kennedy's public rift with Hoover occurred only later, in 1966, triggered by his successor Nicholas Katzenbach's decisions during 1966 court proceedings involving Fred Black.

Indicted and convicted for income tax evasion, Black appealed his conviction to the Supreme Court. During the appeal, Justice Department officials disclosed to the Court that, in 1963, the FBI had bugged Black's office and hotel room (prior to Black's indictment). This disclosure to the Court soon precipitated a major rift between Attorney General Katzenbach and FBI Director Hoover when the Supreme Court justices demanded that the Justice Department submit a brief outlining the legal authority for the FBI's bugging of Black.

Since 1954, FBI officials had installed surveillance microphones without the attorney general's prior knowledge and approval, relying on Attorney General Brownell's broadly worded directive of May 1954. Issued to govern FBI "national security" bugging activities, Brownell's directive had subsequently been interpreted by FBI officials as also authorizing microphone installations during FBI investigations of organized crime leaders. But Katzenbach had not approved such expansion to include criminal investigations (and, in 1965, had issued new rules subjecting FBI microphone surveillance to stricter departmental oversight standards). After consulting his predecessors (Brownell, Rogers, and Kennedy), he refused to comply with Hoover's insistence that the Justice Department's brief to the Court affirm that the FBI's bugging of Black had been authorized by the Justice Department.

Katzenbach's refusal posed delicate political and policy problems—made even more delicate because of the changed political climate of the 1960s, when privacy rights commanded heightened public and congressional support and government surveillance activities were viewed skeptically by the media and by Congress. Infuriated by Katzenbach's unwillingness to defend the FBI's bugging of Black, Bureau officials worked behind the scenes with sympathetic members of Congress and the Johnson White House, suggesting that Katzenbach's refusal to brief the Court that FBI microphone surveillances were authorized by the attorney general had, as its purpose, protection of the reputation of former Attorney General Robert Kennedy. (The FBI's bugging of Black occurred during Kennedy's tenure.) These contacts, really amounting to an end-run on the attorney general, succeeded. Hoover was able to capitalize on President Johnson's widening political rift with then-Senator Robert Kennedy. In one such initiative, FBI Assistant Director Cartha DeLoach approached Supreme Court Justice Abe Fortas, who had been (and remained) a political confidant of the president (and had been appointed to the Court by Johnson), and thus was responsive to proposals that could promote Johnson's political interests. Concluding that "the entire matter boiled down to a continuing fight [between Kennedy and Johnson] for the presidency," Fortas and DeLoach discussed various options. Ultimately, Fortas drafted a plan, which Johnson at first considered, to have the president create a special committee to review the Justice Department's brief. Johnson eventually rejected this plan. Immediately made aware that his resistance to Hoover's demand had complicated his relations with both the FBI and the White House, Katzenbach soon resigned as attorney general to accept appointment as under secretary of state shortly after the Court's ruling in the Black case. His decision confirms the reality of the FBI director's independence, and demonstrates how Hoover's direct access to the White House (as well as support from powerful members of Congress) undermined Katzenbach's ability, as attorney general, to impose his authority over the FBI.

The Katzenbach-Hoover contretemps was exceptional—as was the public conflict of 1966–68 between Hoover and former Attorney General Robert Kennedy over whether Kennedy had known and authorized FBI wiretapping and bugging activities. Dating from 1941, attorneys general had avoided challenging the FBI director, in effect allowing Hoover free rein to conduct FBI operations. FBI officials welcomed the freedom this gave them to expand the FBI's

political containment role. Indeed, no attorney general was directly briefed about—and none directly authorized—the COINTELPROs and the various other information dissemination programs launched by FBI officials since 1946 (see pages 29–30), in some cases, leaking to members of Congress and the media information that undermined the political interests of incumbent administrations. An October 1971 Oval Office meeting highlights the deference the Bureau was given by the attorney general. At this meeting, President Richard Nixon, Attorney General John Mitchell, and key White House aides discussed whether to demand Hoover's resignation, having concluded (in Nixon's words) that Hoover "ought to resign" and "we may have on our hands a man who will pull down the temple with him, including me." The participants agreed that only the president could directly approach Hoover to propose that he retire. Despite his formal role as Hoover's superior, Attorney General Mitchell concluded that he could not initiate such a request.

Mitchell's hesitancy did not stem from the absence of any formal power by attorneys general over the FBI. Indeed, prior to his resignation, Katzenbach had, in 1965–66, abandoned his predecessors' policy of benign neglect and had instituted strict rules governing FBI wiretapping and bugging practices—rules that were refined by his successor, Ramsey Clark. FBI Director Hoover was required to submit written justifications for all planned FBI taps and bugs, to seek the attorney general's reauthorization every six months for approved taps and bugs, and to create a special ELSUR index listing all individuals whose conversations had been intercepted. These rules contributed to a marked decline in FBI "national security" wiretaps (from 519 in 1945 and 244 in 1963, to 82 in 1968) and bugs (from 186 in 1945, to 100 in 1962, to 0 in 1967 and 9 in 1968). Privately, FBI officials bitterly resented Katzenbach's and Clark's stricter reporting rules; moreover, they did not report all of their bugs. Justice Department officials, Bureau officials privately protested, leaked "confidential information to the press and have demonstrated a propensity for going forward and advising the courts whenever they have knowledge" of an FBI microphone installation. The reality of FBI independence is confirmed by the fact that of the 738 microphones that FBI agents installed between 1960 and 1966, the Justice Department (as recorded in an FBI memorandum of May 27, 1966) was informed of only "158 of these sources."

Post-Watergate Attorneys General

Congressional investigations of 1975–76, in which FBI abuses of power were publicized, again altered the FBI–attorney general relationship and resulted in the reinstitution of the attorney general's supervisory authority. To preclude the recurrence of the publicized abuses, in March 1976, Attorney General Edward Levi issued new guidelines governing FBI "domestic security" investigations. Like Attorney General Stone's restrictions of 1924, Levi's guidelines limited FBI investigations to law enforcement and firmly established the attorney general's supervisory responsibility. Levi's successor, Griffin Bell, continued this practice of strict oversight. Learning of the FBI's illegal break-in activities of 1970–74, Bell initiated a grand jury investigation that resulted in the indictments of former FBI Acting Director L. Patrick Gray III, former FBI Acting Associate Director W. Mark Felt, and former FBI Assistant Director Edward Miller. Bell's action signaled a change in departmental policy—illegal activities would not be tolerated, and the attorney general intended to monitor FBI operations more closely to ensure compliance with the law.

The recurrence of "national security" concerns in the aftermath of the Iranian hostage crisis and the Soviet invasion of Afghanistan, and the election of Ronald Reagan to the presidency in 1980, once again altered the FBI–attorney general relationship. In 1983, Attorney General William French Smith issued new guidelines granting greater leeway for the FBI to conduct "domestic security/terrorism" investigations. At the same time, Smith reduced the attorney general's oversight role.

This more permissive stand has remained a constant since then—reaffirmed in 1995 in the aftermath of the bombing of the Alfred P. Murrah Federal Building in Oklahoma City, when President Bill Clinton and Attorney General Janet Reno issued new rules to "clarify" (with the intent of affirming) the FBI's authority to investigate "terrorist" activities. Reno's willingness to defer to FBI Director Louis Freeh was based on mutual trust, but their relationship became strained in the aftermath of a scandal publicized in 1996, in which it was revealed that, in 1993, low-level Clinton White House aides had requested (and received) FBI files on hundreds of former and holdover Reagan-Bush White House employees. In response to these revelations, the FBI director and the White House issued new guidelines to require the submission in writing of all White House name-check requests, with a senior White House official describing the purpose of the request.

The White House

1936–63

As a minor investigative division of the Department of Justice, the original Bureau of Investigation had no direct relationship with the White House. Presidents may have been interested in the vigorous prosecution of antitrust, interstate commerce, or espionage laws; nonetheless, they relied on the attorney general and senior Justice Department officials to supervise the Bureau and to promote the administration's policy interests. This relationship first changed during the presidency of Franklin Roosevelt.

Committed to curbing crime, in 1933–34, President Roosevelt endorsed Attorney General Homer Cummings's Twelve Point Crime Program and attendant publicity efforts to promote an enhanced federal law enforcement role. Concurrently, in 1934, the president requested an FBI investigation to ascertain whether the activities of American fascists were influenced by German agents. By 1936, the president's concerns broadened to include both the American communist and fascist movements, specifically whether Soviet and German agents supported and directed these radical movements. The resultant presidential initiative to expand FBI surveillance fundamentally changed the FBI–White House relationship.

In August 1936, President Roosevelt invited FBI Director Hoover to the White House. At this meeting, Roosevelt requested an FBI report on the extent to which American fascists and communists "may affect the economic and political life of the country." These movements, the president believed, "were international in scope" and "Communism particularly was directed from Moscow." Insisting that the matter be handled quite confidentially because he was unwilling to seek legislation authorizing FBI investigations of "subversive activities," Roosevelt verbally directed Hoover to conduct the necessary investigations and to coordinate them with the military and naval intelligence services. The president's purpose was not to prosecute American fascists and communists for suspected espionage or sabotage but to ascertain whether radical activists were subservient to foreign governments. This initiative, with authority deriving from secret executive directives, expanded FBI investigations beyond federal crimes (such as espionage, bank robbery, and interstate prostitution and auto theft) to include suspicious political activities. In time, FBI investigations expanded further, even when Congress had prohibited the use of intrusive investigative techniques.

Thus, in May 1940—despite congressional legislation of 1934 banning wiretapping—Roosevelt secretly authorized FBI wiretapping during "national defense" investigations. Concurrently, also dating from 1940, the White House formally invited FBI reports on the politics and associations of conservative and radical critics of the president's foreign policy.

Thereafter, the FBI–White House relationship was determined by the prevailing presidential policy and political interests. Presidents regularly requested FBI investigations of varying sensitivity; some strictly personal. Concerned about a potential scandal involving Kermit Roosevelt, a close relative, President Roosevelt in 1941 requested FBI assistance to ensure that his cousin received medical treatment (for a venereal disease he had contracted from his mistress). The White House hoped that the FBI's discreet surveillance in locating Kermit Roosevelt could enable family members to preclude the disclosure of this affair. More often, presidential requests were politically motivated, as in the case of a 1940 request by Roosevelt for an FBI investigation to ascertain whether former Republican President Herbert Hoover had contacted leaders of the Vichy France government to obtain information that could affect the 1940 presidential elections. The president had learned that former president Hoover and his aide Lawrence Rickey had allegedly contacted French officials to ascertain whether Roosevelt "had made definite commitments" to send U.S. troops to assist France "in the present war." At the time, the United States was officially neutral, and Roosevelt's Republican critics questioned whether the president's foreign policy could undermine U.S. neutrality and lead to U.S. involvement in the ongoing European War.

President Roosevelt's successor, Harry Truman, likewise welcomed FBI intelligence reports. His most dramatic action involved a request in 1945 that the FBI wiretap White House aide Edward Prichard, prominent Washington attorney Thomas Corcoran, and syndicated columnist Drew Pearson (FBI officials declined to tap Pearson). Truman's request had been triggered by a Drew Pearson column, which reported information pertaining to a sensitive foreign policy initiative, and a series of FBI reports describing the insubordinate actions of Roosevelt holdovers on the White House staff and in executive agencies. The president's objectives were to foreclose future leaks and to ensure that all high-level administration officials (some of whom were holdovers from Roosevelt's presidency) were loyal to him. The FBI's wiretap of Corcoran, which was continued into

1946 and reactivated in 1948, provided the White House with information about the plans of liberals in Congress, the Democratic National Committee, reporters, and Supreme Court justices to promote liberal domestic and foreign policy objectives (fearing that Truman would advance more conservative initiatives). FBI Director Hoover's assistance was not confined to this code-named White House Security Survey program. The FBI director regularly forwarded unsolicited reports to the Truman White House detailing the political strategies of the president's liberal and radical critics, as well as information about potential "scandals" that might adversely affect the president's political interests. Concurrently, in 1946, President Truman secretly expanded FBI wiretapping authority (allowing its use during investigations of kidnapping and of "subversive activities") and in 1948 approved a secret preventive detention program (having decided that Congress was unlikely to approve legislation authorizing the listing and detention of "dangerous" citizens and alien residents). This underlying unwillingness to rely on legislatively authorized investigations also underpinned a 1950 decision of the Truman administration. Following congressional enactment of the Internal Security Act authorizing a preventive detention program, Truman administration officials concluded that these standards for listing and detaining potentially dangerous citizens and aliens were "unworkable," preferring those proscribed under the recent 1948 program. Accordingly, Attorney General J. Howard McGrath directed the FBI to ignore the congressionally mandated standards and to instead base current and future preventive detention investigations on the administration's secretly authorized program.

The FBI–White House relationship assumed another dimension during the Roosevelt and Truman years, one contradicting the FBI's seeming subservience when promoting the president's intelligence interests. In 1942, FBI agents broke into the offices of the radical American Youth Congress (AYC) and photocopied its records, including Eleanor Roosevelt's extensive correspondence with AYC officials. Briefed on this discovery, FBI Director Hoover demanded a report on the first lady's correspondence. In 1948, FBI officials provided damaging information about President Truman's former association with Kansas City Democratic boss Thomas Pendergast and about the administration's internal security policies to Republican presidential nominee Thomas Dewey, information that was incorporated in Republican campaign literature. FBI officials also covertly assisted the House Committee on Un-American Activities in

1947–48 and Senator Joseph McCarthy in 1950–52, then involved in highly partisan attempts to raise public doubts about the adequacy of the Truman administration's internal security policies. Additionally, in August 1952, FBI officials provided derogatory information about Democratic presidential nominee Adlai Stevenson to an operative whom the Republican National Committee had hired "to do the official [1952] Republican biography of Governor Stevenson."

This multifaceted relationship of assistance and insubordination continued during the Eisenhower years. FBI officials voluntarily forwarded to the Eisenhower White House detailed intelligence about the activities of the administration's liberal and radical critics (and by the late 1950s, information about the president's right-wing opponents, notably the John Birch Society) and conducted security clearance investigations of presidential appointees (expanding upon the loyalty-security program that President Truman had instituted in March 1948 for individuals employed in federal agencies and departments). Sharing Eisenhower's commitment to strengthening the nation's internal security, FBI officials also wittingly assisted Republican activists who continued to exploit public doubts about the Roosevelt and Truman administrations' commitment to purging "Communists in Government." This assistance ranged from public support (FBI Director Hoover's November 1953 appearance with Attorney General Brownell to endorse Brownell's charge that former President Truman had, in 1945–46, knowingly ignored FBI reports that raised questions about the loyalty of presidential appointee Harry Dexter White) to privately assisting the publicity efforts of members and staff of the Senate Internal Security Subcommittee and prominent governors. The FBI's covert assistance to the Senate Internal Security Subcommittee and to governors was terminated in 1955 after some of the recipients breached the FBI's condition of confidentiality. At the same time, FBI officials closely monitored rumors about immoral activities of White House aides and even of President Eisenhower—in one instance attempting to verify a rumor that Eisenhower had resumed an affair with his World War II military aide Kay Summersby.

The FBI–White House relationship changed with the inauguration of the Kennedy administration. Until 1961, FBI Director Hoover had been able to bypass the attorney general to command direct access to the White House. Given Attorney General Robert Kennedy's familial relationship with the president, this independence could not be sustained. In addition, Attorney General Kennedy insisted on being informed about all White House contacts with the Justice Department. As a result, during Kennedy's presidency, FBI reports intended for the White House were forwarded through the attorney general, while FBI political intelligence investigations were initiated only when specifically requested by either the attorney general or the White House. Thus, unlike previous presidencies, the most sensitive FBI operations were known to the attorney general during the Kennedy administration. These included FBI wiretapping of reporters Lloyd Norman and Hanson Baldwin (suspected of being recipients of leaked information about planned presidential decisions) and monitoring House Agricultural Committee members and staff and Department of Justice and Agriculture employees (whom the president and attorney general feared might successfully retain an import sugar quota for the Dominican Republic, thereby subverting presidential foreign policy initiative).

FBI officials did not blindly accept this subordinate status. In a subtle reminder of the Bureau's intelligence capabilities, FBI Director Hoover signaled to Attorney General Kennedy (and thereby the White House) the FBI's awareness of rumors about President Kennedy's various affairs (involving Judith Campbell Exner, Pamela Turnure, Marie Novotny, Ellen Rometsch, Durie Malcolm, and Alicia Purdom). Hoover did so without conveying the fact that the FBI was purposefully collecting such information and sought to verify the allegations. The only information that Hoover reported to the Kennedys had either been obtained through public sources (allegations reported in the right-wing media) or, in a most delicate case, uncovered through authorized wiretaps of crime bosses Sam Giancana and John Roselli (recording Judith Campbell Exner's series of attempts to contact President Kennedy).

1963–72

With Lyndon Johnson's accession to the presidency, Director Hoover regained direct access to the White House. More than any of his predecessors, President Johnson was personally interested in FBI intelligence. His concerns ranged from personal safety (that he might be a target for assassination) to doubts about the loyalty of Kennedy appointees who remained on the White House staff and in the Justice Department. Hoover unhesitantly provided Johnson advice about security matters and forwarded to him a series of reports detailing instances of the divided political loyalties of aides aligned with Attorney General Robert

Kennedy. This relationship soon shifted to subservience, occasioned by Hoover's approach of the mandatory retirement age of 70 in January 1965.

By a May 1964 executive order, President Johnson waived the federal employee mandatory retirement rule for Hoover. However, the waiver was not unconditional; in consequence, Hoover's continued tenure depended on Johnson's approval. Hoover thereafter found it difficult to turn down even the most brazenly partisan presidential request. These ranged from dispatching a special FBI squad to the 1964 Democratic National Convention (held in Atlantic City, New Jersey) that monitored civil rights activists and their liberal allies; to monitoring the 1966 hearings on the administration's Vietnam War policy conducted by the Senate Foreign Relations Committee; to monitoring the contacts of members of Congress and congressional staff with Soviet and Soviet bloc embassies in Washington; to assisting designated cabinet officials and members of Congress by providing them with FBI reports and writing speeches that questioned the loyalty of the administration's anti–Vietnam War critics; and finally to providing the White House with derogatory personal and political information about the president's critics in the media and the public.

Johnson's demands, and Hoover's compliance, refined the FBI–White House relationship to one whereby the FBI acted as the president's intelligence arm. This role was further expanded during Richard Nixon's presidency. Dating from 1940, Hoover had regularly submitted FBI reports describing the suspicious political and personal associations of radical activists and the president's various critics. This reporting role was rationalized in 1969 under a special program code-named INLET. FBI officials, moreover, serviced a number of extremely sensitive White House requests (notably, forwarding a report detailing the illicit sexual activities of members of the Washington press corps in 1970, and in 1969–71, wiretapping members of the White House and National Security Council staffs and prominent Washington reporters). Although Hoover was willing to honor White House requests (while creating a record that the initiative came from the White House), since 1966, he had decided it was too risky politically to have FBI agents continue to use illegal investigative techniques.

His caution complicated the FBI–White House relationship during the Nixon administration. The FBI director's self-imposed restrictions of 1965–66 on FBI investigative practices provided the impetus for Nixon's formulation of

the so-called Huston Plan. Convinced that Hoover's restrictions on the uses of "clearly illegal" investigative techniques had subverted the FBI's ability to acquire information that could discredit militant civil rights and anti–Vietnam War activists, White House aides and their allies in the intelligence community devised an elaborate plan in June 1970 to rescind these restrictions and ensure the FBI's direct subservience to the White House.

Following the White House's formal approval of the Huston Plan, FBI Director Hoover nonetheless remained concerned that the FBI's use of requested "clearly illegal" investigative techniques could be discovered and thereby could harm the FBI's reputation. Hoover's concern had been triggered by the fact that President Nixon had not directly authorized the FBI to conduct recommended "clearly illegal" activities, the authorization memorandum having been sent under the signature of a junior White House aide, Tom Charles Huston. To protect the Bureau, in the event that FBI activities become known, Hoover advised Attorney General John Mitchell of his intention to create a record whenever the FBI complied with the president's program. Mitchell immediately briefed Nixon about Hoover's plans. Aware that this would subvert his interest in deniability, Nixon ordered the recall of the Huston authorization memorandum.

Thereafter, the FBI–Nixon White House relationship deteriorated, and the president hesitated to rely on the FBI to conduct politically sensitive operations. For example, following the *New York Times*'s unauthorized publication of the Pentagon Papers in 1971, when White House aides sought derogatory information about Daniel Ellsberg (identified as responsible for leaking of the Pentagon Papers) the Nixon White House did not request Hoover's assistance. Instead, unexpended funds left over from the 1968 presidential campaign were used to hire former CIA operatives to break into the office of Ellsberg's psychiatrist.

Relations with Hoover had become so tense by October 1971 that President Nixon and his top political aides privately debated how to ensure the FBI director's retirement. Fearing that Hoover would refuse to step down on his own, and knowing that he could command support from conservatives in the media, Congress, and the public, President Nixon decided reluctantly to delay demanding Hoover's resignation until after the 1972 presidential election.

Hoover's death in May 1972 resolved this problem. President Nixon appointed a senior Justice Department official, L. Patrick Gray, as FBI acting director. The president expected, and indeed pressured, Gray to service White House political interests. Gray's ineptness—particularly evident in his requests for FBI reports on members of Congress, his destruction of sensitive documents given to him by White House aides, and his initial willingness to limit the FBI's investigation of the Watergate break-in—created internal tensions within senior FBI ranks over this blatant politicization of the Bureau. Gray's actions rendered his continued tenure vulnerable when Congress, in 1973, convened hearings to consider his confirmation as FBI director (under congressional legislation of 1968, the FBI director thereafter had to be confirmed by the Senate). When Gray's destruction of documents given to him by the White House became known during the resultant hearings, Gray withdrew his candidacy for confirmation.

1973 to the Present

Disclosures of Gray's actions and of the Nixon White House's earlier political uses of the FBI between 1969 and 1973 provoked a change in the FBI–White House relationship. At first, the arrest and indictment in 1972 of seven individuals associated with President Nixon's re-election campaign (for breaking into the Democratic National Committee's headquarters in the Watergate office complex) had not been a major political issue. Senate hearings in 1973 changed that. These hearings raised questions about President Nixon's role in an attempted cover-up and, as well, uncovered the Nixon White House's political uses of the FBI (notably, the break-in of the office of Ellsberg's psychiatrist, the Huston Plan, and the wiretapping in 1969 of reporters and of NSC and White House aides). President Nixon's refusal to turn over requested Oval Office tapes and the hiring of the special counsel (appointed to investigate criminal activities by Nixon White House and campaign officials) led the House, in 1973–74, to initiate hearings on a resolution to impeach President Nixon. The earlier Senate hearings into the Watergate affair and the House impeachment investigation focused public attention on President Nixon's abuses of the FBI and other intelligence agencies. These revelations, combined with other abusive FBI practices that were becoming public at the time (notably, the FBI's COINTELPROs, its attempts to discredit civil rights leader Martin Luther King Jr., and that former FBI Director Hoover had maintained a secret office file containing

dossiers on prominent Americans), led the House and Senate to establish, in 1975, special committees to investigate the extent of the FBI's "illegal, improper, or unethical activities" and "conduct of domestic intelligence or counterintelligence operations against United States citizens"; the "nature and extent" of executive oversight of FBI activities; and the FBI's authority to conduct non-criminal investigations and resort to "surreptitious entries [break-ins], surveillance, wiretaps, or eavesdropping, illegal opening of the United States mail, or the monitoring of United States mail."

The resultant investigations of 1975–76 uncovered the heretofore secretive nature of the abusive presidential-FBI relationship: whether the fact that secret presidential directives had authorized the FBI's past illegal activities, or how presidents since Franklin Roosevelt had used the FBI for political purposes. By 1975, Congress had abandoned its former deference to challenge executive secrecy and the president's claimed right to authorize intrusive investigative techniques. Indeed, although Congress had legalized wiretapping under the 1968 Omnibus Crime Control and Safe Streets Act, subject to court-approved warrants, even this law contained a large loophole: the president's constitutional powers "were not limited by this warrant requirement from taking such measures as he deems necessary to protect the Nation against actual or potential attack or other acts of a hostile power, to obtain foreign intelligence information deemed essential to the security of the United States or to protect national security information against foreign intelligence activities. Nor . . . limit the constitutional power of the President to take such measures as he deems necessary to protect the United States against the overthrow of the Government by force or other unlawful means, or against any other clear and present danger to the structure or existence of the Government."

When written in 1968, this broad exemption had elicited little congressional opposition. Yet, the ensuing revelations of how President Nixon had interpreted this language—combined with the Church and Pike Committees' disclosures of wiretapping abuses—led Congress to enact legislation rejecting a presidential claimed inherent right to authorize national security wiretaps. The Foreign Intelligence Surveillance Act of 1978 extended the court-authorized warrant requirement to "foreign intelligence" and "foreign counterintelligence" wiretaps, which had to be reviewed and approved in secret by a special court (presidents alone could not determine when such use was permissible). Congress, moreover, instituted other legislative restrictions to preclude future abuses; in 1974, narrowing the FBI's and CIA's exemptions from the 1966 Freedom of Information Act's mandatory disclosure requirements; in 1976, establishing permanent House and Senate intelligence committees to oversee the intelligence agencies; and in 1992, creating a special review board to order the release of FBI and CIA documents pertaining to the Kennedy assassination. In addition, FBI investigations of domestic security and criminal activities were subjected to close scrutiny by House and Senate judiciary subcommittees.

Nonetheless, the special FBI–White House relationship was not wholly severed. Presidents continued to seek FBI security clearance investigations for their appointees (to the White House staff and the cabinet). Furthermore, the FBI's sole authority to conduct noncriminal investigations derived from executive directives issued by attorneys general Edward Levi in 1976 and William French Smith in 1983. These directives authorized the FBI to investigate militant radical activists—even critics of the president's foreign policy (which during the Reagan presidency included proponents of the nuclear freeze movement and opponents of the El Salvador government, and during the Bush presidency included Arab American opponents of the Gulf War with Iraq). It remains unclear whether presidential directives authorizing the FBI to investigate "terrorism," "collect foreign intelligence or support foreign collection" requirements, conduct "such other intelligence activities as the President may from time to time request," or protect classified information "against foreign intelligence activities" have meant that the FBI continues to forward helpful political intelligence to the White House.

The FBI–White House relationship again provoked controversy in 1996. That year, it was disclosed that Anthony Marcecha, a low-level Clinton White House aide, had, in 1993–94, requested FBI files on approximately 900 individuals, including 400 former and holdover Bush and Reagan administration employees. While senior White House officials claimed that these files had been inadvertently requested, the names having been based on a dated Secret Service list of White House employees who needed clearance for access to the White House, the ease by which this request had been processed (submitted by a low-level White House aide and handled by low-level FBI personnel) indirectly confirmed that the FBI remained responsive to the White House.

The United States Congress

1908–45

Theoretically, the FBI's investigative responsibilities are defined by Congress. When enacting laws proscribing certain activities (whether bank robbery, extortion, or espionage), Congress has expanded the FBI's investigative responsibilities. Conversely, Congress has prohibited specific investigative activities (such as when it banned wiretapping in 1934). When approving appropriations or conducting oversight hearings, Congress is able to review FBI operations, raise questions about FBI priorities and methods, and impose limits on FBI activities (by not appropriating funds, by reducing FBI funding, or by barring specified uses of appropriated funds). These powers have rarely been exercised to preclude abusive practices, even when highly publicized in 1923–24 or 1975–76. Rather than legislating restraints, Congress deferred to the executive branch, with the result that the scope of, and limits to, FBI operations has been restricted only by executive directives. Furthermore, despite congressional skepticism over the Bureau's future role at the time of the agency's creation in 1908, since 1909, Congress's oversight role has been reactive, and not continuous.

Ironically, in 1907–08, Congress's actions, intended to preclude the creation of a "secret" national police, became the impetus for Attorney General Bonaparte's 1908 order creating the Bureau. In 1907–08, Congress rejected Bonaparte's request to fund a special investigative division in the Department of Justice and, moreover, approved an appropriation rider barring Justice Department officials from hiring Secret Service agents for short-term investigative needs. These appropriation restrictions seemingly demonstrated congressional opposition to a federal bureau of investigation. Attorney General Bonaparte nonetheless unilaterally created such a force while Congress was in recess, funding it through departmental contingency monies. Afterward, in 1909, Bonaparte convinced congressional leaders that this special investigative force was needed to further the Justice Department's authorized prosecutive responsibilities, and that its investigations would be confined to antitrust and interstate commerce violations. Willing to accept these assurances, Congress's sole action in 1909 was to adopt an appropriation rider limiting the newly established force to investigating "crimes against the United States."

In the ensuing years, Congress expanded federal law enforcement responsibilities through legislation such as the Mann Act of 1910, the Espionage Act of 1917, and the Dyer Act of 1919. Concurrently, Congress increased Bureau appropriations from $329,984 in 1911 to $2,272,658 by 1919. However, despite the expansion of the Bureau's role, no formal congressional oversight system was instituted to review how Bureau officials utilized appropriated funds or how Bureau operations were conducted.

By 1924, publicity of the Bureau's recent abusive practices again provoked controversy. These practices included the Bureau's arrest of prominent New Yorkers during "slacker" raids of 1918, the planning and execution of the Palmer Raids of 1920, and the monitoring in 1923–24 of congressional critics of the Harding administration. In response to these disclosures, only isolated members of Congress in 1918, 1920, 1921, and 1924 protested the Bureau's abuses of power and violations of privacy rights. As a body, Congress did not legislatively proscribe Bureau authority. The sole restrictions to preclude any future recurrence of abuses were imposed by Attorney General Harlan Stone in May 1924: banning Bureau wiretapping, dissolving the wartime General Intelligence Division, and prohibiting Bureau investigations of political activities. As in 1909, Congress deferred to the attorney general.

By the 1930s, Congress abandoned an earlier concern about a federal law enforcement threat to limited government and privacy. Instead, it viewed an expanded FBI role as essential to curbing a serious "crime wave" involving ruthless gangsters sweeping the nation. In a series of laws enacted between 1932 and 1934, federal law-enforcement powers were expanded to cover bank robbery, kidnapping, extortion, and fraud, while Congress also increased Bureau appropriations (from $2,775,000 in 1933 to $5,000,000 in 1936). Some members of Congress worried that federalizing crime would undermine states' rights and limited government; nonetheless, the most biting criticism, expressed by Senator Kenneth McKellar of Tennessee, centered on FBI Director Hoover's personal courage and the effectiveness of his leadership.

During the late 1930s, moreover, Congress also sought to curb "un-American" activities by creating a special House Committee on Un-American Activities (which conducted highly publicized hearings intended to publicize threats to the nation's internal security) and by proscribing radical conduct and associations (through the Smith Act, the Foreign Agents Registration Act, and the Hatch Act). Congress's actions, however, were not the catalyst to the FBI's surveillance of "subversive" activities; rather, this expansion resulted from secret presidential directives of 1936, 1939, and 1940. Executive directives proved crucial in other respects. For example, although Congress banned wiretapping in 1934 and resisted the Roosevelt administration's lobbying efforts of 1941 to amend that act to authorize "national defense" wiretaps, FBI wiretapping continued, its authority deriving from a secret executive directive of May 1940. In addition, FBI officials instituted a secret Custodial Detention program in 1939 to identify and list aliens and citizens for possible detention in the event that the United States went to war, a secret program whose sole authority derived from the attorney general, Robert Jackson.

In consequence, during the 1930s and 1940s, Congress was uninformed about both the scope and targets of FBI internal security operations, an ignorance stemming from a long-term practice of deferring to the attorney general. By then, Congress no longer worried whether the FBI was too powerful and instead welcomed expanding FBI investigations as essential to curb violent crimes and foreign threats to the nation's security. Indeed, Congress increased FBI appropriations from $6,578,076 in 1939 to $24,965,000 in 1942. Furthermore, congressional leaders abandoned any pretense of monitoring FBI operations when the chairman of the House Appropriations Subcommittee, Clarence Cannon, executed a liaison agreement with FBI officials in 1943 under which FBI agents were assigned to assist the Appropriations Subcommittee's staff in reviewing all federal agencies' budgetary requests and expenditures of appropriated funds.

1945–75

Congress continued its practice of deference after 1945. In 1947, FBI Director Hoover testified publicly for the first time before the House Committee on Un-American Activities (HUAC) concerning the dangers of communist subversives, and thereafter regularly testified during annual appropriation hearings conducted by the House Appropriations Subcommittee. Through these hearings, the leadership of Congress provided the FBI director with a forum to promote the Bureau's interests and to express to Congress and the public his conception of the seriousness of the threat for the nation's internal security. Committee members raised no hard questions about FBI priorities or methods and routinely approved recommended appropriations—even, on occasion, increasing funding beyond what was requested.

This shared concern about the communist threat changed FBI-congressional relations during the Cold War era. Beginning informally in 1946, FBI officials covertly assisted the HUAC staff in exposing and publicizing the communist menace. FBI assistance ranged from providing background information on prospective witnesses to be called by the committee, to recommendations on hiring staff counsel and investigators, to reports recounting communist influence (whether in the Hollywood movie industry or the trade union movement). FBI officials also forged a "confidential relationship" with former FBI agents who were employed on the committee's staff, from whom they obtained advance notice of planned committee hearings and witnesses. This relationship underscores the ambiguous character of the FBI-HUAC relationship, complicated at times by such occurrences as when HUAC staff and members publicly revealed the FBI's covert assistance (which had been rendered on the assurance of confidentiality) or when the committee sought to enhance its own stature as protector of the nation's internal security (an image that threatened the FBI's carefully crafted monopoly). Nonetheless, the committee's acquiescence to FBI officials' insistence on secrecy, and to the FBI determining the level of assistance it would provide, became the standard of the 1950s and 1960s.

In contrast to the informal HUAC-FBI relationship, in March 1951, FBI officials forged a formal liaison program with the Senate Internal Security Subcommittee (SISS), whereby SISS agreed to focus its hearings on "matters of current internal security significance . . . [and also] to help the Bureau in every possible manner." Under this program, the FBI conducted name checks on prospective SISS witnesses, submitted reports on targeted organizations, and provided the subcommittee with summary memoranda "with appropriate leads and suggested clues." In return, SISS forwarded to the FBI any confidential information it had uncovered. SISS's agreement to focus on "current" inquiries was intended to avert HUAC's by-then controversial reputation for partisanship and the perception that HUAC's purpose was to discredit the loyalty of officials in the Roosevelt and Truman administrations. Republican victories in the 1952 presidential and congressional elections, ironically, led to a reassessment of this relationship.

In 1953–54, the new Republican chairman of SISS, William Jenner, moved quickly to focus on the Truman administration's security procedures. In highly partisan hearings of 1953, the subcommittee had explored "interlocking" subversive influences in executive agencies and

departments of the 1940s. This indirect attack on the preceding Democratic administratations assumed a more direct, confrontational stance when the subcommittee, in November 1953, provided President Eisenhower's attorney general, Herbert Brownell, with a forum to document charges he had made in a speech earlier that month in Chicago, alleging that former president Truman had harmed the nation's security when, in 1946, he had appointed Harry Dexter White to the International Monetary Fund (and in doing so, had ignored FBI reports questioning White's loyalty). FBI Director Hoover's controversial joint appearance with Brownell during these hearings, combined with the adverse publicity precipitated when SISS staff extolled their access to FBI files, caused FBI and Justice Department officials to reassess the FBI-SISS liaison program. In 1954, Deputy Attorney General William Rogers ordered that, thereafter, FBI assistance to SISS should be confined to "public source" information. In 1955, FBI officials instituted an "informal" relationship, wherein information would only be given to the more trusted members of the subcommittee, notably, Senator James Eastland.

FBI officials' complicated relationships with HUAC and SISS mirrored another controversial relationship with Congress's most notorious member, Senator Joseph McCarthy. Dating from 1950, FBI officials secretly provided McCarthy with information to sustain his charges that the nation's internal security crisis was the result of the Truman administration's "softness toward communism." To preclude discovery of this assistance, FBI files were never actually given to the senator; instead, he was provided summaries of information in "blank memorandum" form (these memoranda were not on FBI letterhead, thus did not identify the FBI as their source).

The FBI's relationship to Senator McCarthy temporarily changed following the 1952 elections, which resulted in Republican control of Congress and the presidency. At first, FBI officials concurred with McCarthy's anticipation of "closer cooperation and more extended use of the FBI and its facilities following the beginning of the new Congress." This included having the Bureau recommend "prospective investigative personnel" for McCarthy's "investigative committee" (the Senate Government Operations Committee), while FBI Director Hoover met with McCarthy to discuss the "over-all plans which he has for carrying on the work of his committee." McCarthy specifically invited Hoover's recommendations whenever "any activity" of the committee and its staff was not "in the best interests of good administration."

This spirit of cooperation was quickly shattered following McCarthy's July 1953 appointment of FBI supervisor Frank Carr as counsel of the subcommittee. McCarthy's staff assistants had originally consulted on this planned appointment. Hoover, at the time, opposed "the appointment of an Agent now in service and engaged upon work dealing with subversive activities," arguing that this would create the impression of a covert relationship, one that "would, no doubt, be seized upon by critics of the Senator and of the FBI as a deliberate effort to affect a direct 'pipeline' into the FBI and that it would make it necessary for the Bureau to be more circumspect in all of its [future] dealings with the McCarthy Committee." When McCarthy nonetheless appointed Carr, Hoover immediately severed FBI relations with McCarthy and his staff.

The covert assistance provided to McCarthy, SISS, and HUAC highlights an aspect of the FBI-congressional relationship: Congress could serve as a forum for the FBI to promote an "educational campaign" to influence public opinion as to the seriousness of the communist threat and the effectiveness of the FBI in protecting the nation's security. This shared anticommunist purpose led Congress, in 1950, to enact the Internal Security (or McCarran) Act. This act included a provision authorizing a program to detain individuals whose presence at large could endanger the nation's security. At the time, the FBI already had underway the Security Index program, a more stringent program authorized under a secret directive issued by Attorney General Tom Clark in August 1948. When establishing the Security Index program, Clark had intentionally not sought legislative authorization—fearing that such a request would provoke an acrimonious public debate. He decided, instead, to wait for an auspicious moment and then ex post facto authorization—thus, a presidential proclamation and a resolution were prepared to be issued following the anticipated outbreak of war, at which time permission likely would be granted quickly. When Congress, on its own (and wholly unaware of this Security Index program), enacted the McCarran Act in September 1950, FBI and Justice Department officials decided to ignore the act's congressionally mandated standards for a preventive detention program. Moreover, when Congress repealed the McCarran Act's preventive detention title in 1971 (responding to public concerns of the Vietnam War period that a prospective "concentration camp" program could lead to the detention of critics of the president's foreign policy), Attorney General John Mitchell approved FBI Director Hoover's recommendation that the FBI continue investigat-

ing individuals "who pose a threat to the internal security of the country" for inclusion on an "administrative" index for anticipated future detention. The failure to do so, Mitchell and Hoover concluded, could embolden radical activists, since "they no doubt [will] feel safer now to conspire in the destruction of the country." Furthermore, they reasoned, the crisis atmosphere following the outbreak of war, if it occurred, could then be exploited to obtain ex post facto congressional authorization for this ongoing effort, now renamed the Administrative Index program.

Because they were committed to a rigorous internal security program, members of Congress were generally willing to defer to FBI officials and the Bureau's positive mystique. Concluding that critical scrutiny of FBI practices and sharp questioning of FBI procedures could make them appear to be undermining the nation's security, members of Congress tacitly accepted the unquestioning deference that the revered FBI director commanded. Their reticence to criticize was reinforced by a fear that the FBI monitored their personal and political activities, a suspicion that was warranted.

During the 1950s, for example, the FBI's Washington field office compiled a series of extremely sensitive reports detailing the potentially embarrassing political and sexual activities of members of Congress—information FBI agents had acquired through public sources, wiretaps, interviews with prostitutes, and from the police vice squad in Washington, D.C. At the same time, FBI officials—first informally, then formally—prepared memoranda summarizing whatever information FBI field offices and FBI headquarters had acquired on recently elected members of Congress. These "summary memoranda" listed biographical data, the individual's positions on law enforcement and other policy matters of interest to FBI officials, and information "concerning allegations of criminal or corrupt practices, subversive activities, and immoral conduct." Technically, these summary memoranda were not files (or dossiers); they were based on non-recorded submissions from FBI field offices, which were not serialized in the FBI's central records system; and they were maintained separate from the FBI's central records system in the Administrative Review Unit. Begun informally, by 1954, this practice was formalized (as described in FBI memoranda outlining this program and its purposes) whereby "a systematic review of data in Bufiles [FBI files] and available reference material was begun on Members of Congress." In 1960, this informal reporting requirement was extended to nonincumbent congressional candidates. FBI memoranda record that the original purpose in preparing these summary memoranda was for the use "only" of FBI Assistant Director Louis Nichols to further his liaison responsibilities with Congress.

1975 to the Present

The Watergate Affair of 1972–73 redefined Congress's relations with the FBI. Revelations that the Nixon White House had used the FBI for political purposes shattered public confidence and caused many members of Congress to reassess their deferential attitudes toward the Bureau. In response, in 1975, special House and Senate committees were established to examine FBI operations, and these committees insisted on access to formerly classified FBI and White House records (see page 154). The committees' investigations revealed that the FBI had conducted politically motivated investigations either pursuant to White House requests or with FBI officials volunteering political intelligence to the White House; that presidents and attorneys general had authorized illegal investigative techniques (ostensibly for "national security" reasons); and that FBI officials had instituted programs to harass and disrupt targeted activists and organizations (predominantly political radicals but including other influential activists such as civil rights leader Martin Luther King Jr.). Their publicized findings caused Congress to establish, in 1976, permanent intelligence oversight committees. Concurrently, between 1976 and 1980, Congress seriously considered enacting a legislative charter defining the parameters of FBI authority.

However, a shift in public and congressional sentiment, occasioned by the Iran hostage crisis and the Soviet invasion of Afghanistan during 1979–80, undercut support for an FBI legislative charter. As had occurred in the past, Congress again allowed the attorney general to set the guidelines which would govern future FBI operations and procedures. Congress continued its oversight role, conducting periodic hearings whenever publicized disclosures suggested FBI abuses of power: hearings on FBI undercover operations and on ABSCAM in 1984, on CISPES in 1988, on the Waco and Ruby Ridge incidents of 1992–93, and on the Filesgate controversy of 1993–94.

At the same time, Congress promoted public access to FBI records—enacting in 1974 key amendments to the Freedom of Information Act of 1966 and in 1992 creating the Kennedy Assassination Records Review Board—and no longer uncritically acquiesced to FBI officials' demands to classify all FBI records.

State and Local Police

The FBI's assigned responsibility to investigate violations of federal statutes did not directly encroach upon local and state law enforcement. However, where the divisions between federal and local or state responsibilities were not sharply defined (auto theft and prostitution, for instance, are both federal and state crimes), some coordination was essential. FBI agents regularly contacted local police officers and sheriffs, seeking their assistance to identify criminal suspects, and at times, recruiting assistance to effect arrests. One consequence of this cooperation was that many FBI agents began their careers in local law enforcement while others retired from the FBI to pursue careers in local law enforcement. This is illustrated in the admittedly unrepresentative career of Clarence Kelley—Kelley retired from the FBI to become police chief of Kansas City and held this position until accepting appointment as FBI director in 1973.

Nonetheless, because one impetus to the FBI's expanded law enforcement role was the belief that local and state police alone could not curb all serious crimes, some tension between FBI and local or state police officials inevitably existed. Tensions arose particularly when the FBI's high-profile role in an investigation resulted in it receiving credit for solving a highly publicized case, such as the Lindbergh kidnapping or the capture of John Dillinger.

If the FBI's relationship with local and state police was characterized by both cooperation and conflict, the Bureau's reputation as the nation's preeminent law enforcement agency nonetheless resulted in part from its role in enhancing the crime-fighting mission of local and state police. In 1924, at a time when the Bureau's public esteem had plummeted following disclosures of abuse of power, Bureau Director Hoover established a Fingerprint Division at Bureau headquarters in Washington, D.C., for use by law enforcement agencies nationwide. This centralized operation was of crucial importance for local and state police throughout the country, solving a key law enforcement problem caused by the mobility of the American population. The cooperative relationship expanded in succeeding years, most notably with the establishment of the FBI Police Training School in 1935 (subsequently renamed the FBI National Academy). A 12-week training course, offered by the FBI to selected police officers, indirectly increased the quality and professionalism of local law enforcement operations. In the 1930s, moreover, FBI officials also began annual publication of the *Uniform Crime Reports*, statistical summaries of national crime trends, and the *FBI Law Enforcement Bulletin,* containing articles on the latest technological and sociological developments in the policing field. FBI field offices, in addition, held periodic seminars, conferences, and specialized schools to offer information on various crime problems—including hostage negotiations, crisis intervention, executive development, and internal security threats. By 1975, 8,173 police officers had graduated from the FBI National Academy; 155 specialized field schools on law enforcement administration and command personnel had been held; and 11,013 law enforcement schools had been sponsored by FBI field offices, which were attended by 343,104 police officers.

Ultimately, the FBI became a national law enforcement clearinghouse, helping to promote the use of the newest technology to identify criminals and ensure successful prosecution. The FBI's Crime Laboratory became a model for how technology could be used to solve crimes, and the FBI's National Crime Information Center (NCIC) provided a comprehensive nationwide link for arrest and identification records developed by local and state police agencies. NCIC centrally maintained and computerized these records, creating a database for use by both federal and by local or state police officials. Lastly, through the World War II Plant Protection Program, and after 1945 through various counterintelligence programs, FBI officials shared with, and received information from, specially trained local and state police "red squads," whose purpose was to gather intelligence on the political and organizational activities of radicals in local communities and defense plants.

Other U.S. and Foreign Intelligence Agencies and Law Enforcement Agencies

Dating from its creation, the FBI was principally responsible for conducting internal security investigations, whether involving espionage, sedition, or treason. Because of overlapping responsibilities dating from the World War I period, FBI officials began to coordinate the Bureau investigations and to share information with military agencies that had been created in the 1880s and had the specific responsibility to counter the attempts of foreign intelligence services to steal U.S. military and diplomatic secrets. Like the FBI, these intelligence agencies lacked

charters clearly defining their responsibilities. Delimitation agreements and liaison guidelines between agencies evolved over time but were not formalized until the 1940s, catalyzed by the international crises precipitated first by World War II and then the Cold War.

In part, the problem of overlapping responsibilities stemmed from the fact that some of these agencies had been created prior to the FBI's establishment—the Office of Naval Intelligence (ONI) was created in 1882 and the Military Intelligence Division (MID) in 1885, and thus these services were already collecting intelligence about foreign agents and their domestic contacts before the Bureau was founded. Other problems accompanied the creation of additional new agencies, either of temporary duration (the Office of Strategic Services, OSS, 1942–45) or permanent, powerful agencies (the Central Intelligence Agency, CIA, created in 1947, and the National Security Agency, NSA, created in 1952).

At the same time that efforts were being coordinated with U.S. agencies, FBI officials forged liaison relationships with allied foreign intelligence agencies (notably, Great Britain's), with the international police agency Interpol, and with various foreign police agencies. Because of the international character of crime, and because of German and Soviet espionage and counterintelligence activities (Nazi Germany during the 1930s and 1940s and the Soviet Union dating from the 1920s), such international cooperation was necessary.

U.S. Intelligence Agencies, 1917–39

When created during the 1880s, the MID and the ONI sought intelligence about the objectives and capabilities of other world powers—essential information for planning military strategy and preparedness. This foreign intelligence role spilled over into domestic surveillance following the outbreak of World War I in 1914, and then with U.S. involvement in that military conflict in 1917. Like their counterparts in the Bureau of Investigation, between 1914 and 1918, MID and ONI officials not only closely monitored foreign diplomats but began to investigate, as well, alien residents and citizens whom they feared might seek to influence U.S. policy or engage in "subversive activities." Thus, their domestic targets included both German activists, and pacifists, socialists, and members of the radical Industrial Workers of the World (IWW). In light of their specific interest in promoting military preparedness and conscription, MID and ONI officials also sought intelligence about critics of a strong military in the United States. The Wilson administration's use of Army and National Guard troops during 1917–18 to curb labor strikes, which could disrupt military production (particularly given the IWW's success in organizing mine workers), also led military and intelligence officials to monitor radical political and trade union activities.

The initiation and need for such intelligence resulted from no master plan. As a result, each agency (the Bureau, MID, and ONI) operated independently, although they did share information. Furthermore, during the World War I period, neither the president nor cabinet officials (heads of the State, War, Navy, and Justice Departments) sought to rationalize intelligence collection and analysis, which ensured a duplication of efforts and heightened bureaucratic rivalries (see Table 4.1).

TABLE 4.1	
THE U.S. INTELLIGENCE COMMUNITY	
Abbreviation	**Title**
ONI	Office of Naval Intelligence (created in 1882)
MID (G-2)	Military Intelligence Division (created in 1885)
FBI	Federal Bureau of Investigation (created in 1908)
SIS	Special Intelligence Service (1940–47)
OSS	Office of Strategic Services (1942–45)
ASA	Army Security Agency (World War II predecessor to NSA)
CIG	Central Intelligence Group (1946–47)
CIA	Central Intelligence Agency (created in 1947)
NSC	National Security Council (created in 1947)
IIC	Interdepartmental Intelligence Conference (created in 1949)
NSA	National Security Agency (created in 1952)

The end of World War I did not bring about the cessation of Bureau, MID, and ONI domestic surveillance investigations. Alarmed by the Bolshevik Revolution of November 1917 and the ensuing Russian Civil War, the Red Scare of 1919–20, postwar labor strikes (3,600 in the year 1919 alone), and the postwar upsurge of black nationalism, ONI,

MID, and Bureau of Investigation officials continued to monitor domestic radical activities during the 1920s and 1930s. Military and naval intelligence officials were deeply troubled by the popularity of pacifist and antimilitary sentiments throughout the interwar period and, following the economic crisis of the Great Depression, by the upsurge of fascist and communist movements. Yet their monitoring efforts were hampered by the sharp reduction in appropriations, forcing each agency to reduce personnel and to share whatever information their agents had developed. ONI and MID officials continued to exploit sources they had developed during the World War I era, whether conservative veterans organizations (the American Legion), patriotic businessmen, newspaper editors, or defense organizations.

In response to the sharp increase in the activities and influence of the American fascist and communist movements during the 1930s, all three agencies regularly reported to the White House (as well as to officials in their own departments) on the potential threat these movements posed to the nation's security interests. These reporting and surveillance efforts were conducted independently until 1939. No concerted attempt was made either by the agencies or the president to ensure a more efficient monitoring system. The one exception occurred in 1936 when ONI officers were allowed to attend the FBI's National Academy for training in surveillance methods and operations.

U.S. and Foreign Intelligence Agencies, 1939–45

In response to the international crisis resulting from the spread of fascism in Europe—and to Germany's efforts to capitalize on fascism's subversive appeal in Europe, the United States, and South America—the Roosevelt administration reassessed the existing intelligence operations. To curb German influence (confirmed by the 1938 arrests of members of the so-called Rumrich spy ring in New York, and by similar German "fifth column" activities in Spain, France, Latin America, and South America), the Roosevelt administration lobbied Congress to increase funding of FBI, MID, and ONI counterintelligence operations. At the same time, the administration streamlined U.S. internal security and counterintelligence operations, to minimize duplication and promote coordination.

Through a series of executive directives of 26 June 1939, 5 June 1940, and 9 February 1942, President Roosevelt assigned the FBI primary responsibility to conduct internal security investigations within the United States. All other agencies were to forward information they obtained to the FBI, while the MID's and the ONI's domestic investigations were confined to military personnel and base security. Concurrently, in June 1940, Roosevelt authorized the FBI to monitor the activities of German agents in Latin and South America, through a newly created Special Intelligence Service (SIS). Through a covert liaison program with the British Security Coordinator, the FBI and other U.S. intelligence agencies (the State Department, the MID, and the ONI) also shared information (obtained through mail opening, break-ins, wiretaps, and physical surveillance) to contain German intelligence activities in the United States and the Western Hemisphere. These various initiatives were expanded and refined to adapt to the changed responsibilities created both by wartime demands following U.S. involvement in World War II in December 1941 and the creation in June 1942 of a new intelligence agency, the Office of Strategic Services (OSS). The OSS's role, as defined by President Roosevelt's executive order, was to collect and analyze "strategic information" and to conduct such "special services" as requested by the joint chiefs of staff.

These developments did not affect the FBI's primary responsibility to conduct the nation's internal security investigations, but the division of authority in the foreign intelligence and counterintelligence areas became blurred. Since it was created after President Roosevelt had already authorized the FBI to conduct intelligence and counterintelligence operations in the Western Hemisphere, the OSS was excluded from that geographic area. In addition, OSS officials encountered opposition from ONI, MID, and State Department officials, who were concerned that this presidentially created agency could undermine their traditional foreign intelligence and counterintelligence authority. Resistance to the OSS eventually led to its termination in September 1945 following the end of World War II. President Truman also terminated funding for the FBI's SIS operations in Latin and South America; eventually, FBI sources and contacts were transferred to the Central Intelligence Agency (CIA) with its creation in 1947.

Throughout the World War II period, FBI agents closely monitored the activities of "well known and suspected" agents of the Axis powers (Germany, Italy, and Japan), Axis-aligned or Axis-occupied powers (Spain, Sweden, and Vichy France), as well as the nation's wartime ally, the Soviet Union. This surveillance included wiretapping foreign embassies and their suspected agents, break-ins to photocopy the documents of foreign embassies and their agents, and (under wartime censorship legislation and in cooperation with international telegraph companies) intercepting telegraphic messages of Axis-aligned and Soviet embassies. Through break-ins of foreign embassies, the FBI acquired copies of code books, tapes, and other information that it shared with the Army Security Agency (ASA), the forerunner of the National Security Agency (NSA), to enable its codebreakers to decipher the confidential messages of Axis-aligned officials and their sources. In 1943, moreover, the ASA initiated an effort code-named the Venona program, under which it attempted to decipher the cable messages sent to Moscow by Soviet consulates in New York and Washington. Working closely with the FBI, ASA codebreakers succeeded first in breaking the Soviet code and then, by 1949, used this information to identify those U.S. citizens and alien residents whom Soviet intelligence officers recruited as Soviet spies—most notably, British physicist Klaus Fuchs and American communists Harry Gold, David Greenglass, and Julius Rosenberg for having conspired to steal U.S. atomic bomb secrets in behalf of the Soviet Union.

U.S. and Foreign Intelligence Agencies, 1945–75

The end of World War II did not mark the end of the U.S. foreign intelligence and counterintelligence mission. The deterioration in U.S.-Soviet relations and the onset of the Cold War precipitated a more intensified effort directed primarily at the Soviet Union and its suspected allies and supporters. To promote U.S. intelligence needs, President Truman proposed (and Congress enacted) legislation in 1947 creating the CIA. The creation of a permanent and independent executive intelligence agency renewed efforts to improve coordination among the various federal intelligence agencies (see Exhibit 4.1).

Having dissolved the OSS in 1945, President Truman initially relied, during 1946–47, on the pre–World War II intelligence agencies (the FBI, the MID, the ONI, and the State Department) to conduct and coordinate intelligence collection and counterintelligence and to provide him with a refined intelligence product and any resources needed to counter any foreign military, diplomatic, or espionage threat. Accordingly, by executive order, the president established in January 1946 the Central Intelligence Group (CIG). Staffed with representatives from the established intelligence agencies and lacking an independent budget, the CIG proved incapable of achieving the desired coordination objectives. Accordingly, the Truman administration drafted and lobbied Congress to enact the National Security Act of 1947,

Exhibit 4.1 *Left to right:* Sam Papich (FBI Liaison to the CIA), J. Edgar Hoover, and Richard Helms (CIA), *Courtesy of the National Archives (65-H)*

creating two new agencies: the National Security Council (NSC), to assist the president in formulating foreign and military policy, and the CIA, to coordinate intelligence information collected separately by the established intelligence agencies. The 1947 act also authorized the NSC and CIA to safeguard classified information, promote counterintelligence, and "perform such other functions and duties related to intelligence affecting the national security as the National Security Council may from time to time direct."

Creation of the CIA raised anew the question of how best to coordinate the intelligence and counterintelligence activities of the CIA, the FBI, the ONI, the MID, the ASA (after 1952, NSA), and the State Department. The CIA might have been authorized to coordinate and analyze intelligence (collected by its agents and forwarded by other intelligence agencies), but the enabling legislation did not preclude conflicts resulting from overlapping responsibilities, particularly given its vague and discretionary "perform such other functions and duties" clause. The act, in addition, empowered the CIA to oversee and review intelligence operations to safeguard national secrets.

Almost immediately, the Truman administration sought to delineate clear divisions of authority in the international intelligence area. These efforts foundered on interagency bureaucratic rivalry. In the case of internal security policy, however, the NSC, in March 1949, created two subcommittees, the Interdepartmental Intelligence Conference (IIC), composed of representatives of the FBI, MID, and ONI, and the Interdepartmental Committee on Internal Security

(ICIS), to effect "more adequate and coordinated internal security." The charter for the IIC recognized the FBI's primacy in the domestic security area by having the FBI director chair the IIC, while delegating to this committee the responsibility for "the coordination of the investigation of all domestic espionage, sabotage, subversion and other related intelligence matters affecting internal security." Under this arrangement, the FBI was exclusively responsible for monitoring domestic radical and subversive activists and organizations (the CIA was barred from conducting domestic security investigations by the National Security Act of 1947, and military involvement in law enforcement was prohibited by the Posse Comitatus Act of 1873).

Under an October 1948 delimitation agreement between the CIA and the FBI, the FBI's "primary responsibility" for domestic security was formally recognized with the CIA's domestic role limited to having the agency's "Office of Policy Coordination to have direct dealings with [foreign] individuals and groups." This domestic monopoly meant that the CIA would have to rely on the FBI to conduct any desired operations that would further the agency's foreign intelligence and counterintelligence responsibilities—such as breaking into, wiretapping, and bugging foreign embassies located in the United States. The ASA and the NSA solicited similar FBI operations to promote the military's codebreaking efforts and thereby advance its foreign intelligence and counterintelligence responsibilities. Such assistance continued to be critical to both the CIA's and the NSA's operations.

This assistance, and the underlying division of responsibilities, broke down during the 1960s. The upsurge of militant anti–Vietnam War dissent and civil rights activism intensified suspicions within the intelligence community and the White House that foreign agents were directing these movements. Their requests that the FBI continue to conduct break-ins and wiretaps at this time encountered resistance from FBI Director Hoover who, in 1965–66, had either reduced or prohibited FBI break-in, wiretapping, bugging, and mail-opening activities. Hoover further compounded this problem when, on February 26, 1970, he terminated direct personal contact between FBI and CIA officials, except at the headquarters level, a restriction that complicated liaison and was eventually modified. Hoover had become infuriated first by the unwillingness (in 1965–66) of Justice Department officials to defend FBI wiretapping and bugging practices and then (in 1970) by a CIA official's unwillingness to cooperate with an FBI inquiry involving the Thomas Riha affair. (A professor at the University of Colorado of Czech descent—and a former CIA consultant—Riha had disappeared and apparently had defected to Czechoslovakia.) Hoover's actions became the catalyst to the abortive Huston Plan, which President Nixon had secretly authorized in June–July 1970.

Delimitation agreements, moreover, could not resolve interagency conflict, given that domestic security and international security operations often overlapped. Thus, CIA officials sought to recruit as sources foreign students attending U.S. universities or business persons involved in foreign investment and export activities (requiring travel to foreign countries). Similarly, the FBI's foreign attaché (Legat) program, under which FBI agents were stationed overseas to promote liaison with foreign police agencies (to obtain assistance in prosecuting individuals involved in criminal enterprises), spilled over to foreign intelligence operations. It proved impossible to exclusively define the FBI's domestic responsibilities and the CIA's foreign responsibilities. As one example of the resulting interagency conflict, the CIA's recruitment during the 1960s of Sam Giancana and John Roselli to assassinate Cuban Premier Fidel Castro compromised the FBI's effort to prosecute these powerful organized crime bosses. In contrast, in 1965, President Johnson turned to the FBI—and not to the CIA—to acquire background information about Dominican Republican political leaders, to be used to ensure an anticommunist government (following a coup overthrowing an unpopular military government), while in 1970, President Nixon authorized the expansion of the FBI's Legat program, having concluded that this expansion would enable the FBI to obtain valuable foreign intelligence. Furthermore, FBI and CIA officials differed in their assessments of the reliability of Soviet defectors Anatoliy Golitsyn and Yuri Nosenko. Golitsyn and Nosenko defected in the early 1960s and offered differing accounts of the relationship between Lee Harvey Oswald (President Kennedy's assassin) and Soviet intelligence. In addition, responding to pressures from Presidents Johnson and Nixon, the CIA initiated in 1967 (then refined and expanded in 1969) an intensive domestic surveillance program, code-named Operation CHAOS, to ascertain whether the protest activities of militant civil rights and anti–Vietnam War activists and organizations were orchestrated and directed from abroad. This program was initiated without coordination with the FBI.

FBI counterintelligence and internal security operations created other problems for other U.S. intelligence agencies, given the FBI's conflicting responsibilities as both a law enforcement and counterintelligence agency. Identifying and containing foreign-directed espionage, and promoting the CIA's and the NSA's foreign intelligence and counterintelligence efforts, required use of clearly illegal surveillance and investigative techniques (notably, foreign embassy wiretaps, bugs, and break-ins). The use of these techniques precluded prosecution under the espionage and internal security laws because the intelligence had been acquired by illegal means. Furthermore, CIA and NSA officials were hesitant to prosecute their own corrupt or disloyal agents, whom they suspected (or concluded) had violated federal statutes, fearing that prosecution would lead to the disclosure of classified information during resultant court proceedings. This conflict between law enforcement and counterintelligence complicated the liaison relations among the U.S. intelligence agencies.

Nonetheless, despite differences in priorities and in interpreting often murky intelligence information, during the Cold War era, FBI officials worked effectively with their intelligence counterparts in the CIA, NSA, MID (or G-2), ONI, and allied foreign intelligence agencies, notably those of France and the United Kingdom. Such coordination promoted the FBI's internal security mission. Close coordination among the FBI, CIA, and NSA, for example, under the code-named Venona program, led to the FBI's apprehension of Soviet spies Judith Coplon, Harry Gold, David Greenglass, Julius Rosenberg, and Rudolf Abel. Furthermore, having obtained the approval of U.S. Post Office officials for a mail-opening program in 1953, under which they opened letters to and from the Soviet Union transmitted through the New York City post office, CIA officials in February 1958 shared with the FBI the results of this program, code-named HTLINGUAL.

This liaison relationship became the subject of congressional interest following the creation of special House and Senate intelligence committees in 1975. Primarily interested in ascertaining the scope, purposes, and legal authority for FBI, CIA, and NSA activities, these congressional committees also explored the nature and effectiveness of interagency liaison, the adequacy of executive oversight, and the need for an enhanced congressional oversight role. Uncovering numerous instances of the intelligence agencies' abuses of power, the committees proposed changes to promote greater coordination and efficiency in intelligence operations.

Reforming and Reorganizing U.S. Intelligence Agencies, 1975–96

The Watergate Affair of 1972–73 and the hearings and reports of the special House and Senate intelligence committees had precipitated concerns both about the U.S. intelligence agencies' abuses of privacy and constitutional rights and the need to improve liaison among the intelligence agencies. In response, Presidents Gerald Ford in 1976, Jimmy Carter in 1978, and Ronald Reagan in 1981 issued directives delineating the intelligence agencies' responsibilities and ensuring more efficient coordination in their domestic intelligence and counterintelligence activities. Ford's 1976 directive prohibited the CIA from engaging in "physical surveillance against United States persons within the United States" unless the person "is reasonably believed to be acting on behalf of a foreign power or engaging in . . . activities threatening the national security." Reagan's 1981 directive modified this limitation to allow the CIA to "conduct counterintelligence activities within the United States, in coordination with the Bureau [FBI], as required by procedures agreed upon" by the CIA director and the attorney general. Presidential directives further clarified each agency's investigative role and vested in the CIA director the responsibility for coordinating interagency activities in the foreign intelligence and counterintelligence areas. A special National Foreign Intelligence Board, chaired by the CIA director, was established to effect "coordination" of national intelligence products and the "maintenance of effective interface" between the various intelligence agencies.

Bureaucratic and personality conflicts, nonetheless, continued but were subordinated to broader policy goals, refined during the 1980s to address the increasingly serious problem of international terrorism. Furthermore, Congress in 1982 enacted so-called "gray mail" legislation—limiting the disclosure of classified information during the prosecution of federal employees and accused spies—thereby subverting an earlier reluctance to prosecute. A dramatic improvement in interagency cooperation and in the apprehension of agency employees recruited as spies ensued—with the notable exceptions of the John Walker, Edward Howard, and Aldrich Ames cases of the 1980s and 1990s.

The Legat Program and Interpol

The FBI also established a liaison relationship with foreign police agencies. The internationalization of crime, particularly after World War II when technological developments increased geographical mobility and communication, necessitated greater cooperation among the various national police agencies. In response, in 1946, Interpol (the International Criminal Police Organization, headquartered in Paris, France) was reorganized. As a participating member, the FBI shared with Interpol information about investigations having international dimensions. This international effort, however, became complicated by the tense crisis of the Cold War, which resulted in reduced contact and cooperation between U.S. and Western European police agencies and their counterparts in Eastern Europe and the Soviet Union. For a time, the FBI's cooperation with Interpol was severed—when, in 1950, the communist government of Czechoslovakia solicited Interpol's assistance to track down 10 Czech political refugees who had fled to West Germany. When the United States rejoined Interpol in 1958, U.S. responsibility was then assumed by the Treasury Department (which was eager to promote international cooperation to further its investigative responsibilities—IRS; Bureau of Customs; Bureau of Narcotics; and Bureau of Alcohol, Tobacco and Firearms). Full FBI cooperation with Interpol resumed only during the 1970s and 1980s, motivated both by the decline in Cold War tensions and the upsurge in international terrorism and international crime syndicates.

Another component of the FBI's foreign police operations was its Legal Attaché (or Legat) program, under which FBI agents were assigned to selected U.S. embassies as legal attachés. Begun during World War II with the creation in 1940 of the FBI's special foreign intelligence branch, SIS, assigned to Latin and South America, this liaison program was further triggered when FBI agents began a coordinated effort in 1940 with British and Canadian intelligence operatives in a coordinated effort to counter German espionage and propaganda activities. Agents stationed in foreign capitals (known within the Bureau as legats) exchanged information concerning security and criminal matters with the host nation's police agencies. Their function was primarily public relations and facilitation, serving as intermediaries to advance each country's law enforcement and security interests (see pages 218–19).

THE TRADITIONS AND CULTURE
OF THE FBI

Tony G. Poveda

Introduction

The traditions and organizational culture of the Federal Bureau of Investigation have been shaped by numerous social forces and historical events. The Bureau's criminal investigative responsibilities have expanded over the years in response to outcries over various crime menaces. Wars and domestic turmoil have similarly promoted an expansion of its intelligence responsibilities. At the same time, scandals in government—both inside and outside the FBI—have periodically forced a rethinking of priorities and policies. And, of course, key personalities have played an influential role in shaping the character of the Bureau, particularly J. Edgar Hoover, the FBI's director from 1924 to 1972.

In its early years (1908–24), the agency's culture was shaped both by the uncertainty of its mandate, as Bureau officials constantly needed to justify the agency's existence, and, more importantly, by the model of private detective agencies, the dominant form of private policing at that time. In the Hoover years (1924–72), the police professionalism movement that emerged in the 1920s and 1930s became the major influence in shaping the FBI's organizational character, whether in the selection of agents or in the virtual autonomy accorded to the Bureau as a federal agency. The modern era (from 1972 to the present) is notable for its emphasis on high technology, undercover operations, and proactive law enforcement. Each of these periods left its mark on the Bureau, with some elements surviving and others falling by the wayside. The accumulation of these influences constitutes the organizational culture and traditions of the Federal Bureau of Investigation.

The Early Years (1908–24)

The only question here before the House is whether we believe in a central secret-service bureau, such as there is in Russia today. . . . I believe that it would be a great blow to freedom and to free institutions if there should arise in this country any such great central secret-service bureau as there is in Russia.

—Congressman George Waldo
of New York, 1908

It is a fact, which everybody recognizes, that there are certain inherent dangers of abuse in any system of police and especially in any system of detective police.

—Attorney General Charles Bonaparte, 1908

The Bureau's Beginnings

The Bureau's establishment in 1908 encountered strong congressional opposition and fears of the threat posed by a national police force. Earlier that year, Congress not only rejected Attorney General Charles Bonaparte's request to create an investigative force within the U.S. Justice Department, it also passed a law prohibiting the Justice Department from borrowing investigative agents from other federal agencies, notably the Secret Service. Members of Congress expressed concern that a Justice Department investigative force might become a secret political police that could be used to spy on citizens, including members of Congress, and that it could ultimately subvert democratic principles of government.

Despite this opposition, about one month after the Sixtieth Congress adjourned, on June 29, 1908, Attorney General Bonaparte, with President Theodore Roosevelt's belated authorization, established a small, permanent detective force in the Department of Justice. Originally designated the Bureau of Investigation, the agency was not given its current name—the Federal Bureau of Investigation—until 1935 (see Table 1.2).

At the time, federal crimes were handled by local law enforcement, and other federal agencies had responsibilities for investigating counterfeiting and post office violations. The Bureau's initial responsibilities were to be limited—investigating crimes on Indian reservations and in the District of Columbia, and handling a few antitrust cases.

The Bureau of Investigation acquired its first real mandate in 1910, when Congress enacted the Mann Act (the White Slave Traffic Act). The Mann Act targeted commercialized vice operations that involved interstate commerce, especially organized prostitution. In its enforcement of this law, the Bureau accumulated a wealth of information related to prostitution, such as the names of public officials who had been paid off, the landlords of brothels, and prominent customers who frequented these establishments. Developing files on the personal affairs of citizens, only marginally related to the prosecution of commercialized vice, had become an important offshoot of this new Bureau mandate. The Bureau's Mann Act operations also often spilled over into noncommercial "immorality," and at times men who took women across state lines for nonmarital sexual relations were arrested (see pages 46–47). Vice enforcement remained an important component of Bureau operations through the 1930s.

Additional responsibility came during World War I, when the Bureau was specifically authorized to locate and apprehend draft-law evaders. Raids were conducted in many cities, known as "slacker raids," for the purpose of rounding up "draft dodgers." In a series of raids in New York City in 1918, about 75,000 men were arrested and jailed. The vast majority of those arrested, however, were eventually released without charges. The Bureau's draft law responsibilities were, of course, terminated with the signing of an armistice in November 1918.

On August 1, 1919, a new division was created within the Bureau, the General Intelligence Division (GID). J. Edgar Hoover, a Justice Department employee in the Alien Enemy section, was appointed head of the GID. This division was created in response to fears that a Bolshevik revolution, like the one that occurred in Russia in November 1917, would sweep the United States. These fears intensified when bombs exploded in eight cities in June 1919, including at the home of Attorney General A. Mitchell Palmer, the most prominent public official advocating a campaign against radicals. The country was concurrently beset by major labor unrest in 1919: a general strike in Seattle, nationwide coal and steel strikes, and a police strike in Boston. These events reinforced fears of a communist takeover, fears promoted by both Attorney General Palmer and the GID. The culmination of this Red Scare was the Palmer Raids of January 1920, planned by Hoover as head of the GID. Over 6,000 persons in 33 cities were rounded up, ostensibly for deportation, under the Immigration Act of 1918 because of their membership in proscribed revolutionary organizations (the Communist Labor Party and the Communist Party). Arrestees who were aliens were subject to deportation, whereas those who were citizens were released. Ultimately, 556 aliens were ordered deported.

The seeds of certain Bureau traditions were planted in these early years. As an agency whose origin was rooted in controversy and congressional opposition, from the beginning, Bureau officials sought to justify the force's existence by promoting alarm over crime or national security menaces and by publicizing concrete accomplishments. Created as an executive agency, but dependent upon Congress for annual appropriations, the Bureau had to carve out a secure place for itself in federal law enforcement. Enforcement of the Dyer Act (officially, the Motor Vehicle Theft Act), passed by Congress in 1919, helped further these goals. Bureau officials publicized impressive statistics on the number of cases solved and the dollar value of stolen vehicles recovered—figures that proved convincing at annual congressional appropriations hearings.

These early years introduced other traditions, as well. The investigation of vice, and later of radical activists, had led Bureau agents to compile extensive dossiers on individuals, recording their private morality or personal opinions—activities and issues that were often outside the Bureau's legal mandate. This early penchant for non-criminal information, which under the directorship of J. Edgar Hoover expanded exponentially, remains today a source of public concern. But in the Bureau's early years, private detective agencies provided the model for the agency's operations; notably, the Pinkerton Detective Agency and the Burns Detective Agency, companies that had originated in the nineteenth century after the Civil War.

The Detective Agency Model

Municipal-level public policing was transformed in the United States around the mid-nineteenth century from the British constabulary system of policing to a paid, uniformed, quasi-military police force (not unlike the police in most U.S. communities today). This urban police model did not, however, become the organizational model for the Bureau of Investigation. The public generally held low esteem for police departments in urban America. New recruits received little, if any, formal training, and the police forces were often instruments of local ward bosses and political machines. To the public, the police at the turn of the century were closely linked both to partisan politics and municipal corruption. Indeed one of the key agenda items of Progressive-era reformers (from 1900 to the beginning of World War I) was the reform of corrupt municipal administration.

Private detective agencies also had their origins in the nineteenth century, created largely in response to the failure of public police to protect corporate interests. These private agencies thrived during the industrial expansion after the Civil War. Detective agencies were hired by major corporations, initially in the mining, steel, and railroad industries, to police their employees. Their services included infiltrating and spying on labor organizations to detect dishonesty and discontent, and they also suppressed strikes, resulting at times in armed confrontations with workers. In the 1870s, for example, the Pinkerton Detective Agency was instrumental in crushing the Mollie Maguires, a secret organization of coal miners who threatened the iron and coal companies' control of the mines in eastern Pennsylvania. Private detective agencies prospered especially during the Progressive era, when they were engaged to counteract the increasingly more militant and radical labor movements like the Industrial Workers of the World (IWW) and the Socialist Party.

At the time of the Bureau's formation in 1908, Attorney General Bonaparte intended for it to function more as a detective force—to conduct investigations necessary to the Justice Department's prosecution of economic crime (antitrust or railroad rate violations)—than as a general police force. Bonaparte also recognized, as did many members of Congress, that the men who performed such work were not always of the highest caliber, but nonetheless, their work was necessary to uncover evidence of criminal conduct. All in all, the private detective agency model seemed most appropriate for the new Bureau of Investigation.

One of the distinguishing features of private detective agencies was their partisanship—after all, they were hired by clients to protect certain interests. This presented a dilemma for Bureau officials. Laws ideally were to be enforced in a neutral and evenhanded manner, or at least conveying the appearance of neutrality, yet even the public policing model at the turn of the century was exceedingly partisan. Private detective agencies alone did not promote the interests of their employers, even municipal police had close ties to urban political machines. The Bureau took shape within the context of this partisan model of policing.

In the beginning, Bureau agents aggressively pursued suspected criminals, conducting raids on vice establishments under the Mann Act and rounding up suspected draft evaders during World War I. Bureau activities first assumed a more partisan character in the postwar years, during the Red Scare of 1919–20. After the formation of the GID, Bureau officials, in effect, conducted a war on radical workers—arresting, jailing, and, in some cases, deporting them. GID records on radical organizations and individuals, provided the evidence cited by Attorney General Palmer in his campaign to promote public fear of an imminent communist revolutionary threat.

The detective agency model became fully institutionalized in 1921, when Attorney General Harry M. Daugherty appointed William J. Burns, formerly head of the Burns Detective Agency, chief of the Bureau of Investigation (see Exhibit 5.1). The most famous detective in the United States since Allan Pinkerton, Burns had an established reputation from solving a number of high-profile cases, notably, the bombing of the Los Angeles Times building in 1910. During Chief Burns's three-year tenure, the Bureau continued to pursue and promote the threat of radicalism, linking labor

Exhibit 5.1   **William J. Burns,**
Courtesy of the FBI

strikes and unrest to foreign communism. Agents spied and infiltrated worker organizations in an effort to document radical influence and sometimes worked closely with private detective agencies, including Burns's own International Detective Agency. During this period, Bureau personnel were often recruited from the ranks of private detective agencies. In its antiradical activities, the Bureau of Investigation, like the private detective agencies that it emulated, functioned as a partisan organization. In 1922, for example, Bureau agents helped break a national railroad strike by responding to Burns's order to investigate whether strikers had violated a court injunction. The resulting arrest and prosecution of some 1,200 strikers contributed to the strike's failure. The line between the strike-breaking activities of the private detective agencies and the law-enforcement activities of the Justice Department's Bureau of Investigation had become thinly drawn.

Illegal Practices, Misuse of Power, and Scandal

The Bureau of Investigation's increasingly partisan pursuit of radical workers and aliens soon generated controversy and criticism. In the wake of the Palmer Raids of 1920, Assistant Secretary of Labor Louis B. Post surfaced as one of the Bureau's most outspoken critics. Since the Immigration Bureau was under his authority in the Labor Department, he made the final decision of whether or not to deport the radical aliens whom Bureau of Investigation and Immigration Bureau agents had rounded up in raids. Under immigration laws of 1917 and 1918, alien residents could be deported for believing in anarchism or revolutionary change, or for belonging to organizations that advocated anarchism or revolution. When reviewing the several thousand alien deportation cases referred to his department following the Palmer Raids, Post insisted on evidence of individual guilt. Moreover, because many of those arrested had been denied access to legal counsel during deportation hearings, Post dismissed the vast majority of cases. Although he had the support of Secretary of Labor William Wilson, Post's actions were attacked by Hoover and Palmer, and in 1921, a House committee considered impeaching him.

As part of his defense against impeachment, Post's lawyer, with the aid of several groups, including the American Civil Liberties Union, investigated the conduct of the raids. The result was a 67-page document, *A Report upon the Illegal Practices of the United States Department of Justice,* which was made public in May 1920. Signed by 12 of the most distinguished members of the legal community, this report sharply accused Justice Department and Bureau of Investigation officials of widespread lawless actions. These included warrantless arrests, illegal searches and seizures, and the misuse of administrative power.

In 1921, the Senate Judiciary Committee also held hearings into the Justice Department's conduct. At these hearings, the attorney general and GID chief Hoover were unable to refute evidence of abuses in the planning and execution of antiradical raids. The combination of this critical scrutiny and the lessening of wartime anxieties served to reduce Red Scare hysteria. Nonetheless, the GID under Burns and Hoover continued to monitor radical activities closely.

A major governmental scandal involving the administration of President Warren Harding soon raised new questions about the Bureau's activities and administration. This so-called Teapot Dome scandal (1923–24) began with allegations that two businessmen had bribed Secretary of the Interior Albert Fall to award them, without competitive bids, leases to two oil reserves—one in Teapot Dome, Wyoming, the other in Elk Hills, California. Although these leases were arranged in 1921, Fall's questionable conduct in favoring the two oil companies became known in 1923. Fall was eventually indicted and convicted of accepting bribes and, in 1931, served one year in prison.

Two Montana senators, Thomas J. Walsh and Burton K. Wheeler, were instrumental in publicizing allegations about these secret leases. During congressional hearings in 1923–24, Walsh and Wheeler also produced evidence of wider corruption involving the Harding administration. Among these was the allegation that Attorney General Harry Daugherty had earlier blocked an investigation into Fall's oil leasing irregularities. In anticipation of future damaging disclosures at the Senate hearings, and to discredit the senators, Daugherty authorized Bureau Chief William Burns to send agents to Montana to investigate allegations of corruption involving Wheeler. At the same time, Bureau agents in Washington, D.C., closely monitored the two senators, their homes, and their families.

During the ensuing Senate hearings, Daugherty refused to testify or to release Justice Department records. President Calvin Coolidge, who had become president following Harding's death the year before, eventually fired Daugherty on March 28, 1924. Tried twice on charges of conspiring to defraud the U.S. government, Daugherty was never convicted. Both trials resulted in hung juries and the charges were eventually dismissed. On April 8, 1924, Coolidge appointed Harlan F. Stone, a former dean of the Columbia Law School and one of the critics of the Palmer Raids, as the new attorney general.

Bureau Chief Burns, who admitted during Senate testimony to having used the Bureau to investigate the two Montana senators, was removed from office about a month after Daugherty was replaced. Burns was never charged with any of the crimes he admitted to before the Walsh and Wheeler committees. On May 10, 1924, Attorney General Stone appointed J. Edgar Hoover, at the time an assistant chief under Burns, acting director of the Bureau.

The Teapot Dome scandal meant more than simply that the heads of the Justice Department and the Bureau of Investigation were replaced. It also signaled the demise of the detective agency model as it had become institutionalized in Bureau operations—partisan investigative activities (notably, the antiradical operations), liaison with private detective agencies, and the recruitment of political appointees or agents of questionable characters (see discussion of Gaston Means on pages 172–73). The incipient traditions of labor spying, of undercover work, and the infiltration of radical political organizations had also come under fire, while serious questions had been raised about the Bureau's legal mandate. For the first time in the Bureau's short history, its policies and internal culture had come under unfavorable public scrutiny.

The Hoover Years (1924–72)

Mr. J. Edgar Hoover and the FBI had developed into an extraordinarily independent agency within our Government. It is hard to exaggerate that. Mr. Hoover, in effect, took orders only from himself, sometimes from an Attorney General, usually a President, and that was it. He had created a kind of kingdom of which he was very jealous. . . . Mr. Hoover built a position which I think is almost unparalleled in the administrative branch of our Government, a combination of professional performance on the job, some element of fear, very astute relations with Congress, and very effective public relations.

—Former Secretary of State Dean Rusk, 1974

When U.S. Attorney General Stone first appointed J. Edgar Hoover acting Bureau director in 1924, the Bureau of Investigation was a scandal-ridden agency. Its chief, William Burns, had been removed for misusing his official position, and even though Hoover had been assistant chief during the Burns-Daugherty era of the early 1920s, he escaped any taint of corruption or abusive conduct. This reputation seems remarkable since Hoover had headed the General Intelligence Division, whose activities against radicals and aliens had generated criticism of the Bureau's practices in the now-controversial Palmer Raids. Nonetheless, Attorney General Stone appointed Hoover acting director and then, sufficiently impressed with Hoover's performance, made this appointment permanent on December 10, 1924. J. Edgar Hoover thus was given the responsibility to head a small and relatively obscure investigative arm of the Justice Department, a division that had fallen into disrepute in its early years. It was his task, and Stone's, to reform the operation and personnel of the Bureau of Investigation and to restore public support for the agency. This meant developing a professional culture among Bureau employees, and at the same time, minimizing popular fears of federal police powers.

Police Professionalism

J. Edgar Hoover's and Harlan F. Stone's administrative reforms were in keeping with the values of the conservative Republican administrations of the late 1920s, the presidencies of Calvin Coolidge (1923–29) and Herbert Hoover (1929–33). As fiscal and states' rights conservatives, Presidents Coolidge and Hoover endorsed a limited role for federal law enforcement. They shared certain progressive views about reform: that rational management techniques would ensure greater administrative efficiency, and that political patronage should not determine the hiring of public servants.

Within the law enforcement profession, a reform movement had also emerged during the 1920s and 1930s—the police professionalism movement, which influenced and shaped Bureau operations and procedures for decades to come. Police professionalism reforms came about to counter the pervasive influence of partisan politics on policing at the turn of the century. Municipal police forces, which were closely linked to ward bosses and political machines, were considered by many reformers to be an integral part of the urban corruption of the late nineteenth and early twentieth centuries. Moreover, there was widespread police misconduct in the everyday enforcement of the law.

The Wickersham Commission

The Wickersham Commission (officially the National Commission on Law Observance and Enforcement), appointed by President Herbert Hoover in 1929, documented this problem of police lawlessness. In its eleventh volume, *Lawlessness in Law Enforcement* (1931), the Commission described misconduct and brutality in police departments across the country. "Third degree" tactics to extract confessions were common; some suspects were even hung by their ankles from second-story windows and beaten to extract confessions. The Wickersham Commission, and its impressively detailed 14-volume report, precipitated a major shift in public attitudes toward law enforcement and the criminal justice system in general, lessening the public's toleration of police misconduct and providing powerful support for the emerging professionalism ideal.

The police reform movement endorsed the elimination of political influences in the functioning of police departments. The reformed departments should be run by administrative experts, and police officers should be recruited based on merit, not as part of the political patronage system. Police executives, moreover, should be strong leaders and operate independent of local politics.

Reforms of 1924

In one of his first reform measures, Attorney General Stone abolished the GID, the division that had been at the center of the Bureau's antiradical activity and abuses of authority during the immediate postwar years. In addition, Stone limited Bureau investigations to violations of federal law, such as the Mann Act or the Dyer Act, and he prohibited any investigation of the political beliefs and opinions of U.S. citizens. However, Hoover evidently circumvented this order. Although radical political groups were not directly investigated by the Bureau, files from 1924–30 confirm that the Bureau received and maintained unsolicited information on radical activities from private citizens and local and state police agencies. Bureau agents also continued to monitor radical publications and press releases. Even so, the Bureau's political surveillance function of the pre-1924 era, involving spying on labor organizations and radical groups, was severely curtailed.

Another of Stone's reforms involved the selection of Bureau personnel. One agent who had been fired two years earlier, Gaston B. Means, symbolized the pre-1924 corruption and the unprofessional staff of the early Bureau. Before World War I, Means had worked for German intelligence while William J. Burns (later to become chief of the Bureau of Investigation) had worked for British intelligence. The two had collaborated when sharing intelligence information from their respective employers, and a friendship developed out of this relationship. When Burns became Bureau chief in 1921, he hired Means for "special assignments," which included spying on Democratic members of Congress. Means acquired notoriety for misusing his Bureau position to sell information from Bureau files and to "fix" federal cases, especially those involving his underworld contacts. Although an extreme case, Means (who ultimately was fired) typified the corruption and patronage of the Bureau in the early era.

Hoover was instructed by Attorney General Stone to remove incompetent agents and terminate the practice whereby agent appointments were based on patronage. Hoover quickly implemented these changes, reviewing personnel files and giving preference in subsequent appointments to those holding law or accounting degrees. Although there were no mass firings, some agents who had obtained their jobs through political influence were removed and others quit on their own. Sixty-one employees left the Bureau in the months following Hoover's appointment, although fewer than half of these were agents.

Training and the FBI National Academy

Training and educating police also constituted an important part of the professionalism movement, which emphasized the importance of specialized knowledge for the performance of police work. Education credentials were also seen as a way to elevate the formerly low status of police. Endorsing these principles, Hoover established a special training school in the Bureau's New York City office to ensure the proper training of agents. This school was later moved to Washington, D.C., in the Department of Justice building and later still to Quantico, Virginia.

In addition to training new Bureau agents, in 1935, Hoover conceived the idea of a National Academy to train police from around the country in the latest law enforcement techniques. The Academy's principal objective was to raise the level of professionalism in law enforcement nationwide, and, indirectly, to establish the Bureau as a model of professionalism for local and state police. Over the years, the Academy's curriculum expanded to include

courses in law, management, communications, behavioral science, terrorism, money laundering, and international crime. The training and expertise of FBI agents remains one of the Bureau's hallmarks and contributes to its elite status in the law enforcement community, and the Academy constitutes one of Hoover's enduring legacies.

The Fingerprint Division and the FBI Laboratory

Hoover's advocacy of upgraded police training and qualifications, strong police executive leadership, insulation of police work from political influence, and emphasis on applying science to law enforcement were all part of the police professionalism movement that shaped the Bureau in the 1920s and 1930s. An important component of this new professionalism and scientific law enforcement was to ensure the more efficient and coordinated use of fingerprints to identify criminal suspects (see Exhibit 5.2). Before 1923, such records were administered by the Bureau of Criminal Identification at the federal prison in Leavenworth, Kansas, which relied on the aid of inmate labor. In 1924, the Bureau of Criminal Identification's approximately one million fingerprint files were transferred to the Bureau's Identification division in Washington, D.C. In 1930, the Bureau was given control over all federal fingerprint files, a collection that grew throughout Hoover's tenure as Bureau director.

To further advance the application of science to law enforcement, in 1932, Hoover established a special crime laboratory at the Bureau's Washington headquarters to provide expert assistance to the Bureau and local law

Exhibit 5.2   **An Early FBI Fingerprint Sorting Machine**, *Courtesy of the FBI*

enforcement agencies in the analysis of physical evidence (see Exhibit 5.3). Physical evidence was key in the solving of several major cases during this period, most notably the Lindbergh kidnapping case of 1932, which gave additional credibility to scientific law enforcement. Although beginning

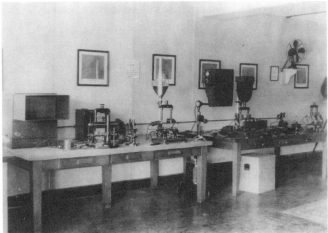

Exhibit 5.3   **The Technical Laboratory in 1932,** *Courtesy of the National Archives (65-LAB)*

with meager resources—a microscope and some ultraviolet light equipment—the crime laboratory's operations eventually expanded to include the analysis of blood and other physiological fluids, hair, soil, clothing fibers, and other types of physical evidence for possible matches with criminal suspects. Laboratory personnel now also examine the authenticity of documents and, on occasion, conduct handwriting analyses. The laboratory also conducts firearms and bullet comparisons and analyzes explosives.

Uniform Crime Reports

In addition, in 1930, Congress authorized the Bureau to collect national crime statistics. The guidelines and manual for crime reporting by local police agencies were initially developed by a special committee of the International Association of Chiefs of Police. This specially appointed group, the Committee on Uniform Crime Reports, identified the seven major crime categories that constituted the nation's crime index: murder/nonnegligent manslaughter, forcible rape, robbery, aggravated assault, larceny, burglary, and auto theft. It further established the basis for measuring these crimes: crimes reported to the police and the number of arrests. Congress assigned to the Bureau the responsibility to collect, record, and publish the statistics that were to be provided by police departments across the country. The participation of local police departments in this national collection of crime data has always been voluntary and, over the years, a larger and larger percentage of police agencies

have participated. Now published annually, these national crime statistics are regularly compiled in a volume titled *Uniform Crime Reports (UCR)*. Until 1973, with the advent of the Justice Department's annual victimization surveys (the National Crime Victimization Survey), the *UCR* offered the only national assessment of the amount and trends of crime in the United States. As the nation's depository for crime statistics, the FBI is placed in a unique position to define and influence the public's perception of the crime problem in the United States.

The development of scientific law enforcement and the professional upgrading of Bureau agents during the 1920s were lasting and positive accomplishments that contributed to the effectiveness of the modern FBI, especially the quality and professionalism of its agents. The administrative reforms that Hoover initiated following his appointment as Bureau director in 1924 transformed the Bureau from an old-style detective agency to a nonpolitical, scientifically grounded law-enforcement organization, operating under the close supervision and control of the FBI director.

G-Men and Public Enemies

The culture of professionalism was at the core of the reforms of Bureau operations in the 1920s and 1930s. Nonetheless, it remained a small and relatively obscure federal agency that continued to be plagued by the uncertainty of its mandate and declining resources. The Great Depression of the 1930s and President Franklin Roosevelt's New Deal policies soon changed this. By the end of the 1930s, the Bureau (renamed the Federal Bureau of Investigation in 1935) had emerged as a prominent law enforcement agency with significantly increased resources and responsibilities. Its image as an efficient crime-fighting organization became an integral part of its professional culture, and its director, J. Edgar Hoover, was considered a leader and spokesman for law enforcement in the United States.

The New Deal and Federal Law Enforcement

This sudden transformation was the indirect by-product of the ideological shift governing President Franklin Roosevelt's New Deal policies in contrast to those of his predecessor, Herbert Hoover. The principle governing President Hoover's responses to the social and economic problems of the Great Depression was, "the best government is that which governs least." Reluctant to commit federal resources to alleviating poverty or promoting economic recovery, Herbert Hoover adhered to the traditional philosophy that local agencies and private efforts would lead to economic recovery, and that direct federal aid to individuals should be avoided. In contrast, President Roosevelt advocated expanding the federal role to deal with the economic crisis of the 1930s, and his New Deal policies entailed an unprecedented expansion of the national government's role in social and economic affairs.

It was this expansion of federal authority that proved to be the further catalyst to the transformation of the FBI. Although the Roosevelt administration's central concern was the need to promote economic recovery from the Great Depression, a related concern involved the crime problem of the 1930s—the menace posed by kidnappers, bank robbers, and gangsters. These gangsters—or "public enemies," as they came to be popularly known—were symptomatic of the era's institutional breakdown and crisis. In the resulting war against the Depression-era gangsters, the forces of the underworld became pitted against those of organized society. The hard times of the Depression, however, had also generated some public sympathy for those who opposed the established order, even if they were violent criminals (see pages 53–58 and 266–68).

Cummings and the Twelve Point Crime Program

The Roosevelt administration's solution to the nation's crime problem followed the same ideological lines as its economic recovery program: expand federal authority and mobilize grass-roots support for federal programs. Crucial to ensuring acceptance of the New Deal crime policy was the need to convince the public that there was a nationwide crime wave, and that the federal government could best apprehend dangerous criminals. The primary responsibility for ensuring the success of this campaign's success rested with Roosevelt's attorney general, Homer S. Cummings.

During the early years of the Depression, many commentators feared that massive unemployment and economic hardship would unleash an enormous crime wave. Cummings exploited this fear by mounting a vigorous anticrime crusade. His speeches stirred public alarm about the threat of an "armed underworld," and he proposed that the country "arm" itself against the "racketeers." In 1934, Cummings convened a major conference on crime in Washington, D.C., as part of this effort to mobilize public support for the Roosevelt administration's crime program. Cummings was the most conspicuous figure in this effort of 1933–35. In fact, journalist Milton Mayer, writing in 1935, aptly characterized the cause of the panic as "Mr. Cummings's crime wave."

In actuality, the nation experienced no crime wave during the 1930s. Statistics confirm that serious crime rose in the early years of the Depression but then, unexpectedly,

it leveled off or, as in the case of murder, actually declined (after the mid-1930s). Nevertheless, Attorney General Cummings's anticrime crusade led to success for the Roosevelt administration in the legislative arena. In 1934, the Seventy-Third Congress added more provisions to the federal criminal code than had all of the previous Congresses. In that year, virtually all of Roosevelt's and Attorney General Homer Cummings's Twelve Point Crime Program was enacted into law, including legislation making federal crimes of bank robbery, interstate flight of felons, murder or assault of federal officials, racketeering, and extortion.

John Dillinger: The Archetypal Public Enemy

Jointly, the Justice Department and the popular media successfully portrayed the responsibility of notorious public enemies for this crime problem, dangerous gangsters who were to be sought out and, in some cases, to be shot on sight (the "shoot to kill" doctrine was advocated by numerous police and Justice Department officials during this time). These gangsters actually were often no more than common criminals who received an inordinate amount of media attention.

The criminal career of one of the most famous of these public enemies, John Dillinger, began with a nine-year sentence for the robbery of a grocery store in Indiana where his net take was nil. In prison, Dillinger met the members of his future gang and, upon his release in 1933, they embarked upon a series of bank robberies and killings that lasted until his death the following year. Despite his rather ordinary criminal career, Dillinger became a symbol for both the media and the Justice Department, and his career became interwoven with the politics of promoting passage of the 1934 crime control acts. Cummings and Roosevelt pointed to Dillinger's criminal acts to marshal support for their Twelve Point Crime Program. Concurrently, the newspapers relished reporting the police bungling of various phases of Dillinger's life as a fugitive (see pages 54–55). The eventual dramatic killing of Dillinger provided the symbolic triumph for the forces of law and order over those of the armed underworld (see Exhibit 5.4).

The exaggeration that transformed ordinary criminals into notorious public enemies was key to congressional approval of the 1934 federal crime legislation. In order to justify federal intervention, there had to be criminals worthy of such attention and a superpolice agency, the Bureau, capable of responding to the challenge. The manufacture of public enemies and the growth of the FBI went hand in hand. Indeed, only because of the general belief in the existence of a crime wave did the Bureau's investigative

WANTED

JOHN HERBERT DILLINGER

On June 23, 1934, HOMER S. CUMMINGS, Attorney General of the United States, under the authority vested in him by an Act of Congress approved June 6, 1934, offered a reward of

$10,000.00

for the capture of John Herbert Dillinger or a reward of

$5,000.00

for information leading to the arrest of John Herbert Dillinger.

DESCRIPTION

Age, 32 years; Height, 5 feet 7-1/8 inches; Weight, 153 pounds; Build, medium; Hair, medium chestnut; Eyes, grey; Complexion, medium; Occupation, machinist; Marks and scars, 1/2 inch scar back left hand, scar middle upper lip, brown mole between eyebrows.

All claims to any of the aforesaid rewards and all questions and disputes that may arise as among claimants to the foregoing rewards shall be passed upon by the Attorney General and his decisions shall be final and conclusive. The right is reserved to divide and allocate portions of any of said rewards as between several claimants. No part of the aforesaid rewards shall be paid to any official or employee of the Department of Justice.

If you are in possession of any information concerning the whereabouts of John Herbert Dillinger, communicate immediately by telephone or telegraph collect to the nearest office of the Division of Investigation, United States Department of Justice, the local addresses of which are set forth on the reverse side of this notice.

                                        JOHN EDGAR HOOVER, DIRECTOR,
                                        DIVISION OF INVESTIGATION,
                                        UNITED STATES DEPARTMENT OF JUSTICE,
June 25, 1934   WASHINGTON, D. C.

                                                           FBI/DOJ

Exhibit 5.4   John Dillinger "Wanted" Poster, *Courtesy of the FBI*

responsibilities and resources expand significantly. Between 1932 and 1935, FBI appropriations increased by 72 percent, and the number of agents doubled to around 600 (see Table 1.1). Furthermore, the FBI's share of the total Justice Department budget increased from about 9 percent to 14 percent during this period. This new authority and increased appropriations placed the Bureau on a firm footing, more so than at any time since its creation in 1908.

Hollywood, the Media, and the G-Man Myth

In the early 1930s, newspapers and movies highlighted an inept police incapable of bringing celebrity criminals to justice. But by 1935, Cummings's crusade had reversed this tide of public opinion, and the media and Hollywood adopted a view more sympathetic to law enforcement. In 1935 alone, seven movies were released about gangsters and federal agents that portrayed federal law enforcement agents—or G-men, as they came to be known— in a favorable light (see pages 267–70).

At about this time, the spotlight in the anticrime effort shifted from Attorney General Cummings to FBI Director Hoover and his agents. The FBI director, as head of a crime-fighting agency, was a better candidate for personifying the crusade than a partisan attorney general. By mid-1933, Hoover fully understood the politics of the anticrime campaign, and his publicity efforts improved the stature of his own law enforcement agency. The turning point in Hoover's attitude toward the media occurred following a shoot-out that came to be known as the Kansas City Massacre. On June 17, 1933, Charles "Pretty Boy" Floyd and two other gangsters ambushed prison escapee Frank Nash while he was being transported in police and FBI custody. In the shoot-out, the gangsters killed one FBI agent and three policemen and wounded two other FBI agents; Nash was also killed. The arrogance of the gangsters and the resulting embarrassment for law enforcement, and the FBI in particular, aroused Hoover's indignation.

In 1933, to offset occasional embarrassing publicity, Hoover began a formal media program in which FBI officials collaborated with a number of free-lance writers and journalists who were provided access to FBI information to prepare articles, speeches, books, and even a comic strip to glorify the Bureau's conquest of the celebrated public enemies of the day. The principal beneficiary of this assistance was the popular writer and journalist Courtney Ryley Cooper. Between 1933 and 1940, Cooper wrote 24 Bureau-approved articles in mass circulation publications, notably *American* magazine. The Hearst press became another of the FBI's faithful glorifiers during the 1930s, designating it "the greatest detective agency in the world." In 1935, Hoover formalized these public relations efforts with the creation of the Crime Records Division. (see pages 229, 271–72, and 344) . This division became the FBI's public relations arm, whose purpose was to have the FBI portrayed as a highly efficient, well-trained, and scientifically run organization, up to the task of catching the nation's most sinister public enemies.

Professionalism

The G-man image that emerged during this period became central to the culture of the FBI in the Hoover era. Although this image derived in large part from the 1930s politics of crime control, FBI officials also turned this positive popular reputation into an internal self-image of professionalism and dedication. The application of science to law enforcement; the careful selection and training of agents; and independent, non-partisan leadership all contributed to the Bureau's new culture of professionalism. This G-man identity also incorporated the idea of an infallible and invincible FBI. If a public enemy was loose in society or a major crime unsolved, it was just a matter of time before the Bureau and its G-men would capture the fugitive or solve the most difficult of crimes—in striking contrast to local law enforcement, at the time still widely perceived as corrupt and inept. Crime menaces were neither too small nor too complex for the Bureau.

The G-man myth was reaffirmed in books, movies, television, and newspaper accounts of the Bureau at work. The 1959 movie, *The FBI Story,* and the television series, "The FBI" (which began in 1965), were two of the more notable productions; both were closely monitored by Hoover. This G-man culture was further embellished during the 1950s and 1960s by publicity concerning the FBI's national security responsibilities, with the Bureau becoming the nation's protector against both crime and the subversion of "the American Way."

"Public enemies" and "G-men" established a pattern that persisted for decades to come: manufacture a crime menace and then convince the public that the FBI could conquer the threat. Whether kidnappers and bank robbers of the Depression era were involved, or communists and subversives of the Cold War, the formula for publicizing and marshaling support for FBI operations was the same.

Domestic Security Intelligence

At the same time that it expanded the FBI's authority in criminal matters, the Roosevelt administration secretly authorized the FBI to resume monitoring radical political activities. Although Attorney General Stone had banned such investigations in 1924, as early as 1934, President Roosevelt ordered a Bureau probe of Nazi groups in the United States. Then, in 1936, Roosevelt directed the FBI to gather intelligence on the fascist and communist movements and their impact on the economic and political life of the country. Both of these were secret assignments. FBI Director Hoover exploited the president's authorizations to reestablish an FBI domestic security capability—a new General Intelligence Section—to conduct ongoing intelligence operations focusing on "subversive" activities.

Franklin Roosevelt's Secret Directives

Congress and the American public did not learn of this expanded authority until the outbreak of World War II, in September 1939, when President Roosevelt publicly directed all local law enforcement officials to turn over to the FBI any information pertaining to espionage, sabotage, violations of the neutrality laws, and subversive activities. In

addition to these domestic security responsibilities, in 1940, President Roosevelt assigned the FBI responsibility for foreign intelligence in the Western Hemisphere (this authority was withdrawn in 1946 following the end of World War II).

The reinstatement of FBI domestic intelligence authority resurrected the tradition of antiradical operations and labor spying of the pre-1924 era. The resumption of intelligence activities also had long-term consequences for the Bureau's organizational culture and for its power and influence as a federal agency. The shift from an agency exclusively concerned with law enforcement to an agency involved in both intelligence and law enforcement meant that FBI operations became much more secretive, less accountable, and, to a greater extent, more lawless.

The Emergence of Domestic Intelligence

As part of the national security apparatus of the federal government during the Second World War and the Cold War period that followed, the FBI conducted intelligence activities that were very different in nature from its law enforcement function. The techniques employed against foreign espionage agents during wartime were also used against suspected domestic national security threats during peacetime. Those considered to be domestic threats were primarily left-wing political groups and persons (communist and socialist groups), although occasionally right-wing groups were also targeted (see Exhibit 5.5). Besides gathering information about their proposed plans and objectives,

Exhibit 5.5   **FBI Anticommunism Exhibit,** *Courtesy of the FBI*

393

EXHIBIT 17

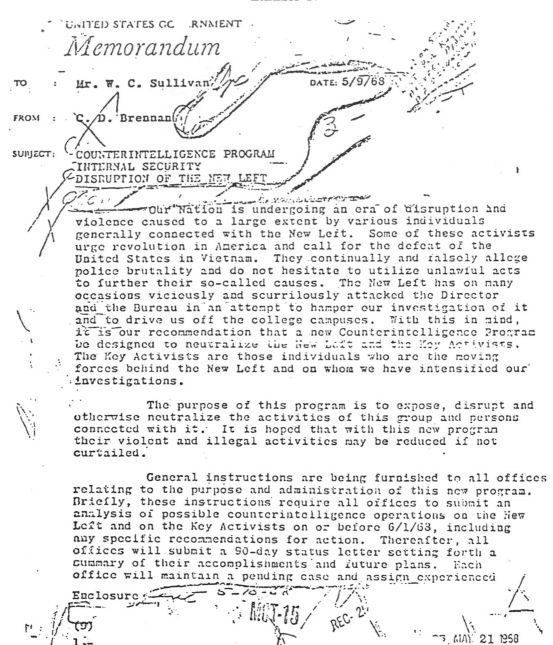

UNITED STATES GOVERNMENT

Memorandum

TO   : Mr. W. C. Sullivan   DATE: 5/9/68

FROM : C. D. Brennan

SUBJECT: COUNTERINTELLIGENCE PROGRAM
          INTERNAL SECURITY
          DISRUPTION OF THE NEW LEFT

Our Nation is undergoing an era of disruption and violence caused to a large extent by various individuals generally connected with the New Left. Some of these activists urge revolution in America and call for the defeat of the United States in Vietnam. They continually and falsely allege police brutality and do not hesitate to utilize unlawful acts to further their so-called causes. The New Left has on many occasions viciously and scurrilously attacked the Director and the Bureau in an attempt to hamper our investigation of it and to drive us off the college campuses. With this in mind, it is our recommendation that a new Counterintelligence Program be designed to neutralize the New Left and the Key Activists. The Key Activists are those individuals who are the moving forces behind the New Left and on whom we have intensified our investigations.

The purpose of this program is to expose, disrupt and otherwise neutralize the activities of this group and persons connected with it. It is hoped that with this new program their violent and illegal activities may be reduced if not curtailed.

General instructions are being furnished to all offices relating to the purpose and administration of this new program. Briefly, these instructions require all offices to submit an analysis of possible counterintelligence operations on the New Left and on the Key Activists on or before 6/1/68, including any specific recommendations for action. Thereafter, all offices will submit a 90-day status letter setting forth a summary of their accomplishments and future plans. Each office will maintain a pending case and assign experienced

Enclosure

(9)

1 -
1 -
1 -
1 -
1 -

REC-24

MAY 21 1968

CONTINUED OVER

Exhibit 5.6   **FBI Memorandum on the New Left Counterintelligence Program**

394

Memo to Mr. Sullivan .
Re: COUNTERINTELLIGENCE PROGRAM

personnel to this program. All proposed counterintelligence
action must be approved at the Seat of Government prior to
instituting it. This new program will be supervised at the
Seat of Government by a Special Agent supervisor in the
Internal Security Section.

RECOMMENDATIONS:

        1) That the Domestic Intelligence Division be
authorized to immediately initiate a coordinated Counterintelligence Program directed at exposing, disrupting, and
otherwise neutralizing the New Left and Key Activists.

        2) That the attached letter setting forth
instructions for the administration and immediate enactment
of the program be forwarded to all offices.

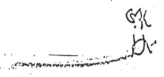

Exhibit 5.6 (continued)

FBI agents also used some of the techniques employed during wartime counterintelligence operations to discredit these groups and prevent them from achieving their political objectives. These tactics included promoting factionalism within a group or between rival groups, and disseminating derogatory information or disinformation about the groups and their members. These actions were conducted secretly, in a climate in which questions of legality and ethics were seldom raised. Assured of secrecy, FBI officials and agents were primarily concerned with whether proposed measures would be effective and whether their actions could be publicly exposed. All such actions were justified as necessary to protect national security (see Exhibit 5.6).

A very different normative environment prevailed in the Bureau's law enforcement operation than in domestic intelligence. The purpose of criminal investigations is to arrest, prosecute, and convict offenders for specific violations of the law. Investigators thus had to follow specific procedural rules relating to arrest, search and seizure, and interrogations. If a criminal case reaches the courtroom stage, the conduct of the investigating agents will be reviewed to ensure that evidence is admissible and that procedural rules were observed. This system of judicial review ensures that the behavior of FBI law enforcement agents and their supervising officials is made accountable— unlike the actions of agents conducting clandestine intelligence operations that never become public.

Domestic intelligence operations radically changed the culture of the FBI in the Hoover era, especially because such work constituted a major component of FBI investigations during the World War II and Cold War eras. By the end of World War II, in fiscal year 1945, the FBI's appropriations had increased to nearly over $44 million, a fivefold increase over fiscal year 1940; 81 percent of this amount was earmarked for "national defense." This rapid growth in intelligence operations meant that a significant segment of FBI activities was governed by a set of standards different from that which governed conventional criminal investigations. This type of work, which depended on secrecy and even lawlessness in the pursuit of targeted groups and individuals, was at odds with the culture of professionalism and the G-man culture that had been cultivated in the Bureau during the 1930s. These two subcultures within the Bureau, the visible world of the G-men, pursuing bank robbers and car thieves, and the hidden world of intelligence, combating communist and subversive menaces, coexisted for several decades in the Hoover FBI.

McCarthyism

A sharply intensified national security panic developed during the 1950s, popularly known as McCarthyism—named after the senator from Wisconsin, Joseph McCarthy. McCarthyism represented a mood of alarm that communists, or their unwitting "dupes," had infiltrated major governmental institutions, particularly those directly affecting national security, such as the U.S. Army and the State Department. This internal threat of communism and its influence on American life became the major focus of FBI activities after 1945. Bureau agents and informers gathered information on the political opinions and activities of groups and individu-

als who were suspected of being communists or under communist influence. The groups under surveillance extended beyond the U.S. Communist Party to include socialist and civil rights organizations—for example, Students for a Democratic Society, the National Association for the Advancement of Colored People, and the American Civil Liberties Union—along with labor unions, university professors, prominent writers, and virtually any organization or person who advocated social change or reform. By 1960, approximately 432,000 files on "subversive" individuals and groups had been opened. Moreover, since 1940, the FBI had been compiling a list of persons whom Bureau officials deemed dangerous to the internal security of the country. In the event of a national emergency, individuals on this list (the Security Index) were candidates for detention, to prevent them from engaging in espionage or adversely affecting the national interest. By the end of 1954, some 26,174 names were on this secret Security Index. Fully two-thirds of the Bureau's annual reports during the early 1950s were devoted to describing the communist menace and the FBI's role in combating it.

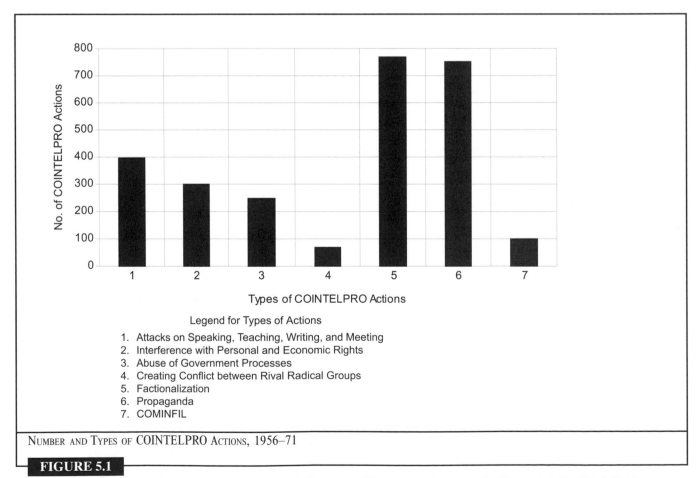

NUMBER AND TYPES OF COINTELPRO ACTIONS, 1956–71

FIGURE 5.1

Source: U.S. Senate. *Hearings before the Select Committee to Study Governmental Operations with respect to Intelligence Activities,* Vol. 6. Washington, D.C.: USGPO, 1975: 370–71.

COINTELPRO

Adopting a more aggressive strategy, in August 1956, FBI officials initiated a covert program against the U.S. Communist Party, the first of 12 counterintelligence programs (known by the acronym of COINTELPRO). These programs aggressively targeted particular domestic political groups, to "disrupt and neutralize" them, to quote from FBI memoranda describing this program's objectives. The FBI's disruptive tactics included placing unfavorable stories about targeted groups in the media; leaking derogatory information to the media and public officials to discredit individuals;

sending anonymous mailings to promote factionalism; directing FBI informants to precipitate controversy; and, in a few instances, creating fictitious organizations as a way to factionalize real organizations and divert their energies and resources.

Although the first COINTELPRO targeted the U.S. Communist Party, this program was soon expanded to a variety of militant groups active during the 1960s, from the Ku Klux Klan on the political right to the anti–Vietnam War movement and black nationalist groups on the political left (see Figures 5.1 and 5.2). In April 1971, FBI officials

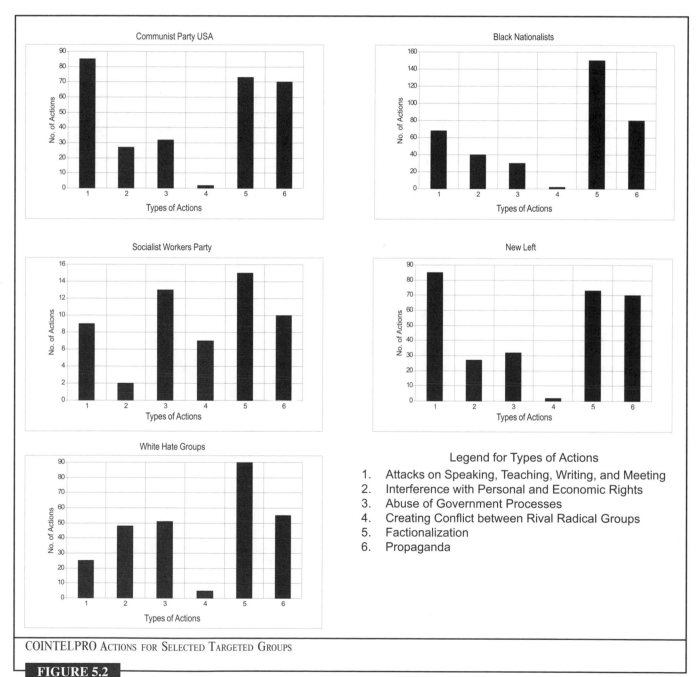

COINTELPRO Actions for Selected Targeted Groups

FIGURE 5.2

Source: U.S. Senate. *Hearings before the Select Committee to Study Governmental Operations with respect to Intelligence Activities,* Vol. 6. Washington, D.C.: USGPO, 1975: 370–71.

formally terminated the COINTELPROs for "security reasons," precipitated by top FBI officials' concerns that these secret programs and their questionable practices might be publicly exposed. Between 1956 and 1971, FBI Director Hoover and high-level FBI officials had approved 2,340 COINTELPRO proposals, with the U.S. Communist Party the target in slightly more than half of these. The FBI's harassment activities and extensive monitoring of dissident political activities throughout the 1960s and into the 1970s constituted a major component of FBI investigative work. In 1976, the U.S. General Accounting Office reported that from 1965 to 1975, intelligence matters utilized 19 percent of Bureau investigative resources.

Increased Appropriations

In addition to altering the organizational culture of the Bureau, the increased involvement in domestic intelligence investigations provided a new source of appropriations and of power for the Bureau within the federal government. Cold War national security concerns enabled the FBI to maintain its budgetary gains of the World War II years, gains that when first authorized had been believed by Congress to be temporary increases to meet specific wartime requirements. Instead, Bureau appropriations sharply increased in the postwar years, almost doubling between 1945 and 1955 (see Table 5.1). Equally important, the FBI successfully maintained its sizable share of the total Justice Department budget, a proportion that fluctuated between 40 and 45 percent during this period. Prior to the war, in contrast, the FBI's share in 1938 of the Justice Department budget had been only 14.7 percent. This enormous expansion of the Bureau's budget was accomplished by exploiting the postwar fears of communism. Insisting that internal security and federal employee loyalty were serious problems, FBI Director Hoover aggressively publicized the communist danger, in part by forging covert ties with congressional committees, such as the House Committee on Un-American Activities (HUAC) and the Senate Internal Security Sub-committee. Furthermore, by ensuring the Bureau's exclusive responsibility for internal security, FBI officials were able, more than any other federal agency, to define who was subversive, disloyal, and dangerous to the state. By 1952, more than 6.6 million federal employees had been subjected to FBI name checks for possible disloyalty.

TABLE 5.1

FBI Appropriations and Relative Size within Department of Justice (DOJ) Budgets, 1938–60

Fiscal Year	FBI Appropriations	FBI Budget As Percentage of Total DOJ Budget
1938	$6,222,976	14.7
1940	$8,639,541	20.6
1945	$44,780,000	42.9
1950	$53,530,000	39.1
1955	$88,930,447	45.2
1960	$116,224,408	42.7

Source: U.S. Bureau of the Budget. *The Budget of the U.S. Government.* Washington, D.C.: USGPO, 1938–60. Appropriations figures are drawn from the "Federal Program by Agency and Account" portion of the budget and reflect actual amounts, not estimates.

Presidents and the FBI

Studies of the FBI's explosive growth after 1940, from the presidency of Franklin Roosevelt to that of Richard Nixon, have shown that FBI Director Hoover and White House officials sometimes used information gathered during FBI intelligence investigations for personal or partisan purposes. This use of intelligence, often to discredit political opponents and their policies, proved to be another instrument in FBI empire-building in every successive presidential administration from Roosevelt to Nixon. At President Lyndon Johnson's request, for example, Bureau agents wiretapped the Mississippi Freedom Democratic Party during the 1964 Democratic convention and furnished the president with information about its delegates' and supporters' activities (Johnson had feared they might disrupt the convention and embarrass him). During Franklin Roosevelt's administration, the FBI monitored the activities of the America First Committee and other critics of the president's interventionist foreign policy. These examples illustrate the kinds of information on public figures that FBI agents under Hoover's close supervision collected voluminously. Such politically sensitive intelligence was double-edged: FBI officials could use the information to curry favor with presidents and other high-level political figures, or to blackmail those who were the subjects of embarrassing discoveries.

FBI Secret Filing Procedures

The FBI, of course, has maintained many types of files. Dating from 1924, FBI Director Hoover kept in his office, separate from the Bureau's central records system, files recording the authorization of illegal investigative techniques and recording the FBI's collection of derogatory information on presidents, cabinet officials, and members of Congress. FBI assistant directors had similar secret files in their offices. These files—with the exception of one of Hoover's two office files and a portion of the office files of two FBI assistant directors— were all destroyed (some at six-month intervals and others immediately following Hoover's death in May 1972). However, not all derogatory information collected by FBI agents was maintained in secret office files. The FBI's main case files also contained extensive files of potentially compromising information on prominent writers, composers, folk singers, actors, business people, civil rights activists, feminists, lesbians, gays, college professors, syndicated columnists, and reporters.

FBI critics long suspected that Hoover used this personal information for political intimidation, but his success in preventing access to FBI records made confirmation impossible. In any event, Hoover did not need to blackmail public officials directly; their suspicion that the FBI possessed damaging information about them became both a boon and a powerful deterrent.

More important, the FBI's expanded authority to conduct domestic security investigations on a wide range of groups and individuals had concurrently enhanced its capacity to illicitly gather political and personal intelligence. The use and misuse of this intelligence by both the White House and the FBI, each with its own self-serving motives, were at the heart of the Bureau's political culture in the Cold War years.

Neither the public nor Congress were aware of the techniques the FBI employed in its covert domestic security operations. Illegal techniques, like break-ins and wiretaps, or highly questionable operations, like COINTELPROs, were conducted in ways to ensure strict secrecy. Beginning in 1942, for example, Hoover instituted a "Do Not File" procedure to ensure that sensitive memoranda were kept out of the Bureau's central records system at headquarters (see Exhibit 5.7). Single copies of such memoranda were prepared, and the FBI director alone decided on their disposition.

In 1958, two years after the first COINTELPRO was initiated, FBI Director Hoover briefed Attorney General William Rogers and Robert Cutler, a special assistant to President Eisenhower, on the existence of the COINTELPRO–Communist Party. Hoover also notified subsequent attorneys general of the FBI's COINTELPROs involving the U.S. Communist Party and the Ku Klux Klan. Hoover's notifications were worded generally, however, and did not disclose questionable FBI techniques, such as the use of informants and anonymous mailings to provoke dissension or adverse press commentary. FBI officials also gave top-secret briefings to the House Appropriations Subcommittee during the FBI's annual appropriation hearings, but it remains uncertain what was disclosed to the favored members of Congress about the FBI's COINTELPROs at those hearings. In any event, FBI officials successfully maintained the secrecy of the FBI's domestic security activities until the early 1970s. Furthermore, those in the executive and legislative branches having oversight responsibilities, although informed of the existence of such operations, never sought details or raised questions about the legality of FBI intelligence actions.

The Intelligence Division Subculture

The FBI's transformation from the G-man agency of the 1930s to an autonomous intelligence agency in the postwar years fundamentally changed its organizational culture. Fueled by national security concerns and the Bureau's expanding domestic security operations, the subculture of the Intelligence Division became a significant component of Bureau organizational life. Unlike the Criminal Investigative Division, the center for FBI crime-fighting, the FBI's Intelligence Division operations were cloaked in secrecy; were less accountable to public scrutiny, including executive and legislative oversight; and spilled over into unethical or illegal conduct. Coexisting with the professional culture of the criminal division was a "counterculture" that developed in the hidden side of the Bureau's intelligence operations. In reverting to the earlier Bureau tradition of antiradical activities and labor spying, the Intelligence Division's clandestine operations inevitably brought it into conflict with the ethics of the professionalism movement, ethics that were based on the ideals of a well-trained and educated

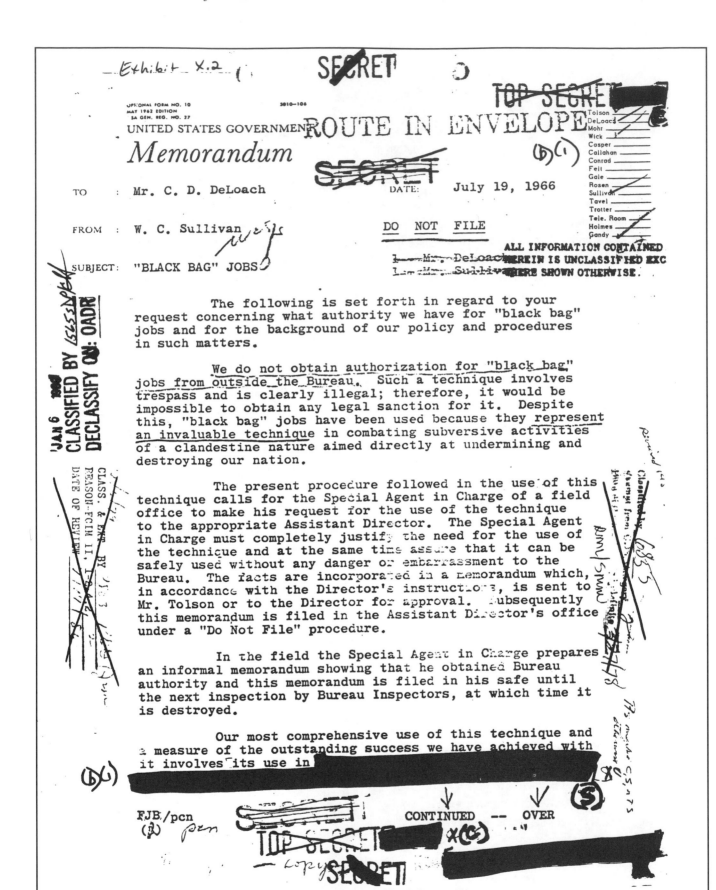

The following is set forth in regard to your request concerning what authority we have for "black bag" jobs and for the background of our policy and procedures in such matters.

We do not obtain authorization for "black bag" jobs from outside the Bureau. Such a technique involves trespass and is clearly illegal; therefore, it would be impossible to obtain any legal sanction for it. Despite this, "black bag" jobs have been used because they represent an invaluable technique in combating subversive activities of a clandestine nature aimed directly at undermining and destroying our nation.

The present procedure followed in the use of this technique calls for the Special Agent in Charge of a field office to make his request for the use of the technique to the appropriate Assistant Director. The Special Agent in Charge must completely justify the need for the use of the technique and at the same time assure that it can be safely used without any danger or embarrassment to the Bureau. The facts are incorporated in a memorandum which, in accordance with the Director's instructions, is sent to Mr. Tolson or to the Director for approval. Subsequently this memorandum is filed in the Assistant Director's office under a "Do Not File" procedure.

In the field the Special Agent in Charge prepares an informal memorandum showing that he obtained Bureau authority and this memorandum is filed in his safe until the next inspection by Bureau Inspectors, at which time it is destroyed.

Our most comprehensive use of this technique and a measure of the outstanding success we have achieved with it involves its use in

Exhibit 5.7 "Do Not File" FBI Memorandum on "Black Bag Jobs"

SECRET

Memorandum to Mr. C. D. DeLoach
Re: "BLACK BAG" JOBS

have been operating this program for twelve years and

year the evaluation of the value of the information obtained
is included in our annual budget. In addition, the intelligence value of the information received has been beyond
calculation.

We have used this technique on a highly selective
basis, but with wide-range effectiveness, in our operations.
We have several cases in the espionage field, for example,
where through "black bag" jobs we determined that suspected
illegal agents actually had concealed on their premises the
equipment through which they carried out their clandestine
operations.

Also through the use of this technique we have on
numerous occasions been able to obtain material held highly
secret and closely guarded by subversive groups and organizations which consisted of membership lists and mailing lists
of these organizations.

This applies even to our investigation of the
Ku Klux Klan. You may recall that recently through a
"black bag" job we obtained the records in the possession of
three high-ranking officials of a klan organization in
Louisiana. These records gave us the complete membership
and financial information concerning the klan's operation
which we have been using most effectively to disrupt the
organization and, in fact, to bring about its near disintegration.

It was through information obtained through our
"black bag" operations that we obtained the basic information
used to compromise and to bring about the expulsion of
William Albertson, the former Executive Secretary of the
Communist Party New York District organization.

Through the same technique we have recently been
receiving extremely valuable information concerning political
developments in the Latin American field, and we also have
been able to use it most effectively in a number of instances

CONTINUED -- OVER

SECRET

Exhibit 5.7 (continued)

SECRET

~~TOP SECRET~~

(b)(1)

Memorandum to Mr. C. D. DeLoach
re: "BLACK BAG" JOBS

recently through which we have obtained information concerning
growing ████████████████ intelligence activities directed
at this country.

        In short, it is a very valuable weapon which we have
used to combat the highly clandestine efforts of subversive
elements seeking to undermine our Nation.

RECOMMENDATION:

        For your information.

*no more such techniques
must be used.*
H (Hoover)

- 3 -

~~SECRET~~

(b)(1)

~~TOP SECRET~~

Exhibit 5.7 (continued)

police force that adhered to the rule of law. Besides encouraging a counterculture of lawlessness, domestic security matters brought politics back into FBI operations. Bureau officials designated which organizations and persons were national security threats and, therefore, the objects of surveillance and/or disruption—in effect, transforming the agency into a political police force.

Disclosures of abuses of authority and improper activities of the FBI (and other U.S. intelligence agencies) first surfaced in the media and in Congress during the early 1970s. These revelations brought this dualism in the Bureau's organizational life to the fore. COINTELPRO, Hoover's secret files, FBI break-ins and mail openings, White House misuse of FBI intelligence for political purposes, and the Bureau's widespread surveillance of U.S. citizens were being revealed for the first time. These revelations ultimately contributed to the unraveling of the FBI of the Hoover era and the demise of its G-man image. The scandal created by these revelations caused FBI officials to initiate a major rethinking of FBI priorities and policies, in both its criminal and intelligence investigations. Out of this scandal and reform, the modern Bureau emerged, with its own distinctive organizational style.

The Modern Era (1972 to the Present)

Thousands came to pay their respects, and an indeterminate number came to make sure [Hoover] was really dead, an assurance denied them by the closed casket.

> —Neil J. Welch (Special Agent in Charge of several FBI field offices), 1984

Our top priority programs are white-collar crime, organized crime and, of course, foreign counterintelligence. We now have guidelines put in place in 1976 by the Attorney General. They have been scrupulously observed. I'm not aware of any single case made against an FBI agent on the grounds of constitutional-rights violations since the guidelines went into effect.

Hiring minorities and women is more than simple justice; it's important to our operation.

> —FBI Director William H. Webster, 1979

Scandals following Hoover's Death

J. Edgar Hoover's death on May 2, 1972, allowed the first step to be made on the road of transition to the modern FBI. For 48 years, Hoover had shaped the direction, policies, and priorities of the Bureau. His name had become inseparable from the FBI in the public mind.

Hoover created a federal agency that was unparalleled in its power and influence. Under his leadership, the Bureau had become insulated from any meaningful legislative oversight, and even within the Justice Department, it had achieved a semiautonomous status, with the attorney general more a peer than a superior in the chain of command. Moreover, for most of those five decades, the FBI was virtually immune from public criticism and scandal. The traditions and organizational culture of the Hoover years had become deeply entrenched in Bureau practice.

Within a few years, an extraordinary set of circumstances transformed this culture. These circumstances converged in the early and mid-1970s. Critical press and congressional inquiries revealed the countercultural side of the Bureau, which senior FBI officials had, until then, concealed from public scrutiny. Public disclosures of lawlessness in the FBI's domestic security operations soon reached the proportions of a major scandal, rendering the G-man image that Hoover had so carefully crafted over the years untenable. Public confidence in the Bureau dropped dramatically during the 1970s. Thus, whereas Gallup national surveys had revealed that 84 percent of the public gave a "highly favorable" rating to the FBI in 1966, this rating fell to 71 percent in 1970; by 1973, approval of the FBI declined further to 52 percent, and to 37 percent in both 1975 and 1979.

These revelations precipitated a critical examination of Hoover's priorities and policies. In its aftermath, the framework for the modern Bureau was established. Domestic security investigations were to have a diminished role. New criminal investigative priorities, such as white-collar crime and organized crime, rose to the top of the agenda. The FBI's autonomy as a federal agency was sharply reduced, and closer Justice Department supervision and congressional oversight was instituted. A new organizational mystique developed, as well, replacing the G-man legacy. The modern Bureau's identity was based on increasing use of state-of-the-art technology and computers, undercover operations, and proactive law enforcement. The FBI, in short, reaffirmed the culture of professionalism, which dated from the police professionalism movement of the 1920s and

1930s. Retaining the standard of highly trained and educated agents, the FBI recruited personnel of diverse ethnic and racial identity, including both women and men. Agents were taught to combat crime proactively, not simply reactively. To do so required that investigations be prioritized; that Bureau personnel identify in advance which criminal organizations to target—and requiring the use of target squads. This approach contrasted with the traditional "reactive" investigations, in which agents responded, after the fact, to reports of crimes—involving the use of case squads. The arsenal of investigative techniques that Bureau agents used to target persons and organizations for investigation now included undercover operations.

Hoover's reputation for not tolerating criticism, within or outside the Bureau, had successfully precluded well-informed criticism. In one instance in 1971, agent Jack Shaw, at the time enrolled in a course at John Jay College of Criminal Justice, made remarks to his instructor that were critical of the FBI. His comments were made in a private letter to the instructor, in which he criticized Bureau personnel practices, especially those relating to promotion and discipline, and questioned the kinds of investigations the FBI pursued. Shaw cautioned his professor to maintain the confidentiality of his letter's contents, fearing that disclosure might result in recrimination and discipline. Little did Shaw realize that his letter's confidentiality had already been compromised because he had it typed in the FBI's typing pool in the New York City field office. A copy of his letter was eventually forwarded to Hoover's desk in Washington, D.C. In response, Hoover ordered Shaw and 15 other agents to withdraw from the course and had Shaw transferred to the FBI's field office in Butte, Montana.

The Media Break-in

Hoover's death, moreover, coincided with a series of disclosures of FBI abuses of authority. One of these came from a break-in of March 8, 1971, at the FBI's resident agency in Media, Pennsylvania, by a radical political group (the Citizens' Commission to Investigate the FBI). The Media break-in proved to be one of the watershed events in FBI history. The stolen documents, which were eventually published, documented the FBI's widespread surveillance of domestic groups, including left-wing organizations and black militant groups. These documents also led to the FBI's secret counterintelligence programs (COINTELPROs) being compromised. Several months after the Media break-in, NBC reporter Carl Stern noticed the caption "COINTELPRO–New Left" on one of the released docu-

ments. Pursuing this clue through a Freedom of Information Act (FOIA) lawsuit, he obtained additional COINTELPRO documents in December 1973 and March 1974. Other FOIA requests and suits followed, eventually resulting in the release of tens of thousands of pages of COINTELPRO files during the 1970s.

Watergate

Investigations into the Watergate scandal (1973–74) documented the Nixon White House's misuse of the FBI and further examples of FBI wrongdoing. During the Watergate hearings, President Richard Nixon had tried to justify his administration's abuses of authority by showing that they had not been unique to his presidency. Previous administrations had employed the FBI for political purposes, including seeking intelligence on their critics in Congress and the media. Nixon's pursuit of this line of defense during a San Clemente news conference, in August 1973, unwittingly disclosed FBI burglaries conducted "on a very large scale" during the Kennedy and Johnson administrations. The following day, the Justice Department confirmed that "black bag jobs," or surreptitious entries, had been "an old, established investigative technique" of the FBI, but claimed that they had been discontinued by Hoover in 1966.

The convergence of these events (along with congressional investigations of 1975–76, see page 195) gave rise to important changes within the FBI, but not without encountering resistance from some of the old-guard veterans of the Hoover era who retained senior administrative positions within the Bureau. Clarence Kelley, who became the first permanent FBI director after Hoover, recounts in his 1987 memoirs the struggle that went on within the Bureau when he curtailed domestic intelligence programs and introduced other reforms. It took three years, Kelley wrote, to change policies and correct abuses; without the impetus to change provided by disclosures and the Watergate scandal, it would have taken even longer.

High Technology and the New Culture of Professionalism

The public first sensed that a new FBI had been forged in February 1980, when the FBI's Operation ABSCAM was leaked to the press. An FBI undercover operation, ABSCAM led to the conviction of one U.S. senator and several members of Congress for accepting bribes from a fictitious Arab sheik (whose "representatives" were FBI undercover agents). Publicity about ABSCAM called attention both to the FBI's use of the undercover technique and the Bureau's new priorities: white-collar crime and public corruption.

The post-Hoover FBI relied increasingly on high technology and undercover operations to fulfill its mission. Moreover, the modern Bureau tackled more complex investigations that encompassed entire criminal enterprises, such as those involved in terrorism and organized crime, while continuing to emphasize well-trained and highly skilled agents. These agents operated in an environment in which guidelines issued by the attorney general and oversight by Congress limited Bureau operations.

The New Priorities

The Hoover FBI had focused on crimes that were relatively simple to investigate and that produced impressive, but misleading statistics—large amounts of stolen property recovered, numerous fugitives located, and a seemingly high percentage of crimes solved. Under Hoover, FBI officials had regularly cited the statistical accomplishments from auto theft, bank robberies, kidnapping, and stolen property cases to demonstrate the FBI's effectiveness when lobbying Congress for additional Bureau appropriations. In the intelligence area, FBI successes during Hoover's tenure are more difficult to measure because of the secrecy shrouding many of these activities. Arrests, prosecutions, and convictions, which FBI officials have maintained accurately measure its law enforcement performance, are inappropriate for evaluating domestic intelligence. The purpose of intelligence investigations is to gain advance knowledge of planned subversive or espionage activities, not to gather evidence for prosecution. A 1976 General Accounting Office (GAO) evaluation of the FBI's effectiveness in the domestic intelligence arena, based on a review of 898 randomly selected cases from 10 field offices for the year 1974, found that only 24 (about 3 percent of the total) were referred for prosecution and 10 were prosecuted, resulting in 8 convictions. The GAO investigation also found little evidence that FBI investigations had resulted in advance knowledge of planned subversive or extremist activities, documenting only 29 instances in which advance knowledge was gained in 17 cases (about 2 percent of the total of 898 cases). The GAO concluded, "Few tangible results are evident."

Under Hoover, the FBI had pursued the same strategy for both criminal and national security matters: publicize the menace of crime and the dangers of communism and subversion, and reassure Congress and the public that the Bureau was protecting the nation. In addition, the FBI had concentrated on those law enforcement and intelligence matters that Hoover deemed most important; conversely,

other areas were avoided. Among the avoided areas were organized crime, white-collar crime, public corruption, and drug enforcement. Hoover also recognized that both organized crime and illicit drug trafficking were politically risky investigative targets. Invariably, these illegal enterprises corrupt public officials, thus law enforcement could encompass the arrest and prosecution of powerful people, not just those involved in the day-to-day criminal operations. Similarly, targeting white-collar criminals could be politically risky given their relationships with powerful members of Congress and within the executive branch.

Enforcing both organized crime and drug trafficking also increases the corruption potential for those policing these activities. Police officers are routinely exposed to the temptations of bribes for nonenforcement of the law, given the substantial profits that can be made by those involved in these illegal enterprises.

Organized Crime

Until 1957, Hoover denied the existence of a "Mafia" and a nationwide organized crime syndicate. He was not oblivious to organized crime, but he claimed that it was a local police problem, outside of the FBI's jurisdiction, and conducted by individual hoodlums. Before the 1960s, Hoover did not endorse the conspiratorial view of organized crime advocated by Harry Anslinger, head of the Federal Bureau of Narcotics, and Senator Estes Kefauver who, as chair of the Special U.S. Senate Committee to Investigate Organized Crime, held hearings on the Mafia in 1950 and 1951. Only after public revelation of a November 14, 1957, Mafia meeting in Apalachin, New York, did FBI Director Hoover begin to increase FBI resources targeting organized crime (see pages 35–37). In response, Hoover at first directed William Sullivan, at the time head of the FBI's Research and Analysis Section, to draft a comprehensive report on the problem of organized crime in America. The result was a two-volume study that concluded that a Mafia existed, and had operated in the United States for many decades. Sullivan's study remained, however, an internal FBI document—although it did lead to an increase in FBI organized crime efforts during the 1960s. In addition, Hoover initiated a special program code-named Top Hoodlum, under which each field office had to designate the top 10 hoodlums in its area for special attention. In these investigations, FBI agents increasingly relied on wiretaps and bugs, which were installed in key Mafia hangouts, the most notable one in Chicago. Information learned from this illegal surveillance, however, could be used only within the Bureau. Ironically, reliance on illegal investigative techniques kept organized-crime cases from being prosecuted. Hoover did not substantially increase FBI resources to fight organized crime. In 1959, for example, only 4 agents in the FBI's New York City field office, whose jurisdiction encompassed 4 of the largest Mafia families in the United States, were assigned full time to organized crime, as compared with 400 who were assigned to domestic security matters. Similarly, when Attorney General Ramsey Clark initiated the federal strike force concept in 1967 as a way to combat organized crime in major cities, few FBI agents were contributed to this joint venture involving numerous other federal law enforcement agencies.

Domestic Intelligence Declines

The Bureau's crime-fighting priorities were first seriously questioned and revised in the mid-1970s. Following this review, some of the investigative areas that the Hoover FBI had shunned became the Bureau's top priorities of the 1970s and 1980s: organized crime, white-collar crime, and illicit drug trafficking. Moreover, during the 1970s, the FBI's top intelligence priorities shifted from domestic surveillance to foreign counterintelligence (FCI). Beginning in October 1982, terrorism (domestic and international) was elevated to a national priority program, and by the late 1980s, violent crime was added to that list.

In this reordering of FBI investigative priorities, domestic intelligence was drastically reduced. Between 1972 and 1978, FBI funding for domestic intelligence investigations declined steadily; it bottomed out in fiscal year 1979, accounting for two percent of the total appropriations allocated to the Bureau's various field programs. Several measures of FBI domestic intelligence highlight this decline (see Figures 5.3 and 5.4): the number of domestic intelligence matters initiated plummeted from 1,454 to 95, the number of pending domestic intelligence matters decreased from 9,914 to 642, the number of agents conducting such investigations were reduced from 788 to 143, and the number of domestic intelligence informants dropped from about 1,100 to 100.

In 1976, FBI Director Kelley assigned Neil Welch, one of the FBI's top field office SACs (Special Agent in Charge), to evaluate the need for the FBI's ongoing domestic security cases. When Welch completed his internal review, only 626 cases remained open of the original 4,868.

FBI Director Kelley then transferred supervisory responsibility for the remaining domestic security investigations from the Intelligence Division to the General Investigative Division, the department in the Bureau that deals with criminal investigations. Kelley later regarded this move as one of his most important changes. This administrative change ensured major changes, given the differing norms of the General Investigative Division and those of the Intelligence Division. Criminal investigations emphasize arrest and prosecution, which are governed by the law of criminal procedure—the rules that agents must follow in their investigative work. These investigative procedures shape the normative environment of the General Investigative Division.

Foreign Counterintelligence

At the same time, Kelley restored foreign counterintelligence to the highest priority within the Intelligence Division. Kelley's emphasis on foreign counterintelligence focused Intelligence Division energies on foreign intelligence services and on foreign extremist or terrorist groups operating within the United States. In October 1982, domestic security became incorporated into a new, intensified FBI terrorism program: "terrorism" or "domestic terrorism" having become new Bureau priorities, replacing the Hoover FBI's "domestic security," "domestic subversion," or "internal security." This decision responded to the heightened concern of the Ronald Reagan administration over both domestic and international terrorism. Beginning in fiscal year (FY) 1983, the share of FBI agent time in the domestic terrorism program, relative to all of the FBI's field programs, increased from 2 percent in FY 1982 to 3 percent, and then to 5 percent in FY 1984, and 6 percent in FY 1986.

Joseph Valachi and La Cosa Nostra

As domestic intelligence declined as an FBI priority, organized-crime enforcement surfaced as one of the top priorities. This change drew on the initiatives of the Kennedy and Johnson administrations during the previous decade. In the early 1960s, Attorney General Robert Kennedy had sought to generate support for legislation to fight organized crime by exploiting the publicity of congressional hearings—notably, the Valachi hearings of 1963. Joseph Valachi, a low-level organized crime figure who became an FBI informant, emerged as the principal witness during the 1963 hearings on organized crime conducted by Senator John McClellan's Permanent Subcommittee on Investigations. Valachi introduced the public to the term "La Cosa Nostra" as the proper designation for the national crime syndicate.

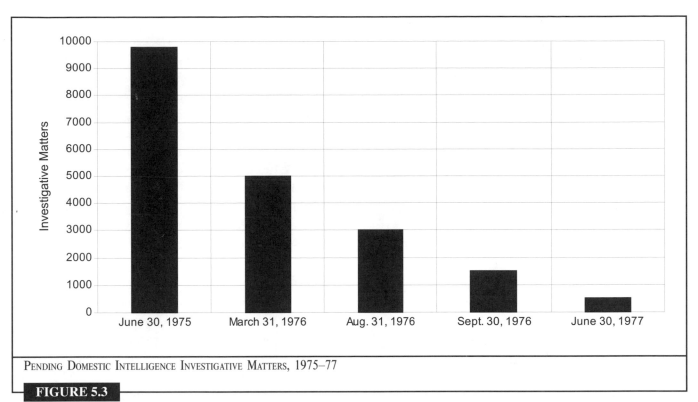

PENDING DOMESTIC INTELLIGENCE INVESTIGATIVE MATTERS, 1975–77

FIGURE 5.3

Source: U.S. Comptroller General. *FBI Domestic Intelligence: An Uncertain Future.* Washington, D.C.: USGPO, 1977, 17–18.

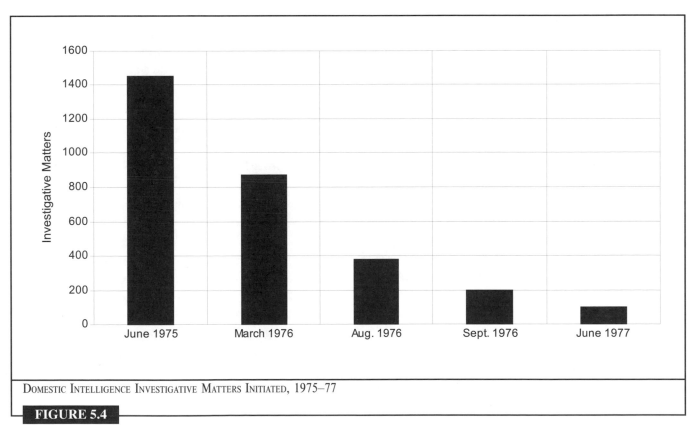

DOMESTIC INTELLIGENCE INVESTIGATIVE MATTERS INITIATED, 1975–77

FIGURE 5.4

Source: U.S. Comptroller General. *FBI Domestic Intelligence: An Uncertain Future.* Washington, D.C.: USGPO, 1977, 17–18.

Following widely publicized hearings, the subcommittee concluded in a public report that a nationwide crime organization operated in the United States, one that descended from the Sicilian Mafia, and that its principal criminal activities involved gambling and narcotics. These hearings (combined with a sharp increase in public concern about "law and order" in reaction to Vietnam War protesters and civil rights demonstrations during the mid-1960s) helped promote passage in 1968 of the Omnibus Crime Control and Safe Streets Act, which incorporated some of the anticrime proposals endorsed by Attorney General Kennedy, particularly legalizing wiretapping.

In its task force report on organized crime in 1967, President Lyndon Johnson's Crime Commission (officially, the President's Commission on Law Enforcement and the Administration of Justice) had also emphasized the organized crime threat and affirmed that a national crime syndicate existed. In this view of the Mafia, or La Cosa Nostra (LCN), a monolithic national organization of criminals operated conspiratorially. This organization was composed mainly of Italian Americans who controlled a variety of illegal enterprises, especially narcotics trafficking and gambling operations. There was a national "commission," but the LCN's day-to-day criminal operations were carried out by elaborate local organizations, called families, whose members were sworn to secrecy and whose traditions derived from Sicily. In 1967, 24 LCN families operated in major cities across the country. Although FBI Director Hoover had acknowledged this problem by the late 1960s, FBI priorities, which focused on domestic security matters, were too deeply entrenched and too much a part of FBI organizational power to substantially alter FBI organized crime activities.

By the 1970s, the view of a monolithic and conspiratorial Mafia had gained unquestioned ascendance. A 1971 Harris poll found that 78 percent of the U.S. public accepted this "alien conspiracy theory" of organized crime. Responding to this changed political climate, FBI officials in 1975 designated organized crime as a top investigative priority and allocated an increasing share of resources to their organized crime program. Between 1975 and 1979, FBI organized crime investigations, as a percentage of total FBI investigations, increased from 4.4 percent to 6.9 percent; by 1979, the organized crime program accounted for 18.2 percent of the total FBI investigative resources.

Nontraditional Organized Crime

FBI officials, moreover, acknowledged that the threat of organized crime extended beyond La Cosa Nostra ("traditional" organized crime) and included a whole range of "nontraditional" groups, including motorcycle gangs, prison gangs, and numerous ethnic organizations involved in illegal enterprises. Whether the illegal activities were organized by Japanese, Cuban, Jamaican, or Colombian criminal groups, or by U.S. street gangs, they were now encompassed under the rubric of "nontraditional" organized crime.

In 1983, President Ronald Reagan established a President's Commission on Organized Crime to ascertain the nature and scope of this crime problem. The president directed the commission to study the role of both traditional and nontraditional organized crime groups. The commission centered on organized criminal organizations' penetration into the legal marketplace. In addition to controlling illegal enterprises, organized crime groups increasingly owned and operated legitimate businesses and distorted other sectors of the economy by theft, extortion, and bribery. The FBI's new emphasis on pursuing organized crime became part of this federal effort to contain such threats in both the legal and illegal sectors of the economy.

White-Collar Crime and Political Corruption

Until the 1970s, white-collar crime investigations had not been an FBI priority, with the exception of bank fraud and embezzlement. Then, in 1974, FBI Director Kelley publicly identified white-collar crime as a "serious problem." For the first time that same year, white-collar crime was designated as a separate program and top priority.

The Justice Department's (and FBI's) concern over white-collar crime and public corruption came at a time of dramatic decline in public confidence in major American institutions, including the press, organized religion, the military, the executive branch of the federal government, Congress, labor unions, and big business. Thus, whereas in 1958, when responding to a University of Michigan national survey, 73 percent of the public expressed trust in the federal government most of the time or always; by 1966, this level of trust had declined to 65 percent; by 1970, the figure had fallen to 54 percent; by 1974, to 37 percent; and by 1978, to 30 percent. National crises over the Vietnam War, civil rights, and Watergate all contributed to these declining confidence levels, as did disclosure of wrongdoing and corruption by those at the top—the political and economic elites. This erosion of trust and confidence in government and other institutional areas provided the background for the Justice

Department's intensified pursuit of white-collar crime, with the Watergate scandal of the Nixon administration providing the immediate context for this new-found priority. In response, high-level FBI and Justice Department officials endorsed white-collar crime prosecution as necessary to restore public confidence in the justice system, in government, and in other mainstream institutions.

Although the FBI had, earlier, investigated crimes that could be designated as white-collar offenses (such as bank fraud and embezzlement, bribery, and antitrust violations), after the 1970s such crimes were reclassified into a formal FBI white-collar crime program and a growing share of the Bureau's investigative resources was allocated to that program. In 1975, 11.7 percent of the FBI's total investigative matters were in the white-collar crime program, and by 1979, this increased to 22.3 percent. Furthermore, public corruption had become this program's top priority.

FBI and Justice Department officials initiated additional steps in 1980 to clarify the white-collar crime program and to delineate a national strategy to address this problem. Public corruption was identified as a major concern, with other priority areas being fraud against the government, crimes against business, crimes against consumers, securities and investment fraud, occupational safety violations, and health and safety violations affecting the general public. Furthermore, FBI agents were authorized to employ undercover operations, when appropriate, to detect white-collar crime, and special Economic Crime Enforcement Units were established throughout the country to coordinate federal investigative and prosecution efforts against fraud and corruption. In fiscal year (FY) 1980, 22 percent of the FBI's agents and 15 percent of its budget were allocated to white-collar crime enforcement.

White-collar crime remained a top FBI priority program throughout the 1980s, with fraud against the federal government and major financial institutions replacing public corruption as the FBI's top concerns. Between 1981 and 1986, however, the appropriations and resources allocated to the white-collar crime program declined as a percentage of total FBI investigations: from 25.3 percent to 19.1 percent.

War on Drugs

FBI attention shifted from white-collar crime to drug trafficking and violent crime as the Reagan administration—and later, the Bush administration—promoted a "war on drugs" as a major domestic policy initiative. Although all activities involving illegal drug use and trafficking were encompassed in the war on drugs of the 1980s, the use of crack cocaine by inner-city youth was singled out for enforcement. Arrest and imprisonment trends in the 1980s document this, with black male arrest rates and imprisonment rates (relative to whites) increasing dramatically during this period, while at the same time, the patterns for serious criminal offenses by race did not change.

In January 1982, drug enforcement was added to the FBI's investigative responsibilities as a joint responsibility with the Drug Enforcement Administration (DEA). Many of the FBI agents transferred in 1982 to narcotics investigations, in fact, came from the Bureau's white-collar crime program. In the uneasy division of labor between the DEA and the FBI, FBI investigations concentrated on the higher levels of the drug trade. By 1986, approximately 10 percent of FBI resources for its field programs were committed to drug enforcement, with drugs becoming one of the FBI's priority programs in August 1987.

The Reagan and Bush administrations' war on drugs closely paralleled a rising public concern over violent crime that began with the urban disturbances and antiwar protests of the 1960s and accelerated in the mid-1980s with official statistics showing a sharp increase in drug-related and other gang violence. As with drugs, criminal violence became part of the politics of crime control of the 1980s, focusing media and policy attention on the crimes of the poor and minorities—street gangs, drug dealers, and other criminal predators in the economic underclass.

Violent Crime

In 1981, shortly after taking office, President Reagan established an Attorney General's Task Force on Violent Crime, which released the first of several federal reports to call attention to the violent crime problem in the United States and to offer recommendations on how best to combat it. The task force report concluded that a small group of repeat offenders were responsible for most violence. Its conclusions shaped federal crime policy of the 1980s and 1990s, the thrust of which was to target chronic offenders with arrest, prosecution, and incarceration and to carve out a larger federal role in combating this problem—rejecting the once-traditional view of violent crime as a local responsibility.

In June 1989, violent crime became another high FBI priority. An assortment of crimes traditionally investigated by the FBI, such as kidnapping, bank robbery, apprehending fugitives, and auto theft, were consolidated into a single project: the Violent Crimes and Major Offenders Program. Task forces were created to work with local law enforcement agencies to combat violent crime. In the early 1990s, Operation Weed and Seed was developed, a program aimed at high-crime neighborhoods. It was based on a strategy of removing criminal elements from high-crime areas and then using federal funds to support community development projects. As of January 1994, 31 cities were participating in the Weed and Seed program.

"Quality over Quantity" and Proactive Strategies

These reordered FBI investigative priorities symbolized the emergence of a new FBI, one that departed from traditions J. Edgar Hoover had established. Under these new priorities, investigative areas that previously had been avoided (like organized crime, drugs, and white-collar crime) were targeted, while other Hoover-era investigative areas (particularly domestic intelligence) experienced sharp reductions. The new FBI also targeted public corruption; although the Hoover FBI had not ignored corruption, it had used its information about corrupt officials for questionable purposes, compiling political intelligence in secret files and using it to curry favor with presidents. These new FBI priorities also signaled a willingness to take on more complex, sophisticated criminal cases, as well as entire criminal organizations—not just individual gangsters and kidnappers.

In addition, these reforms resulted in a major shift in how the new FBI conducted its investigations, what FBI Director Clarence Kelley called the "quality over quantity" approach. This represented a major departure from the earlier approach to investigations, in which agents were organized into case squads (bank robbery, auto theft, etc.) and were assigned to investigate individual cases whenever specific crimes were reported to the FBI. Under this new investigative strategy, first adopted in 1975, crime targets were selected in advance— particular organized crime figures, or corruption among county supervisors in Mississippi, for example—and an investigative approach was then developed to penetrate that particular criminal activity. In this manner, cases would be developed for arrest and prosecution based on priorities set by Bureau officials, and these priorities would direct the flow of resources into the most important cases.

Neil Welch was one of the pioneers in developing such target squads within the FBI. As the special agent in charge (SAC) of the FBI's Detroit and Philadelphia field offices, Welch organized field agents into case squads and target squads. The target squads would identify the key individuals,

groups, and organizations suspected of involvement in ongoing criminal activity, especially top-priority criminal activity, like organized crime and white-collar crime. During the mid-1970s, this concept, which underlay FBI Director Kelley's quality over quantity approach, was extended to all of the FBI's field offices, marking a shift in FBI operations from those of a reactive to an increasingly proactive law enforcement agency.

Proactive law enforcement brought to the modern FBI a different investigative strategy, and also a new organizational style. U.S. law enforcement had formerly followed a reactive approach, wherein police would respond to citizen reports of crime or would create a visible presence in the community, like random police patrol, to deter crime. During Hoover's tenure, the FBI had adopted this reactive model, with agents (in case squads) responding to cases brought to their attention by complaining citizens. Agents had also responded to Hoover's personal priorities and idiosyncratic concerns when selecting cases and when deciding which investigative matters were to receive the most emphasis. In contrast, under a proactive style of law enforcement, the police more aggressively seek to discover law violations. In this new professional culture, agents are increasingly called upon to identify priorities, to engage in long-range planning and forecasting trends, to anticipate crime, and sometimes even to target potential, high-risk offenders and to develop strategies to investigate those targets.

Undercover Operations

Undercover activities became one of the early manifestations of this proactive style. Such operations were virtually nonexistent during Hoover's tenure; he had a long-standing policy that prohibited agents from going undercover. FBI agents were instead required to recruit informants or to seek the FBI director's authorization to install wiretaps (or use other intrusive investigative techniques) during investigations of criminal or subversive activities. The first undercover operations of the 1970s involved antifencing "sting" operations, in which agents and local police set up bogus businesses in high-crime districts in anticipation of receiving stolen property from local criminals. Ten such sting operations were conducted in 1975 and 1976 with funding from the Law Enforcement Assistance Administration (LEAA). Beginning in the mid-1970s, sting operations, the quality over quantity approach, and proactive policing became part of the culture of the modern FBI.

FBI Oversight

The Church and Pike Committees

The series of revelations of Hoover's abuses that first surfaced in the mid-1970s precipitated public and congressional demands for reforming FBI intelligence activities, and one means of doing so involved restoring executive control over the Bureau and its domestic intelligence operations. The inquiries conducted by the select committees of the U.S. Senate and House in 1975–76, the Church and Pike Committees, respectively, marked the beginning of this process. Initiated in response to allegations of misconduct by the FBI and other intelligence agencies (notably, the CIA), the resultant hearings uncovered and documented in extensive detail the scope of FBI abuses. In 1976, both select committees issued detailed reports containing a series of recommendations that became the framework for future reform of FBI operations. These recommendations included reorganizing the Intelligence Division by reducing domestic security cases and transferring supervisory responsibility to the General Investigative Division. The committees also called for an FBI legislative charter, which would, for the first time in the Bureau's history, involve Congress in establishing legal boundaries for FBI operations. An FBI statutory charter could delineate the powers, functions, and responsibilities of the agency, leaving to the discretion of the president and the attorney general the specific rules governing how authorized investigations were to be conducted.

The Levi and Smith Guidelines

The Church and Pike Committee recommendations for an FBI legislative charter were not immediately implemented, coming as they did during the midst of the 1976 presidential campaign. Concurrently, the Ford administration drafted guidelines to govern FBI domestic security investigations, which formally went into effect on April 5, 1976. These guidelines, known as the Levi Guidelines after Attorney General Edward Levi, clarified the standards for the conduct and external review of FBI domestic intelligence operations: when investigations could be initiated, and the responsibility of the attorney general to supervise and authorize such investigations. Under these guidelines, the FBI could initiate a preliminary investigation merely on the basis of allegations that an individual or group "may be engaged in activities which involve or will involve the violation of federal law," such as promoting violence or planning to overthrow the U.S. government. When conducting a preliminary investigation, FBI agents were to use only certain techniques, such as examining FBI files or public records and conducting

interviews. Such investigations were to be limited to a 90-day period and were to be for the purpose of either refuting or verifying the original allegations or information. Should the resulting FBI investigation verify the allegations, FBI agents could then initiate a full investigation of the individual or group. These investigations were subject to review by the Justice Department within 180 days, and continued FBI full investigations would at least annually have to be authorized in writing by the department, as warranted. Intrusive investigative techniques (such as the use of informants, mail covers, and wiretaps) could be employed during full investigations.

In the early 1980s, the Levi Guidelines came under sharp scrutiny from Reagan administration officials and many conservative members of Congress who believed that the Bureau's investigations of terrorist activities in the United States were being severely restricted. Following hearings by the Senate Subcommittee on Security and Terrorism (chaired by Senator Jeremiah Denton), Attorney General William French Smith issued new "domestic security/terrorism" guidelines in March 1983 that broadened FBI investigative authority. The Smith Guidelines empowered FBI agents to initiate investigations of individuals who might simply have advocated criminal activity or whose statements indicated an apparent intent to commit a crime or violence. Furthermore, under the Smith Guidelines, groups that might have temporarily been inactive could be continuously monitored and Justice Department officials need not review annually and stipulate in writing that continued investigation was warranted.

The Levi and Smith Guidelines became the sole standards governing FBI domestic security operations, as Congress never enacted an FBI legislative charter.

In the late 1970s, Congress held hearings on four proposed FBI charter laws. The National Intelligence Act of 1980, the Carter administration's charter proposal, would have codified the system already in effect under executive orders and attorney general guidelines instituted between 1976 and 1978. More restrictive measures to preclude politically motivated investigations were opposed by conservatives as hamstringing the FBI and harming national security interests. Conflicts between liberals, moderates, and conservatives—over whether COINTELPRO-type activities should be prohibited, whether a judicial warrant should be required for FBI intrusive investigative techniques, and whether civil remedies should be provided for charter violations—delayed congressional action. The FBI charter legislation suffered further blows first when the Carter administration reassessed the value of charter legislation in response to the foreign policy crises in 1980 in Iran and Afghanistan and then when Republican presidential candidate Ronald Reagan demanded instead the "unleashing" of the intelligence agencies. After 1981, Congress never seriously considered again any of the FBI charter proposals.

Congressional and Presidential Oversight

There remained, however, a second matter. The Church and Pike Committees had also found that Congress's oversight of FBI operations had been extremely cursory and had recommended that both houses of Congress take this oversight responsibility much more seriously. The Senate did, in May 1976, and the House followed, in July 1977, by establishing permanent intelligence committees to monitor the foreign intelligence and counterintelligence activities of the FBI and the other U.S. intelligence agencies. Oversight of the FBI's domestic activities (criminal and domestic security), however, remained the province of existing subcommittees of the House and Senate Judiciary Committees. The resulting oversight role, however, proved to be more episodic than ongoing, evolving in response to changes in the membership of the Intelligence and Judiciary Committees and triggered by occasional revelations of questionable FBI operations.

Since the mid-1970s, presidents have also periodically issued executive orders to regulate the scope and purpose of FBI intelligence and domestic security activities, thereby asserting their powers and authority in this arena. Presidents Gerald Ford (in 1976) and Jimmy Carter (in 1978) issued such directives. These directives reaffirmed that the exclusive mission of the CIA was foreign intelligence and that of the FBI was domestic intelligence. In 1981, President Ronald Reagan modified Ford's and Carter's restrictive orders; his own order allowed the CIA to conduct foreign intelligence investigations at home under certain circumstances. All three presidents authorized the FBI to monitor specified conduct of dissident Americans at home and abroad and to infiltrate domestic political groups under certain circumstances, especially if an FBI investigation could establish a foreign connection to their activities. These executive orders were complemented by guidelines governing FBI conduct issued by the attorney general. Portions of these attorney general guidelines remain classified.

These administrative reforms more effectively integrated the FBI within the executive branch of government, especially the Justice Department and the intelligence community. FBI operations also were subject to closer scrutiny by the Congress. FBI officials could no longer operate with independence and autonomy. This normative environment constitutes an integral part of the modern FBI's culture of professionalism, wherein FBI operations are much more accountable both to the executive branch and the Congress, and are predominantly based on the rule of law.

Diversity among Agents

At the time of FBI Director Hoover's death in May 1972, only 1.6 percent of all FBI agents were minorities: out of a total force of 8,659, 63 were black, 62 Hispanic, 15 Asian Americans, and 3 Native Americans. There were no female agents. These numbers had been even smaller before the emergence of the civil rights movement of the 1960s, when pressure mounted on FBI officials to hire more agents from minority groups. Prior to 1960, only five black agents were employed by the FBI, most of whom performed personal service tasks for Hoover, such as chauffeuring or performing outdoor chores at his home in Washington, D.C. These black personnel had served in this capacity for many years.

Although the Hoover FBI had been almost exclusively white and male, its recruitment base was even more selective. During the Bureau's early years, agents were primarily white and Protestant, many coming from the South. Beginning in 1940, Catholic appointments increased, especially Catholics of Irish descent. The typical agent was a white male, 34 years of age, with a wife and two children. His father was a businessman who was moderately well off, but not rich. In high school, the agent had earned above-average grades and was a good athlete. He went on to a state university, earned a bachelor's degree, and later entered law school. Agent turnover, moreover, was much lower than that of the federal work force as a whole and private industry. In 1955, for example, the monthly turnover rate for all federal employees was 1.8 percent, and for private industry, 3.3 percent. By comparison, the FBI's monthly turnover rate was 0.5 percent. Twenty years later, agent turnover continued to be low, with the average agent's period of service being 16 years and 3 months and, again, the typical agent being a white male, predominantly Catholic and Irish, solidly middle class, and yet rarely from a wealthy background. Although geographically representative, agents disproportionately came from rural and small-town America. There were few agents who were Jewish or members of other ethnic minorities, and there were no women.

The Bureau's biased selection of agents reflected the values and background of FBI Director Hoover. Having grown up in a segregated Washington, D.C., at the turn of the century, Hoover held turn-of-the-century Southern racial attitudes and a conservative Christian world view. Given his authoritarian management style, these values were translated into FBI culture, and Hoover did not tolerate deviation from this conservative, Southern, small-town vision of America and of the FBI. His intolerance extended even to the personal characteristics of his agents, and he closely monitored their choice of clothing and life style.

Agent selection began to change in the post-Hoover FBI, albeit gradually. During L. Patrick Gray's brief tenure as acting FBI director in the months following Hoover's death, the FBI began recruiting female agents. Clarence Kelley (1973–78), the first permanent FBI director after Hoover, substantially modified Hoover's personnel practices, especially his treatment of agents, and reformed the policies governing the evaluation and promotion of employees. Career boards of high-ranking FBI officials were established to ensure fairer and less arbitrary personnel decisions. FBI Director Kelley also endorsed the hiring of more female and minority agents. Nonetheless, not until William Webster became FBI director in 1978 were women and minority agents actively recruited. During Webster's tenure (1978–87), the number of minority agents more than doubled, from 413 to 943. In addition, the first African American agent was appointed to a high-level Bureau position, executive assistant director. The number of female agents also increased dramatically, from 147 to 787.

Succeeding FBI Directors William Sessions (1987–93) and Louis J. Freeh (1993–) supported affirmative action policies. Early in his tenure, however, Sessions encountered serious allegations of FBI racism and discrimination, especially in assignment and promotion practices. Lawsuits brought on behalf of black, Hispanic, and female agents publicly raised issues of internal discrimination and harassment (see pages 135–37). Settlement of these cases and a commitment to diversity ensured that near the end of Sessions's term as director, in February 1992, 12.6 percent of the 10,422 FBI special agents were minorities (see Figure 5.5). Female agents constituted 11.3 percent of special agents, 12.5 percent of whom were minorities (see Figure 5.6). However, only three of these agents (minorities or females) headed one of the FBI's 56 field offices.

At his nomination hearing before the Senate Judiciary Committee in 1993, Louis Freeh reiterated his commitment to ensuring diversity in FBI ranks to meet the changing nature of crime in the United States and in the world. His pledge to recruit more women and minorities produced a

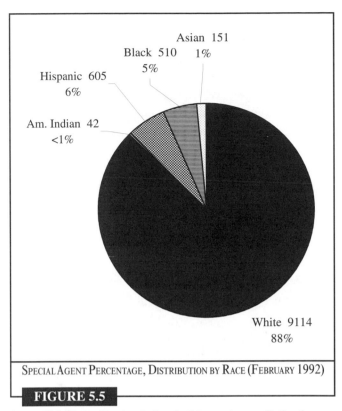

SPECIAL AGENT PERCENTAGE, DISTRIBUTION BY RACE (FEBRUARY 1992)

FIGURE 5.5

Source: U.S. House. *Hearings before the Subcommittee on Civil and Constitutional Rights* (March 1992). Washington, D.C.: USGPO, 1993: 182.

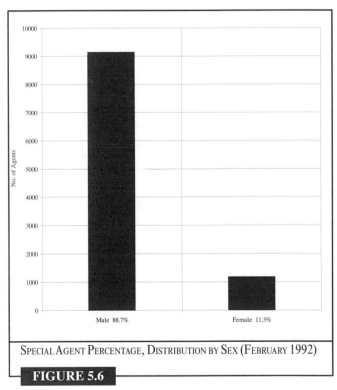

SPECIAL AGENT PERCENTAGE, DISTRIBUTION BY SEX (FEBRUARY 1992)

FIGURE 5.6

Source: U.S. House. *Hearings before the Subcommittee on Civil and Constitutional Rights* (March 1992). Washington, D.C.: USGPO, 1993: 183.

new agent class of November 1994 that numbered 24 women and ethnic minorities: 9 women, 5 African Americans, and 1 Hispanic. Freeh also named to his top echelon of assistant directors the first woman (and then in October 1995, the first black woman) the first Hispanic, and the second and third African Americans.

Under FBI affirmative action policy, agents are recruited from the broadest population base and are promoted in an unbiased manner. The backgrounds and experiences of diverse groups are necessary for the manifold types of operations conducted by the modern FBI, whether undercover operations against organized crime figures, the pursuit of terrorists in foreign countries, securities violations on Wall Street, investigations of drugs and violence in the inner cities, or enforcing civil rights laws. Diversity among agents has become an important component of the culture of the modern Bureau.

The New FBI Mystique

Psychological Profiling
When the dark side of the Hoover FBI first surfaced in the 1970s—with the public disclosure of abuses of authority in FBI domestic security operations and in the political misuse of the Bureau—the mystique and tradition of the G-man collapsed. Before long, however, a new public image began to develop, beginning with the publicity surrounding Operation ABSCAM and heightened awareness of FBI undercover operations. Other new approaches and tech-

niques also shaped the emerging new mystique. One such method was the development of psychological profiles of serial killers, as was done at the Bureau's National Center for the Analysis of Violent Crime (NCAVC) at Quantico, Virginia. An investigative technique developed by FBI personnel, profiling aids in identifying the probable personality and behavioral characteristics of serial offenders, based upon an analysis of the crime scene and victims (see Table 5.2). NCAVC provides this service to local and state police agencies. Public awareness of this FBI method was heightened by the 1991 movie, *The Silence of the Lambs.*

National Crime Information Center (NCIC)
The FBI also began to develop computer files on wanted persons, missing persons, criminal histories, and stolen property, for use by local and state law enforcement agencies through the Bureau's National Crime Information Center (NCIC). Initiated in 1967 with terminal connections to 15 police agencies, the NCIC has become a national repository for criminal records, containing 17 different kinds of files (as of January 1997) consisting of more than 10 million records, and an additional 24 million criminal history records are in the Interstate Identification Index, which is also accessible through the NCIC. NCIC computer files have become an invaluable source for law enforcement officials and have helped locate fugitives, stolen vehicles, guns, securities, and stolen property that can be identified by serial numbers. This system has been regularly modernized. The

---

TABLE 5.2

PROFILE CHARACTERISTICS OF PERPETRATORS OF ORGANIZED AND DISORGANIZED MURDERS

Organized	Disorganized
Average to above-average intelligence	Below-average intelligence
Socially competent	Socially inadequate
Skilled work preferred	Unskilled work
Sexually competent	Sexually incompetent
High birth order status	Low birth order status
Father's work stable	Father's work unstable
Inconsistent childhood discipline	Harsh discipline as child
Controlled mood during crime	Anxious mood during crime
Use of alcohol with crime	Minimal use of alcohol
Precipitating situational stress	Minimal situational stress
Living with partner	Living alone
Mobility with car in good condition	Lives/works near crime scene
Follows crime in news media	Minimal interest in news media
May change jobs or leave town	Significant behavior change (drug/alcohol abuse, religiosity, etc.)

Source: "Crime Scene and Profile Characteristics of Organized and Disorganized Murders." *FBI Law Enforcement Bulletin* 54 (August 1985): 19.

NCIC's current upgrading of the national computer information system for law enforcement—the NCIC 2000 project—is expected to be fully operational by 1999.

Since the initiation of the NCIC in 1967, concerns have been raised about the potential costs and consequences of the establishment of such a computer database by the federal government. The chief and underlying concern centers on government intrusion into citizen privacy. Skeptics have questioned what kind of files should be stored in the NCIC computer, whether the records will be accurate and complete, how the NCIC computer will be linked to other computer databases, and whether persons and organizations not involved in criminal justice work will also have access to those files. How much should the government know about its citizens, and what will government officials do with the information? The advent of computers ensures that such information can be stored and shared much more efficiently than in the past. Computer databases, such as the NCIC, are based on the premise that accurate and complete information is being provided and retained. To the extent, however, that criminal history files (arrest and disposition records) are flawed, computerized records systems can magnify the harm resulting from their use. For example, persons who are erroneously listed in the NCIC's wanted person file or who are incorrectly identified as having a criminal record (citing arrest but not the fact of non-conviction) will be negatively affected whenever law enforcement agencies or prospective employers with access to the NCIC act on the basis of such inaccurate or incomplete files. All of these problems are not yet fully resolved. Nonetheless, NCIC 2000 is a technological upgrade in disseminating criminal history records to police officers in the field, and it provides better-quality information to the law enforcement community—thereby permitting police to identify more quickly and accurately fugitives and missing persons through fingerprint and photo transmissions.

DNA Analysis

Beginning in the 1980s, moreover, the FBI Laboratory pioneered the application of DNA analysis to crime investigations, one of the major advances in forensic science since the introduction of fingerprint analysis. DNA (deoxyribonucleic acid), which is present in all human cells, can be identified in physical evidence derived from human tissue and fluids, like blood, hair, and semen. By matching the DNA pattern or profile on suspects with the DNA pattern on evidence found on victims and at the crime scene, FBI forensic scientists can determine, within a certain range of probability, whether a suspect was present at the scene of the crime. The chance of two individuals having the same DNA pattern is remote.

Computerization

Not all elements of this high-tech image are entirely new. Hoover had always prided himself on establishing the FBI's Laboratory Division in 1932, and on having made the FBI the nation's repository for fingerprints, both criminal and civil, since 1924. The use of science in criminal investigation was part of the G-man culture, and it was a critical component in the professionalism initiated by Hoover in 1924. By the 1970s, however, many criminologists, law enforcement officials, and political commentators concluded that the Bureau had not kept pace with technological and scientific advances. For example, when Clarence Kelley became FBI director in 1973, he found the FBI's computers and data management systems to be "antiquated." According to Kelley, they were not even comparable to the computers of the Kansas City police force, where he had been police chief. A few years later, in 1980, a panel of computer experts evaluated the Bureau's NCIC as having "obsolete equipment resulting in deteriorating service," and as lacking "competent and professional computer managers for the system." These recognized deficiencies were quickly rectified.

In 1972, the FBI's Identification Division began to automate its 94 million criminal fingerprint files. This long-term project, called Automated Identification Division System (AIDS), developed techniques for reading and searching fingerprint cards rather than processing them manually. This ensured a much shorter turnaround time in the processing of fingerprint inquiries from law enforcement agencies around the country. These AIDS files became accessible in 1983 to local and state law enforcement agencies through the NCIC computer. As of 1993, the Bureau had on file the fingerprints of 196 million people—107 million of which were criminal files (the rest mainly from FBI background checks on applicants for federal jobs).

In addition, FBI officials initiated a Revitalization and Relocation Project to become operational by the end of the 1990s. Under this project, an entirely electronic system will be developed to record and transmit fingerprints. The Integrated Automated Fingerprint Identification System (IAFIS) will eliminate the need for fingerprint cards; live-scan fingerprinting at the local level will then be electronically processed and transmitted to a state identification bureau. If no identification is made, the digitized images of fingerprints will then be transmitted to the FBI's Identification Division, where the data will be processed and a response returned to the local booking station within minutes. This initiative will enable the Bureau's CJIS Division (Criminal Justice Information Services) to serve as the nation's fingerprint repository and as a center for the compilation and dissemination of criminal history records for criminal justice officials throughout the country through the NCIC computer. Eventually, fingerprint identification and Criminal Justice Information Services are to be relocated from Washington, D.C., to Clarksburg, West Virginia.

In 1981, the FBI formulated a long-range automated data processing (ADP) plan to computerize all functional areas of the FBI in the ensuing 10 years. Under this strategy, computer technology would be applied to investigations, law enforcement services, and management. One of these applications involved developing a computer program, PROFILER, to produce statistical profiles of serial violent criminals. FBI agents at the NCAVC, in addition, developed VICAP (Violent Criminal Apprehension Program), a national database on specified unsolved violent crimes, as reported by local police agencies. Operating as a pointer system, VICAP alerts law enforcement officials in one part of the country to unsolved violent crimes with similar patterns occurring in other parts of the country.

FBI officials have further adapted computer technology to crime investigation in what is known as artificial intelligence (AI). Computer programs codify the knowledge and experience of experts into a database, which can then be applied to investigative decisions. In the summer of 1986, the first of these expert systems, nicknamed Big Floyd, was employed successfully to solve a number of labor racketeering cases.

Undercover Operations

Beginning with the antifencing operations of the mid-1970s, FBI investigations have increasingly relied on the use of undercover techniques. Under these techniques, bogus businesses would be set up to provide opportunities for crime whenever agent investigations uncovered suspected patterns of ongoing illegal activity. In Operation Recoup, for example, a 1981 investigation of stolen car racketeering, FBI agents created a bogus used car business in which FBI undercover agents acted as intermediaries in the sale of stolen cars. This operation allowed undercover agents to identify and gather evidence on those who were involved in this illegal enterprise. (It also led to the loss of title by more than 250 innocent purchasers of these stolen vehicles.) By 1984, the undercover technique had been extended to most

crimes under the FBI's jurisdiction, including white-collar crime, public corruption, and organized crime. As a result, FBI undercover operations increased sixfold, from 53 in fiscal year (FY) 1977 to 316 in FY 1983. Appropriations increased even more sharply, from $1 million in 1977 to $12.51 million in 1984. These amounts include the special costs of undercover activities (such as informants and lease expenses) but not agent salaries and normal overhead expenses.

Assistance to State and Local Police

FBI operations were further modernized in the 1990s, especially in the identification and information services the FBI provides to local, state, and other federal law enforcement agencies. Providing services and assistance to local law enforcement has been a long-standing practice of the FBI. This has included specialized training for select police officers at the FBI National Academy (since 1935), assisting local and state investigations in the Identification Division (ID), and helping to locate fugitives or missing persons through access to the NCIC computer (since 1967). In 1993, three of these service areas (the NCIC, ID, and *Uniform Crime Reports*) were consolidated in a new Criminal Justice Information Services (CJIS) Division in anticipation of new developments in this area of Bureau operations.

Communications Assistance for Law Enforcement Act of 1994

Under FBI Director Louis Freeh, and with the support of the Clinton administration, the FBI also lobbied for legislation to ensure Bureau access to telephone and computer communications in this age of high technology. Traditional wiretapping has become more difficult because, increasingly, telephonic messages are transmitted digitally. The Communications Assistance for Law Enforcement Act of 1994 ensured that the FBI will have access to digital communications. Bureau officials, nonetheless, must work with the telecommunications industry to develop the surveillance features that companies must make available to the FBI. This legislation, first proposed by the Bush administration, once again raises the long-running debate over how to balance personal privacy concerns with national security and public safety.

Summary

From the years of the Hoover FBI to the modern FBI, each crime menace and national security threat has left its mark on the culture and traditions of the Bureau. The gangsters of the Great Depression; the spies of World War II; the communists and subversives of the Cold War; the Klan violence, black nationalism, and the New Left of the 1960s all became part of the culture and mission of the Hoover FBI. In the modern FBI, organized crime, white-collar crime, terrorism, drugs, criminal violence, and international crime have both added to and altered that culture. Social forces and historical events, like the Great Depression of the 1930s, World War II, and the Cold War, have also been pivotal in shaping the FBI's organizational character, especially in expanding its authority in times of crisis and defining its mission and priorities. Government scandals, both inside and outside the Bureau, such as the Palmer Raids, Teapot Dome, and the Watergate affair, have also influenced FBI policies and sometimes forced FBI officials and members of Congress to rethink established policies and priorities. Finally, influential public figures have also determined the traditions and culture of the FBI, most notably, the FBI's former director, J. Edgar Hoover, and a succession of presidents and attorneys general.

Continued Professionalism

One of the enduring themes in the history of the FBI is the making of a law enforcement agency whose central values are rooted in the police professionalism movement of the 1920s and 1930s. This movement emphasized the selective recruitment and training of personnel, strong police executive leadership, the insulation of police work from political influence, and the application of science and technology to law enforcement. Over the decades, FBI officials' adherence to this model of professionalism varied, but the ideal remained central to their decisions and proposed reforms.

Since the reforms instituted by Attorney General Harlan F. Stone in 1924, when he instructed Acting Director Hoover to remove incompetent agents and eliminate the practice of appointing agents based on political patronage, the selection of Bureau personnel has been central to the shaping of a distinctive culture and tradition within the FBI. These reforms meant that only the most qualified persons having expertise in law enforcement and government service would be selected and that these recruits would then receive the most modern training. Although during Hoover's tenure recruitment was limited to white males from small-town America, the modern FBI has gradually diversified the ranks of its agent force.

Furthermore, since 1935, the FBI National Academy has been the centerpiece of the Bureau's commitment to training both its own agents and selected local and state police officers from around the country in the latest law enforcement techniques (see pages 231–32 and 254–56). FBI officials expanded this training service in 1995 when opening the International Law Enforcement Academy in Budapest, Hungary, modeled on the FBI National Academy, for training police from eastern European countries.

Two other ideals of the police professionalism movement have shaped FBI culture and traditions—those of strong executive leadership and insulation from political influence. Clearly, J. Edgar Hoover exemplified strong executive leadership. Although the power of subsequent directors has been diminished by the 1968 legislation limiting their terms of office to 10 years and by the subordination of their authority to the attorney general, the FBI director remains a dominant figure in the law enforcement and intelligence community.

Decreased Autonomy

A closely related development has been the change in the Bureau's autonomy as a federal agency within the executive branch. During Hoover's tenure, the FBI evolved into a uniquely independent and powerful federal agency, insulated from outside controls by the longevity and secret decisions of its director. The reforms of the post-Watergate era made the FBI a more integral part of the Justice Department and, more generally, of the executive branch of government. As a result, the modern FBI is more responsive to the policy directions of the prevailing presidential administration and less vulnerable to a director pursuing an independent agenda. In addition, closer oversight of the modern Bureau by both Congress and the attorney general reduces the opportunity for either FBI directors or presidents to misuse FBI resources for political purposes.

Science and Technology

The final element of the professionalism model, the application of science and technology to law enforcement, is at the core of the new FBI. What began in the 1930s with the FBI crime lab and consolidation of the nation's fingerprint files has evolved into an agency that has made science and technology a central part of its investigative methods. The modern FBI is computerized, using computer databases on criminal history records, profiling, DNA, and other high-tech initiatives in its investigative work—even fingerprints will soon be entirely electronic in their recording, storage, and transmission. This feature, along with the expanding use of undercover operations, is integral to the FBI's recent emergence as a high-tech, proactive law enforcement agency.

New Priorities

During the 1990s, FBI resources shifted to focus on yet another wave of crime and national security threats. Drugs and violent crime remain top priority investigative areas, with a special focus on violent street gangs and organized criminal groups. Once the traditional responsibility of local law enforcement, these crimes now constitute part of the FBI's mission, and FBI officials increasingly work more closely with local, state, and other federal agencies to combat violent crime and drug trafficking. By 1992, approximately 1,900 agents were assigned to the Bureau's violent crime program.

In the FBI's investigation of white-collar crime, fraud in financial institutions and health care fraud have emerged as top priority initiatives. The savings and loan (S&L) scandal of the late 1980s and early 1990s, which involved massive theft and embezzlement by high-level officials in the S&L industry, prompted this attention to financial fraud. Likewise, the Clinton administration's desire to reform health care coverage and to contain rising health care costs produced the health care fraud initiative.

The bombing of the World Trade Center in New York City in February 1993 and the bombing in April 1995 of the Alfred P. Murrah Federal Building in Oklahoma City resulted in the emergence of international and domestic terrorism as major FBI domestic security concerns. These dramatic terrorist acts precipitated both congressional and executive demands to clarify FBI authority in terrorism investigations and provided the catalyst for a Clinton administration initiative (unsuccessful in 1995) to pressure Congress to enact counterterrorism legislation to expand FBI intelligence-gathering capabilities.

The FBI's investigation of the Oklahoma City bombing also illustrated the modern Bureau's distinctive style. The vehicle identification number (VIN) of a truck that had been destroyed in the bombing was obtained from a fragment of its axle and was traced by FBI investigators through a computer database maintained by the National Insurance Crime Bureau, which stores the VINs of some 300 million vehicles. The computer had a record of the destroyed vehicle (a 1993 Ford truck) and disclosed that it had been sold to Ryder Rental of Miami. From the Ryder branch office in Kansas, where the vehicle was rented, FBI agents followed other leads that enabled them to identify two suspects. Computers were then used to create more lifelike composite drawings of the suspects. About 90 minutes after the bombing, an Oklahoma state trooper used the FBI's NCIC

computer to determine whether the man he had just arrested, Timothy McVeigh, had any outstanding warrants—which he did not. The trooper had arrested McVeigh for driving a car without a license plate and for carrying a concealed weapon, not realizing at the time that McVeigh would soon become the prime suspect in the Oklahoma bombing case. Two days later, when NCIC officials entered McVeigh's name into the NCIC computer, having by then identified him as a possible suspect, they learned that he had been arrested by the Oklahoma trooper. Agents were then able to track McVeigh to the Noble County Jail in Oklahoma where, quite fortuitously, he was still being held in custody.

By the mid-1990s, the FBI's law enforcement jurisdiction extended to over 250 federal laws, 38 of which were enacted after 1976. Some of those federal statutes extend federal law enforcement responsibilities to international cases when U.S. citizens are victims of specified overseas crimes (for example, terrorism). This internationalization of federal law enforcement agencies points to a recent trend wherein FBI resources have been increasingly extended abroad, as international crime, especially terrorism and drug trafficking, necessitates that the Bureau's jurisdiction become more global. In a 52-page report submitted to Congress in June 1996, the FBI detailed its plans for overseas expansion by the year 2000. Plans include an increase in the number of agents stationed abroad, from 70 to 129, and a doubling in the number of foreign cities where agents are permanently present, from 23 to 46.

Conclusion

The modern Bureau has evolved from what had been a detective-style agency in its early years, with limited responsibilities and an uncertain mandate, to one of the most powerful agencies in the federal government during the Hoover years, to an organization in the modern era with expanding responsibilities and authority in a wide variety of investigative areas, including the international arena. Throughout this history, the traditions and culture of the FBI have evolved. The dominant cultural ethos of the Bureau remains rooted in the ideals of the police professionalism movement, with its emphasis on highly trained personnel, the insulation of law enforcement from politics, and the application of science and technology to investigations. But coexisting with this culture of professionalism has been a counterculture of lawlessness that has manifested itself at different times: the antiradical activities and labor movement spying of the Palmer era, the widespread surveillance of Americans and COINTELPROs of the Hoover years, and the occasional excesses of the modern era, such as the 1980s investigation of CISPES (Committee in Solidarity with the People of El Salvador), the shoot-out at Ruby Ridge, Idaho, in August 1992, and the April 1993 raid on the Branch Davidian compound at Waco, Texas. In the more recent incidents—the CISPES case, Ruby Ridge, and Waco—FBI officials were subject to strong public and congressional criticism, including allegations that FBI officials had been overzealous in their pursuit of these groups or individuals, and had authorized the use of excessive force.

The coexistence of professional and lawless traditions has even surfaced in the FBI's Crime Laboratory, which has an international reputation as a state-of-the-art facility. Responding to allegations of lax procedures by Frederic Whitehurst, a chemist in the explosives unit, the Justice Department's inspector general conducted an 18-month internal inquiry. In its April 1997 report, many of Whitehurst's criticisms of laboratory procedures were corroborated in interviews with other employees: the mishandling of evidence, the role of non-scientists in the management of the lab, and the occasional altering of lab findings to support the prosecution. An undetermined number of criminal cases, federal and local, may be jeopardized by the published reports concerning faulty lab procedures. In January 1997, four supervisors, including the heads of the chemistry and explosives unit, were transferred to other duties as part of an overhaul of the FBI Crime Laboratory. In addition, in October 1997, FBI Director Freeh appointed a new head of the FBI lab, Donald Kerr, a nuclear physicist.

These vicissitudes of the cultures of professionalism and lawlessness are central to understanding the history of the FBI. The FBI's major scandals and the succeeding periods of reform have corresponded to the rise and fall of these two cultures. Professionalism and lawlessness remain an integral part of the modern Bureau. Their ebb and flow offer insights into the traditions and culture that have shaped both FBI organizational behavior and the wider public policy context in which Bureau operations have been conducted.

ORGANIZATION AND
DAY-TO-DAY ACTIVITIES

Susan Rosenfeld

Introduction

The mission of the FBI is to uphold the law through the investigation of violations of federal criminal law; to protect the United States from foreign intelligence and terrorist activities; to provide leadership and law enforcement assistance to federal, state, local, and international agencies; and to perform these responsibilities in a manner that is responsive to the needs of the public and is faithful to the Constitution of the United States.

—FBI Mission Statement, 1998

The Federal Bureau of Investigation (FBI) is the principal investigative arm of the Department of Justice. To fulfill its responsibilities, it gathers and reports facts, locates witnesses, and compiles evidence in those criminal and civil matters in which the federal government has, or may have, jurisdiction. Information from FBI investigations is presented to the appropriate U.S. attorney or other Department of Justice official who decides whether federal prosecution or some other action is warranted.

The Bureau's basic authority derives from Title 28, *United States Code*, Section 533, which authorizes the attorney general to "appoint officials to detect . . . crimes against the United States." In addition, the FBI has, under law, exclusive or concurrent jurisdiction over specific violations that occur within the United States and its possessions or to American citizens abroad. Under Title 28, Section 533, Paragraph 3, the Bureau[1] is also authorized "to conduct investigations regarding official matters under the control of the Department of Justice and the Department of State as may be directed by the Attorney General." Under this statutory provision, and subsequent executive orders, the FBI has conducted background security checks on federal officials, employees, and contractors and has gathered intelligence about activities perceived to jeopardize the national security. Since the early 1970s, top priority has been assigned to those areas under the FBI's jurisdiction perceived to affect society the most. In 1997, these priorities consisted of counterterrorism, drugs/organized crime, foreign counterintelligence, violent crimes, and financial crimes. In addition, the Bureau investigates matters where

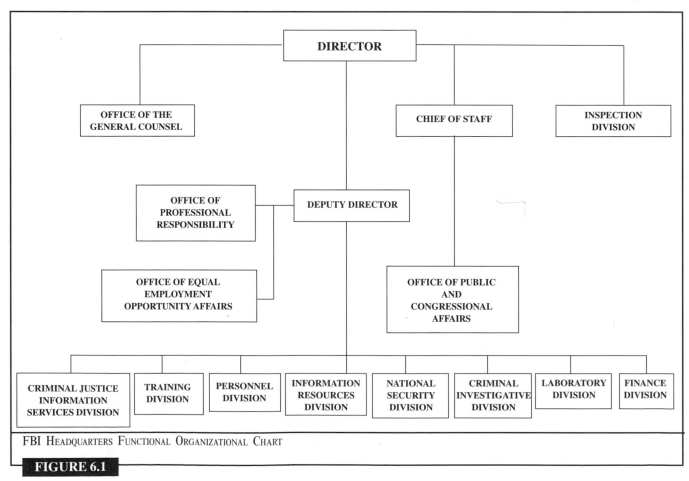

FBI HEADQUARTERS FUNCTIONAL ORGANIZATIONAL CHART

FIGURE 6.1

Source: FBI Web Site <http://www.fbi.gov>.

no prosecution is contemplated. For example, under the authority of several executive orders, the FBI conducts background security checks concerning nominees to sensitive government positions.

In addition, the FBI assists other law enforcement agencies worldwide. It does this through its cooperative services such as fingerprint and DNA identification, laboratory examinations, and police training. Law enforcement information is also collected, coordinated, and disseminated through its *Uniform Crime Reports* and the National Crime Information Center (NCIC). Through its legal attaché (Legat) offices, the FBI provides liaison to assist law enforcement agencies internationally in investigations that cross national boundaries and that either involve American interests abroad or foreign interests in the United States. FBI representatives sit on many national and international committees involving criminal and noncriminal law enforcement matters.

This work is carried out through the FBI's central headquarters (FBIHQ) in Washington, D.C. (see Figure 6.1). In 1996, FBIHQ consisted of the director (Louis J. Freeh) and the director's personal staff; a deputy director (Weldon Kennedy); four offices, three headed by an inspector in charge (the fourth, the Office of the General Counsel, is headed by the general counsel—Howard Shapiro), which report either to the deputy director or to the chief of staff (Robert Bucknam); and nine divisions, each headed by an assistant director.

FBIHQ also includes the FBI Academy in Quantico, Virginia, where most of the Training Division is located, along with the Engineering Research Facility of the Information Resources Division and a number of Laboratory Division functions. The other major off-site headquarters facility is the new Criminal Justice Information Services Division, with its principal functions carried out near Clarksburg, West Virginia.

FBIHQ manages the Bureau as a whole, and performs centralized administrative, training, and laboratory functions. Most of the FBI's investigatory work, however, its local liaison activities, and certain training functions take place in the field. In 1997, the FBI had 56 field divisions (see the Appendix at the end of this chapter), consisting of headquarters offices and approximately 400 resident agencies. The New York City and Washington divisions are metropolitan field offices, with an additional layer of metropolitan resident agencies. In 1997, the FBI had approximately 10,100 special agents and 13,600 other employees who perform professional, administrative, technical, clerical, craft, trade, or maintenance operations with approximately 30 percent assigned to FBIHQ and 70 percent on field installations. The FBI also maintains a site on the Internet's World Wide Web: <http://www.fbi.gov> (see Exhibit 6.1).

A Brief History of the FBI's Organization

The FBI began in 1908 as an unnamed force of special agents (see pages 3–4 and Table 1.2). Its first head, Stanley W. Finch, attempted to organize the force into a headquarters with field units in New York and in Chicago. Within days of becoming attorney general in March 1909, George Wickersham named this force and its support staff the Bureau of Investigation. Finch, as the Bureau's head, now bore the title of chief. His assistant, A. Bruce Bielaski, handled the day-to-day affairs in Washington and took charge when Finch was traveling. Within the next few years, two additional field offices were opened in California and Texas. Each field office had a head, variously called a "superintendent" or a "special agent in charge." The field offices coordinated so closely with the U.S. attorneys in their regions that at first there was some confusion as to their actual chain of command. Despite the growth in field offices, the Bureau itself remained small (34 special agents in 1908, 234 in 1916; see Table 1.1). The early Bureau had jurisdiction over only a few crimes, most notably bank fraud, antitrust violations, and crimes on Indian reservations.

In 1910, Congress passed the Mann Act outlawing transporting women across state lines for "immoral purposes." Then with the Mexican civil wars of 1913–17, the Bureau's work expanded through its jurisdiction over neutrality violations when various of the warring factions created bases in the United States. During World War I, the Bureau—using its own agents with the government-approved assistance of members of the American Protective League—sought saboteurs, spies, and draft deserters. Further adding to Bureau responsibilities, Congress passed the Dyer Act in 1919, in which the Bureau was involved whenever a stolen motor vehicle crossed state lines. The Lindbergh Law of 1932 allowed the Bureau to take the lead in presumed kidnappings after seven days on the theory that the kidnapper had, by then, probably transported the victim over state lines (this was changed, in 1957, to one day).

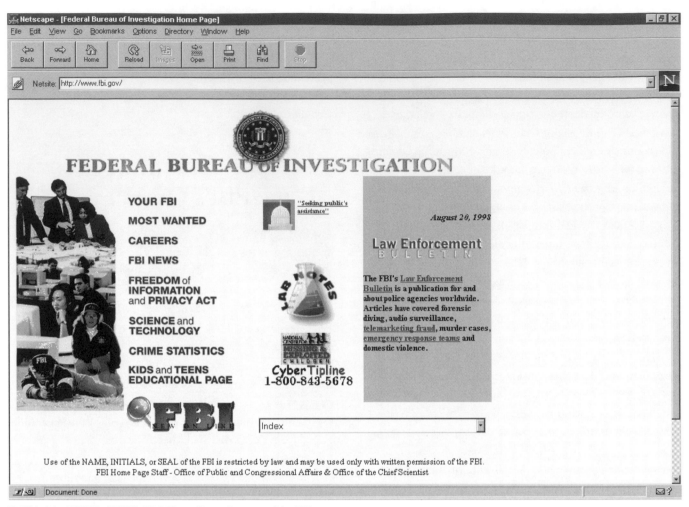

Exhibit 6.1   **FBI World Wide Web Home Page**, *Courtesy of the FBI*

In 1919, the Department of Justice established the General Intelligence Division (GID), also called the Radical Division. Its nominal head, Francis P. Garvan, was a Department of Justice official, and J. Edgar Hoover, the future FBI director, was designated his assistant. In reality, Hoover controlled the operation.

At the start of President Warren G. Harding's administration in 1921, the new attorney general, Harry M. Daugherty, appointed his friend, William Burns, as Bureau director. Burns, who previously headed his own detective agency, became the first Bureau leader to use the title "director." Burns spent most of his time in New York City, where he instituted an informal training program for new special agents. As a result, the day-to-day running of the Bureau headquarters fell to Hoover, who was then the assistant director. During Burns's administration, the Bureau grew from 346 special agents to 441 special agents. He accomplished this, in part, by relaxing special agent qualifications and by appointing his friends as "dollar-a-year men" who were allowed to carry Bureau badges.

Attorney General Harlan F. Stone replaced Burns in May 1924, appointing Hoover acting director. In addition, Stone abolished the GID and required the Bureau to limit its investigations to violations of federal law. On December 10, 1924, Stone named Hoover director. Hoover's appointment signaled a number of changes. First, Hoover made special agent qualifications more stringent, favoring applicants with legal or accounting experience. He then fired special agents who were unqualified. To make certain that Bureau personnel complied with laws and regulations, the new director instituted a system of inspections. Hoover also consolidated the Bureau's fingerprint collections in 1924, established a formal training program in 1928, and started the Bureau's laboratory in 1932. The following year, President Franklin Delano Roosevelt moved the Bureau of Prohibition (formerly in the Department of Treasury) with the U.S. Bureau of Investigation (the Bureau's title since July 1, 1932) into the renamed Division of Investigation. Attorney General Homer Cummings designated Hoover as director of both merged bureaus. This short-lived reorganization ended in

1934, and the following year, the Division of Investigation established its identity as the Federal Bureau of Investigation (see Table 1.2).

In 1933, at the beginning of the New Deal, five individuals, all of whom reported to Hoover, led the Bureau. Immediately subordinate to the director were two assistant directors—Harold Nathan, in charge of investigations, and Clyde Tolson, in charge of personnel and administration. Below them stood three inspectors: Hugh Clegg, in charge of investigations and violations of federal law; James S. Egan, in charge of accounting and preparation of accounting evidence; and John J. Edwards, in charge of the Technical Laboratory and identification (fingerprint and criminal history) matters. The latter three also supervised periodic field inspections.

By the summer of 1934, Congress had passed new crime legislation significantly expanding federal jurisdiction. In response, the FBI expanded to 30 field offices; in FBIHQ, the two assistant directors oversaw six numbered divisions; and the number of agents increased from 353 (in 1933) to 391. The three investigative divisions, supervised by Harold Nathan, were organized by type of violation, whereas the three divisions handled by Clyde Tolson were separated by function. Within the next few years, the six divisions were listed by name, and the two assistant directors were promoted to "assistant to the director," and division heads carried the title "assistant director."

As of 1941, Assistant to the Director Tolson handled the administrative and services divisions, consisting of

- Division One, Identification, headed by Assistant Director D. M. Ladd, which included Identification Proper and the Technical Laboratory
- Division Two, Training and Inspection, headed by Assistant Director Hugh Clegg, which included the Training Schools; Employees' Conferences; Inspections; and the World War II–related section, FBI Law Enforcement Officers Mobilization Plan for National Defense
- Division Three, Personnel and Budget, headed by Assistant Director W. R. Glavin, which handled Personnel, Budget and Accounting, and Cartographic Sections
- Division Four, Administrative, headed by Assistant Director Louis B. Nichols, which included the Crime Records Section, the Communications Section, the Files Section, the Mechanical Section (which handled photographic work for the Bureau and prepared

Bureau publications duplicated on copy machines like mimeographs), as well as sections for Mail Reviewing and Tours

The other assistant to the director, Edward A. Tamm, handled

- Division Five, National Defense, headed by Assistant Director Percy E. Foxworth
- Division Six, Investigative and Accounting, handled by an acting assistant director

These investigative divisions had responsibility for federal law violations, 54 of which fell under the Investigative and Accounting Division, which also included court of claims and missing persons cases. In the cases of violations that came under the primary jurisdiction of other government agencies, such as firearms, income tax, and narcotics, the FBI merely transmitted any information it developed to the appropriate department (a practice that continues today for violations falling outside of the FBI's jurisdiction). In the mid-1930s, President Roosevelt reauthorized the establishment of a General Intelligence Division to meet the Bureau's increased internal security responsibilities of monitoring the rise of fascism and communism. The National Defense Division handled 14 categories of security-related investigations, including "civil rights and domestic violence," a responsibility that continued into the 1960s. During the crisis of World War II, by 1940, almost all FBIHQ divisions ran two shifts covering 24 hours each day.

In 1943, the FBI was again reorganized in response to increased wartime responsibilities. Division Two, Training and Inspection, and Division Six, Investigative and Accounting (headed by Assistant Director Alex Rosen) remained unchanged. Division One, Identification, lost the Technical Laboratory; it became Division Seven, headed by Assistant Director E. P. Coffey, who reported to Assistant to the Director for Investigations Edward A. Tamm. Assistant Director Glavin's division, Division Three, was renamed Administrative to include the Mechanical Section of the old Division Four. Division Four, now called Records and Communications, headed by Assistant Director Nichols, renamed the Files Section to Records and the section handling the mail became the Mail Review and Dispatch Unit. Assistant to the Director Tamm now handled three sections: Division Five, renamed the Security Division, with added wartime responsibilities such as Alien Enemy Control, and Divisions Six and Seven.

A new clandestine branch, the Special Intelligence Service, was temporarily created in 1940 with the responsibility to run intelligence operations in Latin America and South America. By this time, Tolson had become associate director, pushing the assistant to the director for administration into the FBI's number-three position and assistant to the director for investigations to number four.

At the end of World War II, the FBI contained eight divisions: the assistant to the director, Administration, headed the Identification, Administrative, Crime Records, Training and Inspection, and Files and Communications Divisions; for the investigative side, the General Investigative Division (formerly Investigative and Accounting), the Domestic Intelligence Division, and the Laboratory. In 1958, Crime Records and Files and Communications were consolidated into the Records and Communications Division. A Special Investigative Division was added to handle, among other responsibilities, organized crime, and by 1962, Crime Records once again became a separate division, and the Training Division was separated from the Inspection Division.

In 1962, the FBI had 10 divisions. Associate Director Clyde Tolson supervised Division Ten, Inspection, headed by W. Mark Felt, and the two assistants to the director, John P. Mohr and Cartha DeLoach. Assistant to the Director Mohr handled administrative functions (Division Three, Administrative, headed by Assistant Director Nicholas P. Callahan; and Division Four, Files and Communications, headed by Assistant Director W. S. Tavel; as well as Division One, Identification, headed by Assistant Director C. Lester Trotter in 1967; Division Two, Training, headed by Assistant Director J. J. Casper in 1967; and Division Seven, Laboratory, headed by Ivan W. Conrad. Assistant to the Director DeLoach handled the three investigative divisions: Division Five, Domestic Intelligence, with William C. Sullivan as assistant director; Division Six, General Investigative, headed by Alex Rosen; and Division Nine, Special Investigative, headed in 1967 by J. K. Gale; as well as Division Eight, Crime Records, headed in 1967 by Robert L. Beck.

Still other changes were made during the mid-1960s. The Administrative Division acquired oversight of an Exhibits Section, successor to the Tour Unit, which had lapsed during World War II, and had a separate Voucher-Statistical Section. Files and Communications gained a Reading Room, and was responsible for ensuring that all outgoing correspondence was error-free. Domestic Intelligence now contained two branches, an Espionage and Research Branch, and an Internal Security and Liaison Branch. Hoover's split with the Central Intelligence Agency in 1970 caused him to abolish the Liaison Branch. Then, in 1971, the Espionage and Research Branch was renamed the Espionage and Racial Branch to include a Racial Intelligence Section; the former Liaison Branch was renamed Internal Security and Research and included a New Left Section.

The Bureau underwent additional reorganization during Hoover's last years as director. In 1971, a legal counsel (Dwight Dalbey) was added to the staff, who reported to the deputy associate director, a new position, established that summer and held by W. Mark Felt. Felt, in turn, reported to Associate Director Clyde Tolson. As deputy associate director, Felt oversaw the Inspection Division, the Legal Counsel, and the Crime Records Division. In September 1971, Hoover, in effect, fired William C. Sullivan, at the time assistant to the director for Investigations, and elevated Alex Rosen to this position. That personnel shift opened up the General Investigative Division to a new assistant director for the first time in 30 years, and Charles R. Bates was appointed. By March 1972, Legal Counsel had become Division Eleven, the Legal Counsel Division, and William D. Soyars Jr. headed the new Division Twelve, the Computer Systems Division, which reported to Assistant to the Director Mohr and handled the Uniform Crime Reporting and Voucher-Statistical Sections.

When L. Patrick Gray became acting director, a number of significant changes were instituted. The chain of command was reduced by removing the positions of assistant to the director following the retirement of Mohr and Rosen, who held those offices. Between himself and the Executives Conference, Gray placed three aides with whom he had worked at the Department of Justice: Daniel "Mac" Armstrong, Barbara L. Herwig, and David J. Kinley, who became executive assistant and both acted as Gray's spokesperson and handled a number of sensitive issues such as wiretap approvals. Gray abolished the Crime Records Division, replacing it with an External Affairs Division, under Robert Russ Franck. Gray made other changes affecting special agent life. He appointed the first women as special agents since the 1920s, Joanne Pierce and Susan Roley, and eliminated many of the day-to-day regulations that Hoover had imposed.

Gray resigned in April 1973, shortly after withdrawing himself from consideration as director, and was replaced by William Ruckelshaus who served as acting director until Clarence M. Kelley took the oath of office as FBI director on July 9, 1973.

In response to controversies unleashed by Watergate, a further reorganization occurred in early 1974. The section on Planning and Evaluation was separated from the Inspection Division and became an office under the administrative control of Associate Director Nicholas P. Callahan, who also oversaw the Inspection Division. In addition, Division Five dropped "domestic" from its name. The next echelon of executives retained the title of assistant to the director—Thomas J. Jenkins for Administration and Edward S. Miller for Investigations—but were renamed (in January 1974) deputy associate director. In April 1974, the Office of Legal Counsel, now headed by John A. Mintz, moved under the assistant to the director–deputy associate director for Investigations.

The Bureau underwent another major reorganization at the end of 1976. The Planning and Inspection Division, headed by Assistant Director Wilburn K. DeBruler, now reported directly to FBI Director Kelley. In addition to the Office of Inspections and the Office of Planning and Evaluation, this division contained the Office of Professional Responsibility (OPR), first established on October 4, 1976. The Files and Communications Division was renamed the Records Management Division and now contained two branches, one to handle records and the other to handle the Bureau's new responsibilities responding to Freedom of Information Act and Privacy Act requests. A Finance and Personnel Division under Acting Assistant Director Richard E. Long was revived to handle budget, accounting, and personnel matters, while the Administrative Services Division (ASD), under Assistant Director Harold N. Bassett, was responsible for Data Processing, the National Crime Information Center (NCIC), Printing and Space Management, Property Procurement and Management, and Uniform Crime Reports. A new Scientific and Technical Services Division headed by Jay Cochran Jr. was divided into Technical Services and FBI Laboratory branches.

Like Gray, Kelley brought in executive assistants from the outside: William L. Reed, former director of the Florida Department of Law Enforcement, and John Coleman, the former head of training for the Kansas City, Missouri, Police Department. Kelley also brought in William Ellingsworth to help with press relations.

In August 1977, FBI Director Kelley created an Office of Public Affairs (OPA) to replace the External Affairs Division; OPA, headed by Inspector Homer A. Boynton Jr., reported directly to Kelley. OPA consisted of a Press Services Office and a Research Section. At approximately the same time, Kelley divided the Scientific and Technical Services Division by reinstating the Laboratory as a division, under Thomas A. Kelleher Jr., and left Assistant Director Jay Cochran Jr. in charge of the new Technical Services Division. A third change merged the Special Investigative and General Investigative Divisions into the Criminal Investigative Division (CID) under Assistant Director Donald W. Moore Jr.

The reorganization instituted in 1977 was made pursuant to a major management change that continues to govern the Bureau's approach to its investigations. Known as "quality over quantity," this program prioritized responsibilities in order to better utilize the FBI's available resources. The new policy formalized the National Priority Programs.

When becoming director on February 23, 1978, William H. Webster initially made no major changes. However, in 1979, he reorganized the eight FBIHQ divisions into three groups, each reporting to one of three newly named executive assistant directors: Investigations (the Intelligence and Criminal Intelligence Divisions), headed by Lee Colwell; Law Enforcement Services (the Identification, Training, and Laboratory Divisions), headed by Donald W. Moore; and Administration (the Administrative Services, Records Management, and Technical Services Divisions), headed by Homer A. Boynton Jr. The Planning and Inspection Division and the Legal Counsel Division continued to report to the FBI director. The director also moved Congressional Affairs out of the Legal Counsel Division merging it with the Office of Public Affairs to become the Office of Congressional and Public Affairs. Its head, Inspector Boynton, was elevated to the position of assistant director, and he reported to the FBI director. Under Webster, the Bureau's budget more than doubled, from approximately $550 million in 1978 to $1.3 billion in 1987, and the number of agents in 1987 reached an all-time high of 9,434.

On January 28, 1982, Attorney General William French Smith granted the FBI concurrent jurisdiction with the Drug Enforcement Administration (DEA) for narcotics violations, and the administrator of the DEA began reporting to the director of the FBI. The first administrator to hold that position was former FBI executive assistant director Francis "Bud" Mullen. The DEA revised its personnel requirements to follow those of the FBI, requiring its agents to be college graduates. Nonetheless, DEA agents and support personnel, unlike Bureau employees, remained under civil service regulations. DEA agents also began training at the FBI Academy in the mid-1980s.

Webster resigned on May 26, 1987, to become director of the Central Intelligence Agency. His successor, William S. Sessions, on July 18, 1988, announced a "realignment of the duties and reporting lines of his three senior executives." Floyd Clarke, executive assistant director for Administration, was named deputy director, and the two other executive assistant directors, John Otto and Oliver B. Revell, became associate deputy directors for Administration and Investigations, respectively.

Revamping the FBI's organizational structure, in 1991, Sessions directed the Office of Public Affairs and the Congressional Affairs Office (which were combined again in 1992 to form the Office of Public and Congressional Affairs), the Inspection Division, the Legal Counsel Division, and the new Quality Management Office (later abolished) to report directly to himself. The Office of Equal Employment Opportunity Affairs reported to the deputy director.

Louis J. Freeh, who replaced Sessions as FBI director in 1993, also instituted a number of changes. He eliminated the associate deputy director positions and reorganized the FBIHQ divisions, including the Office of Equal Employment Opportunity Affairs, such that all reported to the deputy director. The Administrative Services Division was divided into the Personnel and Finance Divisions, each headed by an assistant director. The former Intelligence Division was renamed the National Security Division and continued to report to the deputy director. The Legal Counsel Division became the Office of the General Counsel, headed by General Counsel Howard Shapiro, whom Freeh brought in from outside the FBI. In addition, Freeh appointed a chief of staff who oversaw the Office of Public and Congressional Affairs. The Office of General Counsel, chief of staff, and the Inspection Division reported to the director. On March 5, 1997, Freeh removed the Office of Professional Responsibility from the Inspection Division and placed it under the deputy director. On October 21, 1997, he named nationally recognized physicist Donald Kerr as head of the Laboratory Division—the first non-agent and professional scientist to head that division.

Position Descriptions

During the Bureau's earliest years, its personnel were divided between special agents, special examiners (later called special accountants), special employees (usually, but not always, non-agent undercover personnel on the Bureau payroll), and clerks. Eventually, the designation "special accountant" was discontinued and the Bureau's accountants thereafter became special agents. The "special employee" designation became obsolete fairly early in the Bureau's history, and by the 1980s, the term "support personnel" had replaced "clerk."

Despite several congressional efforts, Bureau agents have remained in the Excepted Service. This has enabled Bureau officials to impose more stringent requirements for Bureau personnel than those under Civil Service and to fire employees at will. In 1939, clerical employees came under Civil Service and had to be selected from the top three Civil Service applicants for a specific opening, but FBI Director Hoover felt that this requirement could obligate the FBI to hire otherwise-qualified applicants who may have been security risks. Hoover succeeded in bringing all FBI employees into the Excepted Service (Title 28, USC, Section 536) by Executive Order 8766 on June 3, 1941, where they have remained ever since. Although FBI executives may belong to the federal Senior Executive Service, certain federal requirements do not pertain to Bureau personnel. Whistle-blowers at any level, however, have certain protections. Today every employee of the FBI holds a Top Secret clearance and must undergo periodic security reviews.

Acting Director See *Director.*

Agent See *Special Agent (SA).*

Assistant Director J. Edgar Hoover, the Bureau's first *assistant director,* was appointed in 1921 as the second-in-rank executive under Director William Burns. In the 1930s, Hoover created the title Assistant to the Director to designate the two top executives under him. The heads of FBIHQ's six divisions then became *assistant directors,* and the title has been used ever since to designate FBIHQ division heads. Assistant directors constitute the Executives Conference.

Assistant Director in Charge (ADIC) Distinguishing them from FBIHQ division heads, *assistant directors in charge (ADIC)* head the New York City and (since October 1993) the Washington, D.C., field offices. The New York office has responsibility for such a large and heavily populated area that it has three Metropolitan Resident Agencies (MRAs), each headed by a special agent in charge, as well as Resident Agencies. They report to the ADIC and the *deputy ADIC*. The Washington, D.C., field office jurisdiction includes a special agent in charge assigned to Quantico, and several assistant special agents in charge based in Washington, D.C. As assistant directors, the ADICs are member of the Executives Conference.

Assistant Inspector   See *Inspector.*

Assistant Inspector in Place   See *Inspector.*

Assistant Legal Attaché   See *Legal Attaché* or *Legat.*

Assistant Office Service Manager (Assistant OSM)   See *Office Service Manager (OSM).*

Assistant Special Agent in Charge (ASAC)   See *Special Agent in Charge (SAC).*

Assistant to the Director   See *Assistant Director.*

Associate Deputy Director   FBI Director Louis J. Freeh abolished the *associate deputy director* position in October 1993. Under FBI Director William Sessions, associate deputy director was roughly equivalent to *assistant to the director* under J. Edgar Hoover, to *assistant to the director–deputy associate director* under FBI Director Clarence M. Kelley, and to *executive assistant director* under FBI Director William H. Webster. All were directly subordinate to the director and to deputy/associate director, providing program direction and control regarding FBI investigations and the administration of FBI matters, programs, and services. The Laboratory Division, the Criminal Investigation Division, the Training Division, and the Intelligence Division report directly to the associate deputy director for Investigations, and the Office of Liaison and International Affairs reports to the associate deputy director through the Criminal Investigative Division and the Intelligence Division. The Administrative Services Division, the Identification Division, the Technical Services Division, the Engineering Research Facility, and the Information Management Division were under the associate deputy director for Administration.

Associate Director *or* Deputy Director   When Clyde Tolson became *associate director* in the 1930s, this title designated the FBI's second in command. FBI Director William H. Webster did not use a second echelon title, and his successors Sessions and Freeh called their number-two executives *deputy director*. The associate director or deputy director oversees the FBI's day-to-day operations and runs the Executives Conference. Certain offices report directly to this official.

Certified Inspector   See *Inspector.*

Chief Clerk   See *Office Service Manager (OSM).*

Chief Inspector   See *Inspector.*

Chief of Staff   FBI Director Louis J. Freeh appointed the Bureau's first *chief of staff,* Robert Bucknam, in October 1993.

Chief Scientist   FBI Director William S. Sessions appointed Joseph Kielman as the FBI's first *chief scientist* in February 1991. The chief scientist advises the Information Resources Division, and the Bureau in general, regarding technology matters. In addition, this officer oversees "an entrepreneurial type of program" to introduce advanced technologies into Bureau operations. The chief scientist also handles liaison with counterparts in other agencies such as the National Security Agency and the Central Intelligence Agency.

Clerk   See *Professional Support Personnel.*

Deputy Assistant Director   Most divisions have at least one *deputy assistant director,* who is second in command to the assistant director. Deputy assistant directors are often designated *inspector in place.*

Deputy Director   See *Associate Director.*

Deputy Legal Attaché   See *Legal Attaché* or *Legat.*

Director *or* Acting Director   The FBI *director,* with the advice and counsel of staff, the deputy or associate director, and other FBI executives, sets major organizational policy, and provides leadership and direction. An *acting director,* appointed by the attorney general or president as an interim official, is authorized to perform all of the duties of the FBI director and functions as head of the FBI in all matters unless a particular statute or executive order requires that the officer undertaking such action be appointed by the president and confirmed by the Senate.

William J. Burns was the first Bureau head to use the title director when assuming that position in 1921, even though several Bureau leaders preceded him. Until 1968, the attorney general appointed the head of the Bureau and theoretically, the attorney general could fire a director at any time. Under Public Law 90-351, passed in June 1968, the FBI directors who followed J. Edgar Hoover were to be appointed by the president, with the advice and consent of the Senate. L. Patrick Gray III was the first presidential appointee (1972), and Clarence M. Kelley was the first presidential appointee to receive Senate confirmation (1973). Under current law, directors may serve a maximum of 10 years (see Table 9.1 on page 311).

Executive Assistant Director (EAD)   *Executive assistant directors (EADs)* served at the second level in the FBI hierarchy under Director William H. Webster. Webster had EADs for Investigations, Administration, and Law Enforcement Services. The assistant directors of each division reported to one of the EADs.

Executives Conference   Also called the *Executive Conference,* the *Executives Conference* consists of the top-level FBI officials, assistant director and above. It meets periodically to review or recommend policy. The second highest Bureau official (currently the deputy director) leads the conference and passes its recommendations on to the FBI director.

Field Agent   See *Special Agent (SA).*

Historian   See *Office of Public and Congressional Affairs.*

Inspector   Used since approximately 1930, *inspector* is the next highest title after supervisory special agent. The first inspectors worked directly under the two assistant directors and reviewed the work of Bureau units and their personnel. There currently are several types of inspectors. The *chief inspector* in the Inspection Division supervises a small staff of full-time inspectors. Service on the Inspection staff is a prerequisite for becoming a unit chief, assistant special agent in charge, or any higher rank within the FBI's management. To fulfill this requirement, special agents serve as *assistant inspectors* (formerly *inspector's aides*). Until the mid-1990s, agents on the Inspection staff, which is based in FBIHQ, served full time for between nine months and a year. FBI Director Louis J. Freeh instituted a system of certified inspectors, requiring six inspections for certification. With this program, an assistant inspector may remain in a field office with the title *assistant inspector in place,* and be detailed to the Inspection staff at FBIHQ for specific short assignments.

Inspector's Aide   See *Inspector.*

Inspector in Charge   The head of an FBIHQ office (as opposed to an FBIHQ division) traditionally holds the rank of *inspector in charge.*

Inspector in Place   To qualify as an *inspector in place,* a special agent must hold the rank either of an assistant special agent in charge in the field or of at least a section

chief in FBIHQ. Inspectors in place, at times, temporarily leave their normal assignments to supervise a segment of an inspection. See also *Deputy Assistant Director.*

Legal Attaché *or* Legat   The heads of the FBI Foreign Liaison Operations are titled *legal attaché,* sometimes contracted to *legat.* Assigned to overseas offices in American embassies, they establish and maintain liaison with the principal law enforcement and intelligence/security services in that host country and in other countries in the geographical territory served by their office. A *deputy legal attaché* and/or one or more *assistant legal attachés* also serve abroad in these offices.

Liaison Officers   Special agents assigned to liaison offices in Honolulu, Hawaii; Miami, Florida; and San Juan, Puerto Rico carry the title *liaison officers.* They have the same responsibilities as legal attachés and their offices conduct liaison with the foreign nations within each office's assigned geographical territory.

Office Service Manager (OSM)   Originally called chief clerk, the *office service manager (OSM)* traditionally holds the highest non-agent administrative position in a field office. The OSM, the *assistant office service manager (assistant OSM),* and their staff oversee support (non-investigative) matters.

Ombudsman   First appointed in 1981, the *ombudsman* addresses problems before they get to the formal grievance stage. Initially open only to special agents, the position was awarded in 1993 to the "best qualified" applicant, whether agent or professional support personnel. In early 1994, Barbara Duffy became the first professional support employee to hold this position. The ombudsman handles inquiries from both agent and support ranks; approximately 50 percent come from agents in the field, 35 percent from the support staff, and 15 percent from FBIHQ agents.

Professional Support Personnel   With few exceptions, throughout its history, the Bureau required its *professional support personnel* (whether professional, administrative, technical, clerical, craft, trade, maintenance, or in another category) to be U.S. citizens and to meet certain educational requirements, the latter depending on the job. In the more recent past, applicants are required to have had specific work experience—a change from the days when the FBI typically hired its non-agent staff out of high school and trained and promoted its personnel from within.

In the earliest days of the FBI, the vast majority of the professional support personnel (then called *clerks*) were men, partially because of the long hours and sometimes dangerous conditions in which they worked. Today, approximately 70 percent are women. Like agents, support personnel are recruited throughout the United States and must meet loyalty and security requirements. Unlike agents, they do not have a mandatory retirement age, and a 40-year FBI career is not unusual. Mildred Parsons, for example, was a Bureau employee for over 57 years. By the 1980s, the FBI began to hire professionally trained support staff for mid-level and even senior-level positions, especially in the scientific and computer fields. These included Al Bayse, a computer specialist who headed the Technical Services Division; his deputy, Carolyn Morris; and Barbara Duffy, the Bureau's first non-agent ombudsman. In 1993, FBI Director William S. Sessions began a program of moving agent supervisors out of FBIHQ and into the field, replacing them with support personnel. His successor, Louis J. Freeh, expanded this program, giving support personnel in professional positions increasing responsibilities and opportunities. These new opportunities included assisting with inspections. Since 1996, non-agents are designated professional support personnel, regardless of their job responsibilities.

In October 1996, the total support staff included almost 10,000 women and over 4,300 men and, of these, 68.4 percent were white, 4.5 percent Hispanic, 24.8 percent black, almost 2 percent Asian, and less than 1 percent American Indian. At least by the late 1950s, the Bureau made an affirmative effort to hire physically handicapped but otherwise qualified support workers. Among the support staff in October 1992, most of those who held college or higher degrees earned them in the social sciences (747) and the fewest (16) in law (in 1994, the Bureau began replacing agent attorneys in FBIHQ with support attorneys). Over 300 support employees held master's degrees and 44 held doctorates.

Relief Supervisor   The *relief supervisor* position is the lowest managerial spot for a special agent in the field and is required experience for any agent aspiring to an executive position.

Retired Annuitant   See *Special Agent (SA)*.

Rotor Clerk   See *Squad*.

Special Agent (SA)   A *special agent (SA)* has limited ("special") responsibilities. Although the FBI has the broadest jurisdiction, by far, of any federal law enforcement agency, agents nevertheless can investigate only those violations that Congress has not assigned to other federal entities, along with those specifically given to the FBI, exclusively or concurrently with other federal, state, or local authorities.

When they enter government service, special agents are assigned Grade GS (General Schedule) 10, and, after their first office assignment, receive additional "availability pay" (formerly called "administratively uncontrollable overtime," or AUO). *Field agents* may advance to GS 13, and supervisory and managerial positions are available in the GS 14–GS 15 or Senior Executive Service (SES). When signing the Federal Pay Reform Act on November 5, 1990, President George Bush raised FBI special agents' pay to be more commensurate with their responsibilities, their actual working time, and their work-related expenses. Based on a demonstration program begun in 1987 in New York, agents' pay in several high-cost cities was raised (previously, an agent received the same pay whether working in New York City or a small-town resident agency). The Federal Pay Reform Act also raised the mandatory retirement age for agents to 57. Since the establishment of the FBI Drug Deterrence Program in the late 1980s, every employee— agent or support—is subject to random drug testing. Through age 35, an SA must pass a physical exam every other year, and annually thereafter. All agents take a fitness test every six months with performance criteria geared to their age.

From the first, agents were expected to be generalists. One reason was to save money. In the 1930s, for example, an agent sent to investigate a case away from his headquarters office often handled all the investigatory leads in that geographic area. Many agents also serve in one- or two-person resident agencies and must handle all leads that come their way. The exceptions—agents whose careers concentrate in one area of expertise—tend to be scientists, who spend most of their Bureau employment in the FBI Laboratory, or those with certain language or other technical skills. From the late 1930s until the 1970s, agents with a flair for public relations worked in FBIHQ in Crime Records or its successor, the External Affairs Division.

Special agent applicants have to be U.S. citizens between the ages of 23 and 37. Candidates must have a degree from an accredited four-year college or university, pass certain physical tests, be drug free, and undergo a selection process that includes a written test, interviews, a thorough background investigation, and a polygraph examination. Candidates can qualify through one of five programs: law, accounting, engineering/science, language, and diversified. The latter category includes college graduates having at least three years of work experience, which could be in the military or law enforcement—or as far removed from investigative work as real estate or dentistry. Each field office has a recruiter, or sometimes a recruiting staff, to advise prospective candidates and handle the application process.

The earliest Bureau agents received no formal training. The first appointees were either already special agents in the Department of Justice or were transferred from the Secret Service. As the Bureau expanded, it accepted those with detective experience or legal training as well as a few who had a "good general education" and some other relevant skill such as foreign language fluency, investigative journalism experience, or even acting ability. Some of the pre–World War I agents possessed several of these qualifications. The early Bureau was small (34 permanent and 5 temporary special agents in July 1909), and all who requested applications, including women, received them. By 1910, most agents had legal training and often had worked previously in the government or in private law offices. Like the famous G-men of later years, the earliest agents lacked civil service protection and could be fired at any time—as some indeed were.

After World War I, special employees who lacked college and sometimes even a high school education were sometimes elevated to special agent status. After his appointment as acting director of the Bureau of Investigation in 1924, J. Edgar Hoover fired these unqualified agents. At that time, less than 17 percent of the investigative personnel possessed legal training, and less than 14 percent had undergone education in accounting. One of the standards Hoover pledged upon assuming the highest Bureau position was that he would require agents to have training in law or accounting. By 1939, over two-thirds of the FBI agents had legal training and over 17 percent qualified as accountants. By 1939, special agents were also required to be between 23 and 35 years old and to have either graduated from a recognized law school and have bar membership or be "expert" in accounting with practical experience. Agents had to pass a rigorous physical examination conducted by Navy physicians, and an exhaustive background investigation into their character and fitness for an investigative career. In 1953, when the Bureau was accepting very few new agents, applicants had to be between the ages of 25 and 40; had to be willing to serve anywhere in the United States, its territories, and Puerto Rico; and had to have graduated from a resident law school with a bachelor of laws degree, or from an accounting school with at least three years of practical accounting or auditing experience.

All women were excluded from candidacy between 1926 and 1972. Nonetheless, the Bureau did accept as special agents certain men who did not meet all the requirements. These exceptions included individuals having desirable language or scientific skills, firearms experts, those with law enforcement or military experience, and even athletes who could strengthen Bureau basketball and softball teams. Male Bureau clerks could also advance to agent status, although they usually had to graduate from college first. Lawyers and accountants continued to be preferred, but the Bureau eventually amended its official qualifications to eliminate those backgrounds as a requirement and sought those with scientific, engineering, computer, and linguistic skills.

Beginning in 1962, the FBI, like other federal agencies, specifically sought to recruit and retain minority agents. L. Patrick Gray, acting director of the FBI, began hiring women as special agents in 1972 (for a list of the first female and minority agents and other female and minority special agents of note, see Table 9.3 on page 313). A strong minority recruitment program was initiated by FBI Director William Webster that included assigning a Hispanic agent and an Asian American agent to the Press Office in FBIHQ to use the minority media to publicize the Bureau's interest in minority applicants. For example, beginning in 1978, the FBI advertised on the Dallas Cowboys Spanish Radio Network, which broadcast throughout the United States.

In January 1997, the FBI had 1,617 women as special agents and 9,199 men. Approximately 85 percent of the total force was white, 6.9 percent Hispanic, 5.6 percent black, 2.2 percent Asian American, and less than 1 percent American Indian. Most agents in October 1992 held degrees in the social sciences (3,261), and the fewest (107) held computer science degrees. Law degrees were held by 1,450 special agents and 1,552 held accounting degrees. Almost 2,000 special agents had master's degrees and over 100 had earned doctorates.

In 1940, the mandatory retirement age for special agents was 62, but these same individuals could return the next day to their normal positions as *retired annuitants*. Among the agents serving beyond retirement age were James E. Amos, one of the Bureau's first black special agents, and Albert D. Mehegan, who appears to have served the longest of any special agent. A mandatory retirement age of 55 was established on January 1, 1978; this was raised in 1990 to 57.

Special Agent in Charge (SAC)　The head of each FBI field office (except the offices in New York City and Washington, D.C.) is designated the *SAC* (pronounced S-A-C). In New York and Washington, the SACs are subordinate to the assistant directors in charge (ADICs). SACs have one or more assistants, each designated *assistant special agent in charge* (ASAC; pronounced A-sack).

Squad　The special agents in the field are organized into *squads*, each headed by a supervisor. Depending on the size of the office and the types of violations frequently encountered, a squad may have several responsibilities, for example, bank fraud and health care fraud, or several squads may investigate the same violation, for example, narcotics or organized crime. Traditionally, each squad's active paper files are maintained by a rotor clerk. Although by the end of 1996 many investigative files were computerized, paper files continue to be handled by rotor clerks.

FBI Headquarters (FBIHQ)

The FBIHQ chain of command begins with the FBI director and deputy director followed by the assistant directors of each division and their agent and support subordinates. All the agents at FBIHQ are considered management and all carry the designation supervisory special agent (SSA). The special agents in charge (SACs) in the field (assistant directors in charge in the New York City and Washington, D.C., field offices) report to the assistant director of the FBIHQ division with primary responsibility for the specific violation being investigated. Although in 1979, every FBIHQ division had at least an office in Washington, D.C., with most in the J. Edgar Hoover Building, the Training Division is located in Quantico, Virginia, at the FBI Academy, and the Criminal Justice Information Services (CJIS) is in Clarksburg, West Virginia.

Administrative Division (Administrative Services Division; ASD)

Until 1993, the Administrative Services Division (ASD) and its predecessors in Division Three managed FBI budget and accounting matters, voucher and payroll functions, the procurement process, property management, and agency space allocation and maintenance requirements. It also handled personnel matters, including recruitment, hiring, staffing, performance evaluations, the employee health assistance and benefits program, and the training of FBI personnel taught by outside vendors and funded through the Government Employees Training Act. In addition, ASD provides printing and supply services for FBIHQ and the field offices, physical security for FBIHQ buildings in Washington, D.C., and Quantico, Virginia, and coordinates the formulation and presentation of FBI budget requests to the Department of Justice, the Office of Management and Budget, and Congress. In 1993, FBI Director Louis J. Freeh split its functions into two separate divisions, the Personnel Division and the Finance Division (see *Personnel Division* and *Finance Division*).

Criminal Investigative Division (CID)

CID investigates matters concerning organized crime, narcotics violations, violent crime, white-collar crime, civil rights matters, fugitives, crimes on government reservations, interstate theft, and applicant investigations.

CID was formed in 1977 by combining the Special Investigative Division, the General Investigative Division, and sections of the Intelligence Division. On June 21, 1989, CID's responsibilities were consolidated under a Violent Crimes and Major Offenders Program (VCMOP), which brought together programs in violent crimes, fugitives, government reservation crimes, and interstate theft. "Violent crimes" include kidnapping, aircraft hijackings, and assaults on federal officers. Domestic terrorism was added to VCMOP on March 3, 1993, "to detect, prevent, and/or react to unlawful, violent activities of individuals or groups whose intent is to overthrow the Government; interfere with the activities of a foreign government in the United States; substantially impair the functioning of the Federal Government, a state government, or interstate commerce; or deprive Americans of their civil rights as guaranteed by the Constitution, laws, and treaties of the United States." The following year, domestic terrorism was moved to the National Security Division.

In June 1992, the Organized Crime and Drug Sections of CID were consolidated into the Organized Crime/Drug Branch to focus resources on investigations of major international and domestic criminal enterprises that control many illegal activities in the United States.

The FBI defines white-collar crime as "those illegal acts that use deceit and concealment rather than the application or threat of physical force or violence to obtain money, property or services; to avoid the payment or loss of money; or to secure business or personal advantages." These crimes are economic fraud; financial institution fraud; fraud against the government, including defense-related fraud and health care fraud; public corruption; and economic crimes. Reorganized in October 1995, white collar crime's priority areas included health care fraud, telemarketing fraud, environmental crimes, public corruption, insurance fraud, bankruptcy fraud, securities and commodities fraud, computer crimes, government fraud, and international money laundering.

In civil rights matters, CID addresses "the actual or attempted curtailment of rights possessed by citizens and inhabitants of the United States under the Constitution and Federal laws." Although the Bureau has had jurisdiction over civil rights matters since its inception, until the mid-1960s, federalism, administration policy, and court decisions severely limited its capabilities. Since that time, statutes and court decisions have bolstered the FBI's authority. The Civil Rights Division of the Department of Justice establishes guidelines for these investigations and maintains responsibility for the enforcement of these statutes.

Since 1994, CID's International Relations Branch has overseen the Legal Attaché (Legat) Program. In so doing, it took over a responsibility formerly held by the Office of Liaison and International Affairs. That branch is also responsible for contacts with other executive branch agencies; with Interpol; with foreign police and security officers based in Washington, D.C.; and with national law enforcement associations.

Drug Demand Reduction Program

This program alerts Americans, especially young people, to the dangers of drug abuse, and educates them about the FBI's role in the war against illicit drugs and the dangers of illegal drugs. The FBIHQ office oversees the field program. Each field office has a Drug Demand Reduction coordinator. The program originated on June 27, 1984, as a joint FBI–Drug Enforcement Administration project, the Sports-Drug Awareness Program, which, under the direction of Attorney General William French Smith, recruited coaches, sports figures, student athletes, and popular television and cartoon characters (for example, Spiderman and Robocop) to serve as role models in the campaign to reduce drug use in high schools. Field offices also "adopt" schools to encourage students to stay away from drugs and engage in more positive activities. On April 18, 1988, FBI Director William S. Sessions established the Drug Demand Reduction Program in the Research Unit, Office of Congressional and Public Affairs. It moved to the CID approximately five years later.

Special Squads

In 1934, FBI Director Hoover authorized special squads, also called flying squads, to capture notorious gangsters, such as John Dillinger, who crossed and recrossed state lines, or to solve kidnappings that came under federal jurisdiction. The special squads worked out of FBIHQ rather than from the field offices. Samuel P. Cowley headed the Bureau's first special squad.

International Relations Branch

Established in 1994, this branch oversees the Legal Attaché Program; is responsible for FBI contacts with other executive branch agencies, Interpol, and foreign police and security officers based in Washington, D.C.; and handles relations with other United States law enforcement agencies.

Legal Attachés (Legats)

Foreign liaison offices, each of which is headed by a legal attaché or legal liaison officer, work abroad with American and foreign police authorities on criminal matters falling within the FBI's jurisdiction. Overseen by the International Relations Branch of the Criminal Investigative Division, the FBI's international investigations role has expanded as the result of congressional application of extraterritorial jurisdiction and the growth in international criminal activity. FBI investigations abroad are approved by the host country and coordinated through the legat with the U.S. Department of State and any other involved agency. Given its expanded extraterritorial responsibilities and the increasing international demands in the prosecution of illicit drug trafficking, organized crime, foreign counterintelligence, terrorism, and financial crime, the FBI maintains liaison with many foreign countries' law enforcement and intelligence/security services. Liaison is governed by executive orders, statutes, attorney general guidelines, and FBI policy. Through its liaison function, the FBI meets its international obligations regarding organized crime, narcotics, international terrorism, foreign counterintelligence, and general criminal matters. Legats also assist foreign police agencies with their legitimate investigative interests in the United States.

In 1997, the FBI had 36 legat offices, of which 3 are U.S. offices that handle liaison with foreign officers in their geographical regions.

- Honolulu, Hawaii
- Miami, Florida
- San Juan, Puerto Rico

The other offices, most of which handle liaison with several foreign countries, are

- Athens, Greece
- Bangkok, Thailand
- Beijing, China
- Bern, Switzerland
- Bogota, Colombia
- Bonn, Federal Republic of Germany
- Bridgetown, Barbados
- Brussels, Belgium
- Buenos Aires, Argentina
- Cairo, Egypt
- Canberra, Australia
- Caracas, Venezuela
- Hong Kong, China
- London, England
- Madrid, Spain
- Manila, Philippines
- Mexico City, Mexico
- Montevideo, Uruguay
- Moscow, Russia
- New Delhi, India
- Ottawa, Canada
- Panama City, Panama
- Paris, France
- Pretoria, South Africa
- Riyadh, Saudi Arabia
- Rome, Italy
- Santiago, Chile
- Seoul, South Korea
- Tallin, Estonia
- Tel Aviv, Israel
- Tokyo, Japan
- Vienna, Austria
- Warsaw, Poland

Foreign legat offices are located in American embassies. Each foreign office is headed by the legal attaché, who is assisted by a deputy and/or assistant legal attaché. Special agents assigned to the Hawaii, Florida, and Puerto Rico offices are designated liaison officers.

Dating from the World War II era, the purpose of the legats was for exchanging "information with the law enforcement agencies of those countries and . . . cooperating in other ways with those agencies." In January 1953, in addition to Madrid, London, Paris, and Mexico City, new legat offices were established in Havana, Cuba, and Rio de Janeiro, Brazil. The FBI had 10 legat offices in 1959, which expanded in 1968 with the opening of offices in Rome and Tokyo. The number of offices increased further under the Nixon administration to include Managua, Nicaragua, and La Paz, Bolivia (both of which were closed after FBI Director Hoover's death), and Singapore (closed in 1975). By March 1971, the Bureau had 17 legal attaché offices. An additional office opened in Manila, Philippines, in January 1972, and another in Brasilia, Brazil, in March 1972. The number declined to 15 by 1975: Bern, Bonn, Brasilia, Buenos Aires, Caracas, Hong Kong, London, Madrid, Manila, Mexico City, Ottawa, Paris, Rome, Tel Aviv, and Tokyo.

Office of Liaison and International Affairs (OLIA)

For over eight years, OLIA provided management and support for the FBI's Legal Attaché Program and served as a liaison with both friendly foreign police and intelligence agencies to support the FBI mission and with other executive branch agencies and foreign government officials in the United States.

When established on November 23, 1986, OLIA combined several FBI liaison programs, thereby enhancing coordination at FBIHQ to carry out the FBI's international responsibilities. Sean McWeeney was its first inspector in charge. OLIA trained legat and liaison office support personnel, prepared budgets, and handled administrative matters. Its Foreign Liaison Unit oversaw the foreign liaison and legat programs and coordinated day-to-day activities. In 1994, CID's International Relations Branch took over OLIA's former responsibilities.

Special Investigative Division

The Special Investigative Division was established in the early 1960s to handle organized crime cases and was headed by Courtney Evans, FBI liaison to the Department of Justice. By 1967, then under the direction of Assistant Director James H. Gale, the Special Investigative Division also supervised cases involving fugitives, carried out criminal intelligence investigations into organized crime, and conducted background investigations on government employees and contractors. At that time, it consisted of a Criminal Intelligence–Organized Crime Section, a Fugitive Section, and an Employees Security and Special Inquiry Section. FBI Director Clarence M. Kelley merged it with the Domestic Intelligence and General Investigative Divisions in 1977 to form the Criminal Investigative Division.

Criminal Justice Information Services (CJIS)

Created on February 24, 1992, CJIS serves as a focal point and central repository for the FBI's criminal justice information services and is a customer-driven organization that provides state-of-the-art identification and information services to local, state, federal, and international criminal justice agencies. Its principal offices and staff are now located in Clarksburg, West Virginia. CJIS responsibilities include the functions of the former Identification Division, the National Crime Information Center (formerly in the Technical Services Division), and the Uniform Crime Reports (formerly in the Information Management Division). It also maintains program management responsibility for the day-to-day operations of the National Crime Information Center (NCIC) and the Uniform Crime Reports programs. By pulling together these functions, CJIS enables the FBI to coordinate all FBI criminal justice information services issues, as well as enhance liaison with the user community.

G. Norman Christensen was appointed the first assistant director of CJIS. Today it has three deputy assistant directors responsible for administrative support services, engineering, and policy and liaison.

By coordinating the statistical service functions, CJIS brings together the Fully Integrated Automated Fingerprint Identification System from the Identification Division, NCIC, and the NCIC 2000 Development Group and User/System Services Section, formerly associated with the Uniform Crime Reports. The Automated Fingerprint Identification System should be in operation in the late 1990s, including 10-print identification, latent fingerprint, subject search, criminal history, document, image, and remote search assistance.

FBI Disaster Squad

The Disaster Squad, currently consisting of approximately 60 non-agent latent fingerprint specialists, helps identify victims of natural disasters and other catastrophes throughout the world. When an agent and a clerical employee died in a plane crash in 1940, FBI representatives arrived at the scene only to discover that no one at the site knew how to identify the bodies. This tragedy marked the beginning of the Disaster Squad. Among the Disaster Squad's more notable achievements are investigations following the Jonestown, Guyana, mass suicide (1978); the eruption of the Mount St. Helens volcano in Washington state (1980); the explosion of the space shuttle *Challenger* (1986); and the destruction of TWA Flight 800 over Long Island (1996). If no FBI source can provide identifying data, the squad seeks information elsewhere, including dental records, employment applications, and driver's license files. To aid in identification, squad members will, if necessary, obtain prints from the victims' personal possessions.

Identification Division

For 70 years, the Identification Division served as the central repository and clearinghouse for fingerprint records, serving over 66,000 users. Following Larry York's retirement as assistant director of the Identification Division on April 30, 1993, it was absorbed by the Criminal Justice Information Services (CJIS). The Identification Division processed millions of fingerprint cards and related data submitted by federal, state, and local criminal justice agencies. For much of its history, the Identification Division was the largest FBIHQ division and, according to a 1947 *Life* magazine article, it employed (at that time) the largest typing pool in the world. In 1996, its automated components moved to Clarksburg, West Virginia, to become a section of CJIS. At that time, it had over 200,000,000 prints on file representing more than 68,000,000 people.

The Identification Division began in 1924 when the Bureau of Investigation consolidated the fingerprint collections of the International Association of Chiefs of Police National Bureau of Identification, formerly housed in Chicago, and the Department of Justice collection of fingerprints, formerly maintained in Leavenworth Prison in Kansas, to establish what was then called the National Division of Identification and Information. At that time, the division contained approximately 810,000 fingerprint cards.

In 1929, the Civil Service Commission began requiring applicants to supply fingerprints and the Bureau assumed responsibility for these prints in July 1932. When checking applicant fingerprints in 1929, the Bureau of Investigation found that 1 out of every 13 applicants had a police record. That number was reduced to 1 in every 41 by 1939, demonstrating the deterrent value of the fingerprint program.

Beginning in 1932, the FBI exchanged fingerprint data with state law enforcement agencies and with agencies in United States territories and 89 foreign countries.

The Single Fingerprint Section and the Civil Identification Section were established in 1933, although the Single Fingerprint Section remained independent of the Identification Division until 1936. In 1939, it contained the prints of over 14,000 of the most notorious known criminals (all other prints were filed according to 10-finger classifications). In 1950, the Single Fingerprint Section changed its name to the Latent Fingerprint Section. Latent fingerprints are not visible to the unaided eye. By 1972, this section's 84 fingerprint examiners had a caseload of 30,339. The Latent Fingerprint Section later moved to the Laboratory Division.

The civil identification file, maintained separately from the FBI's criminal identification files, enabled agents to identify amnesia victims, unknown deceased individuals, and victims of disasters. For many years, lasting into the 1950s, FBI Director J. Edgar Hoover campaigned to have Americans file their fingerprints with the FBI (see Exhibit 8.3 on page 270). He encouraged many celebrities—from Shirley Temple to former president Herbert Hoover—to contribute their prints and thereby publicize and endorse the program.

By the 1930s, the volume of fingerprint information had increased to a point that the Bureau began using mechanical searching devices (see Exhibit 5.2). Fingerprints were filed not by name but by classification. By 1940, the largest classification group had been transferred to "punch cards" enabling the FBI to search 400 fingerprints within 2 minutes instead of the 45 minutes that a manual search would have required. In 1953, the Identification Division used a "speed photo transceiver." This machine enabled the Bureau to receive, by photograph, fingerprints from similarly equipped law enforcement agencies.

Following the Japanese attack on Pearl Harbor in December 1941, the Departments of War and Navy sent their fingerprint files to the FBI. The Bureau had checked the prints of all Army officers and enlisted personnel since 1934, and after 1936, those of the Navy and Marine Corps. Fearing a catastrophic event (like a bombing), New York City sent the FBI several hundred thousand sets of fingerprints that residents had contributed voluntarily, and the Office of Civil Defense sent approximately five million sets of fingerprints of employees of public utilities throughout the United States. In addition, the Bureau continued to receive prints from the armed services, war industry employees, and the

federal civil service. The division's space needs expanded so drastically in response to World War II submissions that it moved to the National Guard Armory in Washington, D.C. (see Exhibit 8.7 on page 281). Compounding its problems of inadequate staffing, by the end of 1943, 644 Identification Division fingerprint employees were lost to military service, requiring the hiring of women. To cope with the extra work, the division even employed high school students part-time.

When the FBI received its 100-millionth fingerprint card in 1946, it became the world's largest repository of fingerprint records. By 1968, the FBI had 190 million sets of fingerprints (many of them duplicates).

To improve the fingerprint-matching process, the FBI initiated research and development of computerized scanning equipment to read and record fingerprint identifying characteristics, called "minutiae." The National Bureau of Standards provided technical and scientific support; the FBI also contracted with North American Rockwell Information Systems for a requirements study to develop a prototype automatic fingerprint reader. This prototype, now on exhibit in the Smithsonian Institution, was built by the Cornell Aeronautical Laboratory and was delivered to the FBI in 1972. In 1973, the FBI began a program to totally automate its fingerprint records. By 1983, the criminal fingerprint files were converted, and the Bureau achieved its goal of complete automation in 1996 with its move to Clarksburg, West Virginia, and the incorporation of the Identification Division into the Criminal Justice Information Services.

National Crime Information Center (NCIC)

The NCIC is a nationwide computerized information system dedicated to serving local, state, and federal criminal justice agencies. Although operated by the FBI, approximately 99 percent of its use is by state, local, and other federal agencies. Its goal is to provide a readily available computerized database of accurate and timely criminal justice data: "Information collected by criminal justice agencies that is needed for the performance of their legally authorized and required functions." The NCIC database includes information in such categories as license plate numbers and stolen vehicles, stolen and recovered weapons, fugitives, missing persons, and stolen securities. In addition, it provides access to criminal histories.

NCIC became operational in January 1967, with 15 agencies using the network. It was part of the Uniform Crime Reports Unit, then part of the Crime Records Division. A criminal histories file, the Computerized Criminal History file, was added in November 1972. The following year, NCIC joined the new Computer Systems Division and in 1992 became a part of the newly formed Criminal Justice Information Services (CJIS) Division. In 1996, CJIS was engaged in creating a new generation of information services called NCIC 2000.

Uniform Crime Reports

To present a statistical picture of crime in America, the FBI collects data monthly from over 16,000 individual law enforcement agencies nationwide on murder, forcible rape, robbery, aggravated assault, burglary, larceny-theft, motor vehicle theft, and arson, to which, in 1992, it added hate crimes. These constitute the Crime Index, which is disseminated in semiannual releases and annual publications showing crime trends, and in special publications.

Uniform Crime Reports began June 11, 1930, with a congressional authorization for the Bureau of Investigation to collect statistics supplied voluntarily by cities and counties throughout the United States. In 1940, 2,552 cities and 1,612 counties reported, including every city having a population over 50,000 (except Bayonne, New Jersey). Circulation for the monthly report reached 16,000. A quarterly bulletin printed by the Government Printing Office was also circulated to those law enforcement agencies contributing statistics and to universities. By 1941, however, the Bureau circulated only the quarterly *Uniform Crime Reports*. In 1957, 6,808 agencies, representing 97 percent of the population of the United States, participated in this program.

Several different divisions supervised preparation of *Uniform Crime Reports*. In the 1980s, it was part of the Office of Congressional and Public Affairs, moving to the Records Management Division when the Office of Congressional and Public Affairs was reorganized in April 1989. When the Records Management Division became the Information Management Division in the early 1990s, the Uniform Crime Reports unit remained with it, and the division became part of CJIS in 1993 as part of the major reorganization of that year.

Director's Office

Director's Office was the formal title used during the late 1970s and 1980s for those offices that reported to the FBI director or the director's second in command.

Domestic Intelligence Division

See *Criminal Investigative Division (CID)* and *National Security Division.*

Finance Division

Created in October 1993 with Burdena Passinelli as its assistant director, the Finance Division handles budget and fiscal matters (see also *Administrative Services Division*).

Flying Squad

See *Criminal Investigative Division (CID).*

General Intelligence Division (GID)

See *National Security Division.*

Honors Intern Program

Started in 1985, the Honors Intern Program introduces undergraduate and graduate students to the FBI to motivate them to consider careers in law enforcement. The program also enhances the visibility of the FBI on college and university campuses. Interns receive specific work assignments, but they also meet with Bureau officials and they visit field offices and the FBI Academy in Quantico, Virginia.

Information Resources Division (IRD)

IRD was inaugurated in October 1993 to handle many of the functions formerly performed by the Technical Services Division and the Information Management Division. Its 2,000 employees provide a wide variety of technical services to support FBI investigations. These services include engineering research and development, automated data processing, telecommunications services, and the development of computer-based information systems. In addition, IRD furnishes essential technical support to FBI field offices and FBIHQ divisions, and designs, develops, distributes, and installs technical support equipment necessary to carry out the FBI's investigative mission.

IRD began in 1972 as the Computer Systems Division. Previously, the FBI had automated its payroll—the first government agency to do so—and after the establishment of the National Crime Information Center, these functions were consolidated into the Computer Systems Division. The Computer Systems Division was combined with the FBI Laboratory in the mid-1970s to create the Scientific and Technical Services Division and was headed by Assistant Director Jay Cochran Jr. The new Technical Services Branch handled the Communications, Engineering, and Special Projects Sections. Shortly thereafter, FBI Director Kelley created the Technical Services Division by reinstating the FBI Laboratory as a separate division. In 1993, the new Technical Services Division became part of IRD.

Engineering Section

Located on the FBI Academy grounds in Quantico, Virginia, the Engineering Section of IRD provides technical support for investigations in field offices, develops strategies and methods to ensure that law enforcement will have continuing capability of monitoring communications, provides electronic surveillance technology and equipment, and handles the security systems in all FBI-controlled space. This section runs a comprehensive training program for technically trained agents and electronics technicians.

Office of Information Systems—Research and Development

This office designed and developed the field office automation system which, by July 1988, was fully operational in all the field offices and supported by regional computer support centers.

Records Management Division

In 1949, the Records and Communications Division, which preceded the Records Management Division, was responsible for maintaining the Bureau's communications system and was the custodian of the Bureau's investigative, personnel, and administrative records. (For information on its Crime Records Section, see *Crime Records Division* under *Office of Public and Congressional Affairs*.) Owing to the FBI's new responsibilities because of the 1974 amendments to the Freedom of Information Act and the 1974 Privacy Act, in 1976, a separate Records Management Division was created. In addition to handling both Freedom of Information Act and Privacy Act requests (see *Office of Public and Congressional Affairs*), the Records Management Division continued its responsibilities for the FBI's files, as well as for declassification and security matters. The Uniform Crime Reports was also assigned to this division *(*see *Criminal Justice Information Services Division*). In 1993, the Records Management Division was absorbed into the Information Management Division.

Inspection Division

The Inspection Division consists of the Office of Inspections and the Office of Planning, Evaluations, and Audits, each headed by a deputy assistant director. Under FBI Director Louis J. Freeh, the Office of Professional Responsibility, formerly part of the Inspection Division, became an inde-

pendent office in 1997 (see *Office of Professional Responsibility*). This division handles appeals from OPR's disciplinary rulings.

One of the oldest units in the FBI, the Office of Inspections conducts in-depth examinations of the FBI's investigative and administrative operations at both FBIHQ and in the field to ensure compliance with established regulations and to make recommendations for improved organizational efficiency and effectiveness. Inspections cover two kinds of violations: "form," relating to procedure, and "substantive," which might adversely affect the outcome of a case. From at least the early 1950s, all agents aspiring to executive positions had to serve on the inspection staff. In 1996, FBI Director Freeh began sending selected support personnel on inspections, as well.

The Office of Planning, Evaluations, and Audits performs several functions. Its Strategic Planning Unit guides the FBI's strategic and long-range planning processes and provides consultation and training services on planning and administrative efforts. Under Program Evaluations Unit auspices, routine and special program evaluations are conducted in order to provide decision-making information for FBI executives. The Audit Unit ensures that FBI financial operations are conducted properly, its financial reports presented correctly, and it complies with applicable federal laws and regulations.

This internal oversight function was initiated by J. Edgar Hoover after he became the Bureau's director. The early inspection system entailed surprise visits in every field office—at first, every few months; later, once a year. Currently, offices are given official notice two or three weeks in advance that an inspection is imminent. Inspections are carried out by a rotating staff of agents (after 1995, by selected non-agent professionals) under the supervision of an inspector.

Laboratory Division

The FBI Laboratory is the only federal full-service forensic science laboratory serving law enforcement. The Laboratory Division currently has five major sections: Investigative Operations and Support (formerly Documents), Scientific Analysis, Special Projects, Latent Fingerprint, and Forensic Science Research and Training. Among this division's responsibilities are the Polygraph Program, the Foreign Language Services Program, the Photographic Equipment

Program, and the Bomb Data Center. Today, the FBI Laboratory handles over 15,000 forensic examinations annually, covering some 200,000 pieces of evidence.

The Laboratory Division also assists the wider federal community, through such services as ongoing field investigations, surveillance photography, and crime scene and evidence examinations. In addition, since 1937, the Laboratory Division has offered its services free of charge to non-federal law enforcement agencies that lack their own forensic services. Its agents and professional personnel are available to testify in court. To use the FBI Laboratory's services, law enforcement agencies agree to accept the laboratory's test results as final, even if the outcome is not the one desired, and must make the results available to the suspect, even if they prove the suspect's innocence.

The Laboratory Division began in 1932 with a borrowed microscope and ultraviolet lights in one room of the Southern Railway Building that doubled as a smoking lounge. Shortly thereafter it acquired a comparison microscope, test tubes, and wax and plaster to make moulages (impressions of shoeprints or tire tracks). It also boasted a one-way glass for observing interviews or other purposes; it appeared to be a mirror on one side but was transparent on the other. At first, the laboratory's only full-time employee was Special Agent Charles Appel, a document examiner who, with the help of Special Agent Francis X. Fay, convinced FBI Director J. Edgar Hoover that the Bureau needed its own crime laboratory.

On October 1, 1933, the Bureau established a reference firearms collection with arms confiscated from persons under investigation for crimes. The collection was put on public display, and—much enhanced—it remains a feature of the FBI public tour. During the 1930s, the Laboratory Division also began keeping small animals, such as rabbits, to use in blood serum testing. A polygraph was added in 1938, and a year later, equipment for carrying out microchemical and spectrographic examinations.

Most crimes investigated by the FBI involve paper. The Document Section (now Investigative Operation and Support) handled this type of evidence. The section first became known to the public through the grand jury testimony of Special Agent Appel in the Lindbergh kidnapping case in 1933, in which he matched the handwriting of Bruno Richard Hauptmann to the handwriting on the ransom notes. By the mid-1990s, this section contained seven units that

break codes; identify the machines that create documents, such as typewriters, photocopiers, and facsimile machines; identify the paper and/or the ink; and compare handwriting.

The Photographic Operations Unit was established in 1935. Later it was split into the Photo Processing Unit, which develops both crime-scene and internal Bureau photos, and the Special Photography Unit, which handles evidence. In 1979, the Special Photography Unit began adapting digital imaging techniques developed by the National Aeronautics and Space Administration for crime-scene work, and another technique, photogrammetry, that the U.S. Geological Survey developed. The laboratory also produces special cameras for surveillance work. The growing use of vidcotape in surveillance cameras and by amateur photographers has produced chilling evidence as crimes are filmed. These are handled in the 1990s by the Video Enhancement Unit.

In 1937, the Technical Laboratory, as it was then called, or Crime Laboratory, as it was referred to popularly, hired its first full-time chemist, William Magee. Among his best-known cases, during World War II, he materialized "invisible" writing on the handkerchiefs of eight Nazi saboteurs in the George Dasch case (see page 60). His knowledge also helped convict the perpetrator of a 1955 airplane bombing over Colorado, the first case of sabotage in modern aviation history.

When the Bureau was reorganized into divisions, the laboratory was assigned to Division One, the Identification Division. It did not attain division status itself until 1943, as Division Seven, with Edmund P. Coffey as its first assistant director.

As the result of a major reorganization in the mid-1970s, the laboratory became a branch, along with Technical Services, in the Scientific and Technical Services Division, headed by Assistant Director Jay Cochran Jr. As the Scientific Branch, it consisted of three sections: Document, Scientific Analysis, and Technical Analysis. Shortly thereafter, FBI Director Clarence M. Kelley divided the Technical Services Division, reinstating the Laboratory Division as a division, under Assistant Director Thomas A. Kelleher.

The Polygraph Unit, formally established in 1978, is also part of the Laboratory Division. Housed in the Document Section, it maintained quality-control responsibility over the field agents trained to conduct polygraph examinations, as well as performing its own tests. Although FBI Director Hoover discouraged polygraphs after a 1938 Florida test implicated an innocent person in a kidnapping, while exonerating the perpetrator, the FBI continued to use the polygraph intermittently until 1964, when Hoover banned its use completely. Polygraph examinations were resumed in special situations beginning in 1971 under the insistence of President Richard Nixon, who wanted to identify the source of leaks of confidential White House information to journalists.

In 1983, the Scientific Analysis Section, with eight units, was the largest section in the Laboratory Division. The Forensic Science Research and Training Center, which opened in 1981 at the FBI Academy in Quantico, Virginia, was part of the Scientific Analysis Section at that time.

The FBI began accepting DNA (deoxyribonucleic acid) evidence on December 1, 1988, in order to aid state and local police agencies with identification. DNA analysis is the most significant of a number of recent advances in the analysis of body fluids, the type of evidence most often recovered from violent crime scenes. Before October 1, 1997, the FBI was able to state only a probability that a DNA sample came from a particular individual. Since that date, using more refined techniques and extremely strict criteria, FBI examiners have been able to state definitely whether an individual is the source of a particular DNA sample. A positive identification from a DNA sample was made in court for the first time in October 1997. In December 1997, a national DNA database of sex offenders went online. It was first used to identify a suspect in an unsolved crime on December 9, 1997.

In 1996, the Department of Justice's Office of Inspector General opened a review of the FBI Laboratory. As a result of its conclusions (presented in 1997) and its ongoing internal review processes, FBI Director Freeh instituted several major changes. Donald Kerr, a physicist with a background in nuclear energy and nuclear security, became, on October 21, 1997, the first non-agent to head the Laboratory Division. Additional non-agent professional scientists were hired to staff its units. For the first time, the FBI also sought independent accreditation. A larger facility for the laboratory is being built in Quantico, Virginia.

Bomb Data Center

Located in Quantico, Virginia, the Bomb Data Center serves as an international clearinghouse for bombing matters and began in the early 1970s as part of the Training Division. Reassigned to the Laboratory Division in 1987, it became part of the Forensic Science Research and Training Center upon its move to Quantico. The Bomb Data Center uses state-of-the-art training for public safety bomb disposal

technicians, develops bomb disposal technology, provides operational support to law enforcement agencies during special events like the Olympics or crisis management situations, and gathers and publishes statistics on the use of explosives and incendiary devices to commit violent crimes. Explosive bombings are illegal detonations of devices constructed with high or low explosive material; incendiary bombings involve actual attempted ignition of a device constructed with flammable materials designed to produce a burning effect. "Use of a bona fide device" distinguishes firebombings from other types of arson.

The Bomb Data Center also supports the development of procedures and equipment used by public safety bomb disposal technicians. Its training programs include the Hazardous Devices School, a responsibility mandated to the FBI by Congress in 1981. The Bomb Data Center also helped develop national guidelines for bomb technicians.

Forensic Science Research and Training Center

As the Laboratory Division's representative at the FBI Academy, the Forensic Science Research and Training Center provides research, training, and operational support in the forensic sciences for Bureau personnel and personnel of other law enforcement agencies and crime laboratories. In addition, the Forensic Science Research and Training Center identifies and sponsors international symposia to promote the sharing of technical and scientific information on forensic topics of contemporary interest. It publishes *Crime Laboratory Digest* quarterly, in cooperation with the American Society of Crime Laboratory Directors.

Legal Counsel and Legal Counsel Division (LCD)

For information on the Legal Counsel and Legal Counsel Division (LCD), see *Office of General Counsel.*

Legal Instruction Unit (LIU)

For information on the Legal Instruction Unit (LIU), see *Training Division.*

National Security Division

Formerly the Intelligence Division, the National Security Division (NSD) is responsible for collecting intelligence and carrying out counterintelligence measures related to national security and international terrorism. Renamed in October 1993, NSD coordinates investigative matters concerning foreign counterintelligence and domestic terrorism and is responsible for the FBI's Security Countermeasures Program. NSD also handles the Development of Espionage and Counterintelligence Awareness (DECA) program, which briefs security officers and employees of U.S. companies and other government agencies engaged in classified work on recent espionage cases and on the factors which often motivate individuals to commit espionage.

During World War I, the Bureau of Investigation had jurisdiction over national security matters such as espionage, sabotage, military-industry plant protection, and neutrality violations. After the war, fears of communism and anarchism, fueled by several bombings, resulted in the creation of the Radical Division in 1918, shortly thereafter renamed the General Intelligence Division. With J. Edgar Hoover as its effective head, the General Intelligence Division collected public-source information on radical groups and individuals and, by 1922, had compiled over 450,000 cards with this information. Responding to criticism of its role in the so-called Palmer Raids, Attorney General Harlan F. Stone abolished the division in 1924. Revived by President Franklin D. Roosevelt in the mid-1930s, it investigated fascist and communist factions in the United States that were perceived to threaten the nation's internal security. Division Five, which handled security matters, became the National Defense Division in 1941, and was renamed the Security Division in 1943.

The wartime Division Five handled investigations related to national security including passport and visa matters, and matters related to aliens, espionage, plant protection, or internal security, and was headed by D. M. Ladd from 1941 until 1949. Beginning in December 1946, Congress authorized the FBI to investigate applicants and employees engaged in atomic energy work, as well as some congressional staff personnel. In response to President Harry S. Truman's Executive Order 9835, promulgated in March 1947, which established the Federal Employees Loyalty Program, the FBI investigated all applicants or current employees at an agency's request, should derogatory information be developed during an initial screening process. The attorney general also directed the Bureau to handle Department of Justice personnel investigations. By December 1953, the division's basic objectives included developing intelligence information concerning the activities of individuals and organizations who aimed to subvert or overthrow the United States government, procuring legal evidence to sustain prosecutions, and ascertaining facts pertinent to the loyalty and security of federal employees and contractors engaged in atomic energy work or other

confidential national defense projects. The FBI's work in this regard increased in response to President Dwight D. Eisenhower's Executive Order 10450 of April 27, 1953, replacing the loyalty program with one that emphasized security. These background investigations were later handled by the Criminal Investigative Division.

The renamed Domestic Intelligence Division was organized in the mid-1960s into two branches: Espionage and Research had separate sections for the Soviet Union, its satellites, Latin America, and all other countries, while the Internal Security and Liaison Branch had sections for Internal Security, Liaison, and Subversive Control. In February 1973, FBI Director Clarence M. Kelley reorganized the intelligence functions of the FBI in response to criticism of the Domestic Intelligence Division's counterintelligence program (COINTELPRO). He created the Intelligence Division to handle foreign counterintelligence matters, while domestic intelligence matters became the responsibility of the General Investigative Division. From approximately 1979 until 1994, a special staff within the Intelligence Division (Office of General Counsel) advised on the legal ramifications of the division's work.

Counterintelligence Program (COINTELPRO)

Initially used against communists, counterintelligence programs (COINTELPROs) consisted of active countermeasures that were designed to disrupt and destroy specified subversive or terrorist organizations. At the request of President Lyndon B. Johnson, the FBI applied a COINTELPRO to the Ku Klux Klan, and these techniques were later used against various "new left" and militant black nationalist organizations that were suspected of terrorism. The FBI discontinued its COINTELPROs in the early 1970s after the existence of the program became publicly known.

Counterterrorism Investigations

The Antiterrorism and Effective Death Penalty Act (Public Law 104-132) of April 24, 1996, defines the federal crime of terrorism as "an offense that . . . is calculated to influence or affect the conduct of government by intimidation or coercion, or to retaliate against government conduct; and is in violation of at least one of a number of federal offenses including destruction of an aircraft, arson, assassination, kidnapping, conspiracy to injure the property of a foreign government, and destruction of communications facilities." Until Congress adopted this meaning, the FBI defined terrorism as "the unlawful use of force or violence against persons or property to intimidate or coerce a government, the civilian population, or any segment thereof, in furtherance of political or social objectives." The FBI is the lead federal law enforcement agency in identifying and neutralizing terrorist threats or investigating terrorist acts committed in the United States or involving American citizens. Its investigations and intelligence collection follow the Attorney General Guidelines on General Crimes, Racketeering Enterprises, and Domestic Security/Terrorism Investigations (the so-called Smith Guidelines). Until the establishment of the National Security Division, domestic terrorism was handled by the Criminal Investigative Division.

Foreign Counterintelligence

Through its National Security Division, the FBI is the lead foreign counterintelligence agency acting within the United States. Its mission is to identify and neutralize the threat posed by hostile intelligence services and their agents in the United States, and the threat posed by those nations, groups, and individuals that seek to foment international terrorism. To accomplish this mission, the FBI uses "penetration, disruption, expulsion, arrest, and prosecution." The Bureau also disseminates intelligence information to the policy-making levels of the federal government and to other executive branch intelligence agencies. With the collapse of the Soviet Union in the early 1990s, the FBI restructured its foreign counterintelligence strategy into "a flexible, centralized, requirements-driven program that targets threats posed by the intelligence activities of traditionally hostile countries and intelligence activities conducted by any foreign power directed against U.S. national security or national interests." While the Central Intelligence Agency is primarily responsible for coordinating counterintelligence matters abroad, the Intelligence Authorization Act of 1990 permits the FBI, in fulfillment of its law enforcement authority, to conduct espionage investigations outside the United States. In addition, the U.S. military, which also has espionage and counterintelligence responsibilities, also coordinates with the Bureau.

Office of Equal Employment Opportunity Affairs

The Office of Equal Employment Opportunity Affairs (OEEOA) monitors all aspects of FBI operations that could affect equality of opportunity for FBI employees and applicants in order to enforce prohibitions against discrimination in employment based on race, color, religion, age, gender (including sexual harassment), national origin, handicapped status, or any reprisals for previous involvement in a protected activity. To carry out this mission,

OEEOA processes complaints and conducts special programs including affirmative action, selective placement for individuals with disabilities, and an Upward Mobility Program. It also handles American Indian/Alaskan Native, Asian American/Pacific Islander, African American, Hispanic, and women's cultural, educational, and commemorative programs.

Initially a section in the Administrative Services Division, in 1989, Equal Employment Opportunity was elevated to an office reporting to the deputy director to ensure greater autonomy and increased access to the FBI director. FBI Director Sessions brought the office head, James R. Perez, from outside the FBI at the senior executive service level. Approximately three years later, Sessions designated Perez inspector in charge, giving him equivalent status with other office heads. Upon Perez's retirement in 1997, FBI Director Freeh named Kathleen Koch (an attorney and formerly special counsel in the Office of Special Counsel) as OEEOA chief.

Office of General Counsel

As part of a major reorganization of October 1993, the FBI's chief legal officer was renamed the "general counsel." In order to give the Bureau, for the first time, a chief legal officer who had both investigatory and litigation experience, Howard Shapiro, a former assistant U.S. attorney, was recruited by FBI Director Freeh from outside the FBI. The new general counsel inherited the apparatus that previously had been the Legal Counsel Division (LCD), which had been under an assistant director. The general counsel and his or her staff furnishes legal advice to the FBI director and other FBI officials, researches legal questions concerning law enforcement matters, and supervises civil litigation and administrative claims involving the FBI, its personnel, and its records. The Office of General Counsel also handles liaison with the Department of Justice and other agencies on legal matters. Freeh initiated a program of bringing non-agent attorneys into this office and sending special agents into the field. A Legal Instruction Unit, formally assigned to the Office of the General Counsel, is located in Quantico, Virginia, where it is part of the FBI Academy.

The legal counsel office was first established in 1971 with Dwight Dalbey as its head. Under FBI Director Clarence M. Kelley, the legal counsel received the title assistant director, and Legal Counsel became a division. Following Dalbey's retirement in 1973, John A. Mintz was appointed the new legal counsel and the unit was demoted to an office reporting to assistant to the director–deputy associate director for Investigations, Edward S. Miller. With a new reorganization in 1974, Kelley once again elevated Legal Counsel to division status, promoting Mintz to assistant director. The Legal Counsel Division then reported to associate director Richard G. Held and FBI Director Kelley. The Office of Congressional Affairs, which had replaced the Congressional Services Section of the External Affairs Division, was shortly thereafter moved into the Legal Counsel Division, as was the Freedom of Information Act Section. In 1976, however, the Freedom of Information Act Section was reassigned to the new Records Management Division, and in 1980, the Office of Congressional Affairs returned to the successor to the External Affairs Division, the Office of Congressional and Public Affairs.

Office of Professional Responsibility

The Office of Professional Responsibility (OPR), staffed by agents, reviews allegations of misconduct within the FBI. For nearly 20 years since its inception on October 4, 1976, OPR was assigned to the Inspection Division. On March 5, 1997, FBI Director Louis J. Freeh established it as an independent office headed by an assistant director and reporting to the deputy director. At that time, OPR was consolidated with the Administrative Summary Unit, which had formerly been located in the Personnel Division. OPR currently consists of two Internal Investigation Units, an Adjudication Unit, and an Administrative Unit. To ensure the independence of reviews, the Inspection Division manages the appellate process over OPR disciplinary rulings.

Office of Public and Congressional Affairs

The Office of Public and Congressional Affairs (OPCA) communicates information on FBI policy, investigations, services, programs, and accomplishments to the news media, Congress, and the public. It consists of several units, including the Congressional Affairs Office and the Freedom of Information/Privacy Acts Unit (FOI/PA).

As the focal point for all FBI contact with the legislative branch, the Congressional Affairs Office advocates the FBI's views on legislation, facilitates congressional oversight, prepares testimony for the FBI director and other officials, provides advice, develops policy, and responds to inquiries from members of Congress and congressional committees. In addition, the Congressional Affairs Office handles inquiries from the Department of Justice, the Office of Management and Budget, and the General Accounting Office.

Other OPCA units communicate information and serve as a liaison to the news media; authors; scholars; film, video, and movie productions; and the general public concerning FBI investigations, policy, operations, and accomplishments. Among the best known television programs made with OPCA cooperation were *America's Most Wanted* and *Unsolved Mysteries*. OPCA also handles the ABC radio show, *FBI, This Week*, a 60-second FBI report that, since 1946, follows in an unbroken stream of FBI radio shows, previously titled *FBI, Washington*. To assist the media, the Press Office prepares news releases and coordinates press conferences and interviews with Bureau officials. Another OPCA unit oversees the FBI director's speech commitments and prepares speeches and testimony for the FBI director and other top executives. In addition, OPCA units publicize the "Top Ten" most wanted fugitives, organize special programs, conduct special research projects, prepare articles and other written material, and maintain a small library and research collection. From 1984 to 1992, OPCA and its public affairs predecessors housed the FBI historian, a professional historian with professorial and archival experience, who handled specialized research, writing, lecturing, and liaison functions. OPCA also handles much of FBIHQ's ingoing and outgoing correspondence, arranges public exhibits, conducts public tours, and produces the FBI's internal employees' publication, *The Investigator*. In November 1996, OPCA acquired jurisdiction over the Freedom of Information/Privacy Acts unit (FOI/PA).

OPCA is the most recent incarnation of the Crime Records Section or Crime Records Division. In 1972, acting director of the FBI L. Patrick Gray III abolished the Crime Records Division, put relations with the media in his own office, assigned the Crime Records Division's correspondence responsibilities to the office of the associate director, and moved the tours function into the Administrative Division. White House name checks went to the General Investigative Division, fugitive publicity to the Special Investigative Division, and the Training Division and Files and Communications Division assumed most of the Crime Records Division's editorial functions.

FBI Director Clarence M. Kelley reversed Gray's action and established the External Affairs Division, putting public contacts once again into a single entity that reported to the assistant to the director–deputy associate director for Administration, Thomas J. Jenkins, and consisted of the Congressional Services and Press Services Offices, Correspondence and Tours, and the Research Section. For a brief time, this division supervised the Freedom of Information Act Section before that section was transferred to the Office of Legal Counsel in 1974. The following year, the Congressional Services Office moved to the renamed Legal Counsel Division. A Crime Resistance Program resided in External Affairs between 1975 and 1979, except for a short period when it reported to the FBI director. In 1977, Kelley created a separate Speech Unit. The same year, however, FBI Director Kelley abolished the External Affairs Division, converting it into the Public Affairs Office containing Media Services and the Research Unit, with an inspector in charge at its head. Its 95 employees became part of the director's office.

Under FBI Director Webster, a series of reorganizations in 1980 brought Correspondence and Tours back into Public Affairs to create, with the inclusion of congressional liaison matters, the Office of Congressional and Public Affairs. By October 1981, the office was headed by an assistant director in charge (later an assistant director), a deputy assistant director was added, and it remained in the director's office. In January 1984, an official historian was hired as part of the Research Unit in the Office of Congressional and Public Affairs. In 1988, the Research Unit expanded the remnants of the Crime Resistance Program into a Drug Demand Reduction Program, renamed the Research/Drug Demand Reduction Program Unit. The following year, the Office of Congressional and Public Affairs once again split into two offices, the Office of Public Affairs and the Congressional Affairs Office, each headed by an inspector in charge. In June 1992, the two offices were reunited, however, as OPCA.

Crime Records Division

Variously known as the Crime Records Section or Crime Records Division, Crime Records handled public affairs for the Bureau for most of J. Edgar Hoover's tenure as FBI director. The significance of a public face for the FBI was stressed by the Department of Justice's first public affairs representative, Henry Suydam, and to J. Edgar Hoover directly by crime writer Courtney Riley Cooper. Under the supervision of Assistant Director Louis B. Nichols during the 1940s and 1950s, the FBI produced its own public relations material, educational brochures, and books on topics like juvenile delinquency or the dangers of communism, as well as influenced movie, radio, and television programs concerning the FBI. In addition, Crime Records responded to criticism of the FBI either directly or through media representatives friendly to the Bureau.

Crime Records evolved from a section known as the Publications Section, which was formed in 1935 to coordinate public affairs interests. This section originally consisted of a Correspondence Unit, a Library and Publications Unit, and a Publicity Unit, with a staff of six special agents, six stenographers, and six typists. The Research Division began on July 13, 1936, absorbing the Publications Section and adding a Crime Statistics Section, as part of the Administrative Division until it officially became the Crime Records Division on September 16, 1938. In 1945, it once again became a section in the Records and Communications Division. In 1953, this section, under Chief Milton A. Jones, had four units: a 5-agent Correspondence Unit, with a clerical staff of 27; the Research Unit, with 9 agents and a clerical staff of 5; the 4-agent Special Productions Unit; and the Library, headed by an agent assisted by 6 clerks. The Publications Unit was established that year to handle *The Investigator* and *The Law Enforcement Bulletin*, which previously were in different units.

In 1958, Crime Records had five units, which processed and responded to incoming general correspondence from the public, handled book reviews, maintained the Bureau library, conducted tours, updated and distributed the *Abridged History of the FBI* and *Significant Dates in FBI History,* conducted research for books published under the director's byline (for example, *Masters of Deceit* in 1958), advised television programs, wrote memoranda and articles on law enforcement topics as well as speeches for Bureau executives, and handled liaison with law enforcement–related associations such as the American Bar Association and the National Association of Attorneys General. In addition, since 1950, it handled the Most Wanted Fugitives program. It became a division once more by January 1959, and in February 1960, it was divided into the Crime Research Section and Correspondence and Tours Section, with a total of 102 employees. The following year, the section assumed responsibility for the *Uniform Crime Reports* (see *Criminal Justice Information Services Division*). In 1971, the division also handled congressional liaison and contained an Administrative Review Unit to consolidate outside contacts. Acting Director of the FBI L. Patrick Gray III briefly renamed the division the Crime Research Division in October 1972, before abolishing the division altogether. At that time, it had 200 employees.

Freedom of Information/Privacy Acts (FOI/PA) Section

The Freedom of Information Act (FOIA) and Privacy Act, in general, entitle the public to request information created and/or maintained by federal agencies and departments. When the FOIA became law in 1966, all FBI records were exempt. Congress broadened the FOIA's mandated disclosure requirements in 1974 by amendments that opened FBI records to review. Concurrently, Congress enacted the Privacy Act of 1974 to bar the government from collecting intelligence information on individuals exercising their constitutionally protected rights.

Individuals may request government information about themselves under either the FOIA or the Privacy Act. In addition, under the FOIA, they may request government information that does not fall under any of the act's specified exemptions. To process FOIA and Privacy Act requests, the FBI employs a large staff of non-agent analysts in FBIHQ, as well as non-agent analysts in the field. Agents and support staff supervise the FOI/PA's units, including the FOI/PA Reading Room in FBIHQ, in which the public may review previously released documents. As of May 1996, FOI/PA received, on average, 50 requests per day. The FOIA resided, at various times, in the offices or divisions handling public or legal affairs. However, it reported to the Records Management Division and its successor, the Information Management Division, for 20 years. In November 1996, the FOI/PA Section moved from the Information Management Division to the Office of Public and Congressional Affairs.

The Investigator

The employees' publication of the FBI, *The Investigator,* began on April 4, 1932, in response to an employee suggestion and was sponsored by the United States Bureau of Investigation Athletic Association (later, the FBI Recreation Association). Its purpose is "to enhance the mission of the FBI and to boost morale by showing cohesiveness of employees working as a team." The first issue, which appeared on May 9, 1932, consisted of a single sheet titled "Bureau Bulletin," and contained a statement from the FBI director and a request for suggestions for its name. At first, it concentrated on sports, but by the second year, interesting cases and personnel sketches were included, and it came out monthly. Staff artists illustrated the early issues, but by 1935, it contained photographs. In the 1950s, photos and stories about employees and their families became prominent. The magazine became an official FBI publication in October 1978, at which time it no longer was made available to retired or former employees.

Most Wanted Fugitives Program ("The Top Ten")

This program, currently handled in the Office of Public and Congressional Affairs, publicizes particularly dangerous fugitives who might not otherwise merit nationwide attention. Initiated on March 14, 1950, the program sought to bring alleged criminals to public attention and to involve the public in tracking and locating fugitives. As of December 1996, 419 of a total of 448 "Top Ten" most wanted fugitives had been apprehended or had surrendered to authorities. Citizen cooperation played a role in 131 of these apprehensions. In 1953, for example, the *Saturday Evening Post* ran an article on the Ten Most Wanted Fugitives program, and as a result, within 24 hours, two of the featured individuals were apprehended. On four occasions, fugitives presumed to be alive were removed from the list when they no longer fit the criteria for inclusion. By 1996, television spots and the Internet were also employed to publicize these fugitives, notably the television shows *America's Most Wanted* and *Unsolved Mysteries*. A significant number of apprehensions occurred as a direct result of these programs, including one individual who turned himself in after seeing his case on the preview advertisements for the program. Similarly, in 1996, the year after the FBI began using the Internet to publicize the most wanted fugitives, Leslie Isben Rogge, then living in Guatemala, became the first apprehension attributable to the FBI's Internet site; see <http://www.fbi.gov/mostwant/tenlist/htm> and <http://www.amw.com>.

Preliminary recommendations of fugitives for inclusion on this list are made by agents in the Criminal Investigative Division familiar with the Bureau's fugitives, personnel in the Office of Public and Congressional Affairs, and agents in the field. The Criminal Investigative Division's assistant director and the Office of Public and Congressional Affairs inspector in charge approve the final list, which then must be approved by the FBI director.

FBI Tour

FBI tours were formally inaugurated on June 30, 1937, to service requests from groups such as the annual Boy Scout Jamboree. Placed in the Crime Records Section, the purpose of the FBI Tour was "to make the public aware of the Bureau's responsibilities and services, and to alert [visitors] to the criminal and domestic security dangers that threatened society" (see Exhibit 5.5). By opening the FBI to the public in this way, FBI Director Hoover also wanted to dispel the idea that the Bureau was a "secret police" agency.

Now attracting approximately one-half million visitors a year, in 1939, an average of 591 persons daily toured the FBI's Identification and Laboratory Divisions. Initially, the

Bureau scheduled tours twice a day, at 10 a.m. and 2 p.m. By 1940, however, tours were conducted as soon as a group of 15 to 20 people gathered. Clerical employees (until 1972, all male) handled the tours on a rotating basis. Conducting tours served as a stepping stone for clerks to become agents. As today, public tours ran only during the FBI's normal working hours. Prior to World War II, when FBIHQ operated six days a week, tours also ran on Saturdays. Tours were suspended completely from 1942 to 1945, and after World War II, with the reinstitution of a 40-hour work week, they ran Monday through Friday. When the Bureau moved to the J. Edgar Hoover FBI Building, new exhibits were added showing the role of women in the FBI and emphasizing some of its more recent priorities, such as civil rights.

Personnel Division

Created in October 1993 from the Administrative Services Division, the division handles personnel matters. Its first head was Manuel "Manny" Gonzalez.

Special Intelligence Service (SIS)

From 1940 to 1946, the FBI's Special Intelligence Service (SIS) collected intelligence in Latin and South America. Under orders from President Franklin D. Roosevelt, its mission was to destroy the Axis espionage and propaganda networks. This was the only period until 1985 in which the FBI had jurisdiction outside of the United States.

Percy Foxworth served as the first head of SIS. At its peak, it had 360 agents and its staff totaled more than 500 in the United States and abroad. Because its operatives had cover identities, and because the Special Intelligence Service was treated as super-secret, its agents were officially removed from the Bureau rolls and are not reported in the total number of agents listed in FBI annual reports. Special Intelligence Service agents were instrumental in shutting down or controlling German radio transmissions, thereby containing the German espionage system. In addition, the Special Intelligence Service helped keep German-sympathizing Latin American countries like Argentina and Chile from becoming allied with the Axis.

Special Squads (Flying Squads)

For information on Special Squads (Flying Squads), see *Criminal Investigative Division (CID)*.

Technical Services Division

For information on the Technical Services Division, see *Information Resources Division (IRD)*.

Training Division

The Training Division administers the FBI Academy located in Quantico, Virginia; conducts and coordinates training for FBI in-service and new agent personnel; and provides training assistance, upon request, to local, county, state, and international law enforcement personnel throughout the world. To accomplish its mission, it conducts training courses at the FBI Academy and provides academy instructors to field divisions for off-site training. These instructors have adjunct status at the University of Virginia, enabling certain students to receive academic credit for their courses. In addition, the FBI Academy provides research, investigative, and operational support to the field, and functions as an international forum for seeking and identifying solutions to current and emerging problems facing the criminal justice system.

The Training Division currently consists of a number of units, several of which report to other divisions. The Administrative Services Unit coordinates classes, supervises all the programs, and is responsible for academy safety and security matters. (The physical plant, however, comes under the jurisdiction of the Facilities Planning, Construction, and Maintenance Unit.) The Economic and Financial Crimes Training Unit conducts training to support white-collar crime and drug-related financial investigations. To help law enforcement personnel and agencies further their investigatory skills, communicate their mission, and conduct training, the Education and Communication Arts Unit provides training in public speaking, media management, informant development, interrogation, and effective writing. The Firearms Training Unit trains all new agent and FBI Academy classes in weapons use, conducts specialized in-service classes for FBI agents, holds classes in the field, manages the annual firearms program, and conducts research and development regarding weapons, ammunition, and related equipment. The Management Science Unit presents classes in managerial instruction for agents and support staff and produces the in-house magazine *Management Quarterly*. Carrying out a variety of responsibilities, the Operations Resource and Assessment Unit designs and conducts research projects related to policy making and operational decisions in the wider law enforcement community; designs, selects, and monitors personnel for undercover operations; evaluates techniques, statistics, and various field operations; and maintains the FBI Academy Library. The Special Operations and Research Unit provides training and research in all of the various components of crisis and major case management within the FBI and serves as liaison with the domestic and foreign crisis management community. Other units include the Behavioral Sciences Services Unit, the Bomb Data Center, the Forensic Science Research and Training Center, the Legal Instruction Unit, and the National Academy Unit.

Many of the earliest agents lacked prior investigative, legal, or accounting experience. Nonetheless, the Department of Justice provided no training. Bureau Director William Burns started the first formal training course for special agents. Lasting only a few days followed by practical work with experienced agents, these early classes were run out of the New York field office.

In 1928, Bureau of Investigation Director J. Edgar Hoover revived and expanded this formal training. This course took place in Washington, D.C., and on the Marine Corps base in Quantico, Virginia. In 1940, new agents attended training school for 14 weeks (16 weeks a year later), including 600 hours of classroom instruction and practical training with experienced agents from the Washington, D.C., field office. When the United States entered World War II, the FBI reduced new agents' training to 8 weeks—6 for National Academy graduates. New agent training returned to 16 weeks by 1953. Varying thereafter, the new agent training time currently is 15 weeks.

Agents did not begin formal firearms training until 1934, when, on June 18, Congress authorized Bureau agents to carry guns. After that year, firearms training, most of which took place at the FBI Academy in Quantico, included revolvers, shotguns, gas guns, automatic rifles, machine guns, and submachine guns. Agents had to be able to fire day or night; from each hand; and while standing, kneeling, lying prone, or in a moving automobile. By 1939, the FBI instituted a "Kidnap-Squad School" to train its Special Squad members (see *Criminal Investigative Division*). Three schools of 30 men each, representing field offices from all over the country, were held in 1939. Beginning in 1934, agents, for the rest of their active career, had to qualify in firearms (in 1939, 12 times a year for sidearms and 7 times a year for heavy arms; in the late 1990s, 4 times a year for a pistol or revolver and 2 times a year for a shotgun or automatic weapon).

In 1942, new agent training included 3 weeks at Quantico and 13 weeks in Washington, D.C. Classes were held from 9:00 a.m. to 9:00 p.m., with one hour each for lunch and dinner; on Saturdays, classes ended at 6:00 p.m., and on Sundays, which Assistant Director Hugh Clegg described as the trainees' day of rest, classes lasted from 1:00 p.m. to 6:00 p.m. In every course, a score of 85 constituted a passing grade. Each student received two large looseleaf notebooks containing *The Manual of Rules and Regulations* and *The Manual of Instructions,* a briefcase with a .38-caliber police revolver, a holster, and an agent badge.

During the 1940s, every new agent was required to return for training after serving between 5 and 12 months in the field. More experienced agents had to take in-service training at least every two years to be familiarized with the latest legal and scientific developments affecting their work. In 1943, agents required in-service training every 18 months. By the 1970s, the intervals increased, owing to cost. Currently, agents return to Quantico periodically for in-service training and also attend specialized regional field classes. They must also pass a fitness test twice a year.

Child Abduction and Serial Killers Unit (CASKU)

Consisting of a unit chief and 12 agents, 9 of whom hold advanced degrees, "CASKU's primary objective is the safe return of the victim." Created by Congress in 1994, this task force is staffed by at least two FBI agents, plus representatives from the Bureau of Alcohol, Tobacco and Firearms; the Drug Enforcement Administration; the Inspection entity of the U.S. Postal Service; the U.S. Customs Service; the U.S. Marshals Service; and the U.S. Secret Service.

Critical Incident Response Group

The Critical Incident Response Group (CIRG) was inaugurated on April 14, 1994, and is located near the FBI Academy in Quantico, Virginia. It consolidates all of the Bureau's units and functions that deal with crisis management, including a tactical component and an operational support and special investigation entity. Headed in 1996 by Robin Montgomery, its first special agent in charge, the CIRG oversees the Tactical Support Branch that includes the Hostage Rescue Team, the Special Weapons and Tactics (SWAT) Training Unit, and the Special Detail Unit. The Critical Response Team serves to back up field office SWAT teams, while the Special Investigations Branch, which includes the Profiling and Behavioral Assessment Unit from the National Center for Analysis of Violent Crime, as well as the units covering Child Abduction and Serial Killers, Crisis Management, Special Operations, and the Undercover Safeguard Unit. In emergency situations, CIRG's SAC also commands other crisis response groups such as the Rapid Start Team, which consists of computer specialists from the Information Resources Division.

Engineering Research Facility

Currently part of the Information Resources Division, but located on the FBI Academy grounds, the Engineering Research Facility's staff includes "technically trained agents," engineers, mathematicians, technicians, analysts, and support services employees.

Executive Training Programs

Drawing on his experience as a police chief, in 1976, FBI Director Clarence M. Kelley inaugurated the 15-day National Executive Institute to meet the needs of the chief executive officers of the largest American law enforcement organizations. A program for mid-sized agency executives, the Law Enforcement Executive Development Seminar, began in 1981, and a one-week National Law Institute for police legal advisers and prosecutors started in 1984.

FBI National Academy

The FBI provides courses of instruction at the FBI Academy in Quantico, Virginia, and throughout the United States, to improve the administrative, investigative, management, and technical capabilities of state and local criminal justice practitioners (see Exhibit 6.2). This course consists of an 11-week multidisciplinary program for seasoned law enforcement managers who are nominated by their agency heads, based on their potential for continuing advancement. Since the opening of the FBI Academy facility in Quantico

Exhibit 6.2 **Official Seal of the FBI National Academy,** *Courtesy of the FBI*

in 1972, four sessions of approximately 250 students each are usually offered each year. The FBI pays all expenses for the students, with the exception of travel expenses for U.S. federal and foreign government personnel.

In addition to its FBI National Academy classes, the Bureau conducts specialized schools and courses for law enforcement officers concerning such criminal justice topics as hostage negotiation, computer crimes, interpersonal violence, criminal psychology, and forensic science. Agents in the field also instruct law enforcement personnel in subjects such as forensic science, identification matters, *Uniform Crime Reports* statistics, arson, death investigation, and instructor development. In 1994, 115,500 police officers received training from the FBI's Field Police Training Program.

First called the National Police Academy, the FBI National Academy (the name changed in 1945) played a major role in professionalizing law enforcement throughout the United States and eventually throughout the world, including Europe (after the 1990s, the former Soviet Union and the formerly communist Eastern European countries), Central and South America, the Caribbean, Africa, Asia, the Middle East, and Oceania.

The first class took place at the U.S. Marine Corps Base in Quantico in 1935, attended by 23 police officers, who took a 12-week course (see Exhibit 7.6 on page 254). From its earliest days, dormitories were provided, giving officers and agents opportunities to exchange experiences on an informal basis. The close relationships that developed have enhanced interagency and FBI-police cooperation worldwide.

When the National Police Academy began, only a few police departments in the United States gave their officers any formal training, and few universities offered criminal justice programs. In many parts of the country, police departments lacked educational or practical requirements. FBI officials sought to remedy this situation by bringing experienced police officers to Quantico for training by experts in forensics and other aspects of investigation. In turn, the graduates would return to their home territories and train other members of their forces. Agents eventually began conducting refresher courses in the field and abroad to keep National Academy graduates current on legal and scientific developments.

When the FBI suddenly needed to expand its agent force with the entry of the United States into World War II, qualified academy graduates were recruited to become agents after an abbreviated training program. By 1943, 131 of the total 704 National Academy graduates held positions in the Bureau. The wartime FBI also ran National Defense Training Schools handled by its 56 field offices. These regional meetings sought to qualify police officers to assist the federal government with such law enforcement matters as Selective Service violations and prostitution around military camps.

In 1972, the FBI National Academy's central facilities were moved out of the Marine Corps area and onto its own campus in a formerly wooded area near the firearms ranges. This enabled the classes to expand fourfold.

Hostage Rescue Team

The Hostage Rescue Team, a special counterterrorist unit, offers a tactical option using trained law enforcement officers. The philosophy behind the Hostage Rescue Team was to create a "special forces" unit that corresponded to the military special forces. Unlike the military, however, Hostage Rescue Team members, as FBI agents, can make arrests and testify in court, and are trained in the legal and constitutional implications of their actions.

In January 1983, Attorney General William French Smith authorized the Hostage Rescue Team in anticipation of four special events the next year: the Democratic and Republican presidential conventions; the New Orleans, Louisiana, World's Fair; and the summer Olympics in Los Angeles. As originally conceived, its 42 agents would work half the time as members of the Hostage Rescue Team and the other half as street agents assigned to the Washington, D.C., field office. The first Hostage Rescue Team head, Danny O. Coulson, was officially an assistant special agent in charge in the Washington, D.C., field office. It soon became apparent that the Hostage Rescue Team was a full-time job, and thereafter, its agents were assigned formally to the FBI Academy. Today, the Hostage Rescue Team is part of the Critical Incident Response Group, with over 90 agents, including an assistant special agent in charge, supervisory special agents, agent staff positions, and approximately 70 agents. The Hostage Rescue Team is structured to respond to a crisis within four hours of the request. In addition, it conducts regular research and development to enhance its tactical capabilities.

FBI Law Enforcement Bulletin

Issued monthly as a service to law enforcement agencies throughout the country, the *FBI Law Enforcement Bulletin* started in 1932. Originally titled *Fugitives Wanted by the Police,* the magazine initially featured only the fingerprint descriptions and classifications of "the most flagrant violators of laws in the United States." The early issues promoted descriptions from those localities that lacked the means to publicize their own most wanted fugitives themselves and also included articles on scientific crime detection and law enforcement. In 1935, the title changed to *FBI Law Enforcement Bulletin.* In 1940, it began including descriptions of missing persons and other useful information for police officers, such as a listing of the license plates from each state and their colors. By 1972, it had achieved a circulation of approximately 74,000 copies a month. Today it not only reaches law enforcement personnel and offices by mail, but is available over the Internet <http://www.fbi.gov/leb/leb.htm>. Its production is supervised by the Legal Instruction Unit, which is assigned to the FBI Academy.

Legal Instruction Unit

Formally belonging to the Office of the General Counsel, the Legal Instruction Unit faculty provides instruction for new agents in both the FBI and the Drug Enforcement Administration, the FBI National Academy, and in-service and specialized schools for agents and other law enforcement agencies. It also supervises the National Law Institute (a one-week course for prosecutors and law enforcement legal advisers), conducts legal research, produces "Legal Digest" articles for *FBI Law Enforcement Bulletin*, publishes monographs and articles for attorneys practicing in a law enforcement environment, and updates the *FBI Legal Handbook.* The Legal Instruction Unit took over publication of *FBI Law Enforcement Bulletin* from the Office of Public and Congressional Affairs in the mid-1990s.

National Center for the Analysis of Violent Crime

The National Center for the Analysis of Violent Crime is a law enforcement–oriented resource center that consolidates research, training, investigative, operational, and support functions to assist those law enforcement agencies confronted with unusual, high-risk, vicious, or repetitive (serial) crimes. Established at the FBI National Academy in Quantico, Virginia, on July 10, 1984, the National Center for the Analysis of Violent Crime received national attention from the Thomas Harris book, *The Silence of the Lambs,* and the movie of the same name. Initially focused on unsolved murders, it uses sophisticated behavioral science techniques and a complex computer model. The unit does not catch criminals itself, but instead advises the investigating agencies, most often local police departments, through the Violent Criminal Apprehension Program. The unit assists in focusing investigations, suggests proactive techniques that might convince a criminal to surface or confess, and formulates strategies designed to elicit a defendant's criminal personality in court. Organizationally, the National Center for the Analysis of Violent Crime is located in the Profiling and Behavioral Assessment Unit of the Forensic Science Research and Training Center.

The center arose in the late 1970s and 1980s from the Behavioral Science Unit, in 1996 called the Investigative Support Unit. Although the profiling technique had its origins in the fiction of Edgar Allan Poe and Sir Arthur Conan Doyle, the first major use of the technique in the United States was in the New York "Mad Bomber" case in 1957, in which psychiatrist James A. Brussel helped the police to narrow their search for a suspect. Behavioral Science Unit instructor Special Agent Howard Teton subsequently consulted Brussel to develop the profiling technique for the FBI. With Special Agent Patrick Mullaney, Teton represented the first wave of modern criminal behavioral science. Two other Behavioral Science Unit instructors, Richard Ault and Robert Ressler, composed the second wave by applying the techniques in a manner more useful to law enforcement worldwide. Special Agents John Douglas and Robert Ressler created a database by interviewing serial killers, which was further refined by Behavioral Science Unit instructor Roy Hazelwood and Ann Burgess of the University of Pennsylvania School of Nursing and associate director of nursing research for the Boston Department of Health and Hospitals.

In the mid-1980s, the Behavioral Science Unit divided into the Behavioral Science Instruction, Behavioral Science Research, and Behavioral Science Investigative Support Units. The Instructional Services Unit contains a criminal-personality profiling division, the Violent Criminal Apprehension Program, and Engineering Services. The National Center for the Analysis of Violent Crime also provides psychological services to FBI employees, students attending courses at the FBI National Academy, and, upon request, law enforcement officers in other agencies in need of debriefing or counseling following critical incidents.

Special Weapons and Tactics (SWAT)

The first FBI in-service for Special Weapons and Tactics (SWAT) training was held July 9, 1973, for agents from field offices in Albuquerque, New Mexico; Denver, Colorado; Kansas City, Missouri; Omaha, Nebraska; Phoenix, Arizona; and Washington, D.C.

Field Divisions

Introduction

Field offices and the resident agencies within their divisions conduct the actual investigations of violations of statutes under the FBI's jurisdiction, as well as follow leads in background investigations and other security matters. The results of their investigations are then furnished for review by the appropriate FBIHQ division. In 1997, the FBI had 56 field divisions (see the Appendix at the end of this chapter), selected according to crime trends, based on the need for regional geographic centralization and the need to manage resources efficiently. With the exception of the New York City and Washington, D.C., field offices, a special agent in charge oversees each field division, aided by one or more assistant special agents in charge (see *Position Descriptions*). Squad supervisors follow assistant special agents in charge in rank and handle the investigative work, while an office service manager, the highest-level support employee, administers the support operations.

The special agent in charge assigns each squad specific violations to investigate, with the violations prioritized according to FBIHQ policy and the most pressing concerns of that field division. Although the FBI did not have narcotics jurisdiction until 1982, in 1972, Acting Director of the FBI L. Patrick Gray III assigned an agent in each field office to ensure that narcotics violation information would be systematically reported to the appropriate agency. Today, offices typically assign agents to be recruiters, media representatives, legal advisers, training coordinators, and Drug Demand Reduction representatives, among other responsibilities. One agent in a smaller office may have a range of responsibilities; the largest offices, on the other hand, may assign several agents as full-time legal advisers, recruiters, or media representatives. In the field, special agents in charge and senior resident agents are directed to become acquainted both with their counterparts in law enforcement agencies and all the important officials and citizens in their area. These officials and citizens are all considered "special contacts," whose cooperation may be essential and who may be useful sources in conducting investigations or for other needs.

In October 1992, the largest field offices were, in order, New York City, Washington, D.C., and Los Angeles; the smallest were Jackson, Mississippi; Mobile, Alabama; and Anchorage, Alaska.

The Bureau's first head, Stanley W. Finch, wanted to create field offices in Chicago and New York in 1908, but was overruled by the attorney general. By August 1920, however, divisional headquarters had been established in

- Atlanta, Georgia
- Baltimore, Maryland
- Chicago, Illinois
- Cincinnati, Ohio
- Kansas City, Missouri
- New York, New York
- Portland, Oregon
- San Antonio, Texas
- San Francisco, California

In 1934, the Bureau had 39 field offices located in major cities, all of which are still in existence today, with the exception of the St. Paul office, which moved to Minneapolis. Five years later, the number grew to 42 offices with the addition of Huntington, West Virginia; Des Moines, Iowa; and Aberdeen, South Dakota. By 1940, 10 new field offices had opened, including Grand Rapids, Michigan; Juneau, Alaska; and Panama, Canal Zone, while Sioux Falls had replaced Aberdeen in South Dakota. Providence, Rhode Island, became a field office in the fall of 1942, followed by Norfolk, Virginia. By 1944, the FBI had 57 field offices, with the addition of Albuquerque and the substitution of Anchorage for Juneau. FBI Director J. Edgar Hoover reinstated the Jackson, Mississippi, field office in 1964, in response to Ku Klux Klan terrorism and civil rights violations. By 1968, the FBI had 58 field offices, and by 1971, the total reached 59. In 1988, the Bureau contracted once again by consolidating the Alexandria, Virginia, and the Washington, D.C., field offices, and later turned the responsibilities of the Butte, Montana, field office to the Salt Lake City, Utah, field office, and the Savannah, Georgia, field office to the Atlanta, Georgia, field office.

Resident Agencies

In addition to the field office, which serves as each field division's headquarters, approximately 400 resident agencies—satellite offices—also handle the workload in the field. A resident agency may consist of one agent, or it may have a dozen or more agent and support employees. The larger resident agencies have a supervisory senior resident agent who manages and coordinates resident agency activities and reports to the field office. Resident agency sites are selected according to crime trends and to ensure the efficient use of available resources. Resident agents located in smaller cities or towns usually become well known in their communities. Many agents trace their desire to join the FBI to their admiration for the local resident agent.

These subsidiary offices report to the special agents in charge of their divisions. Some resident agencies are the size of small field offices. Many, however, have only one resident agent. In multiple-agent offices, the agent with the longest service holds the title of senior resident agent. This position is not comparable to that of special agent in charge, who, with field office supervisors, has responsibility for the resident agents. Instead, the senior resident agent handles administration and coordination, as well as supervises the support staff. Resident agencies are found both in population centers and in places likely to produce leads. For example, major airports may contain resident agencies to handle interstate transportation of stolen property, theft from interstate shipment, or other violations likely to occur at a transportation hub. Some resident agencies are near college campuses that do classified research or that have a significant population of foreign students. Others are on or near large federal reservations, where all crimes are federal crimes. While the largest resident agencies may have squads, just like field offices, most resident agents must be true generalists and handle all the leads that come their way.

In 1971, after an activist group calling itself Citizens' Commission to Investigate the FBI broke into the Media, Pennsylvania, resident agency and stole unsecured documents, FBI Director J. Edgar Hoover ordered the closure of 100 of the Bureau's 536 resident agencies.

Field Offices

Some of the notable FBI field offices are discussed below (see also the Appendix at the end of this chapter).

Albany, New York

The Albany field office was established prior to October 1918. In 1924, the Albany office, then located in the Federal Building, absorbed the Springfield, Massachusetts, field office and handled western Massachusetts. The Albany office was closed on March 21, 1925, and its territory was divided among the Boston, Buffalo, and New York City offices. The Albany office reopened December 13, 1939, in response to the greater responsibilities brought on by World War II. Today, its territory covers eastern New York state north of Dutchess County, and Vermont.

Anchorage, Alaska

The Juneau, Alaska, field office preceded the Anchorage office; it opened May 25, 1937, while Alaska was a United States territory. At that time, no public telephone communication existed between Alaska and the "lower 48" states. Calls had to be made from the Army Signal Corps Office, and mail was delivered by boat from Seattle three or four times a week. The Department of Justice authorized a direct telephone line in July 1937. Although a lack of funds forced its closing in November 1938, the Juneau office reopened in July 1939.

The Anchorage office opened as Alaska's field office February 20, 1944, and Juneau became a resident agency. On June 22, 1970, its communications improved with the installation of a Telex machine, and further improved when, in the 1980s, it became linked with other Bureau computers through the Field Office Information Management System.

Among its major cases, the Anchorage office handled the investigation of the largest oil spill in U.S. history, which occurred when the supertanker *Exxon Valdez* collided with a reef in Alaskan waters. The investigation, one of the first federal investigations of a major environmental crime, resulted in criminal and civil convictions.

Burdena G. Pasenelli was the first woman to become a special agent in charge with her appointment to the Anchorage field office in May 1992.

Atlanta, Georgia

The Atlanta field office opened in 1920. One of the FBI's best-known cases concluded in 1981 when a Fulton County (Georgia) grand jury returned a two-count indictment against Wayne Williams, a serial murderer who allegedly killed a number of Atlanta boys, although he was tried and convicted of only two murders. On December 7, 1989, Atlanta absorbed the Savannah, Georgia, field office, which had been in existence for 50 years.

Butte, Montana

The Butte field office, legendary as the outpost to which FBI Director Hoover banished personnel for disciplinary reasons, later became a popular office of preference. While its opening date has not been ascertained, the first reference to it appears in 1913. The Butte office closed in the late 1920s, and Montana investigations were handled by the Portland, Oregon, field office into the 1930s, when FBI Director Hoover reestablished it. In 1989, it lost its status as a field office and became a resident agency in the Salt Lake City

field division. On January 18, 1995, the resident agency closed but the office reopened as an Information Technology Center.

In 1948, Butte's geographical territory included the states of Montana and Idaho, Yellowstone and Glacier National Parks, seven Indian reservations, the Custer Battlefield National Monument, and three U.S. Air Force Strategic Air Command bases. It also handled liaison with the Canadian provinces of Alberta and Saskatchewan. At one point, Butte had 14 resident agencies.

The secretary for Butte's special agent in charge for 40 years, Myrtle Dreyfus, may hold the distinction of being the first female acting special agent in charge. On December 8, 1941, all the agents, including the special agent in charge, were occupied rounding up German and Japanese aliens who might pose a danger, with the United States officially at war. With no one else in the office, she handled the teletypes, and signed at least one document "Acting Special Agent in Charge Dreyfus."

From the 1940s through the 1970s, approximately 30–40 agents were assigned to Butte at any one time. Because the Atomic Energy Commission had a huge facility in the Idaho desert, the Butte office handled its applicant investigations. During this period, over 50 agents worked in the Butte office.

Houston, Texas

The Houston field office opened in July 1940, with a territory covering Texas from the Louisiana border to Beaumont and south almost to the Mexican border. During the office's early years, the agents primarily spent their time investigating criminal cases, often cooperating with the Texas Rangers on bank robberies and other cases. Their work expanded with the development of the Johnson Space Center of the National Aeronautics and Space Administration in the 1960s.

Jackson, Mississippi

The Jackson field office reopened in 1964 in response to President Lyndon B. Johnson's insistence that the FBI play a greater role in combating the civil rights violations and outright terrorism directed toward African Americans in general and white civil rights workers in the state. Johnson sent FBI Director J. Edgar Hoover in the presidential plane to personally open the office and to talk to state and local law enforcement executives. From 1964 to 1971, approximately 250 acts of violence per year in Jackson's territory warranted the FBI's attention, including 10 murders and numerous church burnings, assaults, and shootings. Although many of these were solved, they did not always result in prosecutions.

Louisville, Kentucky

Although opened initially in July 1924, the Louisville field office was closed within nine months when the Cincinnati and Indianapolis offices opened and took over its responsibilities. In 1935, a highly publicized kidnapping occurred in Kentucky, that of wealthy heiress Alice B. Stoll, and as a result, the Louisville field office reopened.

New York, New York

The New York field office is responsible for conducting criminal and counterintelligence investigations within the five boroughs of New York City and the counties of Dutchess, Nassau, Orange, Putnam, Rockland, Suffolk, Sullivan, and Westchester. New York's regional Computer Crimes Squad is responsible for investigations into computer intrusions for the northeastern United States. The New York office head is designated assistant director in charge and is assisted by a deputy assistant director and, in 1996, three special agents in charge. In addition to resident agencies, the New York field office has two metropolitan resident agencies, Brooklyn-Queens and New Rochelle. Decentralization provides greater operational efficiency and service to the public by placing investigative personnel and support facilities closer to major centers of their work.

The New York office opened in 1910 as one of the first established field divisions of the Bureau of Investigation. Until relocating to its present space in the Jacob Javits Building at 26 Federal Plaza in 1979, the New York office moved several times. The office consisted of 24 special agents and 12 support personnel in 1923; 22 years later, the office staff consisted of 1,234 special agents and 544 support personnel.

The New Rochelle metropolitan resident agency opened on April 1, 1976. In 1981, the office had 80 agents and 36 clerical employees. The office covered the Newburgh, New York, resident agency as well as the Bronx, Westchester, and five northern counties, an area of over 500 square miles with a population of approximately 3,000,000.

When the Brooklyn-Queens metropolitan resident agency opened on April 10, 1978, it was the largest resident agency in the FBI, with approximately 100 agents in five squads and 35 support staff to handle the two boroughs, which have a population of over 4.5 million.

Richmond, Virginia

The Richmond field office in October 1978 initiated the pilot program for Field Office Information Management System. This program did not include all field offices until June 30, 1988, when the Las Vegas office came online.

San Juan, Puerto Rico

The San Juan field office was established in 1940, and by 1987 had approximately 100 agents and 70 support personnel assigned to its headquarters in San Juan and to the St. Thomas resident agency. The San Juan field office also handles liaison with Haiti, the Dominican Republic, the British Virgin Islands, Dominica, St. Lucia, St. Vincent, Barbados, the Grenadines, Grenada, Trinidad and Tobago, and the French colonies of Montserrat, Guadeloupe, and Martinique. In the late 1980s, responsibility for liaison for many of these offices was transferred to the new Bridgetown, Barbados, legal attaché office.

Washington, D.C.

Called the Washington field office (WFO) from its earliest days—in order to distinguish it from FBIHQ—WFO was briefly renamed the Washington Metropolitan Field Office when it merged with the Alexandria, Virginia, field office in 1988. Alexandria then became a metropolitan resident agency, and Tysons Corner, Virginia, became a second metropolitan resident agency. The Washington, D.C., field office reverted to its former name, the Washington Field Office, in October 1996, and in 1997, it moved into new offices in northwest Washington. This office is headed by an assistant director in charge.

Regional and Other Satellite Centers

Firearms Training Facility

In spring 1995, the Firearms Training Facility opened at Fort Dix, New Jersey. This state-of-the-art center is dedicated to the proposition that "no more names be added to the wall"—meaning both the Law Enforcement Memorial in Washington, D.C., and the Wall of Honor in the Administration Building of the FBI Academy in Quantico, Virginia. This facility annually conducts over 3,000 staff-days of agent training and 1,000 staff-days for police, and it plans to double the number by the late 1990s.

Information Technology Centers

The FBI's two Information Technology Centers are located in Savannah, Georgia, and Butte, Montana, in former field office headquarters facilities. Headed by professional support personnel, the Information Technology Centers provide information processing services to support field investigative and administrative operations.

Regional Computer Support Centers

Regional Computer Support Centers provide FBIHQ and field offices with computer services that do not require on-site handling. Inaugurated in the 1980s and located in Pocatello, Idaho, and Fort Monmouth, New Jersey, the Regional Computer Support Centers are the late-twentieth-century version of the typing pool. An assistant special agent in charge supervises each facility.

International Law Enforcement Academy

On June 16, 1995, 33 officers from former Eastern Bloc countries completed training in the first session of the International Law Enforcement Academy in Budapest, Hungary. This event marked the beginning of a new FBI program to promote police professionalism in the new democracies of former communist states. Designed for five sessions each year, each class of approximately 50 students is limited to three countries, in order to minimize interpreter and translation requirements. The classes are taught in English, target middle management, and focus on the investigative process, ethics, leadership, the rule of law, professionalism, and current law enforcement issues. Teachers, who include representatives of other federal agencies as well as the FBI, use a course developed at the John Jay College of Criminal Justice, "Human Dignity and the Police," to help the transition from totalitarianism to democracy. Each session is monitored by University of Virginia and FBI project managers.

National Computer Crime Squad

The FBI's National Computer Crime Squad investigates violations of the Federal Computer Fraud and Abuse Act of 1986. To qualify as a violation under that act, crimes must have occurred across multiple state or international boundaries. These violations include intrusions into computers used for government, financial, and most medical purposes, as well as "federal interest" computers, defined as "two or more computers involved in [a] criminal offense, which are located in different states." (In other words, a commercial computer that is the victim of an intrusion, coming from

another state is a "federal interest" computer.) The crimes investigated by the National Computer Crime Squad include telephone company intrusions, major computer network intrusions, network integrity and privacy violations, industrial espionage, pirated computer software, and other crimes in which the computer is a major factor in committing the criminal offense.

Outside Investigative and Intelligence Organizations

American Protective League

Businessman Albert M. Briggs began the American Protective League in March 1917 by offering to help expand the World War I domestic spying capability of the federal government. Its 260,000 members, who received no training, were to report potential saboteurs, spies, and draft dodgers (called "slackers") to the Bureau of Investigation. In return, the Bureau supplied these "private eyes" with badges that identified them as auxiliaries of the Department of Justice. The plan became controversial when, in 1918, the U.S. Army enlisted the help of American Protective League members to help round-up slackers in major urban areas. Of the alleged slackers apprehended by APL members and their Bureau supervisors in New York City, all of whom were held for hours in crowded and unsanitary conditions, the vast majority turned out either to have legitimate reasons—like age—for not possessing draft registration cards, or simply did not have their cards with them. The New York press heaped well-publicized criticism onto the American Protective League for its overzealous activities in these detentions. At the war's end, the Department of Justice disbanded its liaison relationship with the American Protective League and the Bureau never again provided overt sponsorship of a similar private organization.

El Paso Intelligence Center (EPIC)

In 1974, several executive branch agencies jointly established the El Paso Intelligence Center (EPIC) as the Southwest Border Intelligence Center in El Paso, Texas. EPIC collects, processes, and disseminates information concerning illicit drug trafficking, alien smuggling, and weapons smuggling. In the beginning, it employed approximately 20 staff people from the Drug Enforcement Administration; the Immigration and Naturalization Service; the U.S. Customs Service; U.S. Coast Guard; and the

Bureau of Alcohol, Tobacco and Firearms. The FBI joined in 1980. By 1983, EPIC also included the Federal Aviation Administration, the U.S. Marshals Service, and the Internal Revenue Service. State agencies also belong to EPIC. It operates 24 hours a day, 7 days a week. In addition to contributing its investigatory skills, the FBI helped enhance EPIC's computer operations and installed a color laboratory to handle the processing needs of its Southwestern offices, as well as the Drug Enforcement Administration's aerial surveillance photography.

FBI Background Investigation Contract Service

The FBI Background Investigation Contract Service employs former Bureau agents to conduct background investigations of prospective special agents, reinvestigations of FBI employees and presidential appointees, and "special inquiries from the White House" (usually background investigations of White House or executive branch applicants).

International Criminal Police Organization (Interpol)

FBI Director J. Edgar Hoover initially supported the International Criminal Police Organization, better known as Interpol, when it was revived after World War II. Interpol was supposed to exclude from its liaison mission matters of political, religious, or racial character. However, as communist-controlled countries became members, U.S. and Soviet mutual suspicions caused the FBI to withdraw in 1950. Hoover continued to oppose the participation in Interpol by any other U.S. government agency until 1958, when the Treasury Department became the United States representative. In 1974, FBI Director Clarence M. Kelley agreed to allow Associate Director Nicholas Callahan to attend an Interpol meeting, the first FBI official above the legal attaché level to do so. The Bureau thereafter continued to have closer relations with Interpol, although it did not officially become a member until the 1980s.

Ironically, the impetus for the FBI's decision to rejoin Interpol officially resulted from a January 1985 change in the Interpol charter to include an acceptance of certain politically motivated crimes. The amended charter allowed Interpol, for the first time since World War II, to circulate warrants for offenses such as kidnapping, bombing, and robbery, even if the crime had a political motivation (an amendment that authorized the organization to investigate terrorists).

Interagency Intelligence Coordinating Committee

The director of the FBI chairs the interagency group that oversees national counterintelligence policy. As a participant, the FBI assists in developing counterintelligence policy, plans, and training programs. It details agents to other government organizations to assist in policy formation and operational support activities. The National Security Division (previously, the Intelligence Division) conducts classes at the FBI Academy for personnel from other federal intelligence agencies as well as selected representatives of foreign intelligence agencies considered friendly to the United States.

An example of the FBI's contribution to intelligence collection and policy is its service on the Intelligence Advisory Committee. This committee prepares national intelligence estimates for the National Security Council (NSC). FBI personnel sat on this committee in order to help coordinate domestic intelligence with foreign intelligence. FBI executives also sat on the U.S. Evaluation Board and the U.S. Communications Intelligence Board, both chartered by the National Security Council. The Bureau also participated on the Interdepartmental Committee on Internal Security, which coordinates "all phases of action in the internal security field."

National Counterintelligence Center

This agency, which became operational on August 1, 1994, and includes FBI agents among its personnel and executives, brings together the federal agencies most concerned with thwarting other countries' intelligence efforts. The chief of the center is a senior FBI executive with operational, counterintelligence, and management experience.

National Drug Intelligence Center

Located in Johnstown, Pennsylvania, the National Drug Intelligence Center collects and consolidates drug-trafficking intelligence developed by law enforcement and other official users. The FBI supports this facility, which is overseen by the Department of Justice.

Office of Investigative Agency Policies

Created by Attorney General Janet Reno in November 1993, this organization brings together the Department of Justice's investigative agencies to promote close cooperation among them on enforcement matters. The FBI director serves as its head.

Special Information Committee of NATO

The Special Information Committee of the North Atlantic Treaty Organization (NATO) is composed of representatives of NATO member countries. In 1953, the FBI was the sole American representative. Its role is to promote the exchange of information among the NATO countries about communist activities, including infiltration of the member nations, the control measures taken, and the legislative steps adopted to protect each country's internal security.

Day-to-Day Life of an FBI Agent

The day-to-day life of a Bureau agent under Attorney General Charles Bonaparte and the Bureau's first head, Stanley W. Finch, differed surprisingly little from that under FBI Director Hoover for most of his tenure. Under Bonaparte, Finch was ordered "to do the work with as few men as possible, keep the force efficient and at work, keep them from soldiering and loafing on the job and keep [the attorney general] posted by . . . daily reports as to what is going on." Each agent was required to file reports daily, including Sunday. "[The attorney general] will not stand for extra allowances, additional pay and two men working where one could do it with a little extra hustling." At this time, accountants were designated special examiners and were not considered the equivalent to agents. Unlike Hoover's agents between 1924 and 1934, all the early agents were issued firearms. Like their successors, these agents were responsible for maintaining their credentials and badge, manuals, and any other property they were issued.

For much of its history, the Bureau had a policy of transferring new agents several times after they "entered on duty" ("EODed") and completed their training. Hoover considered it undesirable to assign an agent near his former home "because there may be political, personal, or fraternal affiliations which might prove embarrassing to him in the performance of his official duties." An effort was made, however, to give veteran agents their "office of preference" (OP) after a number of years. In contrast, FBI Director Clarence Kelley allowed agents to stay as long as five years in their first office, and to select a "zone of preference" that would put them within 500 miles of their OP, if they could not get into the OP itself. Now that the FBI employs married couples, both of whom are agents, it attempts to assign them to offices within a reasonably close geographical area.

Initially, an agent's regular work week included a half day on Saturday, but totaled 39.5 hours. Just prior to 1943, the government expanded its regular work week to 40 hours over 5 days. Starting in 1943, at the height of World War II, "seat of government" (SOG) employees—that is, those working in Washington, D.C., at FBIHQ—began putting in regular work weeks of 48 hours, and in addition put in uncompensated overtime. The attorney general, at the end of 1943, approved a 60-hour week for Identification Division clerks on a voluntary basis. Approximately 50 percent of the workers agreed to put in the additional hours. Working at least 6 10-hour days a week and receiving overtime pay for between 48 and 60 hours, they, like all other Bureau employees under Hoover, put in additional hours of work, "voluntarily." In 1938, for example, the Bureau's approximately 670 agents put in 777,359 hours of overtime. Eventually, the Bureau regularized the procedure for agents as administratively uncontrollable overtime—AUO—and qualifying agents began to receive regular compensation for their extra hours. Under FBI Director Freeh, this procedure was modified in order to regularize pay, benefits, and holidays. It is now called availability pay.

Hoover set strict rules for agents' conduct: "I want FBI men to be models of the clean, manly life. . . . I want them to set the example in their own communities." During Hoover's tenure, investigatory agents were not supposed to do paperwork at their desks during regular hours, only during the "voluntary" overtime that Hoover imposed. In order to write reports and complete paperwork during the day, agents would retreat to such places as the public library or even coffee shops.

An FBI agent is presumably always on call, and, for most of the Bureau's history, was required to carry a weapon at all times. From the Bureau's inception, agents carried firearms. Hoover halted this practice in 1924 after an agent was found to have violated a state antifirearms law. A special agent in charge could grant special permission, nevertheless, for an agent to carry a weapon. In response to the 1933 Kansas City Massacre, Congress, on June 18, 1934, authorized all Bureau agents to carry weapons.

Although some special agents in charge relaxed some of the Bureau's strict dress restrictions in the field, others enforced them to the letter. For example, by the late 1960s, when white shirts in the workplace were an outdated style, many field offices allowed agents and support staff alike to wear colored shirts. But whenever a field agent made an arrest, he would be sure to have his suit coat on and a snap-brim fedora on his head. The media could show up and photograph the scene, and "you never knew when Hoover was watching." In the summer, straw hats replaced the fedoras. Suits and ties were required, and the tie had to be the same color as the suit lining. "It was part of the mystique. Part of the Bureau. When you walked in and sat down and talked to somebody, there was no doubt they knew you were the FBI," explained a retired agent.

Infractions of any rule could bring a letter of censure. Because these letters could hold up promotions or raises for as much as six months, the letters were taken seriously. Certain Bureau executives became notorious for issuing them for trivial offenses such as grammatical or spelling errors in letters that an agent had proofread (the typist was also censured). According to one agent, the letters of censure went out over Hoover's signature and usually began "'I am amazed and astounded . . .' [or similar] 'doomsday' language." On the other hand, good work on a case or in the public affairs area could earn a letter of commendation, often accompanied by a cash award.

When he became acting director of the FBI, L. Patrick Gray eliminated some of the more onerous day-to-day restrictions that Hoover had imposed. Among the changes, he allowed agents to wear colored shirts, relaxed the stringent weight requirements, and abolished "time in the office" statistics and daily reports. He also permitted coffee drinking and snacking in the office and allowed resident agents to take Bureau cars home with them. Gray's transfer policy also became more flexible. In addition, he instituted a voluntary physical fitness program for agents, giving them three hours of work time a week for exercise. Kelley abandoned the program, but FBI Director William H. Webster reinstated it.

During Hoover's time, as today, agents interested in becoming executives begin with a stint as relief supervisors in the field, and often supervisory work in FBIHQ. Until the mid-1990s, an executive track required several months on the Inspection staff in FBIHQ before an appointment as assistant special agent in charge (ASAC). FBI Director Louis J. Freeh modified the inspection requirement somewhat to allow an assistant inspector in place to remain in his or her regular position and be detailed for a few weeks at a time for specific inspections.

An agent may chose not to take that career path, and many, in fact, prefer to stay in the field rather than go into management, which often entails frequent moves. Those seeking executive positions usually transfer from small field offices to FBIHQ, then to larger field offices, and their career may end as a special agent in charge (SAC) in a large office or as a unit chief, section chief, deputy assistant director, or assistant director in one of the FBIHQ divisions.

Since the early Hoover years, the Bureau has given its personnel, which it considers "the FBI family," opportunities to get together outside of work. A major vehicle for these activities is the FBI Recreation Association (FBIRA). In both FBIHQ and the field, agent and support employees participate in intramural and interagency athletic competitions under FBIRA auspices. Interagency athletics were considered so important in the 1930s that Hoover occasionally waived educational and other requirements to recruit exceptional basketball or baseball players. The FBI baseball team won the government agency league on at least one occasion, in 1936. In 1949, the Bureau boasted that "more than twenty-seven teams would be needed to outfit former pigskin stars who joined the ranks of the FBI," including former All-American Texas Christian University and Philadelphia Eagles player Special Agent Davey O'Brien. Ten years later, former New York Giants pitcher James M. Tennant was assigned to the New Haven, Connecticut, field office. In 1978, the Indianapolis, Indiana, field office put together its first women's softball team. The following year, the nation's best marksmen came to Beltsville, Maryland, to compete in a pistol competition. Four FBI agents, from four different field offices, received first-place rankings in the Police Combat Championship competition. Today's teams are often composed of both agent and non-agent personnel.

A career in the FBI is not without dangers. As of 1997, 33 agents had been killed in the line of duty, and another 13 died in work-related circumstances.

When employees retire or resign, they may have to be escorted while in FBI space and must use the Freedom of Information Act to acquire copies of what they wrote while on the job. But they can continue their Bureau associations through the Society of Former Special Agents of the FBI and the FBI Alumni Association. As one former agent wrote, "Many times one is asked what is the one thing you enjoyed the most while being an FBI Agent. With very little thought, the answer comes back, meeting and working with the greatest people in the world. Little did we all realize when we were sworn in as FBI Agents, we were beginning a long *journey of friendship* that would never end."

FBI Alumni Association

The FBI Alumni Association, previously the Society of Former FBI Women, was so named in 1994 after the women's organization began to admit male members, including former special agents, starting in 1992.

FBI Recreation Association (FBIRA)

The FBIRA seeks to promote morale and camaraderie amongst its members through athletic, recreational, and welfare activities. First called the Recreation Association, the FBI Recreation Association began December 5, 1931, "to promote and encourage athletics as a means to better health, to stimulate fair play, and to create a better understanding of each other." In 1979, the FBIRA added a store to generate funds to promote these activities. Today the FBIRA is a nonprofit organization consisting only of present FBI employees and is governed by a board of directors.

J. Edgar Hoover Foundation

A private organization founded in 1965 with a million-dollar endowment contributed by Schenley Industries president Lewis S. Rosenstiel, its general purpose is "to further the values of the Director." Headquartered in Valley Forge, Pennsylvania, it annually gives college scholarships, known as the J. Edgar Hoover Living Memorial.

Society of Former Special Agents of the FBI

"The Society" began in June 1937, with the adoption of a constitution and bylaws and the selection of officers. Incorporated in New York state, its charter members were John O'Connell, Charles J. Scully, John Manning, Francis X. Fay, Mike Glynn, "Matty" Horan, Frank Kilmartin, Wayne Merrick, Bob Reed, John Brann, John Haas, and Charlie Noble. Scully served as its first president. Members had to serve as special agents for at least one year, and had to be "men of good moral character . . . and who served with due fidelity to their oaths of office and with loyalty to the service and to their fellow agents." Former female special agents who fulfilled the other requirements also became eligible for membership when they left the Bureau.

In addition to performing a social function, the society helps other society members and aids the FBI. The society assists its members and their families by providing comfort and other assistance when there are deaths in a family through its foundation, which aids those in need directly or through scholarships.

In April 1938, the society decided to publish a journal, *The Grapevine.* Its first issue, which was mimeographed, came out on July 14 of that year, with John A. Murphy as its first editor. It was published as a printed magazine for the first time in January 1954. Gordon A. Philips and Karl G. Hastedt served as its editor and managing editor respectively until 1984, when Lawrence J. Heim took over. He remained the editor until his death on October 28, 1996. The current editor is Hillary Robinette, who served as an agent from 1969 to 1989.

Society of Former FBI Women

The Society of Former FBI Women began in May 1973 when Frances Artley Newby founded the organization as a way to enable former women employees of the FBI to maintain social contact and make new friends. By 1987, it had 1,200 members and 26 chapters.

In 1992, the organization voted to accept former male employees, including former agents, with full rights and privileges. The first man to join was Phillip B. Carr, president of the Society of Former Special Agents of the FBI, who had served the Bureau as both clerk and agent. In 1994, the organization changed its name to the FBI Alumni Association in recognition of this new policy.

Notes

The author thanks the staff of the Research/Communications Unit of the FBI for providing many of the research materials used in this chapter.

1. The public and FBI personnel alike use "the Bureau" as a synonym for the FBI in general, and it is so used here. However, field personnel *also* use "the Bureau" as a synonym for FBIHQ. Even more confusing, when field employees use the term "headquarters," they usually mean the field office headquarters for the geographical division (as opposed to resident agencies or other units within the division). The "field office," technically, is the main office of the field division, while the "division" refers to its total geographical jurisdiction. However, "field office" is used frequently both in and out of the FBI to mean "field division." Field offices, on the other hand, are never referred to as "field divisions."

Appendix
FBI Field Offices

ALABAMA

Birmingham Field Office
Room 1400
2121 8th Avenue N.
Birmingham, Alabama 35203
(205) 252-7705

Mobile Field Office
One St. Louis Centre
1 St. Louis Street, 3rd Floor
Mobile, Alabama 36602
(334) 438-3674

ALASKA

Anchorage Field Office
101 East Sixth Avenue
Anchorage, Alaska 99501
(907) 258-5322

ARIZONA

Phoenix Field Office
Suite 400
201 East Indianola Avenue
Phoenix, Arizona 85012
(602) 279-5511

ARKANSAS

Little Rock Field Office
Suite 200
Two Financial Centre
10825 Financial Centre Parkway
Little Rock, Arkansas 72211
(501) 221-9100

CALIFORNIA

Los Angeles Field Office
Suite 1700, Federal Office Building
11000 Wilshire Boulevard
Los Angeles, California 90024
(310) 477-6565
http://www.fbi.gov/fo/la/lahome.htm

Sacramento Field Office
4500 Orange Grove Avenue
Sacramento, California 95841
(916) 481-9110
http://www.fbi.gov/fo/sc/fbisc.htm

San Diego Field Office
Federal Office Building
9797 Aero Drive
San Diego, California 92123
(619) 565-1255

San Francisco Field Office
450 Golden Gate Avenue 13th Floor
San Francisco, California 94102
(415) 553-7400

COLORADO

Denver Field Office
Federal Office Building, Suite 1823
1961 Stout Street, 18th Floor
Denver, Colorado 80294
(303) 629-7171

CONNECTICUT

New Haven Field Office
Room 535, Federal Office Building
150 Court Street
New Haven, Connecticut 06510
(203) 777-6311

DISTRICT OF COLUMBIA

Washington Metropolitan Field Office
1900 Half Street, SW
Washington, D.C. 20024
(202) 252-7801

FLORIDA

Jacksonville Field Office
Suite 200
7820 Arlington Expressway
Jacksonville, Florida 32211
(904) 721-1211

Miami Field Office
16320 Northwest Second Avenue
North Miami Beach, Florida 33169
(305) 944-9101

Tampa Field Office
Room 610, Federal Office Building
500 Zack Street
Tampa, Florida 33602
(813) 273-4566

GEORGIA

Atlanta Field Office
Suite 400
2635 Century Parkway, Northeast
Atlanta, Georgia 30345
(404) 679-9000

HAWAII

Honolulu Field Office
Room 4307, Kalanianaole Federal Office Building
300 Ala Moana Boulevard
Honolulu, Hawaii 96850
(808) 521-1411

ILLINOIS

Chicago Field Office
Room 905
E. M. Dirksen Federal Office Building
219 South Dearborn Street
Chicago, Illinois 60604
(312) 431-1333

Springfield Field Office
Suite 400
400 West Monroe Street
Springfield, Illinois 62704
(217) 522-9675
http://www.fbi.gov/fo/si/spfldfbi.htm

INDIANA

Indianapolis Field Office
Room 679, Federal Office Building
575 North Pennsylvania Street
Indianapolis, Indiana 46204
(317) 639-3301

KENTUCKY

Louisville Field Office
Room 500
600 Martin Luther King Jr. Place
Louisville, Kentucky 40202
(502) 583-3941

LOUISIANA

New Orleans Field Office
Suite 2200
1250 Poydras Street
New Orleans, Louisiana 70113
(504) 522-4671

MARYLAND

Baltimore Field Office
7142 Ambassador Road
Baltimore, Maryland 21244
(410) 265-8080

MASSACHUSETTS

Boston Field Office
Suite 600
One Center Plaza
Boston, Massachusetts 02108
(617) 742-5533

MICHIGAN

Detroit Field Office
26th Floor
P. V. McNamara Federal Office Building
477 Michigan Avenue
Detroit, Michigan 48226
(313) 965-2323

MINNESOTA

Minneapolis Field Office
Suite 1100
111 Washington Avenue, South
Minneapolis, Minnesota 55401
(612) 376-3200

MISSISSIPPI

Jackson Field Office
Room 1553, Federal Office Building
100 West Capitol Street
Jackson, Mississippi 39269
(601) 948-5000

MISSOURI

Kansas City Field Office
Room 300, U.S. Courthouse
811 Grand Avenue
Kansas City, Missouri 64106
(816) 221-6100
http://www.fbi.gov/fo/kc/kcpage.htm

St. Louis Field Office
Room 2704
L. Douglas Abram Federal Building
1520 Market Street
St. Louis, Missouri 63103
(314) 241-5357

NEBRASKA

Omaha Field Office
10755 Burt Street
Omaha, Nebraska 68114
(402) 493-8688

NEVADA

Las Vegas Field Office
700 East Charleston Boulevard
Las Vegas, Nevada 89101
(702) 385-1281

NEW JERSEY

Newark Field Office
1 Gateway Center, 22nd Floor
Newark, New Jersey 07102
(201) 622-5613

NEW MEXICO

Albuquerque Field Office
Suite 300
415 Silver Avenue, Southwest
Albuquerque, New Mexico 87102
(505) 224-2000
http://www.fbi.gov/fo/aq/aqhome.htm

NEW YORK

Albany Field Office
Suite 502, James T. Foley Building
445 Broadway
Albany, New York 12207
(518) 465-7551
http://www.fbi.gov/fo/alfo/alfohome.htm

Buffalo Field Office
One FBI Plaza
Buffalo, New York 14202
(716) 856-7800
http://www.fbi.gov/fo/bffo/bffohome.htm

New York Field Office
26 Federal Plaza, 23rd Floor
New York, New York 10278
(212) 384-1000
http://www.fbi.gov/fo/nyfo/nyfohome.htm

NORTH CAROLINA

Charlotte Field Office
Suite 900
400 South Tyron Street
Charlotte, North Carolina 28285
(704) 377-9200

OHIO

Cincinnati Field Office
Room 9023
550 Main Street
Cincinnati, Ohio 45273
(513) 421-4310

Cleveland Field Office
Room 3005
Federal Office Building
1240 East 9th Street
Cleveland, Ohio 44199
(216) 522-1400

OKLAHOMA

Oklahoma City Field Office
Suite 1600
50 Penn Place
Oklahoma City, Oklahoma 73118
(405) 842-7471

OREGON

Portland Field Office
Suite 401, Crown Plaza Building
1500 Southwest 1st Avenue
Portland, Oregon 97201
(503) 224-4181
http://www.fbi.gov/fo/pd/portlnd/htm

PENNSYLVANIA

Philadelphia Field Office
8th Floor
William J. Green Jr. Federal Office Building
600 Arch Street
Philadelphia, Pennsylvania 19106
(215) 829-2700

Pittsburgh Field Office
Suite 300
U.S. Post Office Building
700 Grant Street
Pittsburgh, Pennsylvania 15219
(412) 471-2000

PUERTO RICO

San Juan Field Office
Room 526, U.S. Federal Building
150 Carlos Chardon Avenue
Hato Rey
San Juan, Puerto Rico 00918
(809) 754-6000

SOUTH CAROLINA

Columbia Field Office
Room 1357
1835 Assembly Street
Columbia, South Carolina 29201
(803) 254-3011

TENNESSEE

Knoxville Field Office
Suite 600
John J. Duncan Federal Office Building
710 Locust Street
Knoxville, Tennessee 37902
(423) 544-0751
http://www.fbi.gov/fo/kx/knoxhome.htm

Memphis Field Office
Suite 3000, Eagle Crest Building
225 North Humphreys Boulevard
Memphis, Tennessee 38120
(901) 747-4300

TEXAS

Dallas Field Office
Room 300
1801 North Lamar
Dallas, Texas 75202
(214) 720-2200
http://www.fbi.gov/fo/dl/dallas.htm

El Paso Field Office
Suite C-600
700 East San Antonio Avenue
El Paso, Texas 79901
(915) 533-7451

Houston Field Office
Room 200
2500 East TC Jester
Houston, Texas 77008
(713) 868-2266
http://www.fbi.gov/fo/ho/houston.htm

San Antonio Field Office
Suite 200
U.S. Post Office and Courthouse Building
615 East Houston Street
San Antonio, Texas 78205
(210) 225-6741
http://www.fbi.gov/fo/sanant/sanant.htm

UTAH

Salt Lake City Field Office
Suite 1200, 257 Towers Building
257 East, 200 South
Salt Lake City, Utah 84111
(801) 579-1400

VIRGINIA

Norfolk Field Office
150 Corporate Boulevard
Norfolk, Virginia 23502
(804) 455-0100

Richmond Field Office
111 Greencourt Road
Richmond, Virginia 23228
(804) 261-1044

WASHINGTON

Seattle Field Office
Room 710
915 Second Avenue
Seattle, Washington 98174
(206) 622-0460

WISCONSIN

Milwaukee Field Office
Suite 600
330 East Kilbourn Avenue
Milwaukee, Wisconsin 53202
(414) 276-4684

BUILDINGS AND PHYSICAL PLANT

Susan Rosenfeld

FBI Headquarters, Washington, D.C. (FBIHQ)

From 1908 to 1975, the FBI's primary offices were in Department of Justice headquarters buildings in Washington, D.C.; these included the Baltic Hotel, the Denrike Building, and the Department of Justice Building on Pennsylvania Avenue. The Bureau also occupied satellite offices in Washington, D.C., in the Old Southern Railway Building. During World War II, the FBI took over the Washington, D.C., National Guard Armory at the end of East Capitol Street for its Identification Division operations. After the war ended, the Identification Division moved to Second and D Streets, SW, a site it shared with the FBI central files until both moved into the J. Edgar Hoover FBI Building during the summer of 1975. In the years before completion of the Hoover Building, other Bureau units occupied offices in the Old Post Office Building on Pennsylvania Avenue and in other nearby buildings.

Department of Justice Headquarters, 1908–75

Baltic Hotel

The Baltic Hotel building on K Street, Northwest (see Exhibit 7.1), housed the Department of Justice in 1908, when the FBI began. The Bureau's first head, Chief Stanley W. Finch, had an office in the Department of Justice headquarters in the Baltic Hotel, but agents worked in the field and either had their own offices or used those of U.S. district attorneys.

Exhibit 7.1   **Baltic Hotel Building,** *Courtesy of the FBI*

Denrike Building

The Denrike Building, located at 1435 K Street at the corner of Vermont Avenue (see Exhibit 7.2), was headquarters for the Bureau of Investigation from 1917 until it moved into the main Department of Justice Building in 1934. Except for the Identification Division and the Laboratory, Bureau headquarters in the Denrike Building occupied the third floor and part of the fourth floor. The Bureau director's office was across the hall from the mail room.

Exhibit 7.2   **Denrike Building,** *Courtesy of the FBI*

Department of Justice Building

Dedicated on October 25, 1934, the Department of Justice Building (see Exhibit 7.3) covers an entire block between Ninth and Tenth Streets and Pennsylvania and Constitution Avenues in downtown Washington, D.C. It contains 7 floors above ground, includes a total of 23.5 acres of floor space, and is serviced by 63 elevators.

The FBI occupied three floors at the Department of Justice Building. On the fifth floor, the offices of FBI Director J. Edgar Hoover and Associate Director Clyde Tolson were located at the corner of Ninth Street and Pennsylvania Avenue. Hoover had a long suite of offices that extended down the Ninth Street side of the building, but his private office was back-to-back with Tolson's, separated by a small vestibule. Two floors above, the FBI Laboratory predominated. A firearms range in the basement served both as a practice area for agents and as the site for the shooting exhibition that climaxed the FBI's public tour.

Initially, exhibits for the public tour, which began in June 1937, ran down the corridor directly across from Hoover's office. The tour route was moved in November

Exhibit 7.3   **Department of Justice Building,** *Courtesy of the FBI*

1958 to an exhibit complex adjacent to the side of the building on Ninth and Pennsylvania Avenue. For awhile, tour groups gathered in the FBI director's reception area, where the visitors could view rifles, the bulletproof vest once used by gangster John Dillinger, and a large collection of autographed cartoons. Later, when tour groups were larger, the building's interior courtyard became the waiting area. The tour started with maps that showed FBI field offices and the law enforcement offices nationwide that contributed fingerprints to the Bureau's Identification Division. Other exhibits featured major cases such as the Lindbergh kidnapping and the prosecution of famous gangsters—and a mock-up of the "crime scene room" used to train new FBI agents. Visitors observed the Identification Division at work on the seventh floor, including the Bureau's two sorting machines for fingerprints (see Exhibit 5.2), an early form of computer. If they wished, visitors could be fingerprinted and could have their cards added to the civil (non-criminal) print collection. In addition, they could view the FBI Laboratory at work and the firearms reference collection. By 1955, the Ten Most Wanted Fugitives program, then five years old, posted pictures of the fugitives on the tour route—and two visitors identified fugitives after having seen the pictures during the tour. During the 1950s and 1960s, exhibits focused on communism and its threat to the United States (see Exhibit 5.5).

Below the director's office on the second floor, a fresco by Henry Varnum Poor depicts the FBI Laboratory and its three pioneers, special agents Edwin R. Donaldson, Charles A. Appel, and Donald J. Parsons. Although document examination was the specialty of Appel, the founder of the laboratory, he is pictured holding a test tube. Donaldson

(with the FBI from 1943 to 1959) was a chemist, and Parsons spent his entire Bureau career (from 1934 to 1961) in the laboratory, including a stint as its assistant director.

Satellite Headquarters Buildings

Old Southern Railway Building

The Old Southern Railway Building at 13th and Pennsylvania Avenues, Northwest, contained the Identification Division, including the Latent Fingerprint Unit, starting in 1924 (see Exhibit 7.4). After the creation of the Laboratory in 1932, it was also housed in this building (see Exhibit 5.3). During the early 1930s, this building also housed the FBI's Crime Statistics and the Mechanical Sections. When the main Department of Justice Building was completed in 1934, these units were moved there to occupy the fifth, sixth, and seventh floors, along with the offices of the FBI director and of other FBI officials.

Exhibit 7.4   **Old Southern Railway Building,** *Courtesy of the FBI*

National Guard Armory

Because of the enormous increase in the number of fingerprints it had to process during World War II, in 1943, the Identification Division moved to the Washington, D.C., National Guard Armory at the east end of Capitol Street (see Exhibit 8.7 on page 281). The FBI occupied the entire building, most of which was used by the Identification Division, although a small portion was used for training. Difficult to heat in winter or cool in summer, this cavernous space was occupied 24 hours a day.

Old Post Office Building

Today a multiuse building containing shops, restaurants, and government offices, the Old Post Office Building housed the Washington, D.C., field office and the Washington, D.C., training classes for the Bureau's new agents from 1928 until the new FBI Academy facility opened in Quantico, Virginia, in 1972. The Washington, D.C., field office moved to Buzzard Point in Southwest Washington in 1978, and then to a new building six blocks from FBIHQ in 1997.

FBI Headquarters, 1975 to the Present

J. Edgar Hoover FBI Building

The first request to move the FBI out of the main Department of Justice building occurred in 1939. World War II, however, precluded the construction of any new federal buildings not related to the immediate war effort. After the war, 6,000 building projects competed for federal funds. Consequently, FBI Director J. Edgar Hoover did not lobby for the funding of a separate FBI facility until October 1961, when he made the request to the head of the General Services Administration (GSA), which handles federal construction. Congress approved the project in April 1962.

The GSA selected Charles F. Murphy and Associates, of Chicago, Illinois, as architects, and Berswenger, Hoch, Arnold, and Associates, of Akron, Ohio, for engineering. (The architecture firm purchased the engineering company while the project was in process.) Final site and design approval for the building had to be made by the National Capital Planning Commission, the GSA, the Commission on Fine Arts, and (after 1964), the Pennsylvania Avenue Advisory Council.

On January 2, 1963, the GSA approved a site bounded by Pennsylvania Avenue, E Street, Ninth Street, and Tenth Street, NW, directly across the street from the main Department of Justice building. The government purchased the land for $41.17 per square foot. Throughout the planning and construction phases, the GSA, although soliciting the opinions of Bureau officials, had the primary responsibility for the project. The GSA, however, had to obtain the approval of the National Capital Planning Commission, the Commission of Fine Arts, and Pennsylvania Avenue Advisory Council.

Initially, the plan approved by the GSA was for a traditional, box-like structure that incorporated the Bureau's request for a design that would allow files to be placed in a central core with offices surrounding it; an arrangement that would enable the files to be accessed quickly by Bureau staff. However, in April 1964, the Pennsylvania Avenue

Advisory Council announced a "grand design" for Pennsylvania Avenue, based on the Champs Élysées in Paris, with broad sidewalks, trees, and architecture designed to accommodate parade viewing. Because the new FBI building would be the first new federal structure on the avenue to take the Advisory Council's plan into consideration, the GSA modified the edifice to make it more in keeping with the Champs Élysées–type boulevard that the Pennsylvania Avenue Advisory Council envisioned. The final design incorporated the Bureau's requests regarding both security concerns and the placement of the files, as well as the aesthetic criteria stipulated by the Commission on Fine Arts and the Pennsylvania Avenue Advisory Council and the requirements of the National Capital Planning Commission. To maintain the Champs Élysées idea, the building along Pennsylvania Avenue is fronted by a broad sidewalk with three rows of small trees and a large courtyard open to the sky. A moat between the sidewalk and building extends along the Ninth, Tenth, and E Street sides of the building, with a driveway extending from Ninth to Tenth Street between the courtyard and the main, E Street side structure. On the other three sides, seven-story wings form the boundary of the courtyard, which has a gated entrance in the middle of the avenue side. To preserve an arcade-like facade, the Ninth and Tenth Streets, and Pennsylvania Avenue sides contain recessed panels on the ground floor spaced between the columns that continue through the open mezzanine to the third floor. The notion of faux columns was abandoned in 1989, and instead, panels depicting historical events were placed into the Pennsylvania Avenue side's recessed areas. These panels were replaced in 1996 by marble siding that restores and highlights the column effect.

Retaining one key feature from the original plan, the main part of the FBI building—which faces E Street—contains a core of files surrounded by offices on its fourth, fifth, and sixth floors. Because the Pennsylvania Avenue Advisory Council wanted the new construction to be conducive to viewing parades, an open second-story mezzanine was designed. The E Street mezzanine area now also holds members of the public waiting to go on the FBI Tour. The building also has specially designed flagpoles over the open mezzanine that can telescope out over the Pennsylvania Avenue sidewalk during parades. The sidewalk along Pennsylvania Avenue originally had three broad steps along its curbs to allow people to better view parades (these steps were removed in 1991).

FBI Director Hoover never met with General Services Administration personnel or members of the architectural firm, and he did not involve himself directly in negotiations concerning the FBI building. Hoover's representatives, assistants to the director John Mohr and Cartha DeLoach, insisted on security measures in the planning and prevailed regarding the building's interior design, but they never formally approved the structure as a whole or its external appearance. In fact, as evidenced in his marginal notes on memoranda concerning the building, Hoover disliked its appearance intensely. When a 1966 newspaper columnist suggested that the building looked like a fort, Hoover penned: "I agree the design is obnoxious." Five years later, he gave the Society of Former Special Agents copies of the architectural drawings, but noted that "it looks like something from Mars." Nevertheless, days before his death, he indicated in an informal note that he would not object if the building were named in his honor.

The major design concept received National Capital Planning Commission approval on October 7, 1964 (see Exhibit 7.5). It consisted of 2,800,876 gross square feet of space and 1,978,728 net square feet of space for 7,090 employees, and included over 1,000 parking spaces. The

Exhibit 7.5   **J. Edgar Hoover FBI Building**, *Courtesy of the FBI*

heights of 107 feet (7 stories) on Pennsylvania Avenue and 160 feet (11 stories) on E Street conformed to Pennsylvania Avenue Advisory Council and District of Columbia regulations. The final cost of constructing the building, completed in 1975, was $126,108,000.

The GSA supervising architect, Karel Yasko, assisted by Ralph Harris, had overall responsibility for the building. Carter Manny had supervisory responsibilities for Murphy and Associates. Murphy and Associates architect Stanislas Gladych, a Polish refugee and admirer of FBI Director Hoover, however, was the building's principal designer. Gladych explained to the Commission on Fine Arts that he wanted the building to "express that feeling of ruggedness and efficiency which he feels are exemplified by the Director and the operations of the Bureau." Responding to criticisms of the building's solid, closed-in features, Gladych stated, "There is something about the FBI that is mysterious . . . Why not say this building has a touch of mystery?"

The poured-concrete exterior specified for the building conformed with an architectural style then in vogue, developed at Yale University (both Yasko and Harris had attended the Yale School of Architecture). To create the facade, builders poured the concrete into reusable steel forms separated by metal ties. The ties remained in the concrete when the molds were removed, producing an architectural feature of evenly spaced "holes" throughout the exterior.

A ground-level courtyard—part of the Pennsylvania Advisory Council's plan for an open area surrounded by shops—was, for awhile, surrounded by barren walls and empty save for a fountain. It now holds benches where employees can relax on their breaks or can sit during outdoor presentations. On August 18, 1978, the FBI's first courtyard concert took place. A memorial designed by sculptor Everett Raymond Kinstler, the J. Edgar Hoover Physical Memorial, is located in the area. Dedicated October 13, 1979, it consists of a bronze statue and the curved wall opposite it. The statue depicts a man standing against an unfurled flag, while two seated figures look up to him. On the base is the FBI motto, "Fidelity, Bravery, Integrity." The curved wall contains a quotation from Hoover: "The most effective weapon against crime is cooperation—the efforts of all law enforcement agencies with the support and understanding of the American people."

In 1991, the FBI added polished uba tuba granite on one of the courtyard walls (on the Pennsylvania Avenue side) to hold a 150-pound solid bronze plaque reproducing the Bill of Rights. The plaque was presented to the FBI by the Judicial Conference of the United States Committee on the Bicentennial of the U.S. Constitution. The FBI was the only executive branch agency to receive this honor.

Terrorism at home and abroad have necessitated further changes in the J. Edgar Hoover FBI Building. Employees and official visitors use computer-controlled badges to gain access to the building. Increased security has resulted in closing all but the Tenth Street pass-through to non-Bureau employees, who must now go through a metal detector and have their belongings x-rayed. To prevent car bombs, since the late 1980s, large concrete objects—designed to double as ornamental planters—have obstructed doorways and gated entrances. These protective "flowerpots" now surround the building's entire perimeter and heavy gates protect the driveways.

On May 4, 1972, two days after J. Edgar Hoover's death, President Richard M. Nixon signed Public Law 92-520 officially naming the new FBI headquarters the J. Edgar Hoover FBI Building. Construction of the building was not completed for another two years. Its first occupants moved in June 28, 1974, although FBI Director Clarence M. Kelley and other top FBI executives did not occupy their seventh-floor suites overlooking Pennsylvania Avenue until many months later. President Gerald R. Ford formally dedicated the building on September 30, 1975. Nonetheless, the last unit did not move into the building until June 1977. By the mid-1980s, headquarters functions had once again outgrown their main offices and were scattered in other structures.

FBI Academy

The 385-acre site of the FBI Academy is located on the U.S. Marine Corps base in Quantico, Virginia, approximately 40 miles south of Washington, D.C. When first established in 1935, the academy was located in barracks at the base (see Exhibit 7.6). In 1972, the academy moved to new facilities on a campus constructed in a wooded area near the firearms range. This new campus formally opened on May 8, 1972. This expanded complex enabled FBI officials to increase graduates from 100 a year to over 1,000. The campus consists of over 20 major buildings for housing dormitories, classrooms, and research, and other training facilities, as well as an auditorium, library, gymnasium, weight room, and indoor swimming pool (see Exhibit 7.7). The site also features indoor and outdoor firing ranges, a track, tennis courts, and the training facility of the Hostage Rescue Team (see Exhibit 7.8). A "town," called Hogan's Alley, is used primarily for training purposes but also houses some offices and services.

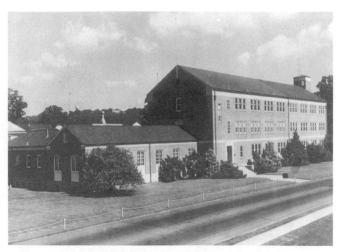

Exhibit 7.6   **Marine Corps Base, Quantico, Virginia,** *Courtesy of the FBI*

In 1985, the Drug Enforcement Administration training facility was established at the academy, and in the mid-1990s, the Engineering Section of the Technical Services Division (now the Information Resources Division) also moved to permanent headquarters on the academy site.

Exhibit 7.7   **FBI Academy, Quantico, Virginia,** *Courtesy of the FBI*

Engineering Research Facility

The Engineering Research Facility was "designed to provide the FBI with the ability to respond to complex investigations against very sophisticated adversaries." Consisting of four interconnected building components comprising 250,000 square feet of space, its first component was completed and occupied in December 1989, with final completion and occupancy occurring in 1993. The Engineering Research Facility contains laboratories, fabrication shops, testing and evaluation centers (to further FBI investigations), as well as classrooms (to train FBI engineers) and offices for officials supervising or assisting in the work of those technicians.

Exhibit 7.8   **Hostage Rescue Team Training,** *Courtesy of the FBI*

Forensic Science Research and Training Center

The Forensic Science Research and Training Center opened in 1981. It provides expert forensic science instruction to state and local crime laboratory personnel, and serves as a specialized facility for FBI Laboratory research personnel. The Forensic Science Research and Training Center facilities occupies one of the buildings in the academy's central complex at Quantico, which also houses offices of the National Center for the Analysis of Violent Crime 60 feet underground in an area that had originally been designed for use as a secure law enforcement headquarters in the event of a national emergency.

Hall of Honor

A joint tribute by the FBI and the Society of Former Special Agents of the FBI, the Hall of Honor is located in the Administration Building of the FBI Academy. It honors past leaders of the FBI. One wall contains a plaque giving tribute to all the men and women of the FBI, bas reliefs of the past FBI directors beginning with J. Edgar Hoover, and the seals of the FBI and the society. Another plaque honors FBI agents who gave their lives in the line of duty (see Table 7.1). In 1991, the Bureau added an additional section dedicated to those local and state police officers who graduated from the FBI National Academy and who lost their lives in the line of duty.

Hogan's Alley

To provide a realistic environment to train both new agents and local and state police attending the FBI National Academy, the FBI created a town setting called Hogan's Alley. This facility has also been used for advanced in-service exercises for special agents (see Exhibit 7.9). Hogan's Alley includes a bank, post office, pharmacy, rooming house, bar/deli, pool hall, motel, trailer park, warehouse area, and a residential street that includes townhouses and apartments. In an allusion to a well-known piece of Bureau history, the movie theater is named the Biograph, the name of the theater at which gangster John Dillinger was apprehended and killed. The town's pawn shop is actually a front for a gambling casino. Some of the buildings are real, such as the restaurant, which is used as a classroom, while other buildings contain offices. However, some structures are simply false fronts or use optical illusions to make them appear to be real buildings. Furnishings for the residential buildings and the cars come largely from property either seized or forfeited through FBI and Drug Enforcement Administration investigations. Although the offices are not used in the crime-scene exercises, arrests, surveillances, and searches take place outside and around them. The people who actually work in the offices in Hogan's Alley help make it a realistic setting as they walk from building to building or drive their cars through the roads. The Practical Applications Unit of the Training Division manages the facility and develops the scenarios. Townspeople are recruited from Quantico or nearby Triangle, Virginia, to act as criminals or hostages. Trainees use deactivated weapons.

Exhibit 7.9   **Agent Training in Hogan's Alley,** *Courtesy of the FBI*

TABLE 7.1

FBI AGENTS WHO DIED IN SERVICE

Name	Birth Date	Death Date
* Edwin C. Shanahan	1898	October 11, 1925
Paul E. Reynolds	September 3, 1899	August 9, 1929
Albert L. Ingle	May 8, 1903	November 24, 1931
* Raymond J. Caffrey	May 15, 1903	June 17, 1933
* W. Carter Baum	July 2, 1904	April 22, 1934
Herman E. Hollis	January 27, 1903	November 27, 1934
* Samuel P. Cowley	July 23, 1899	November 28, 1934
Nelson B. Klein	April 3, 1898	August 16, 1935
Wimberly W. Baker	January 10, 1910	April 17, 1937
Truett E. Rowe	March 25, 1904	June 1, 1937
William R. Ramsey	October 5, 1903	May 3, 1938
Hubert J. Treacy Jr.	January 13, 1913	March 13, 1942
* Percy E. Foxworth	November 29, 1906	January 15, 1943
Harold Dennis Haberfeld	February 8, 1912	January 15, 1943
Richard Blackstone Brown	April 2, 1916	July 14, 1943
Joseph J. Brock	April 30, 1908	July 26, 1952
John Brady Murphy	November 15, 1917	September 26, 1953
Richard Purcell Horan	April 20, 1922	April 18, 1957
Terry R. Anderson	January 19, 1924	May 17, 1966
Douglas M. Price	January 14, 1941	April 25, 1968
Anthony Palmisano	November 3, 1942	January 8, 1969
* Edwin R. Woodriffe	January 22, 1941	January 8, 1969
Gregory W. Spinelli	March 8, 1949	March 15, 1973
Jack R. Coler	January 12, 1947	June 26, 1975
Ronald A. Williams	July 30, 1947	June 26, 1975
Trenwith S. Basford	October 5, 1916	August 25, 1977
Mark A. Kirkland	August 8, 1944	August 25, 1977
Johnnie L. Oliver	May 8, 1944	August 9, 1979
Charles W. Elmore	May 26, 1945	August 9, 1979
Jared Robert Porter	March 15, 1935	August 9, 1979
Terry Burnett Hereford	July 24, 1948	December 16, 1982
Robert W. Conners	October 12, 1946	December 16, 1982
Charles L. Ellington	December 20, 1946	December 16, 1982
Michael James Lynch	September 21, 1947	December 16, 1982
* Robin L. Ahrens	May 6, 1952	October 5, 1985
* Jerry L. Dove	January 19, 1956	April 11, 1986
* Benjamin P. Grogan	February 26, 1933	April 11, 1986
James K. McAllister	July 14, 1951	April 18, 1986
Scott K. Carey	July 16, 1952	May 10, 1988
L. Douglas Abram	April 10, 1942	January 19, 1990
John L. Bailey	November 17, 1942	June 25, 1990
Stanley Ronquest Jr.	October 1, 1939	March 11, 1992
Martha Dixon Martinez	January 10, 1959	November 22, 1994
Michael John Miller	May 31, 1953	November 22, 1994
William Christian Jr.	July 19, 1946	May 29, 1995
Charles Leo Reed	Janaury 31, 1951	March 22, 1996

Note: Names preceded by an asterik are the subjects of biographical entries (see Chapter 9).

Source: The Federal Bureau of Investigation.

Thomas Jefferson Dormitory

Dedicated in 1989, the 12-story Thomas Jefferson dormitory on the FBI Academy campus in Quantico is so named in recognition of the partnership between the academy and the Thomas Jefferson–founded University of Virginia. Designed as both dormitory and conference center, it accommodates 250 students in private rooms (the other two dormitories have double rooms), a conference center fully equipped for audiovisual presentations, and an extensive food service area. The dormitory also houses the main entrance for visitors to the academy campus. One floor has a special security-controlled series of conference rooms and class-rooms for classified work.

Criminal Justice Information Services

On May 25, 1990, Congress appropriated $185 million to fund a special Identification Revitalization and Relocation Project. This appropriation funded the construction of a satellite facility to house the Criminal Justice Information Services, formally created on February 24, 1992, to incorporate and consolidate in one unit the old Identification Division, the National Crime Information Center (NCIC), and the Uniform Crime Reports. The Criminal Justice Information Services facilities are located in Harrison County, near Clarksburg, West Virginia.

On January 31, 1991, the FBI purchased from 14 landowners 986 acres of land in 13 parcels located in Harrison County, West Virginia, near Clarksburg, at a cost of $3.5 million. Work on the permanent facility began with a groundbreaking ceremony on August 23, 1991. In the interim, and until the new building was completed, a temporary office was located in the Clarksburg Post Office Building. Opened on March 4, 1991, and headed by Supervisory Special Agent Otis G. Cox and staffed by nine other employees, this office was used to test, hire, and train West Virginia personnel, as well as to expedite the automation of the FBI's 8.8 million manual records that had been compiled and processed by the Identification Division. By October 1991, the staff of the office had increased to approximately 100. A second satellite facility opened in 1992. This facility was designed to accommodate up to 1,000 employees over two shifts, whose job was to convert the backlog of fingerprint cards to an automated mode and to add dispositions information (e.g., convictions or parole)

to the NCIC criminal history records that had also been converted from manual to automatic records. Eventually, these offices will be retired when construction of the Clarksburg facility is completed.

Field Offices

The geographical distribution of field divisions is based largely on the outlines of federal court districts. Regardless of size, the headquarters of each field office has a similar layout. The heads of the office (the special agent in charge and assistant special agent in charge, and in New York City and Washington, D.C., the assistant director in charge) have private suites. Supervisors and the office service manager (formerly chief clerk) also have their own offices, which may be rooms or may be cubicles walled off from the "bull pens" in which most of the agents have their desks. Each office has a gun vault, a cable room for storing crypto-graphic and electronic surveillance equipment, a "radio room" in which electronic surveillance is monitored, a file room, and a special file room (or a locked section of the file room for code-word or other highly classified or highly sensitive material). "Rotor clerks," stationed near the applicable squad, also maintain the office's active (that is, current) paper files. Prior to the widespread use of computers, each office also devoted an area to the typing pool. In addition, those field offices dealing in particularly sensitive work (such as counterintelligence or counterterrorism) maintain separate secure areas that are accessible only through coded doorways.

Access to working areas is restricted, but all the offices have a reception area, sometimes cordoned off by bullet-proof glass. Agents often use rooms off the reception area for interviews or other purposes as this avoids having to bring individuals who are not FBI employees into the office proper.

The following paragraphs describe only those field offices presenting special physical-plant features (see also pages 235–38 and the Appendix at the end of Chapter 6).

Butte, Montana

In 1948, the Butte field office was located on the third floor of the Federal Building on North Main Street. In 1951, the office moved to the Thornton Building in downtown Butte, where it remained for 20 years, at which time it returned to the Federal Building. Downgraded to a resident agency in 1989, the Butte office was converted in 1995 into an Information Technology Center.

Jackson, Mississippi

In 1964, FBI Director J. Edgar Hoover designated this resident agency and former field office as the headquarters office for the Jackson, Mississippi, field division. He did so in response to pressure from President Lyndon B. Johnson to put a strong federal presence in Mississippi, then the scene of racial terrorism. Just days after the disappearance of civil rights workers Andrew Goodman, James Chaney, and Michael Schwerner, President Johnson ordered FBI Director J. Edgar Hoover and Associate Director Clyde Tolson to travel to Jackson (in a presidential plane) to open the office. Johnson intended this opening to be a media event, to highlight an intensified federal presence and symbolize a new commitment to racial justice and desegregation. The new headquarters office at the time consisted of three empty floors of a building. With private help, the local FBI constructed a "Potemkin village" near the front door, consisting of fake walls that appeared to be a suite of offices. The media event came off without a hitch, and no one questioned how the FBI managed to construct a suite of offices in five days.

New York, New York

The New York office, one of the Bureau's first field divisions, first opened in 1910 and was located in the Old Post Office Building on the site of the present City Hall Park, near the Woolworth Building. It moved in 1923 a few blocks away to 15 Park Row; in 1924, to the SubTreasury Building on the corner of Wall and Nassau Streets; in 1930, to 370 Lexington Avenue in the Grand Central Terminal area in 1936, back to the United States Courthouse, Foley Square; and then, in 1952, to 290 Broadway, where it occupied an entire building. This space proved insufficient, and in 1956, the New York office was moved to the newly renovated former Lincoln Warehouse at 201 East 69th Street. Since 1980, it has occupied the top stories of the Jacob Javits Federal Building near Foley Square.

Phoenix, Arizona

Beginning in one room with one agent and one clerk in 1919, the Phoenix office had, until 1939, alternated between field office and resident agency status. Since that time, it has occupied five different sites. In 1988, it was moved, at the time comprising a staff of 107 agents and 71 support personnel, into 36,000 square feet of office space on the

fourth and fifth floors of a large office building. This building was named for FBI Special Agent Robin Ahrens, who was killed in the line of duty in Phoenix in October 1985.

San Diego, California

On April 5, 1995, new offices housing the San Diego field division were dedicated in that city's Kearny Mesa section. The office is named in honor of Special Agents Charles W. Elmore and J. Robert Porter, who had been assigned to the El Centro resident agency. The two agents were slain by James Maloney, a suspected associate of the new left terrorist Weathermen group, who then killed himself.

Washington, D.C.

In 1943, the Washington, D.C., field office (almost always referred to as WFO to distinguish it from FBIHQ) was located in the Wardman Building, on K Street between Vermont Avenue and Fifteenth Street. For many years, this office was housed in the Old Post Office Building located two blocks west of the main Department of Justice building on Pennsylvania Avenue. Later, it relocated to Buzzard Point in southwest Washington. On August 22, 1997, it moved into new offices in northwest Washington, six blocks from FBIHQ. The new Federal Bureau of Investigation–Washington Field Office Memorial Building is dedicated to the memory of five WFO agents who were killed in the line of duty. Constructed by the General Services Administration, it provides 305,000 gross square feet on eight levels above ground with a three-and-a-half-level garage for 500 cars below ground. Both its exterior and interior conform to security requirements that the FBI put in place following the 1995 bombing of the Oklahoma City federal building.

Designed by Skidmore, Owings, and Merrill, it features a vaulted penthouse roof and an offset portico designed to fit with the geometry of its Judiciary Square neighbors. Included within it are office space, filing facilities, training areas, a food service facility, and evidence storage and review space. The operations of this building are fully computerized and contain many energy-saving devices, including a programmable lighting system.

Other FBI Facilities

Computer Facilities

The FBI's largest investment for hardware is for computer facilities and workstations. Two major computer facilities, in addition to a specialized computer center, are housed within the J. Edgar Hoover FBI Building. All three of these computer facilities are staffed continuously. The backbone of their operational support consists of mainframe computers. The FBIHQ computer center itself houses five large-scale computers and two medium-scale (mini) computers. In addition, the Fort Monmouth, New Jersey, facility (serving the northeast region) and the Pocatello, Idaho, facility (serving the western region) provide access to the Field Office Information Management System. Each of these facilities contains two mainframe computers.

Legal Attaché Offices

Legal attaché offices are located in the U.S. embassies in the countries to which they are accredited.

International Law Enforcement Academy

On June 16, 1995, 33 officers from former Eastern Bloc countries completed training in the first session of the International Law Enforcement Academy in Budapest, Hungary. This session marked the beginning of a systematically taught course in police professionalism for the new democracies of the former communist states of Eastern Europe. The academy is housed in the current Hungarian National Police Training Academy, a complex of buildings built in 1899 as headquarters and barracks for the Royal Hungarian mounted police. Its facilities include dormitories (housing six or seven to a room), classrooms, a gymnasium, computers, a photo laboratory, a library, a cafeteria, and two indoor tennis courts.

FBI-Related Facilities

J. Edgar Hoover Law Enforcement Museum

Not an official FBI museum, this repository holds a major collection of J. Edgar Hoover memorabilia. Located in the 33rd Degree Masons House of the Temple at 1733 Sixteenth Street, Washington, D.C., the museum is open to the public. Its collection of over 3,000 artifacts includes FBI memorabilia from the 1920s to the present, as well as personal memorabilia of former FBI Director Hoover.

Society of Former Special Agents of the FBI

On October 17, 1992, the headquarters of the Society of Former Special Agents of the FBI was opened in Quantico, Virginia. Until its own building was completed, the society was housed temporarily in space provided by the U.S. Marine Corps at 301 Potomac Street in Quantico. The new Society of Former Special Agents Headquarters, now located in the Marine Corps Association Building, was dedicated on September 22, 1993. Velma and John Doig of Alma, Minnesota, funded this office complex with a $170,000 contribution. John Doig had been an FBI special agent from 1940 to 1961.

Note

The author wishes to thank the staff of the Research/Communications Unit of the FBI for providing many of the research materials used for this chapter.

THE FBI IN AMERICAN POPULAR CULTURE

Richard Gid Powers

Introduction

The FBI is a ubiquitous presence in American culture today. A crime is hardly a crime unless the FBI gets involved. National security cases are the Bureau's responsibility. A political scandal would be pitiful indeed if it did not rate an FBI investigation. Movies and television shows, political thrillers, and murder mysteries all raid the FBI for heroes, victims, and even villains. For almost a century, the FBI has been a fixture in American culture.

The FBI's public image is the residue of American culture's century-long curiosity about the Bureau, its famous cases, and its legendary director, J. Edgar Hoover. Its place in American life only partly depends on how it does its job. The country's collective memories of the FBI's role in American life since the 1930s prevent Americans from seeing the Bureau with any degree of clarity; the public rarely knows whether it is reacting to the real or the legendary FBI, a legend that still calls up complicated and conflicting emotions of pride, fear, and fascination.

The FBI first burst into American popular culture during the sensational gangster cases of the mid-1930s, when FBI Director J. Edgar Hoover emerged as a national hero and his G-men as the stars of Hollywood, radio, the comics, pulp magazines, and even bubble gum cards. During World War II, Hoover's Bureau patrolled the home front. FBI publicity assured Americans that they were safe from Japanese spies and Nazi saboteurs. During the tense crisis years of the Cold War, the FBI campaigned against communist subversion in government, labor, the schools, and the entertainment industry. FBI agents gathered evidence in some of the most sensational internal security cases in American history. To millions of Americans, the FBI was the nation's last line of defense against its enemies. To its critics, however, the FBI and its powerful director loomed as repressive forces stifling dissent and preventing rational discussion of issues. This counter-image was reinforced during the Vietnam War following revelations about the Bureau's controversial programs to suppress antiwar and black power radicalism. In the wake of Vietnam and Watergate, congressional committees investigated, exposed, and denounced the Bureau's once popular efforts to suppress communism's domestic sympathizers.

During the 1990s, popular culture has continued to exploit the public's interest in the Bureau's cases and has continued to use the FBI as the symbol of scientific crime detection and professional law enforcement. Nonetheless, the recent stereotype of the FBI as a conspiracy against civil liberties often eclipses the older image of the heroic G-man standing guard against the nation's foes. As a result, the FBI has come to figure in the conspiracy theories of both left and right. Popular entertainment during the 1980s and 1990s exploits this sinister view of the Bureau, a perspective that had once been confined to the far left.

With popular culture littered with the debris of old FBI symbolism, predicting which of the FBI's conflicting images American popular culture will exploit next has become almost impossible. By the 1990s, films and television stories (and the popular press) were sometimes portraying an FBI at war with the citizenry, and sometimes, a technologically proficient FBI at war with the underworld. Sometimes weird combinations drawn from all the warring stereotypes were woven together to form an image of the postmodern popular culture FBI, a cultural construct that challenges the interpretive skills of even the most ingenious students of American culture.

Before the G-Man: Cultural Background

The FBI did not really enter American popular culture until 1935, when the New Deal gangster wars of the previous two years spurred Hollywood to produce a cycle of G-men movies. But when popular culture finally noticed the FBI, the Bureau's climb to mythic status was amazingly swift. That rise could happen only because the public was already familiar with the cultural needs that the Bureau was called upon to satisfy during the Great Depression, and with the way earlier popular heroes had satisfied those needs. There were poets before Homer, and there were detective heroes in popular culture before the FBI.

Early Crime Entertainment

Modern crime entertainment originated in the souvenirs sold to spectators at public executions like those outside London's Newgate Prison during the early eighteenth century. At Newgate, vendors ("patterers") sold cheap one-page ballads that recounted the condemned man's account of the temptations that had led him into crime, along with an appeal to profit from his example and avoid his fate.

The immediate and staggering popularity of crime entertainment occurred in tandem with society's increasing reluctance to take part in the actual punishment of criminals, and the end of public executions. Crime literature, beginning with nineteenth-century crime "exposés" like Eugene Sue's

Mysteries of Paris, Ned Buntline's *Mysteries of New York,* and crime magazines like the *Police Gazette,* filled a gap when the law enforcement process, due to legal professionalization and middle class sentimentality, stopped providing the real thing: the souvenir became the substitute (see Exhibit 8.1).

Exhibit 8.1   *Police Gazette* **Illustration**

Cultural Theories of Crime Entertainment

The relationship between the fictional and the historical in law enforcement can also be understood in the light of social scientific theories about the cultural function of crime and punishment. The classic interpretation is Emile Durkheim's *Division of Labor in Society,* which argues that cultures must be united to survive. To create that unity, cultures stage communal spectacles to awaken a sense of community among their members. Durkheim called these ceremonies "rituals." Among the most important of these solidarity-affirming spectacles for Durkheim was the ritual of crime and punishment. He argued that crimes, by offending the

collective conscience ("the totality of beliefs and sentiments common to average citizens of the same society"), remind citizens that they actually do have a collective conscience; that they actually form a moral community.

According to Durkheim, just as the crime and the criminal help unite a society, so does the punishment of the criminal. The hero of the law, who captures and punishes the criminal, also becomes a key figure in forging cultural unity. Taken together, then, crime and punishment, the criminal and the hero of the law, combine to form a powerful ritual of cultural solidarity, along with such other unifying forces as work, elections, sports, and wars.

Early Heroes of the Law

The public's enthusiasm for rituals of crime and punishment created a public role for heroes of the law that J. Edgar Hoover and his G-men would later fill. The first pop culture detective hero to appear in the English-speaking world was Jonathan Wild, the "Thief-Taker General of England," who was both the Al Capone and the J. Edgar Hoover of the eighteenth century. Operating before the establishment of a police force in London, Wild set himself up at the Old Bailey, where, for a price, he returned stolen goods he had recovered to their rightful owners. When it was discovered that he himself controlled the criminal gangs that had stolen the goods, however, he was arrested and executed.

As soon as official police forces came into existence, such as the Bow Street Runners in 1749 and Sir Robert Peel's Scotland Yard in 1829, the popular press turned their officers into celebrities, and popular writers transformed them into the action heroes of fictional adventures. Just as the "Newgate novels" improved upon accounts of real crime and punishment by streamlining them into traditional ballads, semi-fictional Bow Street memoirs, such as John Wright's *Mornings at Bow Street* (1825) and *More Mornings at Bow Street* (1827), and Scotland Yard memoirs, such as *Recollections of a Detective Police-Officer* by "Waters" (William Russell), made real detectives the figures of popular mythology.

More than any other historical detective, Eugene Vidocq, founder of the French Sûreté and inspiration for Edgar Allan Poe's path-breaking fictional detective, was the model for popular culture's detective hero. Before beginning his career in law enforcement, Vidocq had been a thief, a circus performer, a galley convict, and a jail-breaker. His 18 years as a detective were even more spectacular, at least according to his enormously popular autobiography, which was published in 1829 in four volumes totaling 1,600 pages. In these memoirs, Vidocq claimed to have arrested 20,000 criminals and portrayed himself as "a master of disguise . . . never worsted in a fight and rarely refused by a woman."

Vidocq carved out a new role for the detective in popular culture, that of narrator of crime stories, another role FBI Director Hoover would later exploit. Vidocq was as famous for the stories he told as for the crimes he solved. That was also true of Allan Pinkerton, the most celebrated American detective of the nineteenth century. Pinkerton's reputation was based as much on the 18 volumes of casebooks his ghostwriters turned out between 1873 and 1886 as on his undeniably impressive accomplishments as a detective. When the FBI's Hoover later began issuing his own ghostwritten casebooks (for example, *Persons in Hiding* in 1938, *Masters of Deceit* in 1958, along with scores of magazine articles and several movies), many contemporary observers thought such literary performances incongruous. But Hoover was only continuing in the popular tradition of the "great detective," who was always a storyteller as well as a hero.

Mystery Stories and the Action Detective Hero

The public's enthusiasm for historical detective heroes was accompanied by a corresponding interest in fictional detectives. For nearly a century before J. Edgar Hoover and his G-men entered popular culture, the reading public had been devouring detective stories. The first fictional detective was Edgar Allan Poe's Dupin, who first appeared in 1841 in "The Murders in the Rue Morgue," published in *Uncle Sam's Magazine,* one of the first popular journals devoted to crime fiction. Poe established a tradition of the cerebrally oriented mystery story, as well as the convention of the idiosyncratic intellectual detective, innovations that eventually culminated in the most famous of all mystery-story detectives, Arthur Conan Doyle's Sherlock Holmes.

The next variation on the detective theme was even more popular than the mystery-story detective. This was the action detective hero, who relies on brawn rather than brains, and who, when he has to use his wits, draws upon them more as an arsenal of technological and scientific wizardry than a machine of pure logic. The first action detective to capture the enthusiasm of American readers was Old Sleuth, the "Giant Detective" narrator of the Old Sleuth Library of detective stories first published in New York's *Fireside*

Companion in 1872. The second was Old Cap Collier, and the greatest of all was Nick Carter, who first appeared in Street and Smith's *New York Weekly* in 1886.

By 1900, the action detective became so popular that he largely displaced the cowboy in pulp magazines. One prolific publisher had over 250 different detective heroes in its lineup. Some pulp magazines were devoted to the adventures of a single hero; others, like "The Jew Detective," catered to the immigrant market. During the second decade of the century, this formula entered the newspaper comic pages with "Hawkshaw, the Detective." In 1931, "Dick Tracy," the greatest action detective comic strip of the twentieth century, brought scientific crime fighting to the comic pages. A year later, radio had its first detective program, "True Detective Mysteries."

The Early Bureau and Popular Culture

Establishing the Bureau

When the Justice Department's Bureau of Investigation was created in 1908, neither the public nor the media knew anything about it. Inaccurate reports said the Treasury Department's Secret Service had been transferred to the Justice Department. Some politicians quickly assumed, either with satisfaction or alarm, that the Bureau was an American version of famous foreign national detective forces, such as Scotland Yard, the French Sûreté, or the Russian tsar's Secret Police. Closer examination would have revealed that the Bureau was more an audit bureau focusing on antitrust cases and federal court budgets than an action-oriented detective agency.

The White Slave Scare

The 1910 White Slave Scare underscored the Bureau's lack of identity; its chief and his agents were popularly referred to as white slave officers, a confusion that persisted until 1913. Enforcement of the White Slave Traffic Act was one of the Bureau's approximately two dozen early responsibilities, but the one that garnered the most publicity. Investigating crimes on Indian reservations involved it most directly in the work popularly associated with the image of a detective. During World War I, the Bureau's investigations of suspected draft evaders and violators of espionage and sedition laws created a brief sensation, but its identity remained ill-defined, and press accounts often referred to its detectives generically as Department of Justice agents.

The Red Scare Raids: The Bureau and the Left

The Red Scare of 1919 and the Palmer Raids of 1920 first focused public attention directly on the Bureau of Investigation. The 24-year-old J. Edgar Hoover, who orchestrated the antiradical drive of those years for Attorney General A. Mitchell Palmer, was determined to turn public opinion against the radical supporters (whether aliens or citizens) of the Bolshevik Revolution. Publicity was essential to this strategy. His Radical Division generated an enormous amount of propaganda: news releases to the mass media, a *General Intelligence Bulletin,* and sensational government-sponsored films that used silent movie melodramas to dramatize the heroism of the Bureau of Investigation operatives who foiled the plots of bomb-throwing radicals.

This sensational antiradical campaign temporarily turned Hoover and Palmer into the men of the hour. But early in 1920, the Red Scare collapsed, nearly costing Hoover his job and creating a lasting image of him and the Bureau as conspirators against civil liberties. After the raids, the public at large soon lost interest in the Bureau, but the American left never forgot its first encounters with Hoover and his detectives. Those initial impressions were thoroughly documented in a 1920 *Lawyers' Report* on the Justice Department's actions during the raids, a brief whose prominent authors included Harvard law professor Felix Frankfurter. Hoover and Palmer were further humiliated during the congressional testimony of Assistant Secretary of Labor Louis Post, who had been threatened with impeachment for his supposed radical sympathies after he set free Hoover's interned alien communists. Post defended himself by attacking his accusers.

The Daugherty Era

The Bureau's reputation was further darkened during the administration of President Warren G. Harding, when Samuel Gompers, head of the American Federation of Labor, denounced what he claimed was a Justice Department conspiracy against labor. Gompers charged that the Bureau had created a network of labor spies to provide Attorney General Harry Daugherty with a pretext for seeking court injunctions to suppress labor unrest. During the scandals surrounding the Interior Department's corrupt leasing of the Navy's oil reserves at Teapot Dome, Wyoming, the Bureau was charged with trying to intimidate the senators who exposed the department's misdeeds. By 1924, when J. Edgar Hoover was finally made director of the Bureau of Investigation, the agency had acquired a sinister and corrupt image in American popular culture, a stereotype that the Bureau's critics exploited to urge that the agency be eliminated, or at least weakened.

Symbol of Professional Law Enforcement

Listening to the Bureau's critics, new attorney general Harlan F. Stone ordered Bureau Director Hoover to keep the Bureau out of the public eye. For the next 10 years, Hoover generally operated within that guideline; the one significant exception was his enormously successful campaign to create an image within the police community of the Bureau as the symbol of scientific law enforcement. The International Association of Chiefs of Police had long lobbied the Justice Department to take over administration of the nationwide fingerprint files maintained at Leavenworth Federal Prison. When this takeover occurred in 1924, Hoover and the Bureau could offer local and state law enforcement a variety of identification services that soon made the Bureau (and the director) indispensable to the police profession.

Even more important for improving the Bureau's image was Hoover's work in professionalizing the nation's police forces. Hoover urged that the police be supplied with more and better education, equipment, and supervision. His campaign made the Bureau's agents the highly admired symbols of the new college-educated, middle-class, law enforcement officer. Despite inevitable friction between federal and local investigators during the 1920s, the FBI's image of progressive law enforcement became a fixture in the consciousness of the law enforcement profession.

When promoting the Bureau as the symbol of law enforcement professionalism, Hoover appropriated an idea that had been gathering strength since the late 1800s: the professionalization of law enforcement and the development of scientific crime detection. (Interestingly, the media discussed parallel developments in Germany, Russia, and England as though there was nothing comparable in this country.) Since its formation in 1893, the International Association of Chiefs of Police (a name it assumed in 1902) had proclaimed that ideal, largely under the direction of the visionary chief of the Berkeley, California, police force, August Vollmer. Vollmer first established a police records system within the Berkeley Police Department and then lobbied for creation of the California State Bureau of

Identification and Investigation, which was eventually established in 1917. Vollmer began training his police officers at his own police academy in 1908, and in 1916, he persuaded the University of California at Berkeley to establish the first university police training program. Vollmer's most important innovation was to recruit college graduates for his police force. His university-trained officers were soon drafted to lead police forces around the country. Thus, when requiring university degrees and advanced legal or accounting education for Bureau recruits, Hoover adopted an already proven method for lifting the status of law enforcement in the eyes of the public.

The publicity the Bureau received during the late 1920s and early 1930s stressed its role in promoting scientific law enforcement. Media portrayals of Hoover and his agents usually contrasted the older breed of corrupt, uneducated, immigrant (largely Irish) cops with this new crop of middle class, Protestant, college-educated agents. Although the Bureau investigated some sensational cases during the 1920s, Hoover's principal mission before the coming of the New Deal was to promote the professionalization of the Bureau and to identify his agency with scientific law enforcement. Years later, he would cite his firing of the notorious Gaston Means, one of the most corrupt figures associated with the old Bureau, to demonstrate how he had reformed and redeemed the Bureau after the dark days of the Harding administration.

The 1930s and the Myth of the G-Man

American popular culture had earlier demonstrated an enthusiasm, even an obsession, with action crime entertainment long before either the FBI or the G-man hero came on the scene. But FBI agents only began to fit smoothly into the roles prepared for them by Nick Carter and Dick Tracy when the Great Depression of the 1930s caused the cultural meaning of crime to change.

The Public Enemy

Depression-era America invented the G-man hero because it had to. Embracing the G-man was one way the country responded to a cultural crisis produced by economic collapse, and the symbol of this crisis was the public enemy, one of the most powerful, dangerous, and ambiguously fascinating figures in American cultural history.

The "public enemy," the celebrity criminal, became a popular fixation because of a perceived breakdown of law and order in the 1920s—"perceived" because the crime statistics of the period, incomplete though they are, do not, in fact, indicate the crime explosion that politicians and the media claimed. In the 1920s, crime had sometimes been viewed almost as a form of entertainment; in the 1930s, it came to be seen as a symptom of moral collapse. It echoed the country's sense of doubt that it could survive the economic collapse with its values intact. The country came to link President Herbert Hoover's unwillingness to lead a national effort against crime with his inability to cope with the economic depression. The crime crisis of the 1930s thus became a symptom of the cultural depression that accompanied the bleak economic outlook, and this was graphically illustrated by the front-page gangster the media labeled the "public enemy." Once the myth of the public enemy gained currency, Americans interpreted every outbreak of crime as further evidence of social demoralization and moral decline. Were Americans to emerge from their state of psychological depression, they would need to find another, more hopeful myth to confront, defeat, and displace the public enemy.

Popular culture's image of the public enemy was a collective representation of the notorious criminals who had become celebrities during the Prohibition era: Johnny Toro, Dion O'Banion, Hymie Weiss, and Klondike O'Donnel in Chicago; Dutch Schultz, Mad Dog Coll, and Legs Diamond in New York; and scores of other big-name gangsters across the country. Dwarfing them all in the public imagination was Al Capone, the boss of the "Chicago firm." The premier symbol of crime during Herbert Hoover's administration, Capone's success in evading the law was seen as shocking proof that crime had produced archetypal figures who were more than a match for a law-abiding society.

By 1930, Al Capone had acquired a worldwide reputation as the new symbol of crime in America—crime that was accepted as an intrinsic part of society, a force in American life that government at all levels was powerless to control. Capone nurtured his reputation by cultivating the bravura crime reporters of the era and becoming a national celebrity—not because he was admired, but because he was grudgingly accepted as representative of his city and his time.

Al Capone and the forces he symbolized quickly became important additions to the American scene. President Hoover was pressured to do something about Capone, ordering the Treasury Department to launch a probe of

Capone's tax returns. This investigation eventually led to a 10-year sentence for tax evasion. The Hoover administration, however, received scant credit for this achievement. Many observers lamented that the law had failed, Capone having been nailed on a technicality rather than for his multitude of more violent crimes. The public did not want technical and legalistic justice, but a poetic justice that punished moral, and not merely legal, guilt—and that Capone's punishment demonstrate the law's victory over crime. Because Capone had become a symbol of crime, the public wanted a symbolic, as well as a legal, victory.

The futile search for the kidnapper of Charles Lindbergh's baby, who was snatched from his Hopewell, New Jersey, home on March 1, 1932, provided a more devastating instance of crime as a symbol of national demoralization. The country interpreted this outrage as an underworld attack on the nation and looked to Washington for an appropriate response. President Hoover, instead, lectured the country about states' rights and the constitutional limits on federal jurisdiction. The Lindbergh case did not stop making news until September 1934, when Bruno Richard Hauptmann was captured, tried the following year, and electrocuted a year later. The shock of the Lindbergh case produced demands for a national campaign against crime. Only one thing would turn back the criminal assault, said a senator, "the fear of Uncle Sam."

Gangster Films and the Cultural Depression

Commercial popular entertainment soon reflected how the Depression public had turned crime into a symbol of national demoralization. Like the newspaper accounts of celebrated crimes, gangster movies of the early 1930s revealed how much the image of the public enemy had become embedded in the popular imagination, had become a symbol of national defeat and despair. More than that, gangster movies showed that American popular culture understood the public enemy as a reproach to the times, and as a preview of what the future held should the nation's morale and commitment to traditional values and institutions continue to decline.

A series of prison pictures captured these concerns— *The Big House* (1930), *Convict's Code* (1930), *Ladies of the Big House* (1931), and *20,000 Years at Sing Sing* (1932). In these movies, jail became a metaphor for life in Depression-era America. As the economic depression worsened, so did national morale. Because prison pictures no longer adequately expressed the public's alienation from authority, the heroes in the next cycle of Depression-era crime movies were no longer merely the innocent victims of injustice— they were outlaws on the prowl.

The first example of this ominous turn in public mood was *Little Caesar* (1930), one of the most famous pictures in movie history, starring Edward G. Robinson as Caesar Enrico Bandello, a Capone-style Chicago gangster. The gangster movies that followed *Little Caesar* depicted an America in which the authority of the law had all but disappeared. The economic debacle had destroyed the moral authority of priest, policeman, politician, and plutocrat, and Hollywood offered the mobster as a plausible claimant to their symbolic station at the helm of society. *Little Caesar*'s Chicago is a legal no-man's-land where the gangster succeeds by being more daring and ruthless than his rivals. The only enemies worth his attention are other gangsters, and the only authority he acknowledges is the "Big Boy." The law is such a dim off-screen presence in gangster movies that the stories make sense only if the audience accepts the existence of an organized American underworld outside the reach of the law with the power to infiltrate and conquer legitimate society. The box office success of *Little Caesar* shows that audiences of that period had no trouble accepting that horrific premise.

Following *Little Caesar*'s success, more than 50 gangster pictures swaggered into the theaters in 1931; movies like *The Gang Buster, Scandal Sheet, The Vice Squad, Hush Money, Star Witness, Undercover Man*, and *The Docks of San Francisco*. Among them, one combined the contemporary mythic power of the gangster formula with the raw energy of one of the most dynamic performers ever to appear on film, James Cagney. In *The Public Enemy*, Cagney, as gangster Tommy Powers, created the definitive characterization of the untamed criminal as the new American hero (see Exhibit 8.2). In addition to Cagney's charisma, *The Public Enemy*'s impact derived from its almost documentary flavor. The story was a thinly fictionalized dramatization of the Chicago gang wars that the national press had turned into folklore. The gangster movies' documentary-like references to real-life personalities and events made the films' departures from the familiar crime and punishment formula (the gangsters met their fate, if at all, at the hands of rival gangsters) all the more disturbing. Warner Brothers recognized the subversive effect of *The Public Enemy* by nervously tacking a printed title onto the film's final frames:

Exhibit 8.2   *Public Enemy, Courtesy of Warner Bros.*

"The end of Tom Powers is the end of every hoodlum. The Public Enemy is not a man, it is not a character, it is a problem we all must face."

The Grassroots Anticrime Crusade

The appearance of the "public enemy" in the news and in the movie theaters had two related consequences. The first was a call for a grassroots campaign against criminals. The second was a demand that Hollywood stop glamorizing crime and hoodlums. Both consequences helped create the myth of the G-man.

Frustrated by President Hoover's failure to respond to the outcry over crime, the public began to propose its own remedies. To a remarkable degree, this grassroots anticrime campaign provided a blueprint for the New Deal's subsequent upgrading of the FBI to the status of a national anticrime strike force. The public called for new laws to combat the new breed of "super criminals," for new "super prisons" to hold them, and for a new "super police force" at the federal level to employ the weapons of science against the new threats to law and order. The public was demanding exactly what the Roosevelt administration soon proposed—a

newly powerful FBI armed with new laws and new prisons to hold any prisoners who might survive the new federal firepower. In popular culture, the comic strips displayed Dick Tracy as the kind of scientific crime fighter who could be just as violent as the public enemies. Films like *Gabriel over the White House* expressed a public desire for the federal government to respond to the crime emergency with emergency measures.

The earlier flood of Hollywood gangster pictures had also led to protests against movie violence. These outcries received the backing of social science research, which suggested that gangster movies were contributing to the crime wave by glorifying crime on the screen and by denigrating police officers and the law. During the summer of 1933, the American Catholic Bishops launched a drive against objectionable movies. This campaign produced the Legion of Decency in April 1934 and a pledge by Catholics to boycott movies that glorified vice or crime. When other religious groups joined the bishops, Hollywood agreed late in 1934 to enforce the Production Code, standards it had drawn up in 1930 but largely ignored. This action all but outlawed the gangster movie, since the acknowledged intent of the code was "to insure above all that crime will be shown to be wrong and that the criminal life will be loathed and that the law will at all times prevail." The code severely limited the criminals' arsenal and banned the movie gangster's favorite weapon, the submachine gun. As the new administration of Franklin Roosevelt began to respond to the public's demands for action against the public enemies, Hollywood found itself unable to profit from the mess it had helped create.

The New Deal War on Crime

American popular culture was now prepared for a federal police force, and the 1932 presidential election produced an administration ready to provide it. The Roosevelt administration had neither planned nor foreseen the transformation of the Bureau of Investigation into a band of national heroes. This unpredictable outcome arose from an unrepeatable set of circumstances adroitly exploited by a group of consummate political craftsmen, among them, Attorney General Homer S. Cummings, Bureau Director J. Edgar Hoover, and the FBI's public relations chief, Louis B. Nichols. The war on crime became one of the Roosevelt administration's most striking successes; it provided a superb way of dramatizing the difference between the New Deal's aggressive, activist approach to social problems and the Herbert Hoover administration's lack of leadership.

Cummings was a hasty replacement for Roosevelt's first choice as attorney general, Senator Thomas Walsh, who died on his way to the inauguration. Cummings quickly turned what might otherwise have been an inconsequential (though sensational) crime in Kansas City into the beginning of the gangster wars that transformed the FBI into an enduring icon of American popular culture.

On June 17, 1933, a prisoner in handcuffs stepped off a train at Kansas City's Union Station and was escorted toward a waiting car. The prisoner was Frank "Jelly" Nash, an escaped convict who was being brought back to the federal prison at Leavenworth by four Bureau of Investigation agents, aided by a police chief from McAlester, Oklahoma, and two Kansas City detectives. As the lawmen opened the door of their car, they were met by a blaze of gunfire. Waiting in ambush were well-known Midwestern gangsters Vernon Miller, Adam Richetti, and Charles "Pretty Boy" Floyd. In an instant, four of the officers, including FBI agent Raymond J. Caffrey, were dead. Two other Bureau agents were badly wounded, and Frank Nash lay dead on the ground, killed in the first burst of gunfire.

Ever since the inauguration, Attorney General Cummings had been working to seize leadership of the grassroots anticrime movement. In speeches before anticrime groups, he endorsed new laws, prisons, and police, and he had already designated Hoover's tiny Bureau as his crime war's mobile anticrime detachment. Cummings immediately recognized the propaganda potential of what the newspapers dubbed the "Kansas City Massacre." He called the murder of Agent Caffrey "a challenge to the government" and ordered all government agencies to work on this case. He characterized the new government effort "a military engagement between the forces of law and order and the underworld army, heavily armed . . . a campaign to wipe out the public enemy [to] proceed until it succeeds." While the nation watched with growing excitement, the Bureau's agents hunted down each new "Public Enemy Number One," a designation created for the Bureau by the media. The list of gangsters so designated included George "Machine Gun" Kelly, "Pretty Boy" Floyd, "Baby Face" Nelson, Alvin "Creepy" Karpis, "Ma" Barker and her sons, and, of course, the ultimate 1930s gangster, bank robber John Dillinger, killed by Bureau agents in July 1934.

A few weeks after the Kansas City Massacre, on July 22, 1933, the most sensational kidnapping of the Roosevelt years, occurred, George "Machine Gun" Kelly and his gang abducted Oklahoma City oilman Charles F. Urschel and demanded a $200,000 ransom. The case became an FBI legend when Bureau publicists subsequently exploited the Urschel case to tag FBI agents with a dramatic new nickname: when FBI agents broke into Kelly's hideout to arrest the notorious criminal, they claimed he pleaded, "Don't shoot, G-men!" and later explained that the word was gangster slang for the FBI. An alternative explanation of the "G-man" tag, but with no more evidence to support it than the FBI's version, was that the term was borrowed from the Irish Republican underground, which had long referred to plainclothes detectives and undercover operatives of the Dublin Constabulary as "G-men." The Constabulary's regular, non-secret force was divided into departments "A" through "F"; "G" was thus assigned to the force's special undercover agents. During Kelly's trial, the prosecution pronounced that "the interest of the nation is focused on the drama now coming to a close in this courtroom. We are here to find an answer to the question of whether we shall have a government of law and order or abdicate in favor of machine gun gangsters. If this government cannot protect its citizens, then we had frankly better turn it over to the Kellys, the Bates, the Baileys [Kelly's accomplices] and the others of the underworld and pay tribute to them through taxes."

Attorney General Cummings deftly exploited each new manhunt to generate support in 1933–34 for his proposed package of anticrime measures to enlarge the jurisdiction of the Bureau and to give it new powers. He had already announced that the old military prison at Alcatraz was to be designated the "super jail" for the public enemies he was rounding up. On April 19, 1934, Cummings released a Twelve Point Crime Program, which, among other provisions, permitted Bureau agents to carry weapons, make arrests, and investigate an array of new interstate crimes.

Cummings also used the manhunt technique against the most sensational criminal of the 1930s, John Dillinger, to dramatize the need for these proposed measures. On January 23, 1934, Dillinger pulled off his famous "wooden pistol" escape from the jail at Crown Point, Indiana. On April 22, he eluded an FBI ambush at the Little Bohemia resort in Wisconsin, killing an agent. Cummings and the Justice Department (and Hoover and the Bureau) bet their reputations that they could capture Dillinger. The nation's top law enforcement officials and the country's most famous criminal prepared for an Old West–style showdown, while the public held its breath. Meanwhile Roosevelt and Cummings adroitly exploited the Dillinger manhunt to ram their anticrime proposals through Congress. On May 18, Roosevelt signed the measures into law, explaining that "these laws are a renewed challenge on the part of the Federal Government to interstate crime. . . . So far as the Federal Government is concerned, there will be no relenting. . . . I stand squarely behind the efforts of the Department of Justice to bring to book every lawbreaker, big and little."

The Bureau got its break on July 21. Anna Sage, who later became famous as the "Woman in Red," approached Melvin Purvis, the special agent in charge of the Bureau's Chicago office. She offered to betray her friend Dillinger in return for Bureau help in getting her favorable consideration during her deportation hearings for having operated a brothel. She told Purvis that the next day, she would be at Chicago's Biograph Theatre with Dillinger. Purvis told his squad, "Gentlemen, you know the character of John Dillinger. If . . . we locate him and he makes his escape it will be a disgrace to our Bureau." Dillinger did not escape. Spotting the gangster leaving the theater, Purvis lit his cigar, the signal for his men to close in, and called out, "Stick 'em up, Johnny." Dillinger sprinted toward an alley and a few seconds later was ripped apart in the agents' crossfire.

In December, Cummings capped his federal war on crime by convening a four-day Attorney General's Conference on Crime, where he called for a sustained law enforcement crusade to unite federal, state, and local law enforcement with the public in a comprehensive drive against crime. Just as significantly, the news and entertainment industries were enlisted in the effort. This conference became the climax of Cummings's career as a crime-buster. By then, popular culture heaped so much glory on Bureau Director Hoover and his men that the rest of the Justice Department was all but forgotten.

The Origins of FBI Publicity: Courtney Ryley Cooper

With the newspapers agog over the war on crime, FBI officials began molding the stories of those cases into a unified myth. Nobody did more to promote this goal than reporter Courtney Ryley Cooper, who in the early summer of 1933 was assigned to find a story at the Bureau for *American Magazine*. Cooper ultimately published 24 stories between 1933 and 1940 (all but one in *American Magazine*), three books (*Ten Thousand Public Enemies*, 1935; *Here's to*

Crime, 1937; and *Persons in Hiding*, 1938), and four movies based on his ghostwriting for Hoover (*Persons in Hiding*, 1939; *Undercover Doctor*, 1939; *Parole Fixer*, 1940; and *Queen of the Mob*, 1940).

Cooper was the first writer to organize all the FBI's activities into one coherent story with all the parts contributing to the impressive effect of the whole. Instead of simply writing up FBI cases or procedures, Cooper looked for ways to link one episode to the next. Seeing the advantage a series of stories on the Bureau would have over isolated articles, he looked always for the "big story" that would give an individual case interest and significance. Cooper's pulp experience had taught him that an adventure story had to have a main character who could carry the reader along on fantastic flights of ego identification. For Cooper, every story had a hero, and the hero of the Bureau story was J. Edgar Hoover (see Exhibit 8.3).

Exhibit 8.3   **Courtney Ryley Cooper** *(left)* **fingerprints J. Edgar Hoover,** *Courtesy of the National Archives*

Once Cooper had his theme, he drew on his experience as a hack writer of pulp adventure stories, action formula movies, and newspaper crime features to keep his readers glued to the page with an exciting stew of mystery, action, exotic locales, and struggles between clear-cut good and evil.

Cooper's first piece on the FBI appeared in *American Magazine*'s August 1933 issue. "Getting the Jump on Crime" was topped by a half-page photo of Hoover working studiously at his desk. Cooper's 4,000-word piece began with a kidnapping in North Carolina and closed with a nationwide manhunt for the killer of an FBI agent. He connected the cases by tracing the chain of information and command that tied the agents in the field to Hoover, their commander in Washington, "the master detective who simply does not conform to any picture of the average crime chaser." According to Cooper, J. Edgar Hoover had created an "amazing police force" unified by "an enthusiastic spirit of team play all through the Bureau":

> The organization became as tightly knit as a baseball team—and Hoover was coach, just as he became the sponsor of the real bureau baseball team, which won local championships. . . . And always before every subordinate is the lure of a place on that big map which hangs on the Director's wall, where push pins, each with a name tag, denote the various Special Agents of the bureau as they are moved about in accordance with their assignments.

Because of the science and teamwork that Hoover had drilled into his agents, his FBI was invincible.

Cooper also unified his stories by referring to FBI Director Hoover's theory that the superstructure of national crime (meaning famous criminals like Dillinger) rested on a foundation of local crime, which meant that big-time gangsters existed only because the local police failed to do their jobs. Celebrity criminals would not exist if local police arrested the small-time criminals who made the exploits of the public enemies possible.

Cooper denied that the theory was an argument for a federal takeover of law enforcement. A national police force, staffed with the corrupt personnel of the local forces, would ruin the Bureau because Hoover's strict standards would be impossible in a unified national force with hundreds of thousands of officers. A national police force, even under the leadership of the FBI, would corrupt the Bureau without redeeming American law enforcement. This theory was the background of Hoover's refusal to admit the existence of any national crime organization, a position that made him look ridiculous after a 1957 New York state police raid of a Mafia conference at Apalachin, New York, uncovered a ruling body that resolved disputes between organized crime families.

The answer to the crime problem, Cooper argued, was for Hoover's FBI to continue doing what it was already doing. The Bureau should take over cases only where federal laws were violated, but more laws should be passed to trigger federal intervention in key areas. The Bureau should provide services that were beyond the capabilities of local forces: fingerprint files, collections of criminals' modi operandi, and facilities for identifying automobiles, guns,

bullets, and blood. Its statistical services would help local police understand their own problems in the context of national conditions. The FBI's ultimate role was as the catalyst for regenerating American law enforcement, and only when the FBI model was adopted throughout the country would American crime fighting become truly effective. To bring this about, the best local police officers should be sent to the Bureau for training. On July 29, 1935, shortly after another Cooper article appeared, the Bureau established the FBI National Academy for that very purpose. Cooper's grand vision portrayed the real importance of an FBI case in a way to persuade the public to adopt the FBI as the model for all law enforcement agencies. Because Cooper promoted this FBI image as the ultimate weapon against crime, publicity became the Bureau's most important product.

Cooper's *Ten Thousand Public Enemies* encouraged Hoover to spread the gospel of scientific law enforcement, to stand before the nation as a "symbol of police professionalism" and the "newly emerging cadre of police professionals." These efforts won Hoover the admiration and gratitude of the police themselves and their most important professional association, the International Association of Chiefs of Police.

What emerged from these earliest Bureau-approved stories of Cooper and others can accurately be called the "FBI formula." The formula approached FBI cases by turning them into illustrations of scientific, professional law enforcement. The idea came to govern all FBI publicity and entertainment. By making publicity central to the Bureau concept of its role in American life, the formula would help shape FBI law enforcement priorities from the 1930s to the present.

The Crime Records Division

Convinced by Cooper of the importance of public relations, FBI Director Hoover expanded the obscure Publications Section, which simply cranked out publications for the law enforcement community, and in 1938 renamed it the Crime Records Division. Crime Records became Hoover's face to the world, and, in many ways, the FBI's most important division. The two men who shaped and headed the Crime Records Division between 1935 and 1970, Louis B. Nichols and Cartha DeLoach, became Hoover's right-hand men, enjoying a rank subordinate only to that of Hoover and his lifelong associate director, Clyde Tolson.

The Crime Records Division put out ghostwritten accounts of the Bureau's great cases, thus casting Hoover in the role of such famous tellers of detective stories as Eugene Vidocq, Allan Pinkerton, and William Burns. *Persons in Hiding* (1938) was followed by scores of magazine articles published under Hoover's byline, and by countless speeches the FBI director gave before civic and professional groups.

Film Censorship and the G-Man Movie

In the mid-1930s, Hollywood intervened in the creation of FBI mythology. Movie makers sorely missed the money they lost when the popular gangster movies were outlawed in 1934. When Attorney General Cummings called on the entertainment industry to join the war on crime, Hollywood saw a chance to cash in, particularly when the International Association of Chiefs of Police sent a delegation to Hollywood in 1934 to demand that the industry help "create a public opinion in favor of cooperating with the police."

The filmmakers asked industry censors for an exemption from the prohibition on gangster movies to make films glorifying the Bureau's battles against the gangs. The Production Code authorities agreed. In 1935, Hollywood produced violent and exciting pictures that featured G-man heroes locked in battle with public enemies. Thus was launched one of the most remarkable phenomena of 1930s popular culture, the Hollywood G-man.

G-Men (1935)
(Directed by William Keighley, with James Cagney, Ann Dvorak, Margaret Lindsay, and Robert Armstrong)

Warner Brothers *G-Men* was the first and most important G-man movie released in 1935 (see Exhibit 8.4). This film established the formula that Hollywood has followed (or has

Exhibit 8.4   *G-Men, Courtesy of Warner Bros.*

been conscious of violating) ever since. Cagney played Brick Davis, a young lawyer who joins the FBI when his law-school roommate is gunned down during a Bureau assignment. Cagney's Davis is tough, smart, and brash—the same character Cagney played on the other side of the law four years earlier in *The Public Enemy*. For character definition, the film reworked old clichés in ways that became permanent fixtures in FBI films—the tensions between job and romance separating Cagney from his girlfriend, conflict between Cagney and a by-the-book superior irritated by Cagney's bravado, and the lessons Cagney learns about the value of methodical procedures and teamwork. When the movie was over, *G-Men* offered the country a new breed of action heroes—college-educated cops armed with science and organization (as well as submachine guns).

The picture labored to recreate scenes already made famous by Justice Department publicity photographs. The audience saw shots of the Justice Department building, peered at bullets and fingerprints through microscopes, visited the FBI gym for boxing and judo instruction, and toured the pistol and machine-gun ranges. The film projected a newsreel-like effect in its coverage of FBI procedures. The script called for reproduction "as accurately as possible" of the widely published photographs of a line of G-men at machine-gun practice, specifying that the guns should be "roaring while Marine Corps sergeants are working with the men." A "grim-faced operative" at the firing range demonstrates the determination of the G-men trainees by firing straight into the camera with the muzzle close to the lens.

G-Men's popular "documentary" episodes became obligatory features of most subsequent FBI pictures. Inspired by these movies, visitors to Washington began to ask to see the real FBI laboratories and firing ranges, and the Crime Records Division began daily tours of the facilities, tours that remain among the most popular tourist attractions in the capital. Hollywood, Washington, and the public all liked these tours, and for the same reason: while watching a movie or taking the tour, citizens could share the agents' point of view, vicariously becoming agents themselves.

Warner Brothers' publicity touted *G-Men* as a "shot-by-shot" dramatization of gangdom's "Waterloo." Scriptwriter Seton Miller and director William Keighley pieced the plot together by cutting and pasting the most famous crime headlines of the previous two years, although some touching up was required to compress two years of history into two hours of film. The Justice Department had corralled famous gangsters from all over the country during 1933 and 1934, but fame was the only thing they had in common. To turn their separate careers into a coherent story, the film's producers had to take a few liberties with the facts.

G-Men's villains were modeled after the three most famous hoodlums of the early 1930s, "Pretty Boy" Floyd, "Baby Face" Nelson, and John Dillinger. Dillinger and Nelson had, for a short time, actually been members of the same gang, and Floyd may have helped them rob a bank in South Bend, Indiana. The film used this tenuous relationship to turn the three into a close-knit gang responsible for the two most famous shoot-outs in FBI history, the Kansas City Massacre of June 17, 1933, and the April 22, 1934, battle with the Dillinger gang at Little Bohemia, Wisconsin. To embellish history a little further, the *G-Men* gang also robbed the Federal Reserve Bank in New York, as well as five small Midwestern banks.

The film's improvement (or embellishment) on history turned the great crimes of 1933 and 1934 into a coordinated assault upon society by an "army of crime," an image that by then was a staple of New Deal political rhetoric. Reworking the Kansas City and Little Bohemia incidents and Dillinger's death to suit their purposes, *G-Men*'s producers also pulled together bits and pieces of other famous cases. The Lindbergh kidnapping is recalled by having the movie's "Pretty Boy" Floyd captured when he passes a marked banknote. Every detail of the Lindbergh case was still so familiar that the audience would have recognized the reference to kidnapper Bruno Richard Hauptmann's use of a marked gold certificate at a Bronx gas station. In *G-Men,* the marked banknote is discovered not at a gas station but at a flower shop, an allusion to the Capone organization's flower shop murder of Chicago mobster Dion O'Banion. The movie also refers to an FBI "Public Enemies List"; the list actually was dreamed up by the Chicago Crime Commission and was informally maintained by the press itself, not by the FBI. By making the public enemies list an official Bureau document, the film made the FBI conform to the image created for it by the era's flamboyant crime reporters.

G-Men telescopes history by making the Kansas City Massacre the immediate cause of the war on crime and the laws that armed the FBI a year later. The movie's recreation of the Kansas City Massacre is quickly followed by a series of newspaper headline dissolves—"Railway Station Massacre . . . 4 Officers slain, 2 wounded . . . Machine Guns Butcher Officers"—until the relationship between the filmed incident and the actual crime is firmly established. These headlines are immediately followed by a shot of the Capitol building and the interior of a congressional committee room where a group of "serious-faced" congressmen are listening to a "grim" and "earnest" speech by the FBI director, in the film named Bruce J. Gregory:

> The state police cannot combat these criminals . . . neither can city police! The law prevents them from following criminals across state lines! With the automobile and aeroplane, these gangs can get from one state to another in a few hours. The Department of Justice is handicapped! . . . A federal agent can't carry a gun! He can't even make an arrest without getting a local warrant first! Gentlemen, . . . if you will back us by national laws with teeth in them . . . that cover the whole field of interstate crime, . . . that let us work to full effect with state police agencies, . . . these gangs will be wiped out!

After a suspenseful pause, the chairman of the committee asks Gregory, "What laws do you need most?" Gregory's reply outlines the Twelve Point Crime Program that Attorney General Cummings had submitted to Congress in the spring of 1934. "Make bank robbery and kidnapping federal crimes!" Gregory tells Congress.

> Make it a federal crime to kill a government agent . . . to flee across the state line to escape arrest or to escape testifying as a witness. Arm governmental agents . . . and not just with revolvers! If these gangsters want to use machine guns—give the special agents machine guns . . . shotguns . . . tear gas and everything else! This is war! . . . I want the underworld to know that when a special agent draws his gun, he is ready and equipped to shoot to kill with the least possible waste of bullets!

From the committee room, the scene shifts to a joint session of Congress and then to another series of newspaper dissolves: "Government Declares War on Crime . . . Congress rushes through new crime laws . . . Department of Justice Starts Drive."

The movie redefined the FBI agent as the latest incarnation of a century-old stereotype in popular entertainment, the action detective hero. The movie G-man was even better than the action detective hero, however, because the FBI agent had scientific training and could rely on the FBI's nationwide organization and up-to-date scientific facilities as reinforcements for his individual derring-do. Most of all, the G-man was commanded by the director himself, the organizer and leader of the G-man's team, the trainer, adviser, and father-figure for the youthfully impetuous heroes. In Hollywood's G-man pictures, the FBI director entered into a compact with the public; this alliance would not be dissolved, until Hoover's death in 1972. After *G-Men,* Hoover and the Bureau could no longer be understood simply in terms of political science and criminology. The FBI had become show business after 1935.

James Cagney as the movie G-man turned the FBI agent into a pop culture hero. Cagney, however, was not the only Hollywood special agent of 1935 and 1936. During those years, G-men movies took the country by storm. Seven more were released in these two years, and all were trumpeted as spontaneous tributes to the country's newest idols: *Public Hero Number One; Whipsaw; Mary Burns, Fugitive; Let 'Em Have It; Show Them No Mercy; Public Enemy's Wife;* and *Special Investigator.*

This mythic image of the FBI, created by Courtney Ryley Cooper and Hollywood, proved to be a tremendous boon for Hoover and the Bureau, making them untouchable icons of American culture. In an unforeseen way, this new image also made Hoover and the Bureau captives of public expectations about action heroes. Although Hoover tried to stress the cultural causes of crime and the importance of character development in young boys in successful crime prevention, the public turned a deaf ear to anything Hoover said that did not conform to this media-produced reputation of "machine gun criminology."

Late in 1935, British censors, having no patriotic investment in the FBI's triumphs, and believing Hollywood had meant what it said with the ban on movie violence, objected to the FBI loophole in the Production Code, and the G-men cycle came to an end. By then, the image of the FBI had been lifted to a height from which it never would descend while FBI Director Hoover lived. No longer history, the FBI had become a legend.

Public Hero Number One (1935)
(Directed by J. Rubin, with Lionel Barrymore, Jean Arthur, Chester Morris, and Joseph Calleia)

G-Men had gone to great lengths to look like a factual dramatization of Justice Department operations. Other G-man films released in 1935 and 1936 pretended to be nothing more than what they were—standard action detective melodramas. Their ads promised audiences the same sex and violence formerly provided by the now-outlawed gangster movies. MGM's *Public Hero Number One* was dutifully advertised as a tribute to the FBI. However, the film leeringly promised an exposé of the love lives of the new heroes: "What are they like? How do they carry

on Uncle Sam's relentless war to end crime? Must they keep love out of their dangerous lives? *Public Hero Number One*'s villain, played by Joseph Calleia, was modeled rather loosely on John Dillinger. The film featured a jailbreak, a run-in with a "crime doctor" (played by Lionel Barrymore), and a shoot-out at a movie theater, all scenes recalling Dillinger's career. These historical tidbits were incidental, however. As played by Chester Morris, the film's G-man hero was really Old Sleuth in a three-piece suit and a snap-brim hat, chasing the same crooks action detectives had chased since dime novel days.

Besides the old disguise plot, the movie offered another relic of dime novel days—a romance between the under-cover detective and a bandit queen (re-costumed as a gun moll). The plot sent Chester Morris undercover, disguised as a convict in gangster Calleia's prison cell. The plan was to break out together so that Calleia would lead Morris to the gang's hideout, but Morris fell in love with Calleia's sister, played by Jean Arthur. *Public Hero Number One* was successful enough to be remade in 1941 with Dan Dailey as the gangster and Donna Reed as his sister.

Whipsaw (1935)
(Directed by Sam Wood, with Myrna Loy, Spencer Tracy, Harvey Stephens, William Harrigan, and Clay Clement)

MGM's second G-man feature of 1935, *Whipsaw,* also featured a G-man hero who puts on a disguise and falls in love with a gun moll. Spencer Tracy was the G-man in disguise, Myrna Loy the gun moll. *Whipsaw* also tried to capitalize on the success of *It Happened One Night* with an imitation of Clark Gable and Claudette Colbert's cross-country romance.

Let 'Em Have It (1935)
(Directed by Sam Wood, with Richard Arlen, Virginia Bruce, Alice Brady, and Bruce Cabot)

The doctors who took care of gangsters' needs were also popular plot devices. These characters were based on the careers of crime doctors Joseph P. Moran and William Loesser, who had become famous during the Dillinger manhunt. In the Edward Small/United Artists production of *Let 'Em Have It,* when the movie's Dillinger-like villain pulls off his bandages after his facelift, he discovers that the plastic surgeon branded the criminal's initials on his forehead as a mark of Cain for all the world to see.

Let 'Em Have It offered audiences the kind of proce-dural details that became the hallmark of official FBI entertainment but which were often lacking in other early G-man films. G-man Richard Arlen's tours of the Bureau's

Washington headquarters are ploddingly paced, but 1935 audiences had an almost superstitious reverence for the scientific criminology sold by the Justice Department and its publicists as a magic cure for crime. Responding to their audiences' enthusiasm about fingerprinting, for example, theaters gave moviegoers a chance to be fingerprinted in the lobby to enlist them in the anticrime crusade. The real FBI soon imitated Hollywood with a 1936 drive to get citizens to send their fingerprints to the Bureau. John D. Rockefeller Jr. was the first volunteer, with Hoover himself taking Rockefeller's prints.

The FBI's scientific gadgets were effective crime fighting tools; they also associated the G-man with the fictional detectives of comics and pulp magazines, who had made audiences expect up-to-date detectives to have spy cameras and bullet-proof cars long before anyone had heard of the FBI. By featuring these gadgets, popular entertainment fit the G-man into the stereotype of the action detective and also helped make the FBI synonymous with scientific law enforcement. Before long, a story that used science to catch criminals was almost certain to make the hero an FBI agent.

Show Them No Mercy (1935)
(Directed by George Marshall, with Rochelle Hudson, Cesar Romero, Bruce Cabot, Edward Norris, Edward Brophy, and Warren Hymer)

The most violent of the 1935 G-man movies was Twentieth Century Fox's *Show Them No Mercy,* written by Kubec Glasmon, scriptwriter for Cagney's *The Public Enemy* (1931). The film was based on the kidnapping of the grandson of Washington lumber tycoon J. P. Weyerhauser. Cesar Romero played a sadistic leader of a gang of villains, and the film reveled in the gang's psychological disintegration under the relentless pressure of the FBI's manhunt.

Mary Burns, Fugitive (1935)
(Directed by William K. Howard, with Sylvia Sydney, Melvyn Douglas, Pert Kelton, Alan Baxter, Wallace Ford, and Brian Donlevy)

Mary Burns had Melvyn Douglas rescue Sylvia Sydney, who played a gun moll unwillingly forced into a life of crime. Kernan Cripps, Ivan Miller, and Charles C. Wilson played G-men.

Public Enemy's Wife (1936)
(Directed by Nick Grinde, with Pat O'Brien, Margaret Lindsay, Robert Armstrong, and Cesar Romero)

Warner Brother's *Public Enemy's Wife* showed Hollywood's ability to find a love interest in the most unlikely places. After declaring that "the Public Enemies are rubbed out or locked up," the film's ads asked, "but what about the girls they left behind?" and then promised the "stark naked truth about the crime war widows left stranded by their mates in the wake of history's greatest manhunt." The special agent hero, played by Pat O'Brien, ends up marrying the former wife of a gangster, played by Margaret Lindsay.

Special Investigator (1936)
(Directed by Louis King, with Richard Dix and Margaret Callahan)

In this film, a mob lawyer switches sides when his FBI agent brother is killed in a shoot-out with gangsters. The film contains some Western scenes, an almost inevitable development once the G-man became a stock character in formula adventures.

G-Man Films of the Late 1930s

Although the G-man craze subsided in Hollywood after the reimposition of the Production Code, FBI heroes continued to appear in films.

Smashing the Rackets (1938)
(Directed by Lew Landers, with Chester Morris, Frances Mercer, Bruce Cabot, and Rita Johnson)

Smashing the Rackets was a crime drama modeled after the career of New York's gang-busting district attorney, Thomas Dewey.

Missing Evidence (1939)
(Directed by Phil Rosen, with Preston Foster, Irene Hervey, and Inez Courtney)

The FBI agent hero of *Missing Evidence* falls in love with a beautiful counterfeiter.

Persons in Hiding (1939)
(Directed by Louis King, with Patricia Morison, J. Carroll Naish, Lynne Overman, William Henry, Helen Twelvetrees, and William Frawley)

Persons in Hiding, a spin-off from FBI Director Hoover's casebook, *Persons in Hiding,* relates the adventures of Bonnie and Clyde.

The Radio G-Man

In July 1935, radio producer, writer, and star Phillips H. Lord negotiated an agreement with FBI Director Hoover to turn Lord's "Radio Crimebusters" show on NBC into an FBI program. Hoover did not like Lord's first efforts to insert G-men into stock melodramatic crime plots, so he asked Courtney Ryley Cooper and his friend, Rex Collier, a *Washington Star* reporter, to turn some of the Crime Records

Division's "Interesting Case" write-ups into radio shows. (Interesting Case memos are still employed by the Bureau to offer to the media its perspective on cases.) The result was "G-Men." Despite the show's excellent ratings, Lord resented the constant censoring and rewriting by his Bureau liaisons. After only 13 weeks, Lord severed the official connection and turned the program into the long-lived "Gangbusters." Lord became frustrated by Hoover's insistence that he adhere to the official FBI formula that Courtney Ryley Cooper had developed. Hoover wanted Lord to downplay or eliminate the derring-do of individual agent stars, and to have the cases solved through science and organization. Even after the break with the Bureau, Lord's "Gangbusters" continued to imply that the show had an official Bureau connection. Each episode ended with "Gangbusters Nationwide Clues" about a prominent fugitive, a feature that appealed to the public to send information on the cases to the police, the FBI, or to "Gangbusters" producers.

The G-Man Pulps

The G-man craze was made for pulp magazines, 128-page monthlies that had replaced nineteenth-century story papers and dime novels as the most popular vehicle for formula adventures. In the wake of Cagney's *G-Men,* such adventure pulps as *Argosy, Blue Book*, *Real Detective*, and *True Detective* began featuring G-man heroes. Two pulps were dedicated almost exclusively to the exploits of the FBI: *G-Men*, which began in October 1935 and stayed with the FBI until the winter of 1953, and *The Feds*, which ran from December 1935 until September 1937. Both publications tried to give their readers a total G-man experience—public enemy adventures; straight-from-the-shoulder information on crime fighting from the director; and tips on FBI training, techniques, and equipment—all wrapped into an escapist myth for young FBI fans. *G-Men*'s feature attraction was almost always a full-length novel starring Dan Fowler, the magazine's own ace G-man hero, together with a bonus assortment of shorter special agent stories. Issues also offered comic strips, cryptography lessons and puzzles, "exposés" of a racket-of-the-month by a "reformed" public enemy, and chatter about the magazine's own G-man club. Each issue usually contained a reprint of a hard-hitting extract from one of Hoover's speeches, normally a press release picked up out of the public domain that *G-Men*'s editors could pass off as written especially for the magazine. A member of the magazine's G-Men club swore "to uphold

the laws of the nation and to do all in my power to aid in their enforcement and to back the efforts of the federal agents in their fight on crime." Members also received a "valuable" bronze badge inscribed "G-Men Club: Special Agent."

The Comic Strip G-Man

From their earliest days, American newspaper comic strips had offered readers stories about crime fighters. The earliest was "Hawkshaw, the Detective," borrowed from Tom Taylor's stage detective thriller of the nineteenth century. Chester Gould's "Dick Tracy" (first published in 1931) had provided a preview of what the FBI agent would require to become a thoroughly modern detective hero: strength, courage, and deductive razzle-dazzle laid on a solid foundation of up-to-date (even futuristic) science.

"Secret Agent X-9"
The FBI's initial foray into the comics came after FBI Director Hoover noticed two comic strips that exploited the FBI's new celebrity but contributed little to the Bureau's image or to law enforcement. The first was "Secret Agent X-9" created by Dashiell Hammett and Alex Raymond, but soon taken over by Charles Flanders and Leslie Charteris (famous later for "The Saint"). The hero, known as X-9, began as a run-of-the-mill action detective, complete with the customary Oriental valet. In 1936, X-9 began to show unsuspected scientific talents, and started to take readers on tours of the FBI headquarters and laboratories. Simultaneously, the Hearst chain (which carried "Secret Agent X-9") began distributing a children's version of "X-9" called "The G-Man" by George Clark and Lou Hanlon.

Hoover was probably bothered that X-9 called his own shots with the rest of the Bureau and its director functioning as back-up. Because Hoover was promoting the idea of the FBI's unique ability to bring the expertise and power of the entire organization to bear on every investigation, he decided to counter X-9's threat to FBI orthodoxy with a strip of his own.

"War on Crime"
"War on Crime" was written by Hoover's friend, *Washington Star* reporter Rex Collier (see Exhibit 8.5). The strip opened in 45 papers across the country on May 18, 1936. Hoover retained absolute authority over every detail of the strip, and thus "War on Crime" provides an unusually revealing look at Hoover's public relations objectives. The director had the newspaper syndicate publicize the strip as an "authentic" presentation of the government's "scientific and ruthless"

Exhibit 8.5 **"War on Crime,"** *Courtesy of Ledger Syndicate/Rex Collier*

warfare against organized crime, The strip portrayed the FBI agent as a new kind of hero, the brainchild of the detective genius who was running the Bureau. Strip after strip detailed the training of special agents in science and weaponry. The initial episodes sent the agents into the war touched off by the Kansas City Massacre, then moved through the great gang-busting cases of 1933 and 1934 toward the FBI's greatest adventure, the manhunt for John Dillinger, who was billed as the "Mad Dog of the Midwest." Rigorously conforming to the FBI's official line, "War on Crime" had the Dillinger case solved exclusively through the use of science, dispensing with the reality of the strokes of luck like the tip from the Woman in Red. The strip expired shortly after the Dillinger episode, a casualty of Hoover's insistence that the whole FBI, personified by himself, be the hero of every case. Comic strip readers wanted heroes, and the free-lance competition had plenty of heroes to offer. One such hero, Captain America, was born in April 1941 in the FBI laboratory. The Justice Society of America (a grand conclave of comic book heroes like the Green Lantern, with occasional guest appearances from Batman and Superman) also involved an FBI connection with occasional tours of the FBI headquarters. These fantasy G-men dispensed with the red tape Hoover wrapped around comic book heroes who wanted real FBI credentials.

From the beginning, American popular culture knew two FBIs. The FBI agents sponsored by the Bureau, in officially sanctioned productions like "War on Crime," radio's "This Is Your FBI," television's "The FBI," and Hollywood's *The FBI Story,* had Hoover's standard-issue organization-man personality. The unofficial G-man created by the entertainment industry was an updated version of the classic American gunfighter—young, lean, and mean, a lawman with style, and a lover besides. Hoover's government issue G-man didn't stand a chance.

Junior G-Men

In Harold Rome's 1937 Broadway musical, *Pins and Needles*, a middle-aged actor in a Buster Brown suit sang a song with a chorus that went, "Gee, but I'd like to be a G-man." Rome was having fun with one of the most intriguing aspects of 1930s popular culture, the Junior G-Man craze.

During the 1930s and early 1940s, the FBI made an even deeper impression on American youths than on their parents. As one kid put it in a letter to FBI Director Hoover, "The only difference between the FBI and the Boy Scouts is

the FBI carries guns and the Boy Scouts use a pen knife." Junior G-Man clubs were for those kids who wanted to join the FBI instead of the Scouts.

Many Junior G-Man clubs were actually organized by advertisers as marketing promotions. The cereal club most closely identified with the FBI was Post Toasties' "Junior G-Man Club," which started out as "Inspector Post's Junior Detective Corps" before evolving into the "Melvin Purvis Law and Order Patrol," named after the FBI agent who caught Dillinger (see Exhibit 8.6). Purvis, who had left the Bureau for show business in 1935, became chief of the Post Toasties club in 1936. Purvis's junior agents could send in their box tops for just about everything a young crime stopper might need: badges, codes and passwords, cap pistols, microscopes, telescopes, and even law-and-order baseball gloves. In their cereal box adventures, Ralston's "Tom Mix's Straight Shooters" also exploited the FBI, as did Quaker Puffed Rice's "Dick Tracy's Secret Service Patrol."

Junior G-Men Movie Serials

The Junior G-Men Saturday afternoon serial was another Hollywood contribution to this kiddie craze. These serials included *Secret Agent X-9*, played by Scott Kolk in 1937 and by Lloyd Bridges in 1945. *Dick Tracy's G-Men* (15 chapters) came out in 1939. Ralph Paige starred in *Flying G-Men* in 1939, and Rod Cameron fought the Japanese Underground in *G-Men vs. The Black Dragon* in 1943. *Junior G-Men,* a 12-part Universal serial starring the Dead End Kids, appeared in 1940. In 1942, the Dead End Kids fought the Japanese fifth column in *Junior G-Men of the Air.* In 1945, Kernan Cripps was a G-man in *Federal Operator 99.* Three more FBI serials appeared after the war: Clayton Moore in *G-Men Never Forget* (1948), Kirk "Superman" Alyn in *Federal Agents vs. Underworld, Inc.* (1949), and Walter Reed in *Government Agents vs. The Phantom Legion* (1951).

Big Little Books

Young Americans could also satisfy their FBI cravings with the Big Little Books, a series of books that were fat (1.5 inches thick) and little (4.5 inches × 3.25 inches), with simple text on one page and a comic frame on the other. *Junior G-Men and the Counterfeiters* (1937) had its kid hero step in to help an injured FBI man. *G-Men on the Crime Trail* was based on "G-Man," Lou Hanlon's comic strip in the *New York Daily Mirror;* the strip's main character was the younger brother of a real FBI agent. The hero of *G-Men on the Job* (1935) was "Young" Bill Lee, Uncle Sam's youngest G-man, a recent graduate from the FBI Academy.

Exhibit 8.6   **Post Toasties Junior G-Man Club,** *Courtesy of General Mills*

Bubble Gum Cards

Six competing series of bubble gum cards were devoted to the FBI. These included National Chicle's 24-card series, "Dare-Devils," and Gum Incorporated's 168-card series, "G-Men and Heroes of the Law." The Dillinger card in the last series showed the gangster in his last moments.

> The outlaw staggered, cleared the sidewalk with a bound, turned into an alley a hundred feet away, as a 45 caliber bullet ripped through his breast. Another found its mark in the same spot. Another tore through his neck and brain, coming out over the right eye. John Dillinger had met his match at last, the end that all killers sooner or later find before the unswerving aim of G-Men who take their trail and track them down.

Gum Makers of America sold a 24-card series called "True Spy Stories." There was also a 90-card set called "American G-Men," and another called "Crime Does Not Pay." Pressner put out a 1936 series called "Government Agents vs. Public Enemies."

Junior G-Man toys included guns, handcuffs, crime laboratory kits, and costumes. Books like Quentin Reynolds's *The FBI* (1954) aimed directly at the juvenile market. Today, G-man juvenilia constitutes a category of collectibles, serviced by price lists, catalogs, and dealers.

World War II and the FBI Front

The FBI's public relations objectives were radically altered during World War II. Before the war, the public had been enlisted in a crusade to reform American law enforcement. The Bureau's wartime public relations goal was to prevent the hysteria that had wracked the nation during the First World War by discouraging amateur saboteur-hunting and counterespionage.

The necessity of this effort became clear in 1938 when Nazi Germany took over Austria. The United States went into a war panic; the American Legion, for example, announced that it was organizing a spy hunt. To calm things down, President Roosevelt had Hoover announce the FBI's completion of an exhaustive study of the American Nazi underground. Hoover's 12-volume report led, on June 20, to the indictment of 18 American Nazis.

While the government's case was being prepared, the Bureau's lead agent in this investigation, Leon G. Turrou, who had infiltrated the Nazi underground, published *Confessions of a Nazi Spy*. A furious Hoover and Justice Department officials obtained a temporary injunction against publication. Published nonetheless, the book was quickly picked up by Hollywood for a sensational movie by the same name.

Confessions of a Nazi Spy (1939)
(Directed by Anatole Litvak, with Edward G. Robinson, Francis Lederer, George Sanders, Paul Lukas, James Stephenson, and Sig Rumann)

In *Confessions of a Nazi Spy,* Edward G. Robinson played the G-man hero, modeled after the undercover career of FBI agent Leon G. Turrou. Although the film glorified the Bureau's work against the Nazi underground, Hoover was far from pleased. The excitement stirred up by the film confirmed, for Hoover and the Roosevelt administration, the volatility of public opinion and how easily international tensions could lead to public turmoil. In response, the FBI director launched a publicity campaign to convince the public to report rumors of subversion, espionage, or sabotage to the FBI, and to refrain from spy hunting themselves. In January 1940, Hoover published a magazine article, "Stamping out the Spies," in which he maintained that a spy menace existed, but was being controlled by the FBI. "This country was never so well prepared to combat espionage activities. . . . This is no time for hysteria, wild rumors, or hair-trigger prejudices."

After the Japanese attack on Pearl Harbor in December 1941, the Bureau worked with Hollywood to reassure the public that the home front, or "FBI Front," as it was sometimes called, was in the best of hands—Hoover's. Wartime films both conveyed this message and the FBI's vigilance and success in apprehending crooks and spies.

The FBI Front (1942)
In 1942, the FBI cooperated with March of Time to make the documentary, *The FBI Front,* which conveyed the message, "Let the FBI handle it," and warned that "on no condition should a citizen attempt to prosecute an amateur investigation of his own." The summary trial and execution of the Nazi saboteurs who landed on Long Island by submarine in 1942 also broadcast this message.

The FBI in Peace and War (1943)
In 1943, FBI officials collaborated with writer Frederick L. Collins on a history of the Bureau called *The FBI in Peace and War*. The book adhered to the Bureau's wartime line of dissuading amateur spy-hunting by dramatizing the FBI's mastery of the counterespionage game.

"The FBI in Peace and War" (1944)
In 1944, Collins double-crossed Hoover when selling radio rights to the book to CBS without the director's permission. This program adopted the standard gang-buster formula, with the characters clearly described as FBI agents. A furious Hoover forced the producers to include the disclaimer that the program was not an official FBI production, and he persuaded Congress to pass legislation making unauthorized use of the Bureau's name illegal.

"This Is Your FBI" (1945)
To maintain control over the Bureau's popular culture image, and counteract Collins's heretical "The FBI in Peace and War," Hoover authorized an official FBI radio show. "This Is Your FBI" premiered on ABC on April 6, 1945, with Hoover introducing its first episode. The president of the show's sponsor, Equitable Life, praised the FBI for protecting the home front. "To the FBI you look for national security . . . and to the Equitable Society for financial security." The theme, in keeping with FBI policy, was "leave it to the FBI." "This Is Your FBI" lasted until 1953.

The G-Man Formula and Wartime
Hollywood continued to produce run-of-the-mill FBI films during the war that tried to adapt the G-man formula to wartime security themes.

Queen of the Mob (1940)
(Directed by James Hogan, with Ralph Bellamy, Jack Carson, Blanche Yurka, and Richard Denning)

This G-man movie was based on the account of the "Ma" Barker case offered by FBI Director Hoover in his casebook, *Persons in Hiding*.

Joe Smith, American (1942)
(Directed by Richard Thorpe, with Robert Young, Marsha Hunt, Harvey Stephens, and Darryl Hickman)

In this film, a munitions worker kidnapped by the Nazis refuses to give up defense secrets and leads the FBI to the spies.

They Came to Blow up America (1943)

(Directed by Edward Ludwig, with George Sanders, Anna Sten, and Ward Bond)

A German American FBI agent infiltrates a network of Nazi saboteurs.

Roger Touhy, Gangster (1944)

(Directed by Robert Florey, with Preston Foster, Victor McLaglen, Lois Andrews, Anthony Quinn, Kent Taylor, Harry Morgan, Trudy Marshall, and Kent Richmond)

Twentieth Century Fox advertised the FBI's cooperation in making this film.

Allotment Wives (1945)

(Directed by William High, with Kay Francis, Paul Kelly, and Otto Kruger)

An FBI agent cracks a plot to cheat military personnel out of their pay.

The House on 92nd Street (1945)

(Directed by Henry Hathaway, with William Eythe, Lloyd Nolan, Signe Hasso, Gene Lockhart, and Leo G. Carroll)

By far the most important of the wartime FBI movies, and a landmark in the history of semi-documentary film making, *The House on 92nd Street* was in some ways the distant model for Oliver Stone's later and differently intended "bio-pics." Produced by Louis De Rochemont of March of Time, *The House on 92nd Street* used documentary techniques, always a mainstay of the FBI formula, to introduce audiences to the hardware of espionage and counterespionage: e.g., two-way mirrors, microfilm, and spy cameras. FBI Director Hoover himself appeared on screen to introduce the movie, which won an Oscar for best original story (see Exhibit 8.7).

Dillinger (1945)

(Directed by Max Nosseck, with Edmund Lowe, Anne Jeffreys, Lawrence Tierney, Eduardo Ciannelli, and Elisha Cook Jr.)

This film presented the mythic Dillinger story, ignoring the more complex historical reality.

Exhibit 8.7   *The House on 92nd Street* (**Showing the Fingerprint Division at the National Guard Armory**), *Courtesy of 20th Century Fox Production*

The FBI's Cold War Image

During the late 1940s and the 1950s, FBI Director Hoover made a staggering number of public appearances, expanding his audiences far beyond the law enforcement community and across the entire spectrum of religious, civic, patriotic, and academic groups. His role in high-profile cases—such as those involving Alger Hiss, Julius and Ethel Rosenberg, and the Smith Act convictions of the leadership of the U.S. Communist Party—made Hoover a public figure almost as prominent as, and certainly more trusted than (at least on the communist issue), President Harry Truman. Indeed, Truman's Republican successor, Dwight Eisenhower, pointedly emphasized that Hoover was in charge of internal security. During these years, Hoover became the symbol of the nation's opposition to domestic communism, for which he was detested by those radicals and liberals who felt that fear of domestic communism was overblown or delusory.

The FBI director's high public profile during the early Cold War years projected his notion of a public figure's proper role. Hoover had been reared during an age when prominent community leaders were expected to take moral stands on issues of public concern. The FBI director had another, more practical reason for stepping forward on the issue of communism: the FBI's responsibility to be prepared for the possible mass internment of enemy sympathizers as had occurred during the previous two world wars. In the event of a U.S. conflict with the Soviet Union, ideology, not ethnic background, would determine who would be rounded up. This situation, Hoover realized, could be as catastrophic for the Bureau's reputation as the 1920 round-ups unless the public was carefully prepared for an operation that could be enormously controversial. In 1946, top FBI executives began a campaign to alert the public to the communist danger to internal security, with the goal of ensuring support for the emergency detention of communists and their sympathizers in case of a war crisis. Bureau officials encouraged Hollywood to make films about the FBI wherein G-man heroes were sent into battle against subversives and spies. Hollywood needed time to shift from enthusiastic support of the wartime alliance with the Soviet Union to this anticommunist, anti-Soviet perspective. For a time, the movie industry cautiously tried to exploit the FBI's relatively apolitical popular entertainment image of the 1930s by recycling the gangster wars, but eventually films were produced that pitted G-man against communist subversives.

Entertainment of the Late 1940s and 1950s

Ride the Pink Horse (1947)
(Directed by Robert Montgomery, with Robert Montgomery, Wanda Hendrix, Thomas Gomez, Andrea King, Fred Clark, Art Smith, Rita Conde, and Grandon Rhodes)

In this *film noir*, FBI agent Art Smith frustrates Robert Montgomery's plan to blackmail gangster Fred Clark during a New Mexican fiesta.

Walk a Crooked Mile (1948)
(Directed by Gordon Douglas, with Louis Hayward, Dennis O'Keefe, Louise Allbritton, Carl Esmond, Onslow Stevens, and Raymond Burr)

The FBI cooperates with Scotland Yard to break up a spy network trying to steal nuclear secrets.

Street with No Name (1948)
(Directed by William Keighley, with Mark Stevens, Richard Widmark, Lloyd Nolan, Barbara Lawrence, Ed Begley, and Donald Buka)

This throwback to the classic G-man movies of the mid-1930s has an FBI agent infiltrating a mob. Richard Widmark gives one of his more notable performances as a psychopathic killer.

Federal Agents vs. Underworld, Inc. (1949)
(Directed by Fred C. Brannon, with Carol Forman, Kirk Alyn, and Rosemary La Planche)

This run-of-the-mill crime drama has the FBI foil a gang of thieves planning to rob archeological treasures.

Mister 880 (1950)
(Directed by Edmund Goulding, with Dorothy McGuire, Burt Lancaster, Edmund Gwenn, Millard Mitchell, and Monor Watson)

In this genial comedy, filmed on location in New York, Burt Lancaster plays an FBI agent on the trail of a counterfeiter.

Southside 1-1000 (1950)
(Directed by Boris Ingster, with Don Defore, Andrea King, George Tobias, and Barry Kelley)

Southside 1-1000 is another hunt for counterfeiters.

FBI Girl (1951)
(Directed by William Berke, with Cesar Romero, George Brent, Audrey Totter, Tom Drake, and Raymond Burr)

An Identification Division clerk tells her FBI supervisor, Cesar Romero, that a mobster is trying to remove his fingerprints from the files.

Government Agents vs. The Phantom Legion (1951)
(Directed by Fred Brannon, with Walter Reed, Mary Ellen Kay, and Dick Curtis)

In this 12-part serial, the FBI chases uranium hijackers.

I Was a Communist for the FBI (1951)
(Directed by Gordon Davis, with Frank Lovejoy, Dorothy Hart, Philip Carey, and James Millican)

Based on the true life adventures of Matt Cvetic, an undercover informant for the FBI, this thriller inspired a radio show the next year. Radio's "I Was a Communist for the FBI," starring Dana Andrews, shared the airwaves with Mutual's "Top Secrets of the FBI," a standard detective melodrama introduced by ex-special agent Melvin Purvis, who was billed as "The Man Who Got Dillinger."

Walk East on Beacon (1952)
(Directed by Alfred Werker, with George Murphy, Finlay Currie, Virginia Gilmore, and George Hill)

This documentary-style espionage film was based on J. Edgar Hoover's *Reader's Digest* account of the Klaus Fuchs atom spy case, "Crime of the Century." The picture was made with full Bureau cooperation.

Pickup on South Street (1953)
(Directed by Samuel Fuller, with Richard Widmark, Jean Peters, Thelma Ritter, and Richard Kiley)

Richard Widmark plays a petty pickpocket who helps the FBI crack a communist spy ring. Thelma Ritter has the notable line, "What do I know about Commies? Nothing. I just know I don't like them."

"I Led Three Lives" (1953)
Television's "I Led Three Lives," based on Herbert Philbrick's best-selling book of the same title, premiered in 1953; it lasted 117 episodes, until 1956. The show recounted Philbrick's nine years as an FBI informant fighting communist infiltration of the labor union movement. (Philbrick also wrote an anticommunist newspaper column and gave lectures on the anticommunist circuit.) Richard Carlson played Philbrick, and each episode began with the same dramatic words: "This is the story, the fantastically true story, of Herbert Philbrick, who for nine frightening years *did* lead three lives—average citizen, high-level member of the Communist Party, and counterspy for the Federal Bureau of Investigation. For obvious reasons, the names, dates, and places have been changed. But the story is based on fact."

Down Three Dark Streets (1954)
(Directed by Arnold Laven, with Broderick Crawford, Ruth Roman, Martha Hyer, Marisa Pavan, and Kenneth Tobey)

Broderick Crawford plays an FBI agent working on three cases left unsolved when his partner is killed. The film relies heavily on formulaic FBI crime lab scenes.

The Atomic Kid (1954)
(Directed by Leslie Martinson, with Mickey Rooney, Robert Strauss, Whit Bissell, and Hal March)

Mickey Rooney survives an atomic bomb test and is chased by spies seeking atomic secrets.

Them (1954)
(Directed by Gordon Douglas, with James Whitmore, Edmund Gwenn, Joan Weldon, and James Arness)

James Arness plays an FBI agent who defends America against giant radioactive ants produced by atomic test fallout in New Mexico.

A Bullet for Joey (1955)
(Directed by Lewis Allen, with Edward G. Robinson, George Raft, and Audrey Totter)

A gangster stalks a scientist who knows atomic secrets.

Invasion of the Body Snatchers (1956)
(Directed by Don Siegel, with Kevin McCarthy, Dana Wynter, Larry Gates, King Donovan, and Carolyn Jones)

Kevin McCarthy discovers aliens stealing the bodies and assuming the identities of citizens of Santa Mira, California. He escapes into a crowded freeway, begging drivers (and the audience) to "call the FBI."

Baby Face Nelson (1957)
(Directed by Don Siegel, with Mickey Rooney, Carolyn Jones, Leo V. Gordon, and Cedric Hardwicke)

Mickey Rooney plays gangster "Baby Face" Nelson, while Leo V. Gordon is John Dillinger.

I, Mobster (1958)
(Directed by Roger Corman, with Steve Cochran, Lita Milan, Robert Strauss, and Lili St. Cyr)

In a new trend, *I, Mobster* treats gangsters as tragic heroes.

Machine Gun Kelly (1958)
(Directed by Roger Corman, with Charles Bronson, Susan Cabot, Barbara Morris, Morey Amsterdam, Wally Campo, Jack Lambert, Connie Gilchrist, and Frank DeKova)

This film provides a Freudian take on gangster psychology—they are weak men dominated by strong molls and moms.

From Saving to Representing America: The Domesticated G-Man

The popular culture FBI in the late 1940s and early-1950s alternated between tired reenactments of the old G-man formula and the early Cold War FBI formula of fighting the communist menace. Usually, but not always, the films made an obligatory gesture toward the science and organization distinguishing the FBI agent from the run-of-the-mill action detective hero.

But in entertainment produced or endorsed by the FBI, something new was happening by the mid-1950s. This change could first be seen in the final episodes of radio's

"This Is Your FBI," which went off the air in 1953. As often as not, that show's FBI agents acted less like action heroes than social workers, who through sympathy and understanding instead of guns or fingerprints caught and reformed criminals. The FBI had discovered a more powerful weapon than force, science, and organization: American values, defined as the virtues of ordinary life—kindness, love of family, religion, and loyalty.

The 1950s also saw the appearance of two well-publicized books about the FBI, which presented very different views of the Bureau to the public.

Federal Bureau of Investigation (1950)

Max Lowenthal's *Federal Bureau of Investigation* was written by a lawyer friend of President Truman. Lowenthal's book charged that the FBI had become what Truman privately called "an American Gestapo." Supplementing the charges the left had accumulated against the Bureau since 1919 with shrewdly chosen congressional statements, Lowenthal suggested that Congress had, from the start, feared that the Bureau would become a secret police at war with civil liberties. Lowenthal's indictment summarized evidence that had long been published in the pages of left-liberal journals like the *Nation,* but by 1950 had been eclipsed by the uniformly positive image created by the FBI's mythmakers.

The FBI Story (1956)

Don Whitehead's *The FBI Story,* a popular history of the Bureau, was written with research help from FBI Assistant Director Louis B. Nichols and the FBI's Crime Records Division. A two-time Pulitzer Prize–winning reporter and supervisor of the *New York Herald Tribune*'s Washington Bureau, Whitehead benefited from access to FBI memos and files that he used to write his remarkably well-organized, accurate, and readable book. Hoover wrote the introduction and lent Whitehead the FBI seal for the book's cover. The book spent 38 weeks on the best-seller lists, was serialized in 170 newspapers, and was eventually the basis for a 1959 Hollywood film.

Exhibit 8.8   *The FBI Story, Courtesy of Warner Bros.*

Whitehead began his story by recounting cases that displayed the Bureau's mastery of science, its agents' bravery, and the organizational structure that enabled it to solve crimes. He described the pre-Hoover years—1908–24—as dark days of repression and corruption, and then dramatized Hoover's reforms of the Bureau in the personal context of the director's confrontation with Gaston Means, whom Hoover had turned into a symbol of everything that until then had been wrong with American law enforcement. Whitehead next briefly and dramatically described the gangster wars of the 1930s. Profiling Hoover's top executives, he emphasized the Bureau's services to the nation's police: the FBI National Academy, the crime labs, the fingerprint files.

Whitehead credited the World War II FBI with preventing the recurrence of the injustices of the World War I years, and then praised the Bureau for "awakening" the nation to the danger of domestic communism during the Cold War. After giving an account of the Bureau's successes against Soviet atomic bomb spy rings, he concluded by blasting Bureau critics for parroting the communist line when attacking the conviction and execution of Julius and Ethel Rosenberg.

Masters of Deceit (1958)

In 1958, soon after of Whitehead's successful book, FBI Director Hoover produced—through his ghostwriters in the Crime Records Unit—*Masters of Deceit,* a best-selling primer on the war against American communism. In *Masters of Deceit,* one of the most remarkable political tracts in American popular culture, Hoover gave readers a survey of domestic and international communism that included a brief summary of Marxist-Leninist history and theory. Hoover depicted communism and Americanism as diametrically opposed ways of life, even warring religions. To prove this theory, he raided the stockroom of popular formulas, showing communists as artificial, man-made monsters at war with God and true humanity. Using metaphors like "Frankensteins," "Draculas," and "Attila the Hun," Hoover portrayed communism as "cannibalistic. Its servants are periodically offered as sacrifices on the Communist altar." To Hoover, the U.S. Communist Party, "was a freak [that] has grown into a powerful monster endangering us all" while Communism was, "more than an economic, political, social or philosophical system. It is a way of life; a false, materialistic, 'religion.' It would strip man of his belief in God, his

heritage of freedom, his trust in love, justice, and mercy. Under Communism all would become, as so many already have, twentieth century slaves."

Hoover extolled the FBI's countermeasures against communist espionage and subversion. But the FBI alone would not be able to save the country.

> We, as a people, have not been sufficiently articulate and forceful in expressing pride in our traditions and ideals. In our homes and schools we need to learn how to 'let freedom ring.' In all the civilized world there is no story which compares with America's effort to become free and to incorporate freedom in our institutions. This story, told factually and dramatically, needs to become the basis for our American unity and for our unity with all free peoples. I am sure most Americans believe that our light of freedom is a shining light. As Americans we should stand up, speak of it, and let the world see this light, rather than conceal it. For too long we have had a tendency to keep silent while the communists, their sympathizers, and their fellow travelers have been telling the world what is wrong with democracy. Suppose every American spent a little time each day, less than the time demanded by the communists, in studying the Bible and the basic documents of American history, government, and culture? The result would be a new America, vigilant, strong, but ever humble in the service of God.

Hoover published another, somewhat more advanced, treatise on the same subject in 1962, *A Study of Communism,* and in 1969, he released another collection of his writings, *J. Edgar Hoover on Communism.*

The FBI Story (1959)

(Directed by Mervyn LeRoy, with James Stewart, Vera Miles, Murray Hamilton, Nick Adams, and Diane Jergens)

The film version of Whitehead's book, which became by far the most popular FBI movie ever made, reached movie theaters in 1959 (see Exhibit 8.8). Produced and directed by Mervyn LeRoy, whose crime film career dated from *Little Caesar* (1930), the movie transformed the FBI's history into the biography of a composite FBI agent, Chip Hardesty, played by Jimmy Stewart.

Had LeRoy simply filmed the book that Whitehead had written, the result would have been an expanded newsreel documentary of the sort Time-Life had done several times for the March of Time series. But Warner Brothers intended this film to be a major release aimed at a mass market family audience. As such, the book's story line was reshaped to suit 1950s conventions for popular entertainment. The movie needed a hero, suitable for the domestic-minded 1950s; such a hero, unlike the life-long bachelor Hoover, required a family. In consequence, instead of an action detective formula or a Cold War spy thriller, LeRoy produced a domestic drama.

This theme corresponded with Hoover's 1950s reshaping of the FBI formula into one that depended on values—American, Christian, and family—rather than bullets to save the nation. The film version of *The FBI Story* replaced the 1930s anticrime crusade with the group dynamics of the Hardesty family; the crises of international and domestic politics registered as shocks to the domestic tranquillity of the Hardesty home.

The movie begins in 1924. New agent Chip Hardesty's girlfriend, played by Vera Miles, refuses to marry him because he works for that "dinky little" inefficient and corrupt Bureau. Add to that a broken office fan, and Jimmy Stewart is one discouraged agent. But there are changes in the air—a new director has taken over, a man who can "make water run uphill." Every major event in FBI history—the gangster raids and the cases of World War II and the Cold War—becomes a Hardesty family crisis. By the end of film, Vera Miles is a gray-haired grandmother who nods and smiles when her ancient G-man (by the film's chronology he would have been at least 60) rushes off to new cases. She has accepted her fate: When marrying Chip Hardesty, she married more than a man: she married the whole FBI.

This new characterization of the G-man hero as model husband and father would have been absurd during the 1930s. Hoover's public relations line of the 1950s recast the G-man's role as the moral center of his family, one more important than on-the-job heroics. As Hoover had stated in *Masters of Deceit*, the country would be saved through faith and not fingerprinting.

The Old FBI Formula in the 1960s

While some films of the 1950s and 1960s reflected this new domestic image, others remained faithful to the old FBI formula of science, organization, and firepower as the principal weapons against spies and criminals.

Jet over the Atlantic (1959)
(Directed by Byron Haskin, with Guy Madison, Virginia Mayo, George Raft, and Llona Massey)
An FBI agent escorts an extradited criminal on a plane.

Pretty Boy Floyd (1960)
(Directed by Herbert Leder, with John Ericson, Barry Newman, and Joan Harvey)
This standard Hollywood shoot-'em-up made an effort at accurate historical recreation of 1930s gangster Floyd's life and times.

Ma Barker's Killer Brood (1960)
(Directed by Bill Karn, with Lurene Tuttle, Tris Coffin, Paul Dubrov, Nelson Leigh, and Myrna Dell)
This film exploits the audience's memories of the big-name public enemies of the 1930s.

That Darn Cat (1965)
(Directed by Robert Stevenson, with Hayley Mills, Dean Jones, Dorothy Provine, Roddy McDowell, Elsa Lancaster, and William Demarest)
Disney weaves an animal adventure into an FBI espionage plot, with comic intent.

"The FBI" (1965)
The FBI's last major venture in mass entertainment during Hoover's directorship was television's "The FBI" (1965), starring Efrem Zimbalist Jr. (see Exhibit 8.9). ABC got its foot in the door for this FBI production by buying the rights to *Masters of Deceit*, even though the resultant television program had little in common with Hoover's book save its emphasis on values over action. Each episode opened and closed with the Bureau seal, and crawl credits thanked "J. Edgar Hoover and his associates for their cooperation in the production of this series." Each month, the show ran a mug shot of one of the top 10 fugitives and an appeal to the public for leads. FBI Director Hoover never appeared as a character on the show, but "The Director's" office was supposedly next door to Efrem Zimbalist Jr.'s office. Hoover did make guest appearances during the commercial segments that kicked off each new season. The series' second year was launched by a clip of Hoover presenting a Freedom Foundation award to the show's sponsor, the Ford Motor Company.

The program was completely controlled by the FBI. Hoover wrote that everyone involved in the show had agreed to give the FBI complete approval over scripts, personnel, and sponsorship. Hoover went to ludicrous lengths to ensure that excessive violence or sexual innuendo never intruded on the show: "Perhaps we are inclined toward Puritanism in an increasingly permissive world," he wrote, "but foremost in our minds from the beginning episode has been the fact that 'The FBI' is telecast into American homes at a 'family hour' on a 'family evening.'" Zimbalist recalled that the FBI director had become so worried about violence that no one

Exhibit 8.9 **"The FBI,"** *Courtesy of Warner Bros.*

was killed during the program's last two or three years. This commitment to family values made "The FBI" the best-liked new show during its first season. At the time of Hoover's death in 1972, 40 million Americans watched the show each week and it was syndicated in 50 countries.

"The FBI" differed drastically from the Bureau-approved entertainment from the 1930s glory days, as again the domesticated G-man of *The FBI Story* was the star. During the 1930s, G-man adventures had given political significance to the action detective formula. In adventure programs of the 1930s, the Bureau entered cases because of a breakdown of local law enforcement. The criminals chased by FBI agents were public enemies, national symbols of crime and of a public hysteria that was portrayed in the movies by mass protest meetings and montages of scare newspaper headlines. No ordinary detective, the G-man embodied the public's wrath, and the nation's determination

to bring crime under control. FBI investigations were the model for what law enforcement should be if the nation's police accepted FBI leadership and coordination, and if an aroused public opinion halted political interference with justice and supported professionalization of the police.

In sharp contrast, the adventures of Efrem Zimbalist's Inspector Erskine were securely contained within the fictive world of the television screen. Television's FBI was no longer a gang-busting outfit leading a national crusade against crime, but another version of Chip Hardesty's family from *The FBI Story, with* an off-screen patriarch (The Director) and an on-screen father figure (Efrem Zimbalist Jr.) with his surrogate family (Philip Abbott as Assistant Director Ward and William Reynolds as Special Agent Colby). Each week's office routine of paper shuffling and chitchat about wives and kids was interrupted by a new crime that the team pulled together to solve.

G-men no longer shot it out with thinly fictionalized gangsters based on notorious real-life public enemies. Gone was the pervading sense of national crisis, the electric atmosphere of anticrime hysteria. Vanished, too, was the drama of an epic conflict between the forces of good and evil, the evangelical atmosphere of an FBI-led revival of American law enforcement. The television G-men instead solved crimes that sometimes seemed to involve merely formal violations of the law and rarely commanded the headlines that had made the old-time G-men dramas resonate between fact and fantasy.

G-men of the 1930s and 1940s were agents of change, of law enforcement reform. The FBI of the 1950s and 1960s, the FBI of Special Agent Chip Hardesty and Inspector Erskine, offered a symbol of the status quo. The show almost inevitably adopted the domestic entertainment formula because that formula ritualized the status quo and treated the outside world as a source of trouble to be resolved either within the family or the office circle. The formula was perfectly suited to an audience with over-whelmingly private interests, an audience that had turned from public affairs to become immersed in private life.

The politicized G-man formula of the 1930s had been abandoned by Hoover and his FBI publicists; this image no longer communicated what they thought necessary to preserve the United States from the threat of communism. That change is also evident when comparing Hoover's speeches of the 1930s with his speeches from the 1950s. In the earlier period, the FBI director had described the FBI as leading a national crusade against crime. In the 1950s, Hoover dutifully served up FBI cases as examples of scientific law enforcement; he cited statistics to prove the fine job the FBI was doing, and flayed the sob-sister parole officers and civil libertarian lawyers. His rhetoric became heated, however, only when he talked about what had become his crusade during his last years at the Bureau—the moral reform of the nation. Faith and family solidarity were the nation's best defenses against crime and communism; the new FBI message emphasized the need for kids to study hard, obey their parents, and attend Sunday school. John Dillinger and "Pretty Boy" Floyd were no longer the central danger. The FBI's new meaning was contained in Inspector Erskine's unfailing politeness and decency no matter what the provocation, not in the number of "would-be crime czars" he put behind bars.

Although this new Bible-quoting choirboy image of the G-man served the Bureau well during the 1950s and 1960s, it could become a time bomb ticking away at the Bureau

headquarters. As long as the G-man was quintessentially a man of action, he could only be discredited by defeat on the field of battle. Under the conventions of American popular culture, it would be irrelevant whether an action hero smokes, spits, or swears—as long as he gets his man. Because this image made the old G-man immune to criticism, the real FBI was protected from its critics. When the G-man was advertised as a saint, he could become vulnerable to every rumor of corruption and could no longer be redeemed through action. The slightest whisper of immorality could be a mortal wound. His respectability is transformed to hypocrisy, his moral message to sanctimoniousness.

Hoover's turning the G-man into a symbol of morality made the Bureau vulnerable to precisely the kinds of allegations that began to surface during the late 1960s and the 1970s. The old G-man had never claimed to be a saint; caught taking a shortcut around the Bill of Rights, he could set things straight by catching another crook or smashing another spy ring. The domesticated FBI agent of the 1950s, whose claim to popular respect was based on his righteousness, could forfeit that claim with the first stain on his cloak of moral perfection.

The Late 1960s and the 1970s

Until the first documented revelations of FBI abuses in the 1970s, the FBI continued to command an image of respectability, so much so that films could develop comic twists when turning FBI straight arrows into straight men.

The President's Analyst (1967)
(Directed by Theodore J. Flicker, with James Coburn, Godfrey Cambridge, and Severn Darden)

Coburn plays the president's analyst, pursued by the FBI and the CIA when he learns about official conspiracies.

"The Name of the Game" (1968)
The hero of this TV series is the editor of *Crime Magazine,* a former FBI agent who uses the power of the press against crime.

Bloody Mama (1970)
(Directed by Roger Corman, with Shelley Winters, Don Stroud, Pat Hingle, Robert DeNiro, and Bruce Dern)

Another film based on the notorious 1930s gang leader, "Ma" Barker, *Bloody Mama* sees Ma's motivation in the fact she was raped by her brothers. The movie's advertisements claimed that "the family that slays together, stays together."

A Bullet for Pretty Boy (1970)

(Directed by Larry Buchanan, with Fabian Forte, Jocelyn Lane, and Astrid Warner)

Rock 'n' roll star Fabian portrays a sympathetic "Pretty Boy" Floyd on his way to becoming Public Enemy Number One.

Clay Pigeon (1971)

(Directed by Tom Stern, with Lane Slate, Tom Stern, Telly Savalas, Robert Vaughn, and Burgess Meredith)

Clay Pigeon was one of the first films to depict an FBI willing to entrap citizens and place them in danger. The circumstances, however—a hunt for an elusive drug dealer—make the Bureau's actions more ambiguous than evil.

Dillinger (1973)

(Directed by John Milius, with Warren Oates, Ben Johnson, Cloris Leachman, Michelle Phillips, Richard Dreyfuss, and Harry Dean Stanton)

Everyone in this movie, particularly Melvin Purvis (Ben Johnson) and John Dillinger (Warren Oates), lives up to his media legend. As each public enemy bites the dust, Purvis lights up a victory cigar.

The FBI Story: The FBI versus Alvin Karpis, Public Enemy Number One (1974)

(Directed by Marvin Chomsky, with Harris Yulin, Robert Foxworth, Kay Lenz, Gary Lockwood, Anne Francis, Cris Robinson, Eileen Heckart, Gerald McRaney, Whit Bissell, and James B. Sikking)

Harris Yulin plays a heroic FBI Director Hoover in pursuit of the public enemy he personally arrested, Alvin Karpis, in a movie that recycles the mythic FBI of the 1930s.

Melvin Purvis, G-Man (1974)

(Directed by Dan Curtis, with Dale Robertson, Harris Yulin, Margaret Blye, and Matt Clark)

This made-for-TV movie puts Melvin Purvis (Dale Robertson) on the trail of the notorious 1930s kidnapper Machine Gun Kelly.

Attack on Terror: The FBI versus the Ku Klux Klan (1975)

(Directed by Marvin Chomsky, with Ned Beatty, John Beck, Billy Green Bush, Dabney Coleman, Andrew Duggan, Ed Flanders, George Grizzard, Peter Strauss, and Rip Torn)

Based on Don Whitehead's FBI-authorized book, *Attack on Terror,* the film covers the FBI's successful hunt for the murderers of civil rights activists Goodman, Chaney, and Schwerner in 1964. Peter Strauss plays the FBI director.

Kansas City Massacre (1975)

(Directed by Dan Curtis, with Dale Robertson and Bo Hopkins)

This made-for-TV movie weaves the 1930s gangster cases into a war between crime and the law, following the lead of James Cagney's *G-Men.*

From Hero to Scapegoat: The G-Man in the 1970s and 1980s

During the 1970s, the Bureau's reputation collapsed, constituting one of the great upheavals in the history of American popular culture. Hoover's reputation (which for all practical purpose was one and the same with the FBI's) had been sacrosanct until the 1960s. Nevertheless, even as early as 1960, some of Hoover's most ardent admirers began to realize that the director was becoming out of touch with a rapidly changing society. Attorney General Herbert Brownell, for example, urged Hoover to retire in 1960 when he turned 65 or risk destroying all he had achieved. Hoover stayed on, however, and indeed his reputation—and the Bureau's—eventually plummeted.

Hoover's Public Relations Disasters of the 1960s

FBI Director Hoover, who for decades had exhibited an unerring sense of who would make the most rewarding targets for the FBI, suffered severe lapses of judgment during the 1960s as he became increasingly isolated and estranged from the social changes sweeping the nation. One such error involved his failure to foresee the outcome of his stands against the youth rebellion of the 1960s. Responding to the Berkeley, California, demonstrations against the House Un-American Activities Committee (HUAC) in 1960, Hoover denounced the demonstrators. Although this stand proved to be popular within Hoover's core constituency, it highlighted the contrast between the aged Hoover and the energetic, youthful activists in a country that increasingly worshipped youth and idealism. Hoover's public feud of 1963 with Martin Luther King Jr. similarly put him at odds with a civil rights movement that, though controversial, had captured the imagination of much of the nation. As student protests against the Vietnam War increased, Hoover turned himself into a national scold. An older generation may have agreed with him; regardless, parents did not like to hear their children criticized.

The FBI Nobody Knows

Dissenters from the orthodox faith in the heroic FBI had always existed. Since 1919, the American left had often criticized Bureau abuses and had attempted to weave rumors of FBI misdeeds into an argument that the FBI constituted a conspiracy against reform, dissent, civil rights, and civil liberties. Magazines like *The Nation* had welcomed these heretics to its pages. Their criticisms had little impact on public opinion outside the ranks of the already-converted. In 1958, for example, an entire issue of *The Nation* was devoted to Fred Cook's excoriation of FBI misdeeds. Cook published a much-expanded version of this piece in *The FBI Nobody Knows.* This critical but selective account of FBI outrages provided an interpretative framework that soon became the conventional wisdom during the 1970s and 1980s—a frightening picture of an out-of-control FBI under Hoover. The lack of any public reaction to Cook's revelations in *The Nation* in 1958 or to his book in 1964 demonstrated that the time was not yet ripe for public acceptance of this countercultural image of the FBI.

The Doorbell Rang (1965)

Rex Stout's *The Doorbell Rang,* a Nero Wolfe mystery based on the story Cook told in *The FBI Nobody Knows* of Hoover's efforts to repress Max Lowenthal's *Federal Bureau of Investigation,* conveyed another critical view of Hoover's FBI. In Stout's novel, Nero Wolfe's client, appalled by the public's indifference to the Bureau's misdeeds, sends copies of Cook's book to government and business leaders. When a furious Hoover tries to retaliate, Nero Wolfe lures the FBI into burglarizing his office. He traps the G-men, confiscates their guns and credentials, and demands and receives immunity for his client. The story ends with Hoover himself ringing the portly detective's doorbell to retrieve his agents' credentials. "Let him get a sore finger," Wolfe decides.

Cook's and Stout's books revealed that, by the early 1960s, iconoclastic views of the FBI commanded a limited market. By the end of the decade, however, as national solidarity began to disintegrate under the shocks of the Vietnam War and riots in the ghettos, some disaffected FBI agents began to publicize their complaints against Hoover, something unthinkable a few years earlier. The first such account was Norman Ollestad's *Inside the FBI* (1968), followed by William Turner's *Hoover's FBI: The Man and the Myth* (1970). In these books, the Bureau was a bizarre world with high-ranking officials and agents forced to act like children to obey the nonsensical rules of a self-infatuated and senile director.

COINTELPRO

On March 8, 1971, a group calling itself the Citizens' Commission to Investigate the FBI broke into the FBI's resident agency in Media, Pennsylvania, and appropriated that office's domestic security files. Circulated to the press,

the files were soon published in a leftist magazine, *WIN,* and revealed FBI covert operations against the Black Panthers, the Students for a Democratic Society, and other groups and individuals—some radical, some not. NBC correspondent Carl Stern observed that one of the reprinted documents carried the unfamiliar caption COINTELPRO. Stern filed a Freedom of Information Act request for FBI files on the "COINTELPRO–New Left." On December 6, 1973, he got the files and began to publicize the FBI's undercover counterintelligence programs (COINTELPROs). The first of these involved a 1956-initiated plan to disrupt the Communist Party; the program was soon expanded to the Ku Klux Klan, the Black Panthers, and the Students for a Democratic Society. FBI Assistant Director W. Mark Felt later called the aftermath of the Media raid, with its revelations of COINTELPRO, "the turning point in the FBI image." The radical left at last could present plausible evidence for what Felt called its "paranoid fear of the FBI, which it hysterically equated with the Soviet secret police." This view of the Bureau, Felt lamented, "seeped into the press and found growing expression among the more bewitched and bothered opinion-makers."

At the time of his death in May 1972, Hoover was working feverishly to hold back mounting criticism of the FBI. Whereas in 1965, 84 percent of all Americans gave the FBI a "highly favorable" rating, by 1970, this rating was down to 71 percent, and by the summer of 1973, it declined further to 52 percent. According to a 1971 poll, only 22 percent of American youths expressed an interest in becoming FBI agents; 69 percent responded that they would not.

The dams burst following Hoover's death in May 1972. The Watergate burglary of June 17, 1972, which ultimately brought down the Nixon administration, further tarnished the FBI's reputation. It was learned during congressional hearings investigating the burglary that L. Patrick Gray, the acting director after Hoover's death, had intentionally destroyed files, some of which implicated the Nixon White House in a plan to forge documents intended to tarnish the reputation of the Kennedy administration.

The Church and Pike Committees

With Hoover dead and unable to retaliate—something for which he was widely feared—liberals in Congress finally began to investigate the FBI. Full-scale probes were initiated in the House (under Otis Pike) and the Senate (under Frank Church). Armed with the power of congressional subpoena, the seal of secrecy that had always protected FBI files was broken. The resultant committee reports, laid out in the form of a brief intended to make the most damaging case possible against the FBI (and other national intelligence agencies), seemed to demonstrate that Felix Frankfurter's *Lawyers Report* of 1920 had rightfully criticized the Bureau—that since its beginnings, the FBI had conspired to violate the constitutional rights of citizens to assemble, to petition the government, and to believe and say what they pleased. The Church Committee highlighted the Bureau's odious persecution of Martin Luther King Jr. and treated the most unjustifiable of the COINTELPRO operations as typical of the FBI's domestic security operations. Although an argument could have been made that the COINTELPROs, bad as they were, were not typical Bureau practices, the country, and particularly the media, was predisposed in the aftermath of the Vietnam disaster to think the worst of the government. The once-revered Hoover and the FBI became scapegoats. In December 1975, a *Time* cover story, "The Truth about Hoover," portrayed Hoover and the FBI as the enemies, not the guardians, of democratic society. In some circles, the FBI began to be blamed for almost everything that had gone wrong in the United States since the Second World War.

It would be a long time before American popular culture abandoned this new negative stereotype of the FBI as a malignant conspiracy against the republic. The Bureau's motto of fidelity, bravery, and integrity was now deemed too ridiculous to mention as anything but a joke. That is how Joseph L. Schott treated the former FBI director when he wrote *No Left Turns* (1975), a humorous account of his years as a special agent, filled with office legends and war stories passed off as history.

Negative Depictions of the FBI

A flood of films and television programs in the late 1970s and early 1980s reflected this newly fashionable negative perspective on the FBI.

Dog Day Afternoon (1975)
(Directed by Sidney Lumet, with Al Pacino, John Cazale, Charles Durning, James Broderick, and Chris Sarandon)

This movie reveals the transformation in the FBI's public image. When Al Pacino gets caught robbing a bank and takes bystanders hostage, a nonviolent resolution to the stand-off being worked out between Pacino and the street-wise New York City cops is undermined by the FBI's mindless, depersonalized, by-the-book procedures, precipitating a blood bath. The point conveyed is that the government—that is, the FBI—imposes a Kafkaesque and brutal logic on events to prevent Americans from solving their problems through native common sense. The film's FBI

embodies all of the forces at war with American values. If being American means having a sense of democracy, then *Dog Day Afternoon*'s FBI is un-American.

R Document (1976)
Best-selling thriller writers also began to cast the FBI as villainous in formula adventures. Irving Wallace's *R Document* portrays the FBI as a criminal conspiracy and its director, closely modeled on Hoover, a pulp-fiction villain. Irving's narrator calls the director "the most dangerous individual in the world" who plots to manipulate the nation's fear of crime in order to suspend the Constitution. The director plans to set up a Committee on National Safety to rule the country by decree. Wallace sets the crimes of his fictional FBI director against the litany of Hoover's outrages, which are assumed to be familiar to his readers.

> Hoover had called Dr. Martin Luther King, Jr., a notorious liar and had wiretapped his telephone to record details of his sex life. . . . He called former Attorney General Ramsey Clark a jellyfish. Hoover had called Father Berrigan and other Roman Catholic antiwar activists kidnappers and conspirators before their cases had been presented to the grand jury. Hoover had slurred Puerto Ricans and Mexicans, insisting people of those two nationalities couldn't shoot straight. Hoover had bugged Congressmen, as well as nonviolent civil rights and antiwar protesters. He had even investigated a fourteen-year-old Pennsylvania boy who had wanted to go to summer camp in East Germany and an Idaho scoutmaster who had wanted to take his troop camping in Russia.

The narrator quotes newspaper columnist and novelist Pete Hamill: "There was no single worse subversive in this country in the past thirty years than J. Edgar Hoover. This man subverted our faith in ourselves, our belief in an open society, our hopes that men and women could live in a country free of secret police, of hidden surveillance, or persecution for political ideas."

The Private Files of J. Edgar Hoover (1977)
(Directed by Larry Cohen, with Broderick Crawford, Dan Dailey, Jose Ferrer, and Rip Torn)

The Private Files of J. Edgar Hoover is probably the most hilarious FBI film ever, a campy history of the FBI that makes comic use of rumors about FBI Director Hoover's homosexual relationship with FBI Associate Director Clyde Tolson and conveys a decidedly disenchanted view of the FBI's legendary cases. Broderick Crawford plays a wacky

J. Edgar Hoover, and there is some incredibly droll dialog between Hoover and Tolson, who is played by Dan Dailey. Rip Torn narrates the film, playing an uptight FBI agent.

The Chancellor Manuscript (1977)

Robert Ludlum's lurid 1977 thriller, *The Chancellor Manuscript,* builds its plot around a struggle to control J. Edgar Hoover's "blackmail files" in the aftermath of the FBI director's death in 1972. In Ludlum's story, Hoover's death is the work of an ultra-secret power elite intent on "guiding" the nation because the pressures of democratic politics have become too much for the public. The villain is a renegade member of this elite who plans to use the files to "make the system work" for disenfranchised blacks. The hero, a writer of best-selling thrillers whom Ludlum seems to have modeled after himself (his work in progress seems to be *The Chancellor Manuscript*), instructs the reader on the scope of Hoover's sins.

> Senators and congressmen and cabinet members [were] made to toe the Hoover line or face the Hoover wrath. . . . Hoover's actions following the assassinations of both Kennedy and Martin Luther King [were disgraceful]. . . . Hoover's use of electronic and telephone surveillance . . . [was] worthy of the Gestapo. No one had been sacro-sanct; enemies and potential enemies had been held at bay. Tapes had been spliced and edited; guilt had come by remote association, innuendo, hearsay, and manufactured evidence.

In *The Chancellor Manuscript*, Hoover's blackmail files not only exist, but had been used, "systematically making contact with scores of subjects he believe[d] are in opposi-tion to policies he favors, threatening to expose their private weaknesses if they do not retreat from their position." The writer-hero intends to write a book to expose Hoover as a "dangerous megalomaniac who should have been forced from office twenty years ago. A master whose tactics were more in tune with the policies of the Third Reich than those of a democratic society. I want people to be outraged by J. Edgar Hoover's manipulations."

In 1978, ABC presented a six-hour television docu-drama on Martin Luther King Jr. that, according to reviewers, similarly depicted Hoover as "a harassing psychopath fighting the specter of black insurrection," and implied that Hoover was "to some degree involved in the King assassination."

The Turner Diaries (1978)

A pseudonymous anti-Semitic conspiracy tract published in 1978 revealed that the far right had joined the far left in demonizing the Bureau. The book's thesis, a racist, right-wing fantasy, portrays an armed citizenry at war with a Washington run by a Zionist conspiracy. Its climax involves a successful plot to blow up the J. Edgar Hoover FBI Building. This bombing apparently inspired Timothy McVeigh's 1995 bombing of the Oklahoma City federal building. McVeigh, and his friends, read *The Turner Diaries* as decrypting the conspiracies that they thought controlled their lives and the rest of late-twentieth-century America. The book offers a weird mirror image to movie producer Oliver Stone's left-wing conspiracy theories (in *JFK* and *Nixon*) and suggests that, by the end of the century, an image of an abusive FBI had been incorporated into the paranoia of the right as well as the left.

Depictions of the FBI in the 1980s

Despite the spate of negative images, many popular films and television shows continued to portray the FBI as a law enforcement agency that faithfully performed its duty to investigate crimes and apprehend criminals. Others, however, began portraying the Bureau's dark side.

Love and Bullets (1979)

(Directed by Stuart Rosenberg, with Charles Bronson, Rod Steiger, and Jill Ireland)

Charles Bronson, in a Marlon Brando impression, is hunted by both the mob and the FBI in a movie filmed on location in Switzerland.

The Ordeal of Patty Hearst (1979)

(Directed by Paul Wendkow, with Dennis Weaver and Lisa Eilbacher)

Weaver is an FBI agent on the trail of the kidnapped newspaper heiress.

The Lady in Red (1979)

(Directed by Lewis Teague, and written by John Sayles, with Pamela Sue Martin, Robert Conrad, Louise Fletcher, Robert Hogan, Laurie Heineman, Glenn Withrow, Christopher Lloyd, and Dick Miller)

Also released as *Guns, Sins, and Bathtub Gin,* this film retells the John Dillinger story from the perspective of the woman who betrayed the gangster.

Follow That Car (1980)

(Directed by Daniel Haller, with Dirk Benedict, Tanya Tucker, and Terri Nunn)

The plot involves kids who help the FBI solve a case.

Gloria (1980)

(Directed by John Cassavetes, with Gena Rowlands and Buck Henry)

Rowlands, a former gang moll, tries to save a Hispanic child from the Mafia killers who had murdered his parents.

"Today's FBI" (1981)

By the late 1970s, the FBI's image in popular culture had suffered such a drastic role reversal that it often it became equated with villainy. These circumstances doomed a new, officially sanctioned, prime-time television show that premiered on October 25, 1981, eight years after Efrem Zimbalist's "The FBI" left the air. The show claimed to offer a "new breed of dedicated, young FBI agents . . . fighting today's crime with tomorrow's weapons!"

"Today's FBI" (see Exhibit 8.10) attempted to resurrect Efrem Zimbalist's Bureau in a way that would appeal to a younger generation, but that also carefully distanced the FBI from any of the misdeeds that had come to light since Zimbalist went off the air. Mike Connors starred, and the cast included a black agent (Harold Sylvester), an "ethnic" agent (Joseph Cali), a woman (Carol Potter), and a country boy (Richard Hill). The show failed because it seemed both pointless and a cover-up—where was the FBI villainy the Church Committee had exposed? In light of the revelations of the 1970s, the virtuous FBI of the past seemed not only too good to be true, but not true at all. The show barely made it through its first season and was canceled before the start of the second.

Exhibit 8.10   **"Today's FBI,"** *Courtesy of ABC Television*

No Place to Hide (1981)

(Directed by John Llewellyn Moxey, with Mariette Hartley, Keir Dullea, and Kathleen Beller)

FBI agents protect a woman stalked by a psychopath.

They Call Me Bruce (1982)

(Directed by Elliot Hong, with Johnny Yune, Ralph Mauro, Pam Huntington, and Margaux Hemingway)

Johnny Yune plays a Bruce Lee–obsessed Chinese chef recruited by the Mafia to carry drugs, on the run from the FBI.

"Hoover" Documentary (1982)

The advertising for this 1982 ABC News retrospective on Hoover claimed that "The Only Power He Couldn't Control Was His Own." By now, the FBI and the late director had sunk lower in the public's esteem than the gangsters and the communists they had once pursued. Some even regarded having been pursued by the Bureau as a badge of honor and to have been an FBI "victim" turned a person into a martyr for civil liberties, no matter his or her original sins.

Strange Invaders (1983)

(Directed by Michael Laughlin, with Paul LeMat, Nancy Allen, Diana Scarwid, Michael Lerner, Louise Fletcher, Wallace Shawn, Fiona Lewis, Kenneth Toby, and June Lockhart)

This parody of 1950s science fiction films has a Midwestern town invaded by aliens while the FBI refuses to believe what is happening.

Best Defense (1984)

(Directed by Willard Huyck, with Dudley Moore, Eddie Murphy, Kate Capshaw, and George Dzundza)

Dudley Moore plays an engineer working on an American super-weapon, Eddie Murphy is the Army officer detailed to test the contraption, and the FBI and KGB stumble over each other.

Cloak & Dagger (1984)

(Directed by Richard Franklin, with Henry Thomas, Dabney Coleman, and Michael Murphy)

An FBI agent about to be murdered slips a note to a boy played by Henry Thomas. Dabney Coleman plays both Henry Thomas's father and the boy's fantasy friend, who happens to be a spy.

To Live and Die in L.A. (1985)

(Directed by William Friedkin, with William L. Petersen, Willem Dafoe, John Pankow, and John Turturro)

Two crooked FBI agents commit robberies while chasing counterfeiter Dafoe.

Falcon and the Snowman (1985)
(Directed by John Schlesinger, with Timothy Hutton and Sean Penn)

Two friends elude the FBI after selling military secrets to the Russians.

F/X (1986)
(Directed by Robert Mandel, with Bryan Brown, Diane Venora, Cliff DeYoung, and Mason Adams)

FBI officials hire a special-effects expert to stage a fake murder of a mobster, then the Bureau tries to kill him to conceal the operation.

Black Moon Rising (1986)
(Directed by Harley Cokliss, with Tommy Lee Jones, Linda Hamilton, Robert Vaughn, and Richard Jaeckel)

Government agents hire a thief to steal design plans for a new car, then pursue him when he fails to turn over the documents.

The Deadly Business (1986)
(Directed by John Korty, with Alan Arkin, Armand Assante, and Michael Learned)

This TV movie tells the true story of a mobster who becomes an FBI informant when his mob boss gets involved in dumping toxic waste.

Raw Deal (1986)
(Directed by John Irvin, with Arnold Schwarzenegger, Kathryn Harrold, Sam Wanamaker, Paul Shenar, Ed Lauter, and Darren McGavin)

Schwarzenegger is an ex-FBI agent who single-handedly wipes out the Chicago mob.

Under Siege (1986)
(Directed by Roger Young, written by reporter Bob Woodward, with Peter Strauss, Mason Adams, Lew Ayres, George Grizzard, Hal Holbrook, E.G. Marshall, David Opatoshu, Fritz Weaver, Paukl Winfield, and Frederick Coffin)

This made-for-TV film about the FBI's war on terrorism has Peter Strauss playing an FBI director.

Manhunter (1986)
(Directed by Michael Mann, with William Peterson and Brian Cox)

Based on Thomas Harris's novel *The Red Dragon, Manhunter* has William Peterson playing FBI agent profiler Wil Graham. Graham tracks down a serial killer known as the Tooth Fairy. Brian Cox makes an appearance as Dr. Hannibal Lector (who makes an unforgettable reappearance in *The Silence of the Lambs)*.

Hoover vs. the Kennedys: The Second Civil War (1987)
(Directed by Michael O'Herlihy, with Jack Warden and Nicholas Campbell)

This TV film portrays FBI Director J. Edgar Hoover as the implacable enemy of President John F. Kennedy and Attorney General Robert F. Kennedy and their civil rights program.

The Hidden (1987)
(Directed by Jack Sholder, with Michael Nouri and Kyle MacLachlan)

Kyle MacLachlan (who later stars in "Twin Peaks") plays an FBI agent assigned to investigate an alien organism that turns honest citizens into criminals.

The House on Carroll Street (1987)
(Directed by Peter Yates, with Kelly McGillis, Jeff Daniels, Mandy Patinkin, and Jessica Tandy)

FBI agent Jeff Daniels teams up with Kelly McGillis to foil a plot to smuggle Nazis into the United States during the early 1950s.

Wisdom (1987)
(Directed by Emilio Estevez, with Emilio Estevez, Demi Moore, Tom Skerritt, and Veronica Cartwright)

The film develops sympathy for a criminal gang being pursued by the Bureau.

The Wild Pair (1987)
(Directed by Beau Bridges, with Beau Bridges, Bubba Smith, Lloyd Bridges, Gary Lockwood, Raymond St. Jacques, Danny De La Paz, Lela Rochon, and Ellen Greer)

FBI agent Beau Bridges works with partner Bubba Smith to arrest racist drug dealers.

Running on Empty (1988)
(Directed by Sidney Lumet, with Christine Lahti, River Phoenix, Judd Hirsch, and Martha Plimpton)

A group of 1960s radicals who had once been involved in political bombings now lives in fear of the FBI.

Betrayed (1988)
(Directed by Costa Gravas, with Debra Winger, Tom Berenger, John Heard, Betsy Blair, and John Mahoney)

Debra Winger plays an FBI agent who goes underground to catch the right-wing extremist murderers of a talk-radio host. The killers are portrayed as the products of a sick society.

Married to the Mob (1988)
(Directed by Jonathan Demme, with Michelle Pfeiffer, Matthew Modine, Dean Stockwell, Mercedes Ruehl, Alec Baldwin, and Joan Cusack)

This black comedy has Matthew Modine playing an FBI agent investigating whether a Mafia wife (Michelle Pfeiffer) murdered her husband.

Patty Hearst (1988)

(Directed by Paul Schrader, with Natasha Richardson, William Forsythe, and Ving Rhames)

Natasha Richardson plays kidnapped newspaper heiress Patty Hearst. After converting to her captors' political radicalism, Hearst escapes from the police siege of the Symbionese Liberation Army headquarters and is pursued and captured by the FBI.

Midnight Run (1988)

(Directed by Martin Brest, with Robert DeNiro, Charles Grodin, Yaphet Kotto, John Ashton, and Dennis Farina)

Robert DeNiro plays a bounty-hunter escorting a bail-jumping accountant (Charles Grodin) back to Los Angeles. They elude rival bounty-hunters, the mob, and the FBI.

Shoot to Kill (1988)

(Directed by Roger Spottiswoode, with Sidney Poitier, Tom Berenger, Kirstie Alley, and Clancy Brown)

FBI agent Poitier recruits a wilderness guide (Tom Berenger) to help track down a fugitive who has faked his wife's kidnapping.

Little Nikita (1988)

(Directed by Richard Benjamin, with Sidney Poitier, River Phoenix, and Caroline Kava)

FBI agent Sidney Poitier tells River Phoenix that the boy's parents are Soviet spies.

J. Edgar Hoover (1988)

(Directed by Robert Collins, with Treat Williams, Rip Torn, David Ogden Stiers, Andrew Duggan, and Louise Fletcher)

Treat Williams plays Hoover in this film based on William C. Sullivan's debunking memoir, *The Bureau: My Thirty Years in Hoover's FBI* (New York: Norton, 1979).

Mississippi Burning (1988)

(Directed by Alan Parker, with Gene Hackman, Willem Dafoe, Frances McDormand, Brad Dourif, and Gailard Sartin)

This film teams a naive young FBI agent (Willem Dafoe) with a Southern agent (Gene Hackman) who believes that local crimes can only be solved through the use of rough local rules. Based on the FBI hunt first for missing civil rights workers Schwerner, Chaney, and Goodman, and then for their killers, the film was criticized by some FBI critics for casting too favorable a light on the FBI's record during the civil rights era.

Feds (1988)

(Directed by Dan Goldberg, with Rebecca De Mornay, Mary Gross, Fred Dalton Thompson, Ken Marshall, and Larry Cedar)

This comedy follows inept FBI recruits on their first cases.

Die Hard (1988)

(Directed by John McTiernan, with Bruce Willis, Alan Rickman, Bonnie Bedelia, Alexander Godunov, and Robert Davi)

A New York City cop (Willis) stumbles into a hostage stand-off in Los Angeles. The situation worsens when FBI agents battle with local police over turf.

The Postmodern FBI in American Popular Culture

The many transformations and mutations in the myth of the FBI inevitably raise the question: will the Bureau ever again have a "normal" popular culture image? Of course, "normal" cannot easily be defined in the case of the FBI. Is the Bureau's normal image the heroic FBI of the 1930s? Is it, instead, an FBI that represents the homely American values that were a religious and patriotic talisman against communism? Is it the FBI as the dark shadow of governmental conspiracies, the dehumanized face of a government at war with its citizens? Is it the cutting edge of law enforcement professionalism and scientific criminology? Or does "normal" mean what it would be for almost any other government agency—an organization charged with a specific job and judged simply by whether it meets those responsibilities?

A definite answer can only be given to this last question. Popular culture's FBI will never devolve to the humdrum level of a "garden variety" government agency. The Bureau now carries so much historical and cultural baggage that an FBI agent's appearance in popular entertainment will invariably convey confusing images of a variously mythic FBI.

Post–Cold War popular culture incorporates all the historical and mythic FBIs that have been born over the past century. Sometimes these contradictory images appear in the same piece of entertainment. Producers of popular entertainment often pick, choose, and combine elements from different, even contrasting, FBI stereotypes, which are sometimes detached from any reference to the myths that produced them. The result is a postmodern pop culture FBI: an FBI constructed out of the debris of the various FBI legends combined in novel ways, sometimes merely for the sake of novelty, sometimes to make an artistic or thematic point. The result can be insightful, amusing, annoying, or merely confusing. The FBI resonates with so many cultural associations that it has become one of the most bankable properties in the pop culture stockroom. Far from fading, the Bureau's presence in American popular culture seems to grow year by year.

The Postmodern G-Man

The postmodern G-man first appeared in American popular culture in the late 1980s with the pattern-breaking television series "Twin Peaks."

"Twin Peaks" (Pilot in 1989; weekly television series, 1990–91)
(Directed by David Lynch, with Kyle MacLachlan, Lara Flynn Boyle, Michael Ontkean, Piper Laurie, Joan Chen, and Sherilyn Fenn)

When the sheriff of Twin Peaks, a lumber town in the Pacific Northwest, requests FBI help to solve the murder of a teenage girl, the popular culture image of the Bureau changed forever. Kyle MacLachlan, as other-worldly Special Agent Dale Cooper, is assigned the case. MacLachlan (Cooper) wanders eerily through the investigation, interpreting clues with New Age guesses and searching the dream world for evidence. The wackier Cooper's investigative techniques are, the better he likes them; his best "thinking" is done when in a trance. Obviously, Lynch (a well-known film director) was playing against the grain of the FBI's traditional popular culture image, and against the conventional expectation that an FBI agent would be devoted to linear logic and the scientific method. Just as obviously, Lynch was fully aware of the tectonic shifts in the public's expectations about the FBI of the previous 20 years, dating from the disintegration of the FBI's image during the 1970s. Lynch was the first to realize the dramatic potential of playing with those changes.

In "Twin Peaks," David Lynch incorporated the most famous features of the pre– and post–Church Committee FBI, perversely reassembling them, reversing the meaning of some features of the FBI image, eliminating others altogether, and recombining what remained in a manner that was at once disorienting, fascinating, and amusing. A techno-klutz, Special Agent Dale Cooper dispenses with the high-tech gadgetry of FBI legend. He keeps in touch with FBI headquarters by dictating reports on a simple cassette recorder and mailing the tapes to his secretary.

Cooper's reliance on ESP as an investigative technique reverses the FBI's legendary devotion to science, and his obsession with interpersonal relations contrasts with the FBI's rationality and impersonality, Bureau traits that popular culture once loved and then hated. Lynch also exploits the FBI's dark side as a feature of modern paranoia:

When back-up agents arrive to help Cooper to, for example, conduct an autopsy, the left's nightmares of a Hooveresque Gestapo, as well as right-wing fantasies of SWAT teams dropping out of black helicopters, are thus reflected.

Agent Cooper's matter-of-fact belief in magic maliciously transforms the old-time FBI's promotion of science as an irresistible, infallible, even supernatural crime-fighting weapon into a scientific form of magic. James Cagney and Jimmy Stewart once wielded their microscopes like witch doctors; in contrast, Agent Cooper seems oblivious to any difference between scientific criminology and his own way of sorting out suspects by tossing rocks at a bottle while reciting their names. In the classic G-men pictures, the FBI represented the relentless march of science against savage ignorance. In David Lynch's FBI, there is no difference between science and New Age goofiness. The postmodern FBI is, on the one hand, a rational organization devoted to science, and, on the other hand, a secret society drenched in the occult: America and "alternative" America, one and indivisible.

In the aftermath of the revolutionary "Twin Peaks," popular culture began to exploit all aspects of the Bureau's by now multifaceted image.

Johnnie Mae Gibson (1989)
(Directed by Bill Duke, with Lynn Whitfield, Howard E. Rollins Jr., Marta DuBois, and Richard Lawson)

J. Edgar Hoover insisted that the FBI conform to his idea of an elite institution, and that meant lily-white and all male. FBI entertainment in the post-Hoover era could create square-peg-in-round hole situations simply by casting agents against these expectations, for example, a female or minority agent. In this made-for-TV film, Lynn Whitfield plays the first female African American FBI agent.

The Mighty Quinn (1989)
(Directed by Carl Schenkel, with Denzel Washington, Robert Townsend, and James Fox)

The Bureau's embodiment of by-the-book law enforcement professionalism is portrayed as a symbol of first-world rote thinking doomed to extinction in the new world of racial and cultural diversity. Xavier Quinn (Denzel Washington) returns to the Caribbean as a police chief whose ability to function in the islands is clouded by his years in the United States and his FBI training. He has to adjust to island ways in this film based on A. H. Z. Carr's novel, *Finding Maubee*.

Tapeheads (1989)

(Directed by Bill Fishman, with John Cusack, Tim Robbins, Doug McClure, and Connie Stevens)

Tapeheads is a comedy about a couple of dimwits (Cusack and Robbins) who start a business taping TV ads and music videos. The FBI's image as squarer-than-square sets up a comic cameo appearance by the Dead Kennedys' Jello Biafra as an FBI agent.

Dead-Bang (1989)

(Directed by John Frankenheimer, with Don Johnson, Penelope Ann Miller, and William Forsythe)

The FBI's lack of imagination and primitive social skills become Los Angeles detective Don Johnson's greatest obstacles in his efforts to solve the murder of a cop.

Mr. Hoover and I (1990)

(Directed by Emile de Antonio, with documentary footage)

The film's director, a militant leftist, muses on the contents of his FBI file, obtained through the Freedom of Information Act. FBI Director Hoover's confused sexual identity is ridiculed as de Antonio vents outrage over the Bureau's surveillance and persecution of people like himself, whom he regards as Hoover's victims, hounded for their social activism. De Antonio assumes his audience shares his dour view of the Bureau, but some viewers' sympathy for de Antonio will waver given his refusal to give the FBI information about members of the radical Weather Underground whom he had interviewed and who were being sought for their involvement in terrorist bombings.

Flashback (1990)

(Directed by Franco Amurri, with Dennis Hopper, Kiefer Sutherland, Carol Kane, Cliff De Young, and Paul Dooley)

In this countercultural view of the FBI, a young Bureau agent (Kiefer Sutherland) is jailed when he tries to arrest a radical fugitive from the 1960s (Dennis Hopper).

A Show of Force (1990)

(Directed by Bruno Barretto, with Amy Irving, Robert Duvall, Andy Garcia, and Lou Diamond Phillips)

A reporter (Amy Irving) discovers that the FBI is behind killings intended to influence the 1978 Puerto Rican elections.

My Blue Heaven (1990)

(Directed by Herbert Ross, with Steve Martin, Rick Moranis, Joan Cusack, Melanie Mayron, Bill Irwin, Carol Kane, and William Hickey)

A moronic FBI agent (Rick Moranis) guards a mob informant (Steve Martin) in the government's witness protection program.

I Come in Peace (1990)

(Directed by Craig Baxley, with Dolph Lundgren, Brian Benben, Betsey Brantley, and Matthias Hues)

This science fiction comedy exploits the FBI's image as the ultimate bureaucracy. Brian Benben plays a staid, methodical FBI agent whose partner is an undisciplined Houston vice cop investigating vampire killings by dope addicts from outer space.

Murder in Mississippi (1990)

(Directed by Roger Young, with Tom Hulce, Blair Underwood, Jennifer Grey, C.C.H. Pounder, and Josh Charles)

This made-for-TV film, based on the Chaney, Goodman, and Schwerner civil rights murders, recycles the heroic FBI image of the Hoover era. Like *Mississippi Burning,* the picture was condemned by FBI critics who charged that the Bureau's role in the Southern civil rights struggles had been nonfeasant at best, if not actually malfeasant.

At Gunpoint (1990)

(Directed by Steven L. Harris, with Frank Kanig, Tain Bodkin, and Scott Claflin)

At Gunpoint was one of the first FBI films to feature the criminal profiling procedures that FBI agents employed during investigations of serial murders. This plot device soon became a staple of FBI entertainment, owing to the public's growing fascination with the softer social sciences employed by law enforcement, in contrast to the more familiar hard sciences of fingerprinting, ballistics, and laboratory analysis.

The Silence of the Lambs (1991)

(Directed by Jonathan Demme, with Jodie Foster, Anthony Hopkins, Scott Glenn, Ted Levine, Anthony Heald, Brook Smith, and Diane Baker)

The Silence of the Lambs is another landmark in the history of the popular culture FBI (see Exhibit 8.11). Jodie Foster, an FBI trainee, is sent to interview convicted serial killer

Exhibit 8.11   *The Silence of the Lambs, Courtesy of Photofest and Orion Pictures*

Hannibal Lector (Anthony Hopkins) for ideas that might help the Bureau catch another murderer. Foster's sincerity and idealism increased applications for appointments as special agents, particularly from young women. The film's depiction of the Bureau's highly refined techniques of criminal profiling (methods developed by Quantico instructor and agent John Douglas, played in the film by Scott Glenn and more fully detailed in Douglas's 1995 bestseller, *Mind Hunter*) reinforced the FBI's traditional association with science, albeit the social sciences.

JFK (1991)

(Directed by Oliver Stone, with Kevin Costner, Sissy Spacek, Kevin Bacon, Tommy Lee Jones, Laurie Metcalf, Joe Pesci, Donald Sutherland, John Candy, Jack Lemmon, Ed Asner, Gary Oldman, and Walter Matthau)

Government conspiracy theory movie plots were hardly novel. For instance, in the 1965 thriller *Seven Days in May*, Air Force General Burt Lancaster attempted a military coup d'état, and in *Three Days of the Condor* (1975), Robert Redford foils a CIA plot to take over the country. Oliver Stone's conspiracy theory in *JFK* was different because it moved from counterfactual fantasy to docu-drama style historical realism. Stone's film only tangentially implicated the FBI (via Jim Garrison) in its high-level plot by right-wing fanatics and military-industrial fascists in the government to kill President Kennedy so that the Cold War could continue, but Ed Asner's brutal FBI agent, who sets up Oswald as a "patsy," suggests that the FBI was at least a willing accomplice (see Exhibit 8.12).

One of the most interesting features of *JFK* is Stone's subversion of the old G-man formula to suit his revisionist ends. G-man movies of the 1930s had obligatory tours of the FBI labs and fingerprint collections, ballistic tests, and

Exhibit 8.12   *JFK, Courtesy of Photofest and Warner Bros.*

firing-range demonstrations. *JFK* has documentary scenes that are almost indistinguishable from those of the old G-man formula, but where the FBI films of the 1930s used documentary footage to demonstrate the government's use of science, organization, and force to battle criminal plots against society, Stone's Jim Garrison, played by Kevin Costner, uses ballistics, fingerprints, and photography to expose criminal plots by the government. Stone's film gains emotional (as opposed to intellectual) power by employing the same pseudo-documentary format that had earlier lent the FBI the prestige of science. The difference is Stone uses the formula to make conspiracy theories look scientific.

JFK was more than an attack on the Warren Commission, which had concluded that Lee Harvey Oswald alone was responsible for assassinating President Kennedy. Stone also charged that since the Second World War, most of the key events of American history (and even world history) had been secretly determined by a militaristic cabal in Washington to suit their fascist ends. Stone called Kennedy's assassination a "coup d'état," the logical culmination of the behind-the-scenes manipulation by the military-industrial complex that had replaced democratic government in postwar America. *JFK* thus adopted the far-left's 1920s stereotype of a conspiratorial FBI, and combined it with the post-Watergate, post-Vietnam counterculture's theory that the domestic and foreign policy horrors of the 1960s and 1970s, and, indeed, the entire Cold War, were the work of power-crazed fascists like FBI Director J. Edgar Hoover.

The nearly simultaneous appearance of "Twin Peaks," *The Silence of the Lambs,* and *JFK* reveals how far the popular culture image of the FBI had strayed from the stereotypes and myths of the 1930s. The contemporary G-man's training in New Age pseudo-science ("Twin Peaks") and social-science techniques *(The Silence of the Lambs)* made him resemble the fantastic super-heroes of comic books and pulp magazines more than the lab-coated special agent of the 1930s formula. When tying the FBI down to everyday reality, popular entertainment the Bureau might place the Bureau at the center of an America controlled by government conspiracies, a nightmare that was now the dark side of American popular culture.

The Dark Wind (1991)

(Directed by Errol Morris, with Lou Diamond Phillips, Gary Farmer, Fred Ward, and Guy Boyd)

Popular entertainment at the end of the twentieth century became increasingly committed to portraying the struggles of previously invisible groups to rediscover their submerged identities, and to enter the elite institutions of American society on their own terms. FBI Director J. Edgar Hoover had carefully crafted and protected the image of the FBI agent as the all-American hero, middle-class, white, Anglo-Saxon, and Protestant. In an increasingly pluralistic society, Hoover's FBI became a symbol of a traditional elite trying to preserve its position. A film like Errol Morris's *The Dark Wind* used the Bureau as a symbol of the inauthentic, alienated self now rejected by minorities like (in this instance) American Indians. A conspiratorial FBI tries to keep Lou Diamond Phillips, playing the Navajo hero of the Tony Hillerman detective story series, from exposing a dope ring operating on Navajo and Hopi Indian reservations. Where earlier FBI entertainment had visited Indian reservations to lend an exotic, almost foreign quality to formula adventures, the FBI is now portrayed as an alien intrusion disrupting a traditional society trying to hold onto its culture and security

Homicide (1991)

(Directed by David Mamet, with Joe Mantegna, W. H. Macy, and Natalija Nogulich)

The civil rights era left the FBI with the reputation of being unenthusiastic about protecting minorities. In this film, the FBI is unable to solve a hate crime case, so police officer Joe Mantegna takes over. He discovers a secret society of Jewish activists, rediscovering his own Jewish identity in the process.

Point Break (1991)

(Directed by Kathryn Bigelow, with Patrick Swayze, Keanu Reeves, Gary Busey, and Lori Petty)

Keanu Reeves is an FBI agent investigating a bank robbery gang called the Ex-Presidents, because they wear rubber masks of Presidents Reagan, Nixon, et al. Reeves infiltrates a group of California surfers headed by Patrick Swayze and feels tempted to chase the waves instead of the clues.

Stone Cold (1991)

(Directed by Craig R. Baxley, with Brian Bosworth, Lance Henriksen, William Forsythe, and Arabella Holzbog)

This movie exploits Brian Bosworth's brief fame as a punk-rebel football star. He plays a suspended cop whom the FBI employs to infiltrate an outlaw motorcycle gang. The film portrays an FBI so out of touch with America that it recruits misfits and psychopaths to police a changing country.

Steele's Law (1991)

(Directed by Fred Williamson, with Fred Williamson, Bo Svenson, and Phyllis Cicero)

In this film, the lack of diversity among FBI agents forces it to go outside its ranks to perform its job. Fred Williamson plays an undercover Chicago cop who helps the FBI combat a gang of Texas criminals.

The 10 Million Dollar Getaway (1991)

(Directed by James Contner, with John Mahoney, Joseph Carberry, Terrence Mann, Karen Young, and Tony Lo Bianco)

This TV drama recreates a high-profile FBI case in a semi-documentary fashion, the notorious Lufthansa robbery at New York's JFK Airport.

The Rain Killer (1991)

(Directed by Ken Stein, with Ray Sharkey, David Beecroft, Michael Chiklis, Tania Coleridge, and Woody Brown)

The police and the FBI track down a killer who commits crimes only when it rains, a plot that recycles old FBI crime-fighting formulas.

Malcolm X (1992)

(Directed by Spike Lee, with Denzel Washington, Angela Bassett, Albert Hall, Al Freeman Jr., Delroy Lindo, Spike Lee, Theresa Randle, and Kate Vernon)

In Spike Lee's bio-pic, the FBI is accused of learning about the impending assassination of Malcolm X by the Nation of Islam, but not intervening to save the black leader. The film exploits the reputation of the Hoover FBI as indifferent to civil rights and hostile toward black Americans in general.

White Sands (1992)

(Directed by Roger Donaldson, with Willem Dafoe, Mary Elizabeth Mastrantonio, Mickey Rourke, Samuel L. Jackson, and M. Emmet Walsh)

Willem Dafoe plays the sheriff of a rural New Mexican town who blunders into an FBI investigation led by black agent Samuel L. Jackson. The film treats a black FBI agent as a novelty.

Honor and Glory (1992)

(Directed by Godfrey Hall, with Cynthia Rothrock, Donna Jason, Chuck Jeffreys, and Gerald Klein)

Cynthia Rothrock, a female FBI agent, cracks a plot to steal a nuclear arsenal. The novelty here is a female agent, particularly one skilled in the martial arts, Rothrock's specialty.

Lady Dragon (1992)

(Directed by David Worth, with Cynthia Rothrock, Richard Norton, and Robert Ginty)

This time, Rothrock plays an FBI agent whose husband is murdered on their wedding day.

Three Ninjas (1992)
(Directed by Jon Turteltaub and Victor Wong, with Michael Treanor, Max Elliott Slade, Chad Power, and Rand Kingsley)

In this children's adventure film, the three sons of an FBI agent are instructed in the ninja arts by their Chinese grandfather, Victor Wong. The boys are kidnapped by a gun-runner whom their father is investigating. The film exploits the novelty of a racially diverse FBI.

Rapid Fire (1992)
(Directed by Dwight H. Little, with Brandon Lee, Powers Boothe, Nick Mancuso, and Raymond J. Barry)

A Chinese American college student (played by Brandon Lee) accidentally witnesses a Mafia murder and the FBI insists that he testify.

Incident at Oglala (1992)
(Directed by Michael Apted, with documentary footage, narrated by Robert Redford)

This documentary examines the American Indian Movement (AIM) uprising at the South Dakota Pine Ridge Reservation in 1975 that resulted in the deaths of two FBI agents and the conviction of AIM leader Leonard Peltier for their murders. The film charges that the FBI framed Peltier.

Thunderheart (1992)
(Directed by Michael Apted, with Val Kilmer, Sam Shepard, and Fred Ward)

In this film, based closely on Apted's documentary *Incident at Oglala,* Kilmer plays an American Indian FBI agent investigating the murder of an Oglala Sioux on the Pine Ridge Reservation. Set in the aftermath of the 1975 AIM uprising, the film forces Kilmer to choose between his loyalty to the Bureau and his outrage at the injustices to Indians perpetrated by white society and the FBI.

Ruby (1992)
(Directed by John Mackenzie, with Danny Aiello, Sherilyn Fenn, Arliss Howard, Joe Cortese, and Marc Lawrence)

In this bio-pic, the relationship of Jack Ruby (Lee Harvey Oswald's assassin) with both the FBI and the mafia are made to support conspiracy theories about President Kennedy's assassination.

In the Line of Duty: The FBI Murders (1992)
(Directed by Dick Lowry, with Ronny Cox, Doug Sheehan, and David Soul)

This made-for-TV film is based on the 1986 Miami shoot-out that cost the lives of two FBI agents and left five others wounded, the most casualties of any incident in FBI history.

Teamster Boss: The Jackie Presser Story (1992)
(Directed by Alastair Reid, with Brian Dennehy, Jeff Daniels, Maria Conchita Alonso, Eli Wallach, Robert Prosky, and Tony Lo Bianco)

This TV film is based on James Neff's *Mobbed Up.* The film recounts the FBI investigation that led to Teamsters' Union boss Jackie Presser's downfall.

Passenger 57 (1992)
(Directed by Kevin Hooks, with Wesley Snipes, Bruce Payne, and Tom Sizemore)

Airline security officer Wesley Snipes intervenes when terrorists succeed in freeing one of their associates from the FBI agents escorting him on a cross-continent flight.

Live Wire (1992)
(Directed by Christian Duguay, with Pierce Brosnan, Ron Silver, Ben Cross, Lisa Eilbacher, Brent Jennings, Tony Plana, Al Waxman, Philip Baker Hall, and Michael St. Gerard)

FBI bomb expert Pierce Brosnan protects a crooked U.S. senator, Ron Silver, from a terrorist played by Ben Cross. Brosnan discovers his wife is having an affair with the senator.

Jennifer 8 (1992)
(Directed by Bruce Robinson, with Andy Garcia, Uma Thurman, Lance Henriksen, Kathy Baker, Graham Beckel, Kevin Conway, and John Malkovich)

A plot twist has the FBI mistakenly suspect Andy Garcia, a Los Angeles cop, of being the serial killer Garcia is trying to capture.

Folks! (1992)
(Directed by Ted Kotcheff, with Tom Selleck, Don Ameche, Anne Jackson, and Christine Ebersole)

An FBI investigation of insider trading in the securities industry disrupts the life of Chicago Stock Exchange trader Tom Selleck.

Deadly Rivals (1992)
(Directed by James Dodson, with Andrew Stevens, Cela Wise, Margaux Hemingway, Joseph Bologna, and Richard Roundtree)

Deadly Rivals has the FBI battling smuggling and corporate espionage.

Twin Peaks: Fire Walk with Me (1992)
(Directed by David Lynch, with Kyle MacLachlan, Lara Flynn Boyle, Michael Ontkean, Piper Laurie, Joan Chen, and Sherilyn Fenn)

Lynch tries to exploit the success of the 1990–91 television series, but the public had already lost interest in the show's fantastic plot and surreal style.

Official and Confidential: The Secret Life of J. Edgar Hoover (New York: Putnam, 1993)

For most of its history, the FBI's image was indistinguish-able from the personal image of FBI Director J. Edgar Hoover. After his death in 1972, that identification inevitably faded, but in February 1993, it was revived with a vengeance. British journalist Anthony Summers (author of conspiracy-minded books about the deaths of John F. Kennedy and Marilyn Monroe) published a sensationalist biography of Hoover. The former director, Summers charged, had been a closeted homosexual (which had long been rumored) who had even participated in orgies at New York City's Plaza Hotel. Hoover was supposedly spotted at these events wearing a "fluffy black dress," high heels, and a "black curly wig," or (on another occasion) a "red dress with a black feather boa." Publicity for the book ballyhooed these sensational "revelations," which were widely disseminated on television in a PBS "Frontline" documentary and in a *Vanity Fair* excerpt. Hoover's alleged cross-dressing at once became a part of popular culture. Comedian and late-night talk show host Jay Leno joked that the former FBI director ought to be called "Gay Edgar Hoover." A character in the hit television comedy "Married with Children" said she was going to solve a mystery the same way as J. Edgar Hoover; she was going to put on a red dress. The *New Yorker* ran a cartoon of one FBI agent asking another, "Has anyone considered that maybe his dress was a disguise?" Even politicians chimed in, with President Bill Clinton, Senate Minority Leader Bob Dole, and even Senator Strom Thurmond tossing off Hoover-in-drag gags.

Most historians and reviewers rejected Summers's more serious claim that Hoover had been blackmailed by the mob, which (Summers said) had come into possession of compromising pictures of Hoover and Clyde Tolson that showed a homosexual relationship between them, Hoover scholars also argued that it was extremely unlikely that the stories of Hoover's cross-dressing had any basis in reality, and further suggested that Hoover's supposed sighting at an orgy existed only in the imagination of Summers's informant, a Hoover-hater of venerable vintage who had been unsuccessfully peddling the same story for years. However, biographers continue to differ on whether Hoover was a homosexual, and if so, whether that had any significant impact on the history of the FBI.

Historians could sputter, but popular culture had a story it was unlikely to ever give up. Once the story had run its initial course, it continued to resurface whenever pop culture needed some tasty flavor for a potboiler. After 1993, as far as American popular culture was concerned, the "Lady in Red" in the history of the FBI was J. Edgar Hoover.

The New Age FBI

Movies like *The Silence of the Lambs* provided a realistic description of advanced FBI techniques like profiling; this kind of psychological approach to crime solving could easily be adapted by popular entertainment to create agent heroes with paranormal resources of mental telepathy, extrasensory perception, and the other powers of the fantastic detectives of comic strips and pulp magazines.

Bureau officials had long oversold scientific crime detection as a kind of modern magic. The New Age FBI was born when a reaction to years of scientific hype began to blur the FBI agent's identity as a man (or woman) of science, and popular entertainment began to use the FBI's scientific image to lend respectability to all manner of pseudo-scientific nonsense.

"The X-Files" (1993)
(Created by Chris Carter, with David Duchovny and Gillian Anderson, and many directors and writers)
The popular culture portrayal of the FBI that left the deepest imprint on the American consciousness of the 1990s was producer and writer Chris Carter's "The X-Files" (see Exhibit 8.13). Fox Network's wildly popular television series debuted on September 10, 1993, and ran on Friday nights until the fall of 1996, when it shifted to Sunday. The show sends FBI agents Fox Mulder (David Duchovny) and

Exhibit 8.13   **"The X-Files,"** *Courtesy of Photofest and Fox Broadcasting*

Dana Scully (Gillian Anderson) to investigate cases involving the extraterrestrial and the paranormal. The show's complicated mythology, driven by Mulder's belief that "the truth is out there" (the show's motto), permits multi-layered plots with rich inter-textual references between episodes. In "The X-Files," the FBI is an organization suffused with paranoia (another of the show's mottoes is "trust no one") and riven by plots and counterplots intended to frustrate Mulder and Scully from learning the facts concealed in the Bureau's "X-Files" on cases too disturbing to be revealed to the public.

The show's ingenious plots and characterizations draw on the entire history of the popular culture FBI. Its fundamental plot device, the war between a government intent on concealing its guilty secrets and citizens determined to learn the truth, recalls the Church Committee's portrayal of FBI Director Hoover as the master blackmailer of American history, using secret files to maintain his power and advance an extremist political agenda. The series also draws on some Americans' belief, in the wake of the Pentagon Papers and the Nixon White House tapes, that the release of government secrets might redeem the national soul and transform American history. "The X-Files" also mixes and matches stereotypes of FBI agents from different periods of popular culture history. Special Agent Dana Scully is a female in a man's FBI; a trained scientist committed to a rational understanding of the world. Her weirdly intuitive partner, Agent Fox Mulder, relies on emotions for his sense of reality. He is the antithesis of male stereotypes and of the FBI agent as a scientific investigator. The FBI in "The X-Files" conceals the government's guilty involvement in illegal operations and experiments, and so Mulder and Scully become targets of murderous plots whenever they get too close to the truth.

FBI officials in Washington are uncomfortable with the "The X-Files" image of the FBI. Nonetheless, the program has reinvigorated the Bureau's mystique as a charismatic agency whose everyday work is charged with the high tension of melodrama. It has even helped recruitment.

A Perfect World (1993)
(Directed by Clint Eastwood, with Kevin Costner, Clint Eastwood, Laura Dern, and T. J. Lowther)

In this film, the Bureau is portrayed as a dehumanized force advancing with robot-like brutality to crush its victims, while overwhelming the efforts by ordinary Americans who seek to get along and find humanistic solutions to legal and moral dilemmas. Kevin Costner is an escaped convict fleeing

Texas Ranger Clint Eastwood. When Costner takes a child hostage, the FBI joins the hunt. In a scene probably patterned after the FBI's controversial role in the death of Vicki Weaver at Ruby Ridge, Idaho, an FBI sharpshooter kills Costner just as he and Eastwood achieve trust and empathy.

Golden Gate (1993)
(Directed by Jon Madden, with Matt Dillon, Joan Chen, Bruno Kirby, and Tzi Ma)

After FBI agent Matt Dillon's investigation of an old man's alleged communist associations drives the man to suicide, the agent falls in love with the old man's daughter, played by Joan Chen. The film shares the countercultural left's long-held views of Cold War anticommunism as simply a pretext for government repression, of the unwarranted and illegal FBI loyalty investigations of the 1950s, and of the victims of these witch-hunts as civil liberties martyrs.

The Firm (1993)
(Directed by Sydney Pollack, with Tom Cruise, Gene Hackman, Jeanne Tripplehorn, Holly Hunter, Ed Harris, Hal Holbrook, Wilford Brimley, David Strathairn, and Gary Busey)

FBI agents contact Tom Cruise when two associates of his law firm are murdered. The Bureau plays a minor role in this film, but its characterization once again stresses popular culture's stereotype of the Bureau as unimaginative and obsessed with regulations and procedures.

In the Line of Duty: Ambush in Waco (1993)
(Directed by Dick Lowry, with Tim Daly, William O'Leary, and Dan Luria)

This made-for-TV account of the FBI's attack on David Koresh's Branch Davidian headquarters in Waco, Texas, humanizes Koresh—despite the government's efforts to brand him an insane extremist. The picture questions the necessity and morality of the final FBI-led assault that left more than 70 Davidians dead, including infants and children.

Undercover Blues (1993)
(Directed by Herbert Ross, with Kathleen Turner, Dennis Quaid, Park Overall, and Tom Arnold)

Quaid and Turner play married FBI agents who, while vacationing in New Orleans with their baby, stumble on an arms-smuggling ring. The film treats the notion of married agents as a novelty, playing against the stereotype of the FBI as a depersonalized bureaucracy.

The Outfit (1993)
(Directed by J. Christian Ingvordsen, with Lance Henriksen, Bill Drago, and Martin Kove)

A renegade FBI agent is caught in the middle of the Legs Diamond–Dutch Schultz beer wars of the 1920s.

Slaughter of the Innocents (1993)
(Directed by James Glickenhaus, with Scott Glenn, Jesse Cameron-Glickenhaus, Sheila Tousey, Darlanne Fluegel, and Zitto Kazann)

Scott Glenn is an FBI agent who is helped by his son during a hunt for a murderous religious fanatic.

No Escape, No Return (1993)
(Directed by Charles T. Kanganis, with Maxwell Caulfield, Dustin Nguyen, and Denise Loveday)

FBI and undercover cops work together to apprehend a drug lord.

Hitwoman: The Double Edge (1993)
(Directed by Stephen Stafford, with Susan Lucci, Robert Urich, and Michael Woods)

Lucci plays two roles in this TV movie—the FBI agent *and* the murderer she is hunting.

The Client (1994)
(Directed by Joel Schumacher, with Susan Sarandon, Tommy Lee Jones, Mary Louise Parker, and Anthony LaPaglia)

Tommy Lee Jones is a federal prosecutor who sends FBI agents after lawyer Susan Sarandon's client, a young boy who has witnessed a murder. The movie's FBI agent is as unsympathetic and relentless a bloodhound as *Les Misérables*'s detective Jabert.

Zero Tolerance (1994)
(Directed by Joseph Mehri, with Robert Patrick, Titus Welliver, Kirsten Meadows, Mick Fleetwood, and Miles O'Keeffe)

Robert Patrick plays an obsessed FBI agent who is driven to kill five seemingly respectable businessmen who run a drug cartel that murdered Patrick's parents. In the postmodern popular culture FBI, the all-American hero is as likely as anyone else to turn into a psychopath.

Shattered Image (1994)
(Directed by Fritz Kiersch, with Jack Scalia, Bo Derek, John Savage, Dorlan Harewood, Ramon Franco, Michael Harris, and Carol Lawrence)

The FBI is on the trail of criminals who kidnapped the owner of a modeling agency in this TV movie.

Holy Matrimony (1994)
(Directed by Leonard Nimoy, with Patricia Arquette, Joseph Gordon-Levitt, Armin Mueller-Stahl, Tate Donovan, John Schuck, and Lois Smith)

Bank robber Arquette hides in a Hutterite colony. She is pursued by the FBI, the symbol of a dehumanized modern world in conflict with a traditional community's human values.

Blank Check (1994)
(Directed by Rupert Wainwright, with Brian Bonsall, Karen Duffy, Miguel Ferrer, James Rebhorn, and Tone Loc)

When the kid in this Disney film innocently fills out a blank check for a million dollars, he is chased by the FBI.

Nixon (1995)
(Directed by Oliver Stone, with Anthony Hopkins, Joan Allen, Bob Hoskins, and Paul Sorvino)

Bob Hoskins plays FBI Director Hoover as an outrageous and predatory homosexual, thoroughly corrupt, working hand-in-glove with the mob to blackmail President Nixon. Surprisingly, the president is sympathetically portrayed as helpless in the face of the power of "the beast," Stone's term for the powerful secret groups (among them, the FBI) that rule America. Stone's Hoover blends biographer Anthony Summers's portrait of Hoover as a transvestite blackmailed by the mob with the theory of another FBI critic, Hank Messick, that Hoover and the mob had worked out a modus vivendi to leave each other alone. This film offers one of the more demonic images of the FBI and its legendary director.

From the Journals of Jean Seberg (1995)
(Directed by Mark Rappaport, with Mary Beth Hurt)

This film is an exposé of the FBI's COINTELPRO persecution of actress Jean Seberg, who allegedly committed suicide because the FBI disseminated derogatory personal information about her relationships with the Black Panthers.

Two If by Sea (1995)
(Directed by Bill Bennett, with Sandra Bullock, Denis Leary, and Yaphet Kotto)

The mob and the FBI compete to retrieve stolen artwork from art thieves Bullock and Leary.

Captain Nuke and the Bomber Boys (1995)
(Directed by Charles Gale, with Joe Mantegna, Joanna Pacula, Joe Piscopo, Martin Sheen, Rod Steiger, and Ryan Thomas Johnson)

The FBI mistakenly concludes that kids, who had found what they believe is a nuclear device, are terrorists.

Dillinger and Capone (1995)
(Directed by Jon Purdy, with Martin Sheen, F. Murray Abraham, Sasha Jenson, and Don Stroud)

"The X-Files" liberated the popular culture FBI from the bounds of probability. This film has John Dillinger, having faked his death at the Biograph, recruited by Al Capone for a late 1930s bank job.

The Rock (1996)

(Directed by Michael Bay, with Sean Connery, Nicolas Cage, Ed Harris, David Morse, William Forsythe, and John Spencer)

Nicolas Cage, an FBI agent-scientist at headquarters in Washington, is goofing off in the FBI Laboratory, waiting for a challenging case. He gets his chance when he is sent to San Francisco to advise field agents involved in hostage negotiations with terrorists who have taken over Alcatraz prison and threaten to poison San Francisco Bay with a supertoxin. Cage is an FBI Clark Kent: a seeming scientific nerd and coward whose real heroism is revealed by circumstances. At first, Cage hopes to use the combat skills he learned at the academy, but it is as a scientist armed with a Ph.D. in biochemistry that is his edge over the special forces veterans with their biological weapons.

In the postmodern FBI, it is no longer enough for the special agent superhero to defend the nation against an underworld conspiracy. *The Rock* also serves up a conspiracy *within* the Bureau. Sean Connery plays a British secret operative, who—as the only man to escape from Alcatraz—knows a secret way onto the island. Connery is being held incommunicado in a federal prison having stolen microfilms documenting the Bureau's guilty involvement in cover-ups of UFO landings, the Kennedy assassination, and so on—all the fixtures of modern paranoia. The movie's demented FBI director plans to get Connery to lead the assault on the island—and then have him killed. Cage and Connery liberate the island, kill the director, and, as the picture ends, are about to release the secrets of the microfilms.

"Millennium" (1996)

(Produced by Chris Carter, directed by David Nutter, with Lance Henriksen and Megan Gallagher)

The hero of this TV series (Lance Henriksen) is an ex–FBI profiler who joins the Seattle-based Millennium Group, a secret organization dedicated to combating a new crime wave that has been spawned by the approach of the new millennium. The lead character combines scientific profiling with an intuition that verges on extrasensory perception, another example of the postmodern FBI formula merging traditional with "alternative" forms of science.

Serial Killer (1996)

(Directed by Pierre David, with Kim Delaney, Gary Hudson, Tobin Bell, and Pam Grier)

This film returns to the criminal profiling theme, as a female FBI agent (Kim Delaney), an expert on serial killers, is stalked by a killer she sent to jail.

Children of Fury (1996)

(Directed by Charles Haid, with Ed Begley Jr., Dennis Franz, Tess Harper, Paul Le Mat, and Kyle Secor)

Dennis Franz is an FBI agent involved in a Waco-like standoff with a polygamous religious cult.

Beavis and Butt-head Do America (1996)

(Directed by Michael Judge, with voices of Michael Judge, Robert Stack, Cloris Leachman, Eric Bogosian, and Richard Linklater)

The two cartoon morons are pursued by an FBI agent obsessed with body cavity searches.

Mulholland Falls (1996)

(Directed by Lee Tamahori, with Nick Nolte, Melanie Griffith, Chazz Palminteri, Michael Madsen, Chris Penn, and Jennifer Connelly)

The FBI investigates a vigilante unit operating within the Los Angeles police force.

Maximum Risk (1996)

(Directed by Ringo Lam, with Jean Claude Van Damme, Natasha Henstridge, Zach Grenier, Jena-Hugues Anglade, and Paul Ben-Victor)

This martial arts adventure has the FBI providing plot complications for Van Damme's battles against the Russian mafia.

Chain Reaction (1996)

(Directed by Andrew Davis, with Keanu Reeves, Morgan Freeman, Rachel Weisz, Fred Ward, and Kevin Dunn)

The FBI pursues Keanu Reeves, a young scientist being framed for murder.

Hollow Point (1996)

(Directed by Sidney J. Furie, with Thomas Ian Griffith, Tia Carrere, John Lithgow, and Donald Sutherland)

FBI agent Tia Carrere and DEA agent Thomas Ian Griffith recruit hit man Donald Sutherland to fight John Lithgow's criminal mob.

Mask of Death (1996)

(Directed by David Mitchell, with Lorenzo Lamas, Rae Dawn Chong, Conrad Cunn, and Billy Dee Williams)

An FBI agent undergoes plastic surgery to chase down a killer.

Public Enemies (1996)

(Directed by Mark Lester, with Theresa Russell, Eric Roberts, Alyssa Milano, Dan Cortese, Gavin Harrison, and Joseph Lindsay)

This TV movie revisits the 1930s gangster wars with FBI agent Melvin Purvis (Dan Cortese) on the trail of "Ma" Barker (Theresa Russell) and her gang.

Face/Off (1997)

(Directed by John Woo, with John Travolta, Nicolas Cage, Joan Allen, Gina Gershon, and Allesandro Nivola)

Nicolas Cage, an ace FBI agent, captures his son's murderer, an international terrorist played by John Travolta, who is half of a Castor-Pollux brother act (character doubles abound in this movie). The terrorist, who has hidden a bomb somewhere in Los Angeles, is now in a coma, so FBI scientists (here about as mad as mad movie scientists ever get) suggest to Cage that they slice off his face and stitch on Travolta's, so he can infiltrate Travolta's gang. Cage agrees, and off he goes, in deep disguise. Travolta recovers, grabs Cage's face out of cold storage, puts it on, and sets after Cage, sending Cage to jail and appropriating Cage's house, wife, and daughter. It is the pop culture FBI at its weirdest, as the G-man returns to his origins as the dime novel's Nick Carter, Master of Disguise.

Donnie Brasco (1997)

(Directed by Mike Newell, with Al Pacino, Johnny Depp, Michael Madsen, Bruno Kirby, James Russo, and Anne Heche)

This is one of the great FBI films. The movie is based on FBI agent Joe Pistone's best-selling 1987 memoir of his six years undercover as a soldier in the New York mafia. Johnny Depp, as "Donnie Brasco," Pistone's undercover alias, gives a brilliant performance as a conflicted hero who suffers from prolonged separation from his wife (Anne Heche) and children. Al Pacino departs from his usual bravura character-izations to portray Lefty Guns Ruggiero, Donnie Brasco's entrée into the mob, as a burned out, pathetic hanger-on who is nonetheless a multiple murderer. In many ways, the film looks back to James Cagney's *G-Men,* in portraying the Bureau as a high-tech bureaucracy that resents its depen-dence on the bravery and resourcefulness of an individual hero like Pistone who excels as an undercover detective because he is an autonomous individual who does not fit into the bureaucratic mold. The film departs somewhat from the book when it depicts Depp assuming the sensibility and even the morality of a mobster, which Pistone denies ever took place. The producers hired an English director, Mike Newell, because they wanted a fresh look at the gangster genre. Newell rejuvenated the formula by returning to the source.

The FBI in American Popular Culture at Century's End

The FBI was in the headlines during the 1990s as frequently and prominently as ever. Bookstores offered new books on the Bureau: critical exposés, celebrations of the FBI's most sensational cases, and detective novels featuring FBI agent heroes and villains. An FBI Web site on the Internet offered downloads of Bureau documents from the speeches of the FBI director to selected files, released under the Freedom of Information Act. The FBI headquarters tour remains one of the most popular tourist attractions in Washington, D.C. After years of denial, the Bureau finally came to terms with the legacy of the Hoover years, taking pride in the positive aspects of its history and enjoying its place in American popular culture. After a long absence, J. Edgar Hoover's portrait reappeared on the tour and in Bureau offices. Patricia Cornwell's Kay Scarpetta detective series, the best-selling detective stories in the world, featured an investigator seeped in FBI lore and involved in complex relationships with FBI agents. Television's weekly "America's Most Wanted," often filmed at the FBI's Washington headquarters, has since 1987 reminded Americans that the Bureau still pursues the country's most dangerous and elusive criminals.

The Bureau's swift solution of the February 23, 1993, bombing of the World Trade Center in New York City and of the April 19, 1995, bombing of the federal office building in Oklahoma City reminded Americans of the Bureau's unsurpassed ability to solve difficult, high-profile cases quickly and effectively. On the other hand, the FBI's handling of the Atlanta Olympic bombing investigation and its performance during the 1995 O. J. Simpson trial, which led to a highly critical Justice Department report on the FBI Laboratory in 1997, tarnished the Bureau's reputation for leadership in scientific criminology.

During the 1980s and the early 1990s, the Bureau won unprecedented victories over organized crime. The FBI's extensive use of legal wiretaps and its innovative use of the Racketeer Influenced and Corrupt Organization (RICO) Act put dozens of "wiseguys" behind bars. Joe Pistone's autobiography, *Donnie Brasco* (1987), and the 1997 movie that told the story of his six years in the Mafia, once again confirmed the resourcefulness and bravery of FBI agents. With the conviction of Gambino crime family boss John

Gotti, the "Teflon Don," the Bureau had put nearly every ranking leader of the Mafia behind bars. "The Teflon Don is covered with Velcro," James Fox, head of the Bureau's New York City office, commented after Gotti's conviction, "and every charge stuck." True crime stories about FBI investigations—Howard Blum's 1993 *Gangland: How the FBI Broke the Mob;* Nicholas Pileggi's 1995 *Casino* (the Bureau's successful investigation of the Las Vegas, Chicago, and Kansas City mafias); Agent Jules Bonavolonta's 1996 *The Good Guys, How We Turned the FBI 'Round and Finally Broke the Mob;* and Peter Maas's 1997 *Underboss*, (the story of Sammy Gravano, whose testimony put John Gotti away)—detailed Bureau successes against an enemy that had for so long eluded its grasp.

On the other hand, some of the Bureau's most highly publicized cases in the 1990s were fiascoes. On August 22, 1992, an FBI sharpshooter shot and killed the wife of white separatist Randy Weaver at Weaver's house in Ruby Ridge, Idaho, after a federal marshal had been killed trying to arrest Weaver for selling sawed-off shotguns to Alcohol, Tobacco and Firearms (ATF) agents. On April 19, 1993, the FBI's elite Hostage Rescue Team stormed the Waco, Texas, compound of Branch Davidian religious cult leader David Koresh, after an ATF assault several months earlier had left 4 ATF agents dead and 16 others wounded. At least 75 Davidians, including Koresh, perished in the blaze that followed the assault.

Randy Weaver was acquitted on most charges stemming from the Ruby Ridge case, and the trial judge severely criticized the Bureau's conduct. The Bureau's own internal investigation finally led to charges in 1995 (later dismissed) against the Bureau's second-highest-ranking official, Larry Potts, and the FBI sharpshooter was indicted on an Idaho state manslaughter charge in 1997. Congressional investigations of the Ruby Ridge and Waco disasters forced FBI Director Louis Freeh to admit serious misjudgment on the part of the Bureau, and he curtailed the activities of the Hostage Rescue Team, by then a fixture of far-right paranoia. (Freeh's admissions were made easier because William Sessions, Freeh's predecessor, had been director during both Ruby Ridge and Waco.)

Since Hoover's death in 1972, FBI officials had tried to rebuild the Bureau's reputation for political nonpartisanship, and under FBI Directors Kelley and Webster, the Bureau had largely regained the trust of Congress and the public. But during the Clinton administration, FBI Director Freeh and the Bureau were attacked for getting too close to the White

House when it was revealed that the Bureau had provided the Clinton administration with files on former members of the Bush and Reagan White Houses (Filesgate) and that it had been overly solicitous of the White House's interests during the investigations of Whitewater and of the death of White House aide Vincent Foster. The Bureau's image took a further beating when the FBI agent assigned to the White House, Gary Aldrich, penned a scurrilous attack on the Clinton administration (*Unlimited Access, An FBI Agent Inside the White House,* 1996). A further uproar occurred when the FBI's chief counsel sent advance galleys of Aldrich's book to the White House, and when the agent-author subsequently had to admit that his most sensational charges against the president's character were mere conjecture.

The FBI still arrests foreign spies, although, with the end of the Cold War, these exploits no longer command attention, particularly since some of the spies are in the employ of the nation's allies and their motives are usually more pecuniary than ideological. And, ironically, the most highly publicized recent spy case involved one of the FBI's own, Special Agent Earl Pitts, who admitted on February 28, 1997, to having sold FBI counterintelligence files to the Russians.

In the 1990s, so many different and contradictory images of the Bureau are in circulation that every new FBI story confirms one or another FBI stereotype. FBI officials find it difficult to present a coherent, unified message to the public. This problem can only frustrate current FBI Director Louis Freeh as he moves the Bureau toward an unprecedented position as leader of international law enforcement, with new liaisons and facilities all over the globe. On the other hand, in postmodern America, public figures no longer are able to communicate with the clarity Americans once expected from their leaders.

Throughout the 1990s, Americans could tune to the Fox Network each week and watch FBI special agents do what the FBI had been doing for more than half a century in popular entertainment: protect the country against public enemies. But now, the FBI agents of "The X-Files" had to protect the public from enemies that Jimmy Cagney or Jimmy Stewart could not have dreamed of in their worst nightmares: mutants, freaks, aliens with fantastic paranormal and extraterrestrial powers, and, worst of all, criminals in the highest offices of the Bureau itself.

Battling conspiracies from within the Bureau as well as from without, Special Agents Mulder and Scully call on unconventional auxiliaries like computer hackers, sort of New Age Junior G-men. Popular culture in the 1990s is worlds removed from the 1930s when Tom Sawyerish agent heroes answered the call of public, Congress, and the White House to follow FBI Director Hoover into battle against John Dillinger, "Pretty Boy" Floyd, and "Baby Face" Nelson. The 1930s FBI represented the national government supported by the public and the media, battling to preserve the country's solidarity and honor against the forces of anarchy and lawlessness. In the 1990s, the forces of anarchy and lawlessness are as likely to come from within the government as from without, and the agents themselves share the public's cynicism about official reality and its suspicions of government cover-ups to hide the truths that are "out there."

And yet, there are constants in FBI entertainment and its popular culture image. From the 1930s to the present, the FBI has remained the preeminent symbol of national law enforcement, and as such reflects public attitudes toward the law, crime, and the government. The Bureau continues to employ America's persistent strategies—science and power—for dealing with all its problems. FBI agents have always been, and remain, the preeminent examples of scientifically trained, professional crime fighters. Producers of popular entertainment therefore cannot ignore the pop culture convention that makes the Bureau synonymous with scientific crime fighting.

For better or worse, the Bureau also represents the American predilection for calling upon overwhelming force to eliminate anything that stands between the national will and its objectives. From the Dillinger ambush to the shoot-outs at Ruby Ridge and Waco, the country expects the FBI to bring whatever force is necessary to enforce the law and capture criminals—even if it often criticizes the results.

Paradoxically, the country is more deeply ambiguous about both science and power than ever, just as it always has been uneasy about authority, law, and government. This paradox makes the FBI's image in American popular culture an unmatched gauge for taking the measure of America's attitude toward its government—and toward itself. The FBI's popular image is a mirror in which Americans have long been able to see reflected an image of themselves. That still is true, and it will remain true for years to come.

BIOGRAPHIES

Susan Rosenfeld

Sources

Much of the information in this chapter is derived from FBI personnel files. However, many details about past Bureau personnel are unavailable. Personnel files of non-executive agents, as well as all the files of applicants who were not accepted, were destroyed during the 1980s under a National Archives–approved program. The National Archives also approved the periodic destruction of computerized personnel files. Many of the files that survived, moreover, had been purged periodically. For example, we know that throughout FBI Director Hoover's tenure, agent personnel included African Americans, Hispanics, Jews, Catholics, Asian Americans, and Native Americans. Thus, we cannot always know whether the "firsts" whose biographies are included in this chapter deserve those designations. We do know, however, that blacks, Hispanics, and Jews conducted investigations and received the same evaluations as their Caucasian and Christian counterparts for most if not all of Hoover's tenure as FBI director.

Other major sources of biographical information include autobiographies, biographies, and monographs about the FBI; FBI press releases and official biographies from the Research/Communications Unit, FBI Headquarters, Washington, D.C.; *The Investigator*, the FBI's in-house magazine; *The Grapevine*, the magazine of the Society of Former special agents; and *Society of Former Special Agents of the FBI*, Turner Publishing Company, 1996. Whenever an individual has written an autobiography or other book about the FBI, that information is included in the biographical sketch. The staff of the FBI's Research/Communication Unit was of inestimable help in providing written material and photographs for this chapter.

Criteria

This chapter contains biographies for individuals whose fame rests on their service or association with the Bureau. Individuals in three main categories are included:

- Top-level executives of the FBI: directors, acting directors, associate directors, deputy directors, executive assistant directors, associate deputy directors, and assistants to the director. See also Tables 9.1 and 9.2.
- Employees associated with FBI "firsts." See also Table 9.3.
- Other notable FBI personnel. See also Table 7.1 on page 256.

TABLE 9.1

LEADERS OF THE FBI AND PREDECESSOR AGENCIES

Leader	Title	Date
Stanley W. Finch	Chief	July 26, 1908
A. Bruce Bielaski	Chief	April 30, 1912
William E. Allen	Acting Chief	February 10, 1919
William J. Flynn	Chief	July 1, 1919
William J. Burns	Director	August 22, 1921
J. Edgar Hoover	Acting Director	May 10, 1924
J. Edgar Hoover	Director	December 10, 1924
Clyde Tolson	Acting Director	May 2, 1972
L. Patrick Gray III	Acting Director	May 3, 1972
William D. Ruckelshaus	Acting Director	April 27, 1973
Clarence M. Kelley	Director	July 9, 1973
William H. Webster	Director	February 23, 1978
John Otto	Acting Director	May 26, 1987
William S. Sessions	Director	November 2, 1987
Floyd Clarke	Acting Director	July 19, 1993
Louis J. Freeh	Director	September 1, 1993

TABLE 9.2

Attorneys General of the United States, 1908–98

Name	Beginning of Service	End of Service
Charles J. Bonaparte	December 17, 1906	March 4, 1909
George W. Wickersham	March 5, 1909	March 5, 1913
James C. McReynolds	March 5, 1913	August 29, 1914
Thomas Watt Gregory	August 20, 1914	March 4, 1919
A. Mitchell Palmer	March 5, 1919	March 5, 1921
Harry M. Daugherty	March 4, 1921	March 28, 1924
Harlan Fiske Stone	April 7, 1924	March 2, 1925
John T. Sargent	March 17, 1925	March 5, 1929
William D. Mitchell	March 5, 1929	March 3, 1933
Homer S. Cummings	March 4, 1933	January 2, 1939
Frank Murphy	January 2, 1939	January 18, 1940
Robert H. Jackson	January 18, 1940	July 10, 1941
Francis Biddle	September 5, 1941	June 30, 1945
Tom C. Clark	July 1, 1945	August 24, 1949
J. Howard McGrath	August 24, 1949	April 7, 1952
James P. McGranery	May 27, 1952	January 20, 1953
Herbert Brownell Jr.	January 21, 1953	November 8, 1957
William P. Rogers	November 8, 1957	January 20, 1961
Robert F. Kennedy	January 21, 1961	September 3, 1964
Nicholas deB. Katzenbach (Acting)	September 4, 1964	February 11, 1965
Nicholas deB. Katzenbach	February 11, 1965	October 2, 1966
Ramsey Clark (Acting)	October 3, 1966	March 2, 1967
Ramsey Clark	March 2, 1967	January 20, 1969
John N. Mitchell	January 21, 1969	March 1, 1972
Richard G. Kleindienst (Acting)	March 2, 1972	June 12, 1972
Richard G. Kleindienst	June 12, 1972	May 24, 1973
Elliot L. Richardson	May 25, 1973	October 20, 1973
William B. Saxbe	January 4, 1974	February 3, 1975
Edward H. Levi	February 5, 1975	January 20, 1977
Griffin Bell	January 26, 1977	August 16, 1979
Benjamin Civiletti	August 16, 1979	January 19, 1981
William French Smith	January 23, 1981	February 1985
Edwin Meese III	March 25, 1985	August 12, 1988
Richard Thornburgh	August 12, 1988	August 15, 1991
William Barr	November 20, 1991	January 15, 1993
Janet Reno	March 12, 1993	

TABLE 9.3

FBI "Firsts"

Name	Description
Ahrens, Robin	First female special agent killed while on duty
Amos, James Edward	One of the first African American special agents
Bachor, Helen	First female assistant legal attaché
Barrow, James W.	One of the first African American agents appointed in the 1960s
Bayse, William A.	First non-agent appointed assistant director
Bryant, Robert M.	First assistant director of the National Security Division
Bucknam, Robert B.	First chief of staff
Burns, William J.	First Bureau executive to use the title "director"
Christensen, G. Norman	First assistant director of the Information Management Division
Clarke, Floyd I.	First deputy director
Clegg, Hugh H.	First head of the FBI National Academy
Coffey, Edmund P.	First assistant director of the Laboratory Division
Dalbey, Dwight	First legal counsel and first assistant director of the Legal Counsel Division
Davidson, Alaska P.	First female special agent
De La Rosa, Julian	First Hispanic special agent in charge
Egan, James S.	One of the first inspectors
Finch, Stanley Wellington	First Bureau head
Gardner, Michelle	One of the first support staffers to be awarded the FBI Shield of Bravery
Garogolo, Michael	One of the first support staffers to be awarded the FBI Shield of Bravery
Glavin, W. R.	First Assistant Director of the Personnel and Budget Division
Glover, John D.	First African American executive assistant director (and earlier, first African American special agent in charge)
Gonzalez, Manuel	First assistant director of the Personnel Division
Houston, Lenore	First female special agent appointed by J. Edgar Hoover
Jones, James Wormley	First African American special agent
Juhasz, R.	One of the first support staffers to be awarded the FBI Shield of Bravery
Jung, Christine M. Karpoch	First female firearms instructor
Kerr, Donald M.	First non-agent to head the FBI Laboratory
Kielman, Joseph	First chief scientist
Lewis, Aubrey C.	One of the first African American special agents appointed in the 1960s
Lopez, Julius M.	First Hispanic special agent in charge
Mathis, Sylvia E.	First African American female special agent
McWeeney, Sean M.	First inspector in charge of the Office of Liaison and International Affairs
Miller, Richard W.	First agent arrested for espionage
Mireles, Edmundo, Jr.	First recipient of the FBI Medal of Valor
Misko, Joanne E. Pierce	One of the first female special agents appointed since the 1920s, and one of the first female supervisors at FBIHQ
Montgomery, Robin L.	First special agent in charge of the Critical Incident Response Group
Moore, Donald W., Jr.	First assistant director of the Criminal Investigative Division
Morris, Carolyn G.	First female deputy assistant director
Mullen, Francis M., Jr.	First executive assistant director for Investigations
Pasenelli, Burdena G.	First female special agent in charge
Perez, James R.	First head of the Office of Equal Employment Opportunity Affairs
Reed, Charles	One of the first support staffers to be awarded the FBI Shield of Bravery
Revell, Oliver B.	First associate deputy director–Investigations
Roley, Susan Lynn	One of the first female special agents appointed since the 1920s
Shanahan, Edwin C.	First special agent to die while on duty
Shapiro, Howard	First non-agent FBI general counsel
Slifco, Julianne	First female legal attaché
Sorola, Manuel	First Hispanic special agent
Tokunaga, Don S.	First Asian American special agent in charge
Tolson, Clyde	First assistant to the director, and first associate director
Wolmer, Karen R.	First blind typist
Woodriffe, Edwin W.	First African American agent killed while on duty

Biographies

Adams, James B. As assistant to the director–associate director for investigations under FBI Director Clarence M. Kelley, Adams testified in 1975 at great length before the U.S. Senate and House committees (the so-called Church and Pike Committees) that were investigating the FBI after alleged civil rights violations by the Bureau were revealed. He received the designation of associate director from FBI Director William H. Webster on April 6, 1978.

Born December 21, 1926, in Corsicana, Texas, Adams was raised in Mexia, Texas. He enlisted in the Army in April 1944. While in the military, he attended the Army Special-ized Training Program at Louisiana State University, the University of Minnesota, and Yale University, where he qualified as a Japanese language interpreter. He served as an interpreter overseas until his discharge in 1946. After receiving his bachelor's degree in 1947 and his law degree in 1949 from Baylor University, Waco, Texas, Adams was appointed assistant county attorney. He was elected a Texas state representative in 1950 resigning, on July 9, 1951, to become a special agent of the FBI.

Adams served in the Seattle, Washington, and San Francisco, California, field offices before returning in 1953 to FBIHQ as a supervisor in the Administration Division and the Training and Inspection Division. He later was appointed a section chief and inspector. Beginning in 1959, he served as assistant special agent in charge of the Minneapolis, Minnesota, field office but soon returned to FBIHQ where he served as personnel officer. In 1972, he was appointed special agent in charge of the San Antonio, Texas, field office. He became assistant director of the Office of Planning and Evaluation in 1974, and then in 1975, assistant to the director–deputy associate director. In that latter position, he had responsibility for all FBI investigative operations. In 1978, Adams was appointed associate director, the second highest position in the Bureau. Among other awards, Adams received the Attorney General's Distinguished Service Award in 1978 and the National Intelligence Distinguished Service Medal in 1979 from the Director of Central Intelligence.

Following his retirement from the FBI in 1979, Adams was appointed executive director of the Texas governor's Criminal Justice Division. Adams became director of the Texas Department of Public Safety and chief of the Texas Rangers in 1980. In addition, he served as chairman of the Governor's Task Force on Traffic Safety and as adviser to the Texas War on Drugs Committee. He retired from state service in 1987.

Ahrens, Robin On October 5, 1985, Robin Ahrens of the Phoenix field office became the first female special agent to be killed in the line of duty. She was wounded October 4 while participating in the arrest of a suspected armored car thief and died the next day. Because of confusion at the time, other agents thought she was an armed associate of the fugitive and shot her. The new building that houses the Phoenix field office, built after the incident, was named for her.

Born on May 6, 1952, in St. Paul, Minnesota, Ahrens graduated from Hudson High School in Hudson, Wisconsin, in 1970. She earned a bachelor of fine arts degree in 1974 from Utah State University. She taught school in Firth, Idaho (near Pocatello), until 1980, when she moved to Virginia. She was awarded a media specialist degree in 1983 from James Madison University in Harrisonburg, Virginia. From 1980 until entering the FBI, she was a media specialist and teacher at the Culpeper County High School in Culpeper, Virginia.

She entered the FBI as an agent on October 14, 1984, but served in a support capacity in the Alexandria, Virginia, office and at the FBI Academy at Quantico, Virginia, while recovering from an injury incurred in training. After com-pleting her training on June 28, 1985, she was assigned to Phoenix as her first field office.

Allen, William E. Attorney General Thomas Watt Gregory appointed William E. Allen acting chief of the Bureau of Investigation on February 10, 1919, following the resigna-tion of A. Bruce Bielaski. Adams held this position until June 30, 1919, when William J. Flynn became head of the Bureau of Investigation.

Amos, James Edward James E. Amos was one of the Bureau's first African American special agents. He served for over 32 years.

Amos was born on January 29, 1879, in Washington, D.C., to Joseph F. and Marie Bruce Amos. After attending high school, he worked as a steam engineer, a telephone repairman, a switchboard operator, a bodyguard for Presi-dent Theodore Roosevelt, and for the William J. Burns International Detective Agency.

On August 24, 1921, during Burns's tenure as director of the Bureau of Investigation, Amos was recruited as a special agent. His salary of six dollars per day and four dollars per diem while away from the office was standard for special agents at that time. Amos participated in a number of investigations, including the infamous Buchalter Gang, the black nationalist Marcus Garvey, and German spy Frederick Joubert Duquesne. He also assisted in the apprehension of the gangster Dutch Schultz. He retired from the FBI on October 15, 1953, and died two months later.

Appel, Charles A. Founder of the FBI's Technical Laboratory and, for many years, the Bureau's unofficial historian, Charles A. Appel is immortalized in a fresco painted on the second floor of the Department of Justice Building, in Washington, D.C.

Born in 1895 in Washington, D.C., Appel trained as an aviator during World War I, graduating as a second lieutenant bombardier in February 1919. He graduated from the George Washington University Law School in 1924, and on October 24, 1924, entered the Bureau of Investigation as an agent. A specialist in document examination, he was authorized to establish the FBI Laboratory in 1932, an institution that Appel had advocated for several years. Appel served as the laboratory's only full-time employee during its first months. During the Lindbergh kidnapping case, he testified before the grand jury regarding the handwriting in the ransom notes. Appel also wrote public and in-house brief histories of the FBI for many years. He retired December 31, 1948. His son, Edward J. Appel, also became an FBI agent.

Bachor, Helen The Bureau's first female assistant legal attaché, Helen Bachor, served in Montevideo, Uruguay, where she died in a car accident. See also *Julianne Slifco*.

Barrow, James W. James W. Barrow, an FBI support employee, was one of two African Americans appointed special agents in 1962, in response to Attorney General Robert F. Kennedy's request that the Bureau hire more qualified minorities as agents (see also *Aubrey C. Lewis*). His appointment marked the beginning of a new era in the Bureau's hiring of African Americans.

Born in New York to George and Ella Barrow, he attended parochial schools in that city and graduated from St. Francis College in Brooklyn, New York, with a degree in psychology. He entered the FBI as a mimeograph operator on July 1, 1959, working in the New York City office while earning his college degree. He was accepted as a special agent while attending law school.

Barrow was appointed a special agent on June 25, 1962, and was assigned to the St. Louis field office, where he worked from October 1962 to June 1963, when he was

assigned to the Bureau Language School to study Spanish. After completing the language course, he was transferred to the Miami field office, where he remained until assigned to the Newark field office in February 1967, to the Detroit field office in September 1970, and in 1972 to the Tampa field office. In 1989, he was one of three Equal Employment Opportunity Counselors in that office.

Baughman, Thomas Franklin (Frank) Frank Baughman entered the General Intelligence Division of the Department of Justice at age 22, on October 22, 1919. He worked in that division with J. Edgar Hoover, whom he had known in law school, and they would continue to work closely for the next decade. While in the General Intelligence Division, Baughman assisted Hoover in overseeing the so-called Palmer Raids during the Red Scare of 1919 and 1920.

Prior to joining the Department of Justice, Baughman received a bachelor of law degree in 1922 and a master of law degree the following year, both from George Washington University. He enlisted in the Army in 1917 and was discharged after the war (having attained the rank of captain) to accept an appointment in the General Intelligence Division in October 1919.

Baughman continued for a time to have a close personal relationship with Hoover during Hoover's early years in the Bureau of Investigation. After Hoover became director, he appointed Baughman a supervisor. Baughman's responsibilities directing the headquarters staff rated him the number-three position, behind Assistant Director Harold Nathan. In 1928, Baughman was promoted to the number-two position in the Bureau. Within a year, however, Nathan regained that spot. When Clyde Tolson became assistant director, Baughman was assigned to be his assistant. This short-lived arrangement ended with Baughman's appointment in the mid-1930s as firearms instructor at the FBI Academy in Quantico, Virginia, where he remained until his retirement in 1949. Baughman died in Florida on September 8, 1971.

Baum, W. Carter Only 29 years old when felled by gangster Lester Gillis ("Baby Face" Nelson) on April 22, 1934, W. Carter Baum was born on July 2, 1904, in Washington, D.C. He entered the Bureau of Investigation on June 30, 1930, and served in the New York and Chicago field offices. As a participant in the hunt for the notorious John Dillinger, Baum and several other agents attempted to ambush Dillinger and his gang at their hideaway at the Little

Bohemia resort in Wisconsin. Instead, the agents were discovered, and as Dillinger and others escaped, Gillis killed Baum.

Baum's wife Mary joined the Bureau as a clerk, April 1, 1935, resigning January 13, 1944. One of Baum's daughters, Edith Carter Baum, worked for the Bureau during the summers of 1949 through 1957.

Bayse, William A. (Al)   Named chief scientist of the FBI in October 1993, William A. Bayse was the first non-agent in modern times to hold the position of assistant director. FBI Director William H. Webster hired him in March 1978 as deputy assistant director, Technical Services Division, specifically to oversee the Bureau's growing automation and telecommunications needs.

Bayse received his bachelor of science degree in physics from Roanoke College in 1958 and continued his graduate studies in engineering and mathematics at the University of Virginia. In 1973, American University awarded him a master of science degree in technology of management (computer systems). He also received a diploma in national security resources management from the Industrial College of the Armed Forces and the professional certificate in data processing, and completed the Program for Senior Managers in Government at the John F. Kennedy School of Government at Harvard University.

Before entering the FBI, Bayse served as an aeronautical research engineer with the National Aeronautics and Space Administration and as a mathematician with the Department of the Army. While employed by the Army, he held several positions, including technical director, command deputy, and civilian assistant to the commander. He served as the Army's deputy chief of staff for logistics, Data Processing Center; and director of methodology, resources, and communication for the United States Army Concepts Analysis Agency, where he received the departmental Decoration for Meritorious Civilian Service. In 1983, he was assigned to the office of the Secretary of Defense for a special research and development assignment.

Bayse's FBI career consisted of directing the Technical Services Division. Under his supervision, the FBI developed knowledge-based expert systems (artificial intelligence) to enhance the Bureau's administrative, investigative, and law enforcement capabilities. Bayse also represented the FBI on the National Security Telecommunications and Information Systems Security Committee where he chaired the Subcommittee on Telecommunications Security. In addition, he chaired the Automatic Data Processing Working Group of the Science and Technology Committee, Office of National Drug Control Policy. Bayse retired from the FBI in 1994.

Belmont, Alan H.   Alan H. Belmont served as assistant to the director in charge of investigations, the number-three position in the FBI, from 1961 until his retirement on December 30, 1965.

Born January 22, 1907, in New York City, Belmont attended high school in San Diego, California. After three years at San Diego State University, he transferred to Stanford University, receiving a bachelor's degree in accounting in 1931. For the next five years, he worked as an accountant in California.

After joining the FBI on November 30, 1936, Belmont served in the Birmingham, Alabama (March to June 1937), and Chicago, Illinois (June 1937 to June 1938), field offices before becoming a supervisor, first at FBIHQ (June 1938 to January 1941) and then in New York City (January 1941 to August 1942). From August 1942 into 1943, he held the position of assistant special agent in charge in Chicago. Appointed special agent in charge of the Cincinnati, Ohio, field office in February, he was transferred to New York City as assistant special agent in charge. Belmont became assistant director of the Domestic Intelligence Division at FBIHQ in February 1950. He was appointed assistant to the director in 1961.

After his retirement in 1965, Belmont became executive assistant to the director of the Hoover Institution of War, Revolution, and Peace at Stanford University. He died in Mountain View, California, on July 30, 1977.

Bielaski, Alexander Bruce   Attorney General George W. Wickersham appointed A. Bruce Bielaski on April 30, 1912, to succeed Stanley W. Finch as chief (director) of the Bureau

of Investigation. Prior to his appointment, Bielaski had served as Finch's assistant and handled many of the day-to-day matters regarding the special agents. He resigned on February 10, 1919, amid controversies regarding his handling of the Bureau's wartime investigations, notably the "slacker" raids.

Exhibit 9.1   **A. Bruce Bielaski,**
Courtesy of the FBI

Binney, David G.   FBI Director Louis Freeh appointed David G. Binney deputy director of the FBI in February 1994. Prior to this appointment, Binney served as assistant director of the Inspection Division (May 1992) and deputy assistant director of the Office of Professional Responsibility (March 1991). Binney's FBI career also included service as special agent in charge of the St. Louis field office (August 1989), chief of the Drug Section at FBIHQ (June 1988), and assistant special agent in charge of the Washington, D.C., field office in March 1985.

Born November 3, 1940, in Rochester, New Hampshire, Binney was raised in Wrentham, Massachusetts. In 1964, he received a bachelor of science degree in engineering from the U.S. Military Academy in West Point, New York. He served in the Army from June 1964 until December 1969, attaining the rank of captain. His service included a tour of duty in Vietnam.

Binney entered the FBI in 1970 and served in the Milwaukee, Wisconsin, and Indianapolis, Indiana, field offices. Binney received a doctor of jurisprudence degree from the University of Indiana Law School in 1976. Transferred to FBIHQ in February 1977, he returned to the field in October 1979, where he served in the New York City field office as a supervisor in the organized crime program until his appointment to the Washington, D.C., field office.

Binney retired from the FBI in December 1994 to become chief of security for the IBM Corporation in Armonk, NY.

Bonaparte, Charles J.   Attorney general from 1906 to 1909, Charles J. Bonaparte appointed the force of special agents that became the Bureau of Investigation, predecessor of the FBI (see Exhibit 1.1). President Theodore Roosevelt had earlier named Bonaparte, a fellow progressive Republican, to the Board of Indian Commissioners (1902) and Secretary of the Navy (1905). Bonaparte also served as an assistant to Attorney General Philander C. Knox, a position that enabled him to "pursue bad men in public office." As a progressive, Bonaparte believed that efficiency and expertise should guide government policies and appointments.

Early twentieth-century progressives endorsed the need for federal intervention to solve the growing social problems of the day, including crime. Through 1908, the Department of Justice had no investigative force of its own—it borrowed agents, usually from the Secret Service, to handle the few federal crimes then under its jurisdiction. In May 1908, however, Congress refused to appropriate money to enable the Department of Justice to continue to pay the salaries of

Secret Service agents temporarily assigned to conduct investigations at the request of the department. In response, Bonaparte used his powers as attorney general to appoint special agents of his own, including 10 former Secret Service agents who, with the Department of Justice's own special agents, reported to the chief examiner. Although the special force did not receive a formal title until 1909, under Attorney General George Wickersham, Bonaparte is credited with founding the investigative agency that became the FBI.

Born in Baltimore, Maryland, June 9, 1851, and a nephew of French emperor Louis Napoleon Bonaparte III, Bonaparte graduated from Harvard College in 1871 and Harvard Law School in 1874. He was a member of Harvard's Board of Overseers and an organizer and president of the National Municipal League. As chairman of the Council of the National Civil Service Reform League, Bonaparte first became acquainted with Theodore Roosevelt at the time the future president was Civil Service Commissioner. On June 28, 1921, Bonaparte died at his estate, Bella Vista, near Baltimore.

Boynton, Homer A., Jr.   FBI Director William H. Webster appointed Homer A. Boynton Jr. executive assistant director for Administration in August 1979, a position he held until his retirement on May 30, 1980.

A native of Hartford, Connecticut, Boynton served in the U.S. Navy before receiving a bachelor of arts degree from the University of Connecticut. He subsequently attended graduate school at the University of Southern California.

Boynton entered the FBI on June 30, 1952, and was assigned to the Philadelphia, Pennsylvania, field office from October 1952 to February 1955, when he was transferred to the New York field office. For the next 17 years, he handled foreign counterintelligence cases. During this New York assignment, he also served as chief administrative officer for three years. In November 1972, Boynton transferred to FBIHQ to head the FBI's foreign operations and liaison with the White House, the Central Intelligence Agency (CIA), and other government agencies. Transferred to the Public Affairs Office in April 1975, Boynton was named inspector in charge of that office. He was promoted to executive assistant director from this position.

Bryant, Robert M.   Director Louis J. Freeh appointed Robert M. Bryant deputy director of the FBI on October 2, 1997. Born in Springfield, Missouri, on June 30, 1943, Bryant was nicknamed "Bear" as a youth for his tenacity fighting a local bully. He received a bachelor of science degree in business administration in 1965 and a law degree in 1968, both from the University of Arkansas.

After entering the FBI in October 1968, Bryant was assigned to the Seattle and Dallas field offices before transferring to FBIHQ in March 1975, where he served as a supervisor in the Criminal Investigative and Records Management Divisions until his assignment to the Inspection staff in September 1977. Upon completion of his inspection work in June 1978, Bryant became a supervisor at the Las Vegas field office.

In August 1980, Bryant was appointed assistant special agent in charge of the Kansas City field office. In March 1985, he became a permanent inspector and shortly thereafter was designated acting chief inspector. In December 1985, Bryant was promoted to special agent in charge of the Salt Lake City field office.

Bryant returned to FBIHQ as deputy assistant director of the Criminal Division in September 1989, serving in that position until July 1991 when he was appointed special agent in charge of the Washington, D.C., field office. While in that position, he headed the cooperative CIA-FBI investigation of spy Aldrich Ames. On October 3, 1993, Bryant again returned to FBIHQ, this time as assistant director of the National Security Division. Freeh appointed him assistant director of the Criminal Investigative Division on March 3, 1997, where he remained until his promotion to deputy director.

Bucknam, Robert B.   FBI Director Louis J. Freeh appointed Robert B. Bucknam as chief of staff. Aged 42 at the time, Buckman was the first person to hold this position in the FBI. He and Freeh became acquainted when Bucknam served as a member of the trial team headed by Freeh during the prosecution of the Pizza Connection case; Bucknam was then an assistant U.S. attorney in the southern district of New York. Bucknam subsequently served as deputy chief of the Criminal Division in the U.S. Attorney's Office, and from 1991 until 1993, was deputy assistant attorney general in the Justice Department's Criminal Division. Just prior to his FBI appointment, Bucknam was the managing director in charge of the Washington, D.C., office of Decision Strategies, an international investigative consulting firm.

Burke, Frank   Appointed the assistant to Bureau of Investigation Chief William Flynn (1919–21), Frank Burke served during the "Red Scare" years following World War I, a time of great political, economic, and social unrest within the United States. Under Burke's supervision, the Bureau of Investigation investigated suspected anarchists, communists, and other radicals.

Burns, William J.   Attorney General Harry M. Daugherty appointed William J. Burns on August 22, 1921, to head the Bureau of Investigation. Burns was the first Bureau executive to use the title of director. Prior to assuming his Bureau of Investigation position, Burns had founded and headed his own private detective agency.

Burns's tenure as Bureau of Investigation director was marred by internal scandal, notably, the Teapot Dome incident that brought down Attorney General Daugherty. As Bureau of Investigation director, Burns instituted training for special agents. Because he spent much of his time in New York, his assistant director, J. Edgar Hoover, handled the day-to-day supervisory activities in Washington, D.C.

Following his dismissal on May 10, 1924, by Attorney General Harlan Fiske Stone, Burns was indicted for "shadowing" jurors, causing a mistrial in the Teapot Dome case that involved Secretary of the Interior Albert Fall. The Court, however, set aside Burns's jail term.

At his death on April 14, 1932, the *Washington Post* called him, "probably the most famous individual in the detective business during his active years."

Caffrey, Raymond J.   Raymond J. Caffrey of the Oklahoma City field office died June 17, 1933, in the Kansas City Massacre. Born May 15, 1903, in McCook, Nebraska, Caffrey was killed while escorting gangster Frank Nash from McAlester, Oklahoma, to the Leavenworth Penitentiary in Kansas. At the Kansas City railroad station, Adam Richetti, Vernon Miller, and Charles "Pretty Boy" Floyd opened fire, killing Nash, Caffrey, two policemen, and the McAlester police chief. The Kansas City Massacre led Congress, in 1934, to enact legislation authorizing agents to carry guns and make arrests.

Callahan, Nicholas P.   Nicholas P. Callahan served as associate director of the FBI from 1973 until 1976, under FBI Director Clarence M. Kelley.

Callahan spent four years as a clerk in the Identification Division, from 1936 until 1939, at which time he was appointed a special agent. After serving in the Dallas, Newark, Baltimore, and Philadelphia field offices, Callahan returned to FBIHQ in 1946 as deputy assistant director (then called "number one man") in the Administrative Division. Two years later, he became an inspector. In 1959, he was promoted to assistant director of the Administrative Division. He remained in that position until his 1973 promotion to associate director. He left the FBI in 1976, having been pressured by FBI Director Clarence M. Kelley to resign for unspecified "abuses of power," probably relating to the cover-up of financial mismanagement that occurred within Callahan's chain of command. Callahan died on November 12, 1997.

Christensen, G. Norman   G. Norman Christensen, whose master of business administration degree emphasized management and information technology, supervised the establishment of the FBI's field office automation system and other technological developments. FBI Director William S. Sessions named Christensen the first assistant director of the Information Management Division.

Christensen was born August 29, 1939, in Salt Lake City, Utah, where he received his early education. In 1965, he graduated from the University of Utah with a bachelor of science degree in civil engineering. He later received his master of business administration degree from George Washington University, Washington, D.C.

Christensen entered the FBI as an agent in July 1965, serving first in the Oklahoma City and then in the Los Angeles field office. In May 1970, he was appointed a supervisor in the Administrative Services Division in FBIHQ. In this position, he oversaw employee computer training and the development of some of the Bureau's internal information systems. When FBI Director Clarence M. Kelley created the Office of Planning and Evaluation in November 1973, Christensen transferred to that unit to assist in long-range planning related to technical developments.

After a stint in the Inspection Division beginning in April 1977, Christensen transferred to the Technical Services Division in FBIHQ, where he was responsible for certain aspects of telecommunications operations. Appointed assistant special agent in charge of the St. Louis field office in January 1979, he was promoted to inspector in place in 1980. He returned to the Technical Services Division in April of the following year as section chief of the Office of Information Systems, Research and Development.

In January 1985, Christensen was promoted to inspector–deputy assistant director (deputy assistant director), Records Management Division. His responsibilities included managing the transition from manual to automated procedures in the records management area. In January 1990, he was promoted to assistant director of the Records Management Division and he became assistant director for the Information Management Division following reorganization of that division.

Clarke, Floyd I.   To replace FBI Director William S. Sessions, whom he fired on July 19, 1993, President Bill Clinton appointed Deputy Director Floyd I. Clarke as acting director of the FBI. During FBI Director Sessions's July 18, 1989, reorganization of the Bureau's top executives, Clarke was promoted to the FBI's first deputy director. With Louis J. Freeh's appointment as FBI director, Clarke returned to the deputy position, and retained it when FBI Director Freeh reorganized his top staff in October 1993. Clarke retired from that position in February 1994.

Clarke was born in Phoenix, Arizona, and raised in Scottsdale, Arizona. He attended George Washington University, Washington, D.C., and joined the FBI as a support employee in 1964. After becoming a special agent, he served in the Birmingham, Boston, Philadelphia, and

Exhibit 9.2   **Floyd I. Clarke,** *Courtesy of the FBI*

Kansas City field offices, where he specialized in violent crime and organized crime matters. In 1977, he was appointed assistant special agent in charge of the Philadelphia field office, serving in that position until his promotion, in 1979, to inspector. Clarke became special agent in charge of the Kansas City field office in 1980.

His assignments at FBIHQ included service in the Identification, Administrative, Inspection, and Criminal Investigative Divisions, as well as work for Attorney General Edward Levi. Dating from 1982 he served as assistant director of the Criminal Investigative Division. During his tenure in that position, the FBI developed its first artificial intelligence capability for criminal investigations, a program named "Big Floyd," after Clarke. This program attempted to replicate the patterns of thought of criminals and helped experienced agents sift through facts and evidence to develop new leads or draw conclusions. In 1989, Clarke was promoted to executive assistant director for Administration, a title he held until the reorganization in which he was elevated to the FBI's second-highest position. From that post, he became acting director of the FBI until September 1, 1993, when Louis J. Freeh became FBI director.

President George Bush named Clarke a Distinguished Executive (1989) and a Meritorious Executive (1990). He also received the Attorney General's Award for Exceptional

Leadership (October 1991), the Attorney General's Distinguished Service Award (January 1992), and the Attorney General's Edmund J. Randolph Award in January 1993.

After his retirement from the Bureau, Clarke became vice president for corporate compliance at MacAndres and Forbes Holdings, Inc. of New York City.

Clegg, Hugh H.   As first head of the FBI National Academy (founded in July 1935 as the FBI National Police Academy) and assistant director of the Training and Inspection Division, Hugh Clegg was influential in professionalizing law enforcement through the FBI's National Police Academy training course for local and state police officers, as well as its training of new FBI agents and its in-service classes for experienced FBI agents.

Born on July 17, 1898, in Mathiston, Mississippi, Clegg was raised in Anguilla, Mississippi. He graduated in 1920 with a bachelor of arts degree from Millsaps College in Jackson, Mississippi, and attended George Washington University Law School. During 1922 and 1923, he taught at the Bennett Academy and Preparatory School in Mathiston, from which he had graduated.

He entered the FBI as an agent on August 12, 1926, and within a short time served as special agent in charge of the Atlanta; Washington, D.C.; and Chicago field offices. In 1932, FBI Director Hoover promoted Clegg to assistant director. Clegg, at that time, held the rank of inspector, one of the first such appointments. In addition to supervising field inspections, his responsibilities included supervising investigations of violations of federal law. In 1935, he became the first head of the new FBI Academy and, as assistant director of the Training and Inspection Divisions, supervised both the academy and FBI inspections. In 1940 and 1941, he went to England to study wartime intelligence operations, communications, law enforcement, civil defense, and security under the British intelligence service.

Following his retirement in 1954, he served as special assistant to the president of the University of Mississippi from 1956 until 1971. After his second retirement, he returned to Anguilla. Clegg died on December 12, 1979.

Coffey, Edmund P.   When the FBI's Technical Laboratory was elevated to the Laboratory Division in 1943, E. P. Coffey was appointed its first assistant director. Born and raised in Connecticut, he attended college and law school in Washington, D.C.

Colwell, William L. (Lee)   FBI Director William H. Webster appointed Lee Colwell as the second executive assistant director for Investigations.

A native of Arkansas, Colwell received his bachelor of science degree from Little Rock University, Little Rock, Arkansas. He became an FBI agent on August 14, 1961. After serving in FBI field offices and in supervisory positions in FBIHQ, Colwell was promoted to assistant special agent in charge of the Portland, Oregon, field office, serving from November 1972 to May 1974, until his appointment to the Surveys and Investigative Staff of the U.S. House of Representatives Appropriations Committee. In February 1975, he was named senior staff coordinator of the FBI's Office of Planning and Evaluation, and in July 1975, he became special agent in charge of the San Antonio, Texas, field office and in September 1976, inspector–deputy assistant director of the Office of Planning and Evaluation in the Planning and Inspection Division. Becoming acting assistant director of the Planning and Inspection Division in October 1977, Colwell received the full appointment in January, a position he held until he succeeded Francis Mullen as executive assistant director for Investigations.

Colwell retired from the FBI in 1985 and moved to Little Rock, Arkansas, to direct the Criminal Justice Institute at the University of Arkansas, Little Rock.

Connelley, Earl J.   Known as E. J. Connelley, this inspector's 34-year career involved him in many of the FBI's most famous cases. One such case, the Alger Hiss investigation of 1948, led Vice President Richard Nixon to write Connelley's widow (following his death on January 20, 1957) expressing his admiration for Connelley's "splendid work" in that investigation. Connelley had earlier participated on the "flying squad" that apprehended gangsters during the mid-1930s and during World War II he supervised major espionage matters.

Born January 31, 1892, and raised in Columbus, Ohio, Connelley joined the Army as a private after U.S. involvement in World War I in 1917. Assigned

Exhibit 9.3   **Earl J. Connelley,**
*Courtesy of the National Archives
(65-F)*

to the Army Signal Corps, he was discharged as a first lieutenant at the end of the war. He then completed his studies in law and accounting in New York and joined the FBI on January 16, 1920. On May 2, 1927, Connelley was promoted to special agent in charge of the St. Louis field office. Subsequently, he served in that capacity in the Seattle, New York City, Chicago, and Cincinnati field offices. He became an inspector on June 10, 1936. On June 24, 1940, Hoover named him "assistant director of Major Investigations in the Field." He retired in 1954.

Cowley, Samuel P. FBI Director J. Edgar Hoover credited inspector Samuel P. Cowley as the person responsible for ending the crime spree of John Dillinger, at the time considered the nation's most notorious gangster.

Cowley was born in Franklin, Idaho, July 23, 1899, and was educated in Preston, Idaho, and Logan, Utah. A Mormon, Cowley conducted missionary work in the Hawaiian islands from 1916 to 1920. In 1925, he received a bachelor of science degree from the Utah Agricultural School, and three years later, a law degree from George Washington University in Washington, D.C. He was a member of both the Utah and District of Columbia bars.

After entering the FBI on March 11, 1929, he served in the Los Angeles; Detroit; Washington, D.C.; Butte; and Salt Lake City field offices before being assigned to FBIHQ in October 1932, where, in January 1934, he became senior administrative assistant to Harold Nathan, assistant director for Investigations.

In 1934, Cowley was ordered to travel to the Midwest to coordinate the Bureau's investigation and apprehension of notorious outlaw John Dillinger and his gang. On July 1, 1934, just prior to Dillinger's death, Cowley was promoted to inspector, putting him in charge of the Bureau's roving "flying squad" dedicated to rounding up gangsters. In addition to the Dillinger gang, Cowley also supervised the hunt for the kidnappers of St. Paul businessman Edward Bremer and the perpetrators of the Kansas City Massacre. This operation ended in the slaying of Charles Arthur "Pretty Boy" Floyd.

Two agents traveling on a highway near Barrington, Illinois, November 27, 1934, recognized gang members John Paul Chase and Lester Gillis ("Baby Face" Nelson), who had killed Special Agent W. Carter Baum earlier that year. Rushing to the scene, Inspector Cowley and Special Agent Herman E. Hollis left their car to chase the fleeing bandits. The fugitives opened fire, mortally wounding Cowley and Hollis, who continued firing and killed Gillis. Cowley died the next day.

Chicago Special Agent in Charge Melvin Purvis had engineered the Bureau's operation leading to the attempted capture (and death) of Dillinger at Chicago's Biograph Theatre. Purvis, however, soon lost favor with Hoover. Cowley, as Hoover's special representative in Chicago, then became the hero in the FBI's official version of the frequently recounted Dillinger story. Thereafter, Hoover insisted that Cowley "mapped the campaign, working from a secret office with unlisted telephones, and it was this campaign which led to Dillinger's death."

Cowley's wife became a clerical employee of the FBI on September 1, 1936, and except for 13 months in 1945 and 1946, she remained with the Bureau until her resignation on July 30, 1948.

Dalbey, Dwight In 1971, FBI Director J. Edgar Hoover named Dwight Dalbey as the Bureau's first legal counsel. Dalbey subsequently was promoted to the first assistant director of the Legal Counsel Division, when the legal counsel's office achieved division status in March 1972.

Born in Clarinda, Iowa, Dalbey received a doctor of law degree in 1940 from DePaul University, Chicago. He entered the FBI as an agent in December of that year. During World War II, he worked undercover in Chile for the Bureau's wartime foreign counterintelligence unit, the Special Intelligence Service (SIS), and helped break two German espionage rings. After the end of the war and the dissolution of SIS, Dalbey served in FBI field offices in Baltimore; St. Paul; Houston; San Juan; Puerto Rico; and Springfield, Illinois.

In 1951, Dalbey was transferred to FBIHQ where, in 1953, he worked in the Research Unit of the Crime Records Section, Records and Communications Division. Dalbey became head of legal research in 1955, and 10 years later received the title inspector.

After retiring in 1973, Dalbey moved to Des Moines, Iowa, in 1976. He died on June 27, 1984.

Davidson, Alaska P. Appointed a special agent by Bureau of Investigation Director William Burns on October 11, 1922, Alaska P. Davidson was the Bureau's first woman agent. She was 54 years old at the time of her appointment. Her starting salary was seven dollars per day, plus four dollars subsistence when traveling. After training in New York, she was assigned to the Washington, D.C., field office. With only three years of public school education, and considered "very refined," she was of limited use to the Bureau, which was interested in women agents primarily for investigations related to the Mann Act. Having pledged upon

Exhibit 9.4   **Alaska P. Davidson,**
Courtesy of the FBI

his appointment on May 10, 1924, as acting director of the Bureau of Investigation to remove all unqualified agents, J. Edgar Hoover demanded that each field office evaluate its personnel. In response, the special agent in charge of the Washington field office stated that his office had "no particular work for a woman agent." Davidson resigned at Hoover's request on June 10, 1924.

De La Rosa, Julian   Designated special agent in charge of the St. Louis field office in March 1988, Julian De La Rosa was the first Hispanic agent to hold that rank since 1960 (see *Julius M. Lopez*).

Born September 12, 1939, and raised in San Antonio, Texas, De La Rosa joined the FBI in a support capacity in 1959 while attending St. Mary's University, San Antonio. After receiving his bachelor of arts degree in 1963, in June of that year he became a special agent. He served in the Minneapolis; Cincinnati; Washington, D.C.; and San Diego field offices. In January 1972, he was appointed a supervisor in the Criminal Investigative Division in FBIHQ. Following an assignment in the Administrative Services Division from May 1973 to February 1977, he transferred to the inspection staff in the Planning and Inspection Division, returning to the Administrative Services Division at the end of the year.

In February 1979, De La Rosa was promoted to assistant special agent in charge of the San Antonio field office, one of the first Hispanic FBI agents to attain that rank. In February 1986, he was promoted to inspector in place. He returned to FBIHQ in November 1986 as chief of the Civil Rights and Special Inquiry Section of the Criminal Investigative Division, where he remained until his appointment as special agent in charge of the St. Louis field office.

DeLoach, Cartha Dekle (Deke)   On December 31, 1965, FBI Director Hoover appointed Cartha D. DeLoach deputy associate director, the number-three position in the FBI. Previously, DeLoach had been assistant director of the Crime Records Division. In addition, he handled liaison with Vice President Lyndon Johnson, a position he continued when Johnson became president. Their relationship was so close that the president had a White House telephone installed in DeLoach's bedroom.

DeLoach was born on July 20, 1920, and was raised in Claxton, Georgia. He graduated from Stetson College with a bachelor of arts degree and attended Stetson Law School, although he never finished his law degree. On August 31, 1942, DeLoach was appointed a clerk in the FBI's Identification Division.

Later that year, on December 14, DeLoach was appointed a special agent and was assigned to the Norfolk, Virginia, field office, serving until August 1943, when he was transferred to the Cleveland, Ohio, field office. After FBI agents lost their draft deferments in 1943, DeLoach left the Bureau to join the Navy in November 1944. He spent his naval service involved in the athletic program at the U.S. Naval Air Station in Norman, Oklahoma. Returning to the FBI after the war, he served in the Akron, Ohio, resident agency, as the sole agent, until being promoted to an agent supervisor in the Security Division (later the Domestic Intelligence Division) at FBIHQ, where he supervised the Atomic Energy Applicant Section. In 1951, he was promoted to inspector and worked in the Training and Inspection Division from December 1951 to October 1953, when he was assigned to work for Associate Director Tolson until March 1954. During the mid- to late 1950s, DeLoach served as the number-two man in the Records and Communication Division, taking over as inspector in charge of the Crime Records Division in January 1959. In April 1959, DeLoach received the full title of assistant director and remained in that position until his promotion to assistant to the director for Investigations in 1965. Considered a potential successor to FBI Director Hoover had President Johnson been reelected in 1968, DeLoach retired on July 31, 1970.

Exhibit 9.5   **Cartha Dekle DeLoach,**
Courtesy of the FBI

After retirement from the FBI, DeLoach moved to New York and became vice president for corporate affairs of Pepsico. He retired from Pepsico in 1985. After that retirement, he relocated to Hilton Head Island, South

Carolina, holding the position of chairman of the board of the Lighthouse Mortgage Corporation.

In 1995, he authored a partially autobiographical history titled *Hoover's FBI: The Inside Story by Hoover's Trusted Lieutenant*.

Douglas, John Although not the originator of criminal-personality profiling, John Douglas is closely identified with this technique through his books, through the portrayal of a character loosely based on him in two Thomas Harris novels, and especially through the Academy Award–winning movie based on Harris's *The Silence of the Lambs*.

Born in the mid-1940s in Brooklyn, New York, Douglas attended school in Hempstead, New York, and later at Montana State University in Bozeman. He joined the U.S. Air Force in 1966 and served in Clovis, New Mexico, while attending Eastern New Mexico University in Portales, where he received a bachelor's degree in psychology and took courses toward a master's degree in industrial psychology. Douglas also earned a doctorate in education.

Douglas entered the FBI as an agent on December 14, 1970, and served in the Detroit and Milwaukee field offices. In 1975, he attended a two-week in-service class on hostage negotiation, where Howard Teton and Patrick Mullaney—the true FBI originators of criminal profiling—were his instructors. In 1977, FBI Director Clarence M. Kelley transferred Douglas to the Behavioral Science Unit at Quantico as Mullaney's replacement. With Robert Ressler, he interviewed numerous serial killers, some just prior to their executions, to develop the database from which the profiling technique was produced. Douglas described the techniques and many of the cases that used them in his 1995 book, *Mind Hunter* (written with Mark Olshaker).

In 1990, Douglas became unit chief of the Behavioral Science Investigative Support Unit, renamed the Investigative Support Unit. He retired in June, 1995, but returned to Quantico as an instructor and consultant. While with the FBI, he wrote two books in criminology, *Sexual Homicide: Patterns and Motives*, with Robert K. Ressler and Ann W. Burgess; and *Crime Classification Manual*, with Robert K. Ressler, Ann W. Burgess, and Allen G. Burgess. He is also author (with Mark Olshaker) of *The Unabomber* (1996), *Journey into Darkness* (1997), and *Obsession* (1998).

Dove, Jerry L. Jerry Dove was killed in action with Benjamin P. Grogan in Miami, Florida, on April 11, 1986, when bank robbers opened fire on the agents as they attempted to thwart a robbery. This tragedy, in which the FBI agents faced suspects carrying assault weapons, led to a change in firearms training and to the development of new weapons for FBI agents.

Born January 19, 1956, in Charleston, West Virginia, Dove earned a bachelor of science degree from Marshall University, Huntington, West Virginia, and a J.D. degree from West Virginia University, Morgantown, in 1981. The following year, he entered the FBI as an agent. Dove served in the Pittsburgh and San Diego field offices prior to his (1984) assignment to the Miami office.

Duckstein, Jessie B. Jessie B. Duckstein appears to have been the second woman appointed special agent. William J. Burns, director of the Bureau of Investigation, named her to that position. On August 11, 1921, Attorney General Harry M. Daugherty appointed Duckstein, a high school graduate in her early 40s at the time of her Bureau career, as a temporary stenographer/typist. Serving in the Bureau's Washington, D.C., headquarters, by July 1923, she had become the confidential secretary to Burns with a salary of $2,200.

In November 1923, Duckstein requested an opportunity to become a special agent. Burns changed her title and she was officially appointed an agent on November 20, 1923. Her headquarters experience was considered an asset when she went into the field. As an agent, her salary became seven dollars per day, plus four dollars per diem while traveling. Duckstein was assigned to the Washington, D.C., field office, where she remained until May 1924. The Washington, D.C., field office special agent in charge, E. R. Bohner, advised FBI Acting Director J. Edgar Hoover that he did not need women agents. Hoover requested Duckstein's resignation on May 26, 1924, and she left the Bureau that day.

Edwards, John J. Inspector in charge of the Technical Laboratory and Identification (fingerprints), John J. Edwards was a member of the Bureau's "Big Five" during the mid-1930s, when the FBI played a key role in bringing the so-called gangster era to an end.

Born in the late 1880s, in Coal Creek, Tennessee, Edwards graduated from George Washington Law School, Washington, D.C. He entered the FBI as an agent November 10, 1931, and was promoted to inspector on December 16, 1932.

Egan, James S. One of FBI Director Hoover's "Big Five" during the mid-1930s when the Bureau was engaged in shutting down notorious gangs preying on the Midwest, Inspector James S. Egan oversaw the internal accounting and preparation of investigative accounting evidence.

Born around 1890, in Omaha, Nebraska, he entered the FBI as an agent on June 6, 1922. In 1927, Egan was promoted to inspector.

Esposito, William J. FBI Director Louis J. Freeh appointed William J. Esposito deputy director early in 1997. He remained in that position until his retirement several months later. Born and raised in New York City, Esposito earned a bachelor of arts degree in political science from the University of South Florida (Tampa) and a master of arts degree from the University of Detroit.

Starting in the FBI as a clerk in FBIHQ in 1964, Esposito became a special agent in 1970. He was assigned to the Monroe resident agency of the New Orleans division and then the Detroit field office, where he was promoted to supervisor, before returning to FBIHQ.

In 1986, Esposito was appointed assistant special agent in charge (ASAC)—first of the Cleveland field office and then the Baltimore field office. As a member of the senior executive service, in 1990, Esposito headed the FBI's white collar crime investigations, the largest investigative program in the Bureau. Within two years, Esposito returned to the field as special agent in charge of the San Diego division. In September 1994, FBI Director Louis J. Freeh appointed him inspector–deputy assistant director of the Criminal Investigative Division (CID), from which he was promoted to assistant director of the division in February 1995. That year, President Bill Clinton awarded Esposito the Presidential Rank of Meritorious Executive. He remained in the CID until his appointment as deputy director. Esposito's wife, Jennifer Anderson Esposito, is a special agent.

Evans, Courtney Courtney Evans served as FBI liaison with the U.S. Senate Labor Rackets Committee, at which time he became acquainted with Robert F. Kennedy, then the committee's chief counsel. When Kennedy became attorney general, FBI Director J. Edgar Hoover appointed Evans as FBI liaison to the new Department of Justice head. His responsibilities included briefing the attorney general on important investigations, such sensitive and controversial matters as the black civil rights movement, and electronic and wiretap surveillance policy. In 1964, Evans resigned from the FBI to practice law.

Fay, Francis X. A founder of the Society of Former Special Agents of the FBI, Francis X. Fay was instrumental in starting the FBI Laboratory and establishing the Bureau's firearms program. He also played a major role in solving the Lindbergh kidnapping case.

During World War I, Fay served in the United States Cavalry. He entered the FBI as an agent in 1922 and served in the Pittsburgh field office during the settlement of the Hatfield and McCoy feud in West Virginia. Subsequently, he worked in the New York field office, where he assisted with the Lindbergh kidnapping case. Retiring from the FBI in 1935, the following year, he became head of security for Macy's Department Store in New York City. Joining the Air Force during World War II, he headed the New York office of the Army Counterintelligence Corps. Fay retired as a full colonel in 1953. He died May 5, 1990.

Felt, W. Mark W. Mark Felt was the number-three ranking official in the FBI from 1971 until FBI Director Hoover's death the following year. He became acting associate director, the number-two position in the FBI, under Acting

Exhibit 9.6 **W. Mark Felt,** *Courtesy of the FBI*

Director of the FBI L. Patrick Gray. During Gray's brief tenure, the investigation of a domestic terrorist group, the Weather Underground, fell within Felt's jurisdiction. His decisions governing this investigation ultimately led to his conviction, in 1980, for authorizing illegal surreptitious entries and bugging the homes of friends and relatives of members of the Weather Underground. On March 26, 1981, President Ronald Reagan pardoned both Felt and Edward S. Miller, former assistant director of the FBI's Domestic Intelligence Division, who also had been convicted of authorizing these actions.

Felt grew up in Twin Falls, Idaho, and attended the University of Idaho, where he received a bachelor's degree in 1935. After studying prelaw for a year, Felt moved to Washington, D.C., to work for Idaho Senator James P. Pope and his successor, D. Worth Clark, attending George Washington University Law School in the evening during his years with the Senate. In 1940, he received his law degree, and following his admission to the District of Columbia bar in 1941, obtained an appointment with the Federal Trade Commission before becoming an FBI agent on January 19, 1942.

Felt's first assignment was to the Houston field office. After three months, he was transferred to San Antonio, and three months later, after attending an in-service training class in Washington, D.C., he was transferred to FBIHQ as a supervisor in the Espionage Section. He remained there for the duration of World War II, working on German espionage. Following the war and after a brief sojourn in Washington, D.C., for in-service training and a special surveillance assignment involving a suspected communist, he was assigned to Seattle where, for two years, he handled mostly general cases, and then spent two years as a firearms instructor. When Congress assigned the FBI the responsibility for conducting background investigations for the Atomic Energy Commission, Felt supervised the investigations of employees at the Hanford, Washington, plutonium facility. In 1954, Felt transferred back to FBIHQ, as an inspector's aide, and then two months later, to the New Orleans field office as assistant special agent in charge. He served in New Orleans for 15 months, then was transferred to the Los Angeles field office, where he also served as assistant special agent in charge. Shortly thereafter, Felt was promoted to special agent in charge of the Salt Lake City field office, a division that included the gambling cities of Las Vegas and Reno, Nevada. There, a year before the Apalachin incident that is usually credited with bringing organized crime to Hoover's attention, Felt investigated organized crime cases. In 1958, Felt transferred to the Kansas City field office where organized crime also constituted a significant part of his work. Felt was assigned to FBIHQ in September 1962, where he served as deputy assistant director (number one man) in the Training and Inspection Division. In that post, he headed the FBI's training programs in Quantico, Virginia, and Washington, D.C. Appointed chief inspector as head of the Inspection Division in November 1964, he served in that position for six years until being appointed deputy associate director. While nominally holding the number-three position, Felt in reality handled the day-to-day management of the FBI because of Associate Director Clyde Tolson's poor health. In 1972, following FBI Director Hoover's death and the appointment of L. Patrick Gray as acting director, Felt was promoted to associate director. As the number-two person in the FBI, Felt became acting director in the hours between Gray's resignation, April 27, 1973, and the appointment of William Ruckelshaus as acting director later that day. On June 22, 1973, Felt retired from the FBI.

During Acting Director Gray's tenure, FBI agents had resumed the use of surreptitious entries to install microphones in the homes of individuals associated with the terrorist Weather Underground organization. Felt had approved a number of such operations in 1972 and 1973. For approving these illegal entries, on April 10, 1978, he, Edward S. Miller, and Gray became the first senior FBI executives ever indicted. On November 6, 1980, Felt and Miller were convicted (Gray's case had been severed from theirs). President Reagan pardoned both former officials shortly after his inauguration. In 1979, Felt's autobiographical *The FBI Pyramid: From the Inside* was published.

Finch, Stanley Wellington　Chief Examiner Stanley W. Finch was appointed the first head of the force of special agents when Attorney General Bonaparte created the Bureau in its earliest form in 1908. As such, Finch is really the FBI's first "director." Moreover, he developed and implemented the concept of a centralized Department of Justice investigatory force.

Exhibit 9.7　**Stanley Wellington Finch,** *Courtesy of the FBI*

Born July 20, 1872, to Phineas and Eleanor Brown Finch in Monticello, New York, Finch attended Baker University in Baldwin, Kansas; the Corcoran Scientific School in Washington, D.C.; and business colleges in Albany, New York, and Washington, D.C. In 1893, he accepted an appointment in the Department of Justice as a clerk, and was subsequently elevated to chief bookkeeper, examiner, special examiner, and then chief examiner. In 1908, he received an LL.B. degree from the National University Law School in Washington, D.C., and an LL.M. degree from the same institution the following year. He became a member of the District of Columbia bar in 1911.

Finch's responsibilities as chief examiner in the Department of Justice initially involved supervising audits of the federal courts. In 1908, Attorney General Bonaparte appointed him head of the new force of special agents. Although the force of special agents officially had been inaugurated by Attorney General Bonaparte, Finch had been the Department of Justice's strongest proponent of Justice having its own investigative unit, and immediately on his appointment, he sought to professionalize this service. He originated, or adopted from other agencies such as the Secret Service, many of the administrative and organizational policies and procedures later identified with J. Edgar Hoover. For example, within two years, legal experience had become a de facto requirement for Bureau agents. From the start, all agents had to write daily reports. Like his famous successor, Finch was parsimonious, and regularly sought ways to run the Bureau more efficiently and for less money. At the same time, he used—and possibly helped create through testimony and writings—the furor over girls and women being forced into prostitution ("white slavery") that led to the Mann Act, the first notable expansion of the Bureau's authority.

After becoming attorney general in March 1909, George Wickersham consolidated the force of special agents into the Bureau of Investigation and named Finch its chief. Finch took a particular interest in the problem of "white slavery," in which naive girls and women were allegedly either lured into a life of prostitution by smooth-talking pimps posing as respectable beaux who promised marriage, or were simply kidnapped and threatened with death if they did not comply. His lobbying efforts convinced Congress in 1910 to pass the Mann Act, which made it a federal crime to transport women over state lines for "immoral" purposes. As a result of the act, the Bureau of Investigation acquired both the jurisdiction and the funds to investigate its violations. In 1912, Finch was appointed the Department of Justice's special commissioner for the suppression of white slave traffic, headquartered in Baltimore. He held that position until his resignation in 1913.

After leaving the Department of Justice, Finch became president of the General Novelty Manufacturing Company, a position he held for approximately two years, after which he became secretary of the General Welfare League in New York. While secretary, in 1918, he edited the *World Welfare Magazine,* later *The World's News.* In 1920, he became president of the National Novelty Company.

In 1922, Finch returned to the Department of Justice, accepting appointment as special assistant to the attorney general in the Anti-Trust Division, where he remained through 1925. Finch then, once again, returned to the business world, becoming president of the United Factories Corporation in 1926, and the following year started his own business, the Finch Corporation. During these years and through 1931, he also had a general law practice. In July 1931, Finch returned to the Department of Justice as an

inspector in the Bureau of Prisons, a post he held until 1934. In January 1935, Attorney General Homer Cummings reinstated him as an audit clerk in the Department of Justice's Division of Accounts. In January 1940, Finch once again served as chief examiner and assistant to the general agent, working in the administrative office of the U.S. Courts, the same position he had held before 1908. He retired later that year. Finch died in 1951.

Flynn, William James   Attorney General A. Mitchell Palmer appointed former chief of the U.S. Secret Service William J. Flynn to be chief of the Bureau of Investigation. Flynn served from July 1, 1919, until the appointment of William J. Burns as his successor on August 22, 1921.

Born in New York City on November 18, 1867, to Michael and Elizabeth Stanton Flynn, Flynn attended public schools. He joined the U.S. Secret Service in 1897, where he remained until 1917, except for a brief absence during 1910 and 1911 when he left to reorganize the New York City detective force. In 1912, Flynn returned to the Secret Service, accepting the appointment as chief, U.S. Secret Service. He left the Secret Service to head a wartime office on September 17, 1918, from which he resigned to accept the position of Director of the Bureau of Investigation in July 1919. During his tenure, the Bureau was involved in a series of controversial investigations of radical activists and anarchists that culminated in the Palmer Raids of January 2 and 6, 1920. Flynn died in 1933.

Foxworth, Percy E.   Assistant director of the New York City field office, Percy E. Foxworth was killed while on a secret mission in Dutch Guiana (Suriname) January 15, 1943.

Born on November 29, 1906, in Purvis, Mississippi, Foxworth attended Mississippi public schools. After studying accounting in Chicago at the LaSalle Extension University and the Walton School of Commerce, he entered the FBI as an agent March 21, 1932. His assignments included the Jacksonville, Oklahoma City, New York City, and Washington, D.C., field offices. He was transferred to FBIHQ where he became assistant chief, Investigative Division. After a temporary assignment as acting special agent in charge in Newark, New Jersey, he was promoted to special agent in charge in the New York City field office. He then returned to FBIHQ as assistant director of the Administrative Division, and later was appointed assistant director of the Domestic Intelligence Division. Following the outbreak of World War II in Europe, FBI Director Hoover named Foxworth as assistant director in charge of the New York field office as well as head of the National Defense Office in New York. In that capacity, Foxworth supervised the FBI's Special Intelligence Service (SIS) activities in South America. While on assignment related to this work, Foxworth and special agent Harold Haberfeld died when their plane crashed. In tribute to his service to the United States, a liberty ship launched in February 1944 was named after him.

Freeh, Louis J. President Bill Clinton appointed Louis J. Freeh, a judge and former special agent, FBI director on July 20, 1993. Freeh formally assumed this office on September 1, 1993. His achievements include a major

Exhibit 9.8 **Louis J. Freeh,** *Courtesy of the FBI*

reorganization of FBIHQ and major changes in the FBI culture. Under his leadership, professional support personnel increasingly replaced agents in specialized and supervisory positions in FBIHQ. As a result, all but a small percentage of the Bureau's agents are assigned to the field, where the major investigatory work takes place. During Freeh's

tenure, the FBI's international role has expanded in response to international terrorism and organized crime. A dramatic example of this change is the 1994 opening of an FBI legal attaché office in Moscow. He has supervised a number of major cases including the terrorist bombing of the Oklahoma City federal building; an explosion during the 1996 Olympics in Atlanta; a takeover of a Montana town by the Freemen, an antigovernment organization; the arrest and conviction of organized crime leaders in the New York City area; and the bombing of an abortion clinic in Birmingham, Alabama.

Born January 6, 1950, in Jersey City, New Jersey, Freeh graduated Phi Beta Kappa in 1971 from Rutgers University. He received his J.D. degree from Rutgers Law School in 1974 and an LL.M. in criminal law from New York University Law School in 1984.

In 1975, Freeh entered the FBI, first serving in the New York City field office and then at FBIHQ where he specialized in organized crime investigations. He resigned from the FBI in 1981 to join the U.S. Attorney's Office for the Southern District of New York as an assistant U.S. attorney.

In this capacity, he became chief of the Organized Crime Unit and was later promoted to deputy U.S. attorney and associate U.S. attorney. He prosecuted some of the most important organized crime cases of that period, including the Pizza Connection case, which involved the Italian mafia. In addition, he prosecuted the VANPAC case, which involved the revenge-bombing murder of a federal judge and the bombing murder of a civil rights leader designed to make the first murder appear to be the work of a racially motivated terrorist.

In 1991, President George M. Bush appointed Freeh a U.S. District Court judge for the Southern District of New York. He held that position until his appointment as FBI director in 1993.

Freeh's various honors include, in 1987 and in 1991, the Attorney General's Distinguished Service Award, the second-highest annual honor given by the Department of Justice. He also received the John Marshall Award for Preparation of Litigation, an annual award by the attorney general, and the Federal Law Enforcement Officers Association Award.

Gandy, Helen W. Helen W. Gandy worked as a secretary and later as an administrative assistant to FBI Director J. Edgar Hoover from his early days with the General Investigative Division in 1919 until his death on May 2, 1972. Gandy took charge of Hoover's office, eventually attaining a high government service grade and administering her own staff. However, she was referred to as "Hoover's secretary" for her entire career with the Bureau. Despite her low-status informal title, Gandy held one of the Bureau's key positions. She functioned as the primary gatekeeper for Hoover's appointments, telephone calls, and correspondence. In

Exhibit 9.9 **Helen W. Gandy,** *Courtesy of the National Archives (65-M)*

addition, she maintained Hoover's two major office files—his "Personal and Confidential" files and his "Official and Confidential" files. Following Hoover's instructions, in the weeks after the FBI director's death she supervised the destruction of the "Personal and Confidential" files, a move that generated a major controversy when this action was discovered by Congress in 1975.

The daughter of F. Dallas and Annie W. Gandy, she was raised in Fairton, New Jersey. After graduating from Bridgeton High School in Bridgeton, New Jersey, Gandy took courses in the Corcoran Art School, George Washington Law School, and Strayer Business College, all in Washington, D.C.

Taking advantage of the opportunities for women created by World War I, she had moved to Washington and, for a brief time, worked as a department store salesperson before joining the Department of Justice in 1918 as a file clerk and messenger. Assigned as a typist to the Bureau of Investigation on March 25, 1918, she worked with Hoover. When Hoover became assistant director of the Bureau of Investigation on August 22, 1921, he telegraphed a vacationing Gandy "to return to Washington as soon as possible." After he became FBI director, Hoover promoted Gandy to secretary. For one of her promotions, he wrote: "If there is anyone in this Bureau whose services are indispensable I consider Miss Gandy to be that person." On August 23, 1937, he added "office assistant (FBI Director's office)" to her title, and on October 1, 1939, named her executive assistant to the director. Hoover continued to promote her to higher grade levels, although her title remained the same. An attorney general once questioned her promotion to a higher grade, because she would then outrank his own secretary. In response, Hoover expressed his regret that the attorney general's secretary was not as deserving as Gandy, but insisted on her promotion. On the occasion of her 25th anniversary with the Bureau, Hoover wrote: "You have been my right arm in the Bureau and when its history is finally written . . . you will occupy an important part of the introduction, in the body, and in the epilogue of this presentation." Hoover also nominated Gandy for several federal awards.

Although she eventually occupied one of the highest grade levels in the federal government, Gandy never became a spokesperson for feminism. She thought that women could work more effectively behind the scenes. As an example, she recounted the way she influenced the FBI to change its strict dress code to allow women to wear pant suits. A lower-level employee formally made the suggestion, and the FBI Executives Conference unanimously opposed it. When the memorandum reached her desk, Gandy brought it in personally to Hoover. He read it and asked her opinion. She indicated that since women were wearing short miniskirts, pants actually were more modest. Hoover agreed with her, and while the FBI's men continued to be required to wear out-of-style white shirts to work, women were allowed to wear pant suits.

Gandy retired from the Bureau the day that Hoover died but continued living in Washington, D.C., until the late 1980s, when she moved to DeLand, Florida. She died July 7, 1988.

Gardner, Michelle   On November 15, 1994, FBI tour leaders Michelle Gardner, R. Juhasz, Michael Garogolo, and security officer Charles Reed of the Personnel Division became the first support employees awarded the FBI Shield of Bravery. On March 18, 1994, Gardner was questioned by a man carrying a gym bag at the tour route entrance. Because the man indicated he was hearing-impaired, Gardner called deaf tour leader Juhasz to help. Gardner and Michael Garogolo then went to lead their regular tour groups but —feeling uneasy—Gardner called security officer Charles Reed, who responded (although on lunch break) because he was closest to the area. The man, complaining about Gallaudet University (a school for the deaf), Congress, and the FBI, started to douse himself with gasoline, which he had brought with him in the bag. As Officer Reed forced him against the side of building, gas spread over the others, who had returned to the lobby when they heard the commotion. The man reached for a lighter, which the tour leaders quickly confiscated. A few minutes later, the man was subdued, handcuffed, and taken away. During this incident, approximately 90 tourists congregated in the area.

Garogolo, Michael   See *Michelle Gardner.*

Gibson, Johnnie M. M.   One of the first black women to serve as a special agent, Johnnie M. M. Gibson became the subject of a made-for-TV movie in 1986.

Gibson received a bachelor's degree in health and physical education and a master's degree in education from Georgia State University. Prior to her FBI career, she taught high school physical education in Marianna, Florida, and, for a time, she was the second woman to serve as an officer in the Albany, Georgia, Police Department. Gibson entered the FBI as an agent in 1976 and worked in the Miami and Washington, D.C., field offices, as well as serving undercover in Los Angeles before being assigned to the Press Office and the Criminal Investigative Division in FBIHQ. Her undercover work included stints as an art appraiser and a nightclub singer. In 1988, she transferred to the Detroit field office as a supervisor. She returned to FBIHQ in 1993, assigned to the Personnel Division.

Glavin, W. R. With his appointment in 1941 as assistant director of the Personnel and Budget Division, W. R. Glavin was the first assistant director to head the principal division that handled administrative matters. In 1943, the responsibilities of this division were expanded to include the Mechanical Section, which did all the Bureau's internal printing, and it was renamed the Administrative Division.

Glavin was born in Mahanoy City, Pennsylvania, and grew up in Pittsburgh, Pennsylvania, where he worked for the Postal Telegraph Company. He joined the Marine Corps after moving to Washington, D.C., in the mid-1920s, and for five years taught business at the Marine Corps Institute. Following his discharge, he attended Southeastern University in Washington, D.C, where he received a B.C.S. degree. On April 6, 1931, Glavin entered the FBI as an agent. Named head of the Chief Clerk's Office in 1936, he was subsequently promoted to inspector. In this capacity, Glavin was among those present when, in 1936, FBI Director J. Edgar Hoover personally arrested gang leader Alvin Karpis in New Orleans, Louisiana. Glavin died on June 19, 1986.

Glover, John D. FBI Director William H. Webster appointed John D. Glover as executive assistant director, at that time, the highest position in the FBI that did not require presidential appointment and Senate confirmation. This appointment culminated Glover's FBI career as the highest ranking African American in the Bureau. Prior to becoming executive assistant director, Glover had served as assistant director of the Inspection Division, beginning in 1982, the first African American to hold this responsibility. Earlier, on February 16, 1979,

Exhibit 9.10 **John D. Glover,**
Courtesy of the FBI

Glover was appointed a special agent in charge of the Milwaukee field office, making him the first black in that position. Glover left Milwaukee to head the Atlanta field office from April 1980 until his appointment in 1982 as assistant director. During his tenure as special agent in charge in Atlanta, he supervised the FBI investigation of the apparent serial murders of black boys, a case known as the Atlanta Child Murders.

Born February 1, 1939, and raised in Miami, Florida, Glover attended Florida A & M University, in Tallahassee, where he earned a bachelor of arts degree in education in 1961. He taught high school in Miami from September 1961 to October 1966, when he became an FBI agent.

Glover's first FBI assignment was the Kansas City field office, where he served until his transfer in February 1968, to the Washington, D.C., field office. In December 1972, he was assigned to the FBI Academy in Quantico as a firearms instructor. He returned to FBIHQ in January 1974 as a supervisor in the Identification Division. After a stint in the Inspection Division from August 1975 to August 1976, he assumed supervisory duties in the Technical Services Division, from which he moved to head the Milwaukee field office.

Glover retired from the FBI in 1989. After retirement, he moved to New York City and became vice president for corporate security of Bristol-Meyers-Squibb.

Gonzalez, Manuel In 1993, FBI Director Louis J. Freeh appointed Manuel "Manny" Gonzalez as the first assistant director of the Personnel Division. Gonzalez spent his early career in the Philadelphia and New York City field offices. As an FBI executive, Gonzalez, according to Freeh, "retained a strong kinship with street Agents and support employees." Freeh assigned him Personnel Division assistant director, with the difficult task of developing and implementing the headquarters down-sizing plan. This plan resulted in the transfer of many FBIHQ special agent supervisors and managers into the field. In addition, Gonzalez helped develop other key personnel policies, including revising the Bureau's disciplinary programs. Gonzalez died in 1994.

Gow, W. Douglas After 26 years in the FBI, W. Douglas Gow became the FBI's second associate deputy director for Investigations. Because of this position, Gow also served as chair of the Terrorism Committee of the International Association of Chiefs of Police, the Chair of the Integrity/Law Enforcement Committee of the President's Council on Integrity and Efficiency, and a member of the advisory board of the Armed Forces Communications and Electronics Association.

Born on September 20, 1936, in West Chester, Pennsylvania, Gow was raised in Glendale, California. He graduated with a bachelor of arts degree from the University of

Redlands, in Redlands, California, in 1959, where he also did graduate work. The following year he joined the Marine Corps and served until 1965, attaining the rank of captain.

Entering the FBI in June 1965, he served in the Denver and Dallas field offices until his transfer to FBIHQ in 1974, where he was appointed a supervisor in the Criminal Investigative Division and participated on the inspection staff in the Planning and Inspection Division.

In April 1977, FBI Director Clarence Kelley appointed Gow assistant special agent in charge of the Phoenix, Arizona, field office. Gow soon returned to the Criminal Investigative Division as section chief, where he remained until his April 1980 appointment as special agent in charge of the Knoxville field office. Three years later, he was appointed special agent in charge first of the Houston field office, and then, in January 1987, of the Washington, D.C., field office. During this time, he served on the board of directors of the Security Affairs Support Association. In November 1989, Gow was promoted to assistant director of the Intelligence Division in FBIHQ, where he remained until his appointment as associate director for Investigations. He received the President's Meritorious Executive Award in 1989 and the Distinguished Executive Award in 1990. Gow retired from the FBI in 1994.

Gray, L. Patrick, III   President Richard M. Nixon appointed L. Patrick Gray III acting director of the FBI on May 3, 1972, shortly after J. Edgar Hoover's death. Gray resigned in April 1973 after admitting that he destroyed evidence in the Watergate case.

Exhibit 9.11   **L. Patrick Gray III,** *Courtesy of the FBI*

Born in St. Louis on July 18, 1916, Gray later moved to Houston, Texas, where he attended a Catholic high school. Afterward, he studied engineering and business administration at Rice University in Houston. After finishing four years at Rice, he was appointed to the U.S. Naval Academy. Commissioned line officer after graduation, he attended submarine school. He served in both the Atlantic and Pacific during World War II, and as a submarine commander and commander of a submarine flotilla during the Korean War. While serving in the Navy, Gray attended the George Washington School of Law, receiving his degree in 1949. He later became the assistant to the Joint Chiefs of Staff, retiring in 1960 to join the personal campaign staff of Republican presidential candidate Richard Nixon. When Nixon lost the election, Gray entered private law practice in New London. Connecticut. He once again joined Nixon's presidential campaign staff in 1968. Upon Nixon's inauguration, Gray became executive secretary to Robert H. Finch, secretary of the Department of Health, Education, and Welfare. Gray resumed private law practice in 1970, but returned to government work in December as assistant attorney general in charge of the Civil Division, where he handled a number of prominent cases related to the anti–Vietnam War effort. At the time of his appointment as the FBI's acting director, Gray was awaiting Senate confirmation for the position of deputy attorney general.

As acting director of the FBI, Gray instituted four administrative changes. First, he appointed the first female special agents since the 1920s. Second, he relaxed a number of the requirements for agents instituted by FBI Director Hoover, such as the strict weight rules, and he permitted agents to wear colored shirts to work (Hoover had required white shirts). Third, he visited all but one of the FBI field offices; this earned Gray high marks from field agents, who felt that Hoover had considered them inferior to his head-quarters staff. FBIHQ agents, however, privately criticized the amount of time Gray spent away from Washington. Last, Gray broke with tradition by hiring assistants from outside the FBI, bringing with him from the Department of Justice three aides who stood between career FBI senior executives and himself. Subsequent FBI directors followed this precedent.

During his brief tenure, Gray appeared to have politicized the FBI director's office by using Republican speech writers and by giving high officials in the Department of Justice information for President Nixon to use in his campaign speeches. During his subsequent confirmation hearings, Gray admitted to having shown to White House counsel John Dean FBI investigative files on the Watergate investigation. On April 5, 1973, he requested that his name be withdrawn from consideration as FBI director. He resigned April 27, 1973, after confessing to Connecticut Senator Lowell Weicker that he had destroyed two folders significant in the Watergate investigation without telling investigators of their existence.

Gray, along with acting associate director W. Mark Felt and assistant director Edward S. Miller, was indicted in 1978 for authorizing illegal surreptitious entries and bugging during an FBI investigation of the terrorist Weather Underground group. Gray denied any knowledge of these matters and succeeded in severing his case from that of Felt and Miller. The government dropped the charges against him on December 11, 1980. After resigning from government service, Gray returned to private law practice in Connecticut.

Greenleaf, James W.   In May 1990, James W. Greenleaf, a 22-year veteran of the FBI, was transferred from a position with the Central Intelligence Agency back to the Bureau to become the second associate deputy director for Administration.

Greenleaf was born December 8, 1941, and raised in Portland, Maine. Graduating in 1964 from Gorham State College, Gorham, Maine, he taught high school science from 1965 to 1967 in South Portland.

In August 1967, Greenleaf entered the FBI and was assigned to the Minneapolis field office. He was transferred to the Norfolk field office in March 1969, remaining until his 1972 assignment to FBIHQ as a supervisor in the Laboratory Division. After serving in the Inspection Division from November 1976 to April 1977, Greenleaf was promoted to assistant section chief in the Engineering Section of the Technical Services Division.

Greenleaf was appointed assistant special agent in charge of the Chicago field office in February 1978. The following June, Greenleaf returned to FBIHQ as the deputy assistant director of the Laboratory Division, winning a promotion to assistant director of that division in February 1980. Greenleaf assumed the same position in the Inspection Division in January 1981. In September 1982, Greenleaf was appointed special agent in charge of the Boston field office. He returned to FBIHQ in August 1986 as assistant director of the Training Division at the FBI Academy in Quantico, Virginia.

In 1989, former FBI director William Webster, then director of the Central Intelligence Agency, appointed Greenleaf to be director of public affairs at the CIA in Langley, Virginia, a post he held until his transfer back to the FBI as associate director for Administration. Later that year, Greenleaf retired from the FBI.

Grogan, Benjamin P.   Benjamin P. Grogan was killed in action with Jerry Dove in Miami, Florida, April 11, 1986, when bank robbers opened fire on the agents who were trying to thwart their crime. This tragedy, in which the FBI agents faced felons carrying assault weapons, led to a change in firearms training for FBI agents and to the development of new weapons for their use.

Born in Atlanta, Georgia, February 26, 1933, Grogan received a liberal arts degree from St. Mary's Manor, Penndel, Pennsylvania, in 1953. Entering the FBI as an agent in the early 1960s, he served in FBI offices in Cincinnati; Steubenville, Ohio; Washington, D.C.; New York City; and San Juan, Puerto Rico, before his assignment to the Miami field office in 1966.

Heafner, Horace J.   With a background in commercial art, Horace J. Heafner spent over 40 years in the FBI, many of them as a visual information specialist in the FBI Laboratory. As part of this work, he mastered the skill of age progression, a technique that helps locate missing children and fugitives. He also developed the FBI Facial Identification Catalogue, a resource used by law enforcement throughout the country. In 1956, he and Special Agent Larry Heim collaborated on a coloring poster intended for first-through third-graders that may have been the first national educational effort aimed at alerting children to the dangers of molesters.

Raised in Charlotte and Whiteville, North Carolina, Heafner subsequently attended art school in Washington, D.C., beginning his Bureau career in the late 1940s. He worked first in the Identification Division and then in the chief clerk's office at FBIHQ. After spending two years in the U.S. Army during the Korean War, he returned to the FBI in 1952 to work in the Administrative Division before transferring to the laboratory. One of his more notable achievements while employed as a specialist in the FBI Laboratory was identifying Patricia Hearst, the kidnapped heiress turned criminal, from bank surveillance camera photographs. Heafner also teamed with firearms expert Robert Frazier to diagram the sequence of events in the 1970 Kent State University confrontation between students and the Ohio National Guard.

After retiring from the FBI in 1988, Heafner continued to serve as an instructor at the FBI National Academy. He also became head of the Imaging Laboratory at the National Center for Missing and Exploited Children.

Heim, Lawrence J.   After a career that encompassed 23 years in the Crime Records and External Affairs Divisions, Lawrence J. Heim became active in the Society of Former Special Agents of the FBI, in several capacities including as editor from 1984 until his death in 1996 of *The Grapevine*, the society's magazine.

Born in Cincinnati, Ohio, Heim graduated from Xavier University. He served in the Army in the Pacific during World War II and he participated in the postwar U.S. occupation of Japan, where he was stationed in both Hiroshima and Nagasaki.

Heim began his FBI career in March 1947. His early assignments included the El Paso and Albuquerque field offices, and the Vancouver and Everett, Washington, resident agencies. Transferred to the Crime Records Division in 1952, his responsibilities included serving as liaison with the media, and, as unit chief in the Publications Unit, editor of the *FBI Law Enforcement Bulletin.* With Horace Heafner, he designed an educational program warning elementary school children of the dangers of child molesters. Heim's public relations responsibilities continued even after FBI Director Clarence Kelley dissolved the Crime Records Division and transferred some of its functions to the External Affairs Division. Heim retired in 1975 but continued to advise journalists, authors, and media producers having questions about the history and operations of the Bureau. In addition to editing *The Grapevine,* Heim served the FBI in his retirement as society chairman of the annual Louis E. Peters Memorial Award Committee, which honors a civilian who has aided law enforcement. Heim died on October 28, 1996.

Held, Richard   Standing six feet, five inches tall, Richard Held was given the name Tall Elk when the Sioux Nation made him an honorary member. He was promoted to associate director of the FBI on July 20, 1976.

Born in Chicago and raised in Seattle, Held graduated from the University of Washington as an accounting major with a B.A. in business administration. He entered the FBI as an agent on January 13, 1941, and served in the Memphis, Cleveland, and Butte field offices before assuming supervisory duties in FBIHQ. After this service, he was appointed assistant special agent in charge of the San Diego field office and then the Butte field office. He was subsequently promoted to special agent in charge of the Mobile and Minneapolis field offices. While in the latter position, which covers the Dakotas as well as Minnesota, he was given honorary membership in the Sioux Nation. His next appointment was special agent in charge of the Chicago field office, from which he was promoted to associate director. He retired on January 31, 1978. His son, also named Richard Held, became an FBI agent.

Hoover, John Edgar   J. Edgar Hoover directed the FBI from his appointment on May 10, 1924, until his death almost 48 years later, May 2, 1972.

Edgar, as he was called since childhood, was born January 1, 1895, and raised in Washington, D.C. His family consisted of his father, Dickerson Naylor Hoover Sr., a civil

Exhibit 9.12   **J. Edgar Hoover,** *Courtesy of the National Archives (65-H)*

servant; his mother, Annie Margaret Scheitlin; his older brother, Dickerson Jr.; and his older sister, Lillian (whose last name after marrying was Robinette). Until the death of his widowed mother in 1938, Hoover lived with her in the Capitol Hill house in which he was born. He then moved to northwest Washington, D.C., where he lived alone (save for a housekeeper and his beloved terriers) until his death.

Skipping a traditional college education, Hoover enrolled in the George Washington Law School, where he attended school at night, earning his LL.B. (1916) and LL.M. (1917). He worked during the day at the Library of Congress.

On July 26, 1917, Hoover joined the Department of Justice. Hoover's first major assignment in the alien registration division involved suspected violators of the Alien Enemy Act. Following the end of military conflict in November 1918, he became an assistant to the attorney general and, in 1919, effective head of the newly created General Intelligence Division, where he collected publicly available information on radicals. From his reading of radical literature, Hoover became convinced that radicals (both anarchists and communists) posed as great a danger to United States security as they had to pre-revolutionary Russia in 1917. He never deviated from this view.

In 1921, the director of the Bureau of Investigation, William Burns, appointed Hoover as assistant director, at that time the second-highest position in the Bureau. Burns, who had previously headed a private detective agency, soon became notorious for hiring political cronies as Bureau agents, as well as other unqualified individuals with limited education. Attorney General Harlan F. Stone, appointed by President Calvin Coolidge on April 12, 1924, to clean up the scandal-ridden Department of Justice, secured Burns's resignation on May 9, 1924. On the following day, Stone named Hoover as acting director of the Bureau. Stone made the appointment permanent on December 10, 1924. Hoover set out to reform the Bureau of Investigation, whose reputation had suffered under Burns. In the next few months, Hoover fired incompetent and undereducated agents, and he revived the requirement of legal training for special agents, as well as ordering background checks, interviews, and physical tests for applicants.

The expansion of federal criminal jurisdiction that had occurred with the Lindbergh Law in 1932 and the New Deal's crime-fighting initiatives of 1933 and 1934 enabled the FBI and J. Edgar Hoover to investigate more crimes and, as important, to assume an increasingly high public profile. Hoover astutely recognized that with greater public recognition came a need to maintain public confidence. He therefore enlisted the help of reporters supportive of the Bureau, and others in the media, to portray invincible G-men and their heroic director.

Hoover also used this resultant prestige to educate the public about the threats to American society that he considered most serious, such as gangsters during the 1930s and communists during the Cold War of the late 1940s through the 1960s. He carried out this education mission through books and articles that carried his byline but were researched and written by agents and support personnel.

In contrast to FBI agents, most of whom had attended college, local and state law enforcement officers during the 1930s typically had little or no professional training. Hoover sought to change this in 1935 by establishing the FBI National Police Academy to train policemen in the methods of conducting professional and scientific investigations. Academy graduates would then return home to train their colleagues.

During Hoover's tenure, presidents regularly requested that the Bureau collect information on their political rivals and critics. Hoover often complied with these presidential requests, and, in addition, brought whatever derogatory or titillating information on government officials came to the FBI's attention. Personally or through his assistants, he told each president about the questionable conduct of various administration officials. In addition, he let high officials know when the FBI possessed derogatory materials about them, assuring these officials that the information would be closely held. Much of this information coming into the FBI on public officials and other people of prominence was maintained in files kept in Hoover's office to limit its

accessibility. No conclusive evidence has surfaced that Hoover initiated surveillance of government officials for other than legitimate purposes.

Before the U.S. entry into World War II, the FBI, using the authority granted by President Roosevelt in the years prior to the Japanese bombing of Pearl Harbor, monitored German spies (and other suspected dangerous aliens) and compiled a list of foreign nationals and citizens (the Custodial Detention Index) for possible detention. Following U.S. involvement in World War II, suspected dangerous aliens were arrested. Because he considered all potential spies and saboteurs to be in custody, Hoover opposed the Roosevelt administration's World War II program interning west coast Japanese and Japanese Americans. He was overruled by Attorney General Francis Biddle and President Roosevelt, who acceded to the advice of the military officials.

After the end of World War II, Hoover spoke frequently about the dangers to the American people of juvenile delinquency and a lax parole system. He is better known, however, for his public campaign against domestic subversion, especially the threat to American security posed by communists and "fellow travelers" (non–Communist Party members sympathetic to the Soviet Union). Because the FBI investigations of the 1940s (during the period of the U.S.-Soviet alliance, as well as during the Cold War) uncovered evidence of communist subversion within the United States, Hoover was convinced that if the FBI and the American people relaxed their guard, communists would gain control of the United States, as they did in Eastern Europe and China. Until the end of his career, Hoover made the war on American communism a personal crusade, and by lending his prestige in support of the view that critics of the government were unpatriotic and pro-communist, Hoover was responsible, in part, for discouraging legitimate dissent.

Hoover's power in the years after World War II seemed so great that his critics then (and later) complained that he could investigate what and how he pleased. Hoover was blamed for the FBI's seeming failure to battle organized crime and protect black civil rights. At the time, Hoover contended that the FBI lacked clear-cut authority under federal laws in both these areas. He was correct. Until the late 1960s, presidents, Congress, the courts, and the American public preferred local to federal crime enforcement. When administration policy, law, and public opinion changed in response to "law and order" concerns of the 1960s, FBI organized crime and civil rights investigations became more aggressive.

The FBI's civil rights successes, however, were overshadowed by Hoover's personal vendetta against Martin Luther King Jr. The FBI director considered King a liar and a hypocrite. In an effort to destroy King's prestige and his position of leadership in civil rights endeavors, Hoover authorized a secret program designed to harass and discredit him (which involved bugging King's office and hotel rooms). The operation against King, first exposed during congressional hearings in the 1970s, probably did more than any other action to compromise Hoover's subsequent reputation.

The King vendetta and other illegal Bureau operations were first revealed in the reform atmosphere that followed the Watergate-related revelations in the mid-1970s. Congressional hearings, as well as FBI documents stolen and selectively released, revealed the truth behind some of the accusations previously leveled at the FBI by its civil libertarian critics. After the 1970s, Hoover's anticommunist crusade came to be considered excessive. These revelations altered the public's perception of Hoover.

With the skepticism of government fostered by Watergate, Hoover's many real achievements were often denigrated or ignored. While biographies of the 1950s lionized Hoover, those of the 1990s emphasize scandalous aspects of his life, with some of the more sensationalist of these having as their basis highly dubious sources.

During J. Edgar Hoover's lifetime, however, the Bureau's known successes, combined with its successful public relations efforts, made Hoover one of the most admired Americans. An attorney general theoretically could have fired Hoover at any time. By 1935, however, attorneys general were unwilling to challenge him. Instead, while maintaining cordial relations with most attorneys general, Hoover often dealt directly with presidents (and often vice versa). J. Edgar Hoover maintained his longevity both because of the requested intelligence assistance he gave each administration and the unshakable public support he commanded from the public, the media, and Congress. Indeed, despite reaching the mandatory retirement age of 70, Hoover was allowed to continue as FBI director when President Lyndon Johnson issued a special executive order on May 8, 1964, waiving this requirement. As his legacy, Hoover left a professionalized American law enforcement community and an FBI respected internationally for its competence and efficiency. President Nixon accorded him a

rare honor by having his body lie in state in the Capitol rotunda, where thousands stood in long lines to pay their last respects.

Hoover never married. At his death in 1972, he left a large share of his property to his close friend and professional associate, Clyde Tolson.

Hottel, Guy   For many years a close associate of J. Edgar Hoover and Clyde Tolson, Guy Hottel served at times as Hoover's personal bodyguard and for a time was special agent in charge of the Washington, D.C., field office.

Born and raised in Virginia and a superb athlete, Hottel played football in college. He roomed with Tolson in the 1920s while they attended George Washington University and during their early Bureau years. For several years during the 1930s and 1940s, Hoover, Tolson, and Hottel traveled and socialized together.

Houston, Lenore   Lenore Houston was apparently the first woman appointed special agent by FBI Director J. Edgar Hoover—and the last. A high school graduate who had completed three years of college and a separate business course, Houston was 45 years old when she entered the Bureau of Investigation as a special employee on January 14, 1924. Her salary was equivalent to that given beginning agents: seven dollars a day, plus four dollars per day when traveling. Assigned to the Philadelphia field office, she handled Mann Act violations. From the first, she indicated her desire to be designated a special agent. After several unsuccessful entreaties to Bureau of Investigation Director William Burns from Congressman Graham of Pennsylvania, Hoover—at the time, the acting director of the Bureau—appointed her on November 6, 1924.

By August 29, 1927, when she transferred to the Washington, D.C., field office, Houston earned $3,100 per annum. Her career in the new office suffered, and she resigned October 20, 1928, effective November 7, 1928. Two years later, she was confined to a hospital because she suffered from hallucinations and vowed to shoot Hoover on her release.

Jenkins, Thomas J.   Thomas J. Jenkins entered the FBI as a clerk in 1934 and was appointed a special agent five years later. FBI Director Clarence M. Kelley appointed Jenkins as the FBI's assistant to the director–deputy associate director for Administration in December 1973. Just prior to his promotion, Jenkins held the position of assistant director, Training Division. He retired in 1976.

Jones, Gustave T. The Special Intelligence Service (SIS) coordinator during World War II in Mexico, Gustave T. "Gus" Jones had earlier helped influence the development of military intelligence on the Mexican border while employed with the Bureau during World War I.

Born in July 1882, Jones served as a private in the Texas Volunteers at age 15 when this unit prepared to enter the Spanish American War in 1898. He became assistant chief of police in San Angelo, Texas, in 1905, where he remained until his appointment as a deputy sheriff in Tom Green County, Texas. In April 1908, Jones joined the Texas Rangers, serving until July 1910, when he joined the U.S. Customs Service as an inspector. Serving on a special detail as a deputy U.S. marshal, Jones enforced United States neutrality policy on the Mexican border. From this position, he transferred to the Immigration Service as an inspector and went undercover in Mexico in a group of alien smugglers.

On September 18, 1917, Jones entered the Bureau as a special agent continuing to serve on the Mexican border. In the early 1920s he became a division superintendent (equivalent to special agent in charge) in Texas. Jones played a key role in the Bureau's 1933 investigation leading to the apprehension of the George "Machine Gun" Kelly in the Urschel kidnapping case. In 1934, Jones helped escort Kelly and gangster Al Capone to Alcatraz. During World War II, Jones became the FBI's Mexico City legal attaché, where he coordinated the Special Intelligence Service until his retirement in 1943. He died on September 28, 1963.

Jones, James Wormley (Jack) Appointed an agent on November 19, 1919, James Wormley "Jack" Jones is believed to have been the first African American special agent in the history of the FBI and its predecessor agencies. Born in approximately 1884 in Fort Monroe, Virginia, Jones attended public schools in Cambridge, Massachusetts; studied at Norfolk Mission College for a year; and spent three years at Virginia Union University.

In January 1905, Jones joined the Metropolitan Police Department in Washington, D.C., where he served as footman, horseman, and motorcycle policeman before being promoted to detective. He joined the Army in 1917. After attending Officer's Training School in Des Moines, Iowa, he was commissioned a captain assigned to the 368th Infantry, where he commanded Company F. In 1918, he went to France, commanding his company in the Vosges Mountains, Argonne Sector, and the Metz front. While in France, he became an instructor and, eventually, senior instructor, 92d

Division, School of Specialists. He resigned from the Army with the end of the war in 1918 and returned to the Washington, D.C., police department.

Bureau of Investigation Director A. Bruce Bielaski appointed Jones a special agent in November 1919. He served in New York City and Pittsburgh. While in the Bureau, he infiltrated Marcus Garvey's Universal Negro Improvement Association and the Blood Brotherhood, two black nationalist organizations suspected of subversion. Jones resigned April 14, 1923, after someone recognized him and he no longer could function effectively undercover. Jones died December 11, 1958.

Jones, Milton A. Milton A. Jones served as chief of the FBI's Crime Records Section during the 1940s through the early 1970s. In that capacity, he supervised FBI public relations, media contacts, and publications, including *FBI Law Enforcement Bulletin,* which was distributed to law enforcement agencies nationwide, and the Bureau's in-house publication, *The Investigator.*

Born January 24, 1913, in Monticello, Kentucky, Jones moved to Bowling Green, Kentucky, in 1928. He earned a bachelor's degree from Western Kentucky University in 1935 and a juris doctor degree from Harvard Law School in 1938. After graduating, he practiced law with the Department of Agriculture in Raleigh, North Carolina.

Jones entered the FBI as an agent on February 6, 1939, and his early assignments included the Des Moines and Cleveland field offices and the Youngstown, Ohio, resident agency. He transferred to FBIHQ in 1940 where he worked in the Records and Communications Division. He received promotion to unit chief of the Crime Records Section in 1944.

After retiring in 1973, Jones lived in Annandale, Virginia. During his retirement, Jones served as the historian of the Society of Former Special Agents of the FBI, writing frequently for the society magazine, *The Grapevine.* Jones died on April 24, 1994.

Joseph, Kenneth E. FBI Director William H. Webster appointed Kenneth E. Joseph as executive assistant director for Law Enforcement Services in January 1980. He held that position until his retirement on November 14, 1980.

Born and raised in Alamosa, Colorado, Joseph served in the U.S. Navy and received a bachelor of arts degree from Adams State College in Alamosa. He entered the FBI as a special agent on September 4, 1951, and was assigned first to the Omaha field office. In October 1952, he was transferred to the Detroit field office. During his service in

Detroit, he received a master of science degree in 1968 from the School of Criminal Justice at Michigan State University and a Ph.D. in 1970 from the university's College of Education. Shortly thereafter, FBI Director Clarence M. Kelley assigned him to FBIHQ as a supervisor in the Training Division. In August 1977, he became assistant director of Training. In 1972, he was appointed an adjunct faculty member of the Division of Continuing Education, University of Virginia.

Juhasz, R.   See *Michelle Gardner.*

Jung, Christine M. Kaporch   Christine M. Jung, then known as Christine Kaporch, was one of the first women to become special agents since the 1920s. In 1978, she became the FBI's first female firearms instructor. She also was the first woman in the FBI to shoot a "possible"—a perfect firearms score.

Jung was born November 12, 1947, in Providence, Rhode Island, and grew up in Syracuse, New York. She received a bachelor of arts degree from the University of Miami, Coral Gables, Florida. Upon graduating in 1969, she joined the U.S. Marine Corps, attaining the rank of captain before leaving in 1972.

After entering the FBI as an agent on April 9, 1973, Jung was assigned to the Newark and Washington, D.C., field offices until her transfer to the FBI Academy in Quantico as firearms instructor. In January 1981, Jung was appointed supervisor of the Counterterrorism Squad in the Alexandria field office, a position she held until June 1986 when she transferred to FBIHQ, where she continued to work in counterterrorism. She was subsequently assigned to the Inspection Division, following which she served for a year as the FBI's ombudsman. In 1991, Jung was promoted to assistant special agent in charge in the New York field office. She resigned December 9, 1995.

Kelley, Clarence M.   Clarence M. Kelley became the FBI's first director after the death of J. Edgar Hoover. During his tenure from July 9, 1973, to February 22, 1978, he implemented a major reorganization within the agency and led a change in Bureau culture, instituting "management by objectives" and emphasizing "quality over quantity" in investigations.

Kelley was born October 24, 1911, and was raised in Fairmount, Missouri (now part of Independence). He was the only child of Clarence Bond Kelley, an electrical engineer, and Minnie Brown Kelley, a homemaker. He attended high school in Kansas City, Missouri, and gradu-

ated with a bachelor of arts degree from the University of Kansas, Lawrence, in 1936 and an LL.B. degree in 1940 from the University of Kansas City School of Law. Shortly before Kelley's graduation from law school, the head of the FBI's Kansas City field office spoke to his class and influenced him to join the FBI.

Entering the FBI as a special agent on October 7, 1940, Kelley worked in Huntington, West Virginia; Seattle; San Francisco; Altoona; Johnstown; Pittsburgh; and Des Moines. In 1942, he was transferred to the FBI Academy in Quantico, Virginia as a firearms instructor. Having concluded that he had to join the military to participate directly in the war effort, two years later Kelley left the FBI to join the Navy. Reapplying to the Bureau in 1946, his petition was accepted and he was assigned to Kansas City, Missouri, his office of preference. Until 1951, Kelley worked in Kansas City as a general criminal

Exhibit 9.13   **Clarence M. Kelley,**
Courtesy of the FBI

investigator and supervisor. That year, he was transferred to FBIHQ as a supervisor in the Investigations Division. Kelley returned to the Kansas City field office six months later because of a reduction in FBIHQ supervisory staff.

In 1953, Kelley was promoted to assistant special agent in charge of the Houston field office. Two years later, he was promoted to inspector and returned to FBIHQ. After nine months of almost constant travel conducting inspections, he requested a transfer back to the field. Hoover appointed Kelley special agent in charge of the Birmingham, Alabama, field office. In 1960, Kelley transferred to the Memphis field office as special agent in charge. In 1961, he resigned in order to become chief of the Kansas City, Missouri, police department.

While Kansas City police chief, he oversaw numerous innovations. His department became the first police department to have its own helicopters and the first to develop a metropolitan area response team. It was also one of the first to use computers extensively, to establish community-based policing, to re-institute foot patrols, and to appoint a special Law Enforcement Intelligence Unit to handle organized crime. In addition, Chief Kelley named a special media representative. These innovations were partly based on Kelley's FBI experiences.

Among his many awards, Kelley received (in 1970) the Veterans of Foreign Wars J. Edgar Hoover Award as the outstanding law enforcement officer of the year. His service to law enforcement during his tenure as police chief included chairing the Florida Governor's Task Force to Evaluate Public Safety and Related Support Services at the 1972 Republican and Democratic presidential nominating conventions, both of which took place in Miami.

President Richard M. Nixon nominated Kelley as FBI director in June 1973, and he was confirmed by the Senate in a 96–0 vote. As FBI director, Kelley handled various Watergate revelations that ended, in 1974, with the resignation of President Nixon. His tenure was complicated in the mid-1970s by hearings conducted by House and Senate committees investigating the intelligence agencies. As FBI director, he was subjected to heavy criticism from Congress and the media for some of the activities that had taken place during Hoover's years. To preclude their recurrence, Attorney General Edward Levi issued new guidelines in March 1976 to prevent excessive domestic surveillance or counterintelligence efforts in the future. Kelley instituted new procedures to implement these restrictions on the FBI's intelligence-gathering activities. In addition, Kelley supervised a number of high-profile investigations, the most prominent of which involved the kidnapping of newspaper heiress Patty Hearst and a siege by Native American activists in Wounded Knee, South Dakota.

Kelley's most lasting legacy as FBI director, however, involved his management changes: he emphasized the "quality" of cases solved rather than the "quantity" of arrests and convictions, and he decentralized management and required each office to prioritize its cases. Under the more stringent standards imposed on government officials in the aftermath of the Watergate scandal, Kelley was criticized for having used Bureau employees to make a few furnishings for his home. President Carter accepted his resignation, effective February 1978.

After leaving the FBI, Kelley returned to Kansas City, Missouri, where he ran a security firm until his retirement. He died August 5, 1997.

Kennedy, Weldon L. FBI Director Louis J. Freeh appointed Weldon L. Kennedy to be deputy director of the FBI on August 8, 1995. At the time, he was special agent in charge of the Phoenix field office.

Born September 9, 1938, in Menlow, Texas, Kennedy received his early education at Edinburg, Texas. He attended the University of Texas in Austin, and Georgia State University in Atlanta, after which he served as an intelligence officer in the U.S. Navy.

After entering the FBI as an agent on July 22, 1963, Kennedy served in the Portland, Newark, Miami, San Juan, and Las Vegas field offices, and in the Technical Services Division in FBIHQ. In 1977, FBI Director Clarence M. Kelley appointed him as inspector's aide in the Planning and Inspection Division. The following year, Kennedy became assistant special agent in charge of the Boston field office and in 1980 was promoted to inspector in the Inspection Division, where he remained until 1982, when he became special agent in charge of the Jackson, Mississippi, field office. In 1985, he became special agent in charge in Atlanta, Georgia, and in 1989, assistant director of the Administrative Services Division in FBIHQ. FBI Director William S. Sessions elevated him to associate deputy director for Administration in July 1992. He became special agent in charge in Phoenix in February 1994. Kennedy retired in 1997.

Kerr, Donald M. On October 21, 1997, FBI Director Louis J. Freeh appointed Donald M. Kerr as the first non-agent to head the FBI Laboratory. A nationally recognized physicist, Kerr was director of the Los Alamos National Laboratory from 1979 to 1985. During those years, the Los Alamos laboratory conducted research for the FBI, and Kerr had also worked with FBI representatives on the National Security Council's executive committee on terrorism. With his appointment as assistant director of the Laboratory Division, Kerr will supervise the development of new laboratory facilities at the FBI Academy in Quantico, Virginia.

Kerr received his bachelor of electrical engineering, master of science in microwave electronics, and doctorate in plasma physics from Cornell University in New York. From 1976 to 1979 he served as assistant secretary and acting assistant secretary of energy for Energy Technology; assistant secretary and acting assistant secretary of energy for Deputy Defense Programs; and held appointments in the Department of Energy's Offices of Classification, Safeguards, and Security. From 1966 to 1976, Kerr conducted research at Los Alamos related to nuclear weapons, and in 1976 he was named deputy manager of the Department of Energy's operations in Nevada.

After leaving Los Alamos, Kerr became president of EG&G, a manufacturing and engineering firm, and then joined Science Applications International Corporation where, in 1993, he became its executive vice president in charge of science and technology. In 1996, he joined Information Systems Laboratories of San Diego as executive vice president. During these years, Kerr also served as a member of the Defense Science Board and chaired the Nonproliferation Advisory Panel for the Director of Central Intelligence. He is a fellow of the American Association for the Advancement of Science.

Kielman, Joseph   FBI Director William S. Sessions appointed Joseph Kielman as the FBI's first chief scientist in February 1991. In 1994, FBI Director Louis J. Freeh named him chief scientist of the Information Resources Division.

Kielman received a bachelor of science degree in physics from Pennsylvania State University. After receiving his doctorate in biophysics, also from Pennsylvania State University, he conducted research at Upstate Medical Center in Syracuse, New York. He entered the FBI in 1984 with the Technical Services Division. Employed in that division's Engineering Section in 1985, he began developing cooperative programs with other federal scientific agencies such as the Advanced Research Projects Agency of the Department of Defense.

Kosterlitzky, Emilio   Born in Moscow on November 16, 1853, Emilio Kosterlitzky emigrated first to Mexico and from there eventually entered the United States. Because of his Mexican background, Kosterlitzky is considered by some chroniclers of Bureau history to be its first Hispanic special agent.

Before immigrating to Mexico, Kosterlitzky had attended military college in St. Petersburg. The recent immigrant enlisted as a private in the Mexican Federal Army. Eventually he became a brigadier general but by the time of his retirement had been demoted to colonel. On March 26, 1917, at age 64, he became a special employee of the Bureau of Investigation. Although he resigned on September 1, 1919, he was rehired as a special agent on May 1, 1922. A language expert, he spoke Russian, Polish, Spanish, French, German, Japanese, Chinese, Korean, and "three Norse languages." Kosterlitzky retired from the Bureau on September 4, 1926. He died March 2, 1928.

Ladd, D. Milton (Mickey)   Appointed assistant to the director, (the number-three position in the FBI) on May 5, 1949, D. M. Ladd held that position until his retirement in 1954. Prior to that appointment, he had served as assistant director of the Domestic Intelligence Division since 1942. According to W. Mark Felt, an agent at the time and later associate director of the FBI, "Much of the Bureau's success in combating German espionage and sabotage [during World War II] was due to his effective leadership."

Exhibit 9.14   **D. Milton Ladd,** *Courtesy of the National Archives (65-F)*

Ladd was born on October 30, 1903. His father was elected senator from North Dakota in 1920, and Ladd went to Washington with him in 1921. After attending George Washington University at night, Ladd graduated with a law degree in 1928. In November of that year, he entered the FBI as an agent and, three years later, was appointed special agent in charge of the New Orleans field office. Over the next eight years, he served as special agent in charge in the St. Louis, St. Paul, Chicago, and Washington, D.C., field offices.

In 1939, Ladd was appointed assistant director of the Technical Laboratory. Two years later, he was transferred to the Security Division (later, the Domestic Intelligence Division) as its assistant director, where he remained through World War II. During his career as head of FBI counterintelligence, he supervised the major World War II– and Cold War–related national security investigations including the cases of Alger Hiss and Julius and Ethel Rosenberg.

Ladd died July 11, 1960, in an auto accident in Sanford, Florida. At the time, Ladd had retired from the FBI and was running for Congress.

Lamphere, Robert   A cryptology and counterintelligence expert, Robert Lamphere was instrumental in identifying major Russian espionage agents, including Judith Coplon and Julius and Ethel Rosenberg.

Born in 1918 and raised in Idaho, Lamphere attended the University of Idaho in an accelerated law program, then transferred to the National Law School (George Washington University) while working for the U.S. Department of the Treasury. He graduated in 1941, and shortly thereafter joined the FBI.

Lamphere was first assigned to the Birmingham, Alabama, field office; seven months later, he was transferred to New York City, where he served from 1942 to 1947. Most of his cases in his first three years in New York involved Selective Service violations. By 1945, his work focused exclusively, as a member of the Espionage Squad, on counterintelligence. In 1947, Lamphere moved to Washington where he worked in developing evidence to ensure the conviction of alleged communist spy Gerhard Eisler. Returning to New York briefly after the conclusion of the trial, Lamphere was permanently transferred to FBIHQ, where he spent the rest of his Bureau career. The major cases on which he worked included the Judith Coplon and Rosenberg espionage cases.

Lamphere played a crucial role in American counterespionage history. In the postwar period, he worked closely with military cryptologists in the National Security Agency (and its predecessor agency, the Army Security Agency) to identify the Soviet intelligence operatives and their American recruits cited in cover names in Soviet consular messages that NSA had intercepted and deciphered. By comparing the deciphered information to FBI intelligence files, Lamphere was able to identify members of the Soviet espionage networks of the World War II and Cold War periods recruited by Soviet intelligence operatives among Americans and their allies. Code-named Venona, this project succeeded in breaking up several Soviet spy rings. The existence and success of the Venona project was publicized in 1995 when the National Security Agency released the decrypted Soviet messages.

Lamphere retired from the FBI in 1955 to accept a position with the Veterans Administration, where he worked on investigations, security, and internal auditing. When he resigned in 1961, he was deputy administrator, the second-highest position in the Veterans Administration. He then worked in the private sector. After retirement, Lamphere wrote *The FBI-KGB War: A Special Agent's Story*, published in 1986 and reissued with three new chapters in 1995. Lamphere has lectured extensively and has served as a discussant in television productions concerning espionage-related issues.

Lewis, Aubrey C.   One of the first two African Americans appointed special agent under Attorney General Robert F. Kennedy's directive to hire qualified minorities, Aubrey C. Lewis entered the FBI as a special agent on June 25, 1962 (see also *James W. Barrow*). The September 1962 *Ebony*

Magazine featured Lewis in an article about the FBI that also promoted Bureau efforts to recruit more minorities ("The Negro in the FBI," by Simeon Booker).

Lewis earned a bachelor of science degree from Notre Dame University in South Bend, Indiana, where he starred on the football team. Assigned to the Cincinnati and New York City field offices, Lewis also qualified as a firearms expert, a defensive tactics instructor, and a "Bureau speaker." He retired from the FBI on October 21, 1967. Shortly thereafter, he joined the Woolworth Company as a vice president.

Lopez, Julius M.   Apparently the first Hispanic to serve as a special agent in charge, Julius M. Lopez attained that position on November 20, 1943, when FBI Director Hoover appointed him to head the San Juan, Puerto Rico, field office. Prior to that promotion, Lopez had been acting special agent in charge since April 17, 1943, and had also served from April 22, 1942, as acting special agent in charge in the Indianapolis field office.

Lopez graduated from Loyola University in Chicago, Illinois, where he starred in football and baseball. He later returned to Loyola as a coach, and then went to the University of Chicago, where he coached All-American halfback Jay Berwanger, winner of the first Heisman Trophy. With famed Chicago coach Clark Shaughnessy, Lopez is credited with developing the "T" football formation.

Joining the FBI as an agent in 1936, he apparently became the first Hispanic "number-one man" (assistant special agent in charge) on October 23, 1941, when appointed to that position in the Memphis field office, where he served until promoted to special agent in charge of the San Juan, Puerto Rico, field office in November 1943. Before retiring in 1960, he also served as special agent in charge in the Jackson, New Orleans, Birmingham, Savannah, Memphis, and Chicago field offices.

After leaving the FBI, Lopez became director of public safety in Biloxi, Mississippi. He died July 14, 1996.

Mathis, Sylvia E.   The first black female agent, Sylvia E. Mathis entered the FBI on February 17, 1976. Born in Durham, North Carolina, she received a law degree in May 1975 and was admitted to the North Carolina bar two months later. Her first assignment was in the New York City field office.

McDermott, John J.   FBI Director Clarence M. Kelley named John J. McDermott acting assistant to the director–deputy associate director in charge of administrative operations in September 1976, and soon thereafter appointed him to the position. Prior to that, McDermott served as assistant director of the Administrative Services Division.

McDermott entered the FBI as an agent in September 1950 and began work in the Knoxville field office. In August 1951, he transferred to the Baltimore field office and in October 1952, he went to New York City. In July 1955, he was promoted as a supervisor in the FBIHQ Domestic Intelligence Division. In June 1960, he moved to the Training and Inspection Division.

In February 1961, McDermott was appointed assistant special agent in charge first of the Minneapolis and then the Washington, D.C., field office. Promoted to special agent in charge of the Alexandria field office in March 1969, he served there until October 1972, when he became special agent in charge of the Washington, D.C., field office. He moved back to FBIHQ in May 1974 as assistant director of the External Affairs Division, and in February 1975, he was designated assistant director of the Files and Communications Division. In May 1976, he became assistant director of the Administrative Services Division. McDermott retired on September 14, 1979, to practice law in Alexandria, Virginia.

McKenzie, James D. "As the chief of the academy for nine years, McKenzie had more impact on training in the modern Bureau than did anyone else," Ronald Kessler wrote in *The FBI—Inside the World's Most Powerful Law Enforcement Agency.* FBI Director William H. Webster named McKenzie assistant director of the Training Division in 1980.

Born in Frostburg, Maryland, and raised in Accident, Maryland, McKenzie received his juris doctor degree in 1965 from the University of Baltimore. He entered the FBI as an agent on July 14, 1960, first serving in the Boston field office and then at FBIHQ before being promoted to assistant special agent in charge first of the Kansas City and then the Miami field office. In July 1978, he was appointed deputy assistant director of the Training Division, from which he was promoted to assistant director. In 1986, he transferred to the Chicago field office as special agent in charge.

McKenzie retired from the FBI on June 29, 1990, to become director of security and safety for the Martin Marietta Corporation.

McWeeney, Sean M. In December 1986, FBI Director William H. Webster appointed Sean M. McWeeney the first inspector in charge of the newly created Office of Liaison and International Affairs at FBIHQ. Creation of this office signified the FBI's recognition of the new problems for law enforcement of criminal activities that cross international boundaries.

McWeeney was born October 10, 1938, and raised in Chicago, Illinois. After graduating from De Paul University in Chicago, he joined the United States Navy and was discharged with the rank of lieutenant in 1965. In June of that year, he received a master's degree in business administration from the University of Rhode Island.

On June 28, 1968, he entered the FBI as an agent, serving in the New Orleans, Oklahoma City, Boston, and New York City field offices before being transferred to the Special Investigative Division at FBIHQ as a supervisor. He worked in the Inspection Division from April 1975 to December 1975, returning to the Special Intelligence Division as a unit chief. In April 1976, McWeeney was promoted to assistant special agent in charge of the Portland, Oregon, field office. He returned to FBIHQ to serve as chief of the Organized Crime Section of the Criminal Investigative Division and in 1986 was promoted to special assistant to the executive assistant director, Investigations.

McWeeney retired from the FBI in 1988 and in 1996 held a position with an international security firm.

Means, Gaston B. Bureau of Investigation Director William Burns hired Gaston B. Means as a special agent on October 28, 1921. He was fired from the Bureau in 1924, and J. Edgar Hoover's publicists used Means's notoriety to exemplify the nonprofessionalism of agents before Hoover became director. A German agent during early years of World War I when the United States was neutral, Means was accused and acquitted of murdering a rich widow, Maude A. King, in 1917. Nonetheless, Burns hired Means, apparently considering his detective abilities more important than his questionable reputation. Because of public criticism of Means's appointment, Attorney General Harry Daugherty suspended him as an agent on February 9, 1922. Nevertheless, Burns continued Means on the payroll as an "informant." Shortly after his appointment as acting director of the FBI in May 1924, J. Edgar Hoover fired Means.

In 1932, Means hoodwinked wealthy Washington socialite Evalyn Walsh McLean into paying him $100,000, on the assurance that it would be used as ransom for the kidnapped Lindbergh baby. Means and an accomplice were convicted of conspiracy to commit larceny in this case. Means died on December 12, 1938, while serving his 15-year sentence.

Mehegan, Albert D.   Albert D. Mehegan served as a special agent from March 20, 1922, until April 30, 1975, retiring at the age of 88. His 53 years with the FBI constitutes the longest tenure of any special agent. Subsequent changes in the Bureau's retirement rules ensure that Mehegan will hold this record permanently.

Born May 2, 1886, and raised in Lafayette, Indiana, Mehegan attended Purdue University, where he starred in baseball and football. In 1909, Mehegan received a bachelor of science degree in mechanical engineering. After graduation, Mehegan taught high school mathematics, coached football, and held several positions in the railway industry that later proved invaluable during his FBI career. He spent World War I with the U.S. Shipping Board, becoming an independent sales engineer at the war's close.

After entering the FBI as an agent, Mehegan was assigned first to Hartford and then the Indianapolis, Detroit, Cleveland, and Cincinnati field offices before beginning his 43-year stay in the Chicago field office. His more notable activities included working undercover in West Virginia with the infamous Hatfield clan. While serving in Chicago, he participated in the investigations of gangsters John Dillinger and "Baby Face" Nelson. For most of his Chicago career, however, he investigated crimes involving theft from interstate shipment and served as the Bureau's Chicago liaison with all the major railroads. The Chicago Railway special agents and Police Association conferred an honorary life membership on Mehegan. He was also instrumental in forming the annual International Railroad Police Academy sponsored by the Association of American Railroads. In his later years, when age limited his investigatory responsibilities, Mehegan became a trusted adviser to less-experienced agents on collecting evidence and preparing court testimony. Mehegan died on January 31, 1983.

Miller, Edward Samuel   As assistant director in charge of the Domestic Intelligence Division in FBIHQ and deputy associate director–assistant to the director of the FBI, Edward S. Miller approved the surreptitious entries to install microphones targeting the families and friends of members of the domestic terrorist organization, the Weather Underground. Miller (along with W. Mark Felt) was convicted on November 6, 1980, of violating the constitutional rights of American citizens when approving these illegal measures. President Ronald Reagan, however, pardoned both FBI officials on March 26, 1981.

Born November 11, 1923, near Pittsburgh, Pennsylvania, Miller received a bachelor of arts degree from Grove City College, Grove City, Pennsylvania. He entered the FBI as an agent November 27, 1950, and served in the Los Angeles and San Francisco field offices. In March 1962, Miller was assigned to FBIHQ in the Administrative Division, where he remained until his appointments first to the Inspection Division in August 1963, and a year later, to the General Investigative Division. Promoted to assistant special agent in charge of the Mobile field office in February 1966, he remained there the rest of the year. He became assistant special agent in charge of the Honolulu field office at the end of 1966 and then in February 1969, of the Chicago field office.

Miller returned to FBIHQ in November 1969, as inspector and deputy assistant director (then called "number one man") in the Inspection Division. On September 9, 1971, he was appointed acting assistant director in charge of the Domestic Intelligence Division (receiving the full appointment in November 1971). He remained in that position until October 1973, when he was promoted to assistant to the director–deputy associate director, a position he held until his retirement in 1974.

Miller, Richard W.   In October 1984, Richard W. Miller became the first FBI agent to be arrested for espionage. At the time of his arrest, he was assigned to counterintelligence work in the Los Angeles field office. On June 26, 1985, prior to the start of his own trial on espionage charges, two Russian émigrés implicated with him, Nikolai Ogorodnikov and his wife, Svetlana, pled guilty to conspiracy to receive sensitive FBI information. Svetlana had requested and received from Miller materials that he knew were being given to the Soviets. Although his first trial ended in a hung jury, Miller was convicted on June 19, 1986, of conspiracy to commit espionage. This conviction, however, was overturned on appeal, April 25, 1989. Tried again, on October 9, 1990, he was once again found guilty in a non-jury trial. Miller was sentenced on February 4, 1991, to 20 years in prison. He was, however, released in 1994.

Mintz, John A.   Appointed the FBI's executive assistant director for Investigations by FBI Director William Webster, John A. Mintz became the FBI's legal counsel at the age of 38.

Shortly after graduating from the University of Chicago Law School in 1961, Mintz entered the FBI as an agent. He worked in the Tampa, New York City, Memphis, Jackson, and Washington, D.C., field offices before being assigned to the Office of Legal Counsel in FBIHQ. Upon the retirement of the Bureau's first legal counsel, Dwight Dalbey, Mintz was promoted to that position, although he did not receive the title of assistant director until 1974. In 1983, Attorney General William French Smith presented him with the John Marshall Award for Support of Litigation. Mintz retired in 1986 to practice law in a private firm in Washington, D.C.

Mireles, Edmundo, Jr.   The first recipient of the FBI's Medal of Valor, Edmundo Mireles Jr. (while severely wounded himself) managed to kill two suspected bank robbers. At the time, FBI agents were attempting to arrest the suspects who, armed with assault weapons, killed two agents, Jerry Dove and Benjamin Grogan, and wounded five others, including Mireles. Mireles's heroism also earned him the Police Officer of the Year Award offered jointly by *Parade* magazine and the International Association of Chiefs of Police. As a result of this incident, the FBI's firearms instruction for agents was changed and agents' weapons were upgraded.

Born in Alice, Texas, and raised in Beeville, Texas, Mireles earned a bachelor of science degree in business administration from the University of Maryland in January 1979. That same year, he entered the FBI, serving first in the Washington, D.C., field office prior to being assigned to the Miami field office in 1985. While recovering from his wounds, he served as an instructor at the FBI Academy in Quantico, Virginia, before returning to Miami. He later transferred to the Omaha field office.

Misko, Joanne E. Pierce   FBI Acting Director L. Patrick Gray named Joanne Misko, then known as Joanne E. Pierce, one of the first two female special agents since the 1920s (see also *Susan Lynn Roley*).

A native of Niagara Falls, New York, Misko received bachelor's and master's degrees in history from Medaille College in Buffalo, New York, and St. Bonaventure in Orleans, New York, respectively. She served 11 years as a Roman Catholic nun with the Sisters of Mercy in Buffalo, during which time she taught U.S. history and economics at Mount Mercy Academy in Buffalo and Madonna High School in Niagara Falls.

She entered the FBI on March 23, 1970, and worked as a researcher at the FBI Academy until appointed a special agent at age 31, on July 17, 1972. As one of her early assignments, she spent seven weeks in South Dakota at the Pine Ridge Indian Reservation. In the late 1970s, she became one of the first female supervisors at FBIHQ. Also assigned to the St. Louis and Washington, D.C., field offices, she spent most of her career in the Pittsburgh field office. To

finish her FBI career, Misko and her husband, Michael Misko, also a special agent, transferred to the Miami field office. Misko retired in September 1994 to work as a bank security official in Boca Raton, Florida.

Mohr, John Philip   From 1959 to July 1972, John P. Mohr held the number-three position in the FBI as assistant to the director for Administration.

Born April 20, 1910, in West New York, New Jersey, Mohr attended school in Kingston, New York, where he captained the football team. He continued playing football while attending American University in Washington, D.C., and later received academic honors while completing his bachelor of law degree from Columbus Law School (Catholic University) in Washington, D.C.

He entered the FBI as an agent October 2, 1939, and was sent to San Francisco for his first field office assignment. In February 1940, he was transferred to the Los Angeles field office, remaining there a year before being assigned as a supervisor in the Administrative Division at FBIHQ on February 22, 1941. In 1947, Mohr was appointed assistant to the FBI's associate director Clyde Tolson, being designated inspector in September of that year. He continued working for Tolson until June 1, 1954, when he was promoted to assistant director of the Administrative Division. He held that position until December 30, 1959, when he became the FBI's assistant to the director for Administration, the position he held until his retirement on July 17, 1972. Mohr died in Virginia, January 25, 1997.

Montgomery, Robin L.   FBI Director Louis J. Freeh appointed Robin L. Montgomery in March 1994 to be special agent in charge of the Crisis Management/Hostage Rescue Team at the FBI Academy in Quantico, Virginia. Consequently, Montgomery became the first special agent in charge of the Critical Incident Response Group, which consolidates all of the Bureau's units and functions that deal with crisis situations.

Montgomery was born July 9, 1945, in Augusta, Georgia. After attending college at the University of Maryland's Munich, Germany, campus, he received his bachelor of science degree in political science from Washington State University, Pullman, Washington, in 1968. He joined the U.S. Marine Corps shortly thereafter and was commissioned as an officer. He was wounded twice while serving in Vietnam and received the Navy Cross, the second-highest medal for valor.

After becoming a special agent in February 1971, Montgomery served in the Baltimore field office until transferring in July 1972 to the Omaha field office. While in that office, he helped investigate the occupation and resultant shoot-out that led to the murder of two special agents on June 26, 1975, at the Pine Ridge Indian Reservation near Wounded Knee, South Dakota. In April 1979, he moved to the Washington, D.C., field office, where, in 1980, he was promoted to supervisor. He joined the Inspection Division in November 1982 prior to an assignment as executive secretary of the FBIHQ Career Board.

In March 1988, Montgomery was appointed assistant special agent in charge of the Philadelphia field office, where he remained until becoming section chief of the Violent Crimes and Major Offenders Section, FBIHQ. On September 30, 1991, Montgomery became special agent in charge of the Portland field office, from which he was promoted to special agent in charge of the Critical Incident Response Group. While Montgomery was in Portland, the governor of Oregon named him to the Board of Public Safety Standards and Training.

Moore, Donald W. Donald W. Moore served as executive assistant director in charge of Law Enforcement Services from August 1979 until his retirement on January 11, 1980.

Born in Washington, D.C., on January 12, 1930, Moore received his early education in Washington, D.C., and Takoma Park, Maryland. In 1955, he received a bachelor of commercial science degree at Southeastern University, Washington, D.C.

Moore entered the FBI on March 14, 1949, as a clerk, and was appointed a special agent in July 1955. After working in the Chicago, Detroit, and Cincinnati field offices, Moore was transferred to FBIHQ in October 1961, where he held supervisory positions in the Special Investigative and Inspection Divisions. In January 1966, he was appointed assistant special agent in charge of the Dallas field office. Returning to FBIHQ in October 1969, he served in the Inspection Division. In August 1970, he was designated special agent in charge of the Richmond field office, and in July 1972, special agent in charge of the New Orleans field office. He was promoted to special agent in charge of the Washington, D.C., field office in May 1974. Moore was promoted to assistant director of the External Affairs Division in February 1975, serving in that position until February 1977, when he became assistant director of the Criminal Investigative Division, from which he received his executive assistant director appointment.

Moore, Roy K. Roy K. Moore served as the first special agent in charge of the Jackson, Mississippi, field office when it reopened in 1964. He handled the investigation of the murders of civil rights workers Michael Schwerner, James Lee Chaney, and Andrew Goodman in the infamous Mississippi Burning case, as well as numerous civil rights–related crimes of violence.

Born on June 11, 1914, in Hood River, Oregon, Moore received his early education in Harrisburg, Oregon. After serving in the U.S. Marine Corps, he joined the FBI in 1938, serving as chief clerk in the Richmond and Miami field offices. While stationed in Miami, he graduated with a bachelor of science degree in accounting from Southern University in that city.

Moore became an agent on October 7, 1940, and worked in the Albany field office from December 1940 until being reassigned in 1942 to the Pittsburgh field office, where he served as resident agent in Erie, Pennsylvania. Transferred to FBIHQ in 1945, he worked in the Security Division's Liaison Section before returning to Erie in 1948.

Moore was promoted to assistant special agent in charge of the Milwaukee field office in 1951, a position he also held in Chicago (1953) and Denver (1955). While in Denver, Moore participated in the FBI's first investigation of an airplane bombing in the United States, which resulted in the conviction and execution of Jack Gilbert Graham. In 1956, Moore became "number one man" (deputy assistant director) of the Identification Division in FBIHQ. He transferred to Charlotte, North Carolina, as special agent in charge in 1958, returning to FBIHQ in 1960 as "number one man" in the Training and Inspection Division. In 1962, he was appointed special agent in charge of the Little Rock, Arkansas, field office. From that position, Moore was detailed to Birmingham, Alabama, in November and December 1963, to investigate the church bombing that took the lives of four black girls.

On July 1, 1964, Hoover appointed Moore head of the reopened Jackson, Mississippi, field office. In addition to supervising the Jackson field office's investigations of the 250 acts of violence that occurred while Moore served as special agent in charge, Moore was assigned temporarily to head the special FBI squad in Philadelphia that worked to solve the break-in at the Media, Pennsylvania, resident agency and other crimes associated with left-wing activists. In September 1971, Moore was appointed special agent in charge of the Chicago field office and in 1972, he supervised a special squad in the Virgin Islands. At his request, he returned to Jackson as special agent in charge in 1973. During that year, he also assisted in the joint FBI–U.S. Marshals–Bureau of Indian Affairs operation to break the forcible occupation of radical Indian activists at the Pine Ridge Reservation near Wounded Knee, South Dakota, in response to President Richard Nixon's order. Having a well-deserved reputation as an able trouble-shooter, Moore once again was dispatched in 1974 to help solve the kidnapping of Reginald Murphy, the editor of the Atlanta, Georgia, *Constitution*.

Moore retired in December 1974 to accept a position as vice president and director of security for the Guaranty National Bank, a position he held until 1982.

Morris, Carolyn G.   The second non–special agent to become an assistant director, Carolyn G. Morris was also the second woman and third African American to hold that position. In addition, she is the first woman to be named deputy assistant director. At her appointment as deputy assistant director in 1984, she commanded the highest position of any woman in the FBI up to that time.

Exhibit 9.15   **Carolyn G. Morris,** *Courtesy of the FBI*

Morris was born in Jackson, North Carolina, and grew up in Gumberry in that state. She graduated *summa cum laude* from North Carolina Central University with a bachelor of science degree in mathematics in 1960, and, in 1963, received a master of arts degree from Harvard University, which she attended on a full National Science Foundation academic fellowship. She also completed postgraduate work in statistics at Virginia Polytechnic Institute (now Virginia Commonwealth University), and studied operations research at the University of Michigan and artificial intelligence at George Washington University.

Prior to joining the FBI, Morris served as a mathematician, systems analyst, and programmer with the Department of the Army; technical adviser to the Tri-Service Medical Information System program; director, Assistant Secretary of Defense; and chief of the Materiel Development Systems Division of the Management Information Systems Directorate in the Department of the Army's Materiel Development and Readiness Command. During her Army career, Morris

was the department's nominee for Federal Woman of the Year in 1972, and she received the 25th Annual Arthur S. Flemming Award in 1973. In 1972, she received the PACE Award for her excellence in mathematical modeling and resource allocation, the Department of the Army's highest award to a civilian holding a rank of GS-14 or lower. In 1992, she received the Presidential Meritorious Executive Award.

When appointed assistant director, William A. Bayse brought Morris into the FBI with him in 1980 to assist in the new Technical Services Division. She first served as chief of the Systems Development Section, where she designed, developed, implemented, and maintained advanced computer-based information systems to support all the Bureau's functional mission areas—Investigative, Administrative, and Law Enforcement. In addition, she directed the division's technology transfer operations in automatic data processing and telecommunications and supervised a staff that included over 100 computer scientists, mathematicians, systems analysts, and programmers. In November 1984, Morris was promoted to a deputy assistant director in the Technical Services Division, a position she held until October 1995, when she became assistant director of the Information Resources Division.

Mullaney, Patrick J.   With Howard Teton, Patrick J. Mullaney developed the FBI's criminal behavior profiling techniques made famous in the Thomas Harris book *The Silence of the Lambs* (and the movie of the same name); see also *John Douglas*.

Born on March 18, 1935, in New York City, he graduated in 1958 from Catholic University in Washington, D.C., with a bachelor's degree in American history. In 1965, he received a master's degree in counseling psychology from Manhattan College in New York City.

Mullaney entered the FBI as an agent on January 31, 1966, and was assigned to the Jacksonville, Los Angeles, and New York City field offices. In March 1972, he was appointed to the instructional staff of the FBI Academy in Quantico, Virginia. While serving at the academy, Mullaney helped develop hostage negotiation techniques and the use of hypnosis. He was responsible for instituting post-traumatic shooting counseling. Transferred to FBIHQ in 1977, he served on the Inspection staff before being assigned to the Terrorism Section of the Criminal Investigation Division.

In 1979, Mullaney was appointed assistant special agent in charge of the Baltimore field office and was later promoted to inspector. As an inspector, he attended the Executive Seminar of the Department of State, from 1981 to 1982. Upon his return to the Bureau, he served as an inspector in the Inspection Division, FBIHQ, until August 1984, when he became senior administrative assistant special agent in charge of the Los Angeles field office. Mullaney retired from the FBI in 1986.

After retirement from the FBI, Mullaney served as director of security for First Interstate Bank and then held the position of assistant director–executive protection with Occidental Petroleum. Since 1994, he has worked as an international security consultant. Active in the Society of Former Special Agents of the FBI, he served as its president in 1996–97.

Mullen, Francis M., Jr. (Bud) FBI Director William H. Webster appointed Francis M. (Bud) Mullen Jr. the first executive assistant director for Investigations in 1980. In that position, Mullen oversaw the Intelligence and Criminal Investigative Divisions. On November 10, 1983, he was appointed administrator of the Drug Enforcement Administration when DEA was placed under the FBI director.

Born in New London, Connecticut, Mullen graduated from Central Connecticut State College. He served in the U.S. Air Force and as a police officer in New London before applying for and being accepted as special agent in May 1962, with the Milwaukee field office his first assignment. From 1963 to 1969, he served in the Los Angeles field office until appointed a supervisor in the Administrative Services Division at FBIHQ. Transferred to the Planning and Inspection Division in April 1972, Mullen held that post until December 1972, when he was reassigned to the Administrative Services Division.

In June 1973, Mullen became assistant special agent in charge of the Denver field office, where he served until January 1975. Returning to FBIHQ, he worked as an inspector in the Planning and Inspection Division. He was appointed special agent in charge first of the Tampa field office in July 1975 and then, in November 1976, of the New Orleans field office. In October 1978, Mullen once again returned to FBIHQ, this time to serve as the inspector–deputy assistant director for organized crime and white collar crime matters in the Criminal Investigative Division. In August 1979, he was promoted to assistant director and then executive assistant director. In July 1981, Attorney General William F. Smith appointed him acting administrator and then administrator of the Drug Enforcement Administration.

Nathan, Harold (Pop) Named assistant director for Investigations on May 1, 1925, Harold "Pop" Nathan was the first person to hold that position. At the time, assistant director was the second-highest office in the Bureau.

Nathan was born in 1880 and raised in New York City. His father and grandfather were in the wholesale produce business. After graduating from the City College of New York with a bachelor of arts degree, Nathan worked for the Navy and Labor Departments before entering the Immigration Service of the Department of Justice.

He entered the FBI as an agent on March 31, 1917, and spent his early Bureau years in the Norfolk, Charleston, and Baltimore field offices. In 1921, he was promoted to special agent in charge of the Baltimore field office, followed by serving as special agent in charge of the Pittsburgh field office. Appointed assistant director in 1925, he held that post until 1941 when he was transferred to become special agent in charge of the San Diego field office. When the assistant director position became more specialized, Nathan served as assistant director of the Identification, Training, and Laboratory Divisions. In 1944, he was transferred to the Richmond field office as special agent in charge.

The following year, he retired from the Bureau to San Francisco. During his retirement years, Nathan often visited both the San Francisco field office and FBIHQ, where he was characterized as "the grand old man of the FBI." He died in San Francisco on July 9, 1963.

Ness, Eliot Well known through television and the movies, Eliot Ness headed a group of U.S. Treasury Department agents who became known popularly as the Untouchables. Their principal target was the mobster Al Capone and his gang. Neither Ness nor his colleagues were FBI agents, but since so many people believe he was, he is included in this biographical section in order to set the record straight.

The son of immigrant Norwegian parents, Peter and Emma Ness, who arrived in the United States in 1881, Ness was born in the early 1900s and raised in Chicago. In 1925, he received a degree from the University of Chicago, where he studied political science, commerce, and business administration.

After two years with a retail credit company, he joined the Treasury Department's Prohibition Bureau in 1929, where he developed a special team of investigators to work with the Secret Six, an organization of Chicago businessmen whose mission was to break the hold gangster Al Capone had on the city through public corruption and illegal distilling. The sobriquet "Untouchables" apparently had its origins in the Treasury agents' reputation for incorruptability, refusing bribes that sometimes equaled their government salaries. Ness received widespread media coverage when he used a reinforced truck to bulldoze Capone's breweries. Following a two-year investigation, Capone was finally convicted of income tax evasion, a crime that—like Prohibition violations—fell under the jurisdiction of the Department of the Treasury.

Transferred to the Alcohol Tax Unit in Cincinnati, Ohio, in the fall of 1934, Ness subsequently became chief investigator for that unit's Enforcement Branch, in Cleveland, Ohio.

Before the end of Prohibition, the Bureau of Prohibition was—during its final months—transferred from the jurisdiction of the Treasury Department to the Department of Justice (where it was incorporated with the Department of Justice Bureau of Investigation) to form the Division of Investigation. This period overlapped with Ness's service in the Prohibition Bureau and was the closest approximation Ness had to being an FBI agent.

After leaving the Treasury Department, Ness became safety director for the city of Cleveland, a position he held from 1935 to 1942, when he left to join the Federal Security Agency in Washington, D.C. In this position, Ness worked to curb prostitution near military bases. In September 1944, he resigned this position to return to Cleveland to become chairman of Diebold Corporation. Following an unsuccessful bid to become Cleveland's mayor in 1947, he returned to the business world. In 1956, he left Cleveland for Coudersport, Pennsylvania, where he worked for the Guaranty Paper and Fidelity Check Corporation.

Ness died May 16, 1957, after working on a rough draft of a book called *The Untouchables,* completed by Oscar Fraley.

Nichols, Louis Burrous   Assistant director of the Crime Records Division for many years, and assistant to the director of the FBI from October 1951 to 1957, Louis B. Nichols is the father of the FBI's public relations efforts and is considered by some to be "the most influential figure in the history of the Bureau" after J. Edgar Hoover.

Born on January 13, 1906, in Decatur, Illinois, and raised in Ohio and Michigan, Nichols graduated from Kalamazoo College, Kalamazoo, Michigan, and received a law degree from the George Washington University School of Law in 1934. During law school, Nichols worked as a public relations officer for the Young Men's Christian Association, the YMCA. He later traced his interest in becoming an FBI agent to a radio program that dramatized Bureau case histories.

Exhibit 9.16   **Louis Burrous Nichols,** *Courtesy of the National Archives (65-F)*

Nichols entered the FBI as an agent July 30, 1934, and was assigned to the Birmingham field office. In March 1935, he was assigned to the Research Section in FBIHQ, and later that year (November) was appointed chief of the Research (Crime Records) Section. Designated inspector in July 1938, he was named assistant to the FBI's associate director, Clyde Tolson, in August 1939. In May 1941, he became the assistant director of the Administrative Division, in which position he supervised the Crime Records Section. This section's name was later changed to the Files and Communications Division. As assistant director, Nichols served as FBI liaison to Congress and the media. He personally was responsible for developing the Bureau's policies regarding the press, radio, films, and eventually television. After 10 years heading the FBI's public affairs operations, Nichols was promoted in October 1951 to the position of assistant to the director.

Rretiring in 1957, he joined Schenley Industries, from which he retired as executive vice president in 1969. In 1965, Nichols convinced Schenley head Lewis S. Rosenstiel to donate $1 million to establish the J. Edgar Hoover Foundation. During his later years, Nichols maintained residences in Florida and Virginia. He died in Miami, Florida, in 1977.

Noisette, Samuel   Samuel Noisette was well known to all visitors to the offices of FBI Director J. Edgar Hoover, whom he escorted into and out of Hoover's office. Noisette entered the FBI April 27, 1927, as a messenger. Following assignments in the Identification and Laboratory Division and the Files Division, he began working in the director's office as a clerk. On March 28, 1954, Hoover named him information receptionist. Noisette achieved the title special agent on June 30, 1957, and that fall received three days of firearms training. He never actually functioned as a special

Exhibit 9.17 **Samuel Noisette** (*left*) **with J. Edgar Hoover,** *Courtesy of the National Archives*

agent conducting investigations, nor had his responsibilities changed, although Hoover often pointed out Noisette to visitors as "proof" that the FBI employed black special agents. (In fact, during Noisette's FBI tenure, a number of African American agents did conduct investigations in the field.) Outside of his FBI duties, Noisette was an artist and held exhibits every year. He retired January 19, 1968.

Otto, John   Attorney General Edwin Meese III named John Otto to serve as acting director of the FBI from May 26, 1987 (when William H. Webster became director of the Central Intelligence Agency) until November 2, 1987 (when William S. Sessions took the oath of office as FBI director).

Exhibit 9.18 **John Otto,** *Courtesy of the FBI*

Born December 18, 1938, and raised in St. Paul, Minnesota, Otto served two years in the U.S. Marine Corps after graduating from high school. After first attending the University of Minnesota, he transferred to St. Cloud State College, St. Cloud, Minnesota, where he received a bachelor of science degree in 1960 and then, from 1961 to 1964, he studied educational administration as a graduate student at the University of Minnesota. During his graduate student years, Otto served on the Ramsey County, Minnesota, sheriff's patrol, working for the Arden Hills, Minnesota, police force on his days off. He also taught social science and physical education in a St. Paul junior high school. In 1963, Otto joined the Oakland, California, police department as a member of the special duty tactical squad.

On October 12, 1964, Otto entered the FBI as an agent, serving in the Dallas and Newark field offices, as well as the Tyler, Texas, and Camden, New Jersey, resident agencies. He relocated in March 1971 to FBIHQ as a supervisor in the Public Affairs Office. From March 1972 to April 1973, Otto worked in the Technical Services Division, after which he transferred to the Planning and Inspection Division. In April 1974, he joined the Criminal Investigative Division where he remained until January 1975, when he was appointed assistant special agent in charge of the Portland field office.

Otto returned to FBIHQ in March 1976 as an inspector in the Planning and Inspections Division. He was appointed special agent in charge of the Minneapolis field office in February 1977 and then of the Chicago field office in February 1978. In August 1979, he was promoted to the position of assistant director of the Planning and Inspection Division, and in January 1981, to executive assistant director for Law Enforcement Services. After serving as acting director, Otto returned to head the Law Enforcement Services when FBI Director Sessions assumed his responsibilities. Otto was appointed associate deputy director for Administration on July 18, 1987.

On April 6, 1990, Sessions awarded Otto the first Medal of Meritorious Achievement, for "extraordinary and exceptional meritorious service in a duty of *extreme* challenge and *great* responsibility." In 1990, after retiring, Otto became a security representative for Delta Airlines in Atlanta, Georgia.

Papich, Sam J.   The son of a Montana copper miner, Sam J. Papich played football for Northwestern University before graduating with an engineering degree in 1936. He worked days at a Chicago insurance firm while attending law school in the evening and playing professional football on weekends.

After entering the FBI in 1941, one of his first assignments was to the Special Intelligence Service (SIS), the FBI's World War II counterintelligence unit. Papich initially worked with Dusko Popov, a controversial double agent who brought the German use of microdots to the Bureau's attention. Following U.S. involvement in World War II with the Japanese attack on Pearl Harbor, Papich was transferred to Latin America, where he worked undercover. After a brief return to the United States after the war to marry (the SIS also having been dissolved), Papich was appointed the FBI's legal attaché in Rio de Janeiro. He was transferred in 1947, at his request, to the San Francisco field office.

In 1952, FBI Director J. Edgar Hoover brought Papich back to FBIHQ to serve as liaison between the FBI and the Central Intelligence Agency (CIA), a position he held for the rest of his FBI career (see Exhibit 4.1). As the FBI's liaison, Papich handled the many controversies that periodically erupted between the two agencies. One of the better known of the 1960s involved their differences over the authenticity of two Soviet defectors: Anatoliy Golitsyn, who predicted the "defection" of a disinformation-carrying intelligence officer, and Yuri Nosenko, who, among other allegations, insisted that the Soviet KGB had no interest in Lee Harvey Oswald, accused assassin of President John F. Kennedy. While the FBI considered Golitsyn a disinformation source and Nosenko a genuine defector, the CIA and its controversial head of counterintelligence, James Jesus Angleton, took the opposite position. As liaison (and friend and neighbor of Angleton), Papich attempted to represent to his FBI superiors the views of the CIA on this and other issues. Relations between Hoover and the CIA had been precarious from the start, but by 1970 had deteriorated—as a result of the Thomas Riha affair—to the point that the FBI director eventually disbanded the FBI's CIA Liaison Office and severed all direct Bureau contact with the agency. Papich, who had spent 18 years attempting to reconcile differences between the two intelligence organizations, retired early in 1970.

Parsons, Mildred C.   Secretary to the assistant director in charge of the Washington, D.C., field office, Mildred C. Parsons served longer than any FBI employee in history. Moreover, she never used her sick leave during her 57-plus years with the FBI.

Parsons was born in Frederick, Maryland, where she graduated from high school. She entered the FBI on September 25, 1939, as a junior clerk-typist in FBIHQ until her transfer on January 24, 1940, to the Washington, D.C., field office. Promoted to stenographer on July 1, 1940, she subsequently became supervisor of the office's Information and Radio Room, squad secretary, and receptionist. She earned a further promotion on July 1, 1949, to secretary to the special agent in charge. She has been secretary to the Washington, D.C., field office's head ever since, having worked for 26 special agents in charge and three assistant directors in charge. (Since October 1993, the head of the Washington, D.C., field office changed from being a special

agent in charge to an assistant director in charge.) In April 1986, Parsons received the Attorney General's Award for Excellence.

Pasenelli, Burdena G. (Birdie)   FBI Director William S. Sessions appointed Burdena "Birdie" Pasenelli to special agent in charge of the Anchorage field office in February 1992, the first female special agent to hold that position.

Exhibit 9.19   **Burdena G. Pasenelli,** *Courtesy of the FBI*

Pasenelli was transferred to FBIHQ in October 1993 to head the Finance Division as the first female assistant director in the Bureau's history. In this position, she was responsible for the FBI's budget of over $2 billion.

Born in South Dakota and raised in Lundon, Washington, Pasenelli attended night school at Washington State University, working four years as a detective with the Seattle police department, and after seven years part-time study, received an accounting degree.

Pasenelli entered the FBI as an agent in 1973, serving first in the Sacramento field office, and later, the Kenosha, Wisconsin, resident agency, and from 1984 to 1987, in the Applicant Unit and Inspection Division in FBIHQ. On July 24, 1989, she was appointed assistant special agent in charge of the Houston field office and was the first woman to hold that position. She served in that position until December 1995, when she was transferred to be the special agent in charge of the Seattle field office.

Perez, Bernardo M.   Bernardo "Mat" Perez—at the time, one of the highest ranking Hispanics in the FBI—initiated a class-action civil rights lawsuit in the 1980s claiming that the FBI discriminated against special agents of Latino heritage. On September 26, 1988, U.S. District Court Judge Lucius D. Bunton agreed with the plaintiffs. The government did not appeal Bunton's ruling. As a result of the suit, the FBI changed its general promotion procedures and its methods of selecting translators.

Perez was born September 26, 1939, and raised in Lone Pine, California. He entered the FBI in 1960 as a messenger in FBIHQ. After graduating from Georgetown University with a degree in Spanish literature, he was appointed a special agent in September 1963 and was assigned first to the Tampa and then to the San Antonio field office. Sent to language school to study Portuguese, Perez was then assigned to the Washington, D.C., field office, where he served for three years before being transferred to the Miami field office. In January 1971, Perez became a supervisor in the Intelligence Division in FBIHQ. He served in Hermosillo, Sonora, Mexico, as a special assistant to the consul general from January 1972, returning to FBIHQ in September 1975 to serve in the Inspection Division. After a brief assignment with the Records Management Division, Perez was appointed a supervisor in the Los Angeles field office in March 1977.

Two years later, Perez was promoted to assistant special agent in charge in San Juan, Puerto Rico. He was elevated to senior assistant special agent in charge of the Los Angeles field office in May 1982, and was subsequently assigned to be assistant special agent in charge in the El Paso field office, a transfer which he viewed as a demotion. He inaugurated a formal complaint, which in time became a class-action discrimination suit on behalf of other Hispanic agents. Following Judge Bunton's ruling, on May 22, 1989, Perez was appointed inspector–deputy assistant director of the FBI Laboratory Division in FBIHQ, and on March 6, 1991, he was promoted to special agent in charge of the Albuquerque field office. He retired in 1994.

Perez, James R.   FBI Director William S. Sessions appointed James R. Perez to be chief of the newly elevated Office of Equal Employment Opportunity Affairs on March 13, 1989. In this capacity, Perez also held the title, "equal employment officer for the FBI." In June 1992, Sessions named him inspector in charge of the Equal Employment Opportunity Affairs office.

Born and raised in East Los Angeles, California, Perez received a degree in history and Spanish from California State University, Fullerton. Prior to his FBI appointment, Perez served for 12 years in the Office for Civil Rights, Department of Health and Human Services. He also held a position with the Community Relations Service, Department of Justice; co-hosted *Perspective,* a San Francisco television series concerning minority issues; directed the Mexican-American Legal Defense and Education Fund; and worked with the United Way of Los Angeles County and the Catholic Youth Organization of Los Angeles and Orange Counties. Perez retired from the FBI on August 12, 1997.

Pierce, Joanne E.   See *Joanne E. Pierce Misko.*

Pistone, Joseph D.   As "Donnie Brasco," Joseph D. Pistone was one of the most successful infiltrators of the Mafia in FBI history. His later testimony about his six years undercover resulted in over 200 indictments and over 100 convictions of organized crime figures. In 1997, a film depicting his exploits, *Donnie Brasco*, was released.

The grandson of Italian immigrants, Pistone was born in Pennsylvania and grew up in that state and in New Jersey. After graduating from college, he first taught social studies in middle school before joining the Office of Naval Intelligence in Philadelphia as a civilian agent.

Entering the FBI as an agent on July 7, 1969, he was assigned to the Jacksonville field office for a year and a half before a transfer to the Alexandria field office. During his Alexandria assignment, Pistone took courses at the FBI Academy in Quantico, Virginia, in gambling investigations and in undercover work and received Special Weapons and Tactics (SWAT) training. In 1974, he transferred to the New York City field office and was soon assigned to undercover work. His major undercover operation targeting organized crime families lasted from 1976 to January 1981. He then went public, testifying in some of the Bureau's best known crime cases. On January 17, 1983, Pistone received the Attorney General's Distinguished Service Award. He resigned from the FBI in 1986.

In 1988, Pistone published *Donnie Brasco: My Undercover Life in the Mafia.* Although he and his family are not in the Justice Department's Witness Protection Program, they have resumed life in a different geographic region of the country and use another family name.

Potts, Larry   FBI Director Louis J. Freeh named Larry Potts as deputy director of the FBI on May 2, 1995. From February 1995 until this appointment, he served as acting deputy director. In 1992, as assistant director of the Criminal Investigative Division, Potts was responsible for the FBIHQ supervision of the FBI agents involved in a siege at the home of Randall Weaver, an antigovernment fugitive in Ruby Ridge, Idaho, in which an FBI sharpshooter killed Weaver's wife. After congressional hearings in 1995 and an internal Justice Department review of the matter, FBI Director Freeh temporarily removed Potts from the deputy director position. Following an intensive two-year inquiry, in August 1997 the Justice Department decided not to bring criminal charges against Potts, having uncovered no incriminating evidence of criminal conduct. Potts, however, was not reinstated as deputy director.

After entering the FBI as an agent May 6, 1974, Potts began his investigative career in Pittsburgh, then was promoted to supervisor in the Denver field office. Potts was appointed assistant special agent in charge of the Boston field office before returning to FBIHQ as a supervisor in the Criminal Investigative Division. In 1990, he was designated inspector in charge of the multiagency task force that concluded a complex investigation (code-named VANPAC) of related mail bomb assassinations in Alabama and Georgia. He returned to FBIHQ to head the Criminal Investigative Division in 1991 until his promotion and suspension as deputy director.

Purvis, Melvin H., Jr.   One of the best known G-men of the mid-1930s, Melvin H. Purvis Jr. claimed responsibility for leading the ambush that resulted in the death of gangster John Dillinger. Purvis was soon forced to resign from the FBI following his refusal to cease his high-profile public activities. Forever after, FBI Director Hoover considered Purvis *persona non grata* and even tried to erase his presence from FBI history.

Born in Timmonsville, South Carolina, on October 24, 1903, to Melvin Horace and Janie Mims Purvis, he graduated from the University of South Carolina in 1925. For two years following graduation, he was an associate in a South Carolina law firm.

Purvis entered the FBI as an agent February 4, 1927. Within five years, he was appointed special agent in charge of the Chicago field office. In that position, he headed the Chicago field office's investigation of the John Dillinger gang. Purvis led one of the two teams that engineered the disastrous raid on the Little Bohemia resort in Rhinelander, Wisconsin, where Dillinger and his cohorts were staying. Forewarned by barking dogs, the gangsters escaped, and in the shoot-out, Bureau agent W. Carter Baum was killed. This fiasco heightened pressure to apprehend Dillinger and, in response, Purvis worked with FBI Inspector Samuel Cowley, whom Hoover had dispatched to Chicago to coordinate the Dillinger operation, and with the police in

Exhibit 9.20   Melvin H. Purvis Jr.,
Courtesy of the FBI

East Chicago, Illinois, to prepare the trap that preceded the slaying of Dillinger outside Chicago's Biograph Theatre on July 22, 1934. Next, Purvis took charge of the successful hunt for gangster Charles "Pretty Boy" Floyd, and personally claimed the credit for killing this Public Enemy Number One.

Hoover had, in the aftermath of the successful trap, signed a note effusively praising Purvis's work in the Dillinger case. The FBI director soon regretted having singled him out, as the press immediately made a hero of Purvis, overshadowing both Hoover's and the Bureau's role. In retaliation, Hoover sent a team of inspectors to review the operations of the Chicago office. The inspection team gave the office and Special Agent in Charge Purvis poor ratings, and Purvis was harassed in other ways until he resigned, August 5, 1935. Hoover then tried to minimize—if not obliterate—Purvis's role in the Dillinger case, promoting Inspector Samuel Cowley—killed in service only a few months after Dillinger's death—as the true hero.

Purvis moved to San Francisco, California, where he joined the Bar and opened a law office. But he did not confine his activities to the practice of law. His picture was used to promote products ranging from automobiles to razor blades. Children identified him with a campaign promoted by the cereal Post Toasties, in which its boxtops could be exchanged for "Junior G-Man" badges, whistles, and toy pistols (see Exhibit 8.6). In 1936, his autobiography, *American Agent,* was published. Then, in 1938, Purvis returned to South Carolina from which he was called into the Army Reserve in 1941 to work in military intelligence during the African and Italian campaigns. He later spent a year as deputy director of the War Crimes Office of the War Department. Discharged from the Army in 1946, he resumed his law practice in Florence, South Carolina, where he also owned radio station WOL and helped organize and operate television station WBTW. During the 1950s, Purvis was twice called to Washington to advise congressional committees. However, Hoover sent unfavorable reports whenever the government tried to offer him a permanent position.

On February 29, 1960, Purvis died in his home from a gunshot wound. Although the Florence County (South Carolina) coroner's report lists the cause of death as unknown, it was thought by many that his death was a suicide, supposedly committed with the same gun he used to kill John Dillinger.

Reed, Charles   See *Michelle Gardner.*

Revell, Oliver B. (Buck) An internationally recognized expert on terrorism and on antinarcotics policies, Oliver B. "Buck" Revell was named the first associate deputy director, Investigations, and served on several interdepartmental advisory bodies concerning counterterrorism.

Exhibit 9.21 **Oliver B. Revell,** *Courtesy of the FBI*

Revell was born December 14, 1938, in Muskogee, Oklahoma, and attended the University of Georgia and East Tennessee State University, from which he received his bachelor of science degree in June 1960. From June 1960 to November 1964, Revell served in the U.S. Marine Corps as an aviator, leaving active duty with the rank of captain. He earned a master's degree from Temple University, in Philadelphia, in 1971; took advanced courses at the FBI Academy in Quantico, Virginia; and studied at the Kennedy School of Government, Harvard University.

On November 16, 1964, Revell entered the FBI as an agent, serving in the Kansas City, Philadelphia, and Tampa field offices before being assigned to the Organized Crime Section of the Criminal Investigative Division at FBIHQ. Revell also served in FBIHQ's Inspection Division and in the Office of Planning and Evaluation.

Revell was promoted in January 1975 to assistant special agent in charge of the Chicago field office. Named an inspector in October 1976, he was transferred to FBIHQ as executive assistant to Associate Director Richard Held. Appointed special agent in charge of the Oklahoma City field office in November 1977, he returned to FBIHQ in August 1979 as deputy assistant director, Criminal Investigative Division, and in June 1980, was promoted to assistant director, Criminal Investigative Division. Revell was transferred in January 1981 to the Administrative Services Division. After heading that division for 14 months, he returned in May 1982 to the Criminal Investigative Division until his appointment as executive assistant director, Investigations, in the mid-1980s, a position he held until July 1989 when FBI Director William S. Sessions reorganized his senior management and Revell became associate deputy

director, Investigations. As associate deputy director, he also handled administration and policy oversight of the training and laboratory functions.

Appointed to the President's Council on Integrity and Efficiency, Revell chaired its Committee on Integrity and Law Enforcement. He also served on the National Security Council's Terrorist Crisis Management Committee, the Attorney General's Economic Crime Council, and the National Foreign Intelligence Board. In addition, he was vice chairman of the Advisory Group/Counterintelligence, and a member of the White House Oversight Working Group on Narcotics and of the Senior Review Group of the Vice President's Task Force on Terrorism.

In 1989, President George Bush awarded Revell the Presidential Rank Award of Distinguished Senior Executive, and the following year, the President's Meritorious Senior Executive Award. FBI Director Sessions awarded him the FBI Medal for Meritorious Achievement in May 1991, and the following month, William H. Webster, as director of the Central Intelligence Agency, awarded Revell the National Intelligence Distinguished Service Medal.

Revell completed his FBI career as special agent in charge of the Dallas field office. He retired in 1994 to head the Revell Group, a global business and security consulting firm. He often has appeared on television news programs as an expert on terrorism.

Roley, Susan Lynn L. Patrick Gray, while acting director of the FBI, named Susan Lynn Roley, a Marine Corps veteran, one of the first two female special agents employed by the FBI since the 1920s (see also *Joanne E. Pierce Misko*).

Born May 13, 1947, in Long Beach, California, Roley attended the University of Maryland, College Park, for a year before completing her studies as a history major at California State College, Fullerton, in 1968. On June 25, 1969, she became a second lieutenant in the U.S. Marine Corps. At the time of her discharge, July 14, 1972, she was a first lieutenant.

She entered the FBI as an agent on July 17, 1972. Her work included reactive assignments such as kidnappings and bank robberies. Roley left the FBI in 1979 to join the Defense Investigative Service, a private firm in Washington, D.C.

Rosen, Alex For over 30 years, Alex Rosen headed the General Investigative Division or its predecessors in FBIHQ.

Born September 14, 1905, in New York City and raised in Cleveland, Ohio, Rosen attended Ohio State University in Columbus, where he received his bachelor's degree, and Columbia University Law School, eventually receiving his LL.B. degree from Cleveland Law School in 1930. He worked as a law clerk while attending school and practiced law for three years after being admitted to the Ohio Bar in 1930.

Rosen entered the FBI as an agent on October 16, 1933, and served in the New York City field office from November 1933 to May 1934, and in the Buffalo field office from May to June 1934, after which he transferred to the Criminal Investigative Division at FBIHQ. Two months later, Rosen was sent to the New Orleans field office, where he remained until July 1935. Returning to Washington, he worked in the Criminal Investigative Division until February 1938, except for eight months between June 1936 and February 1937, when he was assigned to the Washington, D.C., field office.

In February 1938, Rosen was appointed assistant special agent in charge of the Cleveland field office and the following year was promoted to special agent in charge of that office. Four months later, on June 17, 1939, Rosen returned to FBIHQ as inspector in the Investigative Division. He was promoted to acting assistant director, Investigative Division, on November 12, 1940, and assistant director of the Investigative and Accounting Division on February 13, 1942, where he remained until a reorganization in February 1961. He then became assistant director of the General Investigative Division, a position he held for 10 more years until his appointment in October 1971 as assistant to the director for Investigations. He retired on June 6, 1972.

Ruckelshaus, William D.   President Richard M. Nixon appointed William D. Ruckelshaus acting director of the FBI on April 27, 1973, following the resignation of Acting Director L. Patrick Gray III. The president never intended for Ruckelshaus to become FBI director; instead, he wanted someone who would be loyal to him (as opposed to a career FBI official) to oversee the Bureau until the Senate confirmed a new FBI director.

Born July 24, 1932, Ruckelshaus attended Princeton as an undergraduate, then the Harvard University Law School. He also served two years in the Army. Elected to the Indiana State Legislature in 1966, he became House majority leader. Two years later, at age 36, he ran unsuccessfully for the Senate. President Nixon then named him assistant attorney general for the Civil Division of the Department of Justice.

Exhibit 9.22   **William D. Ruckelshaus,** *Courtesy of the FBI*

In 1970, he became the first administrator of the Environmental Protection Agency, from which post he was tapped to become acting director of the FBI.

When Clarence M. Kelley was confirmed by the Senate as FBI director, Ruckelshaus left to become deputy attorney general, a position that involved continuing contact with the Bureau. He resigned from this post during the "Saturday Night Massacre" of October 20, 1973, rather than follow President Nixon's order to fire Special Prosecutor Archibald Cox, who was demanding access to the White House audiotapes that recorded the president's conversations in the Oval Office with his top staffers concerning the Watergate break-in and cover-up. Ruckelshaus then established a private law practice in Washington, D.C.

Sessions, William Steele   President Ronald Reagan named federal district judge William S. Sessions as director of the FBI on July 24, 1987. On September 25, 1987, the Senate confirmed him with a 90–0 vote, and he took the oath of office on November 2, 1987.

Born May 27, 1930, in Fort Smith, Arkansas, Sessions completed his early schooling in Kansas City, Missouri. He entered the U.S. Air Force in 1951, and after being commissioned in 1952, served as an airborne radar intercept instructor until his discharge in October 1955. Graduating from Baylor Law School, Waco, Texas, in November 1958, Sessions was admitted to the Texas Bar the following year and began private practice in Waco. He became section chief of the Government Operations Section of the Justice Department's Criminal Division in September 1969, where he served until August 1971, when he became U.S. attorney for the western district of Texas. Nominated by President Gerald Ford to be district judge for the western district of Texas in 1974, Sessions served in El Paso until December 1979, when he was brought to San Antonio to replace District Judge John H. Wood, who had been assassinated. Sessions became chief judge for the western district of Texas in February 1980, a position he held until his appointment as FBI director.

As FBI director, Sessions reorganized the Bureau's senior staff, creating a new post, deputy director, with responsibility for day-to-day operations and assisted by two associate deputy directors. Sessions also implemented the instructions of the federal court that found that the Bureau had discriminated against its Hispanic special agents, and averted a similar lawsuit from black special agents by instituting personnel and policy changes. With the end of the Cold War and the breakup of the Soviet Union in the late 1980s and early 1990s, Sessions redeployed agents formerly engaged in counterintelligence work to handle violent and white collar crimes.

Exhibit 9.23   **William Steele Sessions,** *Courtesy of the FBI*

During his tenure as FBI director, Sessions was criticized within the FBI for violations by his wife, Alice, and his assistant, Sarah Munford, of Bureau regulations and federal and state laws. Among these violations were minor breaches of security by Alice Sessions, the use of federal funds and federal property to construct a fence around the Sessionses' Washington residence, and use of federal funds for personal trips. An investigation conducted by the Justice Department's Office of Professional Responsibility confirmed the alleged violations. Although no criminal charges were brought against Munford or the Sessionses, President Bill Clinton fired Sessions on July 19, 1993, when he refused to resign.

Shanahan, Edwin C.   Edwin C. Shanahan, the first Bureau agent to die in the line of duty, was killed on October 11, 1925, when fugitive car thief Martin James Durkin shot him in the chest.

Born in Chicago, Illinois, in 1898, Shanahan attended high school and then served in the U.S. Army during World War I. He entered the Bureau of Investigation as a special agent in February 1920 and worked his entire career in the Chicago field office.

After shooting Shanahan, Durkin was apprehended by Bureau agents in St. Louis, Missouri, on January 20, 1926. He was subsequently convicted on federal car theft charges, for which he received 15 years in prison. He was also tried

by the state of Illinois on murder charges (of Shanahan), was convicted, and received 35 years. Serving the sentences consecutively, with time off for good behavior, he was imprisoned a total of 28 years.

Shanahan's son Dennis became an FBI agent on August 16, 1948, and retired in 1976.

Shapiro, Howard   In 1995, FBI Director Louis J. Freeh appointed Howard Shapiro, then aged 33, as the FBI's general counsel, the first individual to hold that position, and the first non-agent to serve as the director's principal legal adviser. With Shapiro's appointment, the Bureau—for the first time—had an individual with extensive litigation experience in its top legal position.

Born in Boston, Massachusetts, Shapiro graduated magna cum laude from Williams College, Williamstown, Massachusetts, in 1982, with a degree in political science and economics. He received his J.D. degree from Yale Law School in 1985. After graduation, he clerked for Judge Pierre N. Leval of the U.S. District Court for the southern district of New York.

Prior to his FBI appointment, Shapiro served as an assistant U.S. attorney in the southern district of New York from 1987 to 1992, during which he investigated and prosecuted financial crimes, narcotics, and organized crimes cases. Shapiro assisted Freeh, then a federal attorney, in the successful prosecution of the man charged with murdering a federal judge in Alabama and a civil rights attorney in Georgia (the VANPAC case). Immediately prior to his Bureau appointment, Shapiro taught criminal law and evidence as an associate professor at the Cornell University Law School, Ithaca, New York. He resigned June 6, 1997.

Skillman, Dorothy S.   From 1938 until 1973, Dorothy S. Skillman served as secretary and administrative assistant to FBI Associate Director Clyde Tolson.

Skillman entered the Bureau on July 27, 1926, as a stenographer. After three months, she was promoted to serve as secretary to Harold Nathan, the Bureau's only assistant director at that time, a position she held until her resignation in May 1934, when she resigned because of Depression-era regulations forbidding married couples to both work for the federal government. She returned to the Bureau six months later as secretary to John Keith, special agent in charge of the Washington, D.C., field office. Her husband's position forced her to resign once again in December 1935. Returning again in December 1937, she became a stenographer for assistant director of the Crime Records Division, Louis B. Nichols, and shortly thereafter was promoted to become his secretary. Approximately six months later, Skillman became secretary to Associate Director Tolson, and her title eventually was changed to administrative assistant. After Tolson retired in May 1972, Skillman remained with the Bureau long enough to supervise the closing of Tolson's office.

Slifco, Julianne   A German-language and foreign counterintelligence specialist, Julianne Slifco became the first female legal attaché (legat) (see also *Helen Bachor*). "Legats" are Bureau agents who handle liaison with foreign law enforcement and intelligence agencies. FBI Director Louis J. Freeh appointed her as legat in Vienna, Austria, in July 1995. Previously, she served as one of the first women appointed as assistant legal attaché, also in Vienna, having been appointed to that position by FBI Director William S. Sessions.

Born November 13, 1950, in Detroit, Michigan, Slifco graduated in 1972 from Oakland University, Michigan, with a bachelor's degree in secondary education, concentrating in English and German. She received a master's degree in German from the University of Michigan in 1975. In addition, she studied German in Germany and Austria at the Lerch Language School, the Goethe Institute (where she held a Fulbright Fellowship), the University of Heidelberg, the Inlinqua School of Language, and the Diplomatic Language Service. Slifco also taught high school English and German for eight years.

On July 27, 1980, Slifco entered the FBI as an agent and was assigned to the Detroit field office. In both Detroit and her next assignment in Jacksonville, Florida, she specialized in white collar crime matters. She began her foreign counterintelligence specialty in the Washington, D.C., field office, where she was assigned in October 1983. In January 1990, she was appointed a supervisory special agent in the Intelligence Division in FBIHQ, where she worked on the John Walker and Jonathan Pollard espionage cases, among others. She was temporarily assigned to Germany in connection with the bombing of Pan Am Flight 103 over Lockerbie, Scotland, in 1988. Before her appointment to Vienna, Slifco also worked in the Bonn legal attaché office.

Sorola, Manuel   Perhaps the first Bureau agent of Hispanic ethnicity, Manuel Sorola entered the Bureau of Investigation on April 27, 1916, as a special employee. He became a special agent on July 1, 1922.

Born December 4, 1880, near San Antonio, Texas, he received his education in public schools and the Alamo Business College, San Antonio. Before joining the Bureau of Investigation, he worked as a bookkeeper, an insurance agent, and an investigator for several southwestern railroads.

Sorola was hired initially because of his fluency in Spanish and his knowledge of Mexican politics. At that time, various Mexican political factions were using the United States as a base for such illegal activities as gun smuggling and other violations of U.S neutrality laws. During his Bureau career, Sorola served in field offices in San Antonio, El Paso, Oklahoma City, New Orleans, Phoenix, and Los Angeles. Placed on limited duty in 1938, he continued to serve in the Los Angeles field office as liaison to local law enforcement agencies until his retirement on January 31, 1949. He died November 19, 1957.

Sullivan, Joseph   FBI Director J. Edgar Hoover dispatched Inspector Joseph Sullivan wherever a special problem existed. For example, in 1964, Sullivan traveled to Mississippi to lead the FBI investigation into the disappearance of three civil right workers, Goodman, Schwerner, and Chaney. Sullivan reportedly was as the model for Inspector Erskine, the fictional FBI agent played by Efrem Zimbalist Jr. on the *FBI* television series of the 1960s.

Sullivan, William Cornelius   One of the most colorful and influential Bureau executives, William C. Sullivan rose to be the number-three person in the FBI. Many Bureau insiders and Washingtonians considered him the logical successor to FBI Director J. Edgar Hoover. Instead, on October 1, 1971,

Hoover fired him for insubordination and suspected disloyalty and changed the locks to Sullivan's office (which a surprised Sullivan confronted when returning to work after a temporary leave). To this day, Sullivan remains the FBI's most controversial official next to Hoover. In part, this controversy resulted from Sullivan's counterintelligence activities, particularly his development and supervision of the FBI's counterintelligence program (COINTELPRO), having the stated purpose to harass, discredit, and undermine radical groups considered by the

Exhibit 9.24   William Cornelius Sullivan, *Courtesy of the National Archives (65-CC)*

FBI to be threats to national security. Second, Sullivan was the source of many of the allegations that were publicized in the mid-1970s that put either Hoover or the Bureau in a negative light. While some of Sullivan's claims were substantiated by congressional investigations and released FBI records, others cannot be verified and some are demonstrably incorrect.

Sullivan was born May 12, 1912, and was raised in Bolton, Massachusetts, where his parents were farmers. After receiving a bachelor's degree in history from American University in Washington, D.C., he taught English in Bolton before enrolling in graduate school in Boston. During his Boston years, he joined the Internal Revenue Service.

On August 4, 1941, Sullivan entered the FBI as an agent and was assigned to the Milwaukee field office, a position he held when the United States entered World War II in December 1941. Owing to its large German population, as well as its active group of communists, Milwaukee presented an excellent opportunity for Sullivan to immerse himself in counterintelligence work. He was transferred to El Paso on January 11, 1942, and shortly thereafter to the Albuquerque resident agency, where he assisted the one other agent in a territory that covered the entire state. In less than a year, Sullivan was assigned to the Philadelphia field office and then to the Baltimore field office, where he remained from August 1942 to May 1943. He then joined the San Antonio field office, where he worked until June 1944. At that time, he transferred to the Domestic Intelligence Division in FBIHQ and supervised various intelligence operations, first in Mexico and Central America at the close of World War II and then as the Bureau began to focus on communist activities in the early Cold War years.

Assigned to the Phoenix field office in August 1953, Sullivan returned to FBIHQ's Domestic Intelligence Division in June 1954. The next month, he was promoted to inspector and then to chief inspector in June 1960. He worked briefly in the Research Section of Crime Records, where he was the principal ghostwriter for *A Study of Communism*, published in 1962 by Holt, Rinehart, and Winston with J. Edgar Hoover named as author. In June 1961, Sullivan was promoted to assistant director of the Domestic Intelligence Division.

In this position, Sullivan directed the intelligence side of the Kennedy assassination investigation for the FBI, as well as supervising the FBI's wiretaps of associates of Martin Luther King Jr. who were suspected of being communists, and eventually King himself. In an effort to

topple King as leader of the black civil rights movement, the FBI authored a threatening anonymous letter to him that accompanied compromising audiotapes made through bugs hidden in his hotel rooms—often interpreted as an effort to induce the civil rights activist to commit suicide. Sullivan has been identified as having approved the letter—if not authoring it—though Sullivan denied any knowledge of the note.

In response to a request from President Nixon's National Security Adviser Henry Kissinger in 1969, Sullivan supervised and maintained in his office the records of the FBI wiretaps of the National Security Council and White House staff members suspected of being involved in leaking sensitive information to the press and of the four reporters (whose phones were also tapped). Sullivan also traveled to Paris and personally oversaw the wiretapping of the residence of columnist Joseph Kraft. "I considered the wiretaps important, legal, and justified," Sullivan later insisted. When their existence was publicly revealed, the so-called National Security Council wiretaps and the Kraft surveillance wiretaps figured prominently first in the Watergate controversy of 1973–74 and then in the so-called Church and Pike Committee inquiries of 1975–76.

In June 1970, FBI Director Hoover promoted Sullivan to the number-three position in the FBI, during a period of social unrest in the United States and when radical extremists in the antiwar and New Left movements were actively planning to threaten lives and property. By that time, Sullivan had become convinced that Hoover's policies subverted an effective FBI campaign against terrorism. In reaction to restrictions that the FBI director had imposed on the FBI in 1965–66 governing electronic surveillance, surreptitious entries, mail opening, and the recruitment of informants (raising the minimum age from 18 to 21), Sullivan, in effect, "god-fathered" the Huston Plan. Under this proposal, which ensured presidential deniability, the FBI, CIA, and NSA would have been authorized to use clearly illegal investigatory techniques. When White House counsel John Dean provided a copy of this plan to the Senate committee investigating the Watergate affair, it precipitated a public debate over presidential use and abuse of the intelligence agencies. At that time, this was not known, and in 1971—after consultation with several FBI executives and other special agents—Sullivan began to criticize the FBI director publicly, hoping to encourage his firing or resignation. Instead, Hoover fired Sullivan.

"In a tidy, neat, Hooverian world, Sullivan maintained a chaotic office and profile. Accordingly, he was tagged Crazy Billy by some," FBI Director Clarence M. Kelley wrote. In Sullivan's book, *The Bureau* (completed by Bill Brown and published posthumously), in later (1975) testimony before congressional committees, and in many interviews (both in 1971 and 1975), Sullivan presented himself as a dedicated agent and depicted the FBI under Hoover as an agency run amuck, portraying the FBI director as an autocratic racist. While some of Sullivan's criticism was apt, many of his allegations have been contradicted either by other knowledgeable agents or released FBI records. (One example is Sullivan's erroneous insistence that until Attorney General Robert F. Kennedy forced the issue, the only black agents employed by the FBI had been Hoover's chauffeurs and office staff—in fact, black agents had been employed since the 1910s.)

In 1972, less than a year after Sullivan left the Bureau, Attorney General Richard Kleindienst appointed him director of the newly created Office of National Narcotics Intelligence in the Department of Justice.

Sullivan retired from this position in June 1973 to a farm in Sugar Hill, New Hampshire. He died of a gunshot wound on November 9, 1977, the victim of a hunting accident.

Tamm, Edward A.   As one of two assistants to the director, Edward A. Tamm was a top FBI official from 1940 until he resigned in 1948 to become a federal judge.

Born on April 4, 1906, in St. Paul, Minnesota, Tamm studied accounting at Mount Saint Charles College in Helena, Montana, and at the University of Montana. Two years after arriving in Washington, D.C., in 1930, he graduated from Georgetown University Law School. His law and accounting background, combined with a high entrance examination score, helped secure an appointment as an FBI agent later that year, even though he was under the minimum age for agents at that time. In addition, Tamm served in the Navy reserve, where he attained the rank of lieutenant commander.

Tamm was soon promoted to special agent in charge in Pittsburgh, replacing Samuel P. Cowley as assistant to assistant director for Investigations Harold Nathan, and in 1934, to assistant director, a position he held until 1940, when he became assistant to the director. He also served as a special adviser to the United States delegation to the United Nations Conference on International Organizations.

In 1948, Tamm resigned from the FBI to become a federal district judge in Washington, D.C. President Lyndon B. Johnson elevated him in 1965 to the U.S. Circuit Court of Appeals. While on the court, Tamm recused himself from cases involving the FBI.

Tamm died on September 22, 1985. His brother, Quinn Tamm, who survived him, also had a notable career within the FBI and afterward.

Tamm, Quinn   In 1938, at age 28, Quinn Tamm became the youngest agent to be appointed inspector by FBI Director Hoover.

Born in Seattle, Tamm graduated from the University of Virginia. He entered the FBI as an agent in 1934 and headed the Identification Division for 17 years before becoming assistant director of the combined Training and Inspection Division. Resigning from the Bureau in 1961—at the time, the head of the FBI Laboratory—he became executive director of the International Association of Chiefs of Police (IACP). Under Tamm, the IACP assumed some law enforcement training responsibilities and characterized itself as the voice of the nation's police. Hoover interpreted the IACP developments under Tamm as threats to the FBI and maintained a feud with him thereafter. Tamm died on January 23, 1986.

Teton, Howard   With Patrick Mullaney, Howard Teton was responsible for bringing criminal behavior profiling to the FBI. The breakthrough that Mullaney personally developed involved using crime-scene evidence to establish the criminal's behavior and motive.

After service in the U.S. Marine Corps, the Orange County (California) Sheriff's Department, and the San Leandro (California) Police Department, Teton entered the FBI as an agent in 1962. In 1969, he began teaching applied criminology in the FBI Academy (later renamed Applied Criminal Psychology). He consulted Dr. James Brussel, who had earlier developed the profile that helped identify New York's "mad bomber" in 1957. He spent most of his FBI career in the Behavioral Science Unit (now the Profiling and Behavioral Assessment Unit), located at the FBI Academy in Quantico, Virginia. Teton retired in 1986.

Tokunaga, Don S.   The first Asian American to hold the positions of assistant special agent in charge and special agent in charge, Don S. Tokunaga had a 20-year career with the FBI.

Born April 5, 1938, in Granby, Colorado, Tokunaga received his early education in Brighton, Colorado. He graduated from Colorado State University in Fort Collins, earning a bachelor of science degree in 1960. For the next five years, he served as a naval flight officer in the U.S. Navy, attaining the rank of lieutenant. In 1973, Tokunaga received a master of science degree in public administration from the University of Southern California.

In March 1968, Tokunaga entered the FBI as an agent, serving first in San Antonio, and in May 1969, transferring to the Los Angeles field office. In May 1974, he became an instructor in the Training Division at FBIHQ. After duties in the Planning and Inspection Division from February to September 1977, Tokunaga transferred to the Administrative Services Division, where he headed the Equal Employment Opportunity Section. In July 1979, he was appointed assistant special agent in charge of the Albuquerque field office, returning to FBIHQ as head of the Special Projects Section of the Laboratory Division in November 1983. In October 1985, he moved to the Forensic Science Research and Training Center at the FBI Academy in Quantico, Virginia, as its section chief. Two months later, Tokunaga was promoted to special agent in charge of the Seattle field office.

Tokunaga retired from the FBI in 1988 to serve as director of security for First Interstate Bancorp and its subsidiary, First Interstate Bank, Limited. In July 1966, he became director of corporate security for Occidental Petroleum Corporation in Los Angeles, California.

Tolson, Clyde The number-two man in the Bureau from shortly after he entered the FBI as an agent in 1928, Clyde Tolson briefly served as acting director in the hours between the death of FBI Director J. Edgar Hoover, May 2, 1972, and the appointment of FBI Acting Director L. Patrick Gray in the afternoon of May 3, 1972. As associate director of the FBI, Tolson handled the day-to-day affairs of the Bureau and chaired the Executives Conference. Tolson and Hoover were close associates, both in

Exhibit 9.25 **Clyde Tolson,**
Courtesy of the FBI

and out of work— eating, traveling, and attending social engagements together.

Born near Laredo, Missouri, May 22, 1900, Tolson was active in high school athletics. In 1917, he moved to Cedar Rapids, Iowa, where he received his bachelor's degree from Cedar Rapids Business College, and then to Washington, D.C., in 1918, where he attended George Washington University at night, eventually receiving a law degree in October 1927. He was admitted to the District of Columbia Bar, and later to the Supreme Court Bar. During his school years, Tolson was class president and served on the university senate. During World War I, he joined the War Department and so impressed Secretary of War Newton Baker that, in 1920, Baker appointed him his confidential secretary. Tolson continued in this position with Baker's successors, John W. Weeks and Dwight F. Davis.

Tolson resigned from the War Department to accept an appointment on April 2, 1928, as a special agent for the Bureau of Investigation. He served in the Washington, D.C., field office for several months, was transferred to Boston, and then returned to FBIHQ as chief clerk, all in 1928. On July 31, 1929, Tolson was appointed special agent in charge of the Buffalo field office, holding this position for one week before being brought back to Washington and promoted to the rank of inspector. On August 16, 1930, only two years after joining the Bureau, Tolson became assistant director for Personnel and Administration, and on July 1, 1936, assistant to the director—the first person to hold that position. His title was later changed to associate director. In this position, he took charge of day-to-day operations and handled all personnel and disciplinary matters. Tolson is to be credited with making Hoover's hierarchical, centralized, administrative system work.

During the 1930s, Tolson played first base on the Bureau's baseball team. He became a lieutenant commander in the Naval Reserve prior to the outbreak of World War II in Europe in 1939. For his contribution to the FBI, on June 2, 1965, he received the President's Award for Distinguished Federal Civilian Service.

The close relationship between Tolson and Hoover has led to speculation that they were homosexual partners. No credible evidence has substantiated this rumor. At work, they were plainly boss and subordinate, with Tolson always calling the director, "Hoover"; away from work, Tolson used Hoover's childhood nickname "Speed."

Tolson's health began to fail in the mid-1960s, and he suffered strokes in 1966 and 1967 that made walking and reading difficult. He could no longer maintain the close attention to detail that had made him such an essential help to FBI Director Hoover, whose own memory and powers of concentration were being affected by age. Tolson's reduced assistance contributed to Hoover's own difficulties as FBI director in his last years.

Tolson retired from the FBI on May 16, 1972, two weeks after Hoover's death. Until his own death on April 14, 1975, Tolson lived in what had been Hoover's house, which had been willed to him.

Turrou, Leon G.   Leon G. Turrou participated in two of the Bureau's highest profile cases during the 1930s, and also wrote some of the earliest exposés of the FBI. Seeking to exploit publicity in one of these cases, he resigned from the Bureau in 1938.

Turrou's first major contribution involved the investigation of the Lindbergh kidnapping in the early 1930s. He questioned suspect Bruno Richard Hauptmann at length, eventually eliciting the handwriting samples that, when compared with the handwriting on the ransom notes, provided the crucial evidence that led to Hauptmann's conviction.

Shortly thereafter, he went undercover in an FBI investigation of the German-American Bund, a pro-Nazi organization. Turrou became a hero when the investigation led to the successful prosecution of Bund members for espionage. A popular movie, *Confessions of a Nazi Spy,* starring Edward G. Robinson, was based on the case. To the FBI and Hoover, however, Turrou was anything but a hero. Turrou had sold his account of the Bund investigation to the *New York Post* before the case came to trial, shortly after resigning from the FBI. (Hoover, however, revised Turrou's FBI file to read that the agent had been fired with prejudice.) Fearing that publicity would compromise the government's interest in monitoring German espionage activities, Attorney General Homer S. Cummings initially persuaded the newspaper not to publish Turrou's memoir. A frustrated Turrou then publicly accused Hoover of having fired him because he had scooped the director. The next year, Turrou published his account of his own undercover activities and the threat of German espionage activities, *The Nazi Spy in America*. During World War II, Turrou joined the Office of Strategic Services, forerunner of the Central Intelligence Agency.

Turrou also published a popular book titled *How to Be a G-Man,* as well as *Where My Shadow Falls: Two Decades of Crime Detection,* which revealed (among other issues) alleged Bureau missteps in its investigation of the Lindbergh kidnapping.

Webster, William H.   William H. Webster was named director of the FBI in 1978. He remained in that position until May 26, 1987, when he became director of the Central Intelligence Agency. Under Webster, the FBI's budget doubled, a significantly more diversified workplace was established, and the FBI's international presence increased. Webster also helped bring about a closer formal relationship between the Drug Enforcement Administration and the FBI. Cognizant of the criticism leveled at the FBI for alleged civil liberties violations, Webster described the Bureau's mission as "Doing the work the American people expect of us, in the way the Constitution demands of us."

Exhibit 9.26   **William H. Webster,** *Courtesy of the FBI*

Born March 6, 1924, in St. Louis, Missouri, Webster received his early education in nearby Webster Groves. In 1947, he received a bachelor of arts degree from Amherst College, Amherst, Massachusetts, and, two years later, a J.D. degree from Washington University Law School. In both World War II and the Korean War, Webster served in the Navy as a lieutenant.

Except for a brief period in 1960–61, when he was a U.S. attorney for the eastern district of Missouri, Webster practiced law with a private St. Louis firm from 1949 to 1969. He also served on the Missouri Board of Law Examiners from 1964 to 1969.

President Richard M. Nixon appointed him a judge of the United States District Court for the eastern district of Missouri in 1970. Three years later, Nixon elevated him to the United States Court of Appeals for the Eighth Circuit, where he remained until becoming FBI director. Webster is a fellow of the American Bar Foundation, the recipient of numerous awards and several honorary degrees, and a member of the National Academy of Public Administration. In May 1985, he became president of the Institute of Judicial Administration.

President Jimmy Carter appointed Webster for a 10-year term as FBI director, to succeed Clarence M. Kelley. He took the oath of office on February 23, 1978. During Webster's tenure, the FBI's organization and investigations underwent several dramatic changes. The Bureau's public corruption investigations included sting operations leveled at members of Congress (ABSCAM) and the judiciary (GREYLORD). Both of these operations utilized wiretaps and video surveillance techniques that were conducted under court orders. Use of court-ordered wiretaps also expanded from 326 between 1977 and 1980, to 733 between 1981 and 1984.

Webster continued the trend of diversifying the FBI's personnel started by FBI Acting Director L. Patrick Gray and FBI Director Clarence M. Kelley, and by the time he left in 1987, the FBI had 350 Hispanic agents, 350 African American agents, and 650 female agents.

President Ronald Reagan appointed Webster as director of the Central Intelligence Agency (CIA) on March 3, 1987, and he assumed this role on May 26, 1987. Webster was expected to restore morale within the agency— and confidence in it from without—following the 1986–87 Iran-Contra scandal. He retired from the CIA in 1991.

Wilt, Frederick L.   While serving as a special agent, Frederick L. Wilt became one of the nation's top track stars, competing in the London Olympics in 1948, and the Helsinki Olympics in 1952. Wilt set the American outdoor record of 14:26.8 for 5,000 meters in 1950 and received the Amateur Athletic Union's James Sullivan Award as the amateur athlete of the year. Two years later, he set the world record of 8:50.7 for two miles. (FBI agent Horace Ashenfelter of the Newark field office came in second.) In 1975, Wilt was inducted into the National Track and Field Hall of Fame.

Born in Pendleton, Indiana, Wilt received a bachelor of science degree from Indiana University and attended the University of Tennessee Law School. During World War II, he served in the U.S. Navy, attaining the rank of lieutenant (j.g.).

Wilt entered the FBI as an agent in 1947, serving in the Atlanta, Seattle, New York City, and Indianapolis field offices and the Lafayette, Indiana, resident agency. Wilt died in Anderson, Indiana, September 5, 1994.

Winstead, Charles B.   Charles B. Winstead is reputedly the Bureau agent who killed the gangster John Dillinger.

Born May 25, 1891, in Sherman, Texas, Winstead attended public schools through the eighth grade before transferring to the Sherman Private School for Boys, which he attended for three years. He also studied typing and shorthand at the Sherman Business College. Before joining the Bureau, he worked as a deputy sheriff in Brownsville, Texas, an Army field clerk, and chief clerk in the office of the U.S. attorney in El Paso.

He entered the Bureau of Investigation as an agent on July 27, 1926, and was immediately assigned to Oklahoma City. Assigned to the "flying squad" that was hunting John Dillinger, on July 22, 1934, Winstead awaited the gangster in the lobby of the Biograph Theatre and was apparently closest to him when Dillinger exited and, suspecting that he was being followed, drew his gun. Before Dillinger could shoot, Winstead felled the gangster with three shots.

As a member of the flying squad, Winstead also participated in the investigations of Lester Gillis ("Baby Face" Nelson), and the Barker-Karpis Gang. He claimed to have killed "Ma" Barker as well, during a Bureau stakeout in Florida in 1935. He was subsequently assigned to the Los Angeles, Birmingham, Dallas, Chicago, El Paso, Jacksonville, Miami, and Orlando field offices. In 1942, he worked in the Albuquerque, New Mexico, resident agency, at the time, the only agent assigned to the state. He resigned the following year and joined the U.S. Army as a captain and assistant director of intelligence. His request to return to the Bureau after the war, however, was refused. Winstead died in Albuquerque on August 3, 1973.

Wolmer, Karen R.   Karen R. Wolmer became the FBI's first blind typist on August 11, 1980, and was employed by the New York City field office.

Blind since birth, she was born and raised in New York City. Wolmer attended Adelphi and New York Universities and received secretarial training from the Lighthouse Association for the Blind. She worked for three and a half years for the Veterans Administration before her FBI appointment.

Woodriffe, Edwin R.   The first African American special agent killed in the line of duty, Edwin R. Woodriffe died January 8, 1969, when he and his partner, Anthony Palmisano, were ambushed in Washington, D.C., by a fugitive bank robber.

Born January 22, 1941, and raised in Brooklyn, New York, Woodriffe graduated from Fordham University in New York City with a bachelor of science degree. He worked as a criminal investigator with the U.S. Department of the

Treasury until May 22, 1967, when he entered the FBI as an agent. After an assignment to the Cleveland field office, Woodriffe was transferred to the Washington, D.C., field office on February 28, 1968.

Zeiss, George   Considered one of the FBI's legendary figures, George Zeiss taught firearms and self-defense at the FBI Academy in Quantico, Virginia, from 1942 to 1977. He acquired a worldwide reputation for trick shooting. He could fire a .38-caliber revolver at the edge of a playing card, tearing it in half with one bullet. In another trick, he used the reflection in a diamond ring to hit targets hanging behind him. Perhaps his most dramatic shot was to fire a .38-caliber bullet at the edge of an ax, splitting the bullet and then breaking two targets.

Zeiss entered the FBI as an agent in 1942. In addition to his other duties, he served as a technical consultant—and actor—for the movie *The FBI Story*. In 1968, Zeiss was sent to London to retrieve Martin Luther King Jr.'s accused assassin, James Earl Ray. Zeiss won numerous honors from law enforcement agencies worldwide, including the French Sûreté and Scotland Yard. Upon his retirement in 1977, Zeiss joined the Wackenhut Corporation.

CHRONOLOGY OF KEY EVENTS

Athan G. Theoharis

September 24, 1789   Congress creates the Office of the Attorney General. President George Washington appoints Edmund Randolph as the first attorney general.

June 22, 1870   Congress creates the Department of Justice, headed by the attorney general, to enforce federal laws.

March 3, 1871   Congress appropriates $50,000 for the "detection and prosecution of crimes" by the Department of Justice. The attorney general appoints the first investigator to conduct special investigations (but not an investigative division within the Justice Department).

May 27, 1908   Congress adopts an appropriations rider for the Department of the Treasury that bars Secret Service agents from conducting investigations beyond enforcing reimbursement and counterfeiting laws and protecting the president (thereby ending the temporary loaning of Secret Service agents to the Department of Justice for specific investigative needs).

June 29, 1908   Attorney General Charles J. Bonaparte creates a permanent Justice Department investigative bureau.

July 26, 1908   Attorney General Bonaparte appoints Stanley W. Finch as head of the Special Agent Force.

March 16, 1909   Attorney General George W. Wickersham renames the Special Agent Force the Bureau of Investigation.

June 25, 1910   Congress enacts the White Slave Traffic (or Mann) Act, expanding the Bureau's interstate crime enforcement responsibilities.

April 30, 1912   Former Examiner A. Bruce Bielaski, who since 1909 had supervised Bureau agents, is appointed Bureau of Investigation chief.

March 20, 1917   Bureau Chief Bielaski agrees to a liaison program with the American Protective League (APL), a private businessmen's organization headquartered in Chicago, wherein APL members provide logistical and other assistance to Bureau agents.

April 6, 1917   Following congressional declaration of war on Germany and Austria-Hungary, President Woodrow Wilson issues a proclamation, based on the 1798 Alien Act, authorizing the Justice Department to apprehend and detain "enemy aliens." Bureau investigations are expanded to assist the department's newly established Alien Enemies Bureau.

June 15, 1917   Congress enacts the Espionage Act. The Bureau begins investigating individuals opposing military conscription or the raising of funds through Liberty Bond drives, sowing dissension in the armed forces, or willfully aiding foreign adversaries.

September 5, 1917   For violating the Espionage Act, Bureau agents arrest the leadership of the Industrial Workers of the World (IWW) at its Chicago headquarters, seizing, as well, IWW literature and records. (These IWW leaders are convicted in 1918.)

September 3, 1918   In New York City, Bureau agents, local police, and American Protective League operatives arrest thousands of "slackers"—draft-age men suspected of not having registered for the draft. The arrests of prominent businessmen who simply failed to carry their draft cards provoke bitter criticism.

February 10, 1919   William E. Allen is appointed Acting Chief of the Bureau of Investigation upon Bielaski's resignation.

June 30, 1919   Attorney General A. Mitchell Palmer directs Assistant Attorney General Francis Garvan to supervise the Bureau of Investigation and appoints former chief of the Secret Service, William J. Flynn, to be chief of the Bureau.

August 1, 1919   Attorney General Palmer creates the Radical Division (later named the General Intelligence Division, the GID) within the Bureau to collect data on revolutionary, pacifist, radical, and other dissident movements. J. Edgar Hoover heads this new division.

September 9, 1919   A Senate committee, chaired by North Carolina Democrat Lee Overman, convenes hearings to ascertain Bolshevik influence over radical organizations in the United States relying, in part, on the testimony of Bureau officials.

October 28, 1919   Congress expands the Bureau's investigative responsibilities when it enacts the Motor Vehicle Theft (or Dyer) Act, which criminalizes transporting stolen motor vehicles across state lines.

November 7, 1919   In cooperation with Immigration Bureau officials, Bureau agents arrest approximately 250 members of the Union of Russian Workers for possible deportation under the 1918 Immigration Act. Under this 1918 law, alien residents can be deported if they are members of organizations that the secretary of labor has concluded are working toward the revolutionary overthrow of the government. On December 21, 1919, 249 of those arrested (which included others arrested by New York City police and anarchists Emma Goldman and Alexander Berkman) are deported to Russia.

December 1, 1919   The first *Bureau Bulletin* is issued—communications posted in field offices outlining Bureau of Investigation policy.

January 2, 1920   Bureau agents, in cooperation with local police, detain thousands of alien residents and citizens who were attending meetings of the Communist Party and the Communist Labor Party in 33 cities. These raids were popularly known as the Palmer Raids, after Attorney General A. Mitchell Palmer. Those arrested include citizens, who are turned over to state authorities for possible prosecution under state anarchist-syndicalist laws, and alien residents, who are interrogated by Immigration Bureau authorities for possible deportation under the 1918 Immigration Act. (Ultimately, only 556 of the arrestees are deported.)

April 27, 1920   In Congress, the House Committee on Rules initiates hearings on whether to impeach Assistant Labor Secretary Louis Post (because of his rulings that precluded the deportation of many of those detained during the Palmer Raids). Post's testimony during the hearings subverts this impeachment attempt and—instead—raises questions about the Bureau's role in the raids.

May 25, 1920   National Popular Government League issues a report criticizing Immigration Bureau and Bureau of Investigation abuses during the Palmer Raids and in the ensuing interrogations of detained alien residents. A companion critical report of the raids is concurrently issued by the Interchurch World Movement, an association of 26 Protestant denominations.

September 28, 1920   Bureau Chief Flynn issues the first *SAC Letter*, thereafter issued periodically to SACs (special agents in charge, the heads of field offices), outlining new or revised Bureau policy.

January 19, 1921   A Senate committee, chaired by Democrat Thomas Walsh, initiates critical hearings into the planning and execution of the Palmer Raids.

August 22, 1921   Attorney General Harry Daugherty appoints the head of a private detective agency, William J. Burns, to be Bureau director and J. Edgar Hoover, at the time the head of the Bureau's General Intelligence Division, to be assistant director.

August 22, 1922   Bureau agents raid a meeting of the Communist Party held in Bridgman, Michigan. Lacking any authority to prosecute those attending this meeting, Bureau agents turn over seized records and other materials to the Michigan state police for prosecution under Michigan's sedition laws.

September 1922   Bureau agents raid the offices of Congressman Oscar Keller (a critic of Attorney General Daugherty's injunction against the railroad workers).

September 1, 1922   Attorney General Daugherty obtains a sweeping injunction against striking railroad workers and directs Bureau agents to obtain evidence to prosecute strikers violating the injunction; 1,200 striking workers are arrested.

1924, day and month unknown   Bureau Director Hoover begins to maintain a special "Official and Confidential File" in his office for sensitive records. At an unknown later date, Hoover creates a second file of sensitive material, the "Personal and Confidential File." At another unknown date, Hoover authorizes FBI Associate Director Clyde Tolson to maintain in his office a "Personal File" containing memoranda that Hoover has sent to senior FBI officials demanding action on certain important but sensitive matters.

March 10, 1924   Following an intensive investigation (that began in September 1922 in response to Louisiana Governor John Parker's request for federal assistance to break the Ku Klux Klan), Klan head Edward Young Clarke pleads guilty to charges of violating the Mann Act. Because state authorities had been unable to indict Klan officials for a series of murders and other crimes, Bureau officials focused on Mann Act violations.

May 1924   A special Senate committee investigates former attorney general Harry Daugherty's abuses of office, including ordering Bureau investigations of congressional critics of the Harding administration's handling of the Teapot Dome scandal.

May 10, 1924   Attorney General Harlan Fiske Stone appoints J. Edgar Hoover Bureau acting director, having demanded the resignation of William Burns on May 9, 1924.

July 1, 1924   Bureau Director Hoover establishes an Investigation Division at Bureau headquarters in Washington, D.C., with the responsibility to create a national registry of fingerprints, Congress having authorized the "exchange of identification records with officers of the cities, counties, and states." The registry consolidates the former Bureau of Identification files—which had, in October 1923, been transferred from Leavenworth, Kansas—with the records of the International Association of Chiefs of Police.

December 10, 1924   J. Edgar Hoover is appointed Bureau director.

February 20, 1925   Bureau Director Hoover reorganizes the Bureau of Investigation, creating six divisions with assigned administrative and investigative responsibilities over the Bureau's nationwide field offices.

March 24, 1925   Bureau Director Hoover authorizes a special OBSCENE letter procedure and creates a separate OBSCENE File for agent reports on "obscene or improper" materials.

October 11, 1925   The first Bureau special agent to die in the line of duty, Edwin C. Shanahan, is killed when attempting to arrest auto thief Martin J. Durkin in Chicago.

August 15, 1926   Bureau agents arrest Major General Enrique Estrada, the former Mexican secretary of war, in California. Agents simultaneously assist the border patrol and local police officers in capturing Estrada's general staff, infantry, armor, artillery, and air force as they prepare to invade Mexico to seize control of the government in Mexico City.

September 15, 1927   The first *Manual of Investigation* is issued, detailing rules and procedures governing Bureau investigations. Regularly revised and updated thereafter, this handbook is issued to all agents, SACs, and supervisors.

January 1928   Bureau officials institute a theoretical and practical training course for new agents. Prior to being considered for retention, new agents undergo a two-month assignment at the Bureau's Washington D.C., field office (and later at the FBI Academy) where their performance is closely supervised and evaluated.

April 2, 1928   Clyde Tolson is appointed a Bureau special agent.

March 27, 1929   Bureau agents arrest Al (Alphonse) Capone in Florida when he fails to respond to a subpoena to appear as a witness in a federal Prohibition case in Chicago. Capone is later convicted of income tax evasion.

June 11, 1930   Congress authorizes the Bureau's National Division of Identification and Information to collect and compile uniform crime statistics for the United States.

December 5, 1931   Bureau employees form the Recreation Association, later renamed FBIRA (the Federal Bureau of Investigation Recreation Association), an organization of dues-paying members formed to promote athletic, social, and welfare activities for all FBI employees.

March 1, 1932   Baby Charles A. Lindbergh Jr. is kidnapped from his parents' home in New Jersey. On March 4, 1932, President Herbert Hoover directs the Treasury Department's Prohibition Unit; the Washington, D.C., Metropolitan Police; and the Bureau of Investigation to assist local police (if requested) in the investigation. Bureau Director Hoover is appointed as coordinator of federal assistance.

March 1, 1932   Bureau officials inaugurate a program to exchange fingerprint data with friendly foreign governments.

May 1932   The first issue of *The Investigator,* an in-house periodical—mimeographed and two pages in length—is released.

June 22, 1932   In response to the Lindbergh kidnapping, Congress criminalizes kidnapping whenever the victim has been transported across state lines.

July 1, 1932   The Bureau of Investigation is renamed the United States Bureau of Investigation.

September 1, 1932   The Bureau begins publishing a periodical, *Fugitives Wanted by Police* (renamed, in October 1935, *FBI Law Enforcement Bulletin*).

October 25, 1932   The first national network radio program based on FBI cases, "The Lucky Strike Hour," begins.

November 24, 1932   Bureau officials establish a laboratory to assist FBI investigations that involved the unprecedented use of microscopes, a large gun collection, watermarks, and automobile tire designs.

June 10, 1933   President Franklin Roosevelt issues an executive order combining the Prohibition Bureau, the Bureau of Identification, and the Bureau of Investigation into a new Division of Investigation within the Department of Justice.

June 17, 1933   While transporting recaptured convict Frank Nash to Leavenworth (Kansas) federal penitentiary, Bureau agent Raymond J. Caffrey, two local police detectives, McAlester (Oklahoma) Police Chief Otto Reed, and Nash are killed in the Kansas City (Missouri) Union Station by Adam Richetti, Vernon Miller, and Charles "Pretty Boy" Floyd (criminal associates of Nash's attempting to rescue him).

July 23, 1933   George "Machine Gun" Kelly and Albert L. Bates kidnap Charles F. Urschel, a wealthy Oklahoma City oil man. Urschel is released after a $200,000 ransom is paid. Following an intensive investigation, Bureau agents apprehend Kelly in Memphis, Tennessee. Kelly reportedly cries, "Don't shoot, G-men!" at the moment of capture.

October 1, 1933   The Division of Investigation establishes a reference collection of firearms taken from persons under investigation.

November 10, 1933   A Civil File of fingerprints of non-arrested individuals is established.

March 20, 1934   Attorney General Homer Cummings lobbies Congress to enact his Twelve Point Crime Program making bank robberies and extortion federal crimes and increasing the Bureau's authority to investigate kidnapping cases. Concurrently, the Justice Department successfully promotes the image of a super-professional and efficient FBI, personified by the G-man. By May 19, 1934, Congress enacts six of the proposed crime laws.

May 8, 1934   President Franklin Roosevelt directs Bureau Director Hoover to monitor "Nazi groups," particularly their "anti-racial" and "anti-American" activities having any "special connection" with "official representatives of the German Government in the United States."

June 18, 1934   Congress empowers Bureau agents to make arrests and carry firearms—previously, agents had been able only to make "citizen's arrests," having to rely on federal marshals or local police officers. To use firearms, agents are required to obtain specific authorization from Bureau headquarters.

June 20, 1934   President Roosevelt signs the Communications Act, Section 605 of which bans wiretapping. In *Nardone v. U.S.,* the Supreme Court rules twice (first in 1937, then in 1939) that this ban applies to federal agents and that if illegally obtained wiretap information is used in a conviction, the case must be dismissed.

July 22, 1934   Bureau agents attempt to arrest John Dillinger (at the time notorious for a string of bank robberies and prison escapes) outside the Biograph Theatre in Chicago. Resisting arrest, Dillinger is shot and killed by agents led by Samuel P. Cowley and SAC Melvin Purvis of the Chicago field office.

September 20, 1934   Bruno Richard Hauptmann is arrested in New York for kidnapping and killing the son of famed aviator Charles Lindbergh. Bureau agents, along with Treasury Department agents and local police, play a key role in identifying Hauptmann.

October 22, 1934   Bureau agents arrest the notorious gangster Charles "Pretty Boy" Floyd.

July 1, 1935   The Division of Investigation is formally renamed the Federal Bureau of Investigation.

July 29, 1935   FBI officials establish the FBI National Police Academy, forerunner of the renamed FBI National Academy. The academy offers a 12-week course in scientific and practical law enforcement methods to selected local and state police officers, first in Washington, D.C., and eventually in Quantico, Virginia.

1936, day and month unknown   FBI Director Hoover authorizes FBI assistance to officials of the National Conference of Bar Examiners concerning the organizational ties and political beliefs of applicants to practice law.

April 30, 1936   FBI Director Hoover personally arrests, in New Orleans, Alvin "Creepy" Karpis, a gangster wanted for the June 1933 kidnapping of St. Paul businessman William Hamm Jr.

August 24, 1936   During a private meeting with FBI Director Hoover, President Franklin Roosevelt requests an FBI report on fascist and communist activities within the United States. As authority, the president relies on a World War I statute permitting FBI investigations at the request of the secretary of state. To meet this condition, President Roosevelt arranges a second meeting the next day between himself, Hoover, and Secretary of the State Cordell Hull. Roosevelt's oral directive alone authorizes FBI investigations of "subversive activities."

September 5, 1936   FBI Director Hoover directs all heads of FBI field offices (SACs) to report "any information relating to subversive activities on the part of any individual or organization, regardless of the source from which this information is received." SACs are cautioned not to initiate any investigation without Hoover's advance approval.

December 15, 1936   FBI Director Hoover leads a raid to arrest, in New York City, gangster Harry Brunette.

November 2, 1938   President Roosevelt approves FBI Director Hoover's proposal to expand FBI counterintelligence activities in coordination with the Military Intelligence Division and the Office of Naval Intelligence. This program is to be conducted in "strictest confidence" and without seeking "additional legislation."

December 2, 1938   As a result of an intensive FBI investigation, Guenther Gustav Rumrich, Johanna Hofman, Otto Voss, and Erich Glaser are convicted of espionage activities on behalf of Germany. Fourteen others who had been indicted disappear before they can be arrested and tried. Arrested in February 1938, Rumrich led a ring of spies seeking industrial and military information for Nazi Germany.

June 26, 1939   President Roosevelt issues a secret directive assigning exclusive responsibility for all "espionage, counterespionage, and sabotage matters" to the FBI, the War Department's Military Intelligence Division (MID) and the Navy Department's Office of Naval Intelligence (ONI).

August 24, 1939   Through an arrangement with syndicated columnist and radio commentator Walter Winchell, FBI Director Hoover arrests, in New York City, Louis "Lepke" Buchalter on narcotics charges. Buchalter surrenders to federal authorities, hoping to avoid prosecution for murder under New York law. New York Attorney General Thomas Dewey, however, secures Buchalter's indictment and conviction for the more serious state murder charge.

September 2, 1939   FBI Director Hoover authorizes a Custodial Detention list of aliens and citizens "on whom there is information available that their presence at liberty in this country in time of war or national emergency would be dangerous" to the nation's security. Hoover subsequently, on June 15, 1940, seeks Attorney General Robert Jackson's approval to list individuals for possible preventive detention.

September 6, 1939   President Roosevelt publicly authorizes the FBI to "take charge of investigative work in matters relating to espionage, sabotage, and violations of the neutrality regulations" and invites police officials to forward relevant information to the FBI.

January 14, 1940   FBI agents arrest 17 members of the pro-fascist Christian Front in New York City for planning a "vast plot" to overthrow the government and establish a fascist dictatorship, including stealing arms and ammunition from a National Guard Armory and making bombs. None of the arrestees are convicted, as defense attorneys successfully challenge the role of the FBI's chief informer, Denis Healy.

February 6, 1940   FBI agents arrest 12 radical activists in Detroit and Milwaukee for having—in 1937—recruited volunteers to fight in support of the Spanish Loyalist government in the so-called Abraham Lincoln Brigade. FBI methods in making the arrests, as well as questions about why the volunteers were under investigation, precipitate criticisms of the FBI's "gestapo" tactics. An ensuing internal Justice Department investigation refutes these criticisms.

April 11, 1940   FBI Director Hoover institutes a special reporting procedure governing senior FBI officials' written communications about especially sensitive and administrative matters. Such reports were to be prepared on colored paper (first blue and then pink) to preclude their serialization in the FBI's central records system. Hoover terminated this reporting procedure in 1950. Thereafter, FBI officials reported such information in "informal" memoranda (plain white nonletterhead paper), which were then maintained in office files until destroyed.

May 21, 1940   President Roosevelt issues a secret directive authorizing FBI wiretapping during "national defense" investigations, subject, in each case, to the prior approval of the attorney general.

June 5, 1940   FBI, MID, and ONI officials conclude a delimitation agreement assigning exclusive responsibility for "internal security" investigations to the FBI, with ONI and MID investigations confined to military and naval personnel and military and naval bases.

June 24, 1940   President Roosevelt secretly assigns foreign intelligence and counterintelligence responsibilities in the Western Hemisphere (Central and South America) to the FBI. A special FBI branch is created, the Special Intelligence Service.

June 28, 1940   Congress enacts the so-called Smith Act prohibiting any individual or organization from advocating the violent overthrow of the U.S. government or belonging to or organizing a group having such a goal.

July 2, 1940   At the request of President Roosevelt, FBI officials attempt to ascertain whether former Republican President Herbert Hoover (or his key aide, Lawrence Richey) had contacted French officials to learn whether the Roosevelt administration militarily assisted the French government while the United States was officially neutral during the Anglo-French war against Germany.

October 17, 1940   Congress passes the Foreign Agent Registration (or Voorhis) Act, requiring all foreign-controlled organizations and groups advocating the overthrow of the U.S. government to register with the Department of Justice.

November 18, 1940   Attorney General Jackson approves FBI Director Hoover's proposal to establish a covert FBI liaison relationship with the American Legion. This American Legion Contact Program recruits tens of thousands of American Legion members as FBI "sources of information" or "confidential national defense informants" to report on suspect activities in their localities.

January 1941   The FBI seal is first used.

June 28, 1941   FBI agents arrest Frederick Joubert "Fritz" Duquesne and 32 others on the charge of spying for Nazi Germany.

June 28, 1941   Congress appropriates $100,000 to fund FBI investigations of all federal employees who might be "members of subversive organizations."

October 1, 1941   FBI Director Hoover authorizes FBI Assistant Director Louis Nichols to maintain a "Confidential File" in his office.

October 23, 1941   Julius Lopez is the first Hispanic American to be appointed assistant special agent in charge. Lopez is promoted on November 30, 1943, to special agent in charge of the San Juan (Puerto Rico) field office, becoming the first Hispanic American to become an SAC.

December 7, 1941   With the Japanese attack on Pearl Harbor and congressional declaration of war (first on Japan and then Germany), President Roosevelt issues an emergency proclamation and Attorney General Francis Biddle authorizes the FBI to detain dangerous enemy aliens.

1942, day and month unknown   FBI Director Hoover authorizes a special "Do Not File" reporting procedure to preclude the discovery of FBI break-ins.

June 12, 1942   Four German saboteurs, led by George J. Dasch, land from a German submarine on the beach near Amagansett, Long Island. A second four-man team of German saboteurs, led by Edward Kerling, lands at Ponte Vedra Beach in Florida on June 17, 1942. On June 19, 1942, Dasch surrenders to the FBI and describes the mission and saboteurs. Within 14 days, the FBI arrests all eight saboteurs. Tried by a military commission, six are sentenced to death, one to life imprisonment, and Dasch (because of his cooperation) to 30 years.

June 22, 1942   Under the code-named RACON program, FBI Director Hoover orders FBI field offices to survey "the extent of agitation among the Negroes which may be the outgrowth of any effort on the part of the Axis powers (Germany, Japan) or the Communist Party." Following an intensive investigation, including monitoring prominent civil rights groups and the black press, a massive report is submitted to Hoover on September 10, 1943.

October 9, 1942   The FBI establishes a radio monitoring station in Clinton, Maryland, with the capability of transmitting to England. Additional monitoring stations are set up in Beaverton, Oregon, and Natick, Massachusetts, which are operated until the creation of the Central Intelligence Agency in 1947. Despite losing its international monitoring role, the FBI continues to maintain a domestic emergency network until the mid-1960s.

January 3, 1943   President Roosevelt issues a directive urging "all patriotic organizations and individuals" to report any information concerning "espionage and related matters" to the FBI.

January 14, 1943   Executive assistant to the attorney general, Ugo Carusi, authorizes FBI Director Hoover to honor American Red Cross requests for name checks on specific individuals. FBI officials subsequently make similar liaison arrangements with the American Bar Association, B'nai Brith, the Boy Scouts of America, the U.S. Chamber of Commerce, Kiwanis International, the Knights of Columbus, Optimists International, Rotary International, the Veterans of Foreign Wars, and the Daughters of the American Revolution.

March 1943   FBI Director Hoover authorizes a liaison program whereby three FBI agents are assigned, on a rotating basis, with a three-year term limit, to assist the staff of the House Appropriations Committee.

July 13, 1943   Attorney General Biddle terminates the FBI's Custodial Detention list. Hoover formally complies with this order on August 14, 1943, but covertly directs FBI officials to change the name to Security Index.

November 18, 1944   Director of the Office of Strategic Services (OSS) William Donovan submits a memorandum to President Roosevelt recommending the creation of a permanent centralized intelligence agency. FBI officials leak a copy of Donovan's memorandum to the *Chicago Tribune* which, on February 9, 1945, publishes a highly critical article on the proposed "super gestapo agency," effectively killing any follow-up action on Donovan's recommendation.

March 11, 1945   OSS agents break into the office of *Amerasia,* a journal of Far Eastern affairs, and discover thousands of pages of classified OSS, Navy, and State Department documents. OSS officials refer this matter to the FBI on March 14, 1945, precipitating an intensive FBI investigation (including wiretapping and breaking into the office of *Amerasia* and the residence of its principal editors and identified sources in the Navy and State Departments). On June 6, 1945, FBI agents arrest six individuals (two *Amerasia* editors, Philip Jaffe and Kate Mitchell; freelance reporter Mark Gayn; and three State Department and Navy Department employees, Emmanuel Larsen, John S. Service, and Andrew Roth) for unauthorized possession of classified documents. Only three of the six arrestees (Jaffe, Larsen, and Roth) are subsequently indicted. None are convicted owing to the OSS's and FBI's illegal investigation practices.

April 16, 1945   The nationwide weekly radio serial, "This Is Your FBI," is launched with the close supervision and cooperation of FBI officials.

July 31, 1945   Responding to a request from the Truman White House, FBI Director Hoover authorizes an investigation of White House employees (captioned White House Security Survey) to ascertain the source of leaks to the news media (specifically, to syndicated columnist Drew Pearson). On August 13, 1945, Hoover submits a detailed report to the president that summarizes the results of the FBI's intensive monitoring of White House employees and their various contacts (this report is based, in part, on FBI wiretaps of White House aide Edward Prichard and prominent Washington, D.C., attorney and liberal Democrat Thomas Corcoran).

September 5, 1945   Igor Gouzenko, a clerk employed in the Soviet embassy in Ottawa, Canada, defects to Canadian authorities. Gouzenko's disclosures of wartime Soviet espionage activities in Canada and the United States lead to an intensified FBI investigation of suspect (U.S.) federal employees.

November 7, 1945   During an interview on this and on succeeding dates with FBI agents, Elizabeth Bentley discloses her role as a courier for a wartime Soviet under-cover operation in Washington, D.C., naming the various federal employees who had provided her with government information (including Harry Dexter White, William Remington, and Nathan Silvermaster). Bentley's charges precipitate a flurry of FBI reports to the Truman administration on those she named, and a grand jury inquiry. The grand jury issues no indictments, and in 1948 Bentley publicly surfaces as a witness before Senate and House investigating committees. The Republican-led committees seek to exploit her testimony to confirm the laxity of the Truman administration's internal security procedures.

February 27, 1946   FBI Director Hoover authorizes a covert "educational campaign" to "influence public opinion." Under this program, FBI officials prepare "educational material which can be released through available channels so that in the event of an emergency we will have an informed public opinion about the seriousness of the Communist threat and their support among liberal elements."

July 17, 1946   President Truman authorizes FBI wiretapping during investigations of "subversive activities" when signing Attorney General Tom Clark's letter to himself. At the time, Truman understands that he is only expanding current FBI wiretapping to include serious crimes "where human life is in jeopardy."

March 22, 1947   President Truman issues Executive Order 9835 establishing the Federal Employee Loyalty Program. The FBI is authorized to investigate applicant and incumbent employees whenever derogatory information is uncovered suggesting that the individual might be disloyal.

May 13, 1947   FBI Director Hoover secretly authorizes FBI officials to provide confidential information to assist the House Committee on Un-American Activities in its planned hearings on communist influence in Hollywood.

March 21, 1948   President Truman issues an executive order requiring federal department and agency heads to obtain the president's prior approval before honoring congressional requests or subpoenas for FBI loyalty reports.

June 29, 1948   Twelve top leaders of the U.S. Communist Party are indicted for violating the Smith Act when seeking to overthrow the U.S. government by violence. Their trial lasts from January 17 through October 14, 1949, and results in their conviction. Their appeal of their convictions and challenge to the constitutionality of the Smith Act, *Dennis v. U.S.,* is rejected by the Supreme Court. In the interim, some of the communist leaders go underground to avoid imprisonment but are eventually apprehended following an intensive FBI investigation.

August 3, 1948   Attorney General Tom Clark authorizes the FBI's secret Security Index program based on FBI Director Hoover's March 8, 1946, recommendation. Under this program, the FBI compiles a list of potentially dangerous individuals who are to be detained in the event of a war or threatened invasion. Clark decides not to seek legislative authorization for this program, opting instead for a strategy seeking ex post facto congressional authorization.

August 3, 1948   In testimony before the House Committee on Un-American Activities, Whittaker Chambers names Alger Hiss (and seven other former federal employees) as having belonged, during the 1930s, to a communist cell in Washington, D.C. Hiss's denial of this charge leads the committee to refer the matter to the Department of Justice to ascertain whether Chambers's allegation or Hiss's denial are perjurious. The grand jury inquiry takes a different tack when Chambers—first on November 17 and then on December 2, 1948—produces classified State Department documents (typed, handwritten, and microfilmed) that he claims to have received from Hiss in 1938. Hiss is indicted

on December 15, 1948, on two counts of perjury. His first trial results in a hung jury; retried, he is convicted on January 21, 1950, sentenced to five years imprisonment, and released in November 1954.

March 4, 1949   FBI agents arrest Judith Coplon, a Justice Department employee, during her meeting with Valentin Gubitchev, a Soviet citizen employed at the United Nations. Indicted for attempting to deliver classified FBI reports to a Soviet official, Coplon's conviction is later reversed (based on questions relating to FBI wiretapping of her before and after her arrest).

June 29, 1949   FBI Director Hoover authorizes a special "JUNE Mail" procedure for specially sensitive FBI reports ("the most secretive sources, such as Governors, secretaries to high officials who may be discussing such officials and their attitudes," or when referring to "highly confidential or unusual investigative techniques," i.e., wiretaps, bugs, break-ins, mail intercepts). These reports were then to be maintained separate from the FBI's central records system in a Special File Room at the FBI headquarters in Washington, D.C. FBI Director William Webster terminates the JUNE Mail procedure in November 1978.

July 8, 1949   FBI Director Hoover authorizes the "Administrative Pages" procedure for reporting "facts and information which are considered of a nature not expedient to disseminate, or which could cause embarrassment to the Bureau, if distributed." Such information is to be included in agent reports on special pages that can be removed whenever the report is disseminated outside the FBI.

July 18, 1949   The National Security Council (NSC) outlines the responsibilities of the two NSC subcommittees responsible for coordinating internal security matters: the Interdepartmental Intelligence Conference (chaired by the FBI director) and the Interdepartmental Committee on Internal Security. President Truman approves this NSC directive on March 23, 1949.

February 2, 1950   Based on information provided by the FBI, British security agents arrest nuclear physicist Klaus Fuchs. Fuchs worked on the Manhattan atomic bomb project during World War II and gave atomic secrets to the Soviet Union. Sentenced to 15 years in jail, on release, Fuchs moves to East Germany, where he resides until his death in 1988.

March 1950   FBI officials begin to provide secret assistance and advice to Senator Joseph McCarthy (and continued to do so until July 1953).

March 14, 1950 The FBI's Ten Most Wanted Fugitives program is instituted.

July 17, 1950 FBI agents arrest Julius Rosenberg (and in August, his wife, Ethel) on charges of atomic espionage (having conspired with David Greenglass and Harry Gold to provide crucial information about the atomic bomb project to the Soviet Union during World War II). Their trial begins March 6, 1951. The Rosenbergs are convicted, sentenced to death by electrocution, and executed at Sing Sing federal prison on June 19, 1953.

September 23, 1950 Congress passes the Internal Security (or McCarran) Act, overriding President Truman's veto. Communist, communist front, and communist action organizations are required to register with a specially created Subversive Activities Control Board; sabotage and espionage laws are tightened; subversive aliens become susceptible to deportation; and subversive citizens are subject to detention. Because the act's preventive detention title differs from the standards that Attorney General Clark secretly instituted in 1948, Justice Department and FBI officials debate whether to conform preventive detention policy with the legislative standards. In October 1950, Attorney General J. Howard McGrath decides that detention listings should continue to be based on the Security Index program authorized in 1948. This procedure continues until Congress repeals the act's preventive detention title in September 1971. Rather than abandon listing dangerous persons, Attorney General John Mitchell authorizes FBI Director Hoover to continue listing individuals for preventive detention but to change the name of this listing from Security Index to Administrative Index.

February 12, 1951 FBI Director Hoover establishes the Responsibilities Program to disseminate to state governors (or their designated representatives) derogatory information about alleged subversives.

March 15, 1951 FBI Director Hoover institutes a liaison program whereby the FBI would process requests from the Senate Internal Security Subcommittee for name checks and other information and, in return, receive any information that subcommittee investigators had learned about subversive activists and organizations.

April 28, 1951 President Truman issues Executive Order 10241 modifying the dismissal standard of the Federal Employee Loyalty Program from "reasonable grounds to believe disloyal" to "reasonable doubt as to loyalty."

June 20, 1951 FBI Director Hoover institutes the Sex Deviates program to purge homosexual employees from the executive, legislative, and judicial branches of the federal government. This program is soon expanded to include disseminating information to university officials and law enforcement agencies.

February 26, 1952 Attorney General McGrath reaffirms the FBI's right to perform wiretaps but requires FBI officials to notify the Justice Department whenever FBI wiretaps are used in cases being considered for possible prosecution. McGrath refuses to authorize FBI microphone installations involving trespass.

March 19, 1953 FBI Director Hoover orders senior FBI officials to destroy, on a regular basis, all contents of their "office files"—every 6 months for FBI assistant directors and every 90 days for FBI supervisors.

April 26, 1953 President Dwight Eisenhower issues Executive Order 10450, instituting a new security program to deny federal employment to those who can not prove their "unswerving loyalty" to the United States.

November 6, 1953 Attorney General Herbert Brownell accuses former president Truman of laxity in handling security matters, citing Truman's appointment of Harry Dexter White as director of the International Monetary Fund, despite having received FBI reports questioning White's loyalty. When Truman denounces Brownell's charges as "McCarthyism" and defends his appointment of White, Brownell arranges to have himself and FBI Director Hoover testify on this matter before the Senate Internal Security Subcommittee on November 17, 1953.

December 15, 1953 President Eisenhower issues a directive reaffirming FBI investigative responsibilities concerning espionage, sabotage, and subversive activities and directing the FBI to investigate all violations of the Atomic Energy Act of 1946.

1954, day and month unknown FBI officials institute a "summary memorandum" procedure to compile background information on members of Congress. Summary memoranda are maintained separately from official FBI records, first in the Research and then in the Administrative unit at FBI headquarters. Prior to the institution of this procedure and continuing after, FBI Director Hoover maintains in his office specially indexed folders on members of Congress.

May 20, 1954 Attorney General Brownell authorizes FBI microphone surveillance (bugging), even when involving trespass, during "national security" investigations.

May 21, 1954   FBI officials unilaterally interpret Brownell's bugging directive to include such practices in criminal cases.

October 27, 1955   FBI Director Hoover authorizes FBI officials to assist reporter Don Whitehead, including offering selected information from FBI files and providing editorial review, to promote his writing of a history of the FBI, *The FBI Story* (a bestseller and eventually a popular movie).

August 28, 1956   FBI Director Hoover authorizes COINTELPRO–Communist Party, a program to "harass, disrupt, and discredit" the Communist Party by promoting dissension among members and disseminating derogatory information about prominent communists to carefully selected reporters, columnists, and public officials.

June 3, 1957   In *Jencks v. U.S.,* the Supreme Court rules that whenever FBI informers testify during a trial, defense attorneys are entitled to review the FBI's confidential pre-trial reports based on information provided by these informers. This ruling becomes controversial, and Congress enacts legislation narrowing access to FBI reports during trial proceedings to the "signed" statements of FBI informers and only that information pertinent to the informer's trial testimony.

June 21, 1957   FBI agents arrest Colonel Rudolf Ivanovich Abel, a Soviet espionage agent, in New York City. Convicted and sentenced to 30 years' imprisonment, Abel is exchanged in February 1962 for captured U-2 pilot Francis Gary Powers.

November 14, 1957   New York state trooper Edgar Croswell uncovers a conference of crime bosses at the secluded estate of Joseph Barbara in Apalachin, New York. Embarrassed by this confirmation of a nationwide crime syndicate, FBI Director Hoover institutes a special program, code-named Top Hoodlum, requiring FBI field offices to develop information about the activities of prominent crime leaders in their area.

1958   The publisher Henry Holt publishes FBI Director Hoover's best-selling exposé of the communist conspiracy, *Masters of Deceit.*

January 1958   FBI officials seek Post Office approval for a mail cover program (under which mail is not opened but the names of senders and recipients are recorded) involving all letters mailed to and received from the Soviet Union. In response, Post Office officials disclose that, since 1953, the CIA has conducted just such a program. Following discus-sions with CIA officials, in February 1958, FBI officials obtain CIA cooperation to provide them copies of mail that has been opened and copied.

1960, day and month unknown   FBI officials extend the "summary memorandum" procedure (see *1954, day and month unknown*) to state gubernatorial candidates and to those seeking election to Congress.

May 1960   The FBI cooperates informally with staff and members of the House Committee on Un-American Activities to publicize the committee's report ("Communist Target—Youth") and movie *(Operation Abolition)*, which question the loyalty and tactics of the committee's critics.

February 16, 1961   Attorney General Robert F. Kennedy authorizes FBI wiretapping of three Department of Agriculture employees, the secretary to House Agriculture Committee Chairman Harold Cooley, and a lobbyist for the Dominican Republic, to ascertain Dominican Republic efforts to amend proposed sugar quota legislation. The FBI resumes this investigation in April–June 1962 when similar sugar quota legislation is being considered by Congress, and at this time wiretaps the office of the Washington, D.C., law firm hired as lobbyist for the Dominican Republic, the residence of the clerk to the House Agriculture Committee, and five Dominican Republic establishments.

June 27, 1961   Attorney General Robert F. Kennedy requests an FBI investigation to identify the source of a leak concerning U.S. planning in Germany reported in a *Newsweek* article; the FBI wiretaps *Newsweek* reporter Lloyd Norman.

August 17, 1961   Attorney General Robert F. Kennedy grants blanket authorization for FBI request letters to telephone company officials to secure "leased lines" for "use in connection with microphone surveillances."

October 12, 1961   FBI Director Hoover authorizes COINTELPRO–Socialist Workers Party to "harass, disrupt, and discredit" this Trotskyite organization.

June 1962   Attorney General Robert F. Kennedy requests an FBI investigation of the source of a leak pertaining to Soviet missile systems published in the *New York Times,* and the FBI wiretaps *Times* reporter Hanson Baldwin and his secretary.

June 9, 1962   President John F. Kennedy assigns supervisory control over all internal security matters to the attorney general, revising policy instituted during Truman's presidency that vested such responsibility to NSC subcommittees, one chaired by the FBI director.

February 15, 1963   FBI Director Hoover orders intensified FBI investigations of organized crime syndicate leaders, cited as La Cosa Nostra, refining the Top Hoodlum program. In September 1963, one of the FBI's key informers, Joseph Valachi, publicly describes La Cosa Nostra's criminal activities during hearings held by the Senate Permanent Investigations Subcommittee, chaired by Arkansas Senator John McClellan.

June 12, 1963   Medgar Evers, the Mississippi field secretary of the National Association for the Advancement of Colored People, is killed outside his home in Jackson, Mississippi. Byron De La Beckwith is arrested but at first is not convicted owing to a hung jury. Reindicted in 1990, De La Beckwith is convicted in 1994.

October 18, 1963   Attorney General Robert F. Kennedy approves an FBI request to wiretap the headquarters of the Southern Christian Leadership Conference and the residence of Martin Luther King Jr. Kennedy approves the King wiretap on the condition that the FBI seek his reevaluation in 30 days, but this reevaluation is never sought. The King wiretap is discontinued in 1965 when Kennedy's successor as attorney general, Nicholas Katzenbach, learns of its existence.

November 22, 1963   President John F. Kennedy is assassinated in Dallas, Texas. President Lyndon Johnson immediately orders the FBI to investigate the murder. Dallas police arrest Lee Harvey Oswald that same day. While in police custody, Oswald is killed two days later by Dallas nightclub owner Jack Ruby. President Johnson orders the FBI to investigate this murder, as well (at the time, the FBI had no authority to investigate presidential assassinations, and both murders were local crimes). To allay public doubts about whether Oswald and Ruby had acted alone, President Johnson establishes a special commission, chaired by Supreme Court Chief Justice Earl Warren, and directs the FBI to assist the commission's staff of investigators.

May 8, 1964   President Johnson issues an executive order waiving, for FBI Director J. Edgar Hoover, the federal requirement of mandatory retirement for federal employees at age 70.

June 21, 1964   Civil rights activists James E. Chaney, Andrew Goodman, and Michael Schwerner are murdered near Philadelphia, Mississippi. Following an intensive FBI investigation, code-named MIBURN, 19 men are indicted under federal civil rights statutes. Only eight are convicted (including Deputy Sheriff Cecil Price and Imperial Wizard of the White Knights of the Ku Klux Klan of Mississippi Sam Holloway).

July 10, 1964   President Johnson directs the FBI to reopen its Jackson, Mississippi, field office (which had been closed in 1946). To dramatize the federal commitment to enforce civil rights laws, Johnson sends FBI Director Hoover in Air Force One to attend the formal opening ceremony.

August 22–23, 1964   Responding to a request from the Johnson White House, FBI Director Hoover sends a special 30-agent squad, headed by FBI assistant director Cartha DeLoach, to monitor developments at the Democratic National Convention in Atlantic City, New Jersey. The squad provides timely detailed reports to the White House on planned demonstrations, the activities of civil rights activists and their delegate supporters seeking to seat the Mississippi Freedom Democratic Party, and attempts to draft Robert Kennedy for the vice presidential nomination.

September 2, 1964   FBI Director Hoover authorizes COINTELPRO–White Hate Groups to "expose, disrupt, and otherwise neutralize the Ku Klux Klan (KKK) and specified other [white supremacist] hate groups."

October 26, 1964   Johnson White House aide Bill Moyers requests an FBI report on members of the Senate staff of Republican presidential nominee Barry Goldwater. The requested report is hand-delivered to the White House on October 28, 1964.

February 3, 1965   The FBI and Secret Service conclude a delimitation agreement ensuring Secret Service access to FBI information essential to protecting the president. The assassination of President John F. Kennedy is the catalyst to this agreement. This agreement is refined in May 1966 following congressional approval in August 1965 of legislation making it a federal crime to assault, kidnap, or kill the president, vice president, and other specified officials.

March 1965   Attorney General Nicholas Katzenbach issues new guidelines to govern FBI wiretapping and bugging. The prior written authorization of the attorney general is required for all FBI wiretaps and bugs, such authorization is limited to six-month periods, and each succeeding six-month period is to be reauthorized by the attorney general.

June 10, 1965   The J. Edgar Hoover Foundation is formally incorporated in Valley Forge, Pennsylvania, funded by millionaire businessman Lewis S. Rosenstiel to "perpetuate the ideas and purpose" to which the FBI director "dedicated his life" and to "safeguard the heritage and freedom of the United States."

September 19, 1965   The American Broadcasting Company (ABC) premiers the first national television network series on the FBI, *The FBI,* starring Efrem Zimbalist Jr. as FBI inspector Lewis Erskine, the show's central character. The series runs until 1974.

February 19, 1966   FBI Director Hoover agrees to a Johnson White House request that the FBI monitor the planned hearings of the Senate Foreign Relations Committee into the Johnson administration's Vietnam policy "with a view toward determining whether [Committee Chair William] Fulbright and the other Senators were receiving information from Communists."

March 14, 1966   President Johnson requests that the FBI monitor and immediately report to him any contacts of members of Congress and congressional staff with Soviet and Soviet bloc embassies. FBI officials submit weekly reports to the White House between May 13, 1966, and January 20, 1969, and resume such reporting to the Nixon White House on July 27, 1970.

June 13, 1966   The Supreme Court demands that the Justice Department outline the legal authority for the FBI's bugging of Fred Black, a criminal defendant appealing his conviction for income tax evasion. The Court's request precipitates a bitter dispute between FBI Director Hoover and Attorney General Katzenbach over FBI bugging authority, following Katzenbach's refusal to affirm that earlier attorneys general had directly authorized FBI bugging during criminal investigations.

July 4, 1966   President Johnson signs the Freedom of Information Act requiring, subject to broad exemptions, the public release of specified federal agency and department records. On November 21, 1974, Congress overrides President Gerald Ford's veto of amendments broadening the act's disclosure requirement and subjecting FBI records to the mandatory disclosure requirement (with specified exemptions). On October 17, 1986, this act is further amended to exempt specified law enforcement investigative

information from mandatory release and to permit FBI officials neither to confirm nor deny that records even existed involving ongoing criminal investigations and FBI informants.

July 19, 1966   FBI Director Hoover bans further FBI break-ins during "domestic security" and criminal investigations.

September 1966   Assistant Attorney General Fred Vinson orders the creation of a special ELSUR Index to record the names of all individuals whose conversations had been intercepted by FBI wiretaps or bugs.

December 1966   Based on information provided by FBI Director Hoover, Republican Congressman H. R. Gross publicly accuses former attorney general Robert F. Kennedy of having authorized FBI bugging, escalating the rift between Kennedy and Hoover that first surfaced publicly during the Supreme Court's review of the Fred Black case.

January 1967   The FBI's National Crime Information Center becomes operational.

August 25, 1967   FBI Director Hoover authorizes COINTELPRO–Black Nationalist Hate Groups to "expose, disrupt, misdirect, discredit, or otherwise neutralize" black nationalist and other militant civil rights organizations and "their leadership, spokesmen, membership and supporters."

April 4, 1968   Martin Luther King Jr. is assassinated in Memphis, Tennessee. Initiating an intensive investigation (on grounds that King's civil rights were violated, as murder was not a federal offense), the FBI identified James Earl Ray as King's assassin. On June 8, 1968, Scotland Yard officials arrest Ray in London, England. Ray pleads guilty to King's murder and receives a life sentence. He subsequently denies guilt and claims to have been the victim of poor defense and a conspiracy to protect the real assassins.

June 1968   Congress enacts the Omnibus Crime Control and Safe Streets Act, providing federal assistance to local and state police. The act legalizes electronic surveillance (wiretapping and bugging) during criminal investigations, subject to a warrant requirement, but stipulates that this requirement is not intended to "limit the constitutional powers of the President" in the national security arena. In addition, the term of the FBI director is limited to 10 years; future FBI directors are to be nominated by the president and confirmed by the Senate.

June 6, 1968 Sirhan Sirhan assassinates Democratic presidential candidate Robert F. Kennedy in Los Angeles, California, on the eve of Kennedy's victory in the California primary. Although Sirhan is immediately apprehended, the FBI initiates an intensive investigation to ascertain whether he acted alone.

October 28, 1968 FBI Director Hoover authorizes COINTELPRO–New Left to "harass, discredit, and disrupt" radical student organizations and their adherents.

October 30, 1968 National Security Council executive secretary J. Bromley Smith requests FBI physical surveillance of the South Vietnamese embassy in Washington, D.C., and Anna Chennault, a prominent Republican. The purpose was to ascertain whether Republican activists were pressuring the South Vietnamese government to adopt a harder line during the negotiations in Paris (France) to end the Vietnam War. A stalemate in these negotiations could further the electoral fortunes of Republican presidential nominee Richard Nixon. On November 13, 1968, President Johnson requests that the FBI check all telephone toll calls to ascertain whether Republican vice presidential nominee Spiro Agnew has called the South Vietnamese embassy or Chennault on November 2, 1968.

May 9, 1969 At the request of President Richard Nixon and National Security Adviser Henry Kissinger, FBI Director Hoover authorizes FBI wiretapping of 17 individuals (members of the White House and National Security Council staffs, State and Defense Department officials, and 4 Washington reporters) to ascertain the source of the leak disclosing U.S. bombing of Cambodia, published in a story by *New York Times* reporter William Beecher. The wiretaps continue through February 1971, when Hoover discontinues them. The FBI never uncovers the source of the leak; the wiretap reports, nonetheless, provide valuable political intelligence to the White House.

November 5, 1969 At the request of the Nixon White House, the FBI investigates syndicated columnist Joseph Kraft to ascertain his sources of information about the Paris peace negotiations to end the Vietnamese war.

November 26, 1969 FBI Director Hoover authorizes the INLET program, providing to President Nixon, Vice President Agnew, and Attorney General John Mitchell intelligence about internal security matters and also "items with an unusual twist or concerning prominent personalities which may be of special interest to the President and Attorney General."

March 31, 1970 Incensed by CIA attempts to ascertain FBI sources relating to Professor Thomas Riha (a CIA source who had disappeared), FBI Director Hoover severs the FBI's liaison relationship with the CIA and cuts back FBI wiretapping, bugging, and mail-opening programs instituted at the request of CIA officials.

May 4, 1970 Four Kent State (Ohio) University students are killed by Ohio National Guardsmen seeking to restore order to the campus following student protests over President Nixon's May 1, 1970, decision to invade Cambodia. The FBI initiates an intensive investigation to ascertain responsibility for the student deaths.

June 5, 1970 President Nixon directs FBI Director Hoover to assist in House minority leader Gerald Ford's effort to impeach Supreme Court Justice William Douglas.

July 23, 1970 Michigan police officials arrest White Panther Party activist Lawrence R. Plamonson, based on information provided through the FBI's National Crime Information Center (NCIC). Plamonson becomes the first individual on the FBI's "Top Ten" fugitive list apprehended through the resources of the NCIC.

July 23, 1970 White House aide Tom Charles Huston sends an "official" memorandum to the directors of the FBI, CIA, NSA, and DIA authorizing "clearly illegal" investigative techniques and subjecting the intelligence agencies to closer White House direction. A special interagency task force appointed by President Nixon on June 5, 1970, had drafted this plan. On July 27, 1970, FBI Director Hoover briefs Attorney General Mitchell about this plan and his intent to record in writing any future FBI action. Mitchell briefs Nixon of Hoover's intentions on July 28; Nixon directs Huston to recall the authorization memorandum.

August 24, 1970 A research lab in Sterling Hall at the University of Wisconsin–Madison is bombed, resulting in extensive damage, one death, and three injuries. Following an intensive FBI investigation, four fugitives (Karleton Armstrong, Dwight Armstrong, David S. Fine, and Leo F. Burt) are indicted.

October 15, 1970 Congress approves the Organized Crime Control Act (also known as the Racketeer Influenced Corrupt Organizations Act, or RICO Act) expanding the FBI's authority to prosecute organized crime leaders.

November 25, 1970   Nixon White House aide H. R. Haldeman asks FBI Director Hoover to provide the White House with a list of Washington reporters who are homosexuals (and "any other stuff"). The requested report is hand-delivered to the White House two days later.

March 8, 1971   A radical anti–Vietnam War group, the Citizens' Committee to Investigate the FBI, successfully burglarizes the FBI's resident agency in Media, Pennsylvania, seizing thousands of pages of FBI files and then disseminating these files to the news media and to selected members of Congress. FBI Director Hoover orders an intensive investigation to identify the perpetrators of this break-in (code-named MEDBURG) and closes 103 of the FBI's 538 resident agencies. In its February 1972 issue, *WIN* magazine, the publication of the War Resisters League, publishes, in their entirety, the purloined FBI documents.

April 28, 1971   FBI Director Hoover terminates the various COINTELPROs, as they had been compromised by the Media break-in.

June 13, 1971   The *New York Times* publishes the first installment of the so-called Pentagon Papers (a classified internal-use history of U.S. policy in Indochina, prepared in 1968 by Defense Department officials). An intensive FBI investigation identifies Daniel Ellsberg as the individual who has leaked the material to the *Times* (and other newspapers).

July 4, 1971   A white supremacist organization opposed to the desegregation of public schools dynamites school buses in Longview, Texas. Following an intensive FBI investigation, two persons are convicted on federal civil rights and conspiracy charges.

September 30, 1971   FBI Director Hoover fires Assistant to the Director William Sullivan and locks him out of his office. Unknown to Hoover, in July 1971, Sullivan (who surreptitiously helped develop the Huston Plan) delivers to Assistant Attorney General Robert Mardian the wiretap transcripts he had maintained in his office (instituted in response to the Beecher article on the bombing of Cambodia) and other sensitive FBI records, ostensibly to prevent Hoover from "blackmailing" the Nixon White House.

October 22–23, 1971   White House officials urge President Nixon to request Hoover's resignation as FBI director (an action which the president had considered and rejected in July 1971).

October 29–30, 1971   Princeton University's Woodrow Wilson School of Politics and International Affairs and the American Civil Liberties Union's Committee for Public

Justice co-sponsor a conference to evaluate FBI practices and policies (resulting in the publication of a critical book, *Investigating the FBI*). Rejecting an invitation to have FBI personnel participate, Hoover instead orders an FBI investigation of the conference, its organizers, and its principal participants, and covertly assists efforts by conservative journalists and members of Congress to impugn the loyalty of conference organizers and participants.

March 20, 1972   NBC reporter Carl Stern files a Freedom of Information Act request for the FBI's COINTELPRO files (which he had learned of through the Media documents). Stern's request is denied but he successfully obtains the files when, on September 25, 1973, Federal Judge Barrington Parker rules favorably on his suit.

April 7, 1972   Richard F. McCoy Jr. hijacks an airplane en route from Denver to Los Angeles; forces the pilot to land at San Francisco airport to retrieve his demanded $500,000 ransom, four parachutes, and his luggage; orders the pilot to resume flight; and parachutes over Provo, Utah. FBI agents apprehend McCoy two days later.

May 2, 1972   J. Edgar Hoover dies.

May 3, 1972   Following the death of FBI Director Hoover, President Nixon appoints L. Patrick Gray acting FBI director. Nominated FBI director in February 1973, Gray withdraws on April 23, 1973, having admitted during Senate confirmation hearings to destroying records that Nixon White House aides had given him in 1972.

May 4, 1972   Helen Gandy, Hoover's administrative assistant, begins reviewing and then shredding the former FBI director's "Personal and Confidential File." In contrast, acting associate director W. Mark Felt incorporates Hoover's "Official and Confidential File" into the FBI central records system.

May 8, 1972   The new FBI Academy opens on the U.S. Marine Corps base at Quantico, Virginia, with the first expanded class (numbering 200 students) held on June 26, 1972.

June 17, 1972   Washington, D.C., police arrest five individuals (James W. McCord Jr., Bernard L. Barker, Eugenio R. Martinez, Frank A. Sturgis, and Virgilo R. Gonzalez) inside the Democratic National Committee headquarters in the Watergate office building. Discovering that the five arrestees had illegally bugged the Democratic headquarters, the Washington police request an FBI investigation the next day. The FBI soon identifies G. Gordon Liddy (a former Nixon White House aide who is an official on Nixon's reelection committee) and E. Howard Hunt Jr. (a former CIA officer who is a White House consultant) as organizers of this break-in. The seven are indicted on September 15, 1972, for conspiracy, burglary, and interception of communications. All but Liddy and McCord plead guilty when the trial begins on January 8, 1973. On January 30, 1973, McCord and Liddy are convicted. Fearing a harsh sentence, McCord charges that Nixon's reelection committee had orchestrated the break-in and a resulting cover-up, triggering a special Senate investigation later that year.

June 19, 1972   In *U.S. v. U.S. District Court*, the Supreme Court rules that the president does not have the constitutional power to authorize warrantless "domestic security" wiretaps. Its ruling implies that presidents might have the power to order warrantless "foreign intelligence" wiretaps.

September 7, 1972   The FBI's Identification Division installs a prototype computerized fingerprint reader system.

October 24, 1972   Congress enacts Public Law 92-539, Protection of Foreign Officials and Official Guests of the United States, to permit FBI investigations of any kidnapping involving foreign officials and official guests. In the first case prosecuted under this statute, Gourgen M. Yanikian is convicted on July 2, 1973, and sentenced to life imprisonment for murdering two Turkish consular officials in Santa Barbara, California, on January 27, 1973.

April 27, 1973   President Nixon appoints William D. Ruckelshaus FBI acting director following L. Patrick Gray's resignation.

June 6, 1973   President Nixon nominates Clarence M. Kelley (at the time, the police chief of Kansas City, Missouri, and a former FBI agent and SAC) as FBI director. Confirmed by the Senate on June 27, 1973, Kelley is sworn in on July 9, 1973.

July 11, 1973   Attorney General Elliot Richardson issues an executive order authorizing the release to historical researchers of closed FBI records over 15 years old.

February 1974   FBI officials launch a program codenamed PRISACT to promote better liaison and coordination with police officials nationwide concerning the activities of militant extremists and revolutionaries held in penal institutions. This program focuses on black nationalists and revolutionaries.

February 4, 1974   Members of the Symbionese Liberation Army kidnap Patty Hearst, the daughter of newspaper publisher William Randolph Hearst, from her Berkeley,

California, apartment. Following an intensive investigation by the FBI and local police, Hearst, William Harris, Emily Harris, Wendy Yoshimura, and Stephen Solian are arrested—a brainwashed Hearst having converted to her kidnappers' philosophy and having participated in a string of robberies.

January 27, 1975   The Senate establishes the Senate Select Committee on Intelligence Activities to investigate the role, authority, and conduct of the various federal intelligence agencies, and specifically the FBI and the CIA. The resulting Senate investigation (both public hearings and published reports) uncovers numerous examples of FBI abuses of power and violations of privacy rights. On May 19, 1976, the Senate establishes a permanent Senate Select Committee on Intelligence with oversight responsibilities over foreign intelligence operations—oversight over the FBI's domestic operations remains the province of the Judiciary Committee.

February 19, 1975   The House creates a companion special committee to investigate the intelligence agencies, at first chaired by Lucien Nedzi and then Otis Pike. On January 29, 1976, the House votes not to release the Committee's final report. When the *Village Voice* obtains and publishes a copy of this report, the House attempts to ascertain the source of this leak but ultimately votes to establish a permanent House intelligence oversight committee.

February 27, 1975   During testimony before the House Subcommittee on Civil and Constitutional Rights, Attorney General Edward Levi discloses that former FBI director J. Edgar Hoover had maintained in his office dossiers containing derogatory information on prominent Americans (including presidents and members of Congress).

June 26, 1975   FBI agents Jack R. Coler and Ronald A. Williams are killed while conducting an investigation on an Indian reservation near Pine Ridge, South Dakota. Following a massive FBI investigation, American Indian Movement leader Leonard Peltier is arrested, convicted, and sentenced to two consecutive life terms for the murders.

September 30, 1975   The J. Edgar Hoover FBI Building in Washington, D.C., is formally dedicated.

February 18, 1976   President Gerald Ford issues Executive Order 11905, broadly outlining the authority and responsibilities of the federal intelligence agencies.

March 10, 1976   Attorney General Edward Levi issues guidelines to govern FBI counterintelligence and domestic security investigations. While the counterintelligence guidelines remain secret, those governing domestic security investigations permit "preliminary" investigations of suspected "terrorist" activities, including advocacy to violate federal laws. Preliminary investigations are limited to a 90-day period. In contrast, "full" investigations require evidence of planned violation of a federal statute and must be authorized annually—and in writing—by Justice Department officials.

March, 17, 1976   FBI agents in New York City discover 25 volumes of documents in the office safe of the New York City special agent in charge, John Malone, pertaining to break-ins conducted by the New York office between 1954 and 1973. Pursuant to FBI Director Hoover's 1942 Do Not File procedure for break-in request and authorization memoranda, these documents should have been destroyed within six months of their creation. A subsequent FBI investigation confirms that no other FBI field office has retained break-in documents.

March 26, 1976   National Archives officials approve an FBI records destruction plan, submitted in May 1975, to destroy all closed FBI field office records. A number of civic organizations file suit challenging this and another plan to purge FBI headquarters records. In January 1980, Judge Harold Greene enjoins the FBI and National Archives from further record destruction and demands that these agencies develop a new plan to preserve FBI records of "historical value."

July 1976   During pretrial hearings in a suit brought by the Socialist Workers Party (SWP), U.S. attorneys disclose that the FBI regularly broke into SWP offices during the 1960s and 1970s. This admission, which contradicts earlier testimony in the trial, is the result of the discovery of break-in documents in the safe of New York SAC John Malone (see *March 17, 1976*).

September 21, 1976   Cuban exile Orlando Letelier, at the time affiliated with the Institute for Policy Studies, and co-worker Ronnie Moffitt are killed when a bomb explodes under their car in Washington, D.C. Following an intensive FBI investigation, Michael Townley, Jose Suarez y Esquivel, and Armando Fernandez Larios are convicted of conspiring to kill Letelier and Moffitt. High officials in the Chilean secret police are also implicated in orchestrating the murders.

October 4, 1976   A special FBI Office of Professional Responsibility is established to review matters relating to ethical or criminal allegations involving FBI personnel.

April 7, 1977   FBI agent John Kearney is indicted for illegal mail-opening, wiretaps, and break-ins during an investigation of radical fugitives (members of the Weather Underground) in New York City during the early 1970s. On April 10, 1978, the Justice Department drops prosecution of Kearney and indicts former acting director L. Patrick Gray, former acting associate director W. Mark Felt, and former assistant director Edward Miller for having authorized the illegal activities conducted by Kearney's squad. Felt and Miller are convicted but are pardoned by President Ronald Reagan on March 26, 1981. Gray petitions to be tried separately, and his case never goes to trial.

January 1, 1978   Under legislation enacted in 1976, FBI agents and officials must retire upon reaching the age of 55.

January 24, 1978   President Jimmy Carter issues Executive Order 12036, instituting stricter rules governing foreign intelligence and counterintelligence activities.

February 23, 1978   William H. Webster is sworn in as FBI director. President Carter nominates the former federal judge for this post on January 19, 1978. Confirmed by the Senate on February 9, 1978, Webster serves until May 26, 1978, when he resigns to accept appointment as CIA director.

April 3, 1978   FBI officials initiate the use of laser technology to detect latent "crime scene" fingerprints.

May 20, 1978   FBI agents arrest Rudolph Chernyayev and Valdik Enger, Soviet citizens employed at the United Nations, on charges of attempting to bribe a U.S. naval officer to obtain Navy secrets. Another Soviet citizen, Vladimir Zinyakin, is also arrested but is released because of diplomatic immunity. Chernyayev and Enger are convicted and sentenced to 10 years' imprisonment.

June 7, 1978   Following an intensive FBI undercover investigation code-named UNIAC, 22 labor union officials and shipping executives are indicted in Miami for kickbacks, embezzling, and other illegal activities. Among those convicted is Anthony M. Scotto, a longshoremen's union leader and reputed organized crime figure.

October 1978   The FBI's Richmond field office is selected as the site for the Field Office Information Management System (FOIMS), a program that becomes fully operational when the Las Vegas office comes online on June 30, 1988.

October 25, 1978 President Carter signs the Foreign Intelligence Surveillance Act, creating a special court to review and approve, in secret, all government requests to install wiretaps and bugs during foreign intelligence investigations.

December 18, 1978 The computerized Intelligence Information System is first used at FBI headquarters.

February 16, 1979 The first African American SAC, John D. Glover, is appointed to that position in the Milwaukee field office. On April 22, 1986, Glover is promoted to executive assistant director.

May 29, 1979 U.S. District Judge John H. Wood is assassinated near his home in San Antonio, Texas. Following an FBI investigation, Charles V. Harrelson and four others are indicted on April 15, 1982, and are convicted in 1983 for murder and conspiring to commit murder.

July 1979 The first Asian American ASAC, Don S. Tokunaga, is appointed to that position in the FBI's Albuquerque field office. Tokunaga is promoted to SAC of the Seattle office in December 1985.

February 3, 1980 News stories publicly reveal the FBI's ABSCAM investigation, in which undercover agents posing as an Arab sheik and his aides attempt to bribe members of Congress to secure political favors. Six U.S. congressmen, one U.S. senator, and numerous state officials are indicted and convicted in one of the first cases to use closed-circuit television during surveillance and as evidence in the trial that followed.

February 9, 1980 The FBI's undercover investigation code-named BRILAB leads to the political corruption and bribery indictments of New Orleans crime boss Carlos Marcello and a former Louisiana state commissioner.

April 21, 1980 The computerized Organized Crime Information System is instituted in the FBI's Detroit field office.

October 3, 1980 The FBI's Identification Division inaugurates a computerized system for searching and processing fingerprint records. Research time is reduced from two weeks to 24 hours in the largest fully integrated, online, 10-print fingerprint system in the world.

January 5, 1981 Attorney General Benjamin Civiletti issues guidelines governing FBI investigations involving bribery of public officials.

March 30, 1981 John W. Hinckley Jr. attempts to assassinate President Ronald Reagan in Washington, D.C., wounding the president, the president's press secretary, a Secret Service agent, and a Washington, D.C., police officer. A subsequent FBI investigation uncovers no conspiracy. Hinckley is indicted on August 24, 1981, but is found not guilty by reason of insanity on June 21, 1982.

June 16, 1981 The FBI Forensic Science Research and Training Center is formally dedicated at the FBI Academy in Quantico, Virginia.

June 21, 1981 Helped by the FBI, Atlanta police arrest Wayne B. Williams for the murder of African American children (there had been 28 unsolved murders). Williams is indicted and convicted for two of these murders and is sentenced to two consecutive life terms.

December 4, 1981 President Ronald Reagan issues Executive Order 12333, outlining new rules governing foreign intelligence and counterintelligence operations. Under this order, when requested by officials of other intelligence agencies, the FBI can "conduct within the United States" investigations to "collect foreign intelligence or to support foreign intelligence collection requirements."

January 28, 1982 Attorney General William French Smith orders the head of the Drug Enforcement Administration (DEA) to report to the FBI director and gives concurrent jurisdiction to the FBI and DEA over narcotics violations.

March 7, 1983 Attorney General Smith issues guidelines to govern FBI "domestic security/terrorism" investigations. FBI investigations to "anticipate or prevent" crime are authorized "when the facts or circumstances reasonably indicate that two or more persons are engaged in an enterprise [to further] political or social goals wholly or in part through activities that involve force or violence and a violation of the criminal law of the United States" or whenever individuals or organizations "advocate criminal activity or indicate an apparent intent to engage in crime, particularly crimes of violence." Smith rescinds current requirements that the attorney general review such investigations annually and in writing to determine whether their continuance is warranted. Instead, FBI officials need only "notify" the Justice Department's Office of Intelligence Policy of such investigations, and the attorney general's oversight role is defined as "may, as he deems necessary, request the FBI to prepare a report on the investigation."

August 1983   FBI officials establish a specially trained Hostage Rescue Team to be deployed in crisis situations to rescue hostages or arrest violent individuals.

November 7, 1983   A bomb is exploded in the U.S. Capitol. Following an intensive FBI investigation, Laura J. Whitehorn, Linda S. Evans, and Marilyn J. Buck plead guilty on September 7, 1990, to conspiring to commit this and seven other bombings in New York City and Washington, D.C. Buck and Evans are sentenced to 10 years in prison each, and Whitehorn to 20 years.

February 6, 1984   The FBI's National Crime Information Center cross references its Missing Person File (operational since October 1, 1975) and its Unidentified Person File (operational since June 30, 1983).

March 15, 1984   Former Deputy Traffic Court Clerk Harold Conn is convicted of bribery as the result of the FBI's GREYLORD investigation of corruption in the Cook County, Illinois, Circuit Court. In subsequent trials, Circuit Judge Wayne Olson pleads guilty to similar charges on July 18, 1985, and lawyers Robert Daniels, Harry Jaffe, and Harlan Becker are convicted of bribery on February 17, 1987. Of the 88 judges, lawyers, clerks, and police officers who are indicted, only 4 are acquitted (although 2 others commit suicide before the start of their trials).

April 9, 1984   Culminating a lengthy organized crime and heroin trafficking investigation (known as the Pizza Connection case), FBI agents document the international connections of organized crime syndicates in the United States and their use of pizza parlors to launder drug money. Eighteen crime leaders are convicted on March 2, 1987, including Gaetano Badalamenti, a former leader of the Sicilian Mafia.

July 10, 1984   The National Center for Analysis of Violent Crime is established at the FBI Academy in Quantico, Virginia. Focusing on unsolved murders, this center employs sophisticated behavior science techniques (profiling) and a complex computer system to assist local and state police authorities.

October 2, 1984   The Joint Italian-American Working Group to Fight Drug Trafficking and Organized Crime holds its first meeting in Washington, D.C. Created in October 1983 by President Reagan and the president of the Italian Council of Ministers, Bettino Craxi, the group promotes cooperation to combat crime. Successes include the extradi-

tion of Michele Sindona (who had been convicted in connection with the collapse of the Franklin National Bank) to Milan, Italy.

October 3, 1984   FBI agents arrest former FBI agent Richard W. Miller, making him the first agent in FBI history to be arrested for espionage. Miller is convicted on June 19, 1986, his co-conspirators (Nikolai and Svetlana Ogorodnikov) having earlier pled guilty to conspiracy to commit espionage.

October 12, 1984   President Reagan signs Public Law 98-473, the 1984 Omnibus Crime Control Act, extending federal criminal jurisdiction to computer crimes and counterfeiting consumer goods and strengthening federal authority to seize and confiscate the assets of drug traffickers.

November 26, 1984   Carolyn G. Morris is appointed deputy assistant director of the Technical Services Division, becoming the first woman to hold such a senior FBI appointment.

March 5, 1985   The bodies of Drug Enforcement Administration officer Enrique Camarena Salazar and a Mexican pilot are found in Guadalajara, Mexico (they had been abducted on February 7, 1985). The FBI's assistance in the investigation leads to the indictment of 22 individuals in Los Angeles and the conviction of 24 in Mexico, including a Mexican police official and a Mexican state police officer.

May 19, 1985   FBI agents arrest former Navy intelligence officer John Walker for giving classified Navy codes to Soviet agents. Walker's (and his accomplices') convictions conclude an intensive investigation code-named WIND FLYER and terminate Walker's 18 years of spying for the Soviet Union.

November 21, 1985   Navy intelligence analyst Jonathan Jay Pollard is arrested for spying for Israel (his wife, Anne Henderson-Pollard, is arrested on the same charges two days later). Pollard pleads guilty on June 4, 1986, to conspiring to receive embezzled government property, and his wife pleads guilty to being an accessory. On March 3, 1987, Israeli Brigadier General Aviem Sella is indicted for recruiting Pollard as a spy and receiving U.S. defense secrets.

November 23, 1985   Former CIA analyst Larry Wu Tai Chin is arrested for spying for the People's Republic of China, dating from 1952. Convicted February 7, 1986, he commits suicide two weeks later.

November 25, 1985 Following an intensive FBI investigation, Ronald W. Pelton is arrested for selling military secrets to the Soviet Union and is sentenced to life imprisonment.

December 30, 1985 Ten members of a white supremacist group, The Order, are convicted on federal racketeering charges for a series of robberies and murders committed to further their plans for a white supremacist revolution. Their trial involves the first use of the Racketeering Influenced and Corrupt Organizations (or RICO) Act against a political movement.

April 11, 1986 FBI agents Benjamin Grogan and Jerry Dove are killed, and five other agents are wounded, during a shoot-out with two suspected bank robbers in Miami, Florida. Both suspects are killed. These are the highest casualties in the FBI's history.

July 28, 1986 FBI agents arrest 13 individuals for plotting to overthrow the government of Suriname. All either plead guilty or decline to contest the charges.

September 9, 1986 Following an intensive FBI investigation code-named ILLWIND, 54 Defense Department and private defense contracting officials are indicted—and in 1989, are convicted—on bribery, fraud, and other charges involving the awarding of government defense contracts. Defense contractors Unisys Corporation and United Technologies Corporation are fined and penalized $190 million and $6 million, respectively.

October 10, 1986 The Nicaraguan military shoots down a Southern Air Transport plane and arrests its sole survivor, Eugene Hasenfus. Hasenfus admits to having transported guns to Nicaraguan rebels (the "Contras") and is tried, convicted, and pardoned in a Nicaraguan court for espionage. An FBI investigation is initiated to ascertain whether Southern Air Transport has been transporting arms at the direction of U.S. officials in violation of U.S. neutrality laws and the so-called Boland Amendment of 1984 prohibiting any funding of the Contras.

November 1, 1986 *El Sharia,* a Beirut (Lebanon) newspaper, reports that the United States government has sold arms to Iran to obtain the release of U.S. hostages held in Lebanon. Because arms sales to Iran are illegal, Attorney General Edwin Meese III initiates an internal Justice Department inquiry. On November 25, 1986, Meese confirms the arms sales to Iran and that some of the proceeds from the sales have been diverted to assist the Contras. Two simultaneous investigations are initiated, one by a special congressional committee in 1987 and the second by Independent Counsel Lawrence Walsh. The FBI plays a key role in these two investigations.

November 18, 1986 Through the cooperation of FBI and Drug Enforcement Administration agents, nine members of the Medellin (Colombia) drug cartel are indicted for smuggling at least 58 tons of cocaine into the United States. None of those indicted are in custody, although on February 4, 1987, the alleged head of the cartel, Carlos Lehder Rivas, is arrested in Colombia and extradited to the United States.

January 5, 1987 Following an intensive FBI investigation, reputed Philadelphia crime boss Nicodemo ("Little Nicky") Scarfo and Philadelphia Councilman Leland Beloff are indicted for conspiring to extort $1 million from a developer. Scarfo and 11 associates are also indicted on April 9, 1987, for the murder of a New Jersey municipal court judge. Scarfo is convicted and sentenced to 14 years imprisonment and a $150,000 fine. On January 11, 1988, Scarfo and 16 associates are indicted for murder, attempted murder, extortion, and other crimes, and are later found guilty.

May 9, 1987 FBI agents arrest three members of the Jewish Defense League for having, since 1984, committed a series of bombings in the New York area—including a September 1986 bombing of the Metropolitan Opera House.

July 24, 1987 President Reagan nominates Federal Judge William Steele Sessions as director of the FBI. Confirmed by the Senate on September 25, 1987, Sessions assumes office on November 2, 1987.

September 13, 1987 FBI agents arrest Fawaz Younis for the 1985 hijacking of a Jordanian plane containing four American passengers. Younis is convicted and sentenced to 30 years' imprisonment.

November 17, 1987 Neo-Nazis Bruce Pierce and David Lane are convicted of violating the civil rights of Denver talk host Alan Berg when murdering him in June 1984. Two other white supremacists, Richard Scutari and Jean Craig, are found not guilty of this charge.

January 1988 Responding to a Freedom of Information Act request, the FBI releases its files on the Committee in Solidarity with the People of El Salvador (CISPES). These reveal that, from 1981 through 1985, FBI agents had closely monitored CISPES and other groups (UAW and NEA locals) and individuals (Catholic nuns and college students) opposed to the Reagan administration's Central America policy.

February 5, 1988   Following a coordinated investigation of the FBI, the Drug Enforcement Administration, and the Customs Bureau, Panamanian General Manuel A. Noriega and 16 associates are arrested on drug smuggling and money laundering charges.

April 1988   Released FBI records confirm that, dating from 1962, under a code-named Library Awareness program, the FBI had asked librarians to identify any individuals having a foreign accent who had borrowed scientific and other specialized periodicals. The program's ostensible purpose was to monitor the foreign intelligence and industrial espionage efforts of foreign agents.

September 26, 1988   Federal Judge Lucius D. Bunton rules that the FBI systematically discriminated against Hispanic agents in promotions and working conditions. In the second phase of this class action suit, Judge Bunton, on May 5, 1989, orders changes in FBI promotion procedures but declines to award back pay to the complainant Hispanic agents.

December 1, 1988   The FBI Laboratory begins accepting deoxyribonucleic acid (DNA) samples for analysis, to aid state and local police agencies in identifying or eliminating subjects of investigation. On September 22, 1989, the Virginia Supreme Court, in the first appeal of a murder conviction based on DNA evidence, upholds the conviction and death sentence of Timothy Wilson Spencer. In a September 1990 ruling, a federal judge in Rutland, Vermont, upholds the use of the DNA test identifying the alleged rapist in a criminal trial.

December 6, 1988   Working with the Drug Enforcement Administration, Navy, Coast Guard, and Customs Bureau in an undercover operation that began in 1985, FBI agents seize millions of dollars of drugs, cash, and property and arrest subjects in seven cities, including two operatives of the Medellin drug cartel. Code-named CATCOM, this operation employs a Miami electronics firm as a front to supply communications devices to narcotics cartels (which intercept the conversations of cartel members).

February 1989   In an undercover operation code-named WHITE MARE, FBI agents and New York City police seize 820 pounds of heroin in Queens, New York, the largest confiscation in U.S. history.

March 28, 1989   In cooperation with other federal and state agencies, the FBI investigates the *Exxon Valdez* disaster of March 24, 1989 (the tanker *Exxon Valdez* had run aground on a reef and discharged 11 million gallons of crude oil in Prince William Sound, Alaska). The Exxon Corporation and Exxon Shipping Company are indicted and plead guilty to environmental crimes.

April 19, 1989   Following an intensive FBI investigation, former Army clandestine warfare specialist Thomas J. Dolce is sentenced to 10 years' imprisonment for giving classified military documents to South African agents.

June 21, 1989   Attorney General Richard Thornburgh authorizes the FBI to arrest suspected terrorists, drug traffickers, and other fugitives abroad, without the consent of the foreign country in which they reside.

July 24, 1989   Burdena G. Pasenelli is appointed assistant SAC, serving in the Houston office. Pasenelli becomes the first female SAC, heading the Anchorage office, beginning on February 24, 1992. On October 13, 1993, she is promoted to assistant director of the Finance Division.

January 18, 1990   FBI and Washington, D.C., police officers arrest Washington, D.C., mayor Marion Barry for cocaine possession. Charged with 14 counts of perjury and cocaine possession, Barry is convicted of only one misdemeanor cocaine possession charge.

March 26, 1990   FBI agents arrest New England crime boss Raymond C. Patriarca and 14 others on a 113-count indictment of murder, racketeering, drug trafficking, gambling, kidnapping, obstruction of justice, and witness intimidation.

June 12, 1990   FBI agent Mark S. Putnam pleads guilty to first degree manslaughter in the death of a Pikeville, Kentucky, woman. Sentenced to 16 years' imprisonment, Putnam is the first FBI agent convicted of a homicide-related crime.

August 1990   FBI Director Sessions agrees to settle suit brought by former FBI agent Donald Rochon, who has alleged racial harassment by other agents and his superiors when assigned to the Omaha, Chicago, and Philadelphia field offices. Sessions agrees to a monetary settlement and disciplines 11 FBI agents for either harassing Rochon or ignoring his complaints.

August 24, 1990   Under an FBI program code-named LOST TRUST, five South Carolina legislators are indicted for vote selling. Ten legislators are eventually indicted with four pleading guilty and resigning their seats and State Representative Luther Taylor being convicted of bribery.

September 1990 FBI Director Sessions appoints FBI agent Jimmy Carter to head FBI recruiting in—and to serve as FBI liaison to—the black community. Carter is the first African American to hold this position.

November 7, 1990 Following an intensive FBI investigation code-named VANPAC, Walter L. Moody Jr. is indicted for the bombing deaths of Federal Judge Robert S. Vance (on December 16, 1989) and civil rights attorney and NAACP official Robert E. Robinson (on December 18, 1989). Moody is convicted and sentenced to two life terms plus 400 years.

January 1991 Under an undercover operation code-named DRAGON CHASE, FBI agents in New York seize 28 pounds of high-quality China White heroin and secure the indictment of 10 individuals in the United States and Thailand (with the main suspect being arrested in Bangkok) for drug trafficking.

January 16, 1991 Following the onset of military conflict with Iraq, FBI agents—anicipating possible terrorist operations within the United States—begin interviewing prominent Arab American leaders.

August 1991 The FBI Laboratory creates a special Computer Analysis and Response Team (CART) to use computers to support FBI investigations.

August 30, 1991 FBI and Bureau of Prisons teams rescue nine hostages held by Cuban refugees at the Talladega, Alabama, federal prison. None of the hostages is hurt and only one inmate suffers injury during this rescue operation.

November 14, 1991 Following an intensive FBI investigation coordinated with foreign police authorities, two Libyan intelligence officers are indicted for the terrorist bombing of Pan American flight 103, which exploded over Lockerbie, Scotland, on December 21, 1988.

November 15, 1991 The Bank of Credit and Commerce International (BCCI) and three BCCI officials (Agha Hasan Adebi, Swaleh Naqvi, and Ghaith Pharaon) are indicted for bank fraud. BCCI pleads guilty to federal and state criminal charges on December 19, 1991, and forfeits $550 million.

January 9, 1992 FBI Director Sessions reassigns an estimated 300 agents from foreign counterintelligence to violent crime investigations in connection with the FBI's Safe Streets program—in light of the dissolution of the Soviet Union on December 25, 1991.

March 11, 1992 FBI officials establish a Criminal Justice Information Services Division, consolidating FBI services to law enforcement and criminal justice agencies. Housed in a new FBI facility in Clarksburg, West Virginia, the new Division incorporates the National Crime Information Center Program, the Integrated Automated Fingerprint Identification System, and the Uniform Crime Reports Program.

April 2, 1992 Following an intensive FBI investigation, John Gotti, the head of the Gambino organized crime family, is convicted of murder and racketeering charges in connection with the 1985 murder of rival crime syndicate boss Paul Castellano.

April 21, 1992 FBI officials and lawyers representing over 300 African American agents reach an agreement in principle to settle a class action racial discrimination suit against the FBI. A final settlement is reached on January 26, 1993.

June 30, 1992 Under an operation code-named GOLD PILL, FBI agents and local law enforcement officers arrest and seize assets in over 50 cities and towns of doctors and other medical providers as a part of a two-year investigation of the health care industry.

July 1992 The FBI Laboratory installs a new database, DRUGFIRE, to store and link specific, unique markings left on bullets after a gun is fired.

August 10, 1992 Under an FBI undercover operation code-named EQUINE, coordinated with the Drug Enforcement Administration, Food and Drug Administration, Postal Service, and Royal Canadian Mounted Police, over 40 individuals in four states and two countries are indicted for using and distributing black market anabolic steroids.

August 22, 1992 Members of the FBI's Hostage Rescue Team accidentally kill Vicki Weaver, the wife of white separatist Randall Weaver, at their home in Ruby Ridge, Idaho. The team had been called in to apprehend Randall Weaver, who was wanted on a gun charge and who had resisted arrest by federal marshals the previous day during a shoot-out that resulted in the death of a marshal, Weaver's wife, and the Weavers' son. The incident provokes a major controversy over why FBI shooting policy had been changed to "shoot on sight." In August 1995, the government agrees to pay $3.1 million to Weaver and his three daughters for the wrongful death of Vicki Weaver and the Weavers' son. Five FBI officials are temporarily suspended under suspicion of having destroyed documents as part of an attempt to cover up responsibility for the change in shooting orders. All are cleared except E. Michael Kahoe, who in October 1997 pleads guilty to obstruction of justice (for destroying, in 1992, an FBI after-action report).

December 1992   FBI officials release the first statistics on hate crimes committed in the United States, as required under the Hate Crime Statistics Act of 1990.

January 6, 1993   Following a lengthy FBI investigation, Charles H. Keating Jr. and his son, Charles Keating III, are convicted of racketeering, bank and securities fraud, and interstate transportation of stolen goods—charges related to the 1989 collapse of American Continental Corporation and its subsidiary, Lincoln Savings and Loan.

February 26, 1993   A bomb explodes in New York City's World Trade Center, triggering a massive FBI investigation leading to the trial and conviction of the Muslim fundamentalists responsible for this terroist attack.

February 28, 1993   Alcohol, Tobacco and Firearms (ATF) agents raid the Branch Davidian compound in Waco, Texas, seeking to arrest the cult leader David Koresh on charges of illegal firearms possession. Alerted to the planned raid, the Davidians' armed resistance results in the deaths of four ATF agents and six Branch Davidians. ATF officials then seek the assistance of the FBI's Hostage Rescue Team to effect the arrests. Following a 51-day standoff, FBI officials raid the compound on April 19, 1993. Rather than surrender, Branch Davidian leaders set fire to the building, resulting in the deaths of 79 members and their children.

March 4, 1993   Culminating a three-year investigation, FBI agents arrest and conduct searches in 13 states as part of an operation code-named DISCONNECT that targeted telemarketing fraud; 123 illegal telemarketing operations, and 548 individuals involved in them, are identified.

April 1993   Following a lengthy investigation initiated in 1991, FBI agents arrest Zein Isa and three other Palestinian Americans in St. Louis, Missouri, for plotting to kill thousands of Jews, blow up the Israeli embassy in Washington, D.C., and smuggle money to the Abu Nidal terrorist organization.

June–July 1993   Following an intensive FBI investigation (including recruiting as an informant and wiring Emad Salem) Sheik Omar Abdel Rahman and 11 Islamic fundamentalists are arrested for conspiring to blow up the United Nations building, the Lincoln and Holland Tunnels, and various federal buildings in New York City. Two of the defendants (Siddig Ibrahim Siddig Ali and Abdo Mohammed Haggag) eventually plead guilty and testify for

the government. On October 1, 1995, Sheik Rahman and the remaining defendants (El-Sayid Nosair, Ibrahim Elgabrowny, Clement Hampton-El, Amir Abdelgani, Fares Khallatalla, Tarig Elhassan, Fadil Abdelghani, Mohammed Salameh, and Victor Alvarez) are found guilty on 48 of the 50 indictment counts.

July 19, 1993   President Bill Clinton dismisses FBI Director Sessions for unethical use of his position for personal gain. FBI deputy director Floyd I. Clarke is designated acting director.

August 9, 1993   A new National Drug Intelligence Center is dedicated in Johnstown, Pennsylvania. Founded in 1992 and including the FBI, ATF, DEA, and Coast Guard, the center consolidates and promotes the sharing of information on drug traffickers.

September 1, 1993   Former FBI agent and federal judge Louis J. Freeh is sworn in as FBI director following a speedy Senate confirmation.

October 12, 1993   FBI Director Freeh streamlines operations at FBI headquarters. Forty-seven management positions are abolished, the Technical Services Division is merged into the Information Resources Division, the Administrative Services Division is divided into the Personnel and Finance Divisions, and an FBI assistant director is assigned to head the FBI's Washington, D.C., field office.

December 1993   FBI officials first use the Internet to post requests for tips in the UNABOM investigation. This investigation (which involves a special UNABOM Task Force comprising agents from the FBI, ATF, and Postal Service) seeks to identify the individual responsible for sending mail bombs that—between May 1978 and April 1995—caused the deaths of 3 individuals and the injury of 23 others.

January 18, 1994   Through a joint operation involving the FBI, Miami (Florida) police department, and Colombian and Ecuadorian authorities, Top Ten fugitive Armando Garcia is arrested in Cali, Colombia. In 1985, as a Miami police officer, Garcia and other police officers stole 800 kilos of cocaine in two separate thefts from boats docked along the Miami River. Garcia pleads guilty to the charges, and at least 18 former Miami police officers are sentenced to imprisonment in connection with the so-called Miami River Cops Scandal.

January 27, 1994 FBI Director Freeh permanently reassigns 600 agents from supervisory and administrative positions to assignments involving the investigation of priority criminal and national security cases.

February 21, 1994 Following an intensive FBI investigation, delayed by the unwillingness of Central Intelligence Agency officials to share information, Aldrich Ames, a 30-year CIA officer, and his wife, Maria del Rosario Casas Ames, are arrested on charges of spying for the Soviet Union. Beginning in 1985, Ames gave Soviet agents the names of 10 Soviet sources recruited by the CIA and the FBI and thousands of classified documents. His espionage activities compromised more than 100 intelligence operations. The identified sources were either killed or imprisoned. On April 28, 1994, Ames and his wife plead guilty to charges of conspiracy to commit espionage and tax fraud (for not declaring as income the money they received from Soviet officials). Ames is sentenced to life imprisonment without parole while his wife receives a sentence of five years and three months' imprisonment.

March 7, 1994 FBI Director Freeh imposes stricter penalties for agent misconduct, requires drug-use polygraph examinations for all job applicants, and prohibits bias based on sexual orientation.

April 18, 1994 FBI Director Freeh increases the FBI's Hostage Rescue Team (HRT) from 52 to 77 and creates a post, SAC for Critical Incident Response, to direct the HRT and other specialists assigned to hostage situations, terrorist incidents, and other emergencies.

May 1994 Congress enacts the Freedom of Access to Clinic Enterprises Act, criminalizing the resort to violence against physicians performing abortions and attacks on abortion clinics.

May 24, 1994 Following an intensive FBI investigation, Mohammad A. Salameh, Nidal A. Ayyad, Ahmed Mohammed Ajaj, and Mahmud Abouhalima are convicted for the terrorist bombing of New York City's World Trade Center building. On February 7, 1995, Ramzi Ahmed Yousef is arrested in Pakistan and turned over to the FBI. Yousef was indicted for the bombing but had fled the country. Later that year, a second fugitive, Abdul Rahman Yasin, is arrested and deported. Both Yousef and Yasin are convicted on November 12, 1997.

June 22, 1994 FBI Director Freeh appoints a delegation of high-level federal law enforcement officials to meet on June 28, 1994, with senior officials of 11 European nations (Russia, Germany, the Czech Republic, the Slovak Republic, Hungary, Poland, Ukraine, Austria, Lithuania, Latvia, and Estonia) to promote international cooperation in major crime investigations.

September 14, 1994 Culminating a three-year international drug-trafficking investigation conducted jointly with Italian authorities, FBI agents in New York arrest 29 individuals for conspiring to obtain and distribute heroin and cocaine. Concurrently, Italian authorities arrest 74 individuals in Italy.

October 7, 1994 Congress enacts the Digital Telephony Act of 1994 requiring the telecommunications industry to permit court-ordered wiretapping in criminal investigations in response to new technology moving from an analog to a digital system of communications.

April 19, 1995 At the Alfred P. Murrah Federal Building in Oklahoma City, Oklahoma, 169 individuals are killed and over 500 wounded in a bombing incident. A massive FBI investigation is initiated to apprehend the perpetrators, leading to the indictment and conviction of Timothy McVeigh and Terry Nichols, former Army recruits holding right-wing anti-government views. The bombing precipitates demands to revise FBI terrorist investigative guidelines and enact new counterterrorism legislation.

October 27, 1995 Carolyn G. Morris is appointed the first female African American FBI assistant director.

March 25, 1996 FBI agents arrest LeRoy Schweitzer and Daniel Petersen, leaders of the extremist anti-government Freemen, on federal bank and check fraud charges. Concurrently, FBI and local and state law enforcement officers blockade a farm near Jordan, Montana, seeking the surrender of other members of the Freemen group, on similar federal fraud charges. Rather than resorting to force to effect their arrest, FBI officials attempt to negotiate their surrender. This strategy succeeds, with the peaceful surrender of 16 holdouts on June 13, 1996. Fourteen of those surrendering are indicted on various federal charges (bank and check fraud, threatening the life of a federal judge, and impeding federal prosecution); others face similar state charges. In July 1998, a federal jury convicts three of the Freemen of financial fraud and three (including Schweitzer and Petersen) of threatening the life of Montana's chief federal judge, Jack D. Shanstrom.

April 3, 1996 FBI agents apprehend Theodore J. Kaczynski, then residing in an isolated cabin in Lincoln, Montana. Originally held in Helena, Montana, on the charge of possession of bombing materials, Kaczynski is soon identified as the so-called Unabomber, based on a tip from his brother and a resultant search of his cabin. The search uncovers evidence linking him to a series of mail bombs involving individuals employed by universities, airlines, and the logging industry. Indicted in Sacramento, California, on June 18, 1996, on charges involving two deaths and two injuries. In January 1998, Kaczynski agrees to plead guilty to the bombing charges in return for a sentence of life imprisonment without parole.

June 11, 1996   Nineteen members of the Genovese crime family (notably Liborio Bellomo, Michele Generoso, and James Ida) are indicted for crimes ranging from murder, extortion, labor racketeering, gambling, loan-sharking, and money laundering to tax evasion. The arrests break the leadership of the most powerful organized crime family in the United States.

September 24, 1996   FBI agents arrest Robert C. Kim, an analyst employed by the Office of Naval Intelligence, on the charge of having passed naval secrets between May and September 1996 to South Korean official Capt. Baek Dong, at the time employed as a naval attaché in the South Korean embassy in Washington, D.C.

October 11, 1996   FBI agents arrest Floyd R. Looker and six other individuals associated with a West Virginia militia group, the West Virginia Mountaineer Militia, on charges of plotting to blow up several government buildings in West Virginia, including the FBI's fingerprint center in Clarksburg, West Virginia.

November 18, 1996   FBI agents arrest Harold J. Nicholson (a former CIA station chief and instructor at the CIA's training school) for selling the names of CIA officers and foreign agents to Russia during the 1990s.

December 18, 1996   FBI agents arrest Earl E. Pitts, an FBI supervisor, on charges of having sold highly secret FBI documents (pertaining to FBI counterintelligence operations) to Russian intelligence officers. Pitts's espionage activities began in 1985 and he came under suspicion in 1995, eventually leading to his arrest.

January 1997   Following a critical report of the FBI's Laboratory by the Justice Department's inspector general, the FBI Laboratory staff is overhauled on January 27, 1997, and four senior staff (including the heads of the chemistry and explosive units) are transferred outside the laboratory. The inspector general's investigation uncovers numerous problems of careless handling of evidence and lax procedures, discoveries that shatter the FBI Laboratory's reputation as a high-tech crime fighting agency and threaten to compromise prosecution of a number of major cases (including the Oklahoma City and World Trade Center bombing cases).

January 23, 1997   An FBI sting operation leads to the indictment of 47 members of the Gambino crime family for disposing of millions of dollars of stolen goods.

February 1997   FBI officials publicly disclose an ongoing investigation into whether Chinese officials attempted to influence members of Congress and made illegal contributions to the Clinton presidential campaign in 1996. This investigation began in 1995, then focusing on allegations that Chinese agents sought to influence members of Congress, and it intensified in 1996, triggered by NSA-intercepted conversations of Chinese officials and Chinese agents.

April 24, 1997   FBI agents arrest four members of a white supremacist group (Shawn Adams, Catherine Adams, Edward Taylor, and Carl Waskom Jr.) for conspiring to commit robbery. The four planned to bomb a natural gas plant to divert law enforcement officials while they robbed an armored car to gain funds to be used for terrorist activities.

July 30, 1997   As the result of a successful sting operation, FBI agents arrest six individuals (including two former and two current Houston city council members) on federal conspiracy and bribery charges.

October 7, 1997   FBI agents arrest three former student radicals at the University of Wisconsin–Milwaukee (Theresa Squillacote, Kurt Stand, and James Clark) for spying for Communist intelligence services (East Germany) during the 1970s.

October 21, 1997   Donald M. Kerr, a nuclear weapons physicist, is appointed to head the FBI Laboratory, the first non–FBI agent to hold this position.

January 21, 1998   Culminating a two-year FBI investigation, 44 law enforcement officers are indicted for taking money to protect cocaine trafficking operations in Cleveland and northern Ohio.

February 26, 1998   FBI officials agree to pay former FBI agent Frederic Whitehurst $1.1 million to settle his lawsuit against the FBI claiming that FBI officials had retaliated against him for his allegations involving corrupt practices in the FBI Laboratory.

ANNOTATED BIBLIOGRAPHY

Books

Adler, Bill. *Kids' Letters to the FBI*. Englewood Cliffs, NJ: Prentice-Hall, 1966.
Reprints letters from children to the FBI.

Alexander, Shana. *The Pizza Connection*. New York: Weidenfeld and Nicolson, 1988.
Detailed account of the FBI investigation of organized crime during the 1980s. It resulted in the conviction of a nationwide crime ring involved in drug-money laundering—a crime ring with connections to the Italian mafia.

Avella, Steven. *The Confident Church: Catholic Leadership in Chicago, 1940–1965*. South Bend: Notre Dame University Press, 1992.
Briefly surveys the covert liaison relationship between Roman Catholic bishops and FBI officials (notably, FBI assistant director Edward Tamm).

Ayer, Frederick. *Yankee G-Man*. Chicago: Regnery, 1957.
A former FBI agent recounts service in FBI.

Bales, James. *J. Edgar Hoover Speaks*. Washington, D.C.: Capitol Hill Press, 1970.
Reprints various statements of FBI Director J. Edgar Hoover concerning the communist threat.

Baron, John. *Breaking the Ring*. Boston: Houghton Mifflin, 1987.
Detailed account of the FBI investigation leading to the arrest and conviction of former Navy intelligence officer John Walker (and his associates) for providing Navy secrets to the Soviet Union.

Belknap, Michal. *Federal Law and Southern Order: Racial Violence and Constitutional Conflict in the Post-Brown South*. Athens: University of Georgia Press, 1987.
Surveys FBI investigations of white supremacists and civil rights activists during the 1950s and 1960s.

Bennett, James, ed. *Control of Information in the United States: An Annotated Bibliography*. Westport, CT: Meckler, 1987.
Identifies selected books, articles, and newspaper stories pertaining to the FBI.

Benson, Robert, and Michael Warner, eds. *VENONA: Soviet Espionage and the American Response 1939–1957*. Washington, D.C.: National Security Agency and Central Intelligence Agency, 1996.
Surveys and reprints documents pertaining to the top-secret Venona project, under which U.S. intelligence agencies intercepted and decoded Soviet consular messages during World War II. The information was subsequently used to apprehend Soviet intelligence operatives. Provides important information on FBI counterintelligence operations, on FBI liaison with the NSA and the CIA, and background on the Judith Coplon and Rosenberg cases.

Bernikow, Louise. *Abel*. New York: Trident, 1970.
Surveys the FBI investigation leading to the apprehension and conviction of Soviet spy Rudolf Abel.

Blackstock, Nelson. *COINTELPRO: The FBI's Secret War on Political Freedom*. New York: Vintage, 1975.
Critical account of the FBI's covert program to harass and disrupt the Socialist Workers Party during the 1960s.

Blum, Howard. *Gangland: The Secret Wars of the FBI's Gambino Squad*. New York: Simon and Schuster, 1992.
Detailed account of FBI undercover investigations of crime syndicates in New York during the 1980s.

Blumenthal, Ralph. *Last Days of the Sicilians: At War with the Mafia*. New York: Times Books, 1988.
Detailed history of FBI organized crime investigations of the 1980s, focusing on the Pizza Connection case.

Branch, Taylor. *Parting the Waters: America in the King Years, 1954–1963*. New York: Simon and Schuster, 1988.
Surveys FBI surveillance of civil rights leader Martin Luther King Jr. and the civil rights movement during the 1950s and early 1960s.

———. *Pillar of Fire: America in the King Years, 1963–1965*. New York: Simon and Schuster, 1998.
Surveys FBI surveillance of civil rights leader Martin Luther King Jr. and the civil rights movement during the mid-1960s.

Bratzel, John, and Leslie Rout. *The Shadow War: German Espionage and U.S. Counterespionage in Latin America during World War II*. Frederick, MD: University Publications of America, 1989.
Detailed history of the role of the FBI's special branch, Special Intelligence Service, in foreign intelligence and counterintelligence in Latin America and South America during World War II.

Braude, Michael, and Howard Lindberg. *Jeff Learns about the FBI*. Minneapolis: T.S. Denison, 1968.
Children's book providing a brief history of the FBI.

Breitman, George, et al. *The Assassination of Malcolm X*. New York: Pathfinder Press, 1976.
Critical history of FBI monitoring of black nationalist leader Malcolm X.

Breuer, William. *Hitler's Undercover War: The Nazi Espionage Invasion of the U.S.A.* New York: St. Martin's Press, 1989.
Detailed history of FBI investigations of German espionage activities in the United States during the 1930s and 1940s.

Buitrago, Ann. *Report on CISPES Files Maintained by FBI Headquarters and Released under the Freedom of Information Act*. New York: FOIA, Inc., 1988.
Critical survey of the FBI's investigation of the Committee in Solidarity with the People of El Salvador (CISPES) and other critics of the Reagan administration's Central American policy during the 1980s.

Buitrago, Ann, and Leon Immerman. *Are You Now or Have You Ever Been in the FBI Files?* New York: Grove, 1981.
Helpful guide outlining how to use the Freedom of Information Act to obtain FBI files and how to interpret FBI acronyms and code words.

Burnham, David. *The Rise of the Computer State*. New York: Random House, 1983.
Reviews the history of the FBI's computerized National Crime Information Center and Interstate Identification Index.

Cagin, Seth, and Philip Dray. *We Are Not Afraid: The Mississippi Murder of Goodman, Schwerner and Chaney*. New York: Macmillan, 1988.
Detailed history of the FBI investigation (code-named MIBURN) leading to the apprehension of the murderers of civil rights activists in Mississippi during the 1960s.

Carpenter, Teresa. *Missing Beauty: A True Story of Murder and Obsession*. New York: Norton, 1988.
Brief account of the role of the FBI Laboratory in solving a murder.

Carson, Clayborne. *Malcolm X: The FBI File*. New York: Carroll and Graf, 1991.
Reprints the FBI file on black nationalist leader Malcolm X.

Charns, Alexander. *Cloak and Gavel: FBI Wiretaps, Bugs, Informers, and the Supreme Court*. Urbana: University of Illinois Press, 1992.
Surveys FBI wiretapping and bugging policy and covert monitoring of Supreme Court justices and clerks.

Churchill, Ward, and Jim Vander Wall. *Agents of Repression: The FBI's Secret War against the Black Panther Party and the American Indian Movement*. Boston: South End Press, 1988.
Critical history of the FBI's surveillance of the Black Panther Party and the American Indian Movement during the 1960s and 1970s.

Clayton, Merle. *The Union Station Massacre: The Shootout That Started the FBI's War on Crime*. Indianapolis: Bobbs-Merrill, 1975.
Detailed history of the Frank Nash case and FBI investigations of gangsters during the 1930s.

Coben, Stanley. *A. Mitchell Palmer: Politician*. New York: Columbia University Press, 1963.
Critical history of the FBI's role in the so-called Palmer Raids of 1919–20.

Conconi, Charles, and Tony House. *The Washington Sting*. New York: Coward, McCann, and Geoghegan, 1979.
Describes FBI undercover operations and liaison with local police.

Cook, Fred. *The FBI Nobody Knows*. New York: Macmillan, 1964.
Critical history of the FBI.

Cooper, Courtney Ryley. *Ten Thousand Public Enemies*. Boston: Little, Brown, 1935.
Popular, sympathetic history of FBI crime investigations during the 1930s.

———. *Designs in Scarlet*. Boston: Little, Brown, 1939.
Popular, sympathetic history of FBI investigations of prostitution during the 1930s.

Corson, William. *Armies of Ignorance*. New York: Dial Press, 1977.
Critical history of the FBI, focusing on the 1930s and 1940s.

Criley, Richard. *The FBI v. The First Amendment*. Los Angeles: First Amendment Foundation, 1990.
Surveys the FBI's monitoring of critics of the House Committee on Un-American Activities.

Cromie, Robert, and Joseph Pinkston. *Dillinger: A Short and Violent Life*. New York: McGraw-Hill, 1962.
Detailed account of the FBI's investigation and shooting of John Dillinger.

Darling, Arthur. *The Central Intelligence Agency: An Instrument of Government to 1950*. University Park, Pennsylvania State University Press, 1990.
In-house history by a CIA employee that briefly surveys the FBI's liaison relationship with the CIA and the Office of Strategic Services.

Davis, James K. *Spying on America: The FBI's Domestic Counterintelligence Program*. New York: Praeger, 1992.
Detailed history of the FBI's controversial COINTELPROs of 1956–71.

Dean, Graham. *Agent Nine Solves His First Case: A Story of Thrilling Exploits of the G-Men*. Chicago: Goldsmith Publishing, 1935.
Children's book detailing the role of FBI agents.

DeLoach, Cartha. *Hoover's FBI: The Inside Story by Hoover's Trusted Lieutenant*. Washington: Regnery, 1995.
A 28-year FBI agent and official (whose assignments included heading the Crime Records Division) provides an "insider" account of the FBI's history during the post-1945 era, most notably during the 1960s.

Demaris, Ovid, ed. *The Director: An Oral Biography of J. Edgar Hoover*. New York: Harper's, 1975.
A series of interviews with former FBI officials, members of the Congress, attorneys general, relatives, and other associates of the former FBI director.

DeToledano, Ralph. *J. Edgar Hoover: The Man in His Time*. New Rochelle, NY: Arlington House, 1973.
Sympathetic biography of FBI Director Hoover.

Diamond, Sigmund. *Compromised Campus: The Collaboration of the University and the Intelligence Community*. New York: Oxford University Press, 1992.
Discusses FBI surveillance of college faculties and students, and FBI covert collaboration with university officials, state governors, and the U.S. Senate Internal Security Subcommittee.

Donner, Frank. *The Age of Surveillance*. New York: Knopf, 1980.
Critical history of FBI surveillance, authority, and investigative techniques and programs.

———. *Protectors of Privilege: Red Squads and Police Repression in Urban America*. Berkeley: University of California Press, 1990.
Brief but critical survey of FBI liaison relationships with local police.

Dorwart, Jeffrey. *Conflict of Duty: The U.S. Navy's Intelligence Dilemma, 1919–1945*. Annapolis: Naval Institute Press, 1983.
Briefly surveys the FBI's liaison relationship with the Office of Naval Intelligence (ONI) during the 1920s and 1930s.

Duffy, Brian, and Steven Emerson. *The Fall of Pan Am 103: Inside the Lockerbie Investigation*. New York: G.P. Putnam's, 1990.
Detailed account of the FBI investigation leading to the indictment of Libyan intelligence officers for the terrorist bombing of Pan Am flight 103.

Dunlop, Richard. *Donovan: Master Spy*. Chicago: Rand McNally, 1982.
Brief survey of the relationship between Office of Strategic Services director William Donovan and FBI Director J. Edgar Hoover during World War II.

Earley, Pete. *Family of Spies: Inside the John Walker Spy Ring*. New York: Bantam, 1988.
Detailed history of the FBI investigation leading to the apprehension and conviction of former Navy intelligence officer John Walker (and his associates) for providing Navy secrets to the Soviet Union.

Elliff, John. *The Reform of FBI Intelligence Operations*. Princeton: Princeton University Press, 1979.
Detailed account of FBI abuses of power and proposed guidelines instituted in 1976 to preclude recurrence.

Felt, W. Mark. *The FBI Pyramid from the Inside*. New York: G.P. Putnam's, 1979.
Insider account by a former FBI agent and SAC (1941–63), promoted to chief supervisor, FBI assistant director, and acting FBI associate director (1963–73).

Fisher, Jim. *The Lindbergh Case*. New Brunswick: Rutgers University Press, 1987.
Detailed account of the FBI investigation in the Lindbergh kidnapping case.

Foerstel, Herbert. *Surveillance in the Stacks: The FBI's Library Awareness Program*. Westport, CT: Greenwood Press, 1991.
Detailed history of the FBI's Library Awareness Program of the 1960s through the 1980s.

Fox, Stephen. *Blood and Power: Organized Crime in Twentieth-Century America*. New York: Morrow, 1989.
Critical history of the FBI's investigation of organized crime.

Garrow, David. *The FBI and Martin Luther King, Jr.: From Memphis to "Solo."* New York: Norton, 1981.
Detailed history of the FBI's surveillance of—and attempts to discredit—civil rights leader Martin Luther King Jr.

Gelbspan, Ross. *Break-ins, Death Threats and the FBI*. Boston: South End Press, 1991.
Critical history of the FBI's surveillance of critics of the Reagan administration's Central American policy during the 1980s.

Gentry, Curt. *J. Edgar Hoover: The Man and the Secrets*. New York: Norton, 1991.
Critical, comprehensive biography of FBI Director Hoover.

Gillers, Stephen, and Pat Watters, eds. *Investigating the FBI*. Garden City: Doubleday, 1973.
Critical essays on FBI history, surveillance, and public relations.

Gilmore, Christopher. *Hoover vs. Kennedys: The Second Civil War*. New York: St. Martin's Press, 1987.
Popular history of the personal and policy conflicts between FBI Director Hoover and President John F. Kennedy and Attorney General Robert F. Kennedy.

Glick, Brian. *War at Home: Covert Action against U.S. Activities and What We Can Do about Them*. Boston: South End Press, 1988.
Critical account of the FBI's COINTELPROs.

Goddard, Donald. *The Insider: The FBI's Undercover "Wise Guy" Goes Public*. New York: Pocket Books, 1992.
An FBI undercover agent recounts his role investigating organized crime syndicates during the 1980s.

Godson, Roy, ed. *Intelligence Requirements for the 1980s: Domestic Intelligence*. Lexington, MA: D.C. Heath, 1986.
Essays critical of attempts in the 1970s to restrict FBI intelligence investigations.

Goldstein, Robert. *Political Repression in Modern America*. Cambridge: Schencken, 1978.
Critical history of FBI surveillance and containment of radical political and trade union activists.

Greenberg, Martin, and Mark Sabljak. *Most Wanted: A History of the FBI's Most Wanted List*. New York: Bonanza Books, 1990.
Popular history of the FBI's Ten Most Wanted Fugitive Program and some of those successfully apprehended.

Greene, Robert. *The Sting Man: Inside Abscam*. New York: Dutton, 1981.
Insider account by an FBI informer involved in the FBI's ABSCAM program of the 1970s, in which members of Congress were investigated for bribery and corruption.

Haines, Gerald, and David Langbart. *Unlocking the Files of the FBI: A Guide to Its Record and Classification System*. Wilmington, DE: Scholarly Resources, 1993.
Specialized guide describing FBI records classification and the scope and contents of discrete records systems.

Hall, Angus. *The Crime Busters: The FBI, Scotland Yard, Interpol: The Story of Criminal Detection*. New York: Verdict Press, 1976.
Surveys FBI liaison relations with foreign police agencies.

Halperin, Morton, et al. *The Lawless State*. New York: Penguin, 1976.
Critical history of FBI surveillance programs and abuses of power.

Harris, Richard. *Freedom Spent*. Boston: Little, Brown, 1976.
Critical history of FBI surveillance of New Left activists during the 1960s.

Hill, Robert. *The FBI's RACON: Racial Conditions in the United States during World War II*. Boston: Northeastern University Press, 1995.
Reprints a lengthy FBI report, and accompanying documents, concerning FBI surveillance of civil rights activists and the black press during the World War II years.

Hoover, J. Edgar. *Persons in Hiding*. Boston: Little, Brown, 1938.
FBI Director Hoover recounts FBI investigation and apprehension of gangsters during the 1930s.

———. *Masters of Deceit: The Story of Communism in America and How to Fight It*. New York: Holt, 1958.
FBI Director Hoover describes the communist threat to U.S. internal security and the FBI's role in addressing that threat.

Howe, Russell. *Sleeping with the FBI: Sex, Booze, Russians and the Saga of an American Counterspy Who Couldn't*. New York: National Books, 1993.
Detailed history of the arrest of FBI agent Richard Miller, charged with giving FBI secrets to Soviet agents in the 1980s.

Hurt, Henry. *Shadrin, The Spy Who Never Came Back*. New York: Reader's Digest Press, 1981.
Details the FBI recruitment of a Soviet agent who later defected to the Soviet Union in the 1960s and 1970s.

Hyde, H. Montgomery. *Room 3603: The Story of the British Intelligence Center in New York during World War II*. New York: Ballantine, 1977.
Reviews the FBI's liaison with British intelligence officers during World War II.

Jacquith, Cindy, and Diane Wang. *FBI vs. Women*. New York: Pathfinder Press, 1977.
Critical history of FBI surveillance of women activists and feminist organizations during the 1960s.

Jeffers, H. Paul. *Who Killed Precious? How FBI Special Agents Combine Psychology and High Technology to Identify Violent Criminals*. New York: Pharos Books, 1991.
Detailed account of FBI investigative procedures, including the new methods of the 1980s (such as profiling), to identify violent criminals.

Jensen, Joan. *Army Surveillance in America, 1775–1980*. New Haven: Yale University Press, 1991.
Surveys the FBI's liaison relationship with military intelligence during World War I, World War II, and the Cold War.

Keller, William. *The Liberals and J. Edgar Hoover*. Princeton: Princeton University Press, 1989.
Critical assessment of the responsibility of liberals and liberalism for FBI abuses of power.

Kelly, John F., and Phillip K. Wearne. *Tainting Evidence: Inside the Scandals at the FBI Crime Lab*. New York: Free Press, 1998.
A critical survey of the quality of forensic work of the FBI Laboratory and its role in recent important cases (UNABOM, Ruby Ridge, and Oklahoma City).

Kessler, Ronald. *The FBI: Inside the World's Most Powerful Law Enforcement Agency*. New York: Pocket Books, 1993.
Popular history of changes in FBI investigative priorities and procedures of the 1970s and 1980s.

———. *Spy vs. Spy: Stalking Soviet Spies in America*. New York: Scribner's, 1988.
Surveys FBI counterintelligence investigations during the 1980s.

Kurins, Andris, and Joseph O'Brien. *Boss of Bosses: The Fall of the Godfather: The FBI and Paul Castellano*. New York: Simon and Schuster, 1991.
Two FBI undercover agents detail FBI investigations of organized crime during the 1980s, focusing on their role in the apprehension of crime boss Paul Castellano.

Lamphere, Robert, and Tom Shachtman. *The FBI–KGB War: A Special Agent's Story*. New York: Random House, 1986.
Former FBI counterintelligence agent Lamphere (active 1941–55) recounts the FBI role in identifying accused spies Judith Coplon, Julius and Ethel Rosenberg, and Kim Philby.

Langum, David. *Crossing over the Line: Legislating Morality and the Mann Act*. Chicago: University of Chicago Press, 1994.
Surveys Mann Act investigations and monitoring of sexual behavior by the Bureau of Investigation.

Lockwood, Brocton, with Harlan Mendenhall. *Operation Greylord: Brocton Lockwood's Story*. Carbondale: Southern Illinois University Press, 1989.
Detailed account of the FBI investigation of the 1980s, known as Operation GREYLORD, which uncovered corruption in the Cook County (Illinois) court system.

Lowenthal, Max. *The Federal Bureau of Investigation*. New York: Sloane, 1950.
Critical history of the FBI.

Lysing, Henry. *Men against Crime*. New York: David Kemp, 1938.
Popular history of the FBI war on gangsters during the 1930s.

Maas, Peter. *The Valachi Papers*. New York: G.P. Putnam's, 1968.
  Surveys the FBI investigation of Joseph Valachi, his recruitment as an informer, and Valachi's public testimony on the organized crime syndicate known as La Cosa Nostra.

MacDonnell, Francis. *Insidious Foes: The Axis Fifth Column and the American Home Front*. New York: Oxford University Press, 1995.
  Surveys FBI investigations of pro-German activities and German espionage during the 1930s and 1940s.

May, Gary. *Undercover: Police Surveillance in America*. Berkeley: University of California Press, 1988.
  Surveys FBI undercover operations and procedures of the 1970s and 1980s, focusing on policy and oversight.

———. *Un American Activities: The Trials of William Remington*. New York: Oxford University Press, 1994.
  Detailed account of the FBI investigation leading to the perjury conviction of William Remington.

McCormick, Charles. *Seeing Reds: Federal Surveillance of Radicals in the Pittsburgh Mill District, 1917–1921*. Pittsburgh: University of Pittsburgh Press, 1997.
  Describes Bureau surveillance of radical labor (IWW) and political activists during the World War I and postwar Red Scare eras.

McKnight, Gerald D. *The Last Crusade: Martin Luther King, Jr., the FBI, and the Poor People's Campaign*. Boulder: Westview, 1998.
  Surveys FBI surveillance of civil rights leader Martin Luther King Jr. and the civil rights movement during the late 1960s, focusing on the Poor People's Campaign of 1968.

Mitgang, Herbert. *Dangerous Dossiers: Exposing the Secret War against America's Greatest Authors*. New York: Donald Fine, 1988.
  Critical history of the FBI surveillance of prominent authors.

Morgan, Richard. *Domestic Intelligence: Monitoring Dissent in America*. Austin: University of Texas Press, 1980.
  Surveys FBI domestic surveillance programs and authority.

Murphy, Patrick, and Thomas Plate. *Commissioner: A View from the Top of American Law Enforcement*. New York: Simon and Schuster, 1977.
  Former New York Police Commissioner (Murphy) briefly recounts police liaison with the FBI and the FBI National Academy.

Murray, Robert. *Red Scare: A Study of National Hysteria, 1919–1920*. Minneapolis: University of Minnesota Press, 1955.
  Detailed history of the FBI role in the planning and execution of the so-called Palmer Raids of 1919 and 1920.

Navasky, Victor. *Kennedy Justice*. New York: Atheneum, 1921.
  Detailed history of the relationship between Attorney General Robert F. Kennedy and FBI Director J. Edgar Hoover during the 1960s, and FBI electronic surveillance policy and authority.

Neff, James. *Mobbed Up: Jackie Presser's High-Wire Life in the Teamsters, the Mafia and the FBI*. New York: Atlantic Monthly Press, 1989.
  Detailed history of the FBI investigation of criminal influence in the Teamsters' Union and the recruitment of Teamsters' Union president Jackie Presser as an informer.

Nelson, Jack. *Terror in the Night: the Klan's Campaign against the Jews*. New York: Simon and Schuster, 1992.
  Details the FBI investigation of Ku Klux Klan activity in Mississippi.

Nelson, Jack, and Ronald Ostrow. *The FBI and the Berrigans: The Making of a Conspiracy*. New York: Coward, McCann and Geoghegan, 1972.
  Critical history of FBI surveillance of Roman Catholic, anti–Vietnam War activists during the 1960s.

Ollestad, Norman. *Inside the FBI*. New York: Stuart, 1967.
  A former FBI agent offers insights into FBI agent training, supervision, and recruitment practices.

O'Reilly, Kenneth. *Hoover and the Un-Americans: The FBI, HUAC, and the Red Menace*. Philadelphia: Temple University Press, 1983.
  Critical history of the FBI's covert relationship with the House Committee on Un-American Activities.

———. *"Racial Matters": The FBI's Secret File on Black America, 1960–1972*. New York: Free Press, 1989.
  Critical history of FBI surveillance of civil rights activists, focusing on the 1960s.

Overstreet, Harry, and Bonaro Overstreet. *The FBI in Our Open Society*. New York: Norton, 1969.
  Sympathetic popular history of the FBI.

Payne, Cril. *Deep Cover: An FBI Agent Infiltrates the Radical Underground*. New York: Newsweek Books, 1979.
  Insider account by an FBI undercover agent of the FBI's investigation of radical organizations during the 1960s and 1970s.

Petersen, Neal, ed. *American Intelligence, 1775–1990: A Bibliographical Guide*. Claremont, CA: Regina, 1992.
  Lists books and articles pertaining to the FBI, not annotated.

Pistone, Joseph. *Donnie Brasco: My Undercover Life in the Mafia*. New York: American Library, 1987.
  A former FBI undercover agent (1969–86) recounts his role in infiltrating La Cosa Nostra, and FBI investigations of organized crime syndicates during the 1970s and 1980s.

Potter, Claire Bond. *War on Crime: Bandits, G-Men, and the Politics of Mass Culture*. New Brunswick: Rutgers University Press, 1998.
  Surveys the FBI's war on gangsters during the 1930s (focusing on Bonnie and Clyde, Alvin Karpis, and John Dillinger) and its impact on the Bureau's role and image.

Poveda, Tony. *Lawlessness and Reform: The FBI in Transition*. Pacific Grove, CA: Brooks/Cole Publishing, 1990.
  Critical history of the FBI detailing the abuses of power during FBI Director Hoover's tenure and the reforms and changes in priorities and procedures instituted in the post-Hoover era.

Powers, Richard Gid. *G-Men: Hoover's FBI in American Popular Culture*. Carbondale: Southern Illinois University Press, 1983.
  Surveys FBI public relations strategy from the 1930s through the 1970s, focusing on popular media (comics, radio, movies, and television).

————. *Secrecy and Power: The Life of J. Edgar Hoover*. New York: Free Press, 1987.
> Biography of FBI Director J. Edgar Hoover as a product of American popular culture.

Preston, William. *Aliens and Dissenters: Federal Suppression of Radicals, 1903–1933*. Cambridge: Harvard University Press, 1963.
> Surveys FBI surveillance of the Industrial Workers of the World (IWW) and other radical activists during World War I and the early 1920s.

Purvis, Melvin. *American Agent*. Garden City: Doubleday, 1936.
> A former FBI agent recounts his role in the investigation and apprehension of John Dillinger and Charles "Pretty Boy" Floyd during the 1930s.

Rachlis, Eugene. *They Came to Kill*. New York: Random House, 1961.
> Discusses the FBI's role in the apprehension of German saboteurs in 1942.

Radosh, Ronald, and Joyce Milton. *The Rosenberg File: A Search for the Truth*. New York: Holt, Rinehart and Winston, 1983.
> Describes the FBI's role in the apprehension of Julius and Ethel Rosenberg and in monitoring Soviet espionage activities during the Cold War era.

Riebling, Mark. *Wedge: The Secret War between the FBI and the CIA*. New York: Knopf, 1994.
> Discusses the bureaucratic conflict underpinning the FBI-CIA liaison relationship under FBI Director J. Edgar Hoover.

Robins, Natalie. *Alien Ink: The FBI's War on Freedom of Expression*. New York: Morrow, 1992.
> Discusses the FBI surveillance of prominent writers and journalists.

Roemer, William. *Roemer: Man against the Mob*. New York: Donald Fine, 1989.
> A former FBI agent recounts his role in monitoring organized crime leaders, including the use of microphone surveillance during the 1950s and 1960s.

Schneir, Walter, and Miriam Schneir. *Invitation to an Inquest*. Garden City: Doubleday, 1965.
> Critical account of the FBI investigation of Julius and Ethel Rosenberg and their prosecution for espionage.

Schott, Joseph. *No Left Turns: The FBI in Peace and War*. New York: Praeger, 1975.
> Former FBI agent (1948–71) offers a critical account of FBI rules and procedures under FBI Director Hoover.

Sentner, David. *How the FBI Gets Its Man*. New York: Avon Books, 1965.
> Journalistic account of FBI investigations involving crime and espionage.

Smith, John Chabot. *Alger Hiss: The True Story*. New York: Holt, Rinehart and Winston, 1976.
> Critical account of the FBI role in the Alger Hiss case.

Stein, Judith. *The World of Marcus Garvey: Race and Class in Modern Society*. Baton Rouge: Louisiana State University Press, 1986.
> Surveys FBI surveillance of Garvey and other black nationalists during World War I and the early 1920s.

Stevenson, William. *A Man Called Intrepid: The Secret War*. New York: Harcourt, Brace, Jovanovich, 1976.
> Describes the secret liaison relationship between the FBI and British security officials during World War II.

Sullivan, William. *The Bureau: My Thirty Years in Hoover's FBI*. New York: Norton, 1979.
> A former FBI agent and senior FBI official (1941–71) offers a critical account of Hoover's directorship of the FBI.

Summers, Anthony. *Official and Confidential: The Secret Life of J. Edgar Hoover*. New York: G.P. Putnam's, 1993.
> Critical, sensational biography of FBI Director Hoover.

Theoharis, Athan. *J. Edgar Hoover, Sex, and Crime: An Historical Antidote*. Chicago: Ivan Dee, 1955.
> Critical history of FBI investigations of sexual activities, subversive activities, and organized crime under FBI Director Hoover.

————. *Spying on Americans: Political Surveillance from Hoover to the Huston Plan*. Philadelphia: Temple University Press, 1978.
> Critical history of FBI surveillance programs, policy, and authority for the period 1936–78.

Theoharis, Athan, ed. *Beyond the Hiss Case: The FBI, Congress, and the Cold War*. Philadelphia: Temple University Press, 1982.
> Critical essays of FBI surveillance policy, programs, and authority during the Cold War era.

————. *The F.B.I.: An Annotated Bibliography and Research Guide*. New York: Garland, 1994.
> Annotated bibliography listing books, articles, congressional hearings, and microfilm collections pertaining to the FBI.

Theoharis, Athan, and John Stuart Cox. *The Boss: J. Edgar Hoover and the Great American Inquisition*. Philadelphia: Temple University Press, 1988.
> Critical biography of FBI Director Hoover.

Toland, John. *The Dillinger Days*. New York: Random House, 1963.
> Detailed account of the FBI's role in the apprehension and shooting of John Dillinger.

Troy, Thomas. *Wild Bill and Intrepid: Donovan, Stephenson, and the Origin of CIA*. New Haven: Yale University Press, 1996.
> Surveys the relationship between the FBI, British intelligence, and the OSS during World War II.

Tully, Andrew. *The FBI's Most Famous Cases*. New York: Morrow, 1965.
> Popular history of some of the FBI's prominent cases.

Turner, William. *Hoover's FBI: The Man and the Myth*. Los Angeles: Sherbourne Press, 1970.
> Critical, insider account by a former FBI agent (1951–61).

Ungar, Sanford. *F.B.I.* Boston: Little, Brown, 1976.
> Critical history of the FBI, including brief sketches of prominent FBI officials.

Villano, Anthony. *Brick Agent: Inside the Mafia for the FBI*. New York: Quadrangle/New York Times Books, 1977.
> Insider account by a former FBI undercover agent (1950–73) discussing FBI criminal investigations and investigative techniques.

Waller, George. *The Story of the Lindbergh Case*. New York: Dial Press, 1961.
   Popular history of the FBI role in the Lindbergh kidnapping case.

Washburn, Patrick. *A Question of Sedition: The Federal Government's Investigation of the Black Press during World War II*. New York: Oxford University Press, 1986.
   Critical survey of the FBI's monitoring of the black press during World War I and World War II.

Weinstein, Allen. *Perjury: The Hiss-Chambers Case*. New York: Knopf, 1978.
   Detailed account of FBI investigations involving Alger Hiss and Whittaker Chambers.

Welch, Neil. *Inside Hoover's FBI: The Top Field Chief Reports*. Garden City: Doubleday, 1984.
   Insider account of FBI investigations and policy by a former FBI agent and SAC (1951–81).

Whitehead, Don. *Attack on Terror: The FBI against the Ku Klux Klan in Mississippi*. New York: Funk and Wagnalls, 1970.
   Journalistic history of FBI investigations of Klan activities during the 1960s.

———. *The FBI Story: A Report to the People*. New York: Random House, 1956.
   Journalistic history of the FBI, based on privileged access to selected FBI documents.

Wise, David. *The American Police State: The Government against the People*. New York: Random House, 1976.
   Critical history of FBI surveillance of political activists.

———. *The Spy Who Got Away: The Inside Story of Edward Lee Howard*. New York: Random House, 1988.
   Critical account of FBI counterintelligence investigations during the 1980s, focusing on the failure to apprehend CIA defector Edward Howard.

Articles

"The American OGPU." *New Republic* 102 (March 11, 1940): 330–32.
   Criticizes the FBI's role in compiling lists of alleged "subversives" and arresting recruiters for the Abraham Lincoln Brigade.

Anonymous. "Washington Gestapo." *Nation* 157 (July 17 and 24, 1943): 64–66, 92–95.
   Two-part series criticizing FBI interviewing and investigations of federal employees.

Belknap, Michal. "The Mechanics of Repression: J. Edgar Hoover, the Bureau of Investigation and the Radicals, 1917–1925." *Crime and Social Justice* 7 (Spring/Summer 1977): 49–58.
   Surveys Bureau surveillance of radicals during World War I and the early 1920s.

———. "The Supreme Court Goes to War: The Meaning and Implication of the Nazi Saboteur Case." *Military Law Review* 89 (1980): 59–95.
   Surveys the FBI arrest of George Dasch and other German saboteurs in 1942.

Bennett, Sara. "New Info Disclosed on Surveillance of Lesbians and Gays." *Quash* (August/September 1982).
   Surveys FBI surveillance of gay and lesbian organizations and their periodicals.

Berman, Jerry. "FBI Spies on Central American Protestors," *Civil Liberties* 363 (Winter 1988): 1, 3.
   Surveys FBI surveillance of CISPES.

Bernstein, Barton. "The Oppenheimer Conspiracy." *Our Right to Know* (Fall/Winter 1984–85): 9–13.
   Surveys FBI surveillance of atomic scientist J. Robert Oppenheimer.

Bird, Kai, and Max Holland. "The Tapping of 'Tommy the Cork.'" *Nation* 242 (February 8, 1986): 129.
   Surveys FBI wiretapping of prominent Washington attorney Thomas Corcoran.

Blecker, R. I. "Beyond 1984: Undercover in America—Serpico to Abscam." *New York Law School Law Review* 28 (1984): 823–1024.
   Critical survey of FBI undercover operations, focusing on ABSCAM.

Bradsher, James. "Researchers, Archivists, and the Access Challenge of the FBI Records in the National Archives." *Midwestern Archivist* 11, no. 2 (1986): 95–110.
   Discusses problems confronting researchers and archivists in accessing and researching FBI records.

Bratzel, John, and Leslie Rout Jr. "Pearl Harbor, Microdots, and J. Edgar Hoover." *American Historical Review* 87 (December 1982): 1342–47.
   Surveys the FBI role in failing to anticipate the Japanese attack on Pearl Harbor.

Brock, David. "Today's FBI: Rating the Remake of the G-Men." *Insight* (February 16, 1987): 8–16.
   Surveys reforms in FBI methodology and investigative priorities instituted by FBI Director William Webster.

Burnham, David. "The FBI." *Nation* 265 (August 11/18, 1997): 11–24.
   Critical survey of FBI surveillance activities and law enforcement record during the 1990s.

Candeloro, Dominic. "Louis F. Post and the Red Scare of 1920." *Prologue* 11 (Spring 1979): 40–55.
   Surveys the Bureau's role in the 1920 Palmer Raids.

Cary, Lorin. "The Bureau of Investigation and Radicalism in Toledo, Ohio: 1918–1920." *Labor History* 21, no. 3 (1980): 430–40.
   Recounts Bureau surveillance of the IWW and discusses the value of FBI records for historians of radical unionism.

Charns, Alex. "Cloak and Gavel: The Secret History of the FBI and the Supreme Court." *Trial Briefs* 21, no. 2 (1989): 46–49.
   Surveys FBI monitoring of the Supreme Court, Supreme Court justices, and Court clerks.

———. "Gavelgate." *Southern Exposure* 18 (Fall 1990): 8–11.
Surveys the FBI's contact of Supreme Court Justice Abe Fortas in the Fred Black case.

Clancy, Paul. "The Bureau and the Bureaus, Part I." *Quill* 64 (February 1976): 12–18.
Surveys FBI covert relationship with reporters.

Cohen, William. "Riots, Racism, and Hysteria." *Massachusetts Review* 13 (1972): 373–400.
Surveys Bureau surveillance during the 1919 race riots.

"The Complete Collection of Political Documents Ripped-Off from the FBI Office in Media, Pa." *WIN* 8 (March 1972).
Reprints FBI documents documenting FBI surveillance of political activists.

Cooper, Courtney Ryley. "Camps of Crime." *American Magazine* 129 (February 1940): 14–15, 130–32.
Surveys the surge in prostitution in motels and FBI White Slave Act investigations.

———. "Crime Trap." *American Magazine* 116 (November 1933): 64–66, 94–98.
Ghost-written by Cooper but carrying FBI Director Hoover's byline, describes the Bureau's 1930s war on gangsters.

Cotter, Richard. "Notes toward a Definition of National Security." *Washington Monthly* 7 (December 1975): 4–16.
A former FBI intelligence official defends FBI internal security practices.

Crewdson, John. "Seeing Red: an FBI 'Commie Hunter' Rebels at Illegal Tactics." *Chicago Tribune Magazine* (March 2, 1986).
Discusses FBI break-in activities during the 1950s.

Croog, Charles. "FBI Political Surveillance and the Isolationist-Interventionist Debate, 1939–1941." *The Historian* 54 (Spring 1992): 441–58.
Surveys FBI monitoring of the America First Committee.

Diamond, Sigmund. "The F.B.I. in the Yard: Hoover Goes to Harvard." *Nation* 253 (October 24, 1981): 393, 405–11.
Surveys FBI monitoring of Harvard faculty and students.

———. "God and the F.B.I. at Yale." *Nation* 230 (April 12, 1980): 422–28.
Surveys FBI surveillance of Yale faculty and students.

———. "Kissinger and the F.B.I." *Nation* 229 (November 10, 1979): 449–66.
Recounts the FBI's covert relationship with Harvard professor Henry Kissinger.

Dion, Susan. "The FBI Surveillance of the Women's International League for Peace and Freedom, 1945–1963." *Journal for Peace and Justice Studies* 3, no. 1 (1991): 1–21.
Surveys FBI surveillance of women's pacifist organization.

———. "Pacifism Treated as Subversion: The FBI and the War Resisters League." *Peace and Change* 9, no. 1 (1983): 43–59.
Surveys FBI surveillance of a pacifist organization during World War II.

Donner, Frank. "Electronic Surveillance: The National Security Game." *Civil Liberties Review* 2 (Summer 1975): 21–23.
Critical survey of FBI wiretapping authority.

———. "The New F.B.I. Guidelines: Rounding Up the Usual Suspects." *Nation* 235 (August 7–14, 1982): 97, 110–16.
Surveys attempts to revise the Levi Guidelines.

Douglas, John, and Alan Burgess. "Criminal Profiling: A Valuable Investigative Tool against Violent Crime." *FBI Law Enforcement Bulletin* 55 (December 1986): 9–13.
Describes FBI profiling strategy.

Dunaway, David. "Songs of Subversion: How the FBI Destroyed the Weavers." *Village Voice* (January 21, 1980): 39–40, 42.
Surveys FBI surveillance of a folk-singing group.

Elliff, John. "Aspects of Civil Rights Enforcement: The Justice Department and the FBI, 1939–1964." *Perspectives in American History* 5 (1971): 605–73.
Surveys FBI investigations of civil rights activities.

———. "The Attorney General's Guidelines for FBI Investigations." *Cornell Law Review* 69 (April 1984): 785–815.
Discusses and contrasts the Levi and Smith Guidelines.

Emerson, Thomas, and David Helfeld. "Loyalty among Government Employees." *Yale Law Journal* 58 (December 1948): 1–143.
Surveys FBI investigations under President Truman's Federal Employee Loyalty Program.

English, Raymond. "A Counterintelligence and Counterterrorism Case: CISPES and the FBI." *Harvard Journal of Law and Public Policy* 12 (Spring 1989): 483–94.
Surveys the FBI investigation of CISPES.

"FBI as Big Brother." *Christian Century* 100 (April 20, 1983): 361.
Recounts FBI surveillance of religious groups.

Gibson, Dirk. "The Making of the Hoover Myth: A Critical Analysis of FBI Public Relations." *Public Relations Quarterly* 33 (Winter 1988): 7.
Surveys FBI public relations strategies.

Gleick, Elizabeth. "Agent of Change: Suzane Doucette Broke the Code of Silence at the FBI and Is Suing Over Sexual Harassment." *People Weekly* 40 (November 1, 1993): 101.
Discusses internal FBI conflict over new hiring practices involving female agents.

Goldwasser, Katherine. "After Abscam: An Examination of Congressional Proposals to Limit Targeting Discretion in Federal Undercover Investigations." *Emory Law Journal* 36 (Winter 1987): 75–77.
Discusses FBI uses of undercover informers.

Gordon, Gregory. "Judge to Halt Destruction of FBI's Investigative Dossiers." *New Jersey Law Journal* 105 (February 7, 1980): 9.
Discusses ruling on FBI/National Archives plan regarding FBI records.

Hazelwood, Robert. "An Introduction to the Serial Rapist: Research by the FBI." *FBI Law Enforcement Bulletin* 56 (September 1987): 16–24.
Discusses FBI strategy to identify serial rapists.

Hill, Robert. "The Foremost Radical among His Race: Marcus Garvey and the Black Scare, 1918–1921." *Prologue* 16 (Winter 1984): 216–22.
Surveys Bureau surveillance of a black nationalist leader and the black press during World War I and the postwar years.

Howlett, James, et al. "The Violent Criminal Apprehension Program." *FBI Law Enforcement Bulletin* 55 (December 1986): 14–22.
Describes FBI strategies to apprehend violent criminals.

Icove, David. "Automated Crime Profiling." *FBI Law Enforcement Bulletin* 55 (December 1986): 27–30.
Describes the FBI's computerized profiling system.

Irons, Peter. "'Fighting Fair': Zechariah Chafee, Jr., the Department of Justice, and the 'Trial at the Harvard Club.'" *Harvard Law Review* 94 (April 1981): 1205–36.
Surveys the Bureau's role in the Palmer Raids and covert efforts to ensure the firing of a Harvard law professor.

"The Jencks Legislation: Problems in Prospect." *Yale Law Journal* 67 (1958 59), 674 99 (note).
Surveys the Supreme Court's ruling in the *Jencks* case and resultant legislation concerning access to FBI informer reports.

Kamen, Al. "Diversity Hits the FBI." *Washington Post* (November 4, 1994): A23.
Discusses the FBI's diversity program and hiring.

Kimball, Penn. "The History of *The Nation* According to the FBI." *Nation* 242 (March 22, 1986): 399–426.
Surveys FBI monitoring of the left-liberal periodical, *The Nation*.

Knoll, Erwin. "Filed but Not Forgotten." *Progressive* 50 (October 1986): 24–25.
Surveys FBI surveillance of the left-liberal periodical, the *Progressive*.

MacKenzie, Angus. "Sabotaging the Dissident Press." *Columbia Journalism Review* (March–April 1981): 57–63.
Surveys FBI monitoring of the underground press during the 1960s.

Marx, Gary. "Some Reflections on Undercover: Recent Developments and Enduring Issues." *Crime, Law and Social Change* 18 (September 1992): 193–217.
Surveys FBI undercover operations.

McGee, Jim. "The Rise of the FBI." *Washington Post Magazine* (July 20, 1997): 11–15, 25–28.
Surveys FBI Director Louis Freeh's tenure and policies.

Mitgang, Herbert. "Annals of Government: Policing America's Writers." *New Yorker* 63 (October 5, 1987): 47–90.
Surveys FBI monitoring of prominent writers.

Neier, Aryeh. "Adhering to Principle: Lessons from the 1950s." *Civil Liberties Review* 4 (November–December 1977): 26–32.
Surveys the FBI's covert relationship with ACLU staff and surveillance of the ACLU.

O'Reilly, Kenneth. "The F.B.I.—HUAC's Big Brother." *Nation* 230 (January 19, 1980): 42–45.
Surveys FBI efforts to contain critics of HUAC.

———. "The FBI and the Politics of the Riots, 1964–1968." *Journal of American History* 75 (June 1988): 91–114.
Surveys FBI investigation of race riots of the 1960s.

———. "Herbert Hoover and the FBI." *Annals of Iowa* 47 (Summer 1983): 46–63.
Surveys President Herbert Hoover's uses of the Bureau.

———. "A New Deal for the FBI: The Roosevelt Administration, Crime Control, and National Security." *Journal of American History* 69 (December 1982): 683–58.
Surveys expansion of the FBI's role and authority under the New Deal.

Pledger, James R. "Hogan's Alley: The FBI Academy's New Training Complex." *FBI Law Enforcement Bulletin* 57 (December 1988): 5–9.
Discusses FBI agent training techniques.

Pogrebin, L. C. "Have You Ever Supported Equal Pay, Child Care, or Women's Groups? The FBI Was Watching You." *Ms.* 5 (June 1977): 37–44; 5 (October 1977): 7–8, 37–44.
Surveys FBI surveillance of the women's liberation movements during the 1960s and 1970s.

Pomerantz, Steven. "The FBI and Terrorism." *FBI Law Enforcement Bulletin* 56 (October 1987): 14–17.
Discusses FBI authority and responses to domestic terrorism.

Poveda, Tony. "The Effect of Scandal on Organizational Deviance: The Case of the FBI." *Justice Quarterly* 2 (June 1985): 237–58.
Discusses internal FBI reforms in the aftermath of revelations of abuses under FBI Director Hoover.

———. "The FBI and Domestic Intelligence: Technocratic or Public Relations Triumph." *Crime and Delinquency* 28 (April 1982): 194–210.
Surveys FBI domestic intelligence activities and proposed reforms.

Powers, Richard. "The G-Man and the Attorney General: Hollywood's Role in Hoover's Rise to Power." *Southwest Review* 62 (Autumn 1977): 329–47.
Discusses the role of movies in creating the myth of the G-man.

———. "J. Edgar Hoover and the Detective Hero." *Journal of Popular Culture* 9 (Fall 1977): 257–58.
Surveys FBI Director Hoover's public relations strategies to ensure a positive image of the FBI.

Pratt, William. "Farmers, Communists, and the FBI in the Upper Midwest." *Agricultural History* 63 (Summer 1989): 61–80.
Surveys FBI surveillance of radical farmer movements during the 1940s and 1950s.

Rauh, Joseph. "Nonconfrontation in Security Cases: The Greene Decision." *Virginia Law Review* 45 (1959): 1175–90.
Surveys *Greene v. McElroy* case and FBI insistence on nondisclosure of FBI informers.

Reaves, Lynne. "Greylord's Uneasy Fallout." *ABA Journal* (March 1984): 35–47.
Critical survey of FBI undercover program GREYLORD, targeting corrupt judges.

Robins, Natalie. "Spying in the Stacks: The F.B.I.'s Invasion of Libraries." *Nation* 246 (April 9, 1988): 481, 498–502.
Surveys the FBI's Library Awareness program.

Rosenberg, John. "Follow-Up: The F.B.I.'s Field Files." *Nation* 228 (March 3, 1979): 231–32.
Discloses FBI–National Archives plan to destroy all FBI field office files.

Rosswurm, Steven, and Toni Gilpin. "The FBI and the Farm Equipment Workers: FBI Surveillance Records as a Source for CIO Union History." *Labor History* 27 (Fall 1986): 485–505.
   Surveys FBI surveillance of CIO unions and the value of FBI records for historians of the labor movement.

Schardt, Arlie. "FBI Conference: A Crack in Hoover's Fortress." *Nation* 213 (November 22, 1971): 526–30.
   Discusses a conference on the FBI held at Princeton that became a catalyst to critical assessment of the FBI during the 1970s.

Schwartz, Richard. "What the File Tells: The F.B.I. and Dr. Einstein." *Nation* 236 (September 3–10, 1983): 168–72.
   Surveys FBI surveillance of the world-famous physicist.

"The Secret Files of J. Edgar Hoover." *U.S. News and World Report* 95 (December 19, 1983): 45–50.
   Summarizes the contents of FBI Director Hoover's secret office file.

Simon, David, and Stanley Swart. "The Justice Department Focuses on White Collar Crime: Promises and Pitfalls." *Crime and Delinquency* 30 (1984): 107–20.
   Surveys FBI white-collar crime program.

Steele, Richard. "Franklin D. Roosevelt and His Foreign Policy Critics." *Political Science Quarterly* 94 (Spring 1979): 15–32.
   Surveys FBI surveillance of conservative critics of President Franklin Roosevelt's foreign policy.

Steinwall, Susan. "Appraisal and the FBI Files Case: For Whom Do Archivists Retain Records?" *American Archivist* 49 (Winter 1986): 52–63.
   Appraises FBI–National Archives proposed record retention plan governing FBI files.

Stowe, David. "The Politics of Cafe Society." *Journal of American History* 84, no. 4 (March 1998): 1384–1406.
   Surveys FBI surveillance of left cultural and night club activities during the 1930s and 1940s.

Theoharis, Athan. "Dissent and the State: Unleashing the FBI, 1917–1985." *History Teacher* 24 (November 1990): 41–52.
   Surveys origins and expansion of FBI domestic surveillance activities.

———. "The FBI and the American Legion Contact Program, 1940–1966." *Political Science Quarterly* 100 (Summer 1985): 271–86.
   Surveys the origins and history of the FBI liaison program with the American Legion.

———. "The FBI's Stretching of Presidential Directives, 1936–1953." *Political Science Quarterly* 91 (Winter 1976–1977): 649–72.
   Surveys FBI political surveillance authority and FBI–White House relationship.

———. "The FBI's War on Gays." *Rights* 37 (April–June 1991): 13–15.
   Surveys FBI surveillance of homosexuals and the Sex Deviates program.

———. "FBI Wiretapping: A Case Study of Bureaucratic Autonomy." *Political Science Quarterly* 107 (Spring 1992): 101–22.
   Surveys FBI wiretapping authority and uses, and the relationships between the FBI, the attorney general, and the president.

———. "The F.D.R. File: J. Edgar Hoover, Eleanor—and Herbert Too?" *Nation* 234 (February 20, 1982): 200–201.
   Surveys FBI surveillance of First Lady Eleanor Roosevelt and President Herbert Hoover.

———. "How the FBI Gaybaited Stevenson." *Nation* 250 (May 7, 1990): 617, 635–36.
   Surveys FBI surveillance of Adlai Stevenson (governor, Democratic presidential candidate, and UN ambassador).

———. "The Presidency and the Federal Bureau of Investigation: The Conflict of Intelligence and Legality." *Criminal Justice History* no. 2 (1981): 131–60.
   Surveys the presidential role in the expansion of FBI authority.

———. "The Truman Administration and the Decline of Civil Liberties: The FBI's Success in Securing Authorization for a Preventive Detention Program." *Journal of American History* 64 (March 1978): 1010–30.
   Surveys the origins and history of FBI preventive detention programs of 1939–72.

Theoharis, Athan, and Elizabeth Meyer. "The 'National Security' Justification for Electronic Eavesdropping: An Elusive Exception." *Wayne Law Review* 14 (Summer 1968): 749–71.
   Surveys legislative and executive proposals regarding FBI wiretapping.

Tonkovich, Emil. "The Use of Title III Electronic Surveillance to Investigate Organized Crime's Hidden Interests in Gambling Casinos." *Rutgers Law Journal* 16 (Spring–Summer 1985): 811–29.
   Surveys the role of the 1968 law legalizing wiretapping and FBI investigations of organized crime.

Vitello, Michael. "The Ethics of Brilab." *Howard Law Journal* 27 (Summer 1984): 902–27.
   Surveys FBI undercover sting operations, and new proactive investigative strategies.

Washburn, Patrick. "J. Edgar Hoover and the Black Press in World War II." *Journalism History* 13 (Spring 1986): 26–33.
   Surveys FBI monitoring of the African American press during World War II.

Webster, William. "An Examination of FBI Theory and Methodology regarding White-Collar Crime Investigation and Prosecution," *American Criminal Law Review* (Winter 1980): 275–86.
   Discusses new procedures and priorities pertaining to FBI investigations of white collar crime.

Williams, David. "The Bureau of Investigation and Its Critics, 1919–1921: The Origins of Federal Political Surveillance," *Journal of American History* 68 (December 1981): 560–79.
   Surveys Bureau monitoring of critics of its role in the 1920 Palmer Raids.

———. "They Never Stopped Watching Us: FBI Political Surveillance, 1924–1936," *UCLA Historical Journal* no. 2 (1981): 5–28.
   Surveys FBI monitoring of political activities during the 1920s and 1930s.

Wilson, James. "The Changing FBI: The Road to ABSCAM," *Public Interest* 59 (Spring 1980), 3–14.
   Surveys shift in FBI investigative priorities to focus on white-collar crime.

Accessible FBI Files
(Congressional Hearings or Microfilm Reprints)

Charns, Alexander, ed. *U.S. Supreme Court and Federal Judges Subject Files*. Bethesda, MD: University Publications of America, 1992.
> Reprints documents from FBI files on the U.S. Supreme Court and on selected Supreme Court justices and federal district court judges.

COINTELPRO: The Counterintelligence Program of the FBI. Wilmington, DE: Scholarly Resources, 1978.
> Reprints FBI files on programs for disruption and harassment of the Communist Party, Socialist Workers Party, white supremacist organizations, black nationalist organizations, and new left organizations.

Communist Infiltration of the Southern Christian Leadership Conference: FBI Investigation File. Wilmington, DE: Scholarly Resources, 1984.
> Reprints documents on the FBI investigation of the SCLC.

FBI File: MIBURN (Mississippi Burning): The Investigation of the Murders of Michael Henry Schwerner, Andrew Goodman, and James Earl Chaney. Wilmington, DE: Scholarly Resources, 1990.
> Reprints the FBI file on the 1964 investigation into the murder of three civil rights activists in Mississippi.

FBI File: Robert F. Kennedy. Wilmington, DE: Scholarly Resources, 1991.
> Reprints the FBI file on Attorney General and U.S. Senator Robert F. Kennedy.

FBI File on the NAACP. Wilmington, DE: Scholarly Resources, 1990.
> Reprints FBI files on the prominent civil rights organization.

FBI File on the Student Nonviolent Coordinating Committee. Wilmington, DE: Scholarly Resources, 1990.
> Reprints FBI files on a militant civil rights organization.

FBI File on the Students for a Democratic Society and the Weather Underground Organization. Wilmington, DE: Scholarly Resources, 1990.
> Reprints FBI files on radical student organizations of the 1960s and 1970s.

Garrow, David, ed. *The Martin Luther King, Jr. FBI File: Parts I and II*. Bethesda, MD: University Publications of America, 1985 and 1987.
> Reprints FBI files on the famous civil rights leader.

House Committee on Government Operations, Subcommittee on Government Information and Individual Rights. *Hearings on Inquiry into the Destruction of Former FBI Director J. Edgar Hoover's Files and FBI Recordkeeping*, 94th Cong., 1st sess., 1975.
> Testimony and reprinted documents pertaining to FBI separate recordkeeping and record destruction procedures.

House Committee on the Judiciary. *Hearings on White House Surveillance Activities and Campaign Activities*, 93rd Cong., 2nd sess., 1974.
> Testimony and reprinted documents relating to resolutions to impeach President Richard Nixon, including political uses of the FBI and abuses of power.

House Committee on the Judiciary, Subcommittee on Civil and Constitutional Rights. *Hearings on FBI Counterintelligence Programs*, 93rd Cong., 2nd sess., 1974.
> Testimony and reprinted documents relating to the FBI's COINTELPROs.

————. *Hearings on FBI Oversight*, ser. no. 2, pt. 1, 94th Cong., 1st sess., 1975.
> Testimony and reprinted documents relating to FBI Director Hoover's secret office files.

House Committee on Rules. *Hearings to Investigate Administration of Louis F. Post Assistant Secretary of Labor, in the Deportation of Aliens*, 66th Cong., 2nd sess., 1920.
> Testimony and reprinted documents relating to the role of the Bureau of Investigation in the Palmer Raids of 1920.

House Select Committee on Assassinations. *Hearings on Assassinations of President John F. Kennedy and of Dr. Martin Luther King, Jr.*, 96th Cong., 1st sess., 1979.
> Testimony and reprinted documents relating to FBI investigations of Kennedy's and King's assassinations.

House Select Committee on Intelligence. *Hearings on U.S. Intelligence Agencies and Activities: Domestic Intelligence Programs*, 94th Cong., 1st sess., 1975.
> Testimony and reprinted documents relating to FBI domestic surveillance activities.

Investigative Case Files of the Bureau of Investigation 1908–1922. Washington, D.C.: National Archives, 1983.
> Reprints all Bureau of Investigation files for the period from 1908 through 1922.

O'Reilly, Kenneth, ed. *FBI File on the House Committee on Un-American Activities (HUAC)*. Wilmington, DE: Scholarly Resources, 1986.
> Reprints the FBI file on relations with the so-called Dies Committee, the permanent House Committee on Un-American Activities, and the renamed House Internal Security Committee.

————. *McCarthy Era Blacklisting of School Teachers, College Professors, and Other Public Employees: The FBI Responsibilities Program File and the Dissemination of Information Policy File*. Bethesda, MD: University Publications of America, 1990.
> Reprints FBI documents on a program to disseminate information to state governors and other prominent personalities and a policy file relating to the dissemination of information outside the FBI.

Senate Committee on the Judiciary, Subcommittee on Administrative Practice and Procedure. *Hearings on Invasion of Privacy (Government Agencies)*, 89th Cong., 1st sess., 1965.
> Testimony and reprinted documents relating to federal agencies' uses of wiretapping, bugging, and mail opening.

Senate Select Committee to Study Government Operations with Respect to Intelligence Activities. *Hearings on Intelligence Activities, Vol. 2, The Huston Plan*, 94th Cong., 1st sess., 1975.
> Testimony and reprinted documents relating to FBI surveillance activities and the Huston Plan.

————. *Hearings on Intelligence Activities, Vol. 6, Federal Bureau of Investigation*, 94th Cong. 1st sess., 1975.
　　Testimony and reprinted documents relating to FBI surveillance programs and activities.

————. *Intelligence Activities and the Rights of Americans*, Final Report, Book II, 94th Cong., 2nd sess., 1976.
　　Surveys FBI surveillance programs, activities, and investigative techniques (wiretaps, informers, bugs, break-ins, and mail opening).

————. *Supplementary Detailed Staff Reports on Intelligence Activities and the Rights of Americans*, Final Report, Book III, 94th Cong. 2nd sess., 1976.
　　Detailed survey of FBI surveillance programs, activities, and investigative techniques.

Theoharis, Athan, ed. *The "Do Not File" File*. Bethesda, MD: University Publications of America, 1990.
　　Reprints FBI documents relating to separate recordkeeping and record destruction procedures and an extant secret office file maintained by FBI assistant director D. Milton Ladd.

————. *FBI Wiretaps, Bugs, and Break-Ins: The National Security Electronic Surveillance Card File and the Surreptitious Entries File*. Bethesda, MD: University Publications of America, 1990.
　　Reprints two sensitive FBI files: one identifying the organizations subject to FBI wiretaps and bugs and the second detailing rules and procedures for conducting break-ins and extant break-in documents involving the FBI's New York City field office.

————. *The J. Edgar Hoover Confidential File*. Bethesda, MD: University Publications of America, 1990.
　　Reprints the secret office file maintained by FBI Director Hoover including folders on prominent Americans (John F. Kennedy, Martin Luther King Jr., Eleanor Roosevelt, Adlai Stevenson, and Joseph Alsop), sensitive investigations (White House Security Survey, Thomas Corcoran, Judith Coplon, and Fred Black), and illegal investigative techniques (wiretaps, bugs, and break-ins).

————. *The Louis Nichols Official and Confidential File and the Clyde Tolson Personal File*. Bethesda, MD: University Publications of America, 1990.
　　Reprints two sensitive office files: one maintained by Assistant Director Louis Nichols and the second by Associate Director Clyde Tolson (the Tolson file contains records only for the period 1965–72).

Theoharis, Athan, and Kenneth O'Reilly, eds. *FBI Filing and Records Procedures*. Wilmington, DE: Scholarly Resources, 1984.
　　Reprints FBI documents relating to separate filing and records procedures.

INDEX

by Athan G. Theoharis